Praise for *Establishing SRE*

"Many enterprises today face the challenge of establish[...] aaS offerings. This book provides a proven step-by-step guide for how this can be done from scratch using Google's SRE methodology. From achieving organizational buy-in to laying down the basic SRE foundations, establishing incident response and implementing a suitable organizational structure—the book contains a wealth of advice for development, operations, and leadership teams!"

—Dr. Peter Schardt, Chief Technology Officer at Siemens Healthcare GmbH

"*Establishing SRE Foundations* is a great introductory guide for anyone new to understanding and implementing Site Reliability Engineering (SRE) in their organization. Vlad creates a solid platform for anyone wishing to understand the SRE approach to building reliability into software services. As well as practical advice on implementing techniques such as SLIs and SLOs, Vlad goes into detail on how to achieve buy-in for SRE adoption and how to modify your organizational setup, rooted in his own experiences of working in a large organization. Those experiences are sorely lacking elsewhere in SRE literature, and when I'm asked in the future about SRE, I'll be referring people to this excellent book."

—Steve Smith, author of *Measuring Continuous Delivery* (2020)

"I very much enjoyed reading this book, even in its early forms. Vlad treats the topic of SRE methodically and in great detail; if you have ever been wondering whether or not someone else has come across your particular issue in an SRE implementation, this book can answer that question and probably has an actionable solution as well. Destined to become a constantly referenced handbook by all those involved in SRE change projects."

—Niall Murphy, co-author of *Site Reliability Engineering* (2016) and *The Site Reliability Handbook* (2018)

"There are an overwhelming number of blogs, books, podcasts, and ad hoc opinions covering the nitty-gritty of SRE toolchains and technology choices. That being said, SRE initiatives rarely fail for technological reasons—they fail for structural or organizational reasons. In *Establishing SRE Foundations*, Dr. Ukis has given us all a detailed, accessible, and actionable blueprint for the structures and practices of a successful SRE organization. It is an excellent book and one I would recommend to anyone looking to establish a scaled-out SRE practice in a complex environment."

—Ben Sigelman, co-founder of Lightstep

"*Establishing SRE Foundations* provides far and away the clearest, most comprehensive, and most actionable roadmap I have seen for driving, scaling, and sustaining SRE in an engineering organization. I cannot recommend it highly enough!"

—Randy Shoup, eBay Chief Architect and former Google Engineering leader

"*Establishing SRE Foundations* is a comprehensive guide for anyone looking to take their software operations to the next level. If you are a beginner, you will learn why SRE is a great methodology for improving operations, what the challenges of introducing SRE are, how to achieve organizational buy-in for SRE, how to lay the foundation for SRE in your teams, and how to drive continuous improvement. If you are an experienced practitioner, you will learn how to set up an error budget policy, enable error budget–based decision-making, and implement a suitable organizational structure. I think the content of the book is spot on and highly recommend it!"

—Vitor dos Reis, Director of Software Engineering at Delivery Hero

"Vlad offers a detailed and comprehensive overview of the transformation to SRE. He covers assessment, organizational structures, technical implementation, communication, and continuation. This book is a clear roadmap for any organization starting or progressing their SRE journey, replete with what to consider, options available, and real-world examples. If you are thinking about starting the SRE Journey, have found yourself stalled along the way, or are looking for more ideas to help you continue the journey successfully, then buy this book."

—Doc Norton, Change Catalyst, OnBelay Consulting

Establishing SRE Foundations

Establishing SRE Foundations

A Step-by-Step Guide to Introducing Site
Reliability Engineering in
Software Delivery Organizations

Vladyslav Ukis

✦ Addison-Wesley

Boston • Columbus • New York • San Francisco • Amsterdam • Cape Town
Dubai • London • Madrid • Milan • Munich • Paris • Montreal • Toronto • Delhi • Mexico City
São Paulo • Sydney • Hong Kong • Seoul • Singapore • Taipei • Tokyo

For information about buying this title in bulk quantities, or for special sales opportunities (which may include electronic versions; custom cover designs; and content particular to your business, training goals, marketing focus, or branding interests), please contact our corporate sales department at corpsales@pearsoned.com or (800) 382-3419.

For government sales inquiries, please contact governmentsales@pearsoned.com.

For questions about sales outside the U.S., please contact intlcs@pearson.com.

Visit us on the Web: informit.com/aw

Library of Congress Control Number: 2022937194

ISBN-13: 978-0-13-742460-3
ISBN-10: 0-13-742460-4

1 2022

Pearson's Commitment to Diversity, Equity, and Inclusion

Pearson is dedicated to creating bias-free content that reflects the diversity of all learners. We embrace the many dimensions of diversity, including but not limited to race, ethnicity, gender, socioeconomic status, ability, age, sexual orientation, and religious or political beliefs.

Education is a powerful force for equity and change in our world. It has the potential to deliver opportunities that improve lives and enable economic mobility. As we work with authors to create content for every product and service, we acknowledge our responsibility to demonstrate inclusivity and incorporate diverse scholarship so that everyone can achieve their potential through learning. As the world's leading learning company, we have a duty to help drive change and live up to our purpose to help more people create a better life for themselves and to create a better world.

Our ambition is to purposefully contribute to a world where:

- Everyone has an equitable and lifelong opportunity to succeed through learning.

- Our educational products and services are inclusive and represent the rich diversity of learners.

- Our educational content accurately reflects the histories and experiences of the learners we serve.

- Our educational content prompts deeper discussions with learners and motivates them to expand their own learning (and worldview).

While we work hard to present unbiased content, we want to hear from you about any concerns or needs with this Pearson product so that we can investigate and address them.

- Please contact us with concerns about any potential bias at https://www.pearson.com/report-bias.html.

*To my wonderful wife, Lina, daughter, Annika,
and son, Jonas*

Contents

Foreword

I first met Vlad Ukis at a QCon conference in London a few years ago. He wanted to recruit me as a consultant to help advise his team at Siemens Healthcare. I worked with the teamplay digital health platform team that Vlad led in Siemens Healthcare over the course of the next year or so, and over that period Vlad and I became friends.

Vlad has done an outstanding job helping the teamplay team, and more broadly Siemens Healthcare to make fantastic progress. The hard-won lessons that he and his team worked through are writ large in the pages of this book.

The teamplay team are applying the advanced, engineering-led, modern version of agile development exemplified by Continuous Delivery, DevOps and SRE, to significant advantage. They demonstrate the applicability of these ideas beyond the bounds of the big web companies that most people tend to think of when we discuss these ideas.

I often see and hear organizations dismiss sometimes important ideas that were popularized by the big web companies with comments like, "Yes, but we aren't <Google, Amazon, Netflix, insert your favorite here>." This is a misreading of why these ideas work in those organizations.

It is not always that the problems in the big web companies are unique. Rather, it is that their scale means that common problems often become limiting more quickly. This means that it becomes essential for them to solve these common problems. These big organizations don't practice Continuous Delivery (CD) and SRE because they are fads. They practice them because they work better than any alternatives that we know and address problems at the heart of all software development.

As an early adopter and promoter of some of these ideas, I think that we have entered a new phase in the evolution of some of these ideas. We are now seeing them being adopted more widely, and to very significant advantage and effect, in all kinds of software development organizations. Automotive, aerospace, telecoms, and medical sectors all have examples of their use. This book makes that clear with an example from a real-world complex software development. It stops people being able to say "SRE is all very well, but we are not Google." It is also a lot more than only that, though.

I think there are very good reasons for the growth of ideas like CD and SRE. Both are true engineering approaches to solving problems. They both try to use measurement and apply scientific style reasoning to solving real-world, practical problems that we all face, whatever the scale of our software development or the nature of the problem. I describe CD as being driven by enabling an experimental approach to software development. SRE is profoundly that too.

I have written about my views on applying engineering thinking to the development of software. I think learning, and evolving, our discipline in this direction is essential to doing a good job. Why does this matter in the context of this book? I think it is important to remember that the "E" in "SRE" means "Engineering"; it is not just the word "SRE". My preferred definition for software engineering is this:

> Software engineering is the application of an empirical, scientific approach to finding efficient, economic solutions to practical problems in software.

SRE thinking is profoundly grounded in the principles at the heart of this definition. It also adopts that other essential aspect of true engineering: We start off assuming that we will make mistakes.

The world isn't perfect. Our software won't always perform as we hope. Every system fails sometimes. SRE puts this kind of thinking front and center, and forces us, as teams and organizations, to think about how we would like our systems to cope—*How much down time is too much?* and *What shall we do when approaching those limits?*

This book does two things and does both extremely well.

At its heart, this book describes how the engineering approach that underpins SRE provides greater clarity and more effective collaboration between the three main strands of development: People focused primarily on the product, its development, and its operation.

SRE provides the glue between these groups, focusing them on what really matters in a way that is collaborative but also leaves each group with enough clarity to inform independent decision-making in their own sphere.

The techniques and principles of SRE are not only clearly defined here, but also the rationale behind them is explained in a way that will stick. This is not some dry definition, this is practical, usable, understanding.

The second thing that this book does is to describe how to start making changes to apply this kind of thinking, and the techniques of SRE, in a preexisting real-world, complex development organization. This is clearly based on much more than a theoretical understanding or interpretation—these are words from a practitioner.

The teamplay team are not dealing with simple software. Their work cannot be easily dismissed, inaccurate as those dismissals usually are, as just being another simple website or online shop. The teamplay team build real software that matters. Their software helps to save lives of patients in hospitals. It integrates world-class medical devices in hospitals with information systems in the cloud that enable new insights and new ways to help people. They adopt these leading-edge techniques, not because they are fashionable but because they work better than anything else that we know how to do so far.

This book will certainly help you understand what ideas like Service Level Indicators (SLIs), Service Level Objectives (SLOs), and Error Budgets really mean; their relationship to one another; and how to apply them. It explores, in some detail, how to organize effective responses to incidents and how to perform good post-mortems after incidents to reinforce learning. It describes effective organizational structures. This is a wide-ranging book for a wide-ranging topic. For me, though, it goes even beyond that.

I am a long-time practitioner of ideas that are incredibly well aligned and close to these ideas. I have read around this subject for several years and thought that I really understood what it was about. But my understanding is deeper now. I really get it and plan to add more use of SRE ideas to the way that I communicate and explain things in my own work. I thank Vlad for that.

There are nuggets in here that inform my own thinking and help me to develop my understanding of what it takes to apply real engineering thinking to software development.

I already knew that in engineering it is all about trade-offs, but Vlad explains this very clearly with examples in an SRE context and describes what some of the common trade-offs are and how to think about them.

I laughed out loud when I read the now blindingly obvious statement that "If you set your SLO to 100%, that means that features are always second priority." Of course, that is true. I knew this, but now I have better words and better models to express it with.

I was delighted and honored to be asked to write a foreword for this book. I confess that I may have written a foreword for it anyway because Vlad is intelligent, thoughtful, and does really good work, but also because he is my friend. I am doubly delighted that I don't need to do this as a favor to a friend, though. I can whole-heartedly recommend this book without any reservation. This is a very good book on an important topic that helps to move the game forward for our discipline! I hope that you enjoy it as much as I have.

—Dave Farley
Independent Software Development Consultant
Founder and CEO of Continuous Delivery Ltd.

Preface

This book is based on a site reliability engineering (SRE) transformation journey from a real software delivery organization in the healthcare industry. The organization runs a cloud-based platform for medical applications and services. The platform is deployed in many data centers and the applications on the platform are used in hospitals around the world. Some of the applications are used when patients are in critical condition. It follows, then, that the platform's reliability is of paramount importance.

But what is reliability? How do you measure it? How do you create an environment where development teams are motivated to invest in reliability? These were the questions I grappled with several years ago when the organization struggled to provide a reliable platform for applications and users alike. High-profile customer escalations were common. People were unaligned regarding backlog prioritization of new features versus reliability work. The operations teams were struggling to operate the product. The development teams happily implemented new features but paid very little attention to how the existing features were running in production. Project management plans were impacted greatly by deployment of large numbers of unexpected hotfixes. High-profile customers called the leadership team demanding that the service be restored or that missing features be delivered. Everyone had an opinion on what needed to be done to improve the situation, until the next outage took place, causing new opinions to emerge.

I had attended the QCon London conference for several years. The conference helped me stay abreast of new trends in software development and operations. SRE was one of the topics at the conference. I was aware of its existence but had not started learning about it. At one of the QCons, an entire track was devoted to SRE. I spent a significant amount of time attending sessions in that track. At the end of the conference, it was clear to me that SRE was gaining momentum in the industry.

While traveling back to work from the conference and looking over my notes, I decided that it was the right time for the organization to try SRE in an attempt to improve operations. There was no other structured approach to doing operations that I had come across. What we tried ourselves without SRE did not yield visible improvements. Many companies at the conference reported being successful, whatever that meant, in doing operations using SRE. Getting started seemed to be easy. It would only take a couple of basic indicators, like availability and latency, the definition of acceptable targets for each service, and alerts on when the targets would be broken.

Once I was back at work, I started thinking about how to drive SRE from within my organizational unit. Thinking deeper, I realized I would need engagement from the entire organization. The questions I had in mind were as follows:

- How would I drum up support for SRE in the organization?

- How would I engage the leadership team?

- How would I engage the operations teams?

- How would I engage the development teams? There was a growing number of them, soon to be 20 or more. So, how would I drive SRE in a growing organization, in a way that would scale with the growing number of teams expected to emerge in the future?

- What is SRE at a deeper level?

- Why does it work?

- How could I learn more about SRE?

- How could I learn enough about SRE to explain it to others quickly and easily?

- Is there an alternative to SRE?

- How could I engage with people who had already introduced SRE in their organizations?

- What are the common pitfalls of introducing SRE in an organization and how would I avoid them?

With these questions in mind, a period of soul searching followed. To cut a long story short, we managed to establish SRE as the central discipline in the organization's development and operations departments. Doing so significantly and measurably improved our ability to operate the global platform.

Moreover, the organization is in touch with many teams that build applications on top of the platform. How to operate those applications effectively is a common question from the teams. We now routinely teach SRE as a preferred method of doing operations. The teams introduce it and use the SRE infrastructure we provide.

During the SRE transformation, we got a chance to visit Delivery Hero in Berlin. They were running operations at a world-class level. It was inspiring to learn from them back then. It was even more inspiring to later see our own teams getting close to being world class.

Along the way, many lessons were learned. Introducing SRE at scale to a development organization that had never done operations and to an operations organization that had never enabled others to do operations is a very significant undertaking. It requires deep, long-term engagement with the development teams providing coaching on their individual journeys toward growing maturity in operational capabilities. At the same time, it requires long-term engagement with the operations teams providing coaching on their journey toward becoming an SRE infrastructure framework provider to enable the development teams to do operations. The transformation is a unique blend of changes in the domains of technology, people, culture, and process on both sides: development and operations.

We started publishing our experience with SRE on InfoQ in a data-driven decision-making article series[1] and later in a corresponding eMag.[2] The SRE article[3] from the series got attention, and I was approached to write a book on SRE transformation. The rest is history.

Publishing with Addison-Wesley is a privilege beyond imagination. While at university studying computer science, I read so many books from Addison-Wesley that I could identify them from a distance in the library. When I was offered the chance to publish a book with Addison-Wesley, I took it without much hesitation.

It is also a privilege to have some knowledge that might be worth publishing in a book in an industry that is very fast paced and where experience is not always valuable. At the same time, because of the pace of the industry and the bias for the new over the existing, it is a bit frightening that the knowledge I have is certainly not complete and will become obsolete quickly. More to the point, I seem to be one of the few people who was never affiliated with Google but has dared to write a book about SRE.

Further, lots of reading and gaining hands-on professional experience on my end led to a growing motivation to write. It is about giving back to the software engineering community at large where numerous authors of great books and talks shaped my thinking over the past decades.

Moreover, I consider it an entitlement in a world full of digital distractions to be able to work on a project that requires the highest levels of concentration. Writing a book certainly falls into this category. Writing this book taught me to stay away from digital distractions and develop an ability to concentrate quickly for longer time spans. It feels like my ability to concentrate is back to where it was before the era of connected devices.

My intention for the book is to support organizations that are starting an SRE adoption journey. The journey is a rewarding but difficult multiyear ride with lots of ups and downs. Adopting SRE means changing the culture, organization, responsibilities, practices, and technology around product operations. Product operations is what matters to users and customers. They only interact with the products in production. So, tending to production better is about directly improving the user and customer experience. How do you tend to production better to measurably improve the user and customer experience? How do you establish SRE as a means to getting there? How do you transform the organization toward SRE? This is what we will explore in the book.

The book is divided into three main parts. In Part I, "Foundations," you will establish a general understanding of SRE, its usefulness, and its place in the overall discipline of software operations. Additionally, I outline the challenge of SRE transformation in an organization new to the topic and explain how an organization's status quo can be assessed in terms of operations and readiness for SRE transformation.

---

1. Ukis, Vladyslav. 2021. "The InfoQ EMag: Effective Software Delivery with Data-Driven Decision Making." InfoQ, March 16, 2021. https://www.infoq.com/minibooks/data-driven-decision-making.

2. Ukis, "The InfoQ EMag."

3. Ukis, Vladyslav. 2020. "Data-Driven Decision Making – Product Operations with Site Reliability Engineering." InfoQ, March 25, 2020. https://www.infoq.com/articles/data-driven-decision-product-operations.

In Part II, "Running the Transformation," the transformation activities get rolling and unfold. For an SRE transformation to succeed, you must achieve proper organizational buy-in from the start. Here, I explain how to achieve this buy-in, initiate the transformation activities in the teams, and implement alerting, on-call rotations, and an appropriate incident response process in the organization. Accomplishing these tasks marks the establishment of the basic SRE foundations in the organization.

Part II continues with discussions about putting the advanced SRE foundations in place, including error budget policy and error budget–based decision-making. Following this, a suitable organizational structure for SRE is created. By the end of Part II, the organization has established the basic and advanced SRE foundations as well as an organizational structure for the long term.

In Part III, "Measuring and Sustaining the Transformation," I discuss how to measure the success of an SRE transformation and sustain the SRE movement. The book concludes with a look at the road ahead for SRE transformation beyond the established foundations.

Table P.1 shows the structural elements found throughout the book. They are embedded in the text and can be used as references on their own.

Table P.1   *Structural elements in the book*

Element	Description
Key Insight	A significant insight generated by the discussion in the book that is important to remember to be used in casual SRE conversations.
SRE Myth	A myth about SRE prevalent in the industry debunked in the book.
SRE Cheat Sheet	A reference of SRE topics to be looked up for a quick reminder.
From the Trenches	A story or insight based on hard-won lessons from the SRE transformation and practice. It is a description of what really worked at an organization in a particular context.

If you have any questions as you read through the book, feel free to reach out to me on LinkedIn.[4] I look forward to hearing from you!

---

4. Ukis, Vladyslav. n.d. "Dr. Vladyslav Ukis LinkedIn Profile Page." LinkedIn. https://www.linkedin.com/in/dr-vladyslav-ukis-5172ba32.

Acknowledgments

First I would like to thank my family. You are the emotional, intellectual, and spiritual foundation of my universe. My wife, Lina, is at the center. Being a UI/UX designer, she managed to listen carefully to me as I talked about a topic as technical as SRE, sometimes saying, "I got it, you do not need to go into more details right now!" It is Lina's enthusiasm, encouragement, and patience that made writing the book possible. Further, our children, Annika, age six, and Jonas, age two, are cheerfully around us. Jonas made it a habit to scroll through various black-cover and white-cover SRE books lying around at home. He might have learned something about reliability from them that could be applied at his age. It is our peace at home that made writing this book possible. Further, my parents; my brother's family; my mother's father, age 102; my uncles' families; my brother-in-law's family; my in-laws; the family of my wife's uncle and their children's families; other more distant relatives; as well as my friends all contribute to the firm family foundation I have that fueled this book project.

Second, as time is one of the most precious resources a person has, I would like to thank you, the reader, for taking the time to read this book. I hope the learnings from the book will shape your thinking about software operations in general and SRE in particular. My intention is to help make your SRE transformation as smooth and fast as possible. Get in touch; I long to find out how your SRE transformation is unfolding!

Siemens Healthineers is the center of gravity for my professional development. Specifically, the Siemens Healthineers teamplay digital health platform[1] has become a career-changing product suite and team. It provides an experimental environment necessary for introducing new ways of working. The new ways of working are tried out, and the ones that work well get adopted way beyond the teams that initially introduced them. This benefits the entire company in the end.

Specifically, a big thank-you goes to the teamplay leadership, Dr. Thomas Friese (previous executive) and Carsten Spies (current executive), for being open and supportive of my writing this book. With the book, SRE is going to be one of the most comprehensively documented processes at teamplay.

The QCon London conference became career defining as well. Literally all big organizational changes to improve technology at teamplay originated from talks, conversations, tracks, and meetings at QCon London. Both Continuous Delivery and SRE transformations originated there.

A big professional milestone for me was to meet Dave Farley at QCon London. He taught me and the entire team at teamplay the value, fundamentals, strategy, and tactics of Continuous Delivery. His way of thinking about Continuous Delivery is rooted in the scientific method. The scientific method is about answering questions using hypotheses that are put to the test with experiments. The application of the scientific method in the context of software development is why Continuous Delivery works. Interestingly, the application of the scientific method in the context of software operations is why

---

1. Siemens Healthineers. n.d. "teamplay Digital Health Platform." Accessed January 11, 2022. https://www.siemens-healthineers.com/digital-health-solutions/teamplay-digital-health-platform.

SRE works. My thanks go to Dave not only for Continuous Delivery but also for introducing me to Pearson.

On that note, a big thank-you goes to the book's executive editor, Haze Humbert, for the trust she put in my ability to write the book. She was very professional and a delight to work with from the moment of our first contact until the book's publication. Moreover, the manuscript reviewer, Niall Murphy, provided deep insights, uncovered flaws, and suggested improvements in a very timely fashion, which upon incorporation made the book so much better. Finally, the development editor, Mark Taber, the copy editor, Audrey Doyle, the production editor, Julie Nahil, the production project manager, Aswini Kumar, and many others made an incredibly effective and efficient team that turned the original manuscript into a high quality book. Thank you so much!

Specifically in the context of SRE, I am endlessly indebted to the teamplay operations engineer, Philipp Guendisch, for his enthusiasm around SRE as a discipline, dedication to driving it, and implementation of the SRE infrastructure at teamplay. It is his wit that made the SRE infrastructure reliable and a pleasure to use. Likewise, my thanks go to the many student interns supporting Philipp with the SRE infrastructure implementation.

My gratitude certainly goes to Google for coming up with the SRE concepts and turning them into a new computer science and software engineering discipline! Some Google insiders said that at the time the first Google SRE book was being written, there was not a single team in the Google SRE department doing things uniformly with other teams. So, compiling these different ways of working in a coherent set of SRE principles and practices was a tremendous task. This was, however, absolutely necessary to push SRE beyond Google. At some point the push reached me and, with that, the Siemens Healthineers teamplay digital health platform. The rest is history.

SRE conversations with Niall Murphy, one of the SRE pioneers at Google, and Steve Smith, one of the original operability thinkers at Equal Experts, shaped my thinking about many SRE aspects. Thank you for the time invested!

Interestingly, I had several people in my early development and early career who were particularly focused on establishing good processes in what they did. My father's father had worked as a chief technologist at a chemistry plant. He spent lots of time explaining to me the processes introduced at the plant to make the operations more efficient and effective over time. Although I did not understand the chemistry behind it, the outcomes of the process improvements were clear and exciting.

My friends during my school years fueled an initially rather modest interest in computer science. It is those collaborative conversations about our early programming attempts on calculators and PCs connected to tape recorders and TVs that ignited the sparks necessary to genuinely dig deep into the discipline.

My physics teacher in school, Vladimir Jakobi, taught the class to openly discuss the process of learning. Learning process sharing and improvement was one of the focus points in his physics lessons. It was unusual but had very positive effects on the students' learning outcomes. It taught me early on that the process of doing a thing right is as important as doing the right thing. Early in my professional career, Karlheinz Dorn at Siemens Healthineers taught me the value of a disciplined process in the context of software architecture.

Moreover, I am very thankful to Prof. Dr. Stefan Jablonski for supervising my bachelor thesis at the University of Erlangen-Nuremberg in Germany, as well as Gerold Herold for supervising my masters thesis at Siemens Healthineers. These signficant projects gave me unique opportunities to grow professionally in technical, interpersonal, and organizational dimensions. The associated thesis write-ups showed me the value and impact of clear technical writing.

Further, big thanks go to Kung-Kiu Lau, my PhD supervisor at the University of Manchester in the UK. It is his endless patience that honed my writing skills. I remember numerous meetings in his office discussing our joint research papers. Me calling out, "How can I explain this to somebody who does not know anything about computer science?" was a rather frequent question in these meetings. Undaunted, Kung-Kiu kept at it until our research papers could be understood by people without a background in what we were writing about. As a result, my writing skills and speed improved over time too.

Writing this book certainly required a strict writing routine to be introduced into a busy professional and family life. Being mentally prepared for the need of such a routine to be put in place and stuck to for a long time simplified the decision to write the book and follow through on all aspects of publishing.

There is an interesting quote about writing by E. L. Doctorow: "Writing is like driving at night in the fog. You can only see as far as your headlights, but you can make the whole trip that way."[2] I can relate well to the quote. It is amazing how much information the brain contains on just a single topic in a condensed and foggy structure, which gets uncompressed on hundreds of pages in a form that can be learned from by others.

Before I embarked on my PhD studies, many people said that doing research would be a unique opportunity to focus on a single topic which would not present itself in my future professional life. I guess that was not quite right. Writing this book certainly allowed me to focus on the subject of software operations as much as I focused on software architecture back in the days of my postgraduate studies.

An anecdote is that the original manuscript of the book was written in Google Docs. As I was writing about SRE, I was thinking about how the Google Docs SLOs might get broken while I was writing. Knowing the level of rigor applied to the SRE process by Google contributed to my peace of mind that even if Google Docs SLOs get broken, the services will be brought back within the SLOs rather soon. Writing about SRE using a word processor operated using SRE by the company that invented and practiced SRE might be one of the best representations of "eating your own dog food."

Finally, this book should serve as an inspiration to the world of writing to my daughter, Annika, who started school in 2021, the year the manuscript of this book was finished. Likewise, it should inspire my son, Jonas, who started learning to read letters the same year, to continue by combining them into syllables, words, sentences, paragraphs, stories, and, finally, books. I enjoyed writing the book and, throughout the process, realized that I might wish to write another one in the future.

These people and organizations influenced me to a great degree. I am very appreciative of being in such an innovative professional and caring family environment. Simply said, you all put me where I am today. Thank you!

---

2. Doctorow, E. L. n.d. "A Quote from Writers At Work." Accessed January 8, 2022. https://www.goodreads.com/quotes/53414-writing-is-like-driving-at-night-in-the-fog-you.

Coming originally from Ukraine, I am compelled to extend my deepest sympathies for the innocent civilians who remain or have been forced to flee Ukraine because of the current war. I stand in solidarity with Ukrainians during this humanitarian crisis. I join the UN General Assembly resolution demanding an end to this Russian offensive in Ukraine.

Vladyslav Ukis
April 2022

About the Author

Dr. Vladyslav Ukis is Head of R&D for the Siemens Healthineers teamplay digital health platform and reliability lead for all Siemens Healthineers Digital Health products. Previously, as software development lead, he drove Continuous Delivery, SRE, and DevRel transformation, helping this large distributed development organization evolve architecture, deployment, testing, operations, and culture to implement these new processes at scale.

Dr. Ukis earned a degree in computer science from the University of Erlangen–Nuremberg, Germany, and later from the University of Manchester, UK. During his career, he has been working on software architecture, enterprise architecture, innovation management, private and public cloud computing, team management, engineering management, portfolio management, partner management, and digital transformation at large.

Part I

Foundations

Software delivery organizations create and maintain software products using three disciplines: product management, product development, and product operations. In product management, decisions about what products to build are made. In product development, decisions about how to build the products are made. And in product operations, decisions about how to operate the products are made.

In the early years of software development, the disciplines of product management, product development, and product operations were rather independent. With the onset of agile delivery, they started working in a more collaborative manner. This enabled software delivery organizations to create products in a more user-centric way and deliver them more incrementally, iteratively, and quickly.

So far, collaboration between development and operations has not been as deep as that between product management and product development. In fact, the two disciplines operate rather independently throughout the industry, leaving much room for improvement.

New software delivery philosophies, such as DevOps, specifically promote deep collaboration between product development and product operations. According to Wikipedia, "DevOps is a set of practices that combines software development (*Dev*) and IT operations (*Ops*). It aims to shorten the systems development life cycle and provide continuous delivery with high software quality."[1] Being positioned at a rather philosophical level, DevOps does not provide an opinionated way of achieving the envisioned collaboration between product development and product operations. It's up to practitioners to determine how the philosophy can be implemented.

Site Reliability Engineering (SRE) is an opinionated framework for implementing the DevOps philosophy. In fact, as stated by Google in the Site Reliability Workbook, "SRE implements DevOps."[2] The "State of DevOps 2021" report by DORA[3] says, "SRE and DevOps are complementary philosophies."[4]

SRE is a new software engineering discipline developed by Google to operate production systems reliably at scale. It has served Google very well: Because of SRE, Google can be operated reliably and cost-effectively. Thankfully, how this is done is well described in the original SRE books[5] by Google.

---

1. Wikipedia. 2021. "DevOps." Last modified March 22, 2022. https://en.wikipedia.org/wiki/DevOps.

2. Beyer, Betsy, Niall Richard Murphy, David K. Rensin, Stephen Thorne, and Kent Kawahara. 2018. *The Site Reliability Workbook: Practical Ways to Implement SRE.* Sebastopol, CA: O'Reilly Media.

3. DORA. n.d. "DORA Research Program." Accessed January 18, 2022. https://www.devops-research.com/research.html.

4. DORA. 2021. "State of DevOps 2021." . https://services.google.com/fh/files/misc/state-of-devops-2021.pdf.

5. Google. 2022. "Google SRE Books." https://sre.google/books.

Inspired by Google's success in operations, many companies around the world started adopting SRE as a discipline, learning from the original Google SRE books.

It turns out that putting SRE in place within an organization that has handled operations differently requires significant organizational, technical, and process changes. This book explains the changes required to establish SRE in an existing product delivery organization.

This part of the book lays the foundation for the SRE transformation. It begins by clarifying the reasons for product operations to implement an SRE transformation: Are there alternatives for doing operations? Why SRE in particular?

Once this understanding has been established, I will discuss the challenges of putting SRE in place, focusing on issues around technology, people, teams, culture, process, and the organization as a whole.

Next, I will define an overall direction for tackling these challenges. How do you get people behind SRE? What technology is needed? What sort of culture transformation needs to be facilitated? How does the software delivery process need to change?

After that, I will give you an understanding of how the business will be improved based on SRE activities and data. Will doing SRE reduce the number of outages? (This would reduce the costs sunk in fixing outages and the revenue lost due to them.) Will doing SRE improve decision-making as to when to invest in reliability versus new-feature development? (This would optimize the capital allocation for better returns on investment.)

Toward the end of the chapter, we will view SRE infrastructure development in a new light: specifically with a product mindset, focusing on developing the infrastructure as a new internal product in the company's portfolio.

Chapter 1

Introduction to SRE

This chapter is an introduction to SRE transformation. I will start by clarifying why SRE should be chosen as a product operations methodology. Following this, I will clearly articulate the challenges of implementing an SRE transformation. The chapter concludes with an outlook of how to drive SRE transformation.

1.1 Why SRE?

A provocative but useful question to ask in the context of SRE transformation is "Why SRE?"

Indeed, an existing product delivery organization has been doing operations in some way. The way operations has been done probably did not lead to satisfactory results. This is why there are deliberations going on in the organization to improve the way the product is being used.

In this context, it is useful to consider the options available to improve operations. Apart from SRE, what are the options? The earlier discussion showed already that DevOps is an overarching philosophy for bringing product development and product operations together. SRE is a concrete opinionated implementation of the DevOps philosophy. Are there other implementations? Can DevOps be implemented in a different way? What else is there in the industry to help run production systems reliably at scale? Let us look at what is available.

1.1.1 ITIL

Along with DevOps and SRE, there is a service management framework known as ITIL, from Axelos. ITIL 4[6] is the latest release of the ITIL framework. According to Wikipedia, the name *ITIL*[7] is a former acronym for Information Technology Infrastructure Library. The acronym is no longer in use as such, but the term *ITIL* still is. Wikipedia defines ITIL as "a set of detailed practices for IT service management that focuses on aligning IT services with the needs of business."[2]

---

6. Axelos. n.d. "ITIL." Accessed January 11, 2022. https://www.axelos.com/certifications/itil-service-management.
7. Wikipedia. 2021. "ITIL." Last modified February 11, 2022. https://en.wikipedia.org/wiki/ITIL.

ITIL describes IT processes, procedures, tasks, and checklists. It is used to demonstrate compliance as well as measure improvement toward that end. ITIL originated from a trend that saw a growing number of IT organizations in the 1980s using an increasingly diverse set of practices. The British Central Computer and Telecommunications Agency (CCTA) developed the set of recommendations as a way to standardize these practices.[8]

ITIL 4 defines seven guiding principles.[9]

1. Focus on value.

2. Start where you are.

3. Progress iteratively with feedback.

4. Collaborate and promote visibility.

5. Think and work holistically.

6. Keep it simple and practical.

7. Optimize and automate.

The overall holistic approach to service management in ITIL 4 rests on four dimensions:

1. Organizations and people: culture, capacity, and competency of the workforce

2. Information and technology: information, knowledge, and technologies for service management

3. Partners and suppliers: relationships with other businesses involved in the design, deployment, delivery, support, and continual improvement of services

4. Value streams and processes: integration and coordination of organizational units

Thus, ITIL is a generic framework for designing the IT function of an enterprise. It is widely used in the industry.

1.1.2 COBIT

Another IT governance methodology is COBIT. According to Wikipedia,[10] COBIT is a framework created by ISACA, the international professional association focused on IT governance.[11] COBIT[12] stands for Control Objectives for Information and Related Technologies. It is "a framework for information technology management and governance. It defines a set of generic processes for the

---

8. Davis, Jennifer, and Ryn Daniels. 2016. "Foundational Terminology and Concepts." In *Effective DevOps. O'Reilly Online Learning*. https://www.oreilly.com/library/view/effective-devops/9781491926291/ch04.html.

9. Gallacher, Liz, and Helen Morris. 2012. *ITIL Foundation Exam Study Guide*. West Sussex, UK: John Wiley & Sons.

10. Wikipedia. 2021. "COBIT." https://en.wikipedia.org/wiki/COBIT.

11. Wikipedia. 2021. "ISACA." https://en.wikipedia.org/wiki/ISACA.

12. ISACA. "COBIT." n.d. Accessed January 11, 2022. https://www.isaca.org/resources/cobit.

management of IT, with each process defined together with process inputs and outputs, key process-activities, process objectives, performance measures and an elementary maturity model."

A core tenet of COBIT is to align business goals with IT goals. This is done based on five COBIT principles:[13]

1. Meeting stakeholder needs

2. Covering the enterprise end to end

3. Applying a single integrated framework

4. Enabling a holistic approach

5. Separating governance from management

ISACA released COBIT in 1996. The latest version, COBIT 2019, was released in 2018. It defines six governance system principles:[14]

1. Provide stakeholder value

2. Holistic approach

3. Dynamic governance system

4. Governance distinct from management

5. Tailored to enterprise needs

6. End-to-end governance system

Thus, COBIT, like ITIL, is an overarching governance framework for designing the IT function of an enterprise.

1.1.3 Modeling

Another approach that can be applied to operations is modeling. How this can be done can be seen in the software security discipline. In security, modeling is applied to find threats. Threat modeling is a risk-based approach for secure system design. It is about finding security threats based on an analysis of system architecture, implementation, and deployment. Once the threats are found, mitigations are defined and implemented.

Similar to threat modeling in security, modeling as a technique can be applied to find operational vulnerabilities. System architecture, implementation, and deployment can be analyzed to find weak spots that would prevent the system from executing well in production. Based on these weak spots, mitigations can be defined. These mitigations can then be implemented.

13. Davis, Jennifer, and Ryn Daniels. 2016. "Foundational Terminology and Concepts." In *Effective DevOps*. O'Reilly Online Learning. https://www.oreilly.com/library/view/effective-devops/9781491926291/ch04.html.

14. Nissen, Christian F. 2019. "Introduction to COBIT 2019 and IT Management." SlideShare IOS. https://www.slideshare.net/ChristianFNissen/introduction-to-cobit-2019-and-it-management-140511572.

The implementation can be in architecture, design, implementation, deployment, operations procedures, and organizational processes.

A model created in this way needs to be updated regularly to take into account the development of new features, changes in infrastructure, and learnings from production outages. So, overall, modeling is a methodology rooted in a regular analysis of system architecture, design, implementation, deployment, and so on from an operational perspective.

Although the modeling approach seems feasible and widely applicable, it does not appear to be broadly used in the industry. It is also not a published and widely recognized operations methodology in its own right.

1.1.4 DevOps

Now that you know what DevOps is, let's explore it in more detail. This will be useful when comparing DevOps with the methodologies just described.

DevOps defines five pillars of success.[15]

1. Reduce organizational silos.

2. Accept failure as normal.

3. Implement gradual changes.

4. Leverage tooling and automation.

5. Measure everything.

This is a generic philosophy for bringing development and operations together. The DevOps philosophy has been widely adopted in the software industry across all domains since 2013. Concrete implementations vary greatly, one of those being the application of SRE methodology.

The DevOps maturity level of an enterprise can be assessed using the CALMS framework. CALMS stands for Culture, Automation, Lean, Measurement, and Sharing. The framework was coined by Jezz Humble, a coauthor of several popular books on DevOps and Continuous Delivery, among other topics.

In terms of culture, DevOps requires shared responsibility for tearing down silos between Dev and Ops. *Automation* in DevOps refers to technical practices around Continuous Delivery, automating as much as possible in the areas of building, infrastructure provisioning, deployment, testing, and monitoring. *Lean* refers to the principles of waste elimination and value stream optimization. These are applied in practice using work-in-progress minimization, batch size limitation, handoff complexity reduction, queue length management, and wait time reduction. In terms of measurement, a DevOps organization collects data on its processes, builds, deployments, failures, feature usage, and so on. The data is systematically used to understand current capabilities and drive measurable improvements. Finally, *sharing* in DevOps refers to shared goals, openness, and information sharing among the development and operations teams.

CALMS is also sometimes used to communicate and negotiate the differences between DevOps and ITIL.

---

15. Hazrati, Vikas. 2019. "The Difference Between DevOps Engineers and SREs." *DZone*, July 29, 2019. https://dzone.com/articles/the-battle-of-devops-and-sre.

1.1.5 SRE

Site reliability engineering is probably the latest methodology for doing operations. It originated within Google in 2004.[16] According to Wikipedia, "SRE is a discipline that incorporates aspects of software engineering and applies them to infrastructure and operations problems. The main goals are to create scalable and highly reliable software systems. According to Benjamin Treynor Sloss, the founder of Google's Site Reliability Team, SRE is what happens when a software engineer is tasked with what used to be called operations."[17]

The SRE principles were postulated by Google in the Site Reliability Workbook.[18] They are described in Table 1.1.

Table 1.1 *SRE Principles*

#	SRE Principle	Description
1	Operations is a software problem.	SRE uses software engineering approaches to doing operations.
2	Manage by service level objectives (SLOs).	Agree on an appropriate availability target for a service.
3	Work to minimize toil.	If a machine can perform a desired operation, then a machine should.
4	Automate this year's job away.	Determine what to automate, under what conditions, and how.
5	Move fast by reducing the cost of failure.	Reduce mean time to repair (MTTR) for common faults to increase product developer velocity.
6	Share ownership with developers.	Developers and SREs have a holistic view of the stack: frontend, backend, libraries, storage, and so on.
7	Use the same tooling, regardless of function or job title.	The team minding a service should use the same tools regardless of their roles in the organization.

There are also three additional principles for practicing SRE.

1. SRE needs SLOs with consequences.

2. SREs must have time to make tomorrow better than today.

3. SRE teams have the ability to regulate their workload.

---

16. Google Cloud Tech. 2020. "The History of SRE." YouTube, July 15, 2020. https://www.youtube.com/watch?v=1NF6N2RwVoc.

17. Wikipedia. 2021. "Site Reliability Engineering." https://en.wikipedia.org/wiki/Site_reliability_engineering.

18. Beyer, Betsy, Niall Richard Murphy, David K. Rensin, Stephen Thorne, and Kent Kawahara. 2018. *The Site Reliability Workbook: Practical Ways to Implement SRE*. Sebastopol, CA: O'Reilly Media.

Thus, the SRE principles are pretty opinionated and often directly prescribe what needs to be done to achieve reliable operations. They are very close to software engineering in talking about minimizing toil, automation, and shared ownership with developers.

Since 2014, SRE has been gaining in popularity in the industry. It is considered a native methodology for operating cloud native systems. The growing number of cloud native systems in operation worldwide may be one of the reasons for SRE's growth in popularity. In general, SRE can be used to operate all kinds of systems, not just cloud native ones.

1.1.6 Comparison

Looking at the searches on DevOps, SRE, ITIL, and COBIT, a trend emerges dating back to 2014. What can be seen in the search patterns is that DevOps and SRE are the operations methodologies with the highest interest. ITIL and COBIT attract the lowest number of searches.

Apart from that, the operations methodologies available in the industry are rather different. ITIL and COBIT are governance frameworks for designing the IT function of an enterprise. Modeling is an approach for deriving good operations practices based on an analysis of system artifacts. SRE is rooted in software engineering and approaches operations specifically from that perspective. DevOps is an overarching philosophy for doing operations.

Because the methodologies are so different, they may not be mutually exclusive. They are, indeed, addressing different needs. This can mean that applying some of them in combination may make sense for a company. For example, it may be useful to have ITIL procedures in place for regulatory compliance handling of customer complaints. At the same time, it might be useful to have SRE in place for proper engagement of developers and operations engineers in operations. As part of SRE activities, some aspects of modeling might also be useful while the system is being initially architected.

Because of the differences in these methodologies, a straightforward comparison of them may be difficult. However, such a comparison is necessary from an envisioned SRE transformation standpoint. Driving an SRE transformation means convincing all relevant people in the organization that SRE is the right choice for the company to do operations. The relevant people are simply everyone in product delivery. To persuade such a numerous and diverse crowd, a convincing argument must be constructed as to why SRE is the right choice. The fact that Google does SRE is not a convincing argument for people to transform their own organization toward SRE. What's required is positioning SRE in the context of other available operations methodologies.

In fact, pointing to Google as a reason to do SRE might backfire. The "not-invented-here" syndrome may kick in. This syndrome is observed when organizations avoid things created by other organizations. According to Wikipedia, "research illustrates a strong bias in organizations against ideas from the outside."[19] To overcome the not-invented-here syndrome when running the SRE transformation, clear fundamental reasons for doing SRE over something else are required.

Therefore, in the following, an attempt is undertaken to compare the operations methodologies in order to gain a better understanding of their positioning in the overall set of operations activities. Initially, the following criteria for comparison are used:

- Whether a methodology represents a governance framework to design an enterprise IT function

---

19. Wikipedia. 2021. "Not invented here." https://en.wikipedia.org/wiki/Not_invented_here.

- Whether a methodology explicitly supports IT regulatory compliance

- Whether a methodology is rooted in IT

Using these three comparison criteria, the methodologies considered stack up as shown in Table 1.2.

Table 1.2 *First Comparison of Operations Methodologies*

Methodology	Governance Framework to Design an Enterprise IT Function	Supports IT Regulatory Compliance	Rooted in IT
ITIL	Yes	Yes	Yes
COBIT	Yes	Yes	Yes
Modeling	No	No	No
DevOps	No	No	No
SRE	No	No	No

ITIL is a governance framework for designing an enterprise IT function. It supports IT regulatory compliance and is rooted in IT. The same applies to COBIT.

Modeling is the opposite. It is not an IT framework for designing an enterprise IT function, nor does it support IT regulatory compliance. It is also not rooted in IT. The same applies to DevOps being a philosophy and SRE implementing the DevOps philosophy.

What can be deduced from the comparison is that ITIL and COBIT are going to serve the chief information officers (CIOs) well. CIOs are typically tasked with running the overall IT function of an enterprise. However, other enterprise functions directly contributing to product delivery, such as product management and product development, are not so much the focus of ITIL and COBIT. Chief technical officers (CTOs) and chief product officers (CPOs) are therefore not going to be served well by ITIL and COBIT.

But should they be? It is about operations, after all. Who needs to be involved in operations? Who from the product delivery organization needs to contribute to operating the product reliably at scale in production? Is it product operations? Is it product development? Is it product management? All of them together? How? In which ways? Based on ITIL and COBIT, it is not clear enough what product management and product development need to do to contribute to reliable product operation at scale.

With these questions in mind, the next set of criteria can be established to further compare the operations methodologies along the lines of whom in the product delivery organization they appeal to. Therefore, the following four comparison criteria can be selected:

- Whether a methodology is appealing to the CIO and operations engineers

- Whether a methodology is appealing to the CTO and software developers

- Whether a methodology is appealing to the CPO and product owners

- Whether a methodology is rooted in software engineering as the core discipline in software product delivery

Table 1.3 shows a comparison of the operations methodologies along these criteria.

Table 1.3 *Second Comparison of Operations Methodologies*

Methodology	Appealing to CIOs and Operations Engineers	Appealing to CTOs and Software Developers	Appealing to CPOs and Product Owners	Rooted in Software Engineering
ITIL	Yes	No	No	No
COBIT	Yes	No	No	No
Modeling	No	Yes	No	No
DevOps	Yes	Yes	Yes	No
SRE	Yes	Yes	Yes	Yes

The ITIL framework is appealing to CIOs and operations engineers. Being rooted in IT, it comes with an IT context. Therefore, it is not very appealing to CTOs and software developers, nor to CPOs and product owners. It is also not rooted in software engineering. The COBIT framework exhibits the same characteristics as ITIL.

When it comes to modeling, ITIL is not very appealing to CIOs and operations engineers, because it addresses only one part of the IT universe. Modeling is going to be appealing to CTOs and software engineers because it is an analytical approach known from the field of security and applied to operations. The CPOs and product owners are not going to be attracted to modeling that much because it analyzes technical artifacts like architecture, implementation, and deployment. These artifacts are not where the product people typically have their expertise. In many cases, the artifacts can only be understood by people with a technical background. Finally, modeling is not rooted in software engineering, but rather in product security. It represents an established procedure in the product security field called security threat modeling.

The DevOps philosophy is appealing to all groups in product delivery: CIOs with operations engineers, CTOs with software developers, and CPOs with product owners. The CPOs with product owners view DevOps as enabling faster software releases. Everyone wants their features more quickly. DevOps supports faster feature delivery.

For CTOs with software developers and CIOs with operations engineers, DevOps is by definition a set of practices that combines development and operations. This is appealing to both groups because it attempts to close the chasm between development and operations that is so typical in the industry. Being a philosophy, DevOps is not rooted in software engineering. Being a set of practices combining development and operations, it does not explicitly include product management, which is an essential part of software engineering.

Finally, when looking at SRE, it will also be appealing to all groups in product delivery. CIOs and operations engineers will view SRE as an enabler to ensuring that software developers are properly engaged in product operations. Moreover, with SRE, operational concerns will be addressed early during the initial product architecture and design phase. Additionally, operational concerns will even be elevated to the product owners' attention. The operational concerns will play a role in product definition and, perhaps most importantly, the capacity distribution of the development team.

The CTOs and software engineers will be attracted to SRE because it is a genuine software engineering discipline. It is about approaching operations as a software engineer. Indeed, SRE is "what happens when a software engineer is tasked with what used to be called operations." It is all about automation, development, measurement, empirical evidence, iteration, and allocating engineering time based on the measurements in production.

The CPOs and product owners will be attracted to SRE because it puts them in the driver's seat to make engineering capacity allocation decisions based on data from production instead of on anecdotes by the technical people. Engineering capacity allocation is a notoriously contentious area. There is never enough engineering capacity in a product delivery organization. This is true regardless of the success of the product. Everybody in the product delivery organization has a unique opinion about where the engineering time should be spent. Likewise, everybody has a unique explanation of why that should be the case.

The operations engineers have lots of complaints from customers. So, from their point of view, the big pile of customer support tickets needs to be brought down to zero by engineers first. This is because it is about the customers. If they are not happy, they will eventually pull the plug and stop using and paying for the product.

The software developers have lots of technical debt in many areas of the product. So, from their point of view, the technical debt has to be paid off first before new features are developed. This is because the system in production might be barely surviving in some areas already, and the maintenance of some system parts might require a very high amount of effort. Adding new features to a technically broken system will render the system unusable to customers and will increase maintenance efforts even further. The technical debt will skyrocket as a result, causing higher interest rates, expressed as more effort to pay the debt off later. So, obviously, the technical debt would need to be cleaned up before new features are added to the system.

The product owners have lots of conversations with customers, users, partners, stakeholders, and company executives. Every party, including the product owners themselves, has plenty of ideas for new features. Premium customers might be especially demanding. The number of premium customers might be growing. However, their requests might take more time to implement, at least according to the technical people. Some feature requests from customers collide with the company executives' opinions of what needs to be put into the product next. The partners have a different view too. Some of them might be as demanding as the premium customers. They might be right in some sense. Some of the partners bring in more revenue than some premium customers. Working closely on the product, the product owners themselves have plenty of ideas they want to get implemented. These will help, but do not necessarily reflect, the views of customers, partners, and executives.

All in all, more features would need to be put into the product as soon as possible. Otherwise, the premium customers might stop promoting the product to peers within their industries. They might even stop paying for the product at some point. Growth in the number of premium customers might subside. The executives might reduce the product delivery organization's budget if they do not get the features they consider essential for company growth. The partners might start looking for other partners in the ecosystem. This might result in diminishing revenue from the partner business.

In this situation, whom should the product owners listen to? Themselves? Customers, executives, and partners? Software developers? Operations engineers? How to solve the conundrum? How to break the tie? This is exactly the nexus where SRE has its strength. It mandates the product delivery organization to align based on production data indicating when to invest in reliability versus features. When used diligently, it is a huge help for the product owners to cut through the noise of opinions, move away from doing service to those who shout the loudest, and ensure the right balance between investments in reliability versus features per time period.

With this line of argument, we can compare the operations methodologies considered earlier using another set of criteria:

- Whether a methodology aligns the entire product delivery organization, consisting of product management, product development, and product operations
- Whether a methodology is opinionated for operations engineers in that it clearly prescribes what they should do
- Whether a methodology is opinionated for software developers in that it clearly prescribes what they should do
- Whether a methodology is opinionated for product owners in that it clearly prescribes what they should do

Table 1.4 compares the operations methodologies along these criteria.

Table 1.4 *Third Comparison of Operations Methodologies*

Methodology	Aligns Product Delivery Org	Opinionated for Operations Engineers	Opinionated for Software Developers	Opinionated for Product Owners
ITIL	No	Yes	No	No
COBIT	No	Yes	No	No
Modeling	No	No	Yes	No
DevOps	Yes	No	No	No
SRE	Yes	Yes	Yes	Yes

ITIL being a framework to govern the IT function of an enterprise does not align a product delivery organization. It is opinionated for operations engineers, as it prescribes what they should do to ensure trouble-free service operations. It is much less opinionated for software developers, let alone product owners. COBIT also being a framework to govern the IT function of an enterprise scores the same as ITIL on the given comparison criteria.

Modeling being a technique does not align a product delivery organization. It is not opinionated for operations engineers or product owners. For software developers, however, it is opinionated in that it prescribes that technical artifacts and processes such as architecture, software design, and deployment should be analyzed for operational risks.

DevOps aims to align a product delivery organization. Where it falls short is in prescriptive guidance for operations engineers, software developers, and product owners.

Finally, SRE also aligns the entire product delivery organization. It does so in a prescriptive manner for all parties involved. That is, SRE implements DevOps in a prescriptive way, and it requires operations engineers, software developers, and product owners to align on service objectives. The service objectives need to be defined in such a way that they reflect how happy the users are with the service. If the objectives are met, the users should be happy. If the objectives are not met, the users are not happy. That is, the objectives can be used as a proxy measure for user happiness.

SRE doesn't just align the product delivery organization on the definition of service objectives. A clear principle for practicing SRE is to assign consequences to the objectives: "SRE needs SLOs with consequences." The corollary of this is that, again, the product delivery organization needs to agree on the consequences of the objectives not being met. The operations engineers, software developers, and product owners need to agree upfront what they will do when the previously agreed objectives are not fulfilled by the services.

What could this mean in practice? If the agreed objectives are not met, the operations engineers see a severe impact on the users. The adrenaline level is high. They want to get the issue fixed as soon as possible to restore service for users.

Moreover, if the agreed objectives are not met, the software developers immediately understand the potential user impact. They know they have been alerted because of severe user impact. This provides motivation to immediately start working on fixing the issue.

Finally, if the agreed objectives are not met, the product owners are prepared to get calls from angry customers. They want to spend engineering time on restoring the service. They understand its importance. It does not require time to reprioritize the team backlog. A shared understanding was established before that the features on the backlog wait until the service has been fixed and brought back within the defined objectives.

1.2 Alignment Using SRE

SRE alignment of the product delivery organization for operational concerns is thus threefold, as shown in Table 1.5.

Table 1.5 *SRE Alignment of the Product Delivery Organization*

1. Joint definition of service objectives	2. Joint definition of consequences of not meeting the defined service objectives	3. Joint execution on the defined consequences of not meeting the defined service objectives

First, SRE alignment is about a joint definition of service objectives. Second, it is about a joint definition of what should happen and who should do what when the service objectives are not met. Third, it is about joint execution on the jointly defined consequences.

To put it another way, SRE forces the product delivery organization to engage with the question of and arrive at an agreement on how reliable everyone involved actually wants the product to be and how much the same people are willing to pay for it.

This is a real strength of the SRE methodology. That kind of alignment of the product delivery organization cannot be found in other operations methodologies. It is exactly the type of alignment needed in order to implement DevOps properly. Each party—product operations, product development, and product management—must play a role to ensure proper service operations that lead to a positive customer experience. Everyone needs to be engaged in operations activities. This is not new to operations engineers, is fairly new to software developers, and is surprising to product owners.

The value of SRE is in bringing these three parties together in an opinionated way in pursuit of continuous product operations that lead to user happiness. Ever since SRE originated at Google, people have been delighted to use Google. In fact, no one is obligated to use Google for online search. However, according to Statcounter,[20] people worldwide have consistently done so, preferring Google to other search engines between 2009 and 2020.

In fact, more than 92% of searches were conducted by people voluntarily using Google between 2009 and 2020. While many factors contribute to this domination of the search market, SRE at Google has played a major role in making sure that when users conduct a search on Google, they get a positive experience.

The alignment of the product delivery organization for doing operations suggested by SRE is also required to reach and sustain the speed of DevOps. Consider how difficult it is to gain speed if the product delivery organization is not aligned on operational concerns. If the operations engineers are the only ones ensuring production operations, they will have a difficult time detecting issues in production before they are reported by customers. This is because the parameters to alert upon have not been aligned with product development and product management. So, the operations engineers are going to set up alerts on generic IT resources, such as memory consumption, CPU usage, queue fill levels, storage consumption, and the like. This kind of alerting, while helpful at times, does not necessarily reflect user happiness while working with the system. So, the user may be unhappy and no alert will be generated. The opposite is also true: The user may be happy and alerts will be generated. This is because the alert definition procedure is not user-centric and does not include all the necessary stakeholders, such as operations engineers, software developers, and product owners.

Once the operations engineers have identified an issue they cannot fix, they need to get the software developers to work on it. This is an ongoing struggle. Why? Because the software developers work on feature backlogs prioritized by the product owners. They commit to the backlog items and want to work on them without being interrupted. When approached by operations engineers to fix the issue in production, the developers might greet them with an eye-roll. First, the developers are out of the production context and fully in the development context. Second, fixing the issue in production means interrupting work on the current backlog item. Third, fixing the issue in production means the commitment to the product owner on the backlog item is likely to be broken. Fourth, it is not quite clear whether fixing the production issue should take precedence over the feature work from the backlog item. What is more important: fixing an existing issue in production to make the current users happy, or implementing a new feature to fulfill some existing sales and marketing commitments?

In order to break the tie, the product owner needs to be consulted for a prioritization decision. To make the decision, the product owner needs to understand the production issue first. How many data centers are affected? How many users are affected? Is the issue a blocker for frequently used workflows in the product? Are there any workarounds? What is the impact on revenue? What is the impact on cost? What is the impact on reputation? What is the impact

---

on customer support? How urgent is the fix to be provided? What is the effort to provide the fix? What is the effort to roll it out? What is the effort to monitor the rollout of the fix? These questions are just the beginning of a quest for the right prioritization decision.

The other side of the coin is the opportunity cost of the backlog item the developer worked on not being delivered on time. If the production issue is fixed first, how would it impact the backlog item's delivery timeline? What is the impact of late backlog item delivery on sales commitments, marketing commitments, partners, and executive stakeholders? Can the backlog be reprioritized in a sensible manner considering the knock-on effect of late delivery of the backlog item in question? Shall the backlog item be de-scoped altogether if it arrives late due to fixing the production issue?

A difficult and long quest for the right prioritization decision is taking place between the operations engineer, developer, and product owner, all while the users in production are being impacted. What happens if one of the parties is away on vacation? Would it lengthen the quest for the right prioritization decision? Does the entire process fulfill the promised speed of DevOps?

Think about it. If a similar scenario unfolded for every production issue at Google, would people use Google Search in the phenomenal way illustrated by the aforementioned search statistics? Probably not.

Figure 1.1 shows how the operations engineers, software developers, and product owner work in an organization unaligned on operational concerns during the feature development and operations life cycle. The work is done in silos during feature development. During production operations, when issues occur, suddenly the operations engineer, software developer, and product owner act as a team and work in a collaborative manner.

The feature development period is shown on the left-hand side of the figure. The operations engineers are manning production. They are not involved in the feature development process. The developers are fully concentrated on feature development. They interact with the product owner to clarify the feature requirements. The product owner is busy detailing the feature, answering developers' questions, working with stakeholders, engaging designers, and possibly conducting user research. When it comes to operational concerns, the three parties work in a completely siloed manner. The operations engineers are working fully on operational concerns of features that are already in production. The developers might be thinking about production

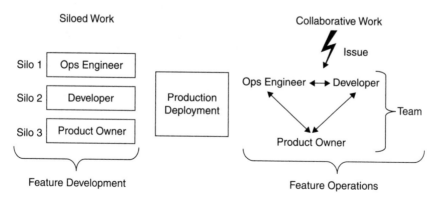

Figure 1.1 *Siloed versus collaborative work during development and operations*

during feature development, but certainly not as one of the most important concerns to address. The product owners' thinking and activities do not include operations.

After production deployment, the feature goes to operations. The operations engineers put their focus on the feature. It just recently arrived in production. They learn as much about it as they can. Suddenly, customers start reporting issues. The operations engineers identify that the recently deployed feature is broken. They get in touch with the developers. The developers get in touch with the product owner. They meet and decide how to proceed, together. They work as a team in a very collaborative manner. This is great. However, they have to do it on every production issue, because there is no fundamental alignment between them about how to handle operational concerns for features. In fact, it was never put in place!

This discussion shows that the organization is not aligned on operational concerns. Without SRE in place, product operations, product development, and product management are not pulling together on operational concerns strongly enough throughout the product life cycle to ensure a positive user experience. What SRE puts in place is an alignment on operational concerns among the three parties throughout the product life cycle. This alignment is one of the important enablers of the speed of delivery in the product delivery organization. It allows the organization to handle operational and development concerns in parallel and at speed. With the proper alignment, both concerns can be handled in such a way that there is enough focus on operations and development without extensive and expensive context switching (Figure 1.2).

SRE is prescriptive about agreements that need to be reached in each stage of the product life cycle. Executing the agreements ensures that product operations, product development, and product management can work in a highly aligned and loosely coupled manner to ensure product operations in production deliver a positive user experience.

While the strength of SRE is alignment of the product delivery organization on operational concerns, its weakness is lack of support for regulatory IT compliance. As we learned in Section 1.1.5, SRE, according to Benjamin Treynor Sloss, the founder of SRE at Google, "SRE is what happens when you ask a software engineer to design an operations team." The software engineers do not have expertise in regulatory IT compliance. This is the strength of ITIL, COBIT, and their practitioners.

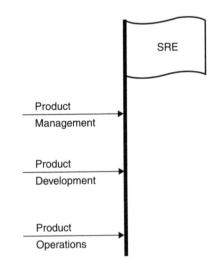

Figure 1.2 *Alignment using SRE*

Because SRE does not provide support for regulatory IT compliance, SRE on its own is not enough to govern the entire IT function of an enterprise. It follows that SRE may well be embedded in ITIL or COBIT implementations. This way, overarching regulatory IT compliance can be achieved using ITIL or COBIT while alignment of product operations, product development, and product management on operational concerns can be achieved using SRE. In other words, SRE does not need to be seen as mutually exclusive with ITIL or COBIT.

The comparison in this chapter showed that SRE is the best operations methodology for aligning the three parties of the product delivery organization—product operations, product development, and product management—to support operational concerns. This alignment is necessary for gaining a DevOps-like speed of delivery. With this key insight, there is a compelling story to tell when facilitating an SRE transformation. A shared understanding of why choosing SRE as the core operations methodology is going to be possible to bring about using the insight.

> **Key Insight:** SRE aligns product operations, product development, and product management on operational concerns.

The next question to explore is why does SRE actually work? What, at a fundamental level, makes the SRE methodology work? Why would it work at organizations other than Google?

1.3 Why Does SRE Work?

To understand why SRE works, we first need to explore how it works in a more detailed manner than before. The following process is at the core of SRE.

1. Define so-called service level objectives (SLOs) for services from the user point of view.

2. Measure in production the fulfillment of the SLOs by the services.

3. If SLOs get broken in production, work to bring the services back within the SLOs, or adjust them.

For example, imagine a service responsible for verifying user credentials. The service exposes some endpoints. The endpoints are used by the service users to get the user credentials verified. The availability of the service endpoints is highly critical. This is because no user can log on to the product if user credentials cannot be verified. Following this, the availability SLO needs to be rather high. For example, it can be set to 99.99% for all endpoints of the user credentials verification service. This means 99.99% of the calls to the endpoints within a given time frame need to succeed for the service to be within its availability SLO.

With the availability SLO definition done before the service is deployed to production, measurements of SLO fulfillment can start right after the service deployment to production. The measurements are supported by the SRE infrastructure that needs to be available. In addition to the measurements, the SRE infrastructure also alerts on SLO breaches.

On arrival of alerts, the SLO breaches are analyzed. On the one hand, if the SLO breaches uncover a real negative impact on users, the user verification service needs to be technically improved so that its endpoints can run within the defined availability SLO. A need to tighten the availability SLO may also be uncovered to get respective SLO breaches sooner in the future. On the other hand, if the SLO breaches only show some technical degradations without much of a negative impact on the user experience, the availability SLO needs to be relaxed.

At the meta level, the preceding process is about creating a hypothesis, testing it, learning from test results, and acting on the learnings. The hypothesis is the SLO definition. It is a conjecture about the minimal level of service required to make service users happy. The test of the hypothesis is done by the SRE infrastructure checking the fulfillment of the SLO and alerting on SLO breaches. The learning from the test results is the analysis of the reasons for SLO breaches to find out whether a real user experience impact occurred. The actions based on the learning are either technical service improvements to bring the service back within the SLO, or SLO relaxation to adjust the minimal level of service required to make the users happy. Additionally, tightening the SLO might be another action to perform.

This process is the exact method scientists have used for centuries to make scientific discoveries. According to Wikipedia, "The scientific method is an empirical method of acquiring knowledge that has characterized the development of science since at least the 17th century. It involves careful observation, applying rigorous skepticism about what is observed, given that cognitive assumptions can distort how one interprets the observation. It involves formulating hypotheses, via induction, based on such observations; experimental and measurement-based testing of deductions drawn from the hypotheses; and refinement (or elimination) of the hypotheses based on the experimental findings. These are principles of the scientific method, as distinguished from a definitive series of steps applicable to all scientific enterprises."[21]

At the heart of the scientific method is the process of defining the hypotheses, putting them to the test, learning from test results, and acting on them. It is a method that has stood the test of time. In fact, the scientific method itself works because it borrows directly from nature where feedback loops are used for auto-controlling entire populations of species with food chains.[22]

The scientific method is applied in all engineering industries. As suggested by the name Site Reliability Engineering, SRE is also an engineering discipline. As with all other engineering disciplines, the scientific method is also at the heart of SRE. Indeed, application of the scientific method in operations is the fundamental reason why SRE really works.

> **Key Insight:** SRE works because of application of the scientific method in operations.

The mechanics of applying the scientific method in software product operations is what makes SRE unique. Every engineering discipline applies the scientific method differently. SRE shows how it can be done in the context of software product operations.

---

21. Wikipedia. 2022. "Scientific Method." https://en.wikipedia.org/wiki/Scientific_method.

22. Neutel, Anje-Margriet. 2014. "Feedback Loops: How Nature Gets Its Rhythms." YouTube, August 25, 2014. https://www.youtube.com/watch?v=inVZoI1AkC8.

1.4 Summary

This chapter started with a question of why SRE would be the best methodology to adopt when it comes to software operations. To answer the question, we explored SRE in the context of other IT frameworks, such as ITIL and COBIT. It turned out that ITIL and COBIT have their strengths in the overarching design of the IT function in an enterprise.

A key insight from this chapter is that SRE is the best methodology for aligning the product delivery organization on operational concerns. It facilitates an appropriate involvement of product operations, product development, and product management in production operations. SRE being the force behind aligned product delivery organizations on operational concerns can be embedded in an ITIL or COBIT implementation for overall IT governance in the enterprise.

As the name Site Reliability Engineering suggests, SRE is an engineering discipline. Engineering disciplines apply the scientific method to problem-solving. So does SRE. It applies the scientific method to software product operations. This is why SRE actually works (and not because it works at Google). This is another key insight to be carried out organization-wide to reinforce the foundations of why it is a good idea to introduce SRE.

Having clarified why SRE actually works, the next very interesting topic to delve into is what and where is the challenge in SRE transformation. This is the subject of the next chapter.

Chapter 2

The Challenge

In Section 1.2, *Alignment Using SRE*, I presented an example of how a product delivery organization works without alignment on operational concerns. The example showed that without alignment, operational concerns are addressed only once production issues occur. This is done using ad hoc urgent meetings involving product operations, product development, and product management. The example is representative and can be generalized to better understand the challenge of SRE transformation.

A product delivery organization unaligned on operational concerns does not weave aspects of operations consistently and evenly throughout the product creation life cycle. Operational concerns are seen by most, as the name suggests, with production operations. Because product operations is the last part in the chain of product management, product development, and product operations, people think about operational concerns as the last thing on their to-do list. This is not a product-centric way of thinking. Users touch the product in production. Therefore, that touch point needs to be centric with all activities in the product creation life cycle. Indeed, product operations needs to be elevated and treated on par with user research, user story mapping, user experience design, architecture, and development.

The consequence of not thinking about production throughout the product creation life cycle can be illustrated using an example from the grocery industry. Imagine that a grocery store chain has a wide variety of products displayed in beautifully designed stores throughout the country, but neglects the checkout counters at the point of sale. The entire supply chain is working flawlessly, but issues arise at the checkout where the customers are trying to purchase their groceries: for example, they might not be able to pay for their groceries quickly, and the checkout queues might be getting longer. The checkout staff might not be able to resolve the issues themselves. The point-of-sale devices are supported by the operations team, which receives an enormous number of support requests. It turns out that the issues are with the software on the devices; the support team cannot resolve the software issues themselves.

While the crisis is unfolding, the developers are happily working on new features for the point-of-sale devices. The product owners are happily specifying additional new features to be handed over to the developers after they finish the current work. The operations engineers are reaching out to the developers, who are not sure whether to prioritize the requests by the operations engineers or the features in development. The developers reach out to the product owners for a prioritization decision. Finally, the operations engineers, developers, and product owners swarm over the problem and decide to fix the product issues with the highest priority.

2.1 Misalignment

Figure 2.1 illustrates the preceding example of how a product delivery organization misaligned on operational concerns works.

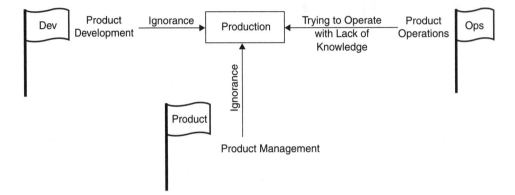

Figure 2.1 *Product delivery organization misaligned on operational concerns*

The left-hand side of the figure shows how product development is working on the feature backlog prioritized by product management. By and large, product development ignores what is going on in production. There is no ongoing visibility into how the system is performing in production. Nor have they set up any alerts to be notified about abnormal situations. Product development's focus is entirely on new feature development. Product operations is not part of their backlog.

Product operations is shown on the right-hand side of the figure. The product operations team is trying really hard to operate the product in production. However, they lack insider knowledge about the product in order to be able to operate it properly. This insider knowledge is with product development. Furthermore, this knowledge is changing quite rapidly with new releases being deployed to production on a frequent basis. Lacking insider knowledge about the product in operation, the operations team sets up alerts on technical resources that are visible outside. These are parameters such as memory consumption, CPU utilization, queue fill levels, disk storage fill levels, and network monitoring, among others. The parameters' thresholds are alerted upon. Once the alerts arrive, the operations team tries to understand whether there is anything wrong with the system. Often, they have to consult the product development team to analyze potential issues. The issue backlog is growing, which frustrates the product operations team. They do not understand product development's attitude toward solving issues in production. If production is where the customers use the product, how on earth can it be less important than anything else?

This frustration reflects a core issue in product delivery organizations that do not excel at operations. In such organizations, being product and user centric means different things to different parties. From a product operations point of view, it means production issues are tackled with the highest priority. From a product development point of view, it means features requested by product owners are developed as quickly as possible. From a product management point of view, it means user stories requested by customers are turned into features in production as quickly as possible. This fundamental misalignment of what it means to be product and user centric when approaching product creation is one of the core reasons for difficulties in operating the product in production to the customer's satisfaction. This is where SRE contributes greatly to aligning the parties in the product delivery organization.

The product management discipline is depicted toward the bottom of Figure 2.1. Product management is very far away from production thinking. In their view, it is a job for product operations to resolve. The product management team are busy talking to executives, stakeholders, customers, partners, and users, trying to figure out where the product fits in the market, identify missed user journeys, pinpoint ways to optimize workflows, and so on. Product management maintains a backlog of features to implement. Although the backlog is prioritized, as mentioned earlier, it doesn't consider product operations requirements. The product management team expects product development to develop and product operations to operate. This is what the names of the departments suggest, do they not?

In essence, the three parties in the product delivery organization operate under three different flags, as depicted in the figure. Product operations is proud to run under the Ops flag; they man production. Product development runs under the Dev flag; they are proud developers of new features. Product management runs under the Product flag; they are all about the product and shape it in a fundamental way: What is it? Who are the customers? What is the competition? What is the product's competitive advantage? What are the most important user journeys? What are the features? What is on the backlog?

It turns out that in a setup like this, no one really owns production operations. Who is it, indeed? Is it product operations? Not really, because they lack the knowledge necessary to truly own production operations. There is no proper continuous knowledge transfer from product development and product management toward product operations, and vice versa.

Is it product development? Certainly not. Their focus is the feature backlog. The feature backlog is void of product operations. Shipping occasional necessary production hotfixes after escalations from product operations is not what owning production operations actually means.

Is it product management? For sure it is not. Their focus is the definition of the product. Their expectation is that product development implements the product and product operations operates it in production. Despite the word *owner* in their title, the product owners do not own the product all the way to and including production.

In this context, it is no wonder that it is precisely in production that the product ends up being neglected. Where there is no ownership, there is no commitment. It would require commitment from all the parties in the product delivery organization to contribute to product operations in production. But how? Who would need to commit to what to establish a meaningful partial ownership of product operations? Would the ownership of product operations be a collective ownership, then? Let us explore these questions in detail.

2.2 Collective Ownership

According to Wikipedia, "collective ownership is the ownership of means of production by all members of a group for the benefit of all its members."[1] The definition shows that everyone needs to benefit from the ownership. In the context of product operations, it means that if collective ownership is to be established in a product delivery organization, the ownership needs to

1. Wikipedia. 2021. "Collective ownership." https://en.wikipedia.org/wiki/Collective_ownership.

benefit all the parties involved. Specifically, if collective ownership of production operations is to be established among product operations, product development, and product management, each party needs to benefit from it.

This is an interesting point to delve into. In the product operations team's view, they own product operations. However, they encounter great difficulties engaging the product development and product management teams in their operations activities. Therefore, product operations will welcome it if the product development and product management teams take partial ownership of production operations.

In the product development team's view, they are feature developers. Shipping new features to production quickly is at the core of their activities. What kind of benefit would they gain if they were to own production operations in some partial manner? What would it look like? Would the backlog contain operational user stories? This is not really feasible, as the operations work is not predictable compared to feature work that can be planned using a feature backlog. What would be beneficial is if the partial ownership of production operations led to insights that would lead to an improved development process augmented by a full operational context. In turn, it would be beneficial if the improved development process led to the reduction of production issues that interrupt feature work.

In the product management team's view, they define the product. The features should be developed by the product development team and operated by the product operations team. What would be the benefit for product management to own production operations in a partial way? To answer this question, customer escalations need to be looked at. Product management particularly dislike customer escalations. Customer escalations disrupt their work, require immediate focus, take a lot of time to justify the product to various stakeholders despite customer dissatisfaction, and chip away the stakeholders' trust. Diminishing stakeholder trust might lead to budget reductions for the product. This is a difficult situation every product owner works to avoid. To be sure, every customer escalation is about an issue in production. So, if the partial ownership of production operations would lead to a reduction of customer escalations, it would be a great and welcomed benefit for product management.

Table 2.1 shows the benefits each party would see in a product delivery organization if a collective ownership of product operations were established.

Table 2.1 *Benefits of Collective Ownership of Production Operations*

	Discipline	Benefit
Collective ownership of production operations	Product operations	Appropriate engagement of product development and product management in operations activities as needed. No more chasing product development and product management on every production issue to decide how to proceed.
	Product development	Appropriate insight in product operations to get to an improved feature development process augmented by the full operational context. Feature development performed with the full context of what is necessary to make the features technically successful in production leads to a reduction of customer escalations. This leads to more uninterrupted time for working on new features.
	Product management	Reduction of customer escalations and time investment to handle them.

Having clarified the benefits a collective ownership of production operations may bring to product operations, product development, and product management, the next question to explore is how to get the benefits. An associated question would be the cost of getting the benefits for each party involved. In other words, in the context of an SRE transformation, how do you implement collective ownership of production operations using SRE with a positive cost–benefit ratio?

2.3 Ownership Using SRE

What does it mean to have partial ownership of production operations using SRE? This question needs to be answered specifically for each party in the product delivery organization.

2.3.1 Product Development

In product development, the benefits of partially owning production operations are rooted in the insights of how the system behaves in production under real user, data, and infrastructure load. The most effective way to continuously learn about a system in production is to observe it in production. This is done using on-call rotations. Traditionally, product operations would go on call for services in production. This way, production insights do not go directly to product development. It follows that product development needs to get involved in on-call rotations for their services in production. Each development team owns some services. For exactly those services, the respective developers would need to be involved in on-call rotations to gain insights from operating the services under real conditions. These insights lead to the following improvements in product development and operations.

- Developers with product implementation knowledge conduct product failure investigations.

- The number of steps in the chain between a production issue occurring and a person with the best knowledge to fix it can be exactly one. The issue can go directly to the developer who implemented the service and can fix it the fastest, provided the alerting is targeted well and there is an agreement with the product owner to fix production issues immediately. The developer can take the learnings from the failure itself, the failure analysis, and the fix into the new-feature development process, supporting infrastructure and debugging tools. This should lead to the product being more operable in the future with less time required to operate it. In turn, it should lead to more time for feature development.

- Developers get to experience the quality of the product in the real world by testing it at production sites. Internal testing is rarely as intensive as the strain a system undergoes in production. Seeing real-world scenarios informs the development of automated test suites and contributes greatly to closing the gap between the internal testing and production scenarios. Thus, confidence is increased in deploying the product to production once the test results from the internal test suites are green. This should lead to fewer failures in production due to scenarios that were untested internally. In turn, it should require less time to fix production issues, leading to more time for feature development.

- Developers gain the knowledge necessary to operate and troubleshoot the product. This informs the development process, among other things, leading to better tools for operations. In turn, it leads to less time spent on troubleshooting production issues, which frees up more time for feature development.

- Developers use the knowledge from product operations in the development of new features. For example, scalability and performance requirements can be learned, and this can often lead to architecture changes. Although making such changes requires a significant amount of work, it is necessary to implement resilience in accordance with the load profiles seen in production. Only then can the system's operational burden (also known as *toil*) reduce, freeing time for more feature development.

- Developers gain a better understanding of the kind of testing and tooling necessary to deliver a product that works well. Test scenarios, test levels, test runs, and test environments need to be designed in such a way that all the testing activities combined address important scenarios the system encounters in production. To be sure, production itself can be one of the test environments with tests running there 24/7. Gaining insight into product operations in production can greatly inform the entire test management process. This should lead to test suites and test runs being more focused on the scenarios taking place in production, which can reduce the amount of time spent on tests that are not effective in catching bugs encountered in production, as well as the rework and maintenance of such tests. Streamlining test management may lead to more time available for feature development.

- Developers have the incentive to implement reliability features and tools for a great product operations experience. This is because if the developers go on call, they actually want to spend as little time as possible dealing with production issues. In this context, they have full control of the situation. It is in their power to implement the product with production operations in mind. Doing this leads to spending as little time as possible on production issues and maximizing the time spent on feature development. This benefits customers and product management alike. Customers also do not want to deal with product failures in production. Rather, they want existing features to work in production and new features added to the product quickly. The product management team, driven by customer requests, wants product development to work on new features.

- Developers with experience in product operations are more highly valued in the industry. Going on call directly contributes to learning the skills necessary to command higher wages in the marketplace.

The idea of going on call for the developers gives rise to a plethora of questions, such as the following.

- Do the developers always need to go on call for their services? No.
- Could the developers go on call only during business hours? Yes.
- Can the on-call responsibility be shared with product operations? Yes.

- What is the best setup for a given organization? It depends.

- Would a development team setup need to be adapted to enable on call? Yes.

- Can developers in a team perform the on-call duties on rotation? Yes.

- Can focused feature development still be done despite going on call? Yes.

- How do you achieve it? It depends.

- Can developers stay developers if they go on call? Yes. They will become better developers. Their skills will be more highly valued in the job market.

These and other related questions will be explored in the book in due course. It is not necessary to answer them in-depth here. For now, I will only outline the scope of the challenge posed by the SRE transformation. What is important to understand at this point is that product development needs to go on call to one extent or another depending on the organizational setup chosen for the organization's SRE implementation.

Without developers going on call to some extent, the benefits of collective ownership of production operations cannot be realized by product development. Feature development is difficult to improve from an operational standpoint without a live feedback loop between the production and development teams. An outage profile in production cannot be sustainably influenced if the feature development team is not well informed using the live feedback loop from production experienced by those who implement the features. In other words, without developers going on call to some extent, things in product development remain the same by and large as far as operational concerns go.

> **Key Insight:** Developers must go on call for some percentage of their time. This can range from very little time to nearly full time.

This key insight is illustrated on the left-hand side of Figure 2.2.

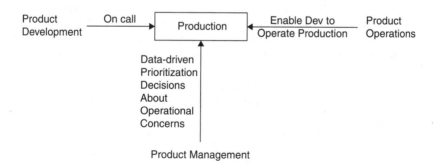

Figure 2.2 *Collective ownership of product operations using SRE*

2.3.2 Product Operations

The product operations discipline is depicted on the right-hand side of Figure 2.2. With developers going on call, the product operations team would need to provide support to enable the developers to do operations.

What kind of support would the developers need? They may never have done operations before, in which case this will be unfamiliar turf for them. Are there trainings for this? Does the operations team provide some onboarding? What does "good" look like in product operations? Is there any documentation available? These are the questions that come to mind for developers when confronted with going on call for the first time.

The entire body of knowledge about product operations is with the operations team. But what kind of knowledge is that? Mostly it is about taking the product as a black box, putting it into the production environment, activating monitoring of IT resources, and alerting on some threshold violations. Developers can learn and understand this. With their insider knowledge of the product, they will also be able to find many more scenarios that can be monitored and alerted upon. The developers' knowledge about the architecture, implementation, configuration, and deployment of the product is an invaluable resource for improving monitoring of the product in production. But how can they utilize that knowledge to improve product operations? How can they bridge the gap between development and operations as suggested by the term *DevOps*?

Let us look more closely at what the developers know. They know how specific routines that contribute to the fulfillment of user requests are implemented. They know the paths the user requests go all the way from the user interface to the deepest service in the service network, and from there to the infrastructure. If the product exposes APIs to customers, the developers also know the paths the API requests take from the API gateway through the network of services all the way down to the infrastructure. Moreover, the developers know which services they implemented versus those implemented by the company and third parties. They know which third-party services are difficult to integrate with, where the domain model of the third-party services is overly complicated and cluttered, where the third-party services are slow occasionally, and where there is simply sporadic behavior that can be explained. The developers also know all this for the internal services of the company, which are the services they depend upon.

Their knowledge does not stop there. The developers and architects know the strengths and weaknesses of their architecture. They know where the architecture limitations lead to performance and scalability issues. They know the circumstances where the performance and scalability issues are likely to exhibit and probably impact the customer. They know the architectural debt in the system and which part of it is planned to be paid off in the near future. They know of any major architectural refactorings that must take place, which are not planned due to the size of the effort involved.

The developers' knowledge goes much further. They know about the infrastructure limitations the product is running on. They know how each service can impact the others; for example, they know what will happen if a particular service in the service network eats up the lion's share of memory in a given area of the infrastructure. They might know some parameters of the container clusters the services are running in and anticipate issues that might occur based on the changing data and user load profiles.

There is yet more to the developers' knowledge. They may know the way the services are deployed: Which infrastructure parameters are set by the deployment infrastructure, and which ones are set in the service at the deployment time, startup time, or runtime. They know which services are deployed independently, which ones use a shared deployment pipeline, and which ones are deployed manually for the time being. They may know the tests running on the deployment pipelines, the quality of those tests, and whether the test results can be trusted. They may know the test management process for a service, the test levels available, the test infrastructure, and any test gaps that exist.

Additionally, the developers might be aware of security implications in the architecture and implementation. Which security vulnerabilities are taken care of? Which are mitigated? Which are known but are not currently taken care of ? Which bugs from penetration testing were not yet fixed?

Finally, the developers know the most painful product areas from a development point of view. What area is the most difficult to integrate with? To test? To speed up? To debug?

This amount of knowledge is staggering to the operations engineers. How do they take all this knowledge from the developers and apply it to product operations? Can it be done with some tool support? What kind of role would automation play here? Does it all sit between the ears of the software developers and cannot be easily repurposed to improve product operations? How can it support the developers effectively?

In other words, the developers know the car engine from the inside. But how do you help them use that knowledge to improve how the car operates?

To approach these questions, we need to turn our attention to how developers make known to the outside world what is going on with the system on the inside. This is done using logging. During development, developers decide what to log and under what circumstances. This way, once the product runs in production, log entries are generated that contain logging information. The log entries stored in, for example, log files or other storage systems can then be analyzed to understand what was going on in the system at runtime. This is the basic process of how developers make known to the outside world what is going on inside a system at runtime. The process is sophisticatedly supported by tools providing all sorts of runtime instrumentation out of the box. That is, the developers' knowledge about the product can be encoded in logs that can be analyzed outside the system.

The next question to ask is what should be logged to improve product operations? Let us imagine, these questions would be answered.

Once that question is answered, we would consider how to log relevant information in a uniform way. What should be the log format? Which log format would lend itself to automated log processing? Would several log formats be required for different operational aspects; for example, one log format for calculating service availability and another for calculating service latency? What about asynchronous operations—how do you log those? Where do you store the logs? Should the logs be stored in regional data centers or centrally? How long should the logs be stored? Let us imagine, also these questions would be answered.

With the answers to these questions, we would next consider how to detect abnormal situations. What should be considered broken availability? What should be considered broken latency? What should be considered insufficient throughput? Which aspects beyond availability, latency, and throughput are important to consider? Let us imagine, these questions would be answered too.

Next, we would want to know how to alert in abnormal situations. Should alerts be generated as soon as the abnormal situation has been detected, or a bit later? Should the alerts be sampled? How do you avoid alert fatigue, in which those who receive the alerts become overwhelmed with too many alerts and stop reacting to them? How do you strike a good balance between alerting people so often that it causes alert fatigue and so rarely that it causes incidents to go unnoticed? What kind of information needs to be included in the alert? Even if these questions would also be answered, there would be more.

The next questions would be about whom to alert—specifically, which developers receive the alert? How do you alert developers in such a way that they do not get distracted from their feature development work? How do you alert developers in such a way that they will actually react to the alerts, provided the alerting does not lead to alert fatigue? Can any developer in general be alerted? What kind of knowledge would a developer need to have to be able to react to alerts within a reasonable time frame and with reasonable effort?

The list of questions can go on. What it shows is that a comprehensive framework that would enable developers to conduct product operations is required. But what is a framework? According to Wikipedia, "a software framework is an abstraction in which software providing generic functionality can be selectively changed by additional user-written code, thus providing application-specific software."[2] So, what is needed in the context of an operational framework is some generic functionality that can selectively be changed. In the context of SRE, a framework like that can be referred to as SRE infrastructure. It needs to provide generic functionality supporting the use cases exemplarily outlined previously, implemented within an SRE context. The generic functionality needs to be selectively changeable to adapt the infrastructure to a specific use within the overall set of SRE activities.

> **Key Insight:** Operations engineers need to provide frameworks to enable developers to do service operations. In an SRE context, such a framework can be referred to as SRE infrastructure.

At the time of this writing, some off-the-shelf tool support for the SRE infrastructure exists, but it is not comprehensive enough to eliminate the need for custom development of missing pieces. Therefore, in all likelihood, building an SRE infrastructure is going to require some custom software development combined with ready-to-use off-the-shelf tools. This means product operations would need to learn to do software development.

The challenge for product operations is lack of experience providing frameworks that enable others to do operations work. The product operations has always conducted operations work in a hands-on manner using existing tools. What is required from product operations now is the enablement of product development to perform service operations. The enablement is done using the envisioned SRE infrastructure. The SRE infrastructure needs to be built using first-class software development techniques.

This is in line with SRE and the words of Benjamin Treynor Sloss: "SRE is what happens when you ask a software engineer to design an operations team." Following this, it should be no surprise that enabling the product development team to do operations work requires the

---

2. Wikipedia. 2022. "Software framework." https://en.wikipedia.org/wiki/Software_framework.

software development team to build a suitable SRE infrastructure. Building frameworks is common in software development. Using frameworks is familiar to software developers. Neither of these will be familiar turf for operations engineers from the product operations discipline.

The following now unfolds as a challenge in SRE transformation.

- Software developers need to learn how to do product operations work by going on call.
- Operations engineers need to learn how to enable software developers to do operations work by developing the SRE infrastructure as a framework.

This is illustrated in Figure 2.3. The two arrows resemble the moves from fencing. It might sound ironic, but this is exactly what needs to happen during SRE transformation.

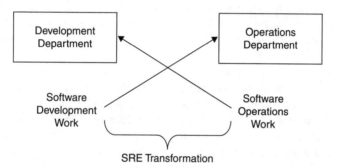

Figure 2.3 *Key SRE transformation challenge*

Neither of those arrows is easy to achieve. However, as evidenced by the growing number of software delivery organizations around the world, it is entirely possible, and will be explored at length in this book.

Figure 2.3 shows what it truly means and takes to implement DevOps. It is about developers doing operations work and operations engineers doing development work. It goes to the heart of both long-standing disciplines, product development and product operations, and shakes their fundamental responsibilities. Truly implementing DevOps takes far more than just achieving good collaboration between product development and product operations.

The difficulties are especially great in traditional software delivery organizations. A development organization that has never done operations and an operations organization that has never enabled others to do operations lack the very foundations on which SRE can be established. Developers do not understand why they should be doing operations. Operations engineers do not provide frameworks to enable developers to do operations. Managers do not promote the endeavor, let alone fund it.

Despite these difficulties, it is well worth the effort to embark on an SRE transformation. The kind of DevOps implementation that can be achieved using SRE is where developers maximize their feature development time while having evidence that the product works well for customers in production. Without SRE, developers maximize their feature development time, ignoring production.

Further, in a DevOps implementation using SRE, operations engineers scale well by providing the SRE infrastructure to the developers, which enables them to do production operations.

Without SRE, the operations engineers are the bottlenecks. They do production operations purely by themselves, regardless of the product quality and insider knowledge available about the product.

2.3.3 Product Management

Having clarified what collective ownership of production operations means for product development and product operations, it is time for such a clarification in the context of product management. What does the product management team need to do to partially own product operations?

Traditionally, product management is pretty far away from product operations. As discussed in Section 2.2, *Collective Ownership*, product management's benefit in getting involved in production operations is to reduce customer escalations. How on earth can product management reduce customer escalations if everything the customers escalate about is a technically broken product? Product owners are not technical experts. They neither implemented nor deployed the product.

To approach this, let us explore what leads to customer escalations. Before a customer gets to the point of picking up the phone and calling customer support to complain, a series of events take place. The customer works with the product and notices something annoying. It might be a sluggish display of data; an inconvenient way of accomplishing a task in too many back-and-forth steps; an action taken, like a button click, that does not result in the action actually performed; or a downright crash with accompanying data loss. Whatever the reason, it is directly linked to the customer having lost so much time or money that they call customer support to release their anger and get help.

Now, could the technical experts—namely, the product development or product operations team—have noticed anything wrong with the product and fixed it earlier? Are product development and product operations set up for such incident detection and resolution? Again, this is technical, so what does it have to do with product management?

Let us dive deeper. Imagine that product development and product operations want to set up incident detection and resolution to detect and fix abnormal situations before customers escalate. How would they go about doing this?

As you saw in Section 2.3.1, *Product Development*, the developers have an enormous amount of knowledge about all sorts of technical aspects regarding the product. The operations engineers have vast experience with customer escalations. They remember a lot of past escalations by heart. They can cluster them. They know by means of anticipation the weak areas of the product that are going to be escalated about soon because product development has not started fixing them. Overall, this is a good mix of knowledge that is brought to the table by product development and product operations. The product development team brings knowledge of technical implementation while the product operations team brings knowledge of the actual issues from production. Taken together, this knowledge can be used to create an incident detection and resolution process rooted in technical implementation and past customer escalations. This is great. It would be a huge leap from ad hoc, unsystematic incident response. It would reduce customer escalations.

The goal, however, is to aim higher. The goal is to create an incident response and resolution process that for every existing and new feature would detect abnormal situations early enough for product development to fix and then to deploy the fixes before customers escalate. This would be a real benefit to product management. To emphasize, the process should work for every existing and new feature, not just for features known to product operations based on the experience of past customer escalations. Also, to emphasize, the developers would allocate their time in such a way that they fix detected issues and deploy the fixes to production before the customers get angry enough to escalate. This means the developers would not just work on the feature backlog prioritized by the product owners. The other prioritization driver would be the product reliability issues detected by the incident response process.

With that, the contribution of product management to the collective ownership of product operations is starting to emerge.

1. Product owners would need to contribute user journey knowledge to the incident detection process. Impaired and broken user journeys should be at the core of incident detection. Which user journeys are the most important ones to detect incidents with? What are the most important steps within a given user journey that must work for the user journey to still make sense? Conversely, which steps of a user journey could fail, and how badly, without rendering the entire user journey broken? Overall, the incident detection process is as good as the defined incidents it can detect. To define detectable incidents well, the user journey knowledge of the product owners, the implementation knowledge of the developers, and the operations knowledge of the operations engineers need to be combined.

2. Product owners would need to understand and agree to the importance of setting up a backlog management procedure in which developers can flexibly allocate time to fix production issues as they are detected by the incident detection process. Traditionally, the product owners prioritize the backlog of user stories, and they want developers to focus on the backlog. To reduce customer escalations, the product owners would want the developers to take immediate action on the issues reported by incident detection.

This now makes sense to the product owners. They were part of and shaped the incident detection definition. They know what the incident detection is going to detect. It is going to detect real broken user journeys and not merely some technical deviations. Now it is easier for the product owners to accept the engineering time being spent on incident resolution. Why? Because spending that time directly contributes to the reduction of customer escalations. If developers do not fix the incidents in production within a reasonable time frame, the customers will still escalate despite the right incidents being detected early enough.

That is, to reduce customer escalations, the following criteria need to be fulfilled.

- The incident detection detects broken and impaired user journeys as defined together by the operations engineers, developers, and product owners.

- The developers prioritize fixing broken and impaired user journeys as they are detected without having to negotiate with product owners every time about the engineering time allocation.

- The developers fix the broken and impaired user journeys in production within a specified time frame before customers get angry and frustrated enough to escalate.

This process is shown in Figure 2.4.

The top left of Figure 2.4 shows the incident detection definition process. It takes as input the implementation knowledge by developers, the operations knowledge by operations engineers, and the user journey knowledge by product owners. The outcome of the incident detection definition process is an understanding of the incidents to detect in production. It is about detection of unhealthy patterns in

- The user journeys from an operational criticality perspective
- The critical service dependencies fulfilling the user journeys
- The critical infrastructure components and their scaling, fulfilling the user journeys

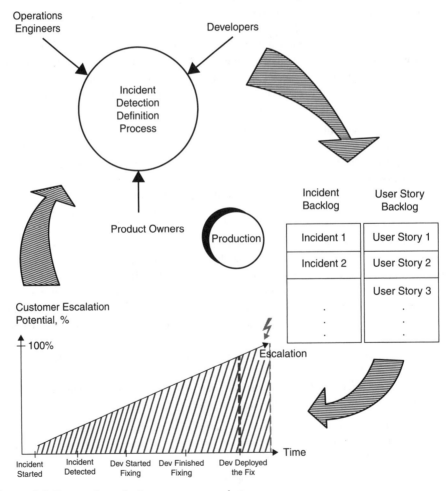

Figure 2.4 *Process for reducing customer escalations*

With the definition of what to look for in production to detect incidents, incident detection can be switched on. The production environment in the middle of Figure 2.4 can now run under monitoring for fulfillment of real user journeys, instead of having monitoring for fulfillment of technical parameters. Monitoring for fulfillment of real user journeys is more targeted to reduce customer escalations, which is product management's benefit in terms of getting involved in product operations.

Once the incident detection process has detected some incidents, it will put them into a backlog. This is shown on the right-hand side of Figure 2.4. The incident backlog exists side by side with the user story backlog. The user story backlog is prioritized by the product owner. The incident backlog also needs prioritization. This prioritization needs to be done as a just-in-time process while the incidents get detected. It also needs to be done very quickly. Lengthy negotiations between the operations engineers, developers, and product owners cannot take place to efficiently prioritize the incident backlog. This means prior agreements among the three parties need to be reached. A good place for timely incident prioritization agreements is the incident detection definition process itself. As part of the process, not only are the incidents defined but also their relative priority can be agreed. These agreements should enable all the people on call, and especially the developers, to make autonomous incident prioritization decisions for a majority of the incidents.

Because the incidents from the incident backlog need to be worked on in a just-in-time manner, the developers working on the incidents cannot work on the user stories from the user story backlog at the same time. Also, just-in-time switching between the incident backlog and the user story backlog leads to a great context switching overhead. Not only is this inefficient, it also places a significant mental burden on the developers. To counter this, there are strategies to setting up development teams in such a way that the ongoing on-call work from the incident backlog and the focused user story work from the user story backlog are well balanced. These strategies will be explored later.

The bottom of Figure 2.4 shows the incident processing timeline. It begins with an incident, shown on the far left. At the time of the incident, the potential for customer escalation is very low. It grows to 100% over time, which is the point to avoid. The goal is to fix the incident before the customer gets angry and frustrated enough to call customer support with an escalation.

After the incident started, it can be detected by incident detection. The next step on the timeline is the point in time when the developer starts working on the fix. Once the issue has been fixed, it needs to be deployed to production. Once it is deployed, the fix needs to be monitored to ensure that the incident has truly been resolved. The goal is to perform the fix deployment and associated monitoring, confirming the incident resolution before the red line of customer escalation.

The incidents that have started may go unnoticed, or be noticed too late or too early by incident detection. Conversely, the incidents may represent false positives. This happens when an incident is reported that does not lead to deterioration in the user experience. All these cases need to serve as input for adjusting the incident detection definition. This is an important part of the overall process. It enables the incident definition adjustments to be done regularly based on the real feedback loop from production. The feedback loop is data driven. This enables the three parties—product operations, product development, and product management—to decide on the incident definitions in an opinion-neutral, data-driven way.

In the context of SRE, such an incident detection and response process is set up using specific mechanisms and terms, such as service level indicators (SLIs), service level objectives (SLOs), and error budget policies. Soon, an exploration of these concepts will begin. Before this exploration, let us summarize the benefits and costs of the collective production operations ownership using SRE.

2.3.4 Benefits and Costs

The analysis in the previous chapter showed what it would take for product operations, product development, and product management to truly work together as a team using SRE methodology. It showed the deep integration among the three parties necessary to implement DevOps using SRE. It takes much more than only a good collaboration among the three parties. Table 2.2 juxtaposes the benefits and costs.

Table 2.2 *Benefits and Costs of Collective Ownership of Production Operations Using SRE*

	Discipline	Benefit	Cost
Collective ownership of production operations using SRE	Product operations	Appropriate engagement of product development and product management in operations activities as needed. No more chasing product development and product management on every production issue to decide how to proceed.	Enabling others to do operations by implementing SRE infrastructure as a framework.
	Product development	Appropriate insight in production operations to get to an improved feature development process augmented by the full operational context. Feature development performed with the full context of what is necessary to make the features technically successful in production leads to a reduction in customer escalations. This leads to more uninterrupted time for working on new features. Additionally, there is a developer skill upgrade valued by the job market.	Doing product operations by being on call during defined times.
	Product management	Reduction of customer escalations and time investment to handle them. Ad hoc involvement in numerous production issues is also reduced, and there is an added ability to make decisions in a data-driven manner about engineering capacity allocation to features versus operational concerns.	Involvement in the incident detection definitions and data-driven prioritization decision-making based on production data.

Now that the benefits and costs of the common ownership of production operations using SRE are clear, let us take a look at the overall picture of what SRE is trying to achieve (Figure 2.5).

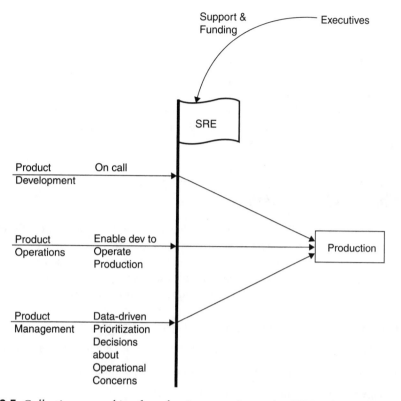

Figure 2.5 *Collective ownership of production operations using SRE*

SRE aligns the product delivery organization on operational concerns under its flag. Product development contributes to production operations by going on call to get firsthand experience with how the product meets customer demands in production. This experience is fed into the new feature and infrastructure development. The result is a maximization of feature development time while ensuring that the product meets customer demands in production.

Product operations makes a contribution by enabling developers to do production operations themselves. This is done through development of the SRE infrastructure as a framework to be used by the developers.

Product management contributes by making data-driven prioritization decisions about the most important user journeys for which the incidents need to be detected. Further, the contribution is in agreements with the autonomous incident backlog prioritization by the people on call. Additionally, the contribution is to be aligned with the data-driven prioritization decisions about reliability enablers to be included in the user story backlog.

The SRE transformation does not come for free. An investment in time, money, and effort is required to align the product delivery organization on operational concerns using SRE. That is why the executives need to also get involved. The executives can contribute twofold to the SRE transformation. First, they need to support the topic. This can be done in all-hands meetings, smaller conversations, and one-on-one discussions. Executive communication regarding

SRE needs to clarify to everyone in the organization that the topic has executive support. This goes a long way toward creating alignment behind SRE at every level of the product delivery organization.

Moreover, the SRE transformation requires some slight investments in tooling and infrastructure. Although they are small scale, these investments need to be done in a timely manner so as not to impede the speed of transformation. In a large enterprise, it could take a significant amount of time to place orders due to supplier selection and data protection processes. Still, it is worth the effort. Voting with one's wallet is a good way for executives to underpin the verbal message of endorsing the SRE transformation.

2.4 The Challenge Statement

With an in-depth understanding of what to strive for during SRE transformation, the challenge statement can be concisely presented. Following is what the challenge is about.

SRE is an operations methodology that aligns the product delivery organization on operational concerns. The key challenge in traditional software delivery organizations is the misalignment on production operations. In such organizations, the following is true.

- Developers do not know why they should be doing operations.
- Operations engineers do not know why developers are not interested in operations.
- Product managers think operations work is done by operations engineers.
- Management does not promote and fund the topic.

In such a software delivery organization, there are no solid foundations on top of which SRE can be built as a practice. The foundations need to be put in place first. This will be a major part of the SRE transformation. The transformation will need to shift stakeholders' mindsets in the following ways.

- Developers should want to be involved in on-call processes to gain enough current operational knowledge to develop features that work well in production.
- Operations engineers should want to enable developers to perform service operations by providing the SRE infrastructure as a framework in order to distribute the operational work throughout the product delivery organization in an optimal way.
- Product managers should want to be involved in operations to help reduce customer escalations by making decisions based on production data. The decisions are about the prioritization of user journeys for which the incidents need to be detected, agreements on incident backlog handling, and prioritization of reliability features.
- Executives should want to enable effective and efficient product operations by promoting SRE and providing appropriate funding in a timely fashion.

Each party in the software delivery organization benefits from SRE. The benefits make it worth undergoing the SRE transformation. The benefits can be used as a beacon to aspire for, unleashing fun on the SRE transformation journey. This book will take you on the journey of transforming a software delivery organization bit by bit into one that does operations the SRE way and enjoys doing so. To get started, in the next section let us look at the general way the SRE transformation can be executed.

2.5 Coaching

A product delivery organization consists of many people who are organized in teams. The SRE transformation process has a clear goal to establish SRE as the central methodology for production operations in the teams. However, running the SRE transformation is not like running a project with predefined milestones to be tracked. Rather, the SRE transformation process is a network of induced changes and feedback on the changes cast in parallel at different teams and individuals. Many teams will be transforming at the same time, but the changes and feedback loops will be unique per team and individual. This is illustrated in Figure 2.6.

Now, how do you set up the SRE transformation process in the way shown in Figure 2.6?

One way to run the SRE transformation is by means of coaching. According to Wikipedia, "coaching is a form of development in which an experienced person, called a coach, supports a learner or client in achieving a specific personal or professional goal by providing training and

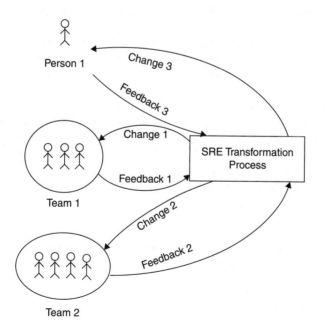

Figure 2.6 *SRE transformation process*

guidance."[3] It follows that coaching works with people and teams on an individual basis. This is the kind of approach needed for being empathetic and structured at the same time when running the transformation.

What makes coaching particularly interesting in the context of the SRE transformation is that it already exists as a discipline at both the organizational and team levels. According to the Institute of Coaching, "Organizational coaching aims at fostering positive, systemic transformation within organizations."[4] Within the broad theme of coaching, organizational coaching is a well-established discipline.

Team coaching, on the other hand, is a more recent and less structured discipline. It gained significance in the past decade. According to TPC Leadership, "team coaching is the art of facilitating and challenging a real team to maximize its performance and enjoyment in service of meaningful organizational goals."[5]

That is, coaching as a discipline with distinct subdomains of organizational coaching and team coaching is going to be a suitable approach for running the SRE transformation. Both types of coaching would be applied simultaneously and would work in tandem. However, when choosing organizational and team coaching as a methodology to run the SRE transformation, the question is, who would do the coaching? Who can act as a coach if the organization is new to SRE? Would external coaches be required? Would it be possible to develop internal coaches? If so, who would develop the internal coaches? Different approaches are possible here.

External coaches can be valuable to bring a fresh experience-based SRE perspective to an organization and quickly establish an understanding of SRE basics across the board. However, SRE coaches with experience doing successful SRE transformations are really difficult to find in the industry. This is because the first original SRE book by Google, *Site Reliability Engineering: How Google Runs Production Systems,* was only published in 2016.[6] Given that SRE transformations are taking several years to achieve in larger organizations, the pool of available coaches is going to be rather small.

Another aspect is that precisely because an SRE transformation takes several years to run in a larger organization, employing external coaches for the transformation time frame is hardly a financially viable option. It follows that coaches for SRE transformation need to be found and grown internally.

Which options would the coaches have to learn about SRE and bring themselves to a level that is necessary to coach others? Both the aforementioned Google book *Site Reliability Engineering* and Google's *The Site Reliability Workbook: Practical Ways to Implement SRE*[7] are a great and necessary starting point. These books will show potential coaches what needs to be done to achieve SRE with the sophistication and scale of Google. Additional books by former Googlers—*Implementing Service Level Objectives: A Practical Guide to*

3. Wikipedia. 2021. "Coaching." https://en.wikipedia.org/wiki/Coaching.

4. David, Susan. 2015. "Introduction to Organizational Coaching." Institute of Coaching, January 13, 2015. https://instituteofcoaching.org/resources/introduction-organizational-coaching.

5. Cardillo, Andrea. 2019. "How Is Team Coaching Different from Group Coaching?" TPC Leadership, July 10, 2019. https://tpcleadership.com/how-is-team-coaching-different-from-group-coaching.

6. Murphy, Niall Richard, Betsy Beyer, Chris Jones, and Jennifer Petoff. 2016. *Site Reliability Engineering: How Google Runs Production Systems.* Sebastopol, CA: O'Reilly Media.

7. Beyer, Betsy, Niall Richard Murphy, David K. Rensin, Stephen Thorne, and Kent Kawahara. 2018. *The Site Reliability Workbook: Practical Ways to Implement SRE.* Sebastopol, CA: O'Reilly Media.

SLIs, SLOs, and Error Budgets[8] and *Real-World SRE: The Survival Guide for Responding to a System Outage and Maximizing Uptime*[9]—provide additional in-depth experience perspectives on SRE.

It is our aspiration that this book in particular will show potential coaches how SRE can be put in place in an organization that has never done operations the SRE way before. Further, the coaches can network with others at relevant conferences and industry events. Two conferences can be of special interest: SRECon[10] by USENIX and the DevOps Enterprise Summit[11] by IT Revolution. These conferences can be a great place to develop relationships with others practicing SRE or running SRE transformations. These relationships might lead to opportunities to visit other companies that are further along in the SRE journey. Seeing is believing, and seeing another company running the SRE process in a sophisticated manner can significantly boost one's own transformation.

Finally, the coaches can learn while running the SRE transformation in their own organization. In a larger organization, teams will inevitably adopt SRE at different speeds. Taking the learnings from the teams that lead the SRE transformation and transporting them to the teams catching up is a very valuable part of coaching. It enables the coach to gain experience and the teams to learn from each other.

> **From the Trenches:** Long-lasting team-based coaching[12] that includes all team members—product owners, architects, developers, operations engineers and, at times, designers—is the most effective way to run the SRE transformation at the team level.

2.6 Summary

Introducing SRE requires changes in product operations, product development, and product management. The biggest change in product operations is the development of the SRE infrastructure as a framework that enables developers to go on call and operate their services in production. The biggest change in product development is to actually get involved in on call and operate the services developed in a real production environment. The delineation of how much developers are on call compared to how much operations are on call will vary by organization.

The challenge of the SRE transformation is that in a traditional software delivery organization, the product operations team has never provided frameworks enabling others to do operations work. Likewise, product development has never done operations work. Thus, there is

8. Hidalgo, Alex. 2020. *Implementing Service Level Objectives: A Practical Guide to SLIs, SLOs & Error Budgets*. Sebastopol, CA: O'Reilly Media.

9. Welch, Nat. 2018. *Real-World SRE: The Survival Guide for Responding to a System Outage and Maximizing Uptime*. Birmingham, UK: Packt Publishing Ltd.

10. "SRECon." 2017. USENIX. August 25, 2017. https://www.usenix.org/srecon.

11. IT Revolution Events. n.d. "DevOps Enterprise Summit 2022." Accessed January 12, 2022. https://events.itrevolution.com.

12. Guendisch, Philipp, and Vladyslav Ukis. 2022. "Employing Agile Coaching to Establish SRE in an Organization." *InfoQ*, August 23, 2022. https://www.infoq.com/articles/establish-SRE-coaching.

a lack of foundation on which SRE can be established. Developers do not understand why they should be doing operations. Operations engineers do not provide frameworks to enable developers to do operations. Managers do not promote the topic, let alone fund it. To drive the SRE transformation throughout the organization, SRE coaches need to be developed and designated.

In the next chapters, the journey of transforming a software delivery organization toward SRE will unfold. To get started, we will learn the basic SRE concepts in the next chapter.

Chapter 3

SRE Basic Concepts

The basic concepts of SRE are not numerous and not difficult to explain, which makes this a good starting point for our SRE transformation journey. The concepts are service level indicators, service level objectives, error budgets, and error budget policies. We touched upon them briefly in Chapter 1 and Chapter 2. In this chapter, we will explore them in more detail.

3.1 Service Level Indicators

Service level indicators (SLIs) are a foundational concept in SRE. All the other concepts build on top of SLIs. In the book *Site Reliability Engineering: How Google Runs Production Systems*,[1] an SLI is succinctly defined as "a service level indicator—a carefully defined quantitative measure of some aspect of the level of service that is provided."

Relevant SLIs for a service are a matter of definition. Typical SLIs include availability, latency, and throughput. Coming up with a relevant set of SLIs for a service is an empirical process. According to the authors of the aforementioned book, they use "intuition, experience, and an understanding of what users want to define service level indicators (SLIs)."

In a Microsoft Tech Community presentation, Jason Hand suggested a hierarchy of popular SLIs[2] that build upon each other to make up the overall reliability of a service. This hierarchy is schematically shown in Figure 3.1. In the figure, the most basic level of reliability comprises availability and latency. That is, a service needs to be available first in order to be reliable. Once available, the service needs to be fast, as measured by low latency.

The availability and latency SLIs are applicable to all services. Other SLIs from the hierarchy apply selectively to the reliability of each service depending on its business and technical domains. One characteristic that applies to all SLIs, though, is that they need to be selected based on customers' perceptions of reliability, not developers' or operations engineers' perceptions. This is hugely important. In

---

1. Murphy, Niall Richard, Betsy Beyer, Chris Jones, and Jennifer Petoff. 2016. *Site Reliability Engineering: How Google Runs Production Systems*. Sebastopol, CA: O'Reilly Media.

2. Microsoft Tech Community. 2019. "Monitoring Your Infrastructure and Applications in Production." YouTube, April 2, 2019. https://www.youtube.com/watch?v=Si6ehIr6kjw.

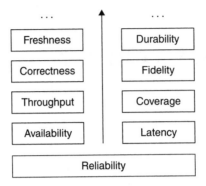

Figure 3.1 Service level indicators hierarchy

order to select the SLIs applicable to a service to measure customer satisfaction, the customers of the service need to be defined in a clear manner.

On top of the availability and latency SLIs in the hierarchy of reliability are the throughput and coverage SLIs. Throughput can mean the number of requests the service processes per time unit or it can mean the amount of data processed per time unit. Not every service needs a throughput SLI, but for some services it is essential. The coverage SLI is also only applicable to certain services. It measures whether a dataset under processing by a service has been processed in full.

Correctness and fidelity comprise another set of SLIs selectively applicable to services based on their business and technical domains. Correctness is about verifying whether the processing did what it was supposed to do. Fidelity is about the feature fidelity available to users: Are all the features available to users as expected, or are some features switched off for some time because of failure in a system part? In other words, the service may still be available, but the feature set offered to customers may be degraded for some time.

The freshness and durability SLIs are also applicable to some services, but not all. Freshness is about the degree to which the data being served for processing is the latest data available. If there is a delay, it can be because the data being served is not the latest data available in the data source. The durability SLI is about measuring whether the data stored in a data store can be retrieved later on.

The book *Site Reliability Engineering: How Google Runs Production Systems*[1] categorizes services based on relevant SLI, as shown in Table 3.1.

To reiterate, the SLIs selected to express service reliability need to be chosen from the customer point of view. The goal is to be able to use the SLIs as proxy measurements of reliability as experienced by customers. The technical experience of the system under strain is not what SLIs are supposed to measure. Rather, the customer experience of the system is what SLIs are supposed to express.

Table 3.1 *System Categories and Relevant SLIs*

System Type	Relevant SLIs	Questions Answered by SLIs
User-facing serving systems	• Availability • Latency • Throughput	• Could we respond to the request? • How long did it take to respond? • How many requests could be handled?
Storage systems	• Latency • Availability • Durability	• How long does it take to read or write data? • Can we access the data on demand? • Is the data still there when we need it?
Big data systems	• Throughput • End-to-end latency	• How much data is being processed? • How long does it take the data to progress from ingestion to completion?

3.2 Service Level Objectives

Whereas SLIs are about customer expectations, SLOs are about how those expectations will be met. The book *Site Reliability Engineering: How Google Runs Production Systems*[1] defines an SLO as "a target value or range of values for a service level that is measured by an SLI." That is, SLOs are defined per SLI.

For example, for the availability SLI, the following availability SLOs could be set:

- 98% availability of a particular endpoint within period of four calendar weeks

- 99.99% availability of another endpoint within a period of four calendar weeks

For the latency SLI, the following latency SLOs could be set:

- 400-millisecond latency for 95% of requests to an endpoint within a period of four calendar weeks

- 250-millisecond latency for 90% of requests to an endpoint within a period of four calendar weeks

Figure 3.2 depicts the relationship between SLIs and SLOs.[3]

An SLI is what is measured; for example, availability or latency. An SLO is the measurement threshold that the service should not break. In Figure 3.2, the SLO sits between the minimum service level of 0 and the maximum service level of 100.

The SLO for an SLI has to be set from the customer perspective. Also, and this is hugely important, in order to set the SLO from the customer perspective, a clear definition of the customer to optimize for is required. Without a clear definition of the customer, an SLO cannot be optimized to reflect the expectations of that particular customer group. Therefore, the SLO will be just a technical measurement that does not reflect the experience of the customer group.

---

3. Rundeck. n.d. "SRE for Everyone: Making Tomorrow Better Than Today." SlideShare IOS. Slide 33. Accessed January 19, 2022. https://www.slideshare.net/Rundeck/sre-for-everyone-making-tomorrow-better-than-today-devops-days-austin-2019.

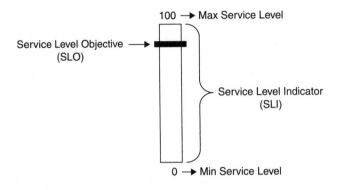

Figure 3.2 *Service level indicator versus service level objective*

A broken SLO such as this will not reflect a broken customer experience. As a result, once the SLO breach is reported, it will not be clear whether engineering time should be spent fixing the service to bring it back within the SLO.

In the example shown in Figure 3.3, the SLI is availability. The SLO is set to 98% availability for a service endpoint. That is, the service endpoint should not fall below 98% availability for a given time frame. This can be measured by determining the success rate of requests to the endpoint in that time frame. The success rate should be at least 98%.

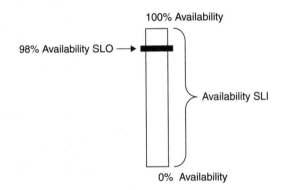

Figure 3.3 *A 98% availability SLO*

This means, in turn, that the team implementing and operating the service needs to ensure that the endpoint's availability for the given time frame does not drop below 98%. The team needs to actively monitor the availability for the endpoint and take operational measures ensuring that its availability does not drop below the SLO of 98%.

Figure 3.4 shows another example. Here, the SLI is latency. The SLO for a service endpoint is that 95% of requests to the endpoint return within 400 milliseconds.

In this example, the team implementing and operating the service needs to ensure that the endpoint's latency for a given time frame does not drop to the point where less than 95% of requests return within 400 milliseconds. The team needs to actively monitor the latency of the endpoint and take operational measures to ensure that its latency does not drop below the SLO of 95% of requests returning with 400 milliseconds.

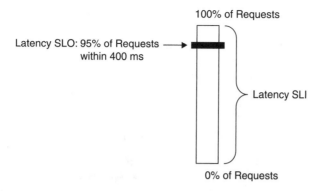

Figure 3.4 *A 95% latency SLO*

To reiterate, the SLOs have to be set from the customer perspective. If an SLO is not set from the customer perspective, it does not reflect customer expectations. In fact, it is disconnected from the customer experience. If such an SLO is broken, it is unclear whether and how the customers are impacted. The corollary of this is that it is unclear what kind of engineering effort and urgency need to be applied to bring the service back within the SLO. To connect the SLO breaches to the customer experience, a clear customer definition is required, from whose perspective the SLO needs to be set.

Furthermore, a perfect SLO does not need to be set right from the beginning. In fact, this should not be the expectation. An initial SLO agreed to by the operations engineers, developers, and product owner is the right starting point. The SLO fulfillment measurements can begin with the initially agreed SLO. Once the SRE infrastructure starts detecting SLO breaches, if any, analyses of the breaches will show whether the SLO strikes a good balance between happy customers and customers who complain. If the SRE infrastructure reports the SLO breaches while the customers are happy (not complaining), the SLO needs to be relaxed. If the SRE infrastructure does not report the SLO breaches while the customers are complaining, the SLO needs to be tightened.

Having learned about SLIs and SLOs, the next SRE concept to explore is error budgets.

3.3 Error Budgets

An error budget is a peculiar concept. Typically, in software development the goal is to avoid errors. If the software has errors, or *bugs,* they need to be fixed. However, an error budget, as the name suggests, gives developers a budget for errors, which seems counterintuitive: If developers are given a budget for errors, there would be even more bugs in the software than there already are! Should the error budget be zero in this case?

To clarify, let us return to the discussion about SLOs from Section 3.2, *Service Level Objective*s. An SLO of an SLI is a service level defined to reflect customer happiness. If a service endpoint is within its SLO, the customers are happy. If a service endpoint does not meet its SLO, the customers are not happy and start complaining about the service. In this context, the SLO automatically determines the error budget available. The error budget is the difference between the maximum service level and the SLO.

Key Insight: error budget = maximum service level – SLO threshold

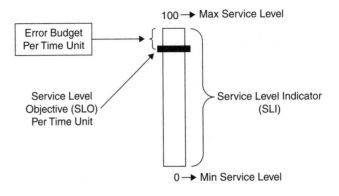

Figure 3.5 *Error budget per time unit*

Figure 3.5 illustrates this concept. The SLO of an SLI is a threshold between the minimum service level of 0 and the maximum service level of 100.

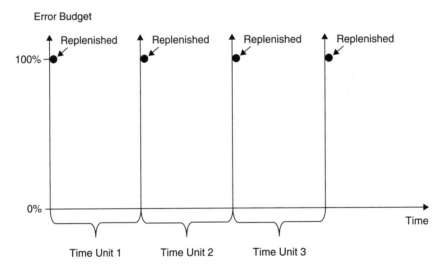

Figure 3.6 *Error budget replenishment*

The error budget is the difference between the maximum service level of 100 and the SLO threshold. Much like a monetary budget, the error budget is allocated per time unit. This means the service endpoint may deplete the error budget within the time unit but should not exhaust it before the time unit ends! That is, staying within the error budget means not exhausting it within the given time unit.

At the end of the time unit, the error budget gets fully replenished. It is similar to a computer game in which a virtual currency is replenished every time the player has reached a new level of the game. Figure 3.6 is a schematic of error budget replenishment.

Regardless of the error budget depletion rate within a time unit, the error budget is fully replenished at the beginning of each time unit. The goal for a service endpoint is not to exhaust the given error budget prematurely, before the end of the current time unit.

The time unit itself can be chosen as a fixed jumping calendar window; for example, a period of four calendar weeks starting from the first calendar week of a year. It can also be chosen as a continuous sliding window; for example, a 28-day window going backward from the current date. The SRE infrastructure needs to track and persistently record error budget depletion by the chosen time unit. This data can later be used for making data-driven decisions based on error budget depletion rates.

3.3.1 Availability Error Budget Example

As an example, let us look at an availability SLO. In Figure 3.7, the availability SLO is set to 98%. Therefore, the error budget is calculated as:

Availability error budget = 100% availability – 98% availability SLO = 2% error budget

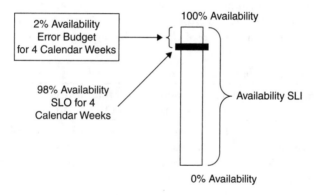

Figure 3.7 *A 2% availability error budget*

The 2% availability error budget from the example gets granted for four calendar weeks. This means a service endpoint with this error budget is agreed to be allowed to be unavailable for a maximum of 2% of the total requests that will be received within the four calendar weeks.

If the service endpoint is exposed to consumers as a public API, this error budget information is very useful for consumers. Depending on the error budget, the consumers need to implement various technical measures to create adaptive capacity between services required to cope with the maximum unavailability of the endpoint. Moreover, when the consumers attempt to determine their own SLOs, the SLOs of the dependent service endpoint play a crucial role. This is because it might not be possible to make the SLO of the consumer service tighter than the SLOs of the dependent service where the dependency is critical (although sometimes it is possible, as stated by Steve McGhee:[4] "You can build more reliable things on top of less reliable things.")

---

4. McGhee, Steve. 2021. "SLO Math." YouTube, May 16, 2021. https://www.youtube.com/watch?v=-lHPDx90Ppg.

3.3.2 Error Budget of Zero

This is now a good point to return to the question posed at the beginning of this section: Should the error budget be zero to make the service always available? Let us explore this. If the error budget is set to zero, it means the SLO is set to 100%. In the preceding example, the availability SLO is set to 100%. Is an availability SLO of 100% great for the service consumers? It might seem to be. Does an availability SLO of 100%, even if it is met, mean the service consumers will experience the service as always available? Unfortunately, no. Why not?

Well, the service is deployed somewhere, and the service consumers are deployed somewhere else. Between the service and the service consumers is a network that consists of many network gear devices, cables, and is dynamic in terms of packet routing. Any of these network components may fail. In the case of a network failure, the service consumers will not experience the service as being 100% available on their end, even if the service itself is 100% available where it is deployed.

Even if the network is not taken into account for the time being and only the point of deployment is considered, can the SLO of 100% availability be met? If so, what would that require? An availability SLO of 100% means the corresponding error budget is 0%. There is no room for errors. All requests to a service endpoint with a 100% availability SLO have to succeed within a given time unit. This, in turn, means the team developing and operating the service must do everything they can to meet the SLO and error budget. Table 3.2 provides an overview of what the team can do to meet a 100% availability SLO, along with intentions and consequences.

Table 3.2 *Team Intentions and Actions with Zero Error Budget*

#	Team Intention	Team Action to Meet the 100% Availability SLO	Assessment of the Action
1	Increase system resiliency to have enough adaptive capacity in the system to meet the SLO.	Implement redundancy, stability patterns for distributed systems, automated health checking, fast failover, zero downtime deployments, defensive (over)provisioning of infrastructure, etc.	Is the ratio of customer experience to engineering effort favorable? Is the increased cost of engineering the service justified by the increased utility of the service to the customers?
2	Increase human capacity dedicated to incident handling to reduce error budget depletion by reducing the time for incident recovery.	Implement on-call rotation in such a way that several people are simultaneously on call to reduce the time to recovery.	Is the increased cost of operating the service justified by the increased utility of the service to the customers?
3	Decrease the likelihood of error budget depletion as a result of outages during or after production deployments.	Avoid updating the service in production; avoid deploying new features, bug fixes, and security patches.	While pushing change to production is a great source of outages, it is necessary to keep the service useful to customers over time. Stagnating services lose customers.

The first team intention is to invest as much as possible in system resiliency so that the system does not deplete the error budget to zero when under strain. As every product owner knows, engineers can work on technical improvements forever. So, in the case of a 100% availability SLO, the engineers will spend a very large proportion of their engineering time on technical means that improve resilience. Depending on the purpose of the service, the increased engineering effort may be justified by the increased utility of the service to the customers. This is something the product owner needs to keep in mind when agreeing to the 100% availability SLO. It might be tempting for the product owner to declare that the service is so important that it needs to be always available. However, the product owner needs to "buy" that 100% availability using the engineering capacity taken away from feature development. This kind of thinking forces the team to strike a balance when defining the SLO. The balance is between the service availability experienced by the customer on the customer device and the service availability at the deployment point worked toward by the team. In all likelihood, a 100% availability SLO is not going to provide so much marginal utility to customers that it would justify a significantly increased engineering effort in an attempt to meet it.

The second team intention is to increase the number of people going on call for the service. This is in pursuit of faster recovery from incidents. Faster recovery from incidents means smaller error budget depletion during the incidents. Since the error budget is zero, there is no budget to deplete. Hence, the team is going to over-provision the human capacity on call. Also here, depending on the purpose of the service, the increased operations effort might be justified by the increased utility of the service to customers. This is another balance the team must strike when negotiating the on-call setup. The balance here is between the potentially decreased time to recovery from incidents and the engineering time available for feature development. Most likely, a 100% availability SLO is not going to provide so much utility to customers that it would justify a significantly increased operations effort in an attempt to meet it.

That is, the first and second team intentions force the team, and especially the product owner, to engage with the question of how reliable they want the service to be and how much they are willing to pay for it. This is a distinct characteristic of SRE application in the organization.

The third team intention is to avoid service updates in production, because every update may lead to an outage. Each outage chips away at the availability error budget, which is zero. This might sound like an absurd idea. However, this is what the team is going to, at least formally, want to do when the availability SLO is set to 100%, leaving no error budget available whatsoever. Yes, the development team, which strives to implement shiny new features, is going to shy away from wanting to deploy these features to production to keep an error budget of zero. This means the error budget of zero does not make sense in practice. Consequently, it means the availability SLO of 100% does not make sense either. There needs to be room for errors expressed as an error budget.

Without an error budget in place, the development team starts acting like a traditional operations team. The traditional operations team did not want any changes in production. "Never touch a running system" is a well-known slogan in the software industry. However, not touching the system leads to the system becoming irrelevant to customers. Becoming irrelevant and losing customers and revenue is not a sign of a successful product.

Therefore, defining an availability SLO of 100% that leaves no error budget whatsoever contradicts the purpose of making the product successful. This statement can be generalized for all SLIs. Defining any SLO of 100% for any SLI leaves zero error budget. This contradicts the purpose of making the service, the product, and the business successful.

> **Key Insight:** An SLO of 100% leaves an error budget of zero. With an error budget of zero, developers do not want to update the service in production, because doing so might lead to an outage. Every outage chips away at the error budget, which is not available in this case. Not updating the service leads to stagnation and irrelevance of the service to customers. That is, an error budget of zero contradicts the purpose of making the service and the product successful.

This is not to say that a service endpoint cannot run without depleting any error budget within a given time unit. In fact, the opposite is true for great services. Great services often run without depleting any error budget within a given time unit. However, the SLOs of those services are not set to 100%, leaving no error budget available by definition. Having no error budget available right from the start would make the development team freeze and not want to achieve the following two goals simultaneously:

1. Implement features that are actually used by customers on a regular basis.

2. Roll out the features and operate them without exhausting the error budget prematurely.

For the service to be successful, these two goals must be achieved simultaneously. In order to motivate the team to achieve these goals, a little bit of error budget needs to be granted from the start. This is done by setting the SLO to a value below 100%. This small error budget plays a big role in unfreezing the team and providing motivation to do production releases both frequently and reliably.

3.3.3 Latency Error Budget Example

Let us now have a look at another error budget example, this one for a latency SLI, as shown in Figure 3.8. Here, the latency SLO is set to 95% of requests to an endpoint to be returned within 400 milliseconds for four calendar weeks.

Following this, the error budget is calculated as follows:

Latency error budget = 100% of requests − 95% of requests within 400 milliseconds = 5% of requests without the 400-millisecond return time cap

The error budget is granted for four calendar weeks. Therefore, the goal of the team developing and operating the service is not to exhaust the error budget prematurely, before the end of a given period of four calendar weeks.

Equipped with a good understanding of error budgets, the next SRE concept to explore is that of error budget policies.

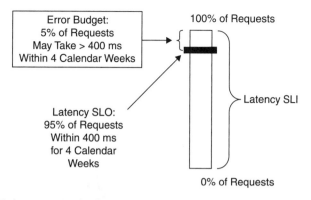

Figure 3.8 *A 5% latency error budget*

3.4 Error Budget Policies

An error budget policy, in its simplest form, is a policy that states what the team developing and operating the services will do to improve reliability when a service exhausts its error budget prematurely. In this context, prematurely means before the end of the time unit for which the error budget was granted. Premature error budget exhaustion can easily happen when planned or unplanned incidents with the service lead to so much error budget depletion that there is no error budget left before the end of the current time unit. Figure 3.9 illustrates such a situation.

The y-axis represents the error budget. The scale of the error budget ranges from a full budget of 100% to a budget debt of –100%. Yes, error budget debt is a real-world situation that is often observed in production with less reliable services. It is by no means bound to the value of –100% and can go much deeper than that. In order not to incur error budget debt, the error budget policy states what will be done to improve service reliability.

The x-axis represents the timeline. It is divided into three consecutive time units of the same duration: time unit 1, time unit 2, and time unit 3. In time unit 1, the error budget is depleted very rapidly. This means there are ongoing incidents in which the service is depleting the error budget. Each time the respective SLO is broken, a tiny bit of the error budget is depleted. The more frequently the SLO is broken, the more frequently the error budget is depleted. In the middle of time unit 1, around 50% of the error budget is depleted. In the second half of time unit 1, rapid error budget depletion continues. It deletes so quickly that, at about 80% of time unit 1, the error budget's zero mark is reached. There is no error budget left for the service endpoint in question. This is the point at which the team needs to enact and execute the error budget policy. It should contain generic steps the team will take to ensure that the error budget will not be exhausted prematurely in the future. In the last 20% of time unit 1, the incidents with the service continue. They lead to a steep error budget depletion so that time unit 1 ends with a –50% error budget shortage.

In time unit 2, the error budget is replenished by the SRE infrastructure automatically. During time unit 2, the error budget depletion rate is not as steep as it was during time unit 1. Throughout time unit 2, only around 20% of the given error budget gets depleted. This means there are some minor incidents with the service, but they do not lead to premature error budget

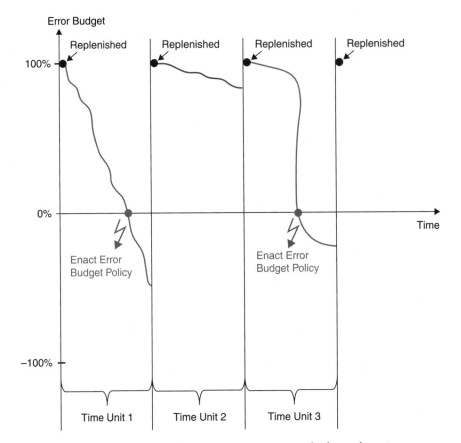

Figure 3.9 *Error budget policy enactment on premature error budget exhaustion*

exhaustion. The gentle error budget depletion rate in time unit 2, after a very steep error budget depletion rate in time unit 1, demonstrates that the measures the team took based on the error budget policy had a positive effect. In other words, enacting the error budget policy led to improved service reliability.

However, in time unit 3, the error budget depletion rate goes up again. At the beginning of this period, the error budget depletion rate is gentle. However, at around 60% into time unit 3, the error budget depletion curve falls off a cliff, dropping from 80% to zero within a very short period. This is typical for major incidents in which some major functionality that is heavily used suddenly stops working. Once the error budget hits the zero mark, it goes into negative territory. The team manages to significantly slow down the depletion rate. At around 90% into time unit 3, the error budget stops being depleted, and time unit 3 ends with an error budget shortage of around −20%.

The SRE infrastructure needs to be able to generate graphs like that shown in Figure 3.9 and alert on the error budget depletion rate. A good alert from the SRE infrastructure states the origin of the SLO breach and the remaining error budget in the given time unit. Based on this information, the people who are on call receiving the alert can quickly assess the priority to be assigned to the alert.

In terms of error budget debt handling, unlike money debt, error budget debt does not accumulate. Rather, the SRE infrastructure provides full error budget debt relief at the beginning of each time unit. However, error budget debt is paid by the service customers. Error budget debt indicates that the customer experience is severely impacted, which may have monetary consequences. The customers may decide to vote with their feet and leave a service that is unreliable.

This is where the error budget policy comes in. In its simplest form, it states an agreement among the operations engineers, developers, and product owner about what the team will do when the error budget is used up prematurely. An error budget policy may contain items such as the following.

- The team will conduct a blameless postmortem to understand the reasons for the premature error budget depletion or exhaustion.

- The team will stop deploying new features to production and only deploy technical reliability improvements until the service is back within its SLO steadily for a period of time.

- The team will review the implementation, architecture, and dependencies of the service to derive reliability measures to be taken.

- The team will assess whether a regulatory notice needs to be submitted to the regulatory bodies to report the service reliability levels and consequences thereof.

- Until the service is steadily within its SLO for a period of time, the team will stop performing production deployments, overriding deployment tool warnings about low levels of error budget that remain available.

- And so on.

An error budget policy is a team-based agreement by the team members applicable to all services owned by the team. An example error budget policy from Google is available in *The Site Reliability Workbook*.[5]

3.5 SRE Concept Pyramid

The pyramid depicted in Figure 3.10 summarizes the SRE concepts discussed in the previous sections. In the pyramid, each lower layer has to be achieved before the layer on top can be reached.

The three lower layers of the pyramid are referred to as the reliability stack in *Implementing Service Level Objectives*.[6] In *Seeking SRE: Conversations About Running Production Systems at Scale*,[7] various SRE implementations from different companies are described. Some companies, like Google, go all the way to the top of the SRE concept pyramid. Others stay at one of the

---

5. Beyer, Betsy, Niall Richard Murphy, David K. Rensin, Stephen Thorne, and Kent Kawahara. 2018. *The Site Reliability Workbook: Practical Ways to Implement SRE*. Sebastopol, CA: O'Reilly Media.

6. Hidalgo, Alex. 2020. *Implementing Service Level Objectives: A Practical Guide to SLIs, SLOs & Error Budgets*. Sebastopol, CA: O'Reilly Media.

7. Blank-Edelman, David N. 2018. *Seeking SRE: Conversations about Running Production Systems at Scale*. Sebastopol, CA: O'Reilly Media.

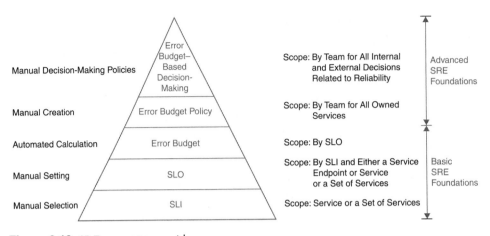

Figure 3.10 *SRE concept pyramid*

lower layers. Illustrating the SRE concepts as a pyramid reflects a smaller number of adopters at each level. The higher up a concept is in the pyramid, the smaller the number of its adopters in the industry.

This is also how it would make sense to drive the SRE transformation. It is about climbing the SRE concept pyramid from the bottom to the top, steadily making improvements along the way. To experience the full benefits of SRE, the top of the pyramid needs to be reached. This should be declared as the goal of the SRE transformation.

In order to put the SRE concept pyramid into a more contextual setting, to the left of the pyramid an indication is provided as to whether a concept is related to manual work or automated calculation. Correspondingly, to the right of the pyramid, an indication of scope can be seen.

At the bottom of the hierarchy are SLIs. They are selected by service to reflect important aspects of service reliability from the customer perspective. While availability and latency are of general use for any service from any domain, other SLIs discussed in Section 3.1, *Service Level Indicators,* such as throughput and correctness, apply selectively depending on the domain the service belongs to. SLIs are selected manually and apply to a service or a set of services.

On top of the SLIs sit the SLOs. They take center stage in any SRE conversation. The SLOs are set by the SLI from the customer perspective and determine a threshold to which to operate the service. If the SLO is below the SLO threshold, customers are happy. If it is above the SLO threshold, customers start complaining. Thus, SLOs are used as a proxy measure of customer happiness. The team developing and operating the service allocates development and operations capacity according to the SLOs agreed to for the service. The tighter the SLOs are, the more time is allocated to technical means that will make the service reliable to the level dictated by the SLOs. The more relaxed the SLOs are, the more time is allocated to new feature development and to pushing the new features to production.

SLOs are set manually. They apply by SLI to a service endpoint, a service, or a set of services. This means several SLOs can be set for each SLI. This also means several SLOs can be set for each service endpoint, service, or set of services. A good example of where several SLOs per service endpoint would make sense is the latency SLI. Sometimes it makes sense to set two latency SLOs for a service endpoint. One SLO would capture the higher latency threshold within which most requests to the endpoint should return (e.g., 95% of requests to the endpoint should return within 700 milliseconds); and the other SLO would capture the lower latency threshold within which a subset of requests to the endpoint should return (e.g., 75% of requests to the endpoint should return within 350 milliseconds).

On top of the SLOs in the SRE concept pyramid sit the error budgets. Error budgets are automatically calculated based on the SLOs. An error budget is the maximum reliability of the service expressed as 100% minus the SLO threshold. Therefore, it is calculated automatically. If the SLO is set for a service endpoint, the error budget is the number of errors the endpoint is allowed to make within a time unit.

The scope of the error budget is the SLO. This means that if several SLOs are set for a service endpoint, the service endpoint has exactly that many error budgets for depletion within a time unit. Each error budget is depleted independently. However, some outages can certainly chip away at several error budgets at once. The SRE infrastructure needs to do an exact tracking of all the error budgets, their depletion levels, the depletion speed, and the error budget levels remaining until the end of the current time unit. This information should be readily available to the people who are on call to help them quickly make decisions about incident priorities. The time units used are the same for all the error budgets.

The SLIs, SLOs, and error budgets represent the foundational elements of SRE. Without all of them in place, an organization cannot be said to practice SRE. Above these foundational elements are more advanced SRE elements. Let us discuss them in some detail.

Just below the top level of the SRE concept pyramid is the error budget policy. This is a declaration by the team developing and operating the service about what they will do if the error budget is depleted or exhausted prematurely. The error budget is granted by time unit. The goal is not to exhaust the error budget before the time unit ends. If the error budget is depleted or exhausted prematurely, the error budget policy is enacted to take measures to increase service reliability. With increased service reliability, the service should stay within its error budget in the future. An error budget policy on top of the hierarchy is essential, because without it existing, being agreed to, and being enacted when needed, the other concepts beneath it do not have as much organizational power. An error budget policy is created manually by a team. Its scope applies to all the services owned by the team.

At the top of the SRE concept pyramid is error budget–based decision–making. This concept goes beyond the error budget policy that states what a team will do if their services deplete or exhaust the error budget prematurely. Error budget–based decision–making is a holistic approach to reliability decision-making. All internal and external team decisions related to reliability are done based on internal and external teams' error budgets at this level of SRE maturity. For example, it is about using the historical SRE data before consuming an API to understand its SLOs and check whether it has been within its SLOs in the target environment, and then using that data to implement the level of adaptive capacity required to mitigate cases when the consumed API is not available, is too slow, and so on. Moreover, after the API has been consumed by a service and the service has been deployed to the target environment, it is about checking whether the service fulfills its SLO. If it does not, the team needs to check whether the SLO of the consumed API needs to be tightened. If it needs to be tightened, a conversation with the team that owns the API needs to be held to explain the new use case based on the error budget data and to ask for an SLO tightening.

Other use cases of error budget–based decision–making can be about decisions on technical features to implement based on projected error budget depletion. Given a choice, should a cache be replaced or a database exchanged? Which of these would deplete less of the error budget? How much error budget would be left at the time of deployment of either feature? Can either feature be deployed in such a way that the error budget is not prematurely exhausted? These are good questions that can be answered as part of error budget–based decision–making.

In fact, projections about error budget depletion can be applied to feature deployments too. For instance, if a feature deployment requires downtime, how long would it be and how much of the error budget would it deplete? How much of the error budget would remain at the beginning of the deployment? At the end of the deployment? This can determine when the feature can be deployed; for example, at the beginning or at the end of an error budget period.

Another use case of error budget–based decision–making is hypotheses of error budget depletion by chaos engineering experiments per environment. In other words, when a team has reached the top of the SRE concept pyramid, they do not just have an error budget policy to guide their actions to make their services stay within the defined SLOs. In addition to that, the team makes any decision related to reliability based on their own error budgets and those of other teams they depend upon. Furthermore, they use error budgets to project the impact of their actions on other teams. Error budgets become a pervasive prioritization tool used in all circumstances related to reliability. An organization like that has institutionalized its error budgets to the point where error budget–based decision–making is practiced at many levels in the organization.

SRE Cheat Sheet:

SLI	What are the service reliability aspects relevant to the customers?
SLO	What are the service reliability thresholds by reliability aspect that indicate the customer pain level leading to escalations?
Error budget	How much room for errors do we have left until the customer pain level is reached where escalations begin?
Error budget policy	In case we did not manage to avoid customer escalations by operating the service within its error budget, what do we do about it?
Error budget–based decision–making	Which data do we use to make team-internal and team-external reliability prioritization decisions?

The concepts from the SRE concept pyramid are related to each other with certain cardinalities. These are shown in Figure 3.11.

The top of the figure shows a set of several services. Each service can have several service endpoints. Each service endpoint, service, or set of services can have several SLOs defined. An SLO is defined for an SLI. Conversely, for an SLI, several SLOs can be defined. Further, several SLIs can be applied to a service. There is a 1:1 relationship between an SLO and an error budget. This is because the error budget is automatically calculated from the SLO. Finally, the error budget policy is a single agreement for a team. A team can practice a way of doing error budget–based

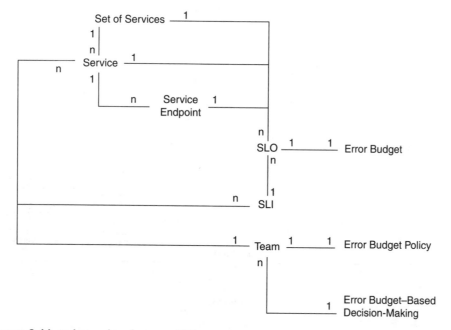

Figure 3.11 *Relationships between SRE concepts*

decision-making and own several services. Certainly, error budget–based decision–making can be practiced by several teams.

With this in-depth understanding of the SRE concept pyramid, the organizational alignment discussed in Section 2.3.4, *Benefits and Costs*, can be explained using SRE concepts. This is the subject of the next section.

3.6 Alignment Using the SRE Concept Pyramid

How do the individual SRE concepts play together to align the product delivery organization with streamlined product operations? Fundamentally, the concepts support the organization to create the alignment before actual production deployment. Going into production deployment as an aligned organization is the key to great product operations. So, what needs to be agreed to before production deployment, and by whom?

Figure 3.12 answers this question. The top of the figure horizontally lists four alignment points. The first alignment point on the left is the selection of SLIs relevant for a service to measure service reliability from the customer point of view. The second alignment point is the setting of appropriate SLOs per SLI to express the reliability thresholds, again from the customer point of view. The third alignment point is the error budget policy determining up front what will be done to improve reliability in case the error budget is depleted or exhausted prematurely. Finally,

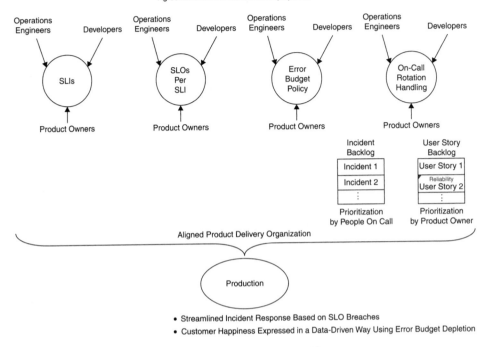

Figure 3.12 *Four alignments using the SRE concept pyramid*

the fourth alignment point is the on-call rotation setup ensuring appropriate ongoing operational support for the service.

The four alignments need to be undertaken and agreed to by the relevant operations engineers, developers, and product owner. It sounds time-consuming, and it might be. But it does not have to be. Especially after initial agreements have been reached in a team, incremental changes can be agreed to rather swiftly. Irrespective of the required time investment, going into production deployment without organizational alignment leads to the chaos discussed in Section 2.1, *Misalignment*. So, taking the necessary time to create the organizational alignment on operational concerns before production deployment is one of the best investments the team can make to ensure a delightful reliability customer experience when using the product.

Let us explore how the alignment can be brought about using SLIs, SLOs, error budget policies, and on-call rotation.

As mentioned earlier, the operations engineers, developers, and product owner need to talk about and agree on the SLIs and SLOs. In this discussion, the developers bring in their knowledge about the service and infrastructure implementation, logging, tracing, and error handling. The operations engineers bring in their knowledge about the infrastructure scaling in production, customer complaints, past incidents, on-call rotation, and the capabilities of the SRE infrastructure. The product owner brings in their knowledge about the user journeys, stakeholders, sales commitments, marketing commitments, deal pipeline, most requested features, customer escalations, and the overall product vision.

What is great about SLIs and SLOs is that the entire conglomerate of this vastly diverse collection of knowledge is forced to be applied to reliability concerns in a structured manner. This

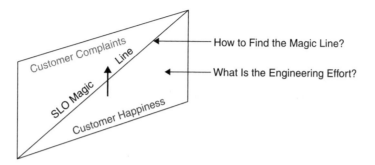

Figure 3.13 *Magic line between customer happiness and customer complaints*

is needed in an attempt to find good SLOs for relevant SLIs to appropriately balance customer happiness with the engineering effort required to achieve it. Figure 3.13 illustrates this.

The SLO magic line[1] runs between customer happiness and customer complaints. If the service is within the SLO, the customers are happy. If the service has broken the SLO, the customers complain. In that context, how do you find the magic line? Initially, without much data at hand, the collective genius of the developers, operations engineers, and product owner needs to be applied to set it in a time-boxed manner.

The SLO definitions should spark very lively discussions, especially if the consequences of setting an SLO are clear to everyone. Setting an SLO determines

- The proxy measure of customer happiness with the service or service endpoint

- The error budget available per time unit

- The effort and time the developers will allocate to implement appropriate service resilience and reliability

- The effort and time the developers and operations engineers will allocate to the service during on-call rotations

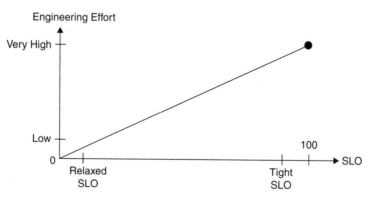

Figure 3.14 *SLO versus engineering effort*

---

1. CernerEng. 2018. "Less Risk Through Greater Humanity, Dave Rensin." Video. YouTube. https://youtu.be/0zqBlRW_6jA?t=1234.

Thus, setting the SLO has far-reaching consequences for time allocation in the team. As shown in Figure 3.14, the tighter the SLO, the higher the engineering effort required to fulfill it.

Despite the fact that setting the SLO leads to far-reaching consequences for time allocation in the team, there needs to be a shared team understanding that setting the SLO is not a decision that is difficult to revise. In fact, the opposite needs to be true. Setting the SLO needs to be seen as an initial SLO decision to be tested in production for spotting true issues with customer experience. Setting the SLO should be the start of a powerful feedback loop from production showing the quality of the decision. This is shown in Figure 3.15.

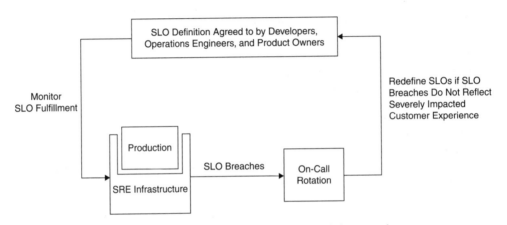

Figure 3.15 *Testing an SLO definition decision using feedback from production*

The SLO definition agreed to by the developers, operations engineers, and product owner is a collective attempt to find the SLO magic line that would balance customer happiness with the engineering effort required to achieve it. The SLO magic line is a hypothesis at this point.

The next step is to test the hypothesis. This is done by letting the SRE infrastructure monitor production for the fulfillment of the defined SLO. Should the SLO be broken, the SRE infrastructure notifies the people on call. They need to analyze the SLO breaches and find out whether they reflect a severely impacted customer experience. If the SLO breaches do not reflect a severely impacted customer experience, the SLO needs to be redefined. The redefinition can now be done with the benefit of having real data and insight from production. It should go without saying that the SLO redefinition needs to be done and agreed to by the operations engineers, developers, and product owner.

Coming back to Figure 3.12, the on-call rotation setup also needs to be agreed to by the three parties. Table 3.4 shows what the agreement needs to include.

Finally, the error budget policy also needs to be agreed to by the developers, operations engineers, and product owner. It needs to state what the team will do to improve service reliability if the service depletes or exhausts its error budget prematurely. The policy applies to all error budgets a service may have.

The agreements on SLIs, SLOs, error budget policies, and on-call setup achieved before production deployment unite the product delivery organization and lay down a great foundation for delivering a delightful customer experience in production on an ongoing basis. Once the

Table 3.4 *On-Call Rotation Setup Agreements*

Agreement Point	Explanation
A general strategy for allocating people to on-call shifts	Who can generally go on call, for which service, at which times, and for how long?
Incident backlog prioritization rules	How can the prioritization of incidents be done autonomously by the people on call? Which criteria should be used for incident prioritization?
User story backlog prioritization rules in terms of reliability	How will the error budget–based decisions be made to prioritize reliability work against customer-facing feature work? Will premature error budget depletion lead to the reliability being prioritized over customer-facing features?

service is deployed to production, the SRE infrastructure continuously detects SLO breaches. The SLO breaches are forwarded to the people on call. The people on call immediately prioritize and analyze them. They fix the incidents as quickly as they can. If SLO breaches do not reflect an impacted customer experience, the people on call set up a meeting with the operations engineers, developers, and product owner to redefine their respective SLOs.

Further, error budget exhaustion is monitored by the SRE infrastructure continuously. When error budgets get depleted or exhausted prematurely, the people on call enact the error budget policy, which contains measures to be taken to improve service reliability. These measures include prioritization of the reliability work over customer-facing feature work for the service in question.

Compare this with the chaos discussed in Section 2.1, *Misalignment*. There were no SLOs, people on call lacked appropriate knowledge of the system, there was no SRE infrastructure, and there were no SLO breaches, no error budgets, no error budget policies, no rules for incident backlog prioritization, and no rules for user story backlog prioritization in terms of reliability. This might result in something more than just chaos. It might result in disarray, confusion, havoc, and more, all taking place at the same time.

How on earth do you introduce SRE in such an organization in order to help the organization? That is the central question of exploration in this book.

3.7 Summary

This chapter explored the basic SRE concepts of SLIs, SLOs, error budgets, error budget policies, and error budget–based decision–making. The concepts were structured as a pyramid to climb during the SRE transformation. In the coming chapters, the journey of transforming the software delivery organization toward SRE will unfold.

There is no broad agreement in the industry yet on how to introduce SRE, organize for SRE appropriately, or run and maintain SRE. This book is an attempt to put a stick in the ground with an opinion on how this can be done. It is going to cause debate. The debate is expected, welcomed, and encouraged. The book is an attempt to show how an SRE introductory program can be executed in a well-structured manner. The book's intention is to advance the software industry in that particular aspect. It is about reducing trial-and-error attempts when introducing SRE and providing a comprehensive overview of aspects that need to be taken care of when running an SRE introductory program.

The book is about establishing the SRE foundations from zero. Because it is about the foundations, it will not contain very advanced SRE practices. These can be found in other books on the subject. Shu Ha Ri is a concept from the Japanese martial arts that describes stages of learning toward mastery. Shu is about learning the fundamentals. Ha is about innovating on the tradition. Ri is about leaving the tradition and creating new, natural ways while not overstepping the fundamentals. This book focuses heavily on the stage of Shu, touches the level of Ha at times, and does not consider the level of Ri.

With an understanding of the book's SRE learning stage, let us start the SRE transformation journey by assessing the status quo of the software delivery organization under transformation.

Chapter 4

Assessing the Status Quo

Imagine a product delivery organization similar to the one presented in Section 2.1, *Misalignment*. In an organization like that, the developers may not understand why they should be doing operations. The operations engineers may not provide frameworks to enable the developers to do operations. The managers may not promote the topic, let alone fund it. What might unite the organization, though, is the desire to finally reduce ongoing high-profile customer escalations of production outages.

Some people in the organization may know that SRE is a good way to bring production operations under control. Thus, the organization may have a very small group of people who want to implement SRE. They might become SRE coaches at some point. Given this, the organization's first step toward SRE would be a clear understanding of where it stands in terms of SRE foundations. To achieve this understanding, several important dimensions need to be analyzed. These include the organization itself, along with its people, technology, culture, and process. Let us look at each dimension in turn.

4.1 Where Is the Organization?

In terms of the organization, the following aspects need to be considered:

- Organizational structure
- Organizational alignment
- Formal and informal leadership

4.1.1 Organizational Structure

The first thing to understand about the organization is how product operations are performed based on an organizational chart depicting boxes of departments and teams. The following questions can guide this analysis.

- Which boxes in the organizational chart are formally responsible and accountable for production operations? Is the responsibility clearly depicted in the organizational chart?
- Does the chart include solid and dotted lines to show who reports to whom in the organization?

- Is the leadership team aligned with the solid and, if applicable, dotted line reporting? Are there other people on the leadership team?

- Which boxes in the organizational chart are actually keeping the product alive in production?

- Which boxes are involved in shipping hotfixes?

- Which boxes are making decisions about prioritization of hotfixes and reliability work?

What the SRE coaches are trying to understand at this point is the status quo. How does the organization cope with production operations at the moment? Given this understanding and the vision of SRE leading to an aligned organization (Section 1.2, *Alignment Using SRE*), the organization's path toward SRE transformation might begin to clear.

The analysis might reveal that the responsibility for production operations is not clearly defined in the organization. More typically, however, it might reveal that the formal responsibility and accountability of production operations is not well aligned with how the organization is actually coping with the responsibility. Those responsible may not have enough control of the matter to be effective and be held accountable. In a traditional software delivery organization with distinct product development, product operations, and product management departments, the responsibility and accountability of production operations will be with product operations. As we saw in Section 2.1, *Misalignment,* this responsibility can hardly be fulfilled given the organization's siloed setup. Figure 4.1 depicts this scenario.

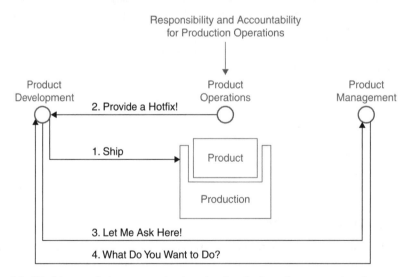

Figure 4.1 *Working mode in an organization that is misaligned on operational concerns*

The product operations team is responsible for production operations. They own the production environment. The product development team ships the product to the production environment. This is where the trouble begins for product operations. With little knowledge about product implementation, they monitor the product using IT resource parameters. Every time a serious issue is flagged, product operations asks product development for a hotfix. The product development team works on the user story backlog prioritized by the product owner. Therefore, working on the hotfix, even if it is actually required, means they must reprioritize the user story backlog. Backlog reprioritization is done by the product owner, so product development tells product operations they will ask product management about backlog reprioritization. Product management is completely out of the loop and needs to be phased in first, before a meaningful discussion about backlog reprioritization can be held.

Thus, the product operations team has so little control of production operations that the responsibility placed on them can hardly be fulfilled. As discussed in Section 2.2, *Collective Ownership,* ownership of production operations needs to be collectively held by product development, product operations, and product management. These three parties contribute to and benefit from collective ownership in their own way (Section 2.3.4, *Benefits and Costs*).

4.1.2 Organizational Alignment

The next thing to understand about the organization is its organizational alignment. How is the organization actually getting production operations done today, irrespective of what is prescribed by the formal organizational structure? Production operations might be done in a misaligned fashion with lots of handovers. But still, how? What is the status quo? The following questions can guide this analysis.

- How does customer support work?

- Who is providing the first level of support in the organization, if any?

- Who is providing the second level of support in the organization, if any?

- Who is providing the third level of support in the organization, if any?

- Are there more than three support levels? How many are there? Who is providing support at each level?

- What is a typical path for a customer support request through the support levels?

- What is the trend of customer support request numbers over the last 12 months?

- What is the average customer support request processing time over the last 12 months?

- How does the release and rollout process work?

- How are the decisions to roll out a hotfix made and by whom?

- How are the decisions to roll out a feature release made and by whom?

- Is regulatory compliance involved in a hotfix or feature release?

- Who creates release plans and rollout plans?

- What kind of coordination is required to do a production rollout?

- Are there release managers to coordinate the production rollout?

- Is there a team or person who typically detects issues in production before the issues make their way through the customer support levels?

The goal here is to understand how all the parties in the organization currently align on operational concerns: customer support, releases, hotfix rollouts, feature rollouts, proactive production monitoring, and so on. How do all these pieces interact today, regardless of their efficiency and effectiveness?

With this understanding, the SRE transformation thinking can be advanced. How do you bridge the gap between the current level of organizational alignment on operational concerns and that of SRE as envisioned in Section 1.2, *Alignment Using SRE?*

For one, the analysis might show that many customer support levels lead to long customer support request processing times. The more support levels there are, the less likely it is that product development can implement all the features required to ensure a positive user experience, simply because they will be spending less time performing service operations and taking the learnings into development. Additionally, the more support levels there are, the greater the chance that information will be lost while on its way to developers. In extreme cases, where developers never go on call, the incentive to implement the product with operations in mind may be close to zero, because the developers and product owners may be fully focused on developing customer-facing features. To counter this situation, the SRE transformation must include incentives for developers to share on-call responsibility with others so that operational concerns are taken into account during service implementation.

> **Key Insight:** The art of SRE transformation is to find the degree to which developers need to go on call for their services to maximize learnings and incentives so that they take into account operational concerns during service development. This is going to be different for each organization.

Further, the analysis might show that the release and rollout processes for hotfixes and features involve lots of handovers between many teams and people. From an operational point of view, it is especially important that hotfix releases and rollouts are done quickly. A good understanding of the current process may lead to insights about what would need to be done during the SRE transformation in order to speed up the release and rollout of hotfixes. Especially in regulated industries, any production release and rollout is subject to regulatory compliance. Ensuring regulatory compliance through automation to speed up release and rollout might be necessary during the SRE transformation.

4.1.3 Formal and Informal Leadership

The final thing to understand about the organization is its leadership. Leadership can be formal and informal. Formal leadership is endowed by the organizational structure evaluated in Section 4.1.1, *Organizational Structure.* Thus, it is easy to identify the formal leaders just by looking at the organizational chart.

Informal leadership consists of people who do not wield formal power but are still great influencers of other people in the organization. Some informal leaders may be more effective at influencing the behavior of others than the formal leaders themselves, especially if they explain the reasons for doing something a certain way from the first principles point of view. They may be effective communicators, and the fact that they do not wield formal power in the organization may play to their advantage. This is because all they have to persuade their colleagues is pure logic and emotion. This breeds authenticity. People do not *have* to follow informal leaders; they only do so because they believe in the suggested course of action.

The following questions can guide this analysis.

- Who is formally in charge of what in the organization?

- Who are the informal influencers in the organization? For which areas?

- Who are recognized experts in the organization? For which areas?

- Which formal leaders are considered great in the organization?

- In general, whom do people follow and not follow in the organization?

- Who are the production heroes involved in all production incidents making the impossible possible?

These questions are important to get answered because all the formal and informal leaders will need to be engaged appropriately during the SRE transformation. The pool of informal leaders might contain some people who would champion SRE as coaches. As discussed in Section 2.5, *Coaching*, SRE coaches will need to be developed from within. Therefore, every opportunity should be used to scout for people who might wish to become SRE coaches to drive the SRE transformation.

With this understanding of the organizational structure, alignment, and leadership, it should be clear how the organization as a whole does production operations today. Additionally, it should provide some food for thought about how the organization would need to operate with SRE as a core methodology for doing production operations.

4.2 Where Are the People?

The next dimension to explore is the knowledge, mindset, and attitudes of the people in the organization. Where are they in terms of understanding how operations is done and should be done? This should be explored by role. In a product delivery organization, the most prominent roles are operations engineer, developer, and product owner. Architects, managers, and executives are also important to consider. The following questions can guide the process of understanding where people are:

- For operations engineers and operations managers:
  - What are your daily tasks?
  - What is the general quality of the product?
  - How do you decide which alerts to set up?
  - Do you know whether these alerts report real issues with the user experience?
  - Do you generally go on call? If so, at what times?
  - Is there an on-call rotation in your team?
  - What do you do if you need a hotfix released and rolled out to production?

○ How are developers involved in production operations?

○ How are product owners involved in production operations?

○ Do you provide a means to enable others to do production operations by themselves?

○ What are the customer support levels in the organization?

○ Who is doing which support level in the organization?

○ How are crises in production managed?

○ How are customer complaint numbers trending over time?

- For developers, architects, and development managers:

  ○ How do you measure the reliability of the product?

  ○ How do you decide which reliability features to implement in the product?

  ○ How do you get the reliability features prioritized?

  ○ Who prioritizes the reliability features?

  ○ What happens if a hotfix needs to be rolled out?

  ○ Does your team do production deployments themselves?

  ○ Do you ever go on call? If so, at what times?

  ○ Is there an on-call rotation in your team?

- For product owners and product managers:

  ○ What is the vision for your product?

  ○ Where is the product currently in fulfilling this vision?

  ○ Who are the users of the product?

  ○ Who are the customers of the product?

  ○ What are the most important user journeys for the users and customers?

  ○ How important is reliability of the product to the users and customers?

  ○ How are customer complaint numbers trending over time?

  ○ How do you do backlog prioritization?

  ○ How are reliability features prioritized?

  ○ Are you involved in production operations?

- For vice presidents and executives:

  ○ What do the customers report about the reliability of the product?

  ○ How does the organization manage production operations?

  ○ Is the organization aligned for doing production operations well?

  ○ Would it be possible to allocate the teams some time for the SRE transformation?

  ○ Is the funding of the product delivery organization appropriate for achieving the required product reliability?

  ○ Is there some budget allocated for additional tooling to improve production operations?

To be sure, only a small number of people in the organization should be interviewed to get a feel for where people are. Big workshops and long meetings are discouraged at this stage of the SRE transformation, as they might make the project appear unnecessarily difficult and therefore discourage people from becoming SRE supporters.

The answers to these questions should provide enough context to understand how people in different roles feel as far as production operations is concerned. This understanding may spark some thinking about the shifts in mindset that would need to take place during the SRE transformation.

4.3 Where Is the Tech?

In terms of the organization's status quo, the next dimension to assess is the technology. This involves looking at all the technical aspects related to production operations. The assessment can be done based on a useful service reliability hierarchy provided by Mikey Dickerson in the book *Site Reliability Engineering: How Google Runs Production Systems*.[1] The hierarchy, shown in Figure 4.2, describes what needs to be in place, and in what order, to achieve service reliability.

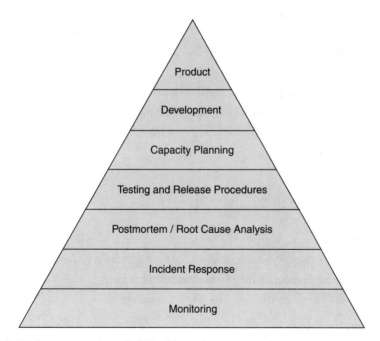

Figure 4.2 *Dickerson's service reliability hierarchy*

---

1. Murphy, Niall Richard, Betsy Beyer, Chris Jones, and Jennifer Petoff. 2016. *Site Reliability Engineering: How Google Runs Production Systems*. Sebastopol, CA: O'Reilly Media. Reprinted by permission of O'Reilly Media, Inc.

The technical aspects of the hierarchy consist of monitoring, testing and release procedures, capacity planning, and development. Let us look at these aspects one by one by outlining the questions to ask for the technical assessment. It will make sense to conduct the technical assessment in a team-based manner, because teams tend to manage their tech in a distinct fashion. However, at this stage of the transformation, only a few people from only a few teams should be interviewed. Coaching every team individually will be done later. For now, only a general understanding needs to be developed. This understanding is needed to estimate the SRE transformation's complexity, duration, and cost. Following are the questions to ask for the technical assessment:

- Logging and monitoring questions:

  ○ Are the services logging?

  ○ Is the logging done in a uniform way?

  ○ Is the logging done by all services using the same logging infrastructure?

  ○ Are the services logging into a single instance of the logging infrastructure by production deployment?

  ○ What instrumentation does the logging infrastructure provide out of the box (e.g., runtime dependency graphs, call durations, etc.)?

  ○ Does the logging infrastructure provide a query language to programmatically query the logs and graph the query results?

  ○ Is anybody looking at the logs? In which cases?

  ○ Are there any metrics over the logs?

  ○ Is there some alerting generated based on logs and metrics?

  ○ How is logging done for asynchronous operations?

  ○ How easy is it to analyze asynchronous operations based on the logs?

  ○ Is there distributed tracing?

- Testing questions:

  ○ Are there tests for services?

  ○ Which tests are manual?

  ○ For automated tests, what are the test levels available for services?

  ○ What is the trigger or cadence of automated test execution by test suite?

  ○ What is the test execution time by automated test suite?

  ○ What is the test execution time by manual test suite?

  ○ Which test suite gets executed in which deployment environment?

  ○ Which tests get executed before a feature release?

  ○ Which tests get executed before a hotfix release?

  ○ After a deployment is done, are automated deployment checks running to verify the deployment procedure?

○ Are automated tests running in production 24/7?

○ Are the tests and test executions trustworthy?

- Release questions:

  ○ Do development teams own deployment pipelines?

  ○ What is the scope of a deployment pipeline? How many services are typically deployed using a single deployment pipeline?

  ○ Are development teams doing production rollouts themselves or are they done by the operations team centrally?

  ○ What are the manual steps for doing a production release?

  ○ Which manual steps ensure regulatory compliance of a production release (document creation, reviews and signatures, approvals, etc.)?

  ○ How often are production releases done on average per team?

  ○ Is there a canary release process in place?

  ○ How long does it take to roll out a service to all production environments, including a canary release?

  ○ Are there standard operating procedures (SOPs) describing how standardized work is done in production (e.g., how to manually scale a resource such as memory)?

- Capacity planning questions:

  ○ Are services running on servers owned by the organization? Are they infrastructure as a service (Iaas) or platform as a service (Paas) solutions?

  ○ Are several services running in a shared infrastructure unit that can only be scaled by the unit as a whole?

  ○ Are services running in containers deployed in clusters, such as Kubernetes clusters, so that infrastructure scaling can be done by the container on demand?

  ○ Is infrastructure scaling done manually, automatically, or semiautomatically?

- Development questions:

  ○ Is the use of HTTP return codes appropriate? For instance, does a "500" error code really mean an internal server error?

  ○ Does the logging infrastructure provide a log query language? If so, do the developers use the log query language on a regular basis?

  ○ Are services built on the principles of the Twelve-Factor App?[2] Are developers aware of them by and large?

  ○ Do services implement any stability patterns for distributed systems from the book *Release It! Design and Deploy Production-Ready Software*?[3] Are developers aware of them by and large?

---

2. Wiggins, Adam. n.d. "The Twelve-Factor App." Accessed January 19, 2022. https://12factor.net.

3. Nygard, Michael T. 2018. *Release It! Design and Deploy Production-Ready Software*, 2nd edition. Raleigh, NC: The Pragmatic Bookshelf.

Interestingly, the preceding questions are not closely related to the technology used by the teams. Rather, to analyze the state of tech in the teams from an operational standpoint, more conceptual matters are important. For example, it does not matter which logging infrastructure is used. What is important about it is whether any logging infrastructure is used consistently in the teams so that a single SRE infrastructure can be built on top of the logs benefiting all the teams. Also, if teams do not consistently use a logging infrastructure, they will have before the SRE transformation can progress any further.

Moreover, it is only important to know whether the logging infrastructure used provides a query language to programmatically query the logs, regardless of the specific query language itself. Having a log query language is important as it enables some parts of the SRE infrastructure to be built more easily. Additionally, incident response will be much faster if people on call can quickly query the logs programmatically (e.g., to rule out potential problem areas or zoom in on suspicious behavior in a part of the system).

For testing, it does not matter which test frameworks and runners are used. What matters is how trustworthy the test results are, how quickly the tests run, in which environments they are executed, and for what kind of releases. This informs how quickly incident response can roll out a change to production. If this is a bottleneck, it would need to be worked on during the SRE transformation.

The same applies to the release, capacity planning, and development questions. It does not matter which release frameworks are used. What does matter, for example, is whether a canary release is done to test the impact of a change in production on a small group of users first. If this is in place, the team's release process will be mature. In all likelihood, it will not need to be touched during the SRE transformation.

Some issues might seem small but will matter a great deal from an SRE standpoint. For example, it is very important for proper HTTP return error codes to be used in all services. This is because service availability calculations are done based on HTTP return error codes. Imprecise HTTP return error codes lead to wrong availability calculations by the SRE infrastructure. Wrong service availability when aggregated over time confuses stakeholders. Teams start investing in increasing availability in the wrong places. API consumers start implementing possibly inappropriate reliability measures to shield themselves from degradations in dependent APIs.

Overall, clarifying the preceding questions should provide enough understanding of the heavy lifting required to elevate the tech to a level appropriate for SRE. No doubt, effort will be required. Depending on the team, the effort might be substantial. That is why the SRE activities need to be prioritized at the portfolio level in the organization. Without clear prioritization of the SRE activities relative to other organizational initiatives, the SRE transformation will not succeed. It might lead to local incremental improvements here and there, but the goal of SRE is systemic alignment of the entire software delivery organization on operational concerns (see Section 1.2, *Alignment Using SRE*), and that goal can only be achieved if the tech is up to par.

4.4 Where Is the Culture?

Numerous books and publications recognize culture as a very important factor influencing all aspects of an organization. Both SRE and SRE transformation are among those aspects that are greatly influenced by organizational culture. The speed with which SRE will be allowed to spread will not be determined by the project plans, executive wishes, or SRE coaches' hopes. Rather, it will be determined by the organizational culture to a great extent.

What is the organizational culture, and how does it influence the SRE transformation? Let us explore these questions in depth.

According to the Longman Dictionary, one definition of culture is: "the beliefs, way of life, art, and customs that are shared and accepted by people in a particular society."[4] Sociologist Ron Westrum defined a popular topology of organizational cultures, often referred to as the Westrum model,[5] which classifies cultures as pathological, bureaucratic, or generative according to how organizations process information: Pathological cultures are power oriented, bureaucratic cultures are rule oriented, and generative cultures are performance oriented. According to DevOps Research and Assessment (DORA[6]), performance-oriented generative cultures also lead to high performance in software delivery. According to the Westrum model, there are six aspects of a generative culture:

1. High cooperation.

2. Messengers are trained.

3. Risks are shared.

4. Bridging is encouraged.

5. Failure leads to inquiry.

6. Novelty is implemented.

These aspects relate very directly to SRE, as outlined in Table 4.1.

It seems like a performance-oriented generative culture would also lead to high performance in SRE. As such, one can assess an organization's current culture through the lens of production operations by analyzing how far away the organization is from the behavior described in Table 4.1.

4.4.1 Is There High Cooperation?

Notorious in the realm of production operations are the walls between product development and product operations. On one side of the wall is product operations, whose goal is to keep production stable. This goal leads them not to want frequent changes in production, because each change may cause instability (or typically does, based on their experience). On the other side of the wall is product development, whose goal is to implement, deploy, and release to production new features requested by product management as quickly as possible. DevOps is trying to break down that wall. So is SRE as an opinionated implementation of DevOps.

---

4. Reprinted by permission of Pearson, Longman Dictionary of Contemporary English. 2014. "Definition of culture." Accessed June 22, 2022. https://www.ldoceonline.com/dictionary/culture.

5. Westrum, R. 2004. "A Typology of Organisational Cultures." *Quality and Safety in Health Care* 13 (suppl_2): ii22–27. https://doi.org/10.1136/qshc.2003.009522.

6. Google. n.d. "Cloud Architecture Center." Accessed January 19, 2022. https://cloud.google.com/architecture/devops/devops-culture-westrum-organizational-culture.

Table 4.1 *Relationship of Westrum's Generative Culture to SRE*

	Westrum's Generative Culture	Relationship to SRE
1	High cooperation.	The purpose of SRE is to align the software delivery organization on operational concerns. This can only be done with high cooperation between product development, product operations, and product management.
2	Messengers are trained.	Service owners whose services deplete error budgets prematurely need to be trained to implement reliability measures to keep the error budgets. People on call resolving incidents are supported in running blameless postmortems viewed as reliability learning opportunities for everyone in the organization.
3	Risks are shared.	Product operations, product development, and product management need to agree on the SLIs, SLOs, error budgets, and on-call rotation setup (Section 3.6, *Alignment Using the SRE Concept Pyramid*). This way, they share the risks of the joint decisions.
4	Bridging is encouraged.	Service SLOs and error budget depletion rates over time need to be made public to create conversations among teams, leading to data-driven decisions about reliability concerns of dependent services. Moreover, during the SRE transformation, regular exchanges between teams need to be facilitated; for example, using an SRE community of practice or lunch and learn sessions.
5	Failure leads to inquiry.	Incident resolution needs to be followed by blameless postmortems.
6	Novelty is implemented.	New insights from production operations need to lead to reliability features being implemented in the product in a timely fashion.

The following questions support the exploration of the quality of cooperation on operational concerns in a given organization.

- What is the relationship between product operations and product development?
- Are there tensions between product operations and product development? If so, what causes the tensions?
- What is the involvement of product management in production operations?
- Is there a working relationship between product management and product operations?
- What is the view of operations engineers on the reliability of the product?
- What is the view of operations engineers on prioritization of the reliability work?
- During an ongoing production incident, how easy is it to involve people from different development teams on demand?

- Are there SLIs and SLOs jointly agreed to by product operations, product development, and product management?

- Are there error budget policies jointly agreed to by product operations, product development, and product management?

- Are the error budget policies enacted on premature error budget depletion?

- Is the on-call rotation setup jointly agreed to by product operations, product development, and product management?

4.4.2 Are Messengers Trained?

The following questions support the exploration of how the organization deals with the messengers of "bad" news from production operations.

- Are teams "shot down" by management for production incidents?

- Are postmortems held after production incidents?

- Do people fear being blamed in postmortems?

- Are people who voice reliability concerns neglected?

- Do production defects lead to scapegoating in the organization?

- Does premature error budget depletion lead to reliability training?

- Are discussions about postmortem summaries viewed as reliability learning opportunities?

4.4.3 Are Risks Shared?

The following questions support the exploration of whether and how risks from production operations are shared.

- Are responsibilities around production operations clearly written?

- Are the written responsibilities around production operations known to the operations engineers? To the developers? To the product owners?

- Do developers share in the risk of production operations? If so, how?

- Do product owners share in the risk of production operations? If so, how?

- Do product operations, product development, and product management make joint decisions and bear shared consequences for the decisions about SLIs, SLOs, error budget policies, and on-call rotation setup?

4.4.4 Is Bridging Encouraged?

The following questions support the exploration of how bridging between teams and individuals about operational concerns is done in the organization.

- Are postmortem summaries readily available for reference by anyone in the organization?
- If you picked a developer randomly, would they know where the postmortems are stored?
- If you picked a product owner randomly, would they know where the postmortems are stored?
- Are postmortems written from a user impact point of view and in a way that can be understood by nontechnical people in the organization?
- Is there a regular exchange about the postmortem content with a wider audience (e.g., lean coffee sessions)?
- Is anybody reading postmortems and learning from them?
- Is there a community of practice (CoP) for operations or, more specifically, SRE?
- Do operations engineers get involved in any product creation activities (i.e., before the product hits production)?
- Do product operations, product development, and product management have regular exchanges to refine SLIs, SLOs, error budget policies, error budget–based decision-making, and on-call rotation setup?

4.4.5 Does Failure Lead to Inquiry?

The following questions support the exploration of how failures in production operations are dealt with in the organization.

- Do hotfixes lead to punishment of teams and individuals by management?
- Who initiates a postmortem?
- Is there a clear set of criteria that an incident must have in order for a postmortem to be initiated?
- Do people feel psychologically safe taking part in a postmortem? How do they know this?
- Are there action items from postmortems that lead to reconsideration of SLIs, SLOs, and error budget policies? If so, how are the action items followed up on? By whom?

4.4.6 Is Novelty Implemented?

The following questions support the exploration of how the organization deals with novelty in the space of production operations.

- Do statistics about services depleting their error budgets prematurely lead to scapegoating in the organization?

- Do statistics about services depleting their error budgets prematurely lead to user story backlog prioritization decisions based on previously agreed error budget policies?

- Are production releases seen as experimentation opportunities used to test previously defined feature hypotheses?

- What is the process of learning from one production release to inform the development of the next production release? Is it structured?

- What is the average lead time for a technical novelty identified in a postmortem to be prioritized in the user story backlogs of teams that need to contribute?

John Shook from New United Motor Manufacturing Inc. (NUMMI), a joint venture between General Motors and Toyota, ran a major culture transformation at the company. In "How to Change a Culture: Lessons from NUMMI"[7] he wrote: "The way to change culture is not to first change how people think, but instead to start by changing how people behave — what they *do*…" Following this, the SRE transformation needs to work on introducing the SRE way of working. As people start doing operations bit by bit in a different way, the organizational culture will change over time. By no means is it expected to be a fast process. Irrespective of the speed, it needs to be a steady process facilitated by the SRE coaches working with all teams on a regular basis.

4.5 Where Is the Process?

The last dimension to assess in the product delivery organization is the overall process of getting production operations done. The process consists of many subprocesses and involves many teams. The following questions can be helpful in developing an understanding of where the process and its subprocesses currently are:

- Customer support:
  - How do the customer support requests reach development teams?
  - What is the interface between customer support and the development teams? Tickets? Regular meetings? ChatOps?

- On-call process:
  - Is there anybody on call for services?
  - What is the availability of the on-call coverage? Is it 24/7?
  - Are there on-call rotations? If there are:
    - Which roles are on the rotations?
    - How is knowledge handover organized when people switch?

---

7. Shook, John. 2010. "How to Change a Culture: Lessons From NUMMI." *MIT Sloan Management Review* 51 (2), 66.

- Is there a primary and secondary on-call person per shift?
- What is the typical duration of an on-call shift?
- Are there runbooks? If so, who keeps them up to date?

- Incident response:
  - For incidents involving several teams, are there incident commanders?
  - Who gets assigned which incident?
  - What is the average incident resolution time?

- Production access control:
  - Is production access needed for humans? If so:
    - Who can get it?
    - How do they request it?
    - How quickly is access provided after a request has been placed?

- Regulatory compliance:
  - How often must the health of deployed services be checked?
  - What artifacts are required to make a production deployment?

- Production deployment:
  - Can a team do a production deployment themselves in an autonomous fashion?
  - Do stakeholders or customers need to be informed before a production deployment can be done?
  - Is there downtime during a production deployment? How long is it on average?
  - How often are production deployments done on average?
  - Is there a definition of production deployment failure?
  - How many production deployments fail on average within a time unit?
  - What is the average production failure recovery time?
  - Are there manual steps to be done to accomplish a production deployment?

- Production release:
  - Is a production release to customers decoupled from a production deployment to a data center? If so, who can make the release to customers and on whose behalf?

- Hotfix deployment:
  - What is the difference in deployment process between a hotfix and feature deployment?
  - Are manual steps necessary to accomplish a hotfix deployment?

- Hotfix release:
  - What is the difference in release process between a hotfix and feature deployment?

- Prioritization:
  - Is there a structured process in place that governs prioritization of reliability work versus user-facing features?

4.6 SRE Maturity Model

Based on the aforementioned considerations in assessing a product delivery organization on various aspects related to production operations, it is possible to create a maturity model for SRE. The maturity model can be used by SRE coaches initially to assess where the organization is before the SRE transformation. Later, once the transformation is underway, the SRE coaches might wish to reassess the organization to check whether different areas are progressing, stagnating, or regressing. Twice yearly might be a reasonable basis on which to conduct a reassessment.

General disadvantages of maturity models apply to the SRE maturity model as well. A maturity model assumes a linear progression path to a fixed destination of excellence. However, running an SRE transformation will be different for each team due to their unique sociotechnical circumstances. A fixed destination of excellence as the highest level in the SRE maturity model is surely not the top of the mountain. Rather, it is a continuous refinement of SRE processes and practices by each team that drives a good and sustainable SRE execution.

Despite these recognized drawbacks, the SRE maturity model might be helpful to the SRE coaches to gain orientation and serve as a guide for action during the SRE transformation. Especially at the beginning of the journey, the SRE coaches find themselves in a world where data-driven decisions about transformation are not yet possible because there is no foundation for it yet. Moreover, the SRE coaches themselves may be relatively new to the topic of SRE transformation. In this context, the SRE maturity model might serve as overview guidance that is difficult for the SRE coaches to obtain otherwise.

Figure 4.3 shows the SRE maturity model in table form, with defined progression levels of regressive, beginner, and advanced. Note that these levels do not need to be followed rigidly by each respective team.

The teams themselves would not benefit much from spending time assessing themselves or from being involved in the assessment in a time-consuming manner. Rather, the purpose of the SRE maturity model is to support the SRE coaches in identifying areas that need their attention most during the SRE transformation.

The SRE coaches should store their assessment results for future reference. Once the SRE foundations are established, a reassessment can be done. The results of the reassessment can then be compared to the results of the original assessment to assess the progress of the SRE transformation.

The maturity model shows at a glance how multifaceted an SRE implementation is. The SRE transformation is multifaceted as well. In the next section, expectations on the SRE transformation are explored. These need to be aligned before the transformation starts to avoid possible disillusionment with the SRE introduction down the road.

4.7 Posing Hypotheses

Different parties in the organization have different views about production operations. Especially when the product delivery organization is struggling with ongoing outages resulting in high-profile customer escalations, opinions abound about how to improve the situation.

SRE Maturity Model		Ranking Key: "0" = Regressive Maturity, "1" = Beginner Maturity, "2" = Advanced Maturity			
		Regressive	Beginner	Advanced	Result
Organization	Structure	0 Siloed Product Delivery Org	0 Departments Collaborate	1 Independent Cross-Functional Teams	2
	Alignment on Operational Concerns	Intransparent	0 Achieved Using Ad-Hoc Meetings Supported by Some Operational Data	Achieved Using Agreed SUs, SLOs, Error Budget Policies and Error Budget Based Decision Making	2
	Formal Leadership	Unaware of SRE	0 Some Support for SRE	1 Full Support for SRE	2
	Informal Leadership	Production Heroes	0 Some Pockets of Operational Knowledge Throughout the Organization	1 Practice SRE Coaching	2
					Average
People	Devs, Architects, Dev Managers	Never On-call	0 Some Insight Into Production Operations	1 Share On-call as Agreed	2
	Ops Engineers, Ops Managers	Always On-call and Siloed	0 Always On-call But Influence Prioritization	1 Share On-call as Agreed	2
	Product Owners, Product Mgrs	Production is Out of Scope	0 Some Production Operations Involvement	1 Error Budget Based Decision Making	2
	Vice Presidents, Executives	Unaware of SRE	0 Some Support for SRE	1 Full Support for SRE	2
					Average
Tech	Logging	Unstructured	0 Some Logs are Structured	1 Structured For Machine Processing	2
	Monitoring	No Alerting	0 Technical Resource Based Alerting	1 Alerts Reflect User Experience Impact	2
	Testing	Untrustworthy	0 Some Test Suites Can Be Trusted	1 Trustworthy	2
	Release	All Services Released Together	0 Some Services Released Independently	1 Independent Service Releases	2
	Capacity Planning	Does Not Exist	0 Haphazard	1 Elastic Capacity	2
	Development	No Adaptive Capacity	0 Some Adaptive Capacity	1 Appropriate Adaptive Capacity	2
					Average
Culture		Pathological	Bureaucratic	Generative	Result
	Cooperation	Low Cooperation	0 Modest Cooperation	1 High Cooperation	2
	Messenger Treatment	Messengers Shot	0 Messengers Neglected	1 Messengers Trained	2
	Risk Sharing	Responsibilities Shirked	0 Narrow Responsibilities	1 Risks Shared	2
	Bridging	Bridging Discouraged	0 Bridging Tolerated	1 Bridging Encouraged	2
	Attitude to Failure	Failure Leads to Scapegoating	0 Failure Leads to Justice	1 Failure Leads to Enquiry	2
	Attitude to Novelty	Novelty Crushed	0 Novelty Leads to Problems	1 Novelty Implemented	2
					Average
Process	Customer Support	Haphazard	0 Dedicated roles	1 On Rotation in Ops Teams	2
	On-call	Does Not Exist	0 Goodwill	1 Shared by Dev and Ops Teams as Agreed	2
	Incident Response	Haphazard	0 On Request by Managers	1 Swarming by People On-call	2
	Production Access Control	Intransparent	0 For Humans and Scripts	1 Only for Scripts	2
	Regulatory Compliance	Manual	0 Automated to Some Degree	1 Automated to a Large Extent	2
	Deployment	Manual	0 Automated to Some Degree	1 Fully Automated	2
	Prioritization of Reliability	Intransparent	0 By Key Opinion Leaders	1 Data Driven Using Error Budget Policies	2
	Decision Making on Reliability	Intransparent	0 By Key Opinion Leaders	1 Data Driven Using SRE Indicators	2
					Average

Figure 4.3 *The SRE maturity model*

Following this, the views and expectations on the SRE transformation will also be different. Before embarking on an SRE transformation, it is important to align the expectations of different roles and stakeholders. This is necessary not only to avoid disappointment, but also to strengthen support for the SRE transformation and the understanding of SRE as a discipline.

The main stakeholders of the SRE transformation are the executives, managers, operations engineers, developers, and product owners. The stakeholders might have exaggerated expectations, which are summarized in Table 4.2.

Table 4.2 *Stakeholders' Exaggerated Expectations of the SRE Transformation*

Stakeholders	Possible Exaggerated Expectations
Executives	Customer churn due to reliability issues will stop within a couple of weeks.
Managers	Conflicts between product operations and product development will come to an end within a couple of months.
Product owners	Ongoing high-profile customer escalations due to production outages will stop within a couple of months.
Developers	Product owners will finally prioritize reliability over features. Operations engineers will stop interrupting the flow of development work.
Operations engineers	Developers will finally implement software with production-grade quality. Product owners will finally prioritize reliability over features.

The SRE coaches need to bring possible exaggerated expectations to a realistic level. In general, this would be done by explaining that the SRE transformation will establish a joint reliability decision-making process for operations engineers, developers, and product owners. The process will be rooted in joint agreements on SLIs, SLOs, error budget policies, and on-call rotation setup. Agreed error budget policies will lay down the criteria for reliability work prioritization. The speed of the SRE transformation cannot be predicted up front. However, a couple of months into the process the first estimates can and will be provided by the SRE coaches.

Next, the SRE coaches should invite some stakeholders to express their expectations in a structured way using hypotheses. Doing so will allow for later tests to determine whether the SRE transformation has succeeded. Hypotheses can be defined based on the approach from hypothesis-driven development.[8]

A hypothesis is posed before the product delivery teams start working on a product capability. It is done in plain English using a three-term expression, <product capability> / <customer outcome> / <measurable signal>, as follows.

- We believe this <product capability>

- Will result in this <customer outcome>

- We will know we have succeeded when we see this <measurable signal>

---

8. Thoughtworks. n.d. "How to Implement Hypothesis-Driven Development." Accessed January 19, 2022. https://www.thoughtworks.com/insights/articles/how-implement-hypothesis-driven-development.

A good place to start with the hypotheses are the motivations for starting the SRE transformation in the first place. Typically, the motivations are represented by the pain areas in the realm of production outages, customer escalations, reliability work prioritization, and organizational alignment on operational concerns. Table 4.3 shows some examples of possible hypotheses for SRE transformation that might be posed by the stakeholders.

Interestingly, driving all the hypotheses shown in Table 4.3 is organization's establishment of the SRE concept pyramid (Section 3.5). This gives rise to a wide range of very diverse outcomes. Following this, the different outcomes are measured using different measurable signals at different time points in the SRE transformation.

It is important to define the hypotheses for SRE transformation with a small group of stakeholders coming from product operations, product development, and product management before the transformation begins. This needs to be facilitated by the SRE coaches and bears the following three advantages.

1. It allows the stakeholders to express their expectations, after alignment, in a structured manner, thinking about how expectation fulfillment can be measured.

2. It builds stakeholder trust in the SRE coaches. It shows that the SRE coaches do not propagate SRE purely out of excitement; rather, they keep a cool head and approach the transformation as a structured experiment whose outcomes need to be backed up by data.

3. The defined SRE transformation hypotheses need to be made public in the organization (e.g., on a public SRE wiki). This allows everyone to see the outcomes sought by the transformation and how outcome achievement will be measured. This builds trust in the SRE transformation process and the SRE coaches executing it.

Table 4.3 *Examples of SRE Transformation Hypotheses*

Stakeholders	Example Hypotheses		
	Capability	*Outcome*	*Measurable Signals*
Executives	SLIs, SLOs, error budgets, and error budget policies established in the organization	Reduction of customer churn rate due to reliability issues	1) The yearly customer churn rate due to reliability issues 12 months into the SRE transformation has been reduced by 50% compared to the previous 12-month period.
Product owners	SLIs, SLOs, error budgets, and error budget policies established in the organization	Reduction of customer escalations	1) A customer escalation is defined unambiguously. 2) The number of customer escalations six months into the SRE transformation has been reduced by 50% compared to the previous six-month period.

Developers	SLIs, SLOs, error budgets, and error budget policies established in the organization	Faster prioritization of reliability work	1) Reliability work is clearly identifiable in team backlogs. 2) The average lead time for reliability work prioritization in the fourth quarter of the SRE transformation is at least 25% shorter than that in the second quarter of the SRE transformation.
Operations engineers	SLIs, SLOs, error budgets, and error budget policies established in the organization	More streamlined organizational alignment on operational concerns	1) Eight months into the SRE transformation developers go on call for their services at defined times and in defined circumstances. 2) Six months into the SRE transformation any development team can be involved in an ongoing production incident within two hours of the request. 3) Twelve months into the SRE transformation the median production deployment failure rate and median production deployment recovery time of the last three months have been reduced by 50% compared to the three months before the transformation started.
Managers	SLIs, SLOs, error budgets, and error budget policies established in the organization	Fewer conflicts between product development and product operations	1) The number of issues brought to the attention of managers concerning production rollouts in the fourth quarter of the SRE transformation is at least 40% less than that in the second quarter of the SRE transformation.
SRE coaches	SLIs, SLOs, error budgets, and error budget policies established in the organization	Superior customer experience in terms of reliability in production is provided at optimized cost	1) Teams can sustain the SRE activities on their own without ongoing coaching 24 months into the SRE transformation. 2) Customer complaints do not occur repeatedly about the same issues for longer than a week 24 months into the SRE transformation. 3) Teams adapt their SLOs and error budget policies regularly on demand 18 months into the SRE transformation.

4.8 Summary

In this chapter, I showed how the status quo of a software delivery organization can be assessed in terms of operational concerns. The assessment can be done along five dimensions: organizational structure, people, tech, culture, and process. The assessment is necessary to understand where the organization stands in terms of practicing product operations. It answers the question: How is product operations done today?

The results of the assessment should give rise to well-grounded thinking about how the organization could be transformed toward SRE. A good way to start on this is to define the end results of the SRE transformation using hypotheses. The hypotheses define the outcomes aspired to be achieved using new organizational capabilities. Importantly, the hypotheses define how the outcomes would be measured. The goal of the SRE transformation is to test the defined hypotheses on an ongoing basis and adapt the transformation approach to meet the outcomes.

Part II

Running the Transformation

By now, a solid understanding of SRE and the organizational status quo has been developed. It is known why SRE is the methodology of choice to improve product operations. Likewise, it is known how far the organization is from running operations the SRE way. In this part of the book, let us hit the ground running and start the SRE transformation!

Chapter 5

Achieving Organizational Buy-In

The SRE transformation will require multifaceted changes in all teams within the product delivery organization. Therefore, the effort needs to be supported through overall organizational buy-in. A guide for achieving organizational buy-in for SRE is the subject of this chapter.

Before delving into the guide, it is important to note that its applicability depends on the organization's culture. The culture heavily influences the way organizational buy-in for SRE can be achieved. The guide in this chapter is especially suitable for rule-oriented (and also performance-oriented) organizational cultures from the Westrum model.[1]

Ways to achieve organizational buy-in for SRE in a power-oriented culture are highly dependent on the behavior of those in power. Individual techniques from the guide in this chapter will be applicable in a power-oriented culture. However, overall buy-in will need to be orchestrated by carefully taking into account the specific behaviors, nuances, relationships, dysfunctions, ways of cooperation, mindsets, and will of the people in power.

5.1 Getting People Behind SRE

Section 3.6, *Alignment Using the SRE Concept Pyramid,* clarified the organizational alignment that is achievable using the SRE concepts. The questions to ask now are: How do you achieve this alignment? Why should people care? How do you motivate them? How do you win their hearts and minds in a consistent way? In other words, how do you launch a sustainable SRE movement in an organization that has never heard of SRE before?

To approach this, let us explore what a movement is. According to the Longman Dictionary, a movement is "a group of people who share the same ideas or beliefs and who work together to achieve a particular aim."[2] An SRE movement, then, would be a group of people working together to advance their shared ideas about software operations.

---

1. Westrum, R. 2004. "A Typology of Organisational Cultures." *Quality and Safety in Health Care* 13 (suppl_2): ii22–27. https://doi.org/10.1136/qshc.2003.009522.

2. Reprinted by permission of Pearson, Longman Dictionary of Contemporary English. 2014. "Definition of movement." Accessed June 22, 2022. https://www.ldoceonline.com/dictionary/movement.

This means that initially, a group of SRE believers needs to exist. This group would have to consist of at least two people, and they would work together to advance their ideas about doing software operations the SRE way.

Section 2.5, *Coaching*, discussed the difficulties of finding external SRE coaches and showed that internal coaches to drive the SRE transformation would need to be developed. It follows that to start an SRE movement, at least two SRE coaches would probably need to be in place initially.

What would this initial group of SRE coaches need to do to get people behind SRE? First, they would need to initiate organizational buy-in for establishing SRE. Discussions similar to the discourse in Section 1.1, *Why SRE?*, need to take place throughout the organization to understand the reasons for the change in operations in general and the change toward SRE in particular. The buy-in needs to be facilitated simultaneously in top-down, bottom-up, and lateral ways in the organization.

To facilitate buy-in from the top down, the SRE activities would need to be incorporated into portfolio management activities. This is because real effort by all teams in a product delivery organization will be required to work on the SRE transformation. Securing this effort requires echoing SRE in the portfolio management activities in an appropriately lightweight manner. Doing this should show where the SRE transformation sits in terms of priority relative to other major initiatives in the organization. This can range from an urgent and immediate "transform while you perform" level of priority, to one in which a unit of time is allocated to SRE activities for a longer period. The latter is more common.

In any case, to achieve SRE prioritization at the portfolio level, engagement with key leaders must be achieved early, before portfolio prioritization decisions are made. The organization's leaders have different backgrounds and tackle different problem areas in their strategic and day-to-day work. Therefore, for SRE conversations to be successful, they need to be tailored to the particular context of a given leader.

To facilitate buy-in from the bottom up, the SRE activities need to be introduced as a methodology for solving current problems, such as outages and chaos in product operations. As clarified in Section 2.5, *Coaching*, individual team coaching is key here. The team coaching sessions need to take place until the team can fully sustain the SRE activities on their own. Running SRE coaching sessions with a team for several years is more the norm than the exception.

To facilitate buy-in laterally, all formal and informal communication between the development and operations managers and their teams needs to reiterate the envisioned SRE setup, once it has been decided upon. It must be clear who is going on call, for which services, in which circumstances, and with which priority relative to everything else that is occurring in the organization. Engaging with managers is an important ingredient of the SRE transformation.

Navigating the organization simultaneously from the top down, from the bottom up, and laterally fuels the SRE movement. You can view this as a marketing campaign. A great marketing campaign is a true story that unfolds across all possible channels. In the case of an online campaign, it can be a story talked about on Instagram, YouTube, Facebook, and Twitter channels. Each channel has its own characteristics and methods of engagement. So, the story is adapted to each channel to fit well in the respective context and methods of user engagement.

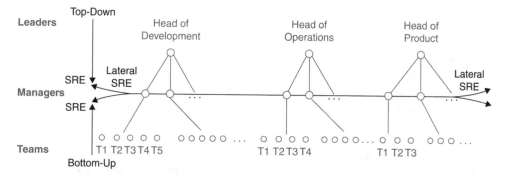

Figure 5.1 *Traditional software delivery organization*

This kind of thinking is required by the SRE coaches trying to create an SRE movement. It might be unnatural for technical people to think in marketing terms and act accordingly, yet this is what is required to drive an SRE transformation. In this context, the most relevant channels are top-down, bottom-up, and lateral conversations throughout the organization. The conversations can be held offline or in any online communication tools the organization might have. What is important is proper engagement of all three channels simultaneously to grow an SRE movement that will sustain itself over time.

This is schematically illustrated in Figure 5.1 using a traditional software delivery organization with a hard split between the development, operations, and product management departments. There are other organizational structures with fewer splits between departments or less pronounced silos. In these organizations, organizational buy-in for SRE might be easier to achieve. The hard split between the departments in Figure 5.1 is chosen for illustration purposes because many traditional enterprises are structured in this way.

A traditional software delivery organization typically has three departments: product development, product operations, and product management. These departments have their own leaders: head of development, head of operations, and head of product. The leaders need to be engaged in getting SRE ranked at the portfolio level of initiatives occurring in the organization. Furthermore, the leaders need to support SRE in their communication with one another and within their respective departments.

The next level of a typical organizational hierarchy consists of development, operations, and product managers. Managers often drive process changes of all kinds. Therefore, some SRE coaches will likely come from this group of people. The managers need to be engaged in creating an understanding of SRE, securing support for it, and ensuring lateral communication about it in the organization. The managers often set goals for the people on their teams. So, getting them engaged in driving SRE is very important to ensure that SRE topics find their way into the goals they set for their teams.

Finally, the bottom level of a typical organizational hierarchy consists of the teams. They need to be coached on an ongoing basis to introduce, develop, and ingrain SRE activities in their daily work. This will require long-term coaching by the SRE coaches. Advancing SRE from the bottom up is the most labor-intensive part of the SRE transformation. It is, indeed, where the transformation happens!

5.2 SRE Marketing Funnel

In marketing, there is a popular model called AIDA[3] for moving consumers through a funnel of cognitive and emotional steps to affect buying behavior. AIDA stands for Awareness → Interest → Desire → Action. First, the consumer's Awareness of a product needs to be captured. One way this can be done is through advertising. Next, the consumer needs to show Interest in learning more about the product. This can be done through, for example, the product website. In the Desire step, the consumer develops a positive attitude toward the product. Finally, the Action step leads to a product purchase.

To achieve organizational buy-in for SRE, the organization needs to undergo a similar series of cognitive and emotional steps until a critical mass of people endorse SRE. Endorsing SRE in this context means being cognitively and emotionally ready for the SRE transformation. Figure 5.2 is an adaptation of the general AIDA marketing funnel to the context of SRE transformation. In the SRE marketing funnel, the steps are Awareness, Interest, Understanding, and Agreement.

With the SRE marketing funnel created, the SRE coaches need to think about how to make the SRE transformation stand out from other initiatives competing for attention from the same stakeholders. How can the marketing for the SRE transformation capture more people's attention than the marketing for other initiatives? How can they frame the SRE transformation in an engaging way? How can they spark interest in SRE? What other initiatives are occurring in the organization that might be adjacent to SRE or can be supported by SRE? Could some activities be done together with these other initiatives to mutually reinforce the messages and get more attention from people in this way? These questions need to be on top of the SRE coaches' minds.

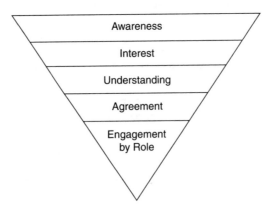

Figure 5.2 *SRE marketing funnel*

3. Wikipedia. n.d. "AIDA (marketing)." Accessed December 15, 2021. https://en.wikipedia.org/wiki/AIDA_ (marketing).

5.2.1 Awareness

Awareness of SRE as a methodology needs to be created. At the time of this writing, many companies and people in the industry are not yet aware of or have only heard of SRE. To drive awareness within the organization, the SRE coaches can organize some lightweight presentations. It is best if there is already some structure for this kind of lightweight learning in the organization, because the audience will already exist and be mentally prepared to learn. For example, lean coffee sessions or lunch and learn sessions would be ideal forums for a short presentation on SRE. To be sure, for the sake of driving awareness, the SRE coaches do not need to create their own presentation materials. Rather, it is better if they use publicly available slides. The following slide decks are freely available online and can be utilized:

- Talk: "Getting Started with Site Reliability Engineering"[4] from DevOps Enterprise Summit London 2018 and associated slide deck by Stephen Thorne

- Slide deck: "SRE for Everyone: Making Tomorrow Better Than Today"[5] from DevOps Days Austin 2019 by Damon Edwards

- Talk: "Monitoring Your Infrastructure and Applications in Production"[6] from Microsoft Ignite Tour 2019 by Jason Hand

The goal of the presentation is to send a message along the lines of "There is an interesting new approach to operations that is practiced by a growing number of companies in the software industry." The presentation may generate additional discussions around the watercooler, at lunch, and in online chats. The presentation should be recorded, and the recording should be named accordingly, tagged with "SRE," and referenced on wiki pages properly for best discoverability in the organization. All of this is important, and should not be underestimated, to spread the message as wide as possible to seed SRE knowledge. Every opportunity should be used to generate a buzz around SRE. No potential conversation should be deemed too small.

The initial buzz is likely to reach developers, architects, and operations engineers. It might also reach development and operations managers. It is less likely to reach product owners in general, although the interest of some product owners with a technical background might be piqued. Finally, the initial buzz is unlikely to reach executives.

5.2.2 Interest

Once the awareness has been seeded, the next step is to get people interested in learning more about SRE. This can be done by sharing the videos mentioned in the previous section in online chats; distributing e-books; and buying SRE books in print, distributing them in offices on-site,

---

4. Thorne, Stephen. 2018. "Getting Started with Site Reliability Engineering." YouTube, July 11, 2018. https://www.youtube.com/watch?v=c-w_GYvi0eA.

5. "SRE for Everyone: Making Tomorrow Better Than Today." SlideShare IOS, May 2, 2019. Accessed January 19, 2022. https://www.slideshare.net/Rundeck/sre-for-everyone-making-tomorrow-better-than-today-devops-days-austin-2019.

6. Microsoft. 2019. "Monitoring Your Infrastructure and Applications in Production." YouTube, April 2, 2019. https://www.youtube.com/watch?v=Si6ehIr6kjw.

and dispatching them to home offices. Additionally, if there is a book club or some technical communities of practice, book discussions can be placed there too. The following books are recommended:

- *Site Reliability Engineering: How Google Runs Production Systems*[7] by Niall Richard Murphy, Betsy Beyer, Chris Jones, and Jennifer Petoff
- *The Site Reliability Workbook: Practical Ways to Implement SRE*[8] by Betsy Beyer, Niall Richard Murphy, David K. Rensin, Kent Kawahara, and Stephen Thorne
- *Implementing Service Level Objectives: A Practical Guide to SLIs, SLOs, and Error Budgets*[9] by Alex Hidalgo
- *Real-World SRE: The Survival Guide for Responding to a System Outage and Maximizing Uptime*[10] by Nat Welch

Also, if there are technical communities of practice—for instance, for developers, architects, operations engineers, or topics like DevOps—the presentation from the previous section should be repeated there in smaller rounds. The smaller rounds are ideal for Q&A sessions where more and more interest for SRE can be generated. Moreover, the technical communities are a good place to share blog posts and newsletters on SRE encouraging people to subscribe. Notably, the *SRE Weekly*[11] newsletter should be recommended by the SRE coaches.

Following this, if the organization has a forum like Scrum of Scrums, it would be worth a try inviting the participants to a dedicated session on SRE. Such a forum will likely be attended by the scrum masters, who are multipliers in the organization. Additionally, it might be occasionally attended by project managers, operations managers, and development managers, all of whom talk to executives in other forums. So, having a conversation about SRE with these groups provides a chance for SRE as a topic to make its way up to the executives.

The Scrum of Scrums participants are typically generally interested in learning about what is going on in the organization. So, a session with them would be about satisfying that interest. It would be about explaining what has happened before, which views about SRE were observed, which pros and cons could be seen if SRE were applied in the organization, and so on. The purpose is also to invite the Scrum of Scrums participants to the ongoing conversation. This is important because they will not endorse the SRE transformation if it falls on them later with full force out of the blue.

As the SRE coaches discuss, present, and distribute more SRE content, people might notice they are the ones pushing the topic. Over time, they might start identifying the SRE coaches

---

7. Murphy, Niall Richard, Betsy Beyer, Chris Jones, and Jennifer Petoff. 2016. *Site Reliability Engineering: How Google Runs Production Systems*. Sebastopol, CA: O'Reilly Media.

8. Beyer, Betsy, Niall Richard Murphy, David K. Rensin, Stephen Thorne, and Kent Kawahara. 2018. *The Site Reliability Workbook: Practical Ways to Implement SRE*. Sebastopol, CA: O'Reilly Media.

9. Hidalgo, Alex. 2020. *Implementing Service Level Objectives: A Practical Guide to SLIs, SLOs, and Error Budgets*. Sebastopol, CA: O'Reilly Media.

10. Welch, Nat. 2018. *Real-World SRE: The Survival Guide for Responding to a System Outage and Maximizing Uptime*. Birmingham, UK: Packt Publishing Ltd.

11. *SRE Weekly*. Weekly online newsletter published by Lex Neva. Available at https://sreweekly.com.

with SRE. This is a great sign, because suddenly, there are people in the organization who can be pointed to whenever anyone has a question around SRE.

5.2.3 Understanding

The next stage of the SRE marketing funnel is development of a deeper understanding about SRE. This can be reached by having detailed conversations about SRE concepts: What are SLIs? What are SLOs? What are error budgets? What are error budget policies? How could something like this work in our organization? How are other companies doing this? These are the topics of discussion to drive understanding.

Through the activities to drive awareness (Section 5.2.1, *Awareness*) and interest (Section 5.2.2, *Interest*), it will be possible to identify people with a special interest in SRE. These are the people who borrow the books distributed in the office, actively ask questions, have discussions with others about SRE, and so on. A couple of dedicated sessions can be held with these people to explore their shared interest in SRE, and more specifically, to find out who knows what about SRE currently, who listened to which SRE talks, who read which SRE books, and who knows people from other companies where SRE has been practiced. These sessions are about deepening the understanding of SRE concepts and seeding community aspects of SRE in the organization. The sessions should be widely advertised in advance in order to attract not only people with an obvious interest in SRE, but also others from the sidelines who did not express an interest before but want to listen or contribute.

5.2.4 Agreement

The next phase of the SRE marketing funnel is achievement of broad agreement in the organization that it would generally be beneficial to have SRE in place to improve product operations. It should be clear, in rough terms, which benefits an introduction of SRE could bring over the current practice of product operations. For example, at this stage, there should be broad agreement about the potential benefits of data-driven decision-making on whether to invest in reliability work versus new features, and about the benefits of improved alignment on operational concerns by operations engineers, developers, and product owners.

To drive this agreement, the SRE coaches can prepare a presentation. Whereas the initial presentation to drive awareness (Section 5.2.1, *Awareness*) was all about others doing SRE, this presentation should summarize in detail the SRE-related activities that have taken place within the organization since the initial presentation. It should list the points on which people in the organization seem to agree, and the open points that generated discussion but did not lead to a conclusion or have not been discussed yet. The presentation should end with next steps. These could be

- Talking to the executives about starting the SRE transformation
- Trying out something new in a team, such as a logging infrastructure with a new log query language
- Setting up a session to deepen the understanding of SRE in a domain-specific area of the product, such as for example, SRE for the new Extract Transform Load (ETL) pipeline being introduced to prepare data for learning by new AI algorithms
- And so on

It is very important to end this presentation on a positive note. For example: "As you can see, SRE offers great potential for the organization. We are determined to explore this potential further!" It should not end with a message such as: "Here is a huge list of things we did not talk about yet. The SRE transformation is going to be a multiyear endeavor. The results cannot be expected soon." The SRE coaches must maintain a positive and upbeat attitude. This will go a long way toward carrying the teams through the ups and downs of the transformation. Moreover, it will help the coaches carry themselves through the difficult journey of transforming the way product operations is done in the organization.

5.2.5 Engagement

The end stage of the SRE marketing funnel is about finishing the marketing campaign by making sure people are ready to engage in SRE activities in their specific role. This can be achieved if the previous stages of the marketing funnel were run through successfully. If people became aware of SRE, it piqued their interest, they developed their own understanding of it, and they agree that it is a helpful methodology for doing operations, they are ready to engage.

Different roles engage in SRE differently. Table 5.1 includes the questions that should be circling in people's minds when they are ready to engage in SRE activities.

Table 5.1 *Questions Indicating SRE Engagement Readiness, by Role*

Role	Questions
Executive	How can I support the SRE initiative?
Manager	What do I need to do to facilitate the SRE transformation?
	How can I enable people?
Developer	What do I need to do to engage in SRE?
Operations engineer	What do I need to do to engage in SRE?
Product owner	What do I need to do to engage in SRE?

For people who are not ready to engage, one or several stages of the SRE marketing funnel would need to be repeated and reinforced. That said, not everyone will agree with SRE. This is especially true before people have seen any results in their own organization. Seeing is believing, and this is not possible at this stage. What is important is broad agreement in the organization that SRE would probably be a good methodology to adopt. If a majority of the people can subscribe to this, the marketing funnel has worked and the SRE coaches deserve a pat on the back!

5.3 SRE Coaches

In the previous sections, SRE coaches were identified as important drivers of the SRE transformation. Before going further on the transformational journey, let us look at the leadership and other qualities an SRE coach needs to have to be accepted by the people. People's trust in SRE coaches is critical for driving the transformation in a streamlined fashion.

5.3.1 Qualities

How do you identify transformational leaders who would enjoy the trust of the people on their teams? Which characteristics would someone need to have to become a transformational leader trusted by the teams? The following list of qualities is representative, although not exhaustive:

- Worked in product delivery for more than three years, ideally within the organization to be transformed

- Demonstrated a track record of shipping products regularly

- Demonstrated a track record of introducing some new ways of working in the organization

- Demonstrated a track record of making some new ways of working stick in a sustainable manner as evidenced by people who adapted their way of doing certain tasks

- Demonstrated a track record of engaging a diverse set of stakeholders to drive an initiative

- Demonstrated a track record of measuring improvements

- Demonstrated a track record of being a nice person to work with

- Has a good relationship with most people in the organization

- Demonstrated tenacity, empathy, persistence, iteration on feedback, experimentation, perseverance, patience, reliability, dependability, endurance, energy, enthusiasm, aspiration, goal orientation, decision-making, communication, creativity, self-motivation, ability to motivate others, openness, learning, honesty, sincerity, niceness, and a bit of charisma

Once the transformational leaders have been identified, an ongoing relationship of trust needs to be maintained as a matter of priority. It is easy to break the trust that people put into transformational leadership. Here are some of the ways this trust can be undermined.

- Establishing unrealistic SRE transformational goals, agreeing to them with the higher-ups in the organization, and presenting them as a given to the teams.

- Getting impatient with the speed of the transformation due to not recognizing that it will be implemented under ongoing product delivery pressures. "Transform while you perform" requires a delicate balance between transformation efforts and product delivery efforts.

- Drumming up and overselling transformation successes when reporting to the higher-ups to the point where the team members recognize that the transformational leaders have lost touch with what is occurring on the ground. This is known as "transformation on paper" syndrome.

- Not attributing successes to those who actually achieved them, but rather presenting them as having been achieved by the transformational leaders.

- Especially with technical topics, involving only certain groups of people on the team in decisions that affect the entire team (e.g., involving only architects in technical decisions on the assumption that they will involve the entire team).

- And so on.

In summary, for the transformation to be successful, it must be driven by those who enjoy the trust of the people undergoing the transformation. Establishing this kind of transformational leadership needs to be high on organizational leaders' priority lists. To be sure, the SRE transformation leaders do not need to have a formal position of power in the organization. It may even be beneficial if they do not, because then it is clear that the teams adopt change based not on compliance with power, but rather on their own newly won conclusions and convictions. This makes change stick in a sustainable way without buy-in issues.

As mentioned earlier in the book, in terms of forming a group of SRE coaches, the best pragmatic setup is a small group of people coming from product operations and product development. This is because most changes will take place in these departments. It is unlikely that someone from product management would become an SRE coach. This is also not necessary, because changes caused by introducing SRE in product management are not as profound as they are in product operations and product development. In general, however, having an operations engineer, a developer, and a product owner as the SRE coaches would be a great, although unlikely, option.

5.3.2 Responsibilities

The SRE coaches need to share responsibilities but also have focus areas. Following is a list of responsibilities to be shared:

- Managerial
  - Managing the project
  - Scheduling meetings
  - Reporting to the executive team
  - Lobbying for an SRE activities budget (to pay for tools, training, conference visits, etc.)
  - Managing procurement of new tools and ongoing licensing
- Strategy
  - Prioritizing the portfolio
  - Creating an SRE adoption strategy for each team and coaching the team along
  - Managing the SRE backlog
  - Managing feature requests for SRE infrastructure
- Technical
  - Running regular team coaching sessions
  - Keeping notes from team coaching sessions in a shared place
  - Knowing the SRE infrastructure, its upcoming features, and its future direction
  - Onboarding teams on the SRE infrastructure
  - Supporting teams with the SLI and SLO definition process
  - Supporting teams with setting up an on-call process and on-call rotations

- ○ Managing troubleshooting requests
- ○ Identifying best practices and cross-pollinating the teams
- Marketing

  - ○ Broadcasting successes (through blog posts, newsletter articles, presentations, etc.)
  - ○ Scouting for opportunities to inject SRE thinking into the daily work of teams and people
  - ○ Taking part in events and meetings within the company to spread the word about SRE
- People

  - ○ Having one-on-one sessions with people on demand
  - ○ Facilitating the creation of SRE backlog items on team backlogs
  - ○ Facilitating a community of practice for SRE
  - ○ Making SRE part of the employee onboarding process
  - ○ Facilitating training for new tools

Despite a long list of responsibilities, being an SRE coach does not have to be a full-time job and instead can be a part-time responsibility. For example, an operations engineer implementing the SRE infrastructure could also be an SRE coach and take on the technical responsibilities from the preceding list. Likewise, a development manager taking on the role of SRE coach could handle responsibilities related to project management, meeting scheduling, executive reporting, procurement, and portfolio management.

When selected in this way, SRE coaches constitute an informal cross-functional group operating throughout the product delivery organization and beyond. In some organizational cultures, such cross-functional groups are taken less seriously than they are within siloed projects. The SRE coaches need to pay attention to this sensitivity. In some situations, they need to secure from leadership a formal announcement to the product delivery organization identifying the appointed SRE coaches who will be working with all the teams.

In terms of achieving organizational buy-in for SRE, the SRE coaches need to work with the organization in a top-down, bottom-up, and lateral manner. In the next sections, I will present a deep dive into how this can be done.

5.4 Top-Down Buy-In

To facilitate top-down buy-in for SRE, it needs to be clear whom to engage with on the executive leadership team. The SRE initiative will require a significant time investment and a moderate monetary investment. Based on this, a list of stakeholders can be compiled. In *Fifty Quick Ideas to Improve Your User Stories*,[12] Gojko Adzic and David Evans recommend that a stakeholder chart be created. A stakeholder chart helps identify people who are directly and indirectly

---

12. Adzic, Gojko, and David Evans. 2014. *Fifty Quick Ideas to Improve Your User Stories*. Woking, UK: Neuri Consulting LLP.

affected by an initiative. People who are indirectly affected are easy to overlook, but they are just as important to engage as those who are directly affected. This is because they might turn out to be supporters or detractors of the initiative, both of which should be known to those driving it.

5.4.1 Stakeholder Chart

To create a stakeholder chart, start by compiling a list of every possible stakeholder in the initiative. The list should include all top-level leaders in the product delivery organization. These are likely to be the head of operations, head of development, and head of product management. In large organizations, these leaders might seem to be far away from the methodologies adopted by the teams, and therefore they might not be considered stakeholders for SRE. This conclusion is incorrect. If the leaders are far away from the day-to-day work, it is even more important to engage with them because they are in charge of initiatives and of time and budget allocations for their departments. They must understand at an appropriate level of detail that the SRE transformation will require time and money in order to judge it. It is the SRE coaches' job to turn these leaders into supporters of the SRE transformation as much as possible.

Another extremely important aspect is that SRE attempts to facilitate alignment on operational concerns between product operations, product development, and product management (see Section 1.2, *Alignment Using SRE*). Can that kind of alignment be achieved if the head of operations, head of development, and head of product management are unaligned? Not really. Can SRE be prioritized well in a list of organizational initiatives if the head of operations, head of development, and head of product management are unaligned? Again, not really. It follows that the top leaders in product delivery must be on the stakeholder list regardless of their flight level.

Once the list of all possible stakeholders has been created, the stakeholders can be categorized in terms of their formal power in the organization and their interest in the initiative (see Table 5.2).[12]

On the left-hand side of the table, the category of formal power is split in two: high formal power and low formal power stakeholders. At the top of the table, the category of interest is split in two: low interest and high interest. Next, the stakeholders can be categorized into four resultant categories. The stakeholders with high formal power but low interest in SRE need to be kept satisfied. Doing this means determining what would make them satisfied in terms of the SRE transformation. The stakeholders with low formal power and low interest in SRE need to be monitored. No action is required with this stakeholder group unless their power or interest changes.

The stakeholders with high formal power and high interest in SRE need to be fully engaged in the transformation. Yes, some senior leaders, especially if they come from a technical background, enjoy being involved in the details of a transformation like this. In these cases, the SRE

Table 5.2 *Stakeholder Chart*

Formal Power Category	Low-Interest Stakeholder	High-Interest Stakeholder
High formal power stakeholder	Keep satisfied	Engage fully
Low formal power stakeholder	Monitor	Keep informed

coaches should ensure their engagement. This does not mean involving the leaders in all of their teams' coaching sessions. Rather, it means discussing with them what level of involvement would be appropriate for them to satisfy their interest on the one hand and not impose constraints on their time on the other hand.

Finally, the stakeholders with low formal power and high interest in the SRE transformation need to be kept informed. This can be done by reaching out periodically via email, including updates in the organization's newsletter, inviting them to presentations intended for a wider audience, and so on.

The SRE coaches are well advised to create an SRE stakeholder chart to identify direct and indirect stakeholders of the transformation. Top-down buy-in in particular requires involving stakeholders who might not be obvious at first but can be uncovered during chart creation. The SRE stakeholder chart does not need to be a private document for the SRE coaches. Rather, it can be shared with some of the stakeholders to get their views and feedback. After all, in a large enterprise, it is easy to overlook people or be unclear about their responsibilities!

Table 5.3 shows an example of an SRE transformation stakeholder chart.

The upper-right quadrant of the chart is where the top leaders of the product delivery organization can be found. Often, these are the head of operations, head of development, and head of product management. The SRE transformation directly influences their departments.

The upper-left quadrant is where a large group of stakeholders can be found. These are people with high formal power but low interest in SRE. For example, the head of legal is not going to be interested in SRE initially. However, when the organization has been developed to the point where there are meaningful SLIs, SLOs, and error budget policies, legal might become interested. This is because the SRE data can be used to inform the so-called service-level agreements (SLAs).

Table 5.3 *Example SRE Transformation Stakeholder Chart*

Formal Power Category	Low-Interest Stakeholder	High-Interest Stakeholder
High formal power stakeholder	Keep satisfied • Head of legal • Head of regulatory affairs • Head of finance • Head of marketing • Head of sales • Head of product delivery organization	Engage fully • Head of operations • Head of development • Head of product management
Low formal power stakeholder	Monitor • Head of procurement • Head of portfolio management	Keep informed • Head of partner management • Other product delivery organizations in the company

SLAs are contractual agreements between the service providers and service consumers. Certainly, legal is involved in contractual negotiations about SLAs. In *Implementing Service Level Objectives*,[9] legal is described as one of the SRE stakeholders because SLA negotiations can be underpinned with SLO data.

In the upper-left quadrant, the head of regulatory affairs can be seen. Here, initial interest in SRE will be low. However, as the practice of SRE grows in the organization, the SRE data will become interesting for regulatory affairs. From a regulatory standpoint, monitoring the health of services in production can be a compliance requirement. For example, ISO/IEC 27001[13] is an international standard for managing information security. It requires appropriate service health monitoring to be evidenced. Doing so with the rigor of SRE is an excellent way to meet this regulatory requirement.

In the upper-left quadrant of the stakeholder chart are the heads of finance, marketing, sales, and the overall organization. These leaders have high formal power in the organization but presumably low interest in SRE. This will probably remain as is. The leaders in this quadrant need to be kept satisfied first and foremost in the sense of the SRE transformation not leading to new issues. In other words, it should not introduce any new legal or regulatory issues, break the organization's budget, or impact marketing and sales initiatives.

In the lower-left quadrant of the chart are the leaders of procurement and portfolio management. SRE is not in their scope. Therefore, no immediate action to engage with these leaders is necessary to advance SRE.

Finally, the lower-right quadrant contains stakeholders who need to be kept informed about how the transformation is unfolding. In this quadrant, the head of partner management can be found. This leader will be interested in SRE because it holds the promise to manage the relationship with partners in a better way. For example, internal and external partners that use public-platform APIs will possibly be able to see some aggregated error budget depletion statistics for relevant data centers. This may contribute to an improvement in trust between the partners over time. In fact, Google set up an entire team for a similar purpose, referred to as Customer Reliability Engineering (CRE).[14] The team offers SRE services to partners for free in exchange for the partners doing the reliability work according to SRE principles and methods.

Another important stakeholder group in the lower-right quadrant of the stakeholder chart are other product delivery organizations in the company. They might be struggling with operations too, not least because they might be new to operating their software in an SaaS fashion. Therefore, these leaders might be very interested in learning from the experience of running an SRE transformation in terms of outcomes and effort required. For them, seeing an SRE transformation succeed would increase their confidence that it will work for them as well because they are part of the same company. A side effect of other departments being interested in SRE and finally adopting it is that a bigger coalition within the company is formed that is lobbying for the same shared resources, such as tools and budgets for operations.

---

13. Wikipedia. n.d. "ISO/IEC 27001." Accessed December 17, 2021. https://en.wikipedia.org/wiki/ISO/IEC_27001.

14. Rensin, Dave. 2016. "Introducing Google Customer Reliability Engineering." Google Cloud, October 10, 2016. https://cloud.google.com/blog/products/gcp/introducing-a-new-era-of-customer-support-google-customer-reliability-engineering.

The stakeholder chart should be revisited on a cadence to adjust for organizational changes and growing SRE maturity level. Revisiting the chart about every six months seems to be a reasonable cadence.

As the head of operations, head of development, and head of product management are the SRE stakeholders with high formal power and high interest, they need to be fully engaged in the SRE transformation. Therefore, getting buy-in from these three stakeholders is of paramount importance. Each of these leaders has unique interests and a unique focus within the scope of product delivery. Let us explore how they can be engaged effectively to achieve buy-in for running the SRE transformation.

5.4.2 Engaging the Head of Development

The primary focus of the head of development is typically the quality and speed of feature delivery. Thus, the following concerns are top of mind for this person:

- Quality of feature delivery
- Speed of feature delivery
- Hiring
- Budget
- Ongoing upskilling
- Relationships with the head of product management, head of operations, and head of the product delivery organization
- Process improvements

From the lens of product operations, SRE would appear in this priority list as part of quality concerns. The head of development feels the pressure of insufficient delivery quality from four angles: the customers directly, the head of the product delivery organization, the head of operations, and the head of product management. It seems like insufficient quality is felt by everyone. In this context, statements like "quality is not negotiable" are nice in theory, but in practice what it really comes down to is a balance between sufficient quality and sufficient feature delivery speed. Now, how do you strike that balance?

Typical answers to this question are to improve the hiring process to hire software engineers who value quality, invest in ongoing upskilling to have the latest knowledge about tools and methods fed into the organization, and have a metrics system in place to steer decision-making. The metrics system can be tricky to create because software quality is not straightforward to measure.

Improving Metrics

A metrics system proposed by Nicole Forsgren, Jez Humble, and Gene Kim in their book *Accelerate*[15] is enjoying growing popularity in the software industry. It consists of four metrics, as shown in Table 5.4.

---

15. Forsgren, Nicole, Jez Humble, and Gene Kim. 2018. *Accelerate: The Science of Lean Software and DevOps: Building and Scaling High Performing Technology Organizations*. Portland, OR: IT Revolution Press.

Table 5.4 *Metrics from Accelerate*

Metric	Explanation[16]
Deployment frequency	How often an organization successfully releases to production
Lead time for changes	The amount of time it takes a commit to get into production
Change failure rate	The percentage of deployments causing a failure in production
Time to restore service	How long it takes to recover from a failure in production

Further, the DORA research program,[17] initiated by some of the *Accelerate* book authors, produced a "State of DevOps 2021"[18] report. In the report, an operational performance metric, reliability, is added to the four metrics of software delivery performance. The report defines reliability as "the degree to which a team can keep promises and assertions about the software they operate." The authors asked respondents to rate their ability to meet and exceed their reliability targets in terms of availability, latency, performance, and scalability.

This is a very good start and a step beyond previous "State of DevOps" reports by DORA that historically only measured availability. From the discussions in the previous chapters, it is clear that SRE can provide concrete measurements of availability and latency as well as add a lot more to measuring operational performance. In fact, in SRE terms, availability and latency are SLIs. There are many more SLIs, such as, for example, throughput, correctness, freshness, and durability, as listed in Section 3.1, *Service Level Indicators*. All of these can be measured against corresponding SLOs.

One aspect of convincing the head of development about SRE is that it can be viewed as an additional source of useful operational metrics that go beyond the *Accelerate* book and are either in line with or go beyond the DORA research program. Using these new metrics, the overall quality of software delivery can be steered in a more precise manner.

Improving Relationships

Additionally, the head of development is interested in good working relationships with the heads of operations and product management. SRE helps here as well, as it has its strengths in bringing about exactly this alignment (see Section 1.2, *Alignment Using SRE*). But how do you convey this to the head of development? You can do this based on the additional operational metrics provided by SRE. So far, the metrics we discussed were used to steer improvements in product development. However, SRE metrics report on the state of production from the user point of view. This is interesting to the head of the product delivery organization, the head of operations, and the head of product management.

---

16. "Use Four Keys Metrics Like Change Failure Rate to Measure Your DevOps Performance." n.d. Google Cloud Blog. Accessed January 20, 2022. https://cloud.google.com/blog/products/devops-sre/using-the-four-keys-to-measure-your-devops-performance.

17. "DORA Research Program." n.d. Accessed January 18, 2022. https://www.devops-research.com/research.html.

18. DORA. 2021. "State of DevOps 2021." Google Cloud. https://services.google.com/fh/files/misc/state-of-devops-2021.pdf.

That is, the SRE metrics can be used to steer conversations about the state of production with the head of the product delivery organization, the head of operations, and the head of product management. Instead of them bringing the bad news to the head of development as lagging indicators of the state of production, the SRE metrics can be used as leading indicators to spark joint conversations about production ahead of time. This can lead to joint decisions about the measures needed to keep production running smoothly being made at the right time, before bigger problems emerge and lead to customer escalations. This can improve relationships with the head of the product delivery organization, the head of operations, and the head of product management. Everybody should be more in touch with product operations and be in a better position to contribute to decisions directly targeted at production improvements.

Figure 5.3 illustrates complaints heard by the head of development in the absence of SRE. Customers use the product in production and send their complaints to the head of the product delivery organization and the head of product management. They, in turn, forward the complaints to the head of development.

The head of operations does production monitoring and also sends respective complaints to the head of development. But with SRE, an entirely new level of decision-making is enabled. It allows the leadership to make timely decisions about reliability based on data from production before the customers complain. This is shown in Figure 5.4.

The SRE infrastructure monitors production and generates appropriate SRE indicators that are coarse-grained enough for the leadership team to understand. This way, joint decision-making is enabled for the head of operations, head of development, head of product management, and head of the product delivery organization. The leadership team's decisions are about allocations of time, budget, and people. For example, they may notice that a particular group of deployed services, such as payment handling services, were barely able to maintain their error budgets in the last three quarters. At the same time, they may notice that the number of customer complaints about payments is growing. Using this data, they can look at the number of services owned by the part of the organization responsible for payment handling. They might find out

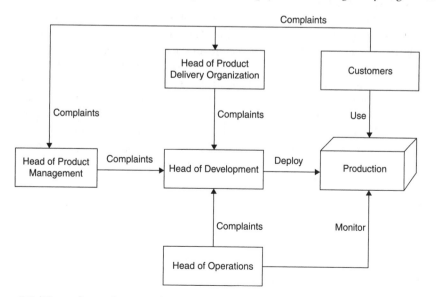

Figure 5.3 *Flow of complaints to the head of development*

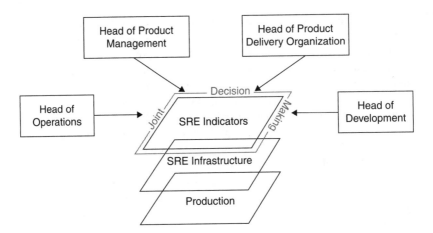

Figure 5.4 *Joint decision-making using SRE indicators*

that this part of the organization owns a number of services that do not stack up with the number of people available. This can spark a conversation about whether the payment handling services should get more people to extend existing teams or form new ones. This, in turn, can spark a conversation about whether this can be done by relocating some people from other teams to the payment handling services or whether a budget request to hire new people has to be raised.

Beyond data-driven decision-making, the SRE introduction can contribute a lot to process improvements: It leads to better insights into production for the entire organization, it enables the organization to act on operational concerns in a data-driven manner ahead of time, and it would push the developers to take greater ownership of the results of their work in production.

Assessing Cost and Effort

So far, so good. But what is the cost of SRE, the head of development might wonder. The answer must be that off-the-shelf infrastructure will be used as much as possible for product instrumentation purposes. The necessary SRE infrastructure add-ons for calculating metrics and enabling developers based on the SRE concept pyramid will be developed and maintained by product operations. Some new tool licenses may be required, but no significant cost position will be added. This should put the mind of the head of development at rest as far as the budget is concerned.

Further, the SRE introduction will require a redistribution of effort for going on call for services in production. A discussion will need to be held between product operations, product development, and product management regarding the on-call setup suitable for the organization. This discussion can lead to any outcome, ranging from the developers always going on call for their services in production to only going on call when their services do not meet a certain service level. Anything in between is also possible using different ways of shared on call between product operations and product development. In any case, the developers will need to be put in a position to go on call supported by the SRE infrastructure and to do so according to the agreed setup. As discussed at length in Section 2.3.1, *Product Development*, having developers on call to the agreed extent provides the necessary live feedback loop feeding the experience of product operations directly into the feature development process. This point illustrates the real human effort of the SRE transformation for product development.

The reaction of the head of development to the developers going on call may vary. If the head of development is following the industry DevOps best practices, they will have anticipated this for a long time. They would be happy that the SRE transformation finally tangibly articulates the need for putting the developers on call to the agreed extent in an attempt to reduce the distance between the developers and production. This would strengthen the ownership of services by the developers. They would implement the services to a lesser extent to satisfy the product owner but to a greater extent to satisfy the customer.

If, on the other hand, the head of development is not up-to-date in terms of the DevOps best practices, they may see the attempt to put the developers on call as a threat posed by product operations to shed some of their workload onto product development. In that case, the entire SRE system based on the SRE concept pyramid will need to be explained in detail along with the advantages of putting the developers on call, as discussed in Section 2.3.1, *Product Development*. The head of development may want to preempt the initial stages of the SRE transformation until on call for developers becomes a topic for discussion. This discussion needs to be guided carefully by the SRE coaches because it is very premature. Many options are possible, which can be discussed, but no choices can be made at this point.

One of the last questions the head of development might have concerns with is who would be driving the SRE introduction. To answer this question, it needs to be conveyed that the SRE coaches would be identified, nurtured, and do the hard work of meeting with each team to introduce the tools and methods. A list of the people who might wish or have agreed to do this contributes to the credibility of the initiative in the eyes of the head of product development.

The last question the head of development might have could be about how the success of the SRE introduction would be measured. The answer is that hypotheses like the ones shown in Section 4.7, *Posing Hypotheses*, will be jointly created by people from product operations, product development, and product management. These hypotheses will contain quantifiable, measurable signals that will guide the transformation and be used to check progress at defined times in a data-driven manner. The fulfillment of the hypotheses will also determine the timeline of the SRE transformation. Also, this should convey the impression of an initiative that will be driven based on ongoing feedback, applying the scientific method.

More than one meeting might be required to get buy-in from the head of development. After the first session, the head of development may want to talk to their direct reports about SRE. They may or may not wish to do this with the SRE coaches. The SRE coaches should be open to either scenario. The same applies regarding discussions with the head of development's peers.

The SRE coaches running the sessions need to bring the buy-in of the head of development to a conclusion by ensuring they will support the prioritization of the SRE transformation against other organizational initiatives at the portfolio level.

5.4.3 Engaging the Head of Operations

The primary concern of the head of operations typically is whether the production system is running well so that there are no customer complaints. Thus, most important to the head of operations are the following concerns:

- State of production
- Customer escalations

- Customer support requests
- Reporting to executive management

In this priority list, SRE would be involved in all four points. However, the state of production would be the most immediate point addressed directly by SRE. This is the starting point of engaging the head of operations. In the current setup, the state of production is likely to be determined by the customer escalations and resource-based alerts set up by the operations teams.

Improving the State of Production Reporting

With SRE, the state of production is determined by the fulfillment of service objectives jointly agreed to by product operations, product development, and product management. Therefore, the objectives will necessarily become more customer-oriented and less technically oriented. The corollary of this is that alerts will reflect negative customer experiences. Receiving such alerts ahead of time and taking appropriate action should reduce customer escalations because more issues should be possible to fix before the customers notice them. Additionally, the reported state of production should be more reliable in terms of reflecting an impacted customer experience. Based on this, the reporting to executive management should also become more reflective of the customer experience.

Furthermore, the SRE infrastructure will generate SRE metrics that will show the fulfillment of the agreed objectives by services over time (error budget depletion). There will be agreements in place between operations engineers, developers, and product owners that will govern the investments in reliability improvements based on the fulfillment of the objectives (error budget policy). The teams will enact the agreements and invest in reliability according to them (error budget–based decision–making). Gone will be the days when obvious reliability improvements will be postponed "forever" in favor of implementing new customer-facing features.

Improving On-Call Setup

In terms of on-call setup, the current situation is likely to be that the operations engineers are doing the entire on-call work. With SRE, an on-call setup will be created by agreement between the operations engineers, developers, and product owners. Gone will be the days when the operations engineers operate a product they did not develop regardless of the service level exhibited by the service. Moreover, the involvement of product owners in the on-call setup definition will ensure that the people on call, and others, required to resolve incidents will be able to do so on the spot without constant renegotiations of backlog priorities by incident.

The envisioned on-call setup with SRE is that the development team takes part in production monitoring as agreed. With that, the development team should aim to be in a position to be the first to detect issues in production. Moreover, the development team should aim to fix the detected issues in production before they are noticed by anyone else. This is illustrated in Figure 5.5.

Furthermore, the development team should make the current issues, their status, and who is working on them transparent within the organization. If the sales and marketing teams are outside the organization, the product status page on the right-hand side of the figure needs to be made accessible to them as well. This reduces the communication overhead and conversations

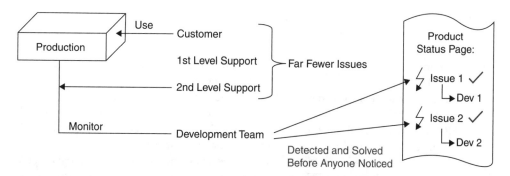

Figure 5.5 *Development team aiming to be the first to detect issues in production*

going on in the organization about production status. A professional status page such as the one for Microsoft Azure[19] or Amazon AWS[20] is the goal with SRE.

Assessing Cost and Effort

Beyond that, the head of operations may have additional questions regarding tools, budget, and people. To know whether the SRE transformation would require new tools, the current tool landscape would need to be analyzed. In general, to implement SRE in the organization the following tool categories would be needed:

1. Logging infrastructure with a log query language to programmatically query the logs

2. Monitoring infrastructure to detect breaches of the agreed service objectives

3. Alerting infrastructure to alarm people on call

4. Visualization infrastructure for metrics reporting

5. On-call management tool

The numbering of the tool categories corresponds to the order of introduction of the respective topics. First, the logging infrastructure needs to be in place so that the development teams can use it to generate logs. The logs can be queried using the log query language. Based on the queries, the monitoring infrastructure can detect the SLO breaches. Next, the breaches need to be dispatched to the people on call in such a manner that the alerts are timely on the one hand but effective on the other hand. After that, visualizations need to be created for SLO breaches and error budget depletions over time for different audiences: teams, managers, and executives. Finally, a professional on-call management tool will be needed to manage on-call rotations within and across teams, departments, and time zones.

The tool stack will require some custom software development. That is, in product operations, software development work will need to be done. For this, a couple of software developers

---

19. Microsoft. n.d. "Azure Status." Accessed January 20, 2022. https://status.azure.com/en-us/status.

20. Amazon Web Services. n.d. "AWS Service Health Dashboard." Accessed January 20, 2022. https://status.aws.amazon.com.

would be needed. Having only one software developer working on the SRE infrastructure is very dangerous because the developer would become the only person with knowledge about the infrastructure used by the entire product delivery organization. One software developer working on the SRE infrastructure means a bus factor[21] of 1. If that person gets hit by a bus, there is no knowledge about the SRE infrastructure left in the organization.

If currently there are no software developers within product operations, a budget request would need to be raised. In terms of time allocation, one software developer will have to work on the SRE infrastructure full time. Depending on the size of the organization, additional SRE infrastructure developers might be able to have other responsibilities in parallel.

As with the head of development, more than one session might be required to convince the head of operations to implement SRE. They are going to wish to discuss it within their department. They might have general questions about the SRE transformation. These can be answered in the same way as with the head of development.

Also, as with the head of development, the SRE coaches need to end the initial engagement with the head of operations by obtaining their agreement to support the prioritization of the SRE transformation at the portfolio level.

5.4.4 Engaging the Head of Product Management

The primary concerns of the head of product management typically are the product-market fit, revenue generated by the product, and product features requested by the customers. Following are their most pressing concerns:

- Feature delivery dates
- Feature specifications
- User experience
- Sales and marketing commitments

Where does SRE appear in this list of concerns? Seemingly, the user experience would be a point influenced by SRE. What about operations and user experience? These two disciplines are not always viewed in an intertwined way by product management. Typically, in product management, under user experience, activities are understood that precede the development work by the developers. These are activities such as thinking about the design, conducting design sprints, developing the information architecture, conducting user research, engaging with UI/UX designers to discuss user interactions, designing UI screens, and so on. These activities are necessary and provide much-needed input to the developers so that they can start thinking about the technologies needed to implement the desired user experience and user interfaces.

Let us explore the term "user experience" for a moment. According to Wikipedia, "user experience (UX) is a person's emotions and attitudes about using a particular product, system or service."[22] The emphasis is on using the product, not thinking about the product, envisioning

---

21. Wikipedia. n.d. "Bus factor." Accessed September 22, 2021. https://en.wikipedia.org/wiki/Bus_factor.

22. Wikipedia. n.d. "User experience." Accessed January 10, 2022. https://en.wikipedia.org/wiki/User_experience.

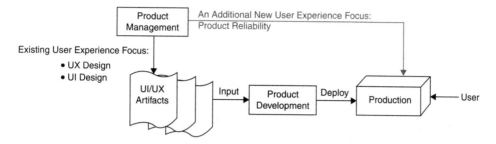

Figure 5.6 *Extended view of the user experience encompassing product reliability*

the product, or even designing the product. Does the user use the artifacts that come out of the design sprints, sessions between the product owners, and UI/UX designers? No. What does the user use, then? The product in production.

It follows that the user experience is as much about the design input to product development as it is about the output, namely the product deployed in production. It also follows that product management needs to extend their viewpoint about the user experience toward the product in production—specifically, the reliability of the product in production. This is illustrated in Figure 5.6.

Product management has an existing user experience focus in UX and UI design. The UX and UI design process generates artifacts as input to product development. The output of the product development process is the product deployed to production. This is where the users access the product. Their entire user experience is based on the product in production. Therefore, product management needs an additional new experience focus: product reliability in production. The combination of the two focuses, UI/UX design and product reliability in production, yields the best user experience in production for the user.

But how do you extend the user experience focus to include product reliability in production? This is where SRE has its strength. It allows the product owner to take part in a structured process together with operations engineers and developers that leads to sufficient product reliability. What do the product owners need to do?

1. Take part in the definition of indicators and objectives for services in production (SLIs and SLOs).

2. Take part in the definition of policies for violating the objectives (error budget policies).

3. Make prioritization decisions based on the policies (error budget–based decision–making).

4. Take part in the definition of the on-call setup for services in production.

The head of product management may have a question regarding the time investment needed by the product owners to take part in the SRE activities. The question might arise because the product owners are typically very busy juggling numerous strains of work within product management. Adding a new type of work, however important it might be, will chip away some time from other work areas. The answer to this question needs to be that the amount of time to take part in SRE activities will be rather limited. Following is the time investment breakdown:

1. SLI and SLO definitions
   - Several meetings with the team to set up initial SLIs and SLOs from the user's point of view
   - Ongoing adjustments of SLOs based on feedback from SLO breaches

2. Error budget policy definition
   - A meeting with the team to set up an initial error budget policy
   - Occasional adjustments of the error budget policy based on feedback after incidents

3. Prioritization decisions based on error budget policies
   - Use of SRE metrics to guide backlog prioritization decisions in terms of reliability

4. On-call setup definition
   - A meeting laying down how on-call support will be ensured for a service: which roles will be going on call, at what times of the day, and with what kind of rotation frequency
   - In the meeting, agreement with operations engineers and developers on the prioritization of the incident backlog by the people on call

Thus, with not a lot of time investment on the product owner side, much can be achieved:

- Influence of the reliability objectives for services (SLOs); for example, by product importance, criticality, customer segments, and so on
- Influence of the policy enacted when the service objectives are not fulfilled
- Reliability work prioritization decision-making based on real data from production reporting on user experience impacts
- Influence of the on-call setup (including its cost); for example, by service importance, criticality, customer segments, and so on

As with the heads of development and operations, it might take several sessions until the head of product management would endorse SRE. Like other leaders, they will discuss the matter within their department. Their questions regarding the conduct of the SRE transformation can be answered the same way as with the heads of development and operations. The head of product management needs to be engaged with by the SRE coaches until an agreement to prioritize the SRE transformation at the portfolio level is achieved.

5.4.5 Achieving Joint Buy-In

The SRE coaches might think that achieving buy-in individually with the head of operations, head of development, and head of product management would be sufficient. This, however, is not the case. A decisive final part of top-down buy-in is joint buy-in by all three leaders. It is one thing to achieve individual agreements, but it might turn out to be a different thing entirely to reach a joint agreement. This is because during the joint discussion about SRE and SRE transformation, all sorts of misunderstandings and new nuances will crop up. Also, it might be the first meeting where the three leaders are discussing a new collaboration mode on operational concerns between them and their respective departments.

Therefore, this meeting is very important, and it should take place before the portfolio prioritization of the SRE initiative takes place. The meeting should be short and led by the SRE coaches. The meeting invitation can be titled "Final joint preparation for SRE prioritization at the portfolio level." Further, the meeting invitation should have three agenda points:

- Recap: What was agreed individually in terms of SRE before?

- Discussion: What will the collaboration of product operations, product development, and product management on product operations using SRE look like?

- Q&A

It is great if the SRE coaches can set the tone of the meeting to be colloquial. This might be achieved with a remark at the beginning that the meeting is being held to take operations in the organization to a whole new level, and why it is needed. Following that, the SRE coaches should repeat individual agreements to the respective leaders. The goal is to reconfirm in a group setting what was agreed to individually before. This already may lead to questions and clarifications. This is because SRE is surely not at the top of the leaders' minds. They have a myriad of other things going on in parallel. Additionally, they might have all sorts of work and interpersonal issues about other topics with each other. All of that needs to be empathized with by the SRE coaches.

Once the individual agreements have been successfully reconfirmed, the SRE coaches need to lay down the future collaboration mode between the leaders and their departments. This should start with the benefits of the new collaboration mode over the current way of doing product operations. In a nutshell, this can go as follows.

- The current alignment of different parts of the organization on operational concerns does not reflect the business's need to provide a superior customer experience with the product in production. SRE provides a framework for aligning the organization on operational concerns.

- Under the SRE framework, operations engineers, developers, and product owners jointly define the important reliability indicators and reliability objectives to be fulfilled by the services. The operations engineers provide infrastructure to measure the fulfillment of the reliability objectives. Together, the operations engineers, developers, and product owners hold themselves accountable to the fulfillment of the agreed reliability objectives using agreed policies.

- Moreover, the organizational alignment is reinforced by joint agreements between operations engineers, developers, and product owners on the on-call setup to be provided for the services.

Further on, in terms of defining freedom and responsibility, the following points need to be stated by the SRE coaches for discussion.

- The operations team will provide the SRE infrastructure to enable others to do product operations and make data-driven decisions about reliability.

- The split of on-call duties between the operations team and the development team will be jointly decided upon during the course of the SRE transformation.

- The SRE metrics for making data-driven decisions about reliability will be used by teams and leadership.

- The SRE coaches will run the SRE transformation with all teams in product operations and product development.

There is no need in this meeting for extensive SRE lingo based on the SRE concept pyramid. The SRE coaches should not try to teach the leadership team about the SRE concepts. The goal of the meeting is to develop a shared vision for SRE that leads to the level of alignment required to get the SRE transformation prioritized at the portfolio level.

In terms of the Q&A, questions about the duration of the SRE transformation and, especially, about the time frame for various visible improvements could be discussed. The conversation needs to lead to clarity for everyone involved that the SRE transformation will be a long-term endeavor with many wins along the way, some of which can be expected in the short term.

The meeting should end with the SRE coaches saying they see everyone being in agreement about the need for the SRE introduction. As a next step, the coaches will put SRE as a topic for prioritization on the portfolio management agenda. They will let the leaders know when the SRE prioritization will be discussed in the portfolio management round.

5.4.6 Getting SRE into the Portfolio

According to the Association for Project Management, "portfolio management is the selection, prioritization and control of an organization's programmes and projects, in line with its strategic objectives and capacity to deliver."[23] Following this definition, the starting point of getting SRE prioritized at the portfolio level in a given organization needs to be a set of the organization's strategic objectives. To be sure, the strategic objectives might not be transparent to everyone in the organization. It is the job of the SRE coaches to find the strategic objectives in order to position SRE in support of some of them. The head of portfolio management will have the current list of strategic objectives.

It may happen that the list of the organization's strategic objectives does not contain a direct reliability, stability, or similar objective, which could be used as a parent for the SRE transformation. In this case, SRE can actually be framed in support of any product-related objective. This is because, according to *The Site Reliability Workbook,* "reliability is the most important feature of any system,"[8] a statement the workbook authors make based on the following argument.

---

23. APM. n.d. "What Is Portfolio Management?" Accessed April 14, 2022. https://www.apm.org.uk/resources/what-is-project-management/what-is-portfolio-management.

- "If a system isn't reliable, users won't trust it."
- "If users don't trust a system, when given a choice, they won't use it."

In other words, reliability is, arguably, the most important feature of a system because without reliability there is no trust, and soon there will be no users. The counterargument would be that it is possible to have a fully reliable system that is not used by anyone. So, a reliable system could have no users. However, when talking about a system that has proven to have a user base, the argument that reliability is the most important feature of the system because it builds trust may well hold true. This argument makes it easy to find one or several organizational objectives that will be supported by SRE.

Once one or more strategic objectives that can serve as parents for the SRE transformation have been found, the next step is to understand how the portfolio management system in the organization handles technical programs like SRE. Some organizations have customer-facing business opportunities and technical programs together in a portfolio backlog of initiatives. In this case, the customer-facing business opportunities and technical programs are treated as the same class of citizens and prioritized against each other.

In other organizations, the portfolio backlog only contains customer-facing business opportunities because they are the ones generating revenue. The technical programs are handled as part of the customer-facing business opportunities they support. In this case, the rank of a customer-facing business opportunity automatically determines the rank of all the technical programs that support it. However, the technical programs are not visible at the business opportunity level of the portfolio backlog in this case.

In any case, the SRE coaches need to briefly meet with the head of portfolio management and explain the SRE transformation to them. They need to know that SRE is an initiative for measurably improving the reliability of the system in production by creating a stronger alignment between product operations, product development, and product management. In turn, the head of portfolio management will be able to briefly explain how the portfolio management process works in the organization. Specifically, they will be able to explain how the technical programs are handled in the portfolio backlog.

If technical programs appear at the business opportunity level of the portfolio backlog, the head of portfolio management will be able to advise the SRE coaches on how they can create the SRE item, fill it in, submit it for prioritization, and link it to one or more strategic objectives it supports. This is shown in Figure 5.7.

Figure 5.7 *Inserting SRE into the portfolio as a dedicated technical program*

The SRE item is marked with the tag "tech" to make it clear that it is a technical program.

If technical programs do not appear at the business opportunity level of the portfolio backlog, the head of portfolio management will be able to provide guidance for making SRE visible in the customer-facing business opportunities supported by SRE. This can be done by adding tags, links, and so on to the respective items in the portfolio backlog. In Figure 5.8, SRE is made part of a business opportunity linked to strategic objective 2. The business opportunity is about scaling a platform to 10 additional territories to, for example, increase revenue and market share.

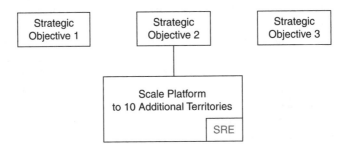

Figure 5.8 *Inserting SRE into the portfolio as part of a customer-facing business opportunity*

The business opportunity is marked with the tag "SRE" to make it known that the SRE transformation will run as part of the work on that particular opportunity. This also means the prioritization of SRE will be done through the ranking of that business opportunity against all other business opportunities.

In any case, it must be possible to easily identify SRE in the portfolio backlog. If the portfolio management system supports it, it should be possible to see SRE as a topic and its current prioritization, if there is any yet, by following a single hyperlink. This makes it easy to share the hyperlink, which will be necessary for alignment.

The SRE coaches promised to the heads of product operations, product development, and product management to get back to them once it becomes clear when SRE prioritization will be discussed in the portfolio round. That date can be obtained from the head of portfolio management. The date along with the link to the SRE item in the portfolio backlog needs to be sent to product delivery organization leadership. In case of a dedicated portfolio backlog item, this gives the leaders a chance to review, comment on, and adapt the item before the prioritization meeting.

The SRE coaches will likely not be in the prioritization meeting, but after the meeting they should be polling for the decision. Ideally, the ranking of the SRE item should be visible by following the same hyperlink that leads to the item. This, however, does not always hold true. Once the ranking of SRE is clear, the SRE transformation has a mandate to unfold in the organization. The SRE coaches have achieved a great milestone and have a reason to celebrate!

The celebration should start by sending a thank-you note to the head of operations, head of development, and head of product management. A good relationship with them is vital for the SRE coaches to run the SRE transformation successfully. Moreover, the SRE coaches should inform all the other people who have shown a particular interest in SRE so far.

5.5 Bottom-Up Buy-In

With top-down buy-in achieved and SRE ranked at the portfolio level, the time allocation to SRE has been understood and justified. The teams can now engage with SRE activities. Team engagement needs to occur in two groups: the operations teams and the development teams. With the development teams, the goal is to engage developers and product owners to establish the SRE concept pyramid (Section 3.5). With the operations teams, the goal is to establish an SRE infrastructure that enables the development and operations teams to do SRE. The SRE coaches need to orchestrate the engagement in such a way that the development of the SRE infrastructure goes hand in hand with its consumption by the development teams.

Unlike with top-down buy-in, bottom-up buy-in is facilitated bit by bit in various coaching sessions over time. This is because the operations and development teams need to learn and experience new ways of working to be employed on a daily basis. It is about changing the professional habits that have been developed over professional lifetimes.

5.5.1 Engaging the Operations Teams

The operations teams are likely to buy into SRE sooner than the development teams. They need to learn how to develop a framework that can be used by others to enable them to do SRE. Enabling others to do SRE is a welcome change for the operations teams because they have always wanted developers to be more involved in product operations instead of "throwing new releases over the fence." At its core, the buy-in challenge for the operations teams is not so much about SRE philosophy, but rather about their own ability to do software development to develop the SRE infrastructure. For this, new skills and experience are required.

With the operations teams, several coaching session themes can be defined, as shown in Table 5.5.

Table 5.5 *Themes of Coaching Sessions for Operations Teams*

Coaching Theme	Short Explanation	Success Measurement
SRE introduction	Introducing the SRE concept pyramid in a team setting, the kind of SRE infrastructure needed, and responsibilities under the SRE framework	The operations engineers understand the SRE concept pyramid, are ready to get started with developing the SRE infrastructure, and know what they need to do under the SRE framework.
Logging infrastructure	Selecting a logging infrastructure that has a comprehensive log query language	A logging infrastructure with a comprehensive query language has been selected, procured, and made available to the development and operations teams.

Coaching Theme	Short Explanation	Success Measurement
Infrastructure to set SLOs for availability and latency SLIs	Implementing infrastructure that is able to store the availability and latency SLO definitions from development teams	Development teams use the infrastructure to set the availability and latency SLOs.
Infrastructure to detect SLO breaches for availability and latency SLIs	Implementing infrastructure that can compare the availability and latency SLO definitions with the actual availability and latency of endpoints	The infrastructure detects the SLO breaches reliably.
Alerting infrastructure	Implementing infrastructure that can alert on SLO breaches in a timely and effective manner	Development teams provide positive feedback regarding the alert timeliness (alert soon but not too soon) and effectiveness (not too many alerts).
Infrastructure to generate graphs for SLO fulfillment by SLI	Implementing dashboards that show SLO fulfillment by SLI over time	Development teams use the SLI/SLO dashboards to view SLO fulfillment over time.
Infrastructure to generate error budget depletion graphs	Implementing dashboards that show error budget depletion over time	Development teams use the error budget depletion dashboards to check the remaining error budget in a given time unit.
Infrastructure to generate graphs for error budget–based decision–making	Implementing dashboards for product owners, managers	Product owners and managers use the dashboards to make error budget–based decisions.
Infrastructure for generic custom SLI definitions	Implementing a facility that can take generic input based on predefined log structures and make a fully fledged SLI out of it	Development teams are using the infrastructure for custom SLI definitions that go beyond availability and latency.
Self-service SLO adaptation tool	Implementing a tool that enables development teams to adjust SLOs on their own	Development teams are using the tool to adjust their SLOs on demand without contacting the operations team.
Self-service configuration of SRE infrastructure	Implementing configuration points in the SRE infrastructure to allow for team-wise and service-wise adaptations	Development teams are using the configurations offered to adjust the alerting algorithm, dashboards, etc.

Coaching Theme	Short Explanation	Success Measurement
Infrastructure for on-call management	Selecting an on-call management infrastructure	An on-call management infrastructure has been selected, procured, and made available to the development teams.
Providing support for the SRE infrastructure	Implementing a process for requesting emergency bug fixes, general bug fixes, and new features and getting onboarding support	Support requests for the SRE infrastructure are not numerous and are fulfilled sufficiently quickly based on feedback from the teams using the infrastructure.

5.5.2 Engaging the Development Teams

The development teams need to learn why using the SRE framework provided by the operations teams is a good idea, how to use it, how to get involved in product operations by going on call, and how to make data-driven decisions about reliability investments. Here, the core of the buy-in challenge is the switch to DevOps where developers do operations work. For this, a new mindset is required. To be sure, a new mindset is required on the side of product owners as well. They need to want the development team to be the first to find out about product issues in production, notify the stakeholders about the issues being taken care of, and fix the issues before customer escalations begin. Is this not quite a departure from the notorious image of the product owner only requiring new features all the time?

The new mindset is illustrated in Figure 5.9. The new standard set by the development teams for themselves needs to be that they are the first to detect incidents, notify the stakeholders about them, and fix the incidents before they lead to customer escalations.

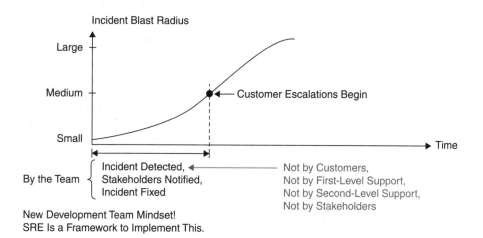

Figure 5.9 *New development team mindset with respect to operations*

That is, the development team's standard demand for themselves needs to be that production incidents are not detected by customers, first- or second-level support, or stakeholders. Rather, they detected them. For this to work, the development teams need to have their own monitoring. This is where the SRE infrastructure provided by the operations teams comes in.

Table 5.6 shows the coaching session themes for the development teams.

Table 5.6 *Themes of Coaching Sessions for Development Teams*

Coaching Theme	Short Explanation	Success Measurement
SRE introduction	Introducing the SRE concept pyramid (Section 3.5) in a team setting, explaining what the SRE infrastructure will provide, and laying down responsibilities under the SRE framework	The developers and product owners understand the SRE concept pyramid, are ready to get started with SRE implementation in their team, and know what they need to do under the SRE framework.
Logging	Ensuring the services are logging using the infrastructure recommended by the operations teams	All services use the same logging infrastructure recommended by the operations teams and log appropriately by production environment.
Queries on logs	Learning the log query language to be able to formulate queries programmatically	Developers are using the log query language to answer questions about the system state in production.
SLOs for availability	Identifying the most important workflows from the customer point of view and setting availability SLOs for endpoints	The development team has agreed on initial availability SLOs and a process for reviewing and adapting them.
SLI/SLO dashboards	Understanding the SLI/SLO dashboards	The development team uses the SLI/SLO dashboards to check SLO fulfillments over time.
Error budget depletion dashboards	Understanding the error budget depletion dashboards	The development team uses the error budget depletion dashboards to view the remaining error budget and its depletion trend.
Error budget–based decision–making dashboards	Understanding the error budget–based decision–making dashboards	The development team uses the error budget–based decision-making dashboards to make error budget–based decisions about reliability investments.

Coaching Theme	Short Explanation	Success Measurement
SLOs for latency	Identifying the most important workflows from the customer point of view and setting latency SLOs for endpoints	The development team has agreed on initial latency SLOs and a process for reviewing and adapting them.
Reacting to SLO breaches	Setting up a procedure in the development team to appropriately react to SLO breaches	The development team reacts to SLO breaches periodically as agreed to by the team.
Determining whether the SLO breaches really report on poor customer experience	Checking whether previously defined SLOs really report on poor customer experiences when they get broken	The development team regularly adjusts the SLOs to make sure they really report on poor customer experiences when they get broken.
Error budget–based decision–making	Understanding how error budgets can be used for making data-driven decisions about reliability investments	The development team practices error budget–based decision-making to steer reliability investment decisions.
Error budget policies	Defining an error budget policy for a team	The development team has defined an error budget policy and enacts it as needed.
On-call rotation	Setting up on-call rotation for a service by defining the roles and people that go on call, at what times, and with which technical knowledge, as well as setting up a handover procedure	The development team practices on call as agreed to between the operations engineers, developers, and product owner.
Additional SLIs	Defining and setting up additional SLIs that go beyond availability and latency (e.g., correctness in queue message processing)	The development team has identified additional SLIs beyond availability and latency, and has set SLOs for them.
Stakeholders	Identifying stakeholders for services	A stakeholder list has been agreed to by the stakeholders.
Incident priorities	Defining incident priorities from the customer point of view; assigning a set of tasks for each incident priority	Incident priorities are used by the people on call to take action accordingly.
Stakeholder notifications	Identifying scenarios important for the stakeholders; setting up stakeholder notifications	Stakeholders receive notifications and provide positive feedback that the notifications make sense and arrive in a timely fashion.

5.6 Lateral Buy-In

The middle managers in the organization need to be engaged as the top-down and bottom-up buy-ins unfold. As soon as there is top-down buy-in, the SRE coaches need to engage with operations managers, development managers, and product managers to explain the agreements that were reached and announce the upcoming portfolio prioritization. Once SRE has been ranked at the portfolio level, the managers have a mandate to establish the SRE-related processes in the teams they are responsible for.

Establishing the processes can only work once the bottom-up buy-ins in the operations and development teams have progressed to the point where it is clear what SRE means for a particular team and some experience with practicing SRE has been gained. That is, SRE needs to be practiced in some ad-hoc manner first to gain experience before it would make sense to institutionalize the practice using organizational processes.

Once the time is ripe to create organizational processes to institutionalize SRE, the SRE coaches need to suggest the processes based on their engagements with all teams across the board. The engagements will uncover what would work where and why, as well as what would not work where and why not. Additionally, the SRE coaches may be aware of people issues in the organization that might need to be resolved before the SRE processes are institutionalized.

The processes need to be written up and shared for comments with the affected teams, which will be the entire product delivery organization. Once comments arrive, they need to be incorporated into the processes. Depending on the number of changes the comments cause, another round of review might be required. Overcommunication is better than misunderstanding. Therefore, in case of doubt, it is better to communicate more than once to avoid the risk of misunderstanding.

Once the processes are finalized, they need to be communicated broadly both verbally and in writing. Table 5.7 outlines the points that the processes need to cover.

Table 5.7 *SRE Process Points*

Process Point	Explanation
On-call setup	Which roles are doing on call for which services and at which times?
Error budget–based decision-making	Which decisions should be made by the teams based on error budgets?
Responsibilities	Who is responsible for what in the realm of product operations?
Freedom and responsibility split	What is the freedom enjoyed by the teams and nonnegotiable responsibilities to be fulfilled by the teams?
Regulatory compliance	Which SRE artifacts are relevant for regulatory compliance? Which SRE artifacts can be relevant during an audit?
Escalation policy	Who breaks the ties if issues cannot be resolved by the people involved?
Change management	How do you request changes to the SRE processes?

Lateral buy-in by the middle managers is expressed using the processes they set up. It is important for the SRE coaches to drive the process and ensure a good balance between formal and informal ways SRE is practiced in the organization.

5.7 Buy-In Staggering

Top-down, bottom-up, and lateral buy-ins of SRE do not necessarily take place at the same time. For instance, in a rather stable product delivery organization with a rule-oriented culture, the three buy-ins could flow sequentially. The flow of persuasion in this case is shown in Figure 5.10.

To start, the SRE coaches engage with the entire organization as part of the SRE marketing funnel (Section 5.2). At this point, SRE buy-in is pretty low across the board. Next, the SRE coaches start engaging heavily with the product delivery organization's leadership. If successful, this elevates the leadership to high levels of top-down buy-in. It culminates in SRE being prioritized at the portfolio level, which provides the mandate to engage deeply with the entire organization.

Following this, the SRE coaches start engaging with the operations and development teams. In a series of coaching sessions over a longer period, the understanding and experience of SRE grows in the teams. If successful, at some point bottom-up buy-in reaches high levels.

This is the point where there is enough experience with SRE in the organization that SRE processes can be institutionalized. To do this, the SRE coaches engage with development, operations, and product managers to establish and communicate the formal processes to manifest SRE in the organization. The managers owning SRE process management is a testimony to high levels of lateral SRE buy-in.

In a less stable enterprise environment, the flow of persuasion may not be linear. It may be a complex and unpredictable set of discussions pursued in parallel. The discussions might involve a political component where some agreements might only be reached tentatively to begin with. The tentative agreements might then have to be sold to others as regular agreements to unlock progress. Finally, the tentative agreements are hardened as the others agree. This type of, sometimes unpleasant, maneuvering might be required in certain organizational cultures to achieve overall buy-in for SRE. This is the art of SRE transformation as opposed to the science of SRE.

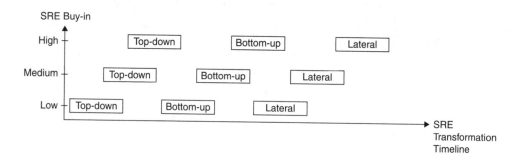

Figure 5.10 *Example SRE buy-in staggering in a stable rule-oriented culture*

5.8 Team Coaching

In Section 2.5, *Coaching*, team coaching is identified as a primary means of driving SRE transformation in the product delivery organization. The SRE coaches need to have a schedule of planned coaching sessions with different teams. Each team session needs to have an agenda sent out in advance.

With the operations teams, the operations engineers who implement the SRE infrastructure and provision associated third-party tools need to take part in ongoing coaching. Additionally, someone in operations needs to act as a product owner for the SRE infrastructure. This person also needs to take part in ongoing coaching.

With the development teams, it is important to coach the following team members as permanent participants: developers, business analysts, and product owners. The UI/UX designers do not need to be involved regularly. However, the SRE coaches should create a welcoming atmosphere in case the designers want to take part in some SRE coaching sessions. What is critical to clarify from the beginning is the involvement of business analysts, if there are any, and product owners. Table 5.8 outlines why it is so important for business analysts and product owners to be part of ongoing SRE coaching sessions.

Table 5.8 *Reasons for Product Owners to Attend the SRE Coaching Sessions*

Reason	Explanation
Team culture	SRE aims to introduce new ways of working and decision-making styles. A joint definition of SLIs, SLOs, error budget policies, on-call setup, and joint data-driven decisions about reliability investments builds a new culture of reliability in the team. However, the culture can only be conceived and blossom when all the team members take part in the SRE introduction process.
Organizational alignment	The strength of SRE is in creating alignment between the operations engineers, developers, and product owners (see Section 1.2, *Alignment Using SRE*). However, the alignment can only be brought about if the business analysis and product owners are part of the ongoing SRE activities.
User perspective	The business analyst or product owner will be the person on the team spending more time than others with product users. When it comes to taking a user perspective to define SLIs/SLOs that can be used as a proxy measure of user happiness, only a person close enough to the users can make the judgment. Otherwise, SLOs will not reflect the level of user happiness, but merely the level of technical soundness of the system. As a result, a broken SLO is not as meaningful and the motivation to fix it is not as clear.

Reason	Explanation
Customer perspective	This is the same as the user perspective, but for customers instead. Customer SLOs might need to be more tightly defined than user SLOs because the level of service provided to those who pay might need to be higher. Again, only a person close enough to the customers can determine the service level that would make them happy.
SLI/SLO understandability	If the business analyst or product owner is not available in the SRE coaching sessions, there are only technical team members, such as developers and operations engineers, taking part in the SLI and SLO definitions. Following this, the SLIs and SLOs that are defined will be technically rooted. The understandability of such SLIs and SLOs will be limited to the technical people. This, however, contradicts the purpose of SLIs and SLOs being the proxy measures of user happiness, which should be understandable for everyone.

If a business analyst or a product owner repeatedly does not take part in ongoing SRE coaching sessions, one of the SRE coaches should invite the person for coffee. Following the approach from Marshall B. Rosenberg's book *Nonviolent Communication*,[24] the SRE coach should steer the conversation along the chain of observations → feelings → needs → requests, in that order.

The SRE coach should start by stating the observations that the business analyst or product owner did not attend the last SRE coaching sessions. Following this, they should describe their feelings about it—for instance, being frustrated, unhappy, uneasy, unsure, or worried. After the feelings are expressed, they should describe the need for the business analyst or the product owner to be available in the SRE coaching sessions based on Table 5.8. The SRE coach should conclude with a gentle request asking the person to join future SRE sessions.

The business analyst or product owner may state that they understand the importance of SRE and of them being part of it, and the only reason they were missing was that they had previous commitments they could not change. In that case, they can discuss with the SRE coach the date at which regular participation will be possible. If, however, the behavior of the business analyst or product owner does not change, the SRE coach should continue the engagement with the rest of the team. The SRE introduction will not reach its full potential in this case, but it will still be beneficial enough to justify the effort.

> **From the Trenches:** At some point, the product owner will want to join the SRE sessions because the team members repeatedly request them to do so or because the business starts requesting contractual SLAs.

During the coaching sessions, the SRE coaches should take notes and store them in a single well-known location. As a team gains SRE maturity, they should gradually take over the note

---

24. Rosenberg, Marshall B., and Deepak Chopra. 2015. *Nonviolent Communication: A Language of Life: Life-Changing Tools for Healthy Relationships*. Encinitas, CA: Puddle Dancer Press.

taking. This is a good step in preparing to reduce SRE coaching to make the SRE activities self-sustaining. After each coaching session, the note taker should send the notes to the entire team. The archive of the notes is useful to see the progress the team has made over time.

5.9 Traversing the Organization

In a large product delivery organization, there may be several operations teams and dozens of development teams. In this setting, which teams should you start with? Which teams should follow? How should you traverse the organization in the most beneficial manner? For the purpose of traversing the organization, the process can be divided into three groups:

- Operations teams

- Development teams that are close to product operations

- Development teams that are far away from product operations

5.9.1 Grouping the Organization

The starting point needs to be the operations team where the SRE infrastructure will be developed. This team needs to understand the SRE concept pyramid (Section 3.5) first. They need to analyze the current logging, monitoring, and alerting infrastructure and see how far it can be used to implement the envisioned SRE infrastructure. What can be used or procured off the shelf? What would definitely need to be developed? Which technologies would need to be used for development? Who from the team can do the development? Who in the team has experience with developing frameworks to be used by others?

Once the operations teams know which logging infrastructure to use for SRE purposes, the coaching sessions with the development teams can start. The development teams can be divided into two groups. One group consists of teams that were close to product operations before the SRE transformation began. These development teams were creating their own alerts for specific conditions, setting up the alerts by production environment, reacting to the alerts on a schedule, and so on. They may not have done all this with the structure and rigor required by SRE, but they were still close to product operations.

These are the development teams who understood DevOps long before the SRE introduction. They are going to be curious about SRE, but they might also be very suspicious and picky about the value-add of SRE compared to the ad-hoc product operations procedures existing in the team. In these teams, the SRE transformation is going to mean a transformation from ad-hoc product operations procedures to standardized SRE practices.

These development teams are good candidates to start the SRE transformation because the foundational mindset is in place. They are doing product operations because they want to know how their services are doing in the real production environment. In these teams, there is no question of why it is not the operations teams who do product operations instead. Also, because these development teams are further ahead already, the first successes with SRE can be achieved more quickly. These can be broadcast in the organization to fuel the SRE movement.

These teams, however, are going to place demands on the operations teams implementing the SRE infrastructure more quickly than other development teams. It is the job of the SRE coaches to balance the timeline of SRE infrastructure demands by development teams with the capacity and speed of the operations teams implementing the infrastructure. This is a delicate balance to strike.

- The development teams cannot be left starving the features in the SRE infrastructure to avoid motivation loss in SRE.
- The operations teams cannot be overburdened with feature requests slowing them down due to too many features being worked on simultaneously and in parallel.

It needs to be taken into account that the operations team may be inexperienced in developing frameworks to be used by others. Therefore, the "first pass yield"[25] for features in the SRE infrastructure cannot be assumed. Rather, several iterations on a feature should be presumed to project more realistic timelines of delivering SRE infrastructure features that will actually be used by the development teams.

The other group of development teams consists of those who are far away from product operations. These teams do not operate their services in production. Rather, they rely on the operations teams to do so and come back with bug reports. In this context, two subgroups can be distinguished. One subgroup is unhappy with the current situation. They want more knowledge about product operations and do not necessarily want the operations team to be the intermediaries between them and production. These teams welcome SRE because it offers a structured way for bringing the development teams closer to product operations.

The other subgroup is happy with the current situation. They fully concentrate on feature development. Product operations is with the operations teams. The operations teams report bugs from production that are fixed by the development teams. The development teams do not feel the need to get more involved in product operations. These are the teams where the foundational mindset needs to be brought about first, before any SRE practices can be introduced. These teams consider the SRE value proposition as a threat to their time. They do not have enough time for feature development. Getting involved in product operations means even less time for feature development!

Figure 5.11 depicts how the product delivery organization can be charted.

The initial traversal of the organization needs to take place left to right in a depth-first manner until the SRE transformation can be executed in parallel in all teams. Interestingly, the demand for the SRE infrastructure is growing the opposite way. The teams on the right generate less demand for SRE infrastructure features than the teams on the left. This is demonstrated in the next section.

5.9.2 Traversing the Organization Versus SRE Infrastructure Demand

The traversal of the organization is shown in Figure 5.12. In the initial SRE introduction period of about two months, the order of team engagement starts with the operations teams, which start building up the SRE infrastructure. Then the teams close to product operations are engaged with. These teams have the right mindset already and can hit the ground running. However, their speed and associated strong SRE infrastructure demand needs to be balanced with the operations teams' capabilities to provide the requested infrastructure.

---

25. Wikipedia. n.d. "First pass yield." Accessed September 29, 2021. https://en.wikipedia.org/wiki/First_pass_yield.

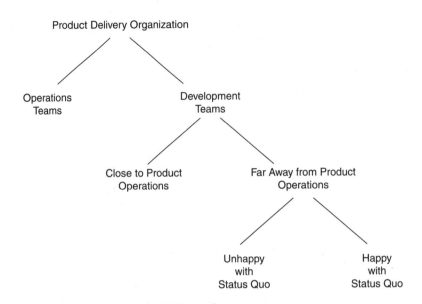

Figure 5.11 *Team classification for SRE transformation*

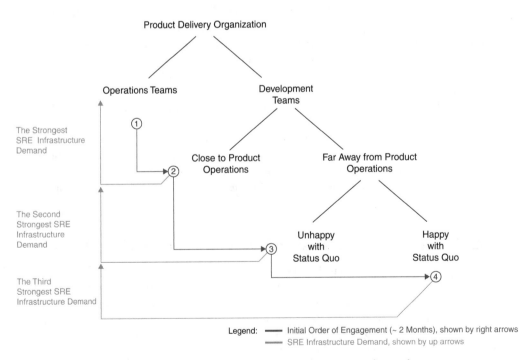

Figure 5.12 *Traversing the organization versus SRE infrastructure demand*

Third, the teams that are unhappy with the status quo of being far away from product operations need to be engaged with. They are waiting for the SRE introduction to improve the status quo. Their mindset will still need to be worked on, but the proposed changes will fall on fertile ground. The technical changes will start relatively slowly. Therefore, demand for SRE infrastructure will be less strong for these teams than for the teams that were close to product operations before the SRE introduction.

Fourth, the teams that are happy with the status quo need to be engaged with. The necessary mindset changes will need to be worked on first, before any technical changes can be taken up. This will take time. Therefore, demand for SRE infrastructure will be weakest for these teams. In all likelihood, by the time these teams are ready to request features in the SRE infrastructure, they will already be available based on previous requests from other teams.

5.9.3 Team Engagements Over Time

Figure 5.13 illustrates team engagements by SRE coaches over time. In the initial phase of the SRE transformation of about two months, the SRE coaches start engaging a limited number of teams. The engagement is done in the order discussed in the previous section. The operations teams go first, followed by the development teams close to product operations. Development teams that are unhappy with being far away from product operations go third, and development teams that are happy with being far away from product go last.

The SRE coaches tune in new teams in the initial phase of transformation as it fits their own capacity, the capacity of the operations teams implementing the SRE infrastructure, and the infrastructure demands by the development teams. Once the SRE coaches detect a point where a basic level of SRE infrastructure is available, they can decide to start running the SRE transformation in parallel in all teams. This, of course, would greatly fuel the SRE movement in the organization. Suddenly, it becomes a topic of conversation for everyone because everyone is doing SRE in some shape or form.

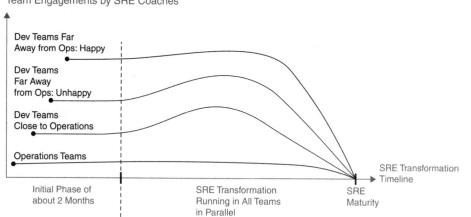

Figure 5.13 *Team engagements by SRE coaches over time*

Following are the prerequisites for starting to run the SRE transformation in parallel in all teams.

- The SRE infrastructure needs to support two SLIs foundational to reliability: availability and latency (see Section 3.1, *Service Level Indicators*).

- The SRE infrastructure needs to support SLO definitions.

- The SRE infrastructure needs to support some basic alerting on SLO breaches.

- The use of the SRE infrastructure needs to be proven by several development teams.

- The ownership of the SRE infrastructure and its maintenance is clear and unambiguous.

- The SRE movement is on the rise, as more and more teams are curious about SRE and are waiting to jump on the bandwagon.

These are the six criteria the SRE coaches can use to open the floodgates and invite all the other teams to join the SRE transformation. This might be intimidating to the SRE coaches because they might need to deal with many more teams than they did during the initial phase of the transformation. However, the SRE coaches need to consider that they already have some experience with onboarding teams to the SRE infrastructure.

Moreover, the SRE coaches need to take into account that the teams will not adopt SRE at the same rate. This can be seen already during the initial phase of the transformation. It will not be different later either. There will always be possibilities to schedule the sessions in such a way that the SRE coaches do not get overwhelmed. After all, they are the ones scheduling the sessions, pacing the team engagements, and aligning the development teams' demands on the SRE infrastructure with the feature delivery capabilities by the operations teams!

Also, at this point, the SRE movement is still nascent. There are not a lot of success stories yet. So, the goal now is to fuel the movement to make it more sustainable. For this, it is worth taking a little risk on the side of SRE coaches and going a little bit into overdrive mode, with the steering wheel still being in their own hands.

From the Trenches: A small number of SRE coaches can handle running an SRE transformation with dozens of teams in parallel. The number of meetings will be high for a couple of months after the initial phase of transformation is over and all teams are steaming ahead in parallel. However, because each team is going to adopt SRE concepts from the SRE concept pyramid (Section 3.5) at different speeds, the number of meetings per week is going to decline soon.

The teams will ask to schedule the coaching sessions considering their other commitments, it might make sense for some coaching sessions to take place after the teams have done their homework, some progress will depend on the SRE infrastructure features currently missing, and so on. Finally, some teams might decide to stop climbing the SRE concept pyramid at lower levels while some other teams might sprint to the top quickly. Both cases would render further involvement of SRE coaches unnecessary, resulting in a reduction in meetings.

In other words, the SRE coaches do not need to fear a large number of teams in front of them. The coaching effort will be distributed naturally as the SRE transformation unfolds.

The potential benefits to opening the floodgates far outweigh the risks. With more teams taking part in the SRE transformation, more opportunities for knowledge sharing arise.

- There will be more success stories to be shared in lean coffee sessions and brown bag lunches.

- A new community of practice (CoP) for SRE might appear to make sense.

- Teams may start having completely new conversations about operational aspects of their services they could not have had before because the operational data provided by the SRE infrastructure was simply not available.

That is, the classical lean mantra of limiting work in progress applies to the initial phase of the SRE transformation (about two months). This is where the SRE coaches should test the waters and onboard new teams carefully. After the initial phase, maximizing work in progress makes sense to fuel the SRE movement in the organization. Without the movement being alive, the entire initiative might not take off at an organizational scale.

In transformational work, maximizing work in progress for the SRE coaches does not lead to an extension in time until the organization has reached SRE maturity. This is because the ultimate goal of the SRE coaches is to make themselves redundant. Every SRE coaching session with every team is a steppingstone in this direction. In fact, maximizing work in progress for the SRE coaches leads to speeding up the point of reaching SRE maturity organization-wide. This is important from the portfolio point of view.

Getting SRE into the portfolio of organizational initiatives was not easy (see Section 5.4.6, *Getting SRE into the Portfolio*). However, it is not easy to keep it there either. Other initiatives get evaluated all the time and compete for a position in the portfolio with all existing initiatives. Without clear signals of success before SRE maturity is reached (see Section 4.7, *Posing Hypotheses*), there is a real risk for the SRE initiative to get prioritized lower or get deprioritized entirely at the portfolio level.

This risk ceases to exist with the achievement of SRE maturity because by that time, the SRE thinking and ways of working have become part of how people in the organization go about operational concerns. In fact, at that point in time, SRE should disappear from the portfolio list of initiatives because the SRE transformation does not need to be driven any longer. SRE is the way operations is done in the organization. There are lots of SRE practitioners, there is SRE documentation and an SRE community of practice (CoP). The SRE infrastructure is owned and maintained. A new team draws on all these resources to set up product operations using SRE because that is how all the other teams do this.

5.10 Organizational Coaching

The discussion in this chapter showed the importance of fueling the SRE movement through information sharing and exchange. These activities embody organizational coaching because they spark serendipitous conversations across teams and roles that make people grow in their understanding of SRE. Conversations like that are important because SRE touches upon all roles in the product delivery organization, and different people practice the same roles in

Table 5.9 *Ways of Sharing SRE Information Across the Product Delivery Organization*

Information	Way of Sharing	Explanation
SRE success stories	Lean coffee sessions, lunch and learn session, engineering blog	In a lean coffee setting, participants need to vote on topics. If SRE gets selected, it indicates a good level of general interest in the topic. Lunch and learns are a good vehicle for spreading positive information in a relaxed atmosphere. Success stories make good content on the organization's engineering blog, if it exists. If it does not, blogging about SRE could be a good starting point.
Bigger postmortems	Lean coffee session	The more people vote on postmortems in a lean coffee setting, the more the culture of learning from other people's mistakes is growing. The interest in postmortem results should grow with the growing SRE maturity in the teams.
Reports on overall SRE progress	Lean coffee session, information radiators	This is meant as a healthy competition among teams and should be reinforced to be understood that way.
Technical discussions	SRE CoP	In a CoP setting, technical ways of working can be effectively shared across the team. Joining an SRE CoP should be made easy to invite people in.
SLAs	All-employee meeting	Contractually agreed SLAs offered by the organization can be effectively broadcast in an all-employee meeting. It should be reinforced that the SLAs were defined based on previous SRE work in respective teams. This kind of communication makes the managers look good about the previous decision to prioritize SRE at the portfolio level.

individual ways. The sharing methods shown in Table 5.9 can be applied for sharing specific pieces of information across the organization.

To foster information sharing beyond forums like lean coffee sessions, lunch and learns, and SRE CoP meetings, the meetings should be recorded if possible. If these meetings take place online, they should be recorded by default. Each recording needs to be tagged with an "SRE" tag if the video-sharing service in use supports it. This way, it should be possible to easily find all the SRE-related recordings by following a single hyperlink.

To report on overall SRE progress, a Kanban board can be used. It should contain typical phases all teams go through on the way toward SRE maturity. Table 5.10 shows an example Kanban board. It is worth noting that each organization should customize such a Kanban board to their unique circumstances.

Table 5.10 *Kanban Board to Visualize SRE Transformation Progress*

1	2	3	4	5	6	7	8	9	...
Induction	Enable logging	Set initial SLOs	React to SLO breaches	Ongoing SLO adjustments	Define error budget policy	Enact error budget policy	Define stakeholders	Enable stakeholder notifications	...
	Team A			Team D			Team I		
			Team B	Team E		Team H			
			Team C	Team F	Team G			Team J	

A Kanban board such as the one shown in Table 5.10 offers four great benefits.

1. It shows a journey from zero to SRE maturity at a glance (the top two horizontal lines on the board).

2. It shows all teams on the SRE adoption journey at a glance (the bottom three horizontal lines on the board).

3. It shows where each team is in terms of SRE adoption journey (individual cells on the board).

4. It shows phases with a high concentration of teams indicating where the majority of the organization is (the steps 4 and 5 on the board). This information might be helpful in order to understand where the most coaching effort or the most team effort might be on the SRE transformation journey.

Having a Kanban board like that on an information radiator rotating organization-wide statistics ensures that the SRE initiative is considered important and jumps out at people casually strolling by. Simple tiny things like that lead to additional conversations about SRE, further fueling the SRE movement.

5.11 Summary

Achieving organizational buy-in for SRE is the first success of the SRE transformation. The buy-in is achieved in a top-down, bottom-up, and lateral manner. Top-down buy-in is about getting product delivery organization leadership to endorse SRE and getting SRE prioritized at the portfolio level of organizational initiatives. Bottom-up buy-in is about engaging with the operations and development teams establishing the SRE concept pyramid (Section 3.5), unlearning old and learning new ways of working. Lateral buy-in is about engaging with operations managers, development managers, and product managers to have them own SRE process management in a formal manner.

With organizational buy-in in place, detailed SRE transformation activities with teams and individuals can finally begin! This is the subject of the next chapter.

Chapter 6

Laying Down the Foundations

In the previous chapter, a solid understanding was developed for how to achieve SRE buy-in at different levels of the product delivery organization. With buy-in in place, executing the SRE transformation now takes center stage. This is a critical point, when the time invested in SRE activities far outweighs the outcomes. It is therefore very important to stage the execution of the transformation in such a way that visible and recognizable outcomes materialize as soon as possible.

6.1 Introductory Talks by Team

Executing the SRE transformation starts with introductory talks about SRE with each team that is being onboarded. The teams are already somewhat familiar with SRE. Their familiarity comes from the SRE marketing activities geared toward creating awareness of and sparking interest in SRE. These activities took place before organizational buy-in for SRE occurred. The time between the SRE marketing activities and the SRE transformation kickoff in a team can be significant, ranging from several weeks to several months.

Therefore, the SRE transformation kickoff in a team needs to start with a presentation geared specifically for the team. It should contain the general SRE introduction from before, and should explain how top-down buy-in was achieved and with whom. The presentation should also explain the portfolio prioritization of SRE and where it is ranked in the list of overall organizational priorities.

For the operations teams, the presentation should contain immediate next steps toward creating the SRE infrastructure. These could be

- Selecting the logging infrastructure
- Choosing a common way to get the availability and latency of service endpoints in all production environments using the logging infrastructure
- Providing a way for developers to set availability and latency SLOs for all production environments
- Providing alerting on SLO breaches in all production environments

For development teams, the presentation should contain next steps toward using the SRE infrastructure to get their hands dirty with SRE. These could be

- Identifying the most important customer use cases fulfilled by the services owned by the team

- Identifying the typical call chains generated by the most important customer use cases

- Thinking through availability and latency requirements for specific service endpoints in the identified call chains that would need to be fulfilled to make customers happy when exercising the respective use cases

- Setting the initial availability SLOs using the SRE infrastructure

- Setting the initial latency SLO using the SRE infrastructure

- Starting to get alerts on SLO breaches from the SRE infrastructure

- Analyzing the alerts to understand whether

  ○ The alerts really represent poor customer experiences

  ○ The SLOs need to be loosened because a worse customer experience would still not lead to customer escalations

  ○ The SLOs need to be tightened because the customer experience detected by the current SLOs is too poor and the customers escalate before an SLO breach is detected

With both the operations and development teams, the SRE coaches need to repeatedly reinforce that the teams will not be left alone. Rather, the whole point of SRE coaching is to guide the teams through the process. Many SRE coaching sessions will be scheduled in the future at a pace suitable for each team.

The introductory session should take about an hour, including time for questions and answers. It should conclude with a note that the SRE coaches will schedule the next session at the earliest time slot suitable for everyone according to their calendars. The session should be recorded to enable missing and future team members to benefit from it later. This and all future coaching session recordings should be tagged with "SRE <team name>." This way, an entire archive of coaching sessions for a team can be collected over time. Where applicable, the recordings can be linked to from future SRE documentation wiki pages to provide an additional and visual way to consume the textual content.

6.2 Conveying the Basics

After the introductory talk, the development team should be ready to start establishing the SRE basics. By now, the SRE terms and their meaning should be familiar and comprehensible. Specifically, the terms from the SRE concept pyramid—SLI, SLO, error budget, error budget policy, and error budget decision-making—should not be foreign to the team members. The SRE coaches should explicitly ask the team whether the terms are clear before moving on.

From the Trenches: SRE coaches might glean a team's hands-on transformation readiness by listening to their conversations or watching the conversations in online chats. They might hear or see statements along the lines of "SR-what?" when referring to SRE; confusing SRE with SRI (hint: the term does not exist) or SLI; or referring to SLOs as "this SL-thingy?" These are good indicators that the basic SRE concepts should be made familiar to the team before moving on with the transformation. Conducting a quick search on Slack or MS Teams to determine a team's readiness might be worth it for SRE coaches.

6.2.1 SLO as a Contract

The team should be clear that an SLO is like a contract guaranteeing that they will engineer a service to the level expected by the user. This is shown in Figure 6.1.

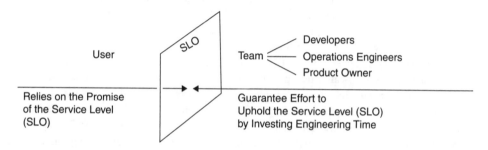

Figure 6.1 *SLO as a contract*

Digging deeper, it should be clear to each team member what they are actually agreeing to. This is based on each team member's role, as shown in Figure 6.2.

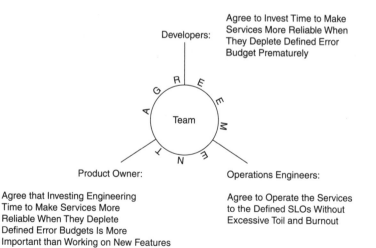

Figure 6.2 *Agreements by role when setting SLOs*

That is, the operations engineers, developers, and product owners need to agree to different things. These should be clear to them before the SLIs are discussed and the SLOs are set.

6.2.2 SLO as a Proxy Measure of Customer Happiness

Another important agreement in the team needs to be the definition of SLIs and SLOs from the user point of view. SLOs need to be used as proxy measures of user or customer happiness. Therefore, it is important to start with the definition of a user for each use case that will be covered by SLIs and SLOs. Understanding whose happiness is being optimized for is a critical requirement to actually make those users happy. Just having a generic user in mind is not sufficient to start an SLI and SLO definition process.

However, when asking a development or operations team to describe the characteristics of a user exercising a particular use case in the software, an answer encountered by the SRE coaches might be that a user is, well, just a user. Having only a generic user in mind when defining SLIs and SLOs does not bear the specific mental model necessary to adopt in an attempt to understand how to make the user happy. Moreover, the lack of such a mental model makes it more difficult to express the user's happiness through proxies like SLIs and SLOs.

In that context, how do you develop the mental model of a user for a specific use case? The work the product owner did together with the UI/UX designers when conceiving the product might well include the definitions of so-called user personas. According to Wikipedia, "a user persona is a fictional character created to represent a user type that might use a site, brand, or product in a similar way."[1] Thus, the user persona definitions may contain enough detail about the users and their context when the product is used. This can be used as a starting point of SLI and SLO discussions.

This kind of conversation is also great to have with the UI/UX designers. If they can allocate time to take part in this SRE discussion, it would enable them to bring the UX viewpoint right at the heart of reliability decisions. However, oftentimes the UI/UX designers have other priorities. This is fine. For the purpose of this conversation, the product owner can, and should, take the lead based on the user personas previously defined together with the UI/UX designers.

6.2.3 User Personas

Based on information by the Interaction Design Foundation,[2] the following details[3] may be contained in a user persona definition.

- Who are the users?
  - What is their demographic?
  - What is their profession?
  - What is their technological environment?

---

1. Wikipedia. n.d. "Persona (user experience)." Accessed December 24, 2021. https://en.wikipedia.org/wiki/Persona_(user_experience).

2. Dam, Rikke Friis. n.d. "Personas – A Simple Introduction." The Interaction Design Foundation. Accessed January 20, 2022. https://www.interaction-design.org/literature/article/personas-why-and-how-you-should-use-them.

3. Veal, Raven. 2020. "How to Define a User Persona." CareerFoundry. December 29, 2020. https://careerfoundry.com/en/blog/ux-design/how-to-define-a-user-persona.

- What are the users' everyday activities?

  ○ What is the users' typical day?

  ○ Are the users taking care of their children?

  ○ What does their typical vacation look like?

- What are the users' needs?

  ○ What do the users need to go about their typical day at home?

  ○ What do the users need to go about their typical day at work?

  ○ What would the users need in the product?

- What are the users' frustrations?

  ○ Are the users performing any tedious jobs?

  ○ Does something the users do take a long time to complete?

  ○ What is the users' environment when using the product?

- What are the users' motivations?

  ○ What causes the user to behave in a certain way?

  ○ What energizes the user?

  ○ What is it about the product that motivates the user?

- What are the users' goals?

  ○ How does the product fit into users' lives?

  ○ Why are they using the product?

  ○ Why are they buying the product?

- What are the barriers preventing the users from achieving their goals?

  ○ What is stopping the users from buying the product?

  ○ What is stopping the users from using the product more?

  ○ What is stopping the users from using the product in a more effective way?

That is, a user persona definition can provide broad context about the user. It can help you understand the user characteristics per relevant use case. This is exactly what is needed in the context of SLI and SLO definitions because they are defined per customer use case and not by the product in its entirety. That is, in the context of SLI and SLO definitions, ideally a user persona per relevant use case is needed. The following user characteristics are especially relevant in the context of SLI and SLO definitions.

- How much time would the user have to spend on the use case? For example:

  ○ Is the user in a hurry trying to catch a train?

  ○ Is the user on a bus waiting for the next stop?

  ○ Is the user boarding a plane in a foreign country?

- What is the overall environment the user is in when exercising the use case? For example:

  ○ Location (e.g., a car)

  ○ Institution (e.g., a hospital)

  ○ Home (e.g., preparing dinner)

- What user needs are being fulfilled by the use case? For example:

  ○ What are the most important characteristics for the use case?

    ○ Correctness?

    ○ Throughput?

    ○ Availability?

  ○ What would cause the user to pick up the phone and complain?

  ○ What would make the user leave the product?

> **Key Insight:** The UX process defines user personas per product. The SRE process to define SLIs and SLOs needs user personas per relevant use case. Well-defined user personas per product from the UX process is a great starting point for defining SLIs and SLOs within SRE.

If there are no user personas defined for a product from the UI/UX point of view, the SRE conversations might be the first attempt to lay down user characteristics in a structured way. This will benefit not only reliability conversations within SRE, but also the product feature definition in general!

> **From the Trenches:** The SRE coaches might encounter pushback from the product owners when it appears that a lot of time is being spent identifying specific service users or specific users for individual customer use cases. However, it is so important to define SLOs from the user point of view that it might be worth trying to insist on the time needed to understand the users in detail. If the product owner does not yield, there is no point in having an open dispute in front of the entire team. The SRE coaches should instead seek a private conversation with the product owner in an attempt to explain that spending the time now will pay big dividends down the road.
>
> If this does not elicit change, the SRE coaches should continue with the SLO definitions with the current understanding of the users. Later, once the SLO breaches start arriving, the team will report that it is unclear what kind of impact the breaches have on the user experience. The need to redefine the SLOs from the user point of view will become evident through the team's experience.

6.2.4 User Story Mapping

Another instrument from the UI/UX world is the organization of user stories in so-called user story maps. The process of creating a user story map is referred to as user story mapping. It is well described in the book *User Story Mapping: Discover the Whole Story, Build the Right*

Product[4] by Jeff Patton. Figure 6.3 depicts the structure of a user story map. On the left-hand side, three main entities of a user story map are shown. These are user activities, user tasks, and user stories.

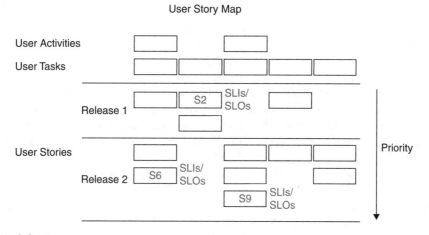

Figure 6.3 *User story map*

The user activities are the backbone of the user story map. They represent the biggest steps the user takes in their journey through the software. An example of a user activity from Gmail could be "compose email." Below the user activities, the user tasks are shown. The user tasks are the skeleton of the user story map; they detail the user activity they belong to and represent the steps the user takes on their journey through the user activity. Examples of user tasks from Gmail could be "type text," "insert image," and "add link."

At the lowest level of the user story map are the actual user stories. The user stories detail the user tasks and represent the steps the user takes on their journey through the user tasks. Examples of user stories from Gmail could be "make text bold," "insert image from cloud storage," and "add a link to a YouTube video."

Organizing the user journeys in a hierarchical way using story maps has proven to be useful for developing a deep understanding of user journeys. This is typically done in the initial stage of product definition as well as every time new functionality is being defined. Ideally, the entire development team, including the product owner and operations engineers, are involved in creating a user story map. This ensures that everyone is focused on understanding the user journey before any design or tech work is done. That work is done later in a very user-centric manner.

Using story maps in the context of SRE is a rather recent practice. In fact, a story map being rooted in the user experience is a great hierarchical model for identifying the most critical points in user journeys. What a user story map does not contain are reliability levels that would be important for the system to guarantee. The reliability levels need to be defined for the most critical user stories. The SRE process of user-centric definitions of SLIs and SLOs is a perfect fit for attaching reliability levels to user stories in a user story map.

---

4. Patton, Jeff, and Peter Economy. 2014. *User Story Mapping: Discover the Whole Story, Build the Right Product*. Sebastopol, CA: O'Reilly Media.

Referring back to Figure 6.3, release 1 contains user story S2. It was identified by the operations engineers, developers, and product owner to be a critical part of the user journey. Therefore, the reliability levels for user story S2 need to be expressed using appropriate SLIs and SLOs. For a simplified example, let us use the user story "make text bold" from Gmail. An acceptable latency of the operation could be defined using latency SLI. The corresponding latency SLO can be set to 99% of operations making text bold to return within 500 ms.

Furthermore, in release 2, two user stories are considered critical by the operations engineers, developers, and product owner: user stories S6 and S9. Also here, the team needs to express the reliability levels required for these user stories using respective SLIs and SLOs. For a simplified example, for the user story "add a link to a YouTube video" from Gmail, an acceptable latency for the appearance of the link and the video preview thumbnail could be defined differently. Also here, the latency SLI can be used. The latency for the link to the YouTube video appearing in the email being composed could be expressed using a latency SLO of 98% of the operations to complete within 400 ms. The latency for the YouTube video preview thumbnail appearing in the email being composed could be expressed using another latency SLO of 96% of the operations to complete within 800 ms.

The advantage of doing this over a user story map is that the team necessarily works in a user-centric manner. If there is no user story map for a product or part of the product yet, the SRE activities of defining SLIs and SLOs from the user point of view can be the impetus for creating one. This will have a broader positive implication on the level of user centricity applied by everyone when doing their specific work later on.

6.2.5 Motivation to Fix SLO Breaches

The definition of SLIs and SLOs from the user point of view is also important because it determines the motivation level the people on call will have when the SLO breaches arrive. If an SLO is defined clearly from the user point of view, it is clear what kind of user experience impact is there when the SLO is broken. As shown by the upper horizontal line on the graph in Figure 6.4, a clear user experience impact by SLO breaches caters to a high motivation to bring the service back within the SLO irrespective of the number of SLO breaches per time unit.

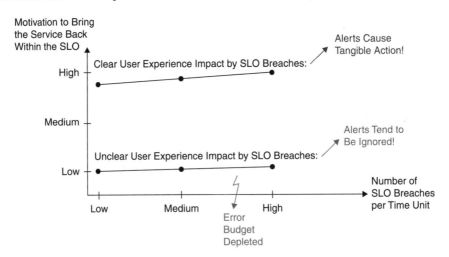

Figure 6.4 *Motivation to bring the service back within the SLO*

The upper horizontal line shows that the people on call are highly motivated to analyze individual SLO breaches when their numbers are low. If a service's error budget has been severely depleted as a result of a high number of SLO breaches, the people on call are even more motivated. However, their motivation to keep the services within the defined SLOs is nearly equally high irrespective of the number of times the SLOs get broken per time unit. No SLO breach is too small. This kind of motivation can only be sustained when the SLIs and SLOs were defined rigorously and uncompromisingly reflecting the user experience.

The lower horizontal line in Figure 6.4 demonstrates the motivation levels by the people on call when the user experience impact by the SLO breaches is not clear. The SLO breaches are like gauges of technical resources in this case. Much like how CPU and memory consumption going over a certain threshold is not clearly connected to the perceived experience by the user, so are the SLO breaches in this case. A broken SLO is most likely a manifestation of something technical. It requires investigation by the people on call to figure out what the breach actually means to the user before a decision can be made as to whether the breach is worth fixing, and if so, how.

This means the people on call are going to spend a disproportionately large amount of time connecting the dots between the alerts on SLO breaches and the user experience. This will keep them busy to the point where not all SLO breaches will be analyzed simply due to time constraints. The overload will cause motivation to plummet. As a result, the lower horizontal line in Figure 6.4 will manifest itself. It is a vicious circle of the SLOs not being defined rigorously from the user point of view, being unclear about the user impact when the SLO breaches arrive, and suffering from alert fatigue because it takes a long time to investigate a single alert. As a result, the people on call start ignoring the alerts on SLO breaches. This is shown in Figure 6.5.

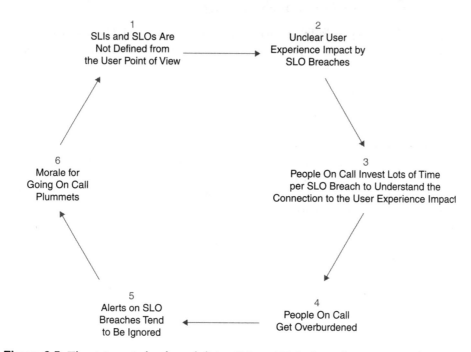

Figure 6.5 *The vicious circle of not defining SLIs and SLOs from the user point of view*

Figures 6.4 and 6.5 show that even exhaustion of the entire error budget does not change the motivation of the people on call the when the SLOs are not defined from the user point of view. It goes up a little but still remains relatively low. It just is not clear what it means when a service has exhausted its error budget prematurely. Did the user abandon the service already? Did the user not notice anything at all? The error budget depletion does not provide the answer. Further, even if an error budget policy exists in the team, it is not going to be enacted because the people on call are overburdened anyway.

Finally, no one wants to go on call in a team like that. Developers do not learn enough by being on call to improve the development process with insights from live production operations. The team is doing SRE but it does not yield the desired results! Doing SRE does not mean doing SRE well. The situation cries out for calling all hands on deck, including the product owner, to redefine the SLIs and SLOs from the user point of view. It is the SRE coaches' job to detect situations like this early enough and to guide the team before morale plummets.

> **From the Trenches:** It is common for development teams to define SLOs initially in such a way that the SLO breaches do not reflect the customer experience impact well. The job of the SRE coaches is to position the first attempt to define the SLOs as merely defining initial SLOs. It should be clear to the team from the start that the initial SLO values are there only to learn from and iterate upon thereafter until every SLO breach indicates an impacted user experience.

6.2.6 SLOs Are Not About Technicalities

The preceding discussion showed that the process of defining SLIs and SLOs is rooted in user experience thinking. This, however, is almost certainly not how the teams view it at the beginning of the SRE transformation. A common viewpoint about SRE is that it is about doing production monitoring in a purely technical manner. This view does not include the need for the SRE process to be started with the user experience. While technical production monitoring is a part of SRE, it is not where the teams need to begin. Rather, they need to begin in the nontechnical realm of the problem: the user experience artifacts, such as user story maps.

The perception of SRE coaches being there for reasons of establishing technical production monitoring needs to be changed at the onset of engagement with a development team. The team's mindset needs to shift to view the SRE process as starting from the user experience and associated artifacts. If this is not done, the process of defining SLIs and SLOs will take place under the mantra of technical monitoring being on top of people's minds.

As discussed earlier, user personas per use case actually need to be on top of people's minds when approaching the SLI and SLO definition process. In fact, as shown in the previous section, it must be the first step of the process to avoid hardship down the road.

Because technical monitoring is an established discipline within computer science and SRE is a relatively new methodology, it might be worth pointing out important differences between the two. These differences are outlined in Table 6.1.

Table 6.1 *Traditional Technical Monitoring Versus SRE*

Traditional Technical Monitoring	SRE
Resource-based alerting	Alerting on SLO breaches
Immediate alerting on thresholds	Alerting algorithm balancing timeliness, effectiveness, and other criteria
Indirect connection between resource states and user experience impact	Direct connection between SLO breaches and user experience impact
No explicit agreement about reactions to alerts	An explicit error budget policy agreed to by the team defining, developing, deploying, and operating the service stating actions to be taken as a reaction to excessive SLO breaches
Data and data visualizations about resource states over time	Data and data visualizations about adherence to the defined SLOs by SLI; data visualizations about service level performance over time intended to be used for decisions about reliability investments

With SLO breaches and reactions to them taking center stage in SRE, it's time to explore classes of errors leading to SLO breaches. It is helpful to understand them before embarking on the SLI and SLO definition journey.

6.2.7 Causes of SLO Breaches

The causes of SLO breaches can be classified into two broad categories:

- SLO breaches caused by a team's own services
- SLO breaches caused by dependent services not owned by the team

Each category can be classified into subcategories, as shown in Table 6.2.

Table 6.2 *Causes of SLO Breaches*

SLO Breach Category	SLO Breach Subcategory	Further Explanations Where Necessary
SLO breaches caused by a team's own services	Own bugs not leading to downtime	Self-explanatory.
	Own unplanned service downtime	Self-explanatory.
	Own planned service downtime	If a needed service level cannot be provided due to the planned service downtime (e.g., during production deployments), it can provide motivation to invest in a zero downtime deployment capability.

SLO breaches caused by dependent services or infrastructure not owned by the team	Bugs in dependent services/infrastructure from own organization	Historical error budget depletion patterns by the dependent services/infrastructure in the target environment can be consulted to make a decision about the service level actually provided in the past. This can inform possible SLOs for the services sitting on top of the dependent services/infrastructure. It also can inform the implementation of stability patterns necessary to uphold the SLOs.
	Bugs in dependent services/infrastructure from a third-party organization	Published SLAs, if any, can be consulted to inform the decision about possible SLOs for the services sitting on top of the dependent services/infrastructure from the third party. It also can inform the necessary implementation of stability patterns to uphold the SLOs.

If there are dependencies between services in the organization, new conversations between teams can take place that were not possible before because the entire discussion about SLIs and SLOs simply did not exist in the organization. The conversations will be about tightening existing SLOs or creating new ones because of new requirements of new services considered to be built on top of existing services. Conversations like these will also advance SRE adoption in more and more teams.

Likewise, if there are dependencies with third-party organizations, new conversations are unleashed. If a third party does not offer published SLAs, they should be requested. If a third party provides an SLA that is not sufficient for a service sitting on top to fulfill their own SLOs, a conversation about tightening the third party's SLO can be initiated. Especially if there are alternative third-party services to use offering different SLAs, the new conversations about the service levels might lead to one third-party service being abandoned for another one.

The discussions about SLIs and SLOs may also lead to changes in the procurement process. It might be decided to only procure services in the future that provide properly published SLAs and data on past adherence to the published SLAs.

6.2.8 On Call for SLO Breaches

At this point, it is not necessary to be very clear about the on-call setup. What needs to be clear is that the SLO breaches will require on-call duty. If SLOs were defined from the user point of view, the SLO breaches will represent a badly damaged user experience. It follows that based on the team's agreement, it is important to spend engineering time to determine why the SLOs broke and to bring the services back within the SLOs in a timely fashion.

It should be clear that without this, the entire SRE approach does not make sense. Generating alerts on SLO breaches and having no one there to react to them wastes more time than doing nothing at all. So, the questions of who will be going on call, for which service, at which time, and on which day will be important. However, these questions do not have to be answered at this point. They will be discussed in due course considering all the options at hand.

What is important now is to convert the theoretical knowledge about SLIs and SLOs gained so far into a concrete set of SLIs and SLOs for real services in production owned by a team.

The next step after this will be to feed the SLO definitions to the SRE infrastructure. This will bring the team to the point where the first SLO breaches will arrive. Only then will the first questions about the on-call setup for SLO breaches become concrete in a team.

That is, now is the time to get your hands dirty and implement the chain SLIs → SLOs → SLO breaches for a set of services owned by a development team. Which SLIs should you start with? This is the subject of the next section.

6.3 SLI Standardization

In *Implementing Service Level Objectives*,[5] the author devotes a great deal of time making sure the right SLIs are selected for a service and reflect the user experience well. This is of great importance, indeed. The SLIs are at the bottom of the SRE concept pyramid (Section 3.5). Getting the SLIs wrong makes the entire pyramid shaky.

Now, every service is different. Moreover, the users of every service are different. It follows that the SLIs that are important for a service to track the user experience well will be different. In Section 3.5, *SRE Concept Pyramid*, a pyramid of SLIs that comprise reliability was presented. The SLIs are an attempt to standardize important indicators that are applicable to a wide range of services. Such standardization is important from two points of view.

1. It establishes a common language for SLIs that can be widely understood and applied to a broad range of services from different domains.

2. It enables the SRE infrastructure to be developed in a generic way.

Both points are equally important. Introducing SRE in a product delivery organization requires new terminology to be learned by lots of people. The more the terminology can be standardized, the easier it will be for the teams to understand and the more quickly it will be adopted. Complicated language can put off even the most open and willing people from adopting SRE. The SRE coaches need to keep this in mind. In conversations, the coaches need to gauge people's readiness to use the terms from the SRE concept pyramid effortlessly. Taking an empathetic approach instead of pushing the SRE terms to be used in every conversation leads to better SRE adoption. Especially with SLIs, terms like availability, latency, throughput, and correctness will be familiar to people in general. However, calling them SLIs is a step that needs to be learned.

The second point is about implementing the SRE infrastructure in a cost-effective and timely manner. This is critically important at the beginning of the SRE transformation. The operations team needs to enable as many development teams as possible with a small SRE infrastructure. The infrastructure needs to be made available quickly to onboard as many development teams as possible in a short amount of time to fuel the SRE movement.

If the SRE infrastructure arrives too late, the development teams can get discouraged from adopting SRE. One of the reasons the SRE infrastructure may come too late is if it attempts to

5. Hidalgo, Alex. 2020. *Implementing Service Level Objectives: A Practical Guide to SLIs, SLOs, and Error Budgets*. Sebastopol, CA: O'Reilly Media.

implement custom features for individual development teams that cannot benefit lots of other teams. Especially at the beginning, only features that benefit nearly all the development teams should be implemented by the SRE infrastructure. This enables a small but necessary economy of scale within the product delivery organization.

> **From the Trenches:** In a larger enterprise, many product delivery organizations are going to coexist. The product delivery organizations may use similar technology stacks. Once SRE has been firmly established in a single product delivery organization within the enterprise, other product delivery organizations might take notice and wish to implement SRE as well. In this case, the existing SRE infrastructure may be largely reused. This provides a greater economy of scale for the infrastructure. Also in this case, the operations team implementing and maintaining the infrastructure starts operating at the enterprise level serving several product delivery organizations at once. Still, even at that level, the SRE infrastructure should implement features that benefit several product delivery organizations at once, as far as possible.

In light of establishing SRE from zero, a ruthless prioritization of features for the SRE infrastructure is necessary to implement the chain SLIs → SLOs → SLO breaches for the first time. It starts with a prioritization of SLIs to support because certainly not all the SLIs from Section 3.1, Service level indicators, can be implemented at once. Nor is it necessary to get SRE going in the organization.

As suggested by the SLI pyramid from Service level indicators, two of the SLIs that are most foundational to reliability are availability and latency. If a service is not available, the service users will not consider it reliable. If a service is too slow, the service users will not perceive it as being reliable either. Users on the internet are used to being served quickly. Therefore, the slogan "slow is the new down"[6] has emerged demonstrating the user perception of slow services. Referring again to the UI/UX domain, according to *Usability Engineering*,[7] already a latency of 1 second represents a noticeable delay!

That is, functionality not being available at all or being available too slowly is at the core of reliability as perceived by users. Availability applies to all services. Latency applies to most services. Therefore, from an economy of scale point of view, implementing the availability and latency SLIs by the SRE infrastructure is going to serve all development teams in the product delivery organization. In all likelihood, these should be the SLIs to start with!

In the remainder of this book, this will be our assumption. However, there might be systems where the two most important SLIs are different. For example, they might be availability and correctness. The key takeaway from the discussion is that SLI selection needs to be based on the percentage of development teams in the product delivery organization that can be immediately served. This is dependent on the domain the product delivery organization is in. A product delivery organization selling tools for data pipelines might have a different set of important SLIs than another product delivery organization selling car dashboard applications.

---

6. Harley, Nick. 2017. "Software Intelligence: Why Slow Is the New Down." *VentureBeat*, April 27, 2017. https://venturebeat.com/2017/04/27/software-intelligence-why-slow-is-the-new-down.

7. Nielsen, Jakob. 1993. *Usability Engineering*. Burlington, MA: Morgan Kaufmann.

With availability and latency assumed as initial SLIs to implement the chain SLIs → SLOs → SLO breaches, the next step for the operations team is to figure out how availability and latency can be measured in a standardized manner. This means the SRE infrastructure needs to offer a generic facility that can measure the availability and latency of some specifically defined sort. For instance, the measurements can be done on the client side or on the server side. Also here, the choice needs to be based on general applicability to the majority of development teams. For example, initially the SRE infrastructure might offer measuring availability and latency of a web service's service endpoints on the server side. However, initially it might not offer measuring the latency of background jobs or serverless functions.

> **Key Insight:** A small selection of about two initial SLIs is required to implement the chain SLIs → SLOs → SLO breaches quickly in the SRE infrastructure. The choice of the SLIs and the offered way of measuring them needs to be based on the number of development teams that can be served immediately. For lots of domains, the two initial SLIs will be availability and latency, initially measured on the server side for web services by endpoint.

6.3.1 Application Performance Management Facility

To measure availability, latency, and other SLIs, the operations team needs to research and suggest an application performance management facility to be used by the development teams. The facility should be off the shelf as much as possible so as not to spend development time on service instrumentations, which can be provided out of the box by existing products. The following products may be used for this purpose: Azure Monitor, New Relic, Dynatrace, and Datadog, among others.

The operations team needs to select the most suitable product, get hands-on experience with it, share the experience with some developers, achieve a joint decision, document it, initiate procurement if applicable, and create documentation for the development teams. The documentation needs to equip a new developer with the knowledge to enable the application performance management facility in a service of a given type. For example:

- Backend service

- Frontend service

- Background job

- Serverless function

The documentation has to be produced with self-service in mind. That is, the developer needs to be enabled in a fully autonomous manner without having to ask questions of the operations team. To that end, SRE should get a new section on the overall engineering wiki. The documentation to enable developers should go into the SRE section of the wiki.

The SRE coaches need to discuss this important point with the operations team. The operations team should not become the bottleneck, holding the development teams' hands to enable the application performance management facility for services of any type. In fact, this is the first step in getting onto the SRE infrastructure. It should be able to be done by new developers on their own quickly.

Moreover, the operations team needs to think about logical partitions inside the application performance management facility to be able to differentiate the measurements by environment as necessary. For example, the organization may have several production environments in different geographies. Additionally, in the future it may make sense to monitor some environments preceding production using the SRE infrastructure to get early feedback on whether the services fulfill their SLOs.

Also, these insights need to be part of the self-service documentation for the developers. In general, developers tend to like to try things out quickly. So, the documentation should put them in a position to quickly dock to the infrastructure any service they might have in any environment it might be deployed. Any service types, environments, or combinations thereof not yet supported by the infrastructure should be clearly listed. There is nothing more frustrating to a motivated developer who wants to get their hands dirty with SRE than to follow documentation that leads to a known issue that is not described.

The SRE coaches should not position the documentation with the operations teams as a means of describing what they have done or what they recommend the development teams do. Rather, the documentation should be positioned as an enabler for making the development teams work autonomously and in a self-service manner. Without appropriate documentation of that quality and detail, not only will the operations team become the bottleneck, but also the overall SRE movement will suffer and lose the appeal drummed up by the SRE marketing funnel. Keeping the self-service documentation up-to-date as the SRE infrastructure changes will be a new way of working to be learned by the operations teams.

6.3.2 Availability

The endpoint availability measurements for the purpose of SLO breach calculations will be based on the HTTP response codes of the service endpoint requests. The SRE infrastructure needs to make public which error codes are considered unavailable endpoints. Moreover, the SRE infrastructure needs to make them configurable by the development team.

When the SRE coaches later engage with the development teams to set the availability SLOs, they need to ensure very explicitly that there is a good discipline in the team for using correct HTTP response codes. Before the SRE introduction, it might not have mattered as much which HTTP response codes were used in some circumstances. However, now that the codes will be used by the SRE infrastructure to calculate the availability of SLO breaches and error budget depletion, it becomes much more important to be precise.

The error budget depletion calculated based on imprecisely used HTTP response codes will lead to skewed error budget depletion calculations. This may lead to wrong conclusions about premature error budget depletion. In turn, this may lead to wrong prioritization of reliability work versus feature work. To avoid this, the SRE coaches need to make it an explicit point to check the HTTP response codes for all service endpoints where availability SLOs will be defined, and clean them up as necessary. This will slow down the process of getting to the point where a team has defined an initial set of availability SLOs. However, it is well worth the wait.

Figure 6.6 illustrates what makes up a successful availability SLI implementation for a service.

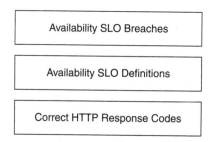

Figure 6.6 *Components for implementing an availability SLI*

It starts with correct HTTP response codes in all endpoints involved in the availability SLO. Once the codes are correct, the availability SLO definitions can be done by the team owning the service. Finally, the SRE infrastructure calculates the actual availability against the availability defined by the SLO. On detection of availability SLO breaches, the infrastructure sends out alerts.

6.3.3 Latency

As mentioned earlier, slow is considered the new down on the internet. Measuring the time that it takes to complete operations as perceived by the user is therefore very important in order to know the perceived performance bottlenecks and work to eliminate them. Thus, the selected application performance management facility needs to support latency measurements in a broad sense.

Further, the considerations about the quality and detail of documentation enabling developers to autonomously and in a self-service manner dock services of any type deployed in any environment apply to latency as well. Again, the SRE coaches need to work on the mindset in the operations teams to treat the self-service documentation as a first-class concern on the same level as implementing technical features in the SRE infrastructure.

In the likely event that the SRE infrastructure would initially offer latency to be measured by web service endpoints, it may be necessary to break down the latency SLOs coming from the user story map at a higher level into individual endpoint-level SLOs. This is another great exercise to do over a story map with the operations engineers, developers, and product owner. The process is shown in Figure 6.7.

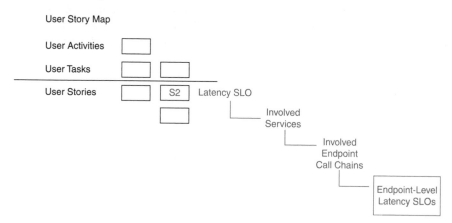

Figure 6.7 *Using a story map to define fine-grained latency SLOs*

The left-hand side of the figure shows the structure of a story map. The story map contains the user story S2. A latency SLO is defined for user story S2. Measuring the latency SLO would require new features in the SRE infrastructure that might not be available initially. In terms of latency, the SRE infrastructure currently provides measurements at the individual web service endpoint level. Therefore, the gap between the latency SLO defined at the user story level in the story map and the individual endpoints needs to be bridged.

The gap is bridged with an analysis of the services involved in user story S2. Once the services are identified, involved endpoint call chains need to be uncovered. The endpoint call chains reveal individual endpoints for which the endpoint-level latency SLOs can be set. The endpoint-level latency is supported by the SRE infrastructure.

In this context, it is worth noting that even if the SRE infrastructure supports coarse-grained latency measurements, a split of the user story–level latency SLO into lower–level endpoint latency SLOs may make sense. The split can be done by service or by team. This is beneficial because of alert targeting for latency SLO breaches. The alert targeting should correspond to the way the on-call responsibilities will be split in the organization. The latency SLO breaches need to be dispatched to the people on call who are responsible for the service or the set of services where the breach occurred, when it occurred.

Apart from that, the operations engineers, developers, and product owner may find it difficult to define latency SLOs at the user story and lower levels. "How long could an operation take for the user to stay happy?" is a difficult question to answer in lots of cases. In situations like that, the SRE coaches need to remind the team that defining a latency SLO, or any SLO, for that matter, merely means defining it initially. The initial latency SLO definition is done in order to kick off a frequent SLO iteration process based on feedback from production in the form of SLO breaches systematically analyzed by the people on call.

Finally, in some cases it may be possible to treat latency SLOs and their breaches as performance tests in target environments. This may be the case where a rigid user and data load profile is not necessarily required to obtain meaningful test results. Some part of the overall "testing in production" strategy might be realized using latency SLOs.

6.3.4 Prioritization

The preceding discussion shows the need for ruthless prioritization in the realm of SLI standardization in order to implement an initial set of useful functionality (the chain SLIs → SLOs → SLO breaches) in the SRE infrastructure in the fastest way possible. The prioritization needs to take place at five levels:

- Initial SLI selection
- Initial way of measuring SLIs
- Initial way of setting SLOs
- Initial way of alerting on SLO breaches
- Initial visualization

The prioritization at all levels needs to be done with two important criteria in mind:

1. Immediate applicability to most development teams in the product delivery organization

2. Minimal viable set of functionalities enabling a development team to get started with SRE in the fastest way possible

This is shown in Figure 6.8.

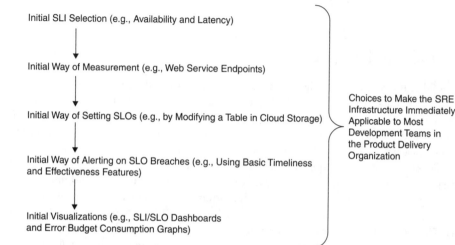

Figure 6.8 *Prioritization of SRE infrastructure features*

Initially, selecting two SLIs, such as availability and latency, will be applicable to most development teams in most product delivery organizations. The initial way to measure availability and latency offered by the SRE infrastructure can be restricted to web service endpoints only. This will be widely applicable to a broad range of development teams too.

Further, the initial way to set the SLOs that are offered could simply be by modifying a table in cloud storage. A more user-friendly interface is not required at the beginning. The developers are familiar with modifying cloud table storage using standard tools by cloud vendors. It will not be a hurdle for them to change the SLO settings this way.

Moreover, the initial way to alert on SLO breaches needs to be a little bit better than pure resource-based alerting. For example, offering basic features of timeliness where not every surpassing of the SLO threshold leads to an alert would go a long way toward reducing alert fatigue. Likewise, offering basic features of effectiveness where not every SLO breach is alerted upon every time, but rather an alert snooze period after an alerted SLO breach is introduced, would also yield great benefits in reducing alert fatigue. More sophisticated alerting features are not needed at this point at all, as no team is reacting to any SLO breach alerts as of now! Getting the teams to react to SLO breaches will be a major exercise and, if successful, a great breakthrough for the SRE transformation and success for the SRE coaches.

Finally, the same logic applies to visualizations initially provided by the SRE infrastructure. All teams need to be able to see time series graphs showing SLO adherence over time and error budget depletion in the current time unit. Providing rudimentary time series graphs with this information is enough to get SRE going in all development teams of any product delivery organization.

Making the graphs broadly available in the product delivery organization exposes a lot of previously private and scattered information about services to be seen publicly in a well-aggregated way. Depending on the organizational culture, the teams may be apprehensive about the potential to be rendered negatively in public by the graphs. The SRE coaches need to address these valid concerns very early on by ensuring that the graphs are not used for individual performance evaluations and assuring the teams that this indeed is the case.

6.4 Enabling Logging

With initial SLIs selected during the SLI standardization process, the next step is to ensure that the services are logging properly for the SLI measurements to be performed in a sensible way. This is an important point that needs to be clarified with the development teams up front. The SRE infrastructure will operate based on logs from production environments. It will not call the services to measure the latency of requests. Nor will it call the services to find out whether they are available (there are ping tools for this). All the calculations of SLI measurements, SLO breaches, and error budgets will be done based on real logs from production environments.

It follows that enabling logging is the next important step on the SRE transformation journey. To start the process, the operations teams need to research and suggest a suitable logging facility. The logging facility needs to work well with the application performance management facility selected. Even better, the application performance management facility might include a logging facility, providing a well-integrated solution.

The resultant overall structure of the SRE infrastructure is shown in Figure 6.9.

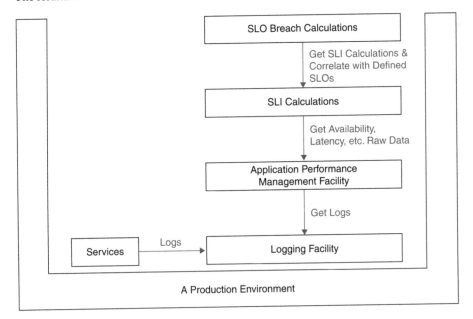

Figure 6.9 *SRE infrastructure components*

Services deployed to a production environment send logs to the logging facility. The application performance management facility obtains the logs and calculates service performance. The SLI calculations obtain the raw data from the application performance management facility required for availability, latency, and other SLIs as defined during the SLI standardization (Section 6.3). On top of the SLI calculations, the calculations of SLO breaches reside. The SLO breaches are correlations of the SLI calculations and defined SLOs.

The logging facility needs to provide logging from all the programming languages used in the product delivery organization. Moreover, it needs to provide a log query language to programmatically query logs. Additionally, it needs to provide visualizations over logs produced using simple language commands. It must be easy to create pie charts, line charts, tables, and so on using the log query language commands provided by the logging facility.

The operations team needs to select the most suitable logging facility, get hands-on experience with it, share the experience with some developers, achieve a joint decision, document it, initiate procurement if applicable, and create self-service documentation for the development teams. Once a development team implements logging in their services using the logging facility, the SRE coaches need to initiate a session with the team. In the session, an operations engineer would need to query the logs to see whether all the services owned by the team appear in all production environments as expected.

Although the development team might think the services are logging, with the help of the operations engineer the team might encounter the following cases:

- Services not logging as expected
- Services logging but to the wrong logical partition of the application performance management facility (e.g., logs from Production JP appearing in Production EU)
- Endpoints discovered that nobody was aware of
- Endpoints missing in a surprising way
- Service names not following naming conventions
- Endpoints not following naming conventions
- And so on

This kind of log sanity checking needs to take place before the logs are fed to the SRE infrastructure for SLI, SLO, and error budget calculations. For the operations engineer, the exercise is also important for the following reason. The SRE infrastructure needs to cluster services by development teams. In a product delivery organization where the development teams were not involved in product operations, it might be that there is no service catalog showing up-to-date ownership of services by development teams. Doing the log sanity checking just described puts the operations engineer in a position to build up the service catalog manually. This is good enough to start with. It is also sufficient for the SRE infrastructure to cluster the services, dashboards, and so on by team.

6.5 Teaching the Log Query Language

In a product delivery organization where development teams did not take part in product operations before, average knowledge of the selected log query language will be rather low. This is because developers did not need to use it on a daily basis. The developers' most important concern was implementation of new product features. The log query language is not needed for that purpose.

With SRE, the development team has two important concerns:

1. Ensuring the services owned are within their SLOs in all production environments

2. Implementing new product features (ideally as experiments using hypothesis-driven development[8])

Ensuring a development team's services are within their SLOs requires reactions to SLO breaches. An SLO breach investigation requires finding product issues using logs. The log analysis has to be done using the log query language.

Such analyses require proficiency with the log query language. In a short amount of time, lots of hypotheses of what the issue might be need to be generated, tested using log queries, discarded, or pursued further. All of these steps require quick formulation of log queries to approach the issue and resolution step by step.

Luckily, the log query languages available as part of commercial logging facilities can be learned quickly by developers because of their general programming knowledge. Examples of log query languages are the Kusto Query Language (KQL) and Prometheus Query Language (PromQL). These query languages enable developers to query logs efficiently, and more importantly, they enable developers to create visualizations based on the logs using specific language commands. Visualizations using bar, column, line, pie, and other charts are supported using single language commands out of the box. This is invaluable support when investigating SLO breaches quickly.

The SRE coaches need to work with the operations teams to compile internal overview wiki documentation about the most applicable and commonly used features of the chosen log query language. The purpose of this documentation is to describe and link to common queries used by the people on call when investigating the SLO breaches. The internal documentation should link to external online language documentation as much as possible for generic explanations of language commands. As always, the documentation needs to be self-service.

Next, the SRE coaches should run sessions with a couple of development teams where an operations engineer with a good command of the log query language would explain it based on the documentation. In the sessions, the operations engineer needs to demonstrate hands-on how some typical SLO breaches can be investigated using a series of queries. The sessions need to be recorded, and the recordings need to be tagged with the tag "SRE" and placed in the internal wiki documentation.

When the time is right for other development teams to learn the log query language, the SRE coaches need to refer to the existing wiki documentation and the recordings. They need to ask the teams to work with the material on their own first. Only then can a session be set up where

---

8. O'Reilly, Barry. 2014. "How to Implement Hypothesis-Driven Development." Thoughtworks, October 18, 2014. . https://www.thoughtworks.com/insights/articles/how-implement-hypothesis-driven-development.

an operations engineer can answer remaining questions by the development teams in an interactive Q&A mode.

This is another step in the direction of reducing the workload of operations engineers and SRE coaches. Teaching and learning the log query language should be instrumented to the point where it is done in a self-service manner. This can be done based on the provided wiki text, video, and external documentation as well as the possibility of having a just-in-time Q&A with someone who has a good command of the language.

6.6 Defining Initial SLOs

With logging services in place and developers able to use the log query language, the foundations for defining SLOs and reacting to SLO breaches are established. The next step the SRE coaches should take with the development team is about actually defining initial SLOs for the services they own. To undertake this step, knowing up front what a good SLO looks like is beneficial. So, what makes a good SLO? Let us explore!

6.6.1 What Makes a Good SLO?

A good SLO:

- Reflects the user experience of a specific step in a specific user journey
- Is defined by the operations engineers, developers, and product owner from the user point of view (e.g., with the help of a story map)
- Is agreed to by the operations engineers, developers, and product owner
- Has been arrived at by an iterative process of
  - Setting an initial SLO based on a hypothesis
  - Measuring the fulfillment of the SLO in production
  - Analyzing the SLO breaches
  - Learning from the SLO breaches whether the user experience is impacted as hypothesized before
  - Adjusting (tightening, relaxing, or redefining) the SLOs as needed based on the learning
  - Repeating the steps until the SLO reflects the user experience well
- When broken, leads to a
  - Fast and clear understanding of how the user experience is impacted
  - Motivation burst among the people on call to take action
- Can be measured by the current SRE infrastructure

In Section 1.3, *Why Does SRE Work?*, a key insight was that SRE works because of the application of the scientific method in software operations. This is exactly the iterative process of arriving at a good SLO described in the preceding list of criteria. The process is illustrated in Figure 6.10.

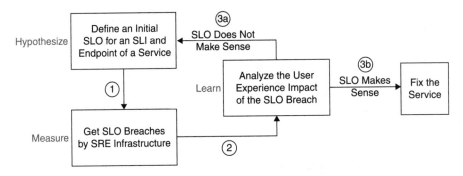

Figure 6.10 *Arriving at good SLOs using the scientific method*

The iterative process starts with adopting the mindset that defining an SLO is not something set in stone. The opposite needs to be true. Defining an SLO always needs to be treated as defining an initial SLO. Defining an SLO always means hypothesizing.

The hypothesis in the form of an SLO undergoes rigorous testing in production. The test results arrive in the form of SLO breaches reported by the SRE infrastructure. This is the process of measuring whether the originally defined hypothesis is true.

The analysis of the SLO breaches embodies the process of learning. It can be learned that the SLO breach did not reflect the user experience impact well. The action in this case is to falsify the hypothesis by declaring that the SLO does not make sense and embarking on the SLO definition process from the beginning. This is shown in step 3a in Figure 6.10.

Alternatively, it can be learned that the SLO breach actually did reflect the user experience impact well. The action in this case is to acknowledge the original hypothesis as being correct and fix the service to bring it back within the SLO. This is shown in step 3b in Figure 6.10.

> **From the Trenches:** Teams tend to define initial SLOs too tightly, aiming for high availability, low latency, and so on. Through the iterative process, the initial SLOs are adapted and tend to be relaxed to reflect a real-world intersection point of acceptable customer experience and the service level the teams are able to uphold.
>
> The SRE coaches do not need to intrude in the lively team discussion taking place when setting the initial SLOs. Even if the coaches see that the suggested initial SLOs tend to be too perfect for the level of reliability provided by the services, they should not interfere with the teams' judgment. It is more important to let the teams learn from their own misconceptions than to avoid the misconceptions in the first place. Additionally, it is more important for the teams to quickly arrive at the realization that the initial SLOs need to be adapted and actually adapt them than to get the initial SLOs closer to reality in the first place. Learning to learn is a vital part of the process!

The only constraint the SRE coaches should apply to the discussion on initial SLOs is time. It might be reasonable to limit the initial discussion to one hour per SLI. All the SLOs set within that hour for an SLI can be submitted to the SRE infrastructure on the same day. This way, soon afterward, the initial iteration in the hypothesize → measure → learn loop can be finished and all further iterations can take place based on real feedback from production!

6.6.2 Iterating on an SLO

The detailed process of iteration on SLOs is outlined in Figure 6.11.

In step 1, all people contributing to a service need to come together in an offline or online meeting. That is, all operations engineers, developers, and product owners need to be present for a good SLO to be defined.

In step 2, the team needs to identify the most important customer use cases fulfilled by the services in question. This can be greatly facilitated by a user story map (see Section 6.2.4, *User Story Mapping*). The user story map already contains all the user journeys. So, a subset of them needs to be selected for setting the SLOs.

In step 3, the team needs to identify typical call chains involved in the most important customer use cases. This step can be greatly facilitated by the logging facility or the application performance management facility. These facilities usually can display call chains over time. The developers can identify the use cases by looking at the displayed call chains.

In step 4, the initial availability SLOs for the endpoints from the typical call chains are defined. This step can be greatly facilitated by looking at the historical availability data for the endpoints. The application performance management facility should have this data available and presentable in tables, graphs, and charts. If it does not, the selected facility was not the right choice!

What the historical availability data can do is provide data regarding the maximum and minimum availability of a given endpoint for a given time period. This data can be used to create a hypothesis about the future availability of the endpoint. This hypothesis can be codified as the initial availability SLO for the endpoint. The initial SLO should not be set tighter than the maximum availability for the endpoint based on historical data. If the historical data shows that an endpoint was never more than 95% available, the initial SLO should not be set to 99%. Doing so would only lead to the people on call being bombarded by availability SLO breaches. This, in turn, would lead to alert fatigue (see Section 6.2.5, *Motivation to Fix SLO Breaches*).

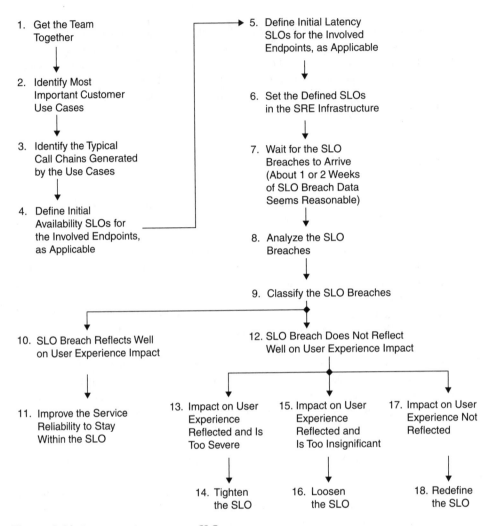

Figure 6.11 *Process to iterate on an SLO*

Looking at the historical availability data for endpoints can also have the positive side effect that, for the first time, many operations engineers, developers, and the product owner will see that kind of data. Seeing lower availability than expected can spark new conversations, which might lead to decisions about investing in reliability improvements. Is it not the goal of SRE to enable data-driven decision-making about investing in reliability versus new features? It is, indeed! Sometimes, in the initial stages of the SRE transformation, this goal can be achieved just by looking at some historical data that was never looked at before.

In step 5, the initial latency SLOs for the involved endpoints are defined. It will not make sense to measure latency everywhere. So, a careful analysis of which endpoints would benefit from having a latency SLO needs to be done. As for availability SLOs, this analysis can be greatly facilitated by the historical latency data of the endpoints. The initial latency SLO for an endpoint should not be set tighter than the minimum latency indicated by the historical data.

For example, if the historical data shows that an endpoint had a latency range between 300 ms and 900 ms for a given time period, it does not make sense to set the initial latency SLO to 200 ms in 80% of the cases. Also here, looking at the historical data for the first time may prompt the team to prioritize reliability improvements they have not thought of before.

In step 6, the defined SLOs need to be set in the SRE infrastructure. Ideally, the development team should be able to do this in a self-service manner. However, if this is not yet possible or is too cumbersome to do in the initial stages of SRE infrastructure development, the operations engineers can take over this step. Doing so more than once will create the correct impression among the development teams that the SRE infrastructure cannot be handled in a self-service manner. Therefore, the SRE coaches need to insist that the operations teams make it their highest priority to make setting the SLOs a self-service operation for the development teams. Only when the SLOs can be set in a self-service manner can the motivation for adjusting the SLOs regularly be sustained with the development teams. If every time a development team wants to adjust an SLO, they have to contact the operations teams, motivation will dwindle rather quickly.

In step 7, the team should wait until the SLO breaches start arriving. A wait of one or two weeks might be reasonable. However, if many SLO breaches arrive sooner than that, there is no need to wait longer to start an analysis of the first SLO breaches. If no SLO breaches arrive within one or two weeks, there might be a bug in the newly developed SRE infrastructure. The SRE infrastructure needs to provide a way for a development team to see the historical data by SLI and SLO based on how the SRE infrastructure decided to generate SLO breaches. SLI/SLO graphs can support this in a good way. However, initially just a table representation of the data should be sufficient.

Also here, it is important to put the development team in a position to rule out certain categories of errors in a self-service manner. They should be able to understand, using self-service facilities, that the reason some SLO breaches were not generated is because the service endpoint was actually within the SLO. Only once this is confirmed can other suspicious infrastructure behavior be discussed with the operations teams implementing the SRE infrastructure.

In step 8, the initial analysis of SLO breaches is performed. This can be a time-consuming activity. It should be carried out in a structured way. The SLO breaches should be grouped by reason, and the reasons should be well described (e.g., on a team wiki). In step 9, a classification of the breaches takes place. The classification is done based on the level on which the SLO breaches reflect the impact on the user experience. If an SLO reflects the impact on the user experience well (step 10), the service reliability needs to be improved (step 11).

If an SLO breach does not reflect the impact on the user experience well (step 12), there are three cases to consider. If the impact on the user experience is reflected and it is too severe (step 13), the SLO needs to be tightened. Tightening the SLO will lead to the SRE infrastructure alerting earlier on the SLO breach at a time when the impact on the user experience is not as severe.

If the impact on the user experience is reflected and it is too insignificant (step 15), the SLO breach was generated at a time when the user experience was not hurt badly enough to take action by the people on call. To let the SRE infrastructure generate the SLO breach at a later point in time when the user experience impact is a bit more significant, the SLO needs to be loosened (step 16).

Finally, in step 17, there is a case when an SLO breach simply does not reflect an impact on user experience. In such a case, something technical is going to be off, but the user does not perceive the technical glitch at all. In this case, the SLO needs to be redefined (step 18).

The entire process is geared toward aligning the SLOs and SLO breaches with the user experience impact. Its aim is to reduce alerts on SLO breaches. Following the process, the people on call should reach a point where every SLO breach makes sense to them because the impact on the user experience is clear. Consequently, the motivation to bring the service back within the SLO should be clear as well.

6.6.3 Revising SLOs

It is the responsibility of the people on call to run through the process continuously. Every SLO definition should be considered a hypothesis to be tested using SLO breaches and their analyses. Apart from that, SLO revisions need to take place in several cases, outlined in Table 6.3.

Table 6.3 *SLO Revision Cases*

SLO Revision Case	Explanation
When someone outside the group of people on call detects an issue with the service they are responsible for	Stakeholders, customers, or anyone else outside the group of people on call can detect issues. The people on call should hold themselves to the high standard of aiming to be the first to detect issues with the services they are responsible for. Therefore, every time someone else detects an issue with one of their services, an SLO revision needs to take place. The goal is not to have as many SLOs as possible. Rather, the goal is to have as many SLOs as necessary to be the first to find out about the reported issue the next time.
Before the first production deployment of a new feature	Initial SLOs need to be defined for new features before their first production deployment so that the features can be monitored. Deploying the new features without SLOs is like flying blind. Customers and stakeholders will be the ones detecting issues with the features, not the people on call. This is not the standard the people on call should hold themselves to. Therefore, the people on call need to call for an SLO definition meeting before new features get deployed to production for the first time.
On a cadence reasonable for the team	Apart from the preceding cases, the people on call should also initiate an SLO-checking schedule for the team. A quarterly cadence might be reasonable. Error budget depletions of services in the previous quarter can be reviewed in the same meeting.

The process of setting and revising SLOs can be supported by default SLOs. What default SLOs are and how they might be set is the subject of the next section.

6.7 Default SLOs

Default SLOs for service endpoints is a concept that can be explored by a team's operations engineers, developers, and product owner. Default SLOs are intended to serve two needs:

- Avoid flying blind when deploying new service endpoints to production

- Avoid disaster scenarios when something is completely broken in production and only users know about it

When a new service endpoint is added to a service, a deliberate discussion needs to take place to determine whether any SLOs for any SLIs would be applicable to the service and would therefore need to be set. However, this discussion might not take place if the team is in a rush to deploy the new functionality to production (among other reasons). Deploying the service to production without having this discussion and without SLOs renders the people on call incapable of monitoring the new service endpoint. It might not need to be monitored. However, this is not known. The team is flying blind in this regard. As a result, the functionality implemented by the newly deployed endpoint may be completely broken in production, and the only people who know about it are the users of the service.

To prevent such a situation, the operations engineers, developers, and product owner may decide to implement so-called default SLOs. A default SLO is defined per SLI per service. It can be defined in such a way that it represents the bare minimum service level that should be fulfilled in any case by all endpoints of the service. For example, for a user-facing service, the default SLOs shown in Table 6.4 could be defined.

Table 6.4 *Examples of Default SLOs*

A User-Facing Service	
Default availability SLO	90% availability for every endpoint
Default latency SLO	1,000 ms latency in 80% of the cases for every endpoint

These default SLOs say that the availability for all endpoints should be at least 90% and the latency should be no longer than 1,000 ms in 80% of the cases.

With default SLOs entering the picture, now there are two SLO flavors.

- Explicit SLOs set through the process discussed in the previous section (see Section 6.6, *Defining Initial SLOs*). Explicit SLOs, if defined, override default SLOs.

- Default SLOs applied implicitly by the SRE infrastructure to all endpoints without an explicit SLO definition.

That is, any endpoint in production that does not have an explicit SLO set for an SLI gets assigned a default SLO defined for the service for that SLI. This way, there is no situation in which the discussion about setting explicit SLOs did not take place before production deployment, and therefore the people on call cannot monitor the endpoint. Nor can they detect even the most disastrous scenarios with the endpoint, leaving the users only with the option to escalate.

Using the preceding example, the SRE infrastructure would apply the availability SLO of 90% and the latency SLO of 1,000 ms in 80% of the cases to every endpoint of the given service that does not have any explicit SLO defined for the availability and latency SLIs, respectively. Certainly, the SRE infrastructure needs to offer a self-service facility to its users to set and make changes to the default SLOs at will. The changes of the default SLOs, and explicit SLOs, for that matter, need to take effect within about an hour after they have been made. Otherwise, the feedback loop between the changes and their effect is not tight enough for avoiding questions about whether the changes really took effect or whether the SRE infrastructure has a problem.

Additionally, the process of defining initial SLOs at the beginning of the SRE transformation can be supported by the default SLOs. In such a situation, there are lots of endpoints in production, possibly thousands clustered in hundreds of services. It is best to define SLOs explicitly for the most important customer scenarios. However, in a large system, this can be very time-consuming.

In an attempt to balance the time spent on high-quality initial SLO definitions versus achieving some reasonable SLO coverage versus bringing an end to flying blind, a careful set of default SLOs might make sense. As always with SRE, the default SLOs need to be jointly decided upon by the operations engineers, developers, and product owner responsible for a given service.

One strategy could be to go for default SLOs initially, and then to gradually replace the default SLOs with explicit ones as proper user-centric discussions about the most important customer use cases take place. A twist to that strategy could be to go with the default SLOs initially and then define explicit SLOs one by one later as part of reacting to default SLO breaches. Whatever the strategy, the goal is for SLOs to be iterated upon until they reflect the impact on user experience well (see Section 6.6.2, *Iterating on an SLO*).

6.8 Providing Basic Infrastructure

As discussed in the previous sections, the basic SRE infrastructure needs to put a development team in a position to iterate on SLOs. In Section 6.3.4, *Prioritization*, a basic set of features for enabling the hypothesize → measure → learn cycle was outlined. The basic features are

1. Ability to set explicit, and default, SLOs for availability and latency (ideally self-service from the beginning)

2. Ability to get alerted on SLO breaches

3. Ability to adapt SLOs (ideally self-service from the beginning)

The infrastructure needs to be implemented in a multitenant way to be able to onboard a large number of development and operations teams. This is an important design choice to consider from the outset. Not only can the current product delivery organization grow in size, but also other product delivery organizations within the enterprise might want to use the infrastructure in the future.

6.8.1 Dashboards

In addition to the three basic features, at some point in the near future the SRE infrastructure should add basic dashboards of the following two types.

- SLI/SLO dashboards. These dashboards answer questions along the lines of "how are our services doing in terms of SLO fulfillment by SLI over time?"
- Error budget depletion graphs. These graphs answer questions along the lines of "how much error budget is left in the current period?"

In terms of multitenancy, the dashboards need to be provided to the development teams in the way shown in Figure 6.12.

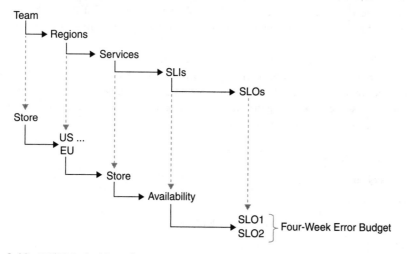

Figure 6.12 *SLI/SLO dashboard structure*

Figure 6.12 shows five hierarchy levels. They are there to meet the needs of multitenancy. Table 6.5 outlines these levels.

Table 6.5 *SLI/SLO Dashboard Hierarchy Levels*

Level	Explanation
Team	A unit to group services, dashboards, and alerts. Each team needs to get a standardized set of dashboards showing their services. However, each team should also be able to see the dashboards of other teams within a product delivery organization.
Regions	A service can be deployed to several regions. A team needs to be able to see the dashboards by region. (For example, if there is an outage in Japan, it should be possible to see at a glance all services deployed in Japan.)

Level	Explanation
Services	Services deployed to the environments under monitoring.
SLIs	A service can have several SLIs selected to be applied. The dashboards need to display graphs by SLI. (For example, if something is slow in Japan, it should be possible to see the latency SLI/SLO dashboards for all services deployed in Japan.)
SLOs	A service can have one or more SLOs set per SLI. It must be possible to see at a glance all the SLOs per SLI as well as across SLIs.

6.8.2 Alert Content

After the basic dashboards are provided by the SRE infrastructure, the next extension can be targeted toward reducing the time it takes to analyze SLO breaches. This can be approached based on the feedback from the people on call. It starts with the information contained in an alert of an SLO breach. An alert should contain as much information as necessary to minimize the time it takes to understand the root causes so that the resolution work can begin.

Alerts on SLO breaches can be augmented with information to reduce the time the people on call spend analyzing the alerts, ruling out potential error causes, and getting to the point where the actual work on resolving the incident can begin (reduce mean time to resolution). The following alert content might be beneficial:

- Endpoint affected
- SLI broken
- SLO broken
- Deployment where the SLO breach took place
- Time when the SLO breach took place
- How far the SLO was broken (e.g., SLO broken by 500%)
- Remaining error budget in the given time unit
- Environment details; for example:
  - Neighborhood: 20 other services are running in the same cluster
  - Memory: 95% memory consumed by the cluster overall at the time of the SLO breach
  - CPU: 90% CPU load in the cluster at the time of the SLO breach
  - Recycling: 3 minutes before the SLO breach occurred container recycling took place
  - Scaling: 10 minutes before the SLO breach occurred the service was rescaled (scale-in, scale-out events)
  - Errors: link to relevant event logs, if applicable
  - Sampling: current log sampling settings

- Information about the state of dependencies of the service:
  - ○ Availability of a dependency
  - ○ Latency of a dependency
  - ○ Error budget state of a dependency
- Snooze time for alerting on this type of SLO breach

Such SRE infrastructure extensions need to be made based strictly on feedback from the teams already reacting to alerts on SLO breaches. It is particularly easy to fall into the trap of implementing infrastructure used by nobody. The extensions need to be prioritized in such a way that the features implemented first are the ones that were requested by and will benefit the largest number of development teams. This is illustrated in Table 6.6.

Table 6.6 *Prioritization of SRE Infrastructure Feature Requests*

SRE Infrastructure Feature Request	Number of Teams That Requested the Feature	Number of Teams That Are Going to Benefit from the Feature	Assigned Priority
Feature A	Requested by 3 teams	Will benefit 20 teams	1
Feature B	Requested by 3 teams	Will benefit 15 teams	2
Feature C	Requested by 2 teams	Will benefit 10 teams	3

The prioritization will not be an exact science, but it should be guided by the logic explained previously.

6.9 Engaging Champions

By now the SRE coaches have engaged with all the operations and development teams taking part in the SRE transformation. During the process, it may have become evident that some people were particularly enthusiastic about SRE. These are the people who talk the most about SRE between sessions. They can talk about SRE for hours and they beam about the new possibilities unlocked by the new practice. These people can truly be referred to as SRE champions.

The SRE coaches should engage the SRE champions and ask them to present the new practice compared to the previous practice of doing operations to a broader audience. For example, a lean coffee session or a brown bag lunch would be a good place to share the experience. If possible, the SRE coaches should record the session. The session should be tagged with "SRE" and uploaded to the company's video sharing service. The link to the video should be put in the SRE section of the engineering wiki.

The champions might become SRE coaches themselves in the future. For instance, if or when another product delivery organization within the enterprise decides to adopt SRE, an SRE champion might wish to take up the role of SRE coach there. (See Section 5.3, *SRE Coaches*, for the qualities an SRE coach needs to possess.)

6.10 Dealing with Detractors

Through the process of engaging with the operations and development teams, the SRE coaches might have seen not only enthusiastic champions but also detractors. This is absolutely normal. Like any other methodology, SRE is not for everyone. Some people have other views on product operations. The detractors should be encouraged to openly express their views. SRE should not become a dogma that cannot be questioned. Rather, questioning should be appreciated while the overall direction of the organization toward SRE is made clear.

6.10.1 Issues with the Cause

For example, some operations engineers might have been trying in vain for years to bring developers closer to production operations, and by this point, they might have given up mentally. To them, trying to create alignment between operations engineers, developers, and product owners is a cause lost. Thus, they welcome the SRE transformation with a sigh and a yawn.

The position of these operations engineers is completely understandable. In fact, their position is the reason for trying to turn things around using the SRE methodology. Trying to convince the disgruntled operations engineers that SRE is a good idea is not going to change their minds. No amount of enthusiasm on the part of the SRE coaches as part of the SRE marketing funnel (Section 5.2) will convince them. Only hard results toward the end of the SRE transformation where it becomes evident that SRE actually brings the topic of production operations under control may do the trick.

During the transformation, though, the SRE coaches need to ensure that the disgruntled operations engineers do not spread negativity around SRE. In fact, SRE is an unproven methodology during the initial period of the transformation. So, there is no objective reason yet to declare failure or success. Given the prioritization of SRE at the portfolio level, a significant number of people in the organization decided to give the methodology a try (see Section 5.4.6, *Getting SRE into the Portfolio*). This needs to be explained to the operations engineers if the SRE coaches detect negative sentiments around SRE being spread in the organization without transparent reasons.

6.10.2 Issues with Alerting

Another reason for the operations engineers to question SRE might be the way alerting is handled. The operations engineers live and breathe resource-based alerting, in which an alert is generated and dispatched to an operations engineer every time a technical threshold is broken. Some operations engineers believe this is all that is needed. In fact, this might be the stronghold of some of the operations engineers.

SRE goes contrary to this belief, which causes tension. It considers resource-based alerting to be technically focused and rather disconnected from the user experience. Under SRE, it is encouraged to start from the user experience using, for example, a user story map; define an SLO reflecting the user experience impact; and explicitly not to alert on every SLO breach. However, SLO alerting is a delicate balance between timeliness, effectiveness, targeting, and other factors in an attempt to only generate alerts for cases in which the user experience will be seriously impacted.

Moreover, with resource-based alerting, alerts are ephemeral. With SRE, the entire corpus of historical data about SLO breaches of different SLIs is retained and used to calculate error budgets and generate error budget depletion dashboards. All of this is done in an effort to elevate the data to the point where error budget–based decision–making is enabled at different levels of the organization (see Section 6.2.6, *SLOs Are Not About Technicalities*).

To some operations engineers, this logic might seem like a fantasyland, with the core issues reported by the resource-based alerts for years. Many of the issues were known for a long time, but not enough action was taken to resolve them. Why on earth would adding some sophistication to the alerting logic change the attitudes of the people in the organization toward operations? It is still the same people after all! Giving them a fancier data landscape will not change their views.

To these disgruntled operations engineers, the heart of the matter is not about new data. Nor is it about new dashboards. None of this is of essence. It is entirely about the people.[9] In fact, it seems there are two choices here: Either continue living with the status quo or attempt to effect a change with the people.

The SRE transformation is an attempt to change the attitudes of the people in the organization toward operations. The entire terminology, methodology, and infrastructure are only a means to this end. SRE transformation will not succeed in every organization. Its success depends *entirely* on the people involved. Explaining this logic in this way might change the opinion of a disgruntled operations engineer.

6.10.3 Issues with Tooling

The operations engineers might provide tools to the developers in an attempt to bring them closer to product operations. However, the developers might never have used these tools. So, once again, the operations engineers find themselves in a difficult position where they attempted to provide something that was ignored in the past. Encouraging these operations engineers to provide an entirely new SRE infrastructure will not work. That is, only the operations engineers who believe in SRE can be selected to work on the infrastructure.

Moreover, there might be people in operations, development, or systems engineering who feel that providing an entire SRE infrastructure will actually discourage the development teams from getting closer to product operations. This is because the development teams then would not set up their own monitoring, create their own dashboards, set up their own alerting, develop their own tools, and so on. In other words, the SRE infrastructure might provide too much service, leaving the development teams in a hands-off position.

Here, the development teams' responsibilities need to be discussed. Given the SRE infrastructure, the development teams are responsible for

- Taking part in the SLI and SLO definition process

- Adapting SLOs continuously to align them with the user experience impact

---

9. Guendisch, Philipp, and Vladyslav Ukis. 2022. "Employing Agile Coaching to Establish SRE in an Organization." *InfoQ*, August 23, 2022. https://www.infoq.com/articles/establish-SRE-coaching.

- Defending the SLOs and staying within the error budgets by
  - Reacting to SLO breaches according to the agreed on call setup
  - Using error budget calculations to prioritize implementations of reliability features
  - Implementing tools, resiliency, and so forth to lighten the workload for the people on call

Making the development teams implement their own SRE infrastructure does not cater to economies of scale. Nor does it cater to the standardization necessary to aggregate the SRE data that enables error budget–based decision–making at different levels of the organization. It is true that making the development teams implement their own monitoring, alerting, and so on would bring them closer to production because it would increase their ownership of these topics. However, it was not achieved before for various reasons, it is not economical at scale, and it will not lead to something as lofty as error budget–based decision–making.

A more effective and efficient approach is to clarify the development teams' responsibilities. Fulfilling these responsibilities certainly will not leave them in a hands-off position! Rather, it will bring them closer to production than they ever were before while realizing the cost efficiencies of a shared SRE infrastructure.

6.10.4 Issues with Product Owner Involvement

It might be common for some product owners not to regularly attend SLO definition sessions. The team starts defining the SLOs, but the product owner is not at the meeting.

This situation is similar to what development teams often experienced when Scrum processes were introduced in the software industry in the early years of the 21st century. Back then, it might be rather common for some product owners not to take part in sprint planning, sprint grooming, or the sprint demo. They did not consider it important to be there, thus prioritizing business-related work over the work with the team. What did the teams do back then? Did they stop the meeting? They did not. They went ahead with the meeting and planned, groomed, or demoed with the people available. The missing product owners had to deal with the consequences of the decisions made without them.

It will be similar with the SLO definitions. The SRE coaches should let the meeting proceed and define the SLOs with the people involved. Behind the scenes, the coaches should work with the missing product owner in an attempt to bring them into the discussion. In any case, the SLOs need to be defined and the SRE transformation needs to continue. Doing so without a product owner will diminish the value of the SLOs, but it will still be a good improvement over not having any!

6.10.5 Issues with Team Motivation

Sometimes a development team defines initial SLOs, does an initial analysis of the SLO breaches, and then falls into a chasm. It can take a really long time for a development team to start reacting to the SLO breaches regularly. It might not be through an on-call rotation setup yet, but some people in the team need to react to the SLO breaches on a regular basis for the SRE process to make sense. The following motivators might be helpful.

- Wait until the first release is deployed to production with general availability and customer escalations begin.

- Wait until an external party requests SLAs.

- Wait until more success is available to share from other teams.

- Wait until other teams and stakeholders overwhelm the team with questions asking why the services they offer are not working.

- Motivate via the need for professional broadcast of service status (similar to the approach taken in Microsoft Azure[10]), saying the organization's goal is to have a similar kind of transparency internally and externally.

> **From the Trenches:** The development and operations teams can get excited by professional service status dashboards (e.g., in Microsoft Azure). Callouts such as "We need to have this kind of dashboard too!" can be used as motivators for establishing meaningful SLOs and reacting to the SLO breaches on a regular basis.

To sum it up, the SRE coaches should deal with detractors mostly in one-on-one sessions and should adopt an empathetic mindset. They should make every attempt possible to convey the reasons for SRE and address the detractors' concerns in an explanatory manner.

The SRE coaches should avoid asking people in formal organizational power to influence someone whose position is not in line with SRE. A formal manager may influence a subordinate more easily than the SRE coaches. However, if influenced by an SRE coach, the person truly acts out of conviction. The motivation is surely intrinsic. It will last longer and cause more action. This is the goal.

6.11 Creating Documentation

Throughout this chapter, I have discussed at length the usefulness of documentation for various SRE use cases. This documentation needs to be publicly accessible, as opposed to being available only on the operations wiki where only operations engineers can access it. This may be a common starting point for the documentation—it emerges where the SRE infrastructure emerges too, namely in product operations. If so, at some point the documentation needs to be moved to a central place that is accessible to everyone. A chapter on the central engineering wiki is a good place to store the SRE documentation.

As mentioned in previous sections, the SRE documentation needs to be created with a self-service user in mind. The documentation shields the operations engineers from anyone who needs to perform common SRE tasks. Without a good shield, the operations team will be drowned in sporadic support requests, which will interrupt their ability to focus on SRE infrastructure implementation.

---

10. Microsoft. "Azure status." n.d. Accessed January 20, 2022. https://status.azure.com/en-us/status.

Therefore, the SRE coaches must point out at the beginning of the initiative the importance of writing self-service documentation. No pull request for the SRE infrastructure should be approved if the documentation is not up-to-date. Before an SRE infrastructure feature goes live, it has to be documented for self-service consumption by the SRE infrastructure users.

The self-service documentation is not just documentation. Rather, it is an accelerator of the SRE transformation and time protection insurance for the operations engineers.

6.12 Broadcast Success

By now a significant time investment was made in SRE activities in all involved operations and development teams:

- HTTP return code improvements

- Logging improvements

- Application performance instrumentation

- Initial SLI selection

- Initial explicit SLO definitions

- Initial default SLO definitions

- Initial SRE infrastructure implementation

- Self-service SRE documentation

Along the way, success stories were surely witnessed. It is time to broadcast these success stories to create awareness of what has been achieved. To be sure, the improvements will not be impressively quantifiable at this point. So, successes like "we reduced the number of customer escalations by 25% in the last month because of SRE practice" will not be possible to declare yet. Still, the groundwork for such successes in the future has been laid. It is worth creating awareness of this!

To prepare the broadcast, a check of the SRE transformation hypotheses should be done (see Section 4.7, *Posing Hypotheses*). Are there outcomes that the teams got closer to? If so, they need to be listed. Are there measurable signals that could be advanced? If so, they need to be listed too. Are any adjustments of the previously defined hypotheses needed based on new learnings? If so, they need to be done and made public. It is important to convey the message that the SRE transformation is executed in a data-driven way under the guidance of hypotheses and measurable signals as feedback loops.

Further, the SRE coaches need to listen to conversations and conduct a search on the instant messaging service used in the organization (e.g., Slack, MS Teams, or Basecamp) to find out how people speak about SRE. The following hints need to be looked for and broadcast as examples of SRE thinking taking root in the organization:

- Development teams saying something like "if we are doing DevOps, then yes, we need to be the first ones getting notice of product issues in production."

- People saying something like "30% of the monthly error budget was depleted by yesterday's outage."

Next, the status quo and the road map ahead need to be shown along the lines of the following:

- 20 out of 20 development teams readjusted HTTP return codes.

- 20 out of 20 development teams docked their services onto the logging and application performance management facilities.

- 15 out of 20 development teams defined initial SLOs for availability and latency SLIs.

- 5 out of 20 development teams react to alerts on SLO breaches.

- 3 out of 20 development teams performed a structured analysis of availability and latency SLO breaches that occurred within a month and derived reliability improvements.

- On the road map, all development teams need the following:

  ○ Definition of on-call setup

  ○ Definition of error budget policies

  ○ Definition of stakeholders

  ○ Broadcast of service status to the stakeholders

  ○ Service status page

Finally, the biggest next steps for the organization need to be defined with an indication of timelines such as the following:

- Completion of the definition of initial availability and latency SLOs in all teams, probably by DD.MM.YYYY

- A structured analysis of availability and latency SLO breaches that occurred within a month of the initial SLO definitions in all teams, prospectively by DD.MM.YYYY

- Definition of on-call setup per team, potentially by DD.MM.YYYY

The broadcast needs to be made during a presentation in a lean coffee or brown bag lunch session led by the SRE coaches. Involving an SRE champion is a great way to show that the initiative took root in the development teams. The session needs to be recorded if possible. It should then be uploaded onto the organization's video sharing service and tagged with "SRE". The link to the recording and the presentation slides needs to be put onto the SRE wiki.

Next, the people the SRE coaches worked with while putting SRE onto the list of portfolio initiatives need to be engaged. The stakeholder chart created before (see Section 5.4.1) should be used to determine the intensity level of engagement required by the stakeholders. To start with, a concise email needs to be composed. It should list the content of the previously created broadcast presentation in one or two paragraphs and link to the page on the SRE wiki containing the presentation slides and the link to the recording. The email should end with an invitation to have a short meeting to discuss how the SRE transformation is going so far. The email should not be used as a rigid template for all stakeholders. Rather, tweaking the content a bit to better fit the frame of mind of a particular stakeholder goes a long way toward having the message received in a positive way.

6.13 Summary

This chapter laid the foundations of the SRE process in the operations and development teams. It discussed the features necessary in the SRE infrastructure developed by the operations teams to get SRE going in the development teams. The infrastructure needs to be developed based on a standardization of SLIs and their measurements initially offered in such a way that it benefits most development teams immediately. Further in the chapter, the mindset and steps necessary in the development teams to define initial SLIs and SLOs were shown. The chapter reinforced iteration as the central technique for arriving at good SLOs. A good SLO reflects the impact on the user experience very well. When a good SLO is broken, the impact on the user experience is clear. This provides a clear motivation for the people on call to fix the service in order to bring it back within the SLO, thus reinstating the user experience.

With good SLOs arrived at by iteration, the next step on the SRE transformation journey is to set up the teams to react to alerts on SLO breaches. This is the subject of the next chapter.

Chapter 7

Reacting to Alerts on SLO Breaches

Reacting to alerts on SLO breaches is an activity at the heart of SRE. It lies exactly between the definition phase where the SLI and SLOs are defined as hypotheses and the acting phase where the reliability measures are implemented as part of learning. It is best to perform this activity when the following criteria apply.

- There are very few alerts on SLO breaches to react to.
- The reaction to an SLO breach can be done very quickly.
- The service can be brought back within the SLO very quickly.

This is the goal. Regardless of where a team is on their way to this ideal, a process for reacting to alerts on SLO breaches needs to be set up. The process is both organizational and technical. Organizationally, it needs to be decided who is reacting to the SLO breaches, for which services, at which times, and for which regions in a multi–data center setup. Technically, it needs to be clear what needs to be done to react to an SLO breach properly, which technical tools can be used, and how redeployments can be done by environment.

Let us begin by selecting deployment environments for which SLO breaches should be reported and reacted to.

7.1 Environment Selection

One of the first agreements the operations engineers, developers, and product owner responsible for a service need to make in the scope of reactions to alerts on SLO breaches is about the deployment environments in question. Which deployment environments should be monitored with SLOs? The answer to this question provides a list of environments where the SLO breaches need to be analyzed.

A natural starting point would be the production environments. In a multiregion setup, many production environments will exist. So, an agreement about the production environments to be monitored with SLOs needs to be reached. A team may start with a single production environment to get their hands dirty and gradually expand coverage of SLO monitoring to more and more production environments until the entire production landscape is covered.

The next set of environments to consider for monitoring with SLOs can be staging environments. If there are multiple staging environments, start with only one. Additional staging environments may be added at a later date.

Finally, even internal environments used for development purposes can be monitored with SLOs. For example, deployments for marketing, security testing, exploratory testing, and other purposes might be monitored with SLOs.

This discussion shows a powerful combination of defining an SLO and deploying it to the chosen set of deployment environments automatically by the SRE infrastructure. The SRE infrastructure should support the deployment of a centrally defined SLO to any set of deployment environments existing in the organization. The set of deployment environments an SLO should be deployed to should be easily changeable in a self-service manner for a development team responsible for the service. This is shown in Figure 7.1.

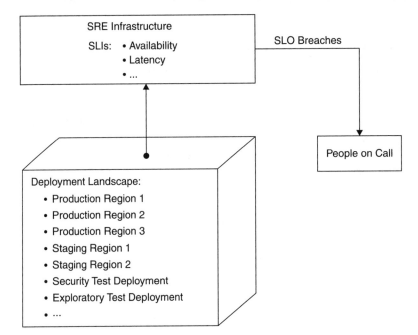

Figure 7.1 *SLO deployment environment selection using SRE infrastructure*

The lower part of Figure 7.1 illustrates the deployment landscape of a given organization. It consists of three production deployments in regions 1, 2, and 3. Additionally, there are two staging deployments in regions 1 and 2. Further, there are test deployments for security testing, exploratory testing, and some others.

The SRE infrastructure on top of the figure supports SLIs such as availability and latency, among others. The SRE infrastructure can detect SLO breaches for all SLIs it supports in any environment from the organization's deployment landscape. Given a list of environments a development team wants to monitor using SLOs, the SRE infrastructure can detect the SLO breaches in all of them and alert the people on call.

Having selected the environments that should be monitored using SLOs, the next thing to clarify is who is responsible for which service in which environment in terms of operations.

7.2 Responsibilities

While the development responsibility for a service can be well defined in an organization, the operational responsibility for the same service might not be as clear. Service development is best done by a single development team. Within an organization, an inner source development model can also be practiced where there is a process for a team to make changes to services owned by another team. A similar level of rigor needs to be applied when defining operational responsibilities for services.

7.2.1 Dev Versus Ops Responsibilities

In general, development responsibilities for a service are different from operational responsibilities for the service. The two types of responsibilities are contrasted in Table 7.1. It is important to note that the tabular splitview of the development and operational responsibilities does not suggest whatsoever that the responsibilities have to be fulfilled by different teams. In fact, the opposite is true. The closer the people fulfilling the two types of responsibilities are situated organizationally (e.g., within a single team), the better the feedback loop from product operations to product development will be, resulting in better product reliability over time.

Table 7.1 *Development and Operational Responsibilities of Service Owners*

Development Responsibilities	Operational Responsibilities
• Requirement engineering	• Production rollout
• Feature prioritization	• Production monitoring
• Feature hypothesis definition	• 8x5 on-call during business hours
• Backlog management	• 16x7 on-call outside of business hours
• User research	• Defending SLOs (reactions to SLO breaches)
• UI/UX prototyping	• Reactions to resource-based alerts (if any)
• User story mapping	• Postmortems
• User story refinement	• Ongoing SLO adjustments
• Architecture	• Reactions to stakeholder escalations
• Testing	• Reactions to customer escalations
• Development	• Creation of error budget policies
• Deployment	• Enacting error budget policies
• Feature hypothesis testing	• Ongoing runbook updates

Generally, many organizational structures can be employed to fulfill the development and operational responsibilities shown in Table 7.1. Each organizational structure has its pros and cons. These are considered in detail in Chapter 12, *Implementing Organizational Structure*.

Furthermore, it is important to note that, culturally, development and operational responsibilities might not enjoy parity of esteem at the beginning of the SRE transformation in a product delivery organization. One of the SRE coaches' tasks is to work with teams and individuals during the transformation to change their perception of operational responsibilities. Indeed, it is the operational responsibilities that ensure the last mile of a truly great user experience in terms of reliability. And, indeed, as mentioned in Section 2.3.1, *Product Development*, the job market rewards more those software developers who have experience fulfilling operational responsibilities well.

As always with SRE, the operational responsibilities need to be agreed to by the operations engineers, developers, and product owner responsible for the service. As part of the agreement, it should be clear who owns each point in the "Operational responsibilities" column in Table 7.1.

7.2.2 Operational Responsibilities

A central aspect of the discussion leading to agreement on responsibilities is whether developers go on call for services they own according to their development responsibilities. Another aspect of the discussion is whether operations engineers go on call. In general, this needs to be clarified per service.

- Who is going on call during business hours? Developers/operations engineers/mix?

- Who is going on call outside of business hours? Developers/operations engineers/mix?

- Who is doing production rollouts? Developers/operations engineers?

- Who is reacting to SLO breaches and resource-based alerts? Developers/operations engineers/mix?

- Who is creating error budget policies, enacting them, doing postmortems, and performing ongoing SLO adjustments? Developers/operations engineers/mix?

- Who is reacting to stakeholder escalations? Developers/operations engineers/mix?

- Who is reacting to customer escalations? Developers/operations engineers/mix?

In other words, the split of operational responsibilities between developers and operations engineers needs to be clearly defined. Note that at this point, it is not advisable to make decisions about the organizational structure. This is because there is very little experience in the organization with splitting the operational responsibilities between developers and operations engineers. Moreover, the operational responsibilities related to the SRE concept pyramid are very new to everyone involved.

Therefore, at this point the organization will start testing the waters by reacting to alerts on SLO breaches, making some decisions based on error budget depletion, and so on. The period ahead is dedicated to learning and adapting. It does not make sense to set up a new organizational structure for SRE at this point. This should be done later, once enough experience with fulfilling SRE responsibilities has been gained.

Thus, an initial agreement between the operations engineers, developers, and product owner is enough to get started and iterate based on learnings from practicing SRE according to the operational responsibilities specified in Table 7.1. It does not matter which departments the developers, operations engineers, and product owner belong to. What matters is an agreement to use swarming across departments to fulfill the SRE responsibilities in a certain way.

7.2.3 Splitting Operational Responsibilities

The operational responsibilities can be split between the developers and operations engineers in many ways. For illustration purposes, three variants of a split are shown in Figure 7.2.

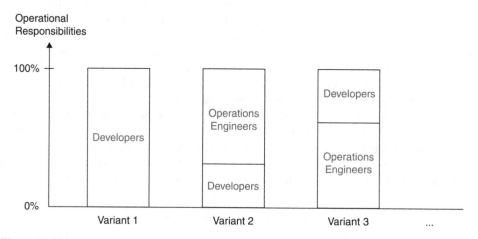

Figure 7.2 *Example variants of splitting the operational responsibilities*

Variant 1 is where the entire set of operational responsibilities is with the developers. This is a classic "you build it, you run it" mode of working. The developers are fully responsible for operating the services they own. They are always on call for their services. The operations engineers only provide the SRE infrastructure. Amazon runs operations this way.

Variant 2 is the opposite of variant 1. The operations engineers take up the bulk of the operational responsibilities. However, they do it only if and when the services they are responsible for fulfill a certain agreed-upon service level. Whenever the services do not fulfill this service level, the operations engineers hand over the operational responsibilities to the developers. As soon as the services fulfill the agreed service level, the operations engineers take back the operational responsibilities from the developers. That is, the operations engineers do the on-call duty for services as long as they fulfill the agreed service level. Otherwise, this responsibility is with the developers. Google runs operations this way.

Variant 3 represents the middle ground between variants 1 and 2. The operational responsibilities are split roughly 50-50 between the developers and operations engineers. They share on-call duty. Facebook runs operations this way.

There are many other ways to split the responsibilities, all of them incarnations of the three variants shown in Figure 7.2. For example, another variant might be to establish a so-called domain on-call rotation. Such a rotation contains selected developers and/or selected operations engineers with the knowledge of all products belonging to a particular product domain. A product delivery organization may cover several product domains with its products. Thus, several domain on-call rotations might be established, one per domain. The SRE coaches need to explain the variants to the operations and development teams. Experimentation should be encouraged to find a setup that is best suited to the unique circumstances of each team. Also, not all the operations responsibilities from Table 7.1 need to be taken up at once. It might be sufficient to start with a subset and extend it as maturity grows.

To begin, each development team (including a product owner) and associated operations engineers need to decide on the initial setup of how they want to try reacting to SLO breaches. Next, the developers and operations engineers need to react to the SLO breaches for a month or two using the agreed initial setup. After that, the SRE coaches need to invite the operations engineers, developers, and product owner to a retrospective to see whether the initial setup needs to be revisited to accommodate the learnings collected in the meantime. This process needs to be carried out several times to iteratively arrive at a setup that works for all parties involved.

Because the process will be carried out team by team, the teams will decide to do the operational responsibility split in different ways. This is great because it maximizes the organizational learning of what works best. The SRE coaches can do cross-team sharing of insights because they are involved in all teams and know the best practices that are crystallizing throughout the organization. Also, because the questions of adapting the organizational structure have not been tackled yet, there is freedom to experiment. Is it not DevOps at its best when operations engineers and developers experiment freely to discover the best way to work together? It is, indeed!

7.3 Ways of Working

Section 7.2, *Responsibilities*, detailed development and operational responsibilities for a service. The two types of responsibilities require application of two unique working modes. The development responsibilities are best carried out in a focus-based working mode. Developers implement features best in a state of flow where they work uninterrupted for a longer period of time. Any interruption leads to loss of context, which takes time to reinstate. The fewer context switches there are, the more efficient the developers will be with feature implementations.

By contrast, the operational responsibilities are rooted in interruptions. Being on call for a service means to be ready for SLO breaches to arrive and start analyzing them immediately to bring the service back within the SLO as quickly as possible. Additional interruptions can be caused by other operational responsibilities, such as reactions to stakeholder and customer escalations.

Now, how do you accommodate the two conflicting working modes within the operations and development teams? Both teams perform development activities. The development teams implement features and go on call to the extent agreed upon. The operations teams implement the SRE infrastructure and also go on call to the extent agreed upon. Both teams find themselves in new terrain. The newness is different by team, as shown in Table 7.2.

Table 7.2 *Necessary Working Modes in Development and Operations Teams*

	Development Teams	Operations Teams
Interruption-based working mode (on call)	New	Familiar
Focus-based working mode (product development)	Familiar	New

While the development teams are new to on-call work, they are very familiar with doing product development work. On the contrary, while the operations teams are very familiar with on-call work, implementing the SRE infrastructure as a product to be used by others is new to them. In the next sections, let us explore how the interruption-based working mode and focus-based working mode can coexist within the operations and development teams.

7.3.1 Interruption-Based Working Mode

The interruption-based working mode will be familiar to operations engineers. However, for developers this will be entirely new territory. Moreover, it will have a profound impact on the way the development team works. As shown in Section 7.2, *Responsibilities*, the developers will have to go on call to the agreed extent. So, changing the way the development teams work to accommodate the interruption-based working mode is necessary.

A good practice for a development team is to divide the team's activities, but not its people, into two groups: development activities and operations activities. The activities correspond to the people's respective responsibilities.

Wherever it is possible and it makes sense, developers should work in pairs to systematically foster knowledge sharing on all topics. Developer pairs on operations activities work in an interruption-based working mode. That is, they are driven by interruptions like SLO breaches and customer escalations.

Developer pairs on development activities work in a focus-based working mode. That is, they are driven by feature implementation. These developer pairs are shielded from interruptions by the developer pairs doing operations. This is shown in Figure 7.3.

The left-hand side of Figure 7.3 shows two developer pairs: pair 1 and pair 2. They are working on development activities, and these activities require focus. Therefore, the interruption-based operations activities are done by another pair. This is pair 3, on the right-hand side of the figure.

Pair 1 applies the driver-navigator[1] style of pairing. The driver is on the keyboard, types in the code, and deals with the intricacies of the programming language used. The navigator takes a slightly more distant approach. This person is thinking more about the low-level software design and reviewing the code as the driver types it. This just-in-time code review is characteristic of pair programming. The driver and navigator switch roles at least once a day.

The same pair programming style is applied to pair 2. The people from pairs 1 and 2 also switch pairs on a regular basis. Whenever possible, this is done per user story completion.

---

1. Wikipedia. n.d. "Pair programming." Accessed January 4, 2022. https://en.wikipedia.org/wiki/Pair_programming.

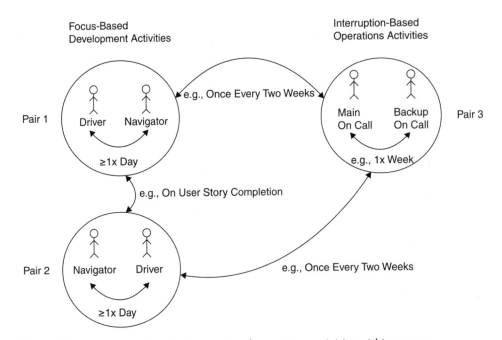

Figure 7.3 *Accommodating development and operations activities within a team*

Pair 3, which is handling operations activities, is structured in a main on-call and backup on-call setup. The main on-call person is the primary person receiving SLO breaches. The backup on-call person only gets the breaches whenever the main on-call person is unexpectedly unavailable. The main and backup on-call people switch roles; for example, once a week.

Importantly, pairs 1 and 3 exchange people on a regular basis. This is the switch between development and operations activities and is done, for example, every two weeks. The same switch is done between pairs 2 and 3. The team needs to determine the regularity of the switch. The following aspects will contribute to this decision:

- Overall number of people in the development team
- Number of people in the development team with the knowledge to go on call (should increase over time)
- Number of people in the development team with the experience of being on call (should increase over time)
- Number of people in the development team willing to go on call (should increase over time)

To reiterate its importance, the following reasons are critical for the developers to go on call.

- Developers with product implementation knowledge do product failure investigations in production.
- Developers get to experience the quality of the product in the real world (i.e., production sites).

- Developers gain the knowledge necessary to operate and troubleshoot the product.

- Developers take the knowledge from product operations into the development of new features.

- Developers gain a better understanding of the kind of testing and tooling necessary to deliver a product that is delightful to operate.

- Developers take holistic ownership of the product they develop by also operating it in production.

That is, cross-pair rotation happens regularly everywhere: in development work and in operations work. The regularity of cross-pair rotation needs to be determined by experience in a particular team for a particular type of work. For example, when it comes to feature implementation, it might make sense to switch pairs on user story completion. Importantly, the developers themselves need to determine the regularity.

Inter-pair rotation happens regularly as well. Also, here the regularity needs to be determined by the developers themselves. For example, when it comes to feature implementation, switching the driver and navigator roles at least once a day would make sense. By contrast, when it comes to on-call rotations, switching the primary and backup on-call people about once a week might be appropriate. It all depends on the context and the domain of the teams as well as their maturity in terms of pairing.

> **From the Trenches:** Development teams might be fearful of the effort that will go into being on call. This is the right fear to have. Depending on the team, initially the effort of going on call might be high. However, this is the right path to learning what it takes to develop services with the reliability appropriate for the use cases exercised in production. This learning leads to services being developed in the future along with the necessary reliability features right from the start. This, in turn, leads to a great reduction of effort going into on call. Over time, being on call goes from constant firefighting to dealing with occasional emergencies.
>
> This is a story the SRE coaches need to tell when introducing on call in an attempt to reduce the fear of on call. The whole purpose of SRE is not to introduce on call to unleash an onslaught of alerts onto developers in the middle of the night. Rather, it is to facilitate the knowledge necessary for understanding reliability as perceived by the user and dispatching the knowledge to the development and operations processes efficiently and effectively. This means the reliability knowledge needs to be with the developers to implement reliability measures appropriate for each customer-facing feature during implementation. Further, it means to alert on SLOs only when the user experience is significantly impacted. Finally, it means to make error budget–based decisions to invest in reliability where and when it is needed most.

It is essential for any development and operations team that develops and operates a product to introduce separation of focus-based working and interruption-based working. Whether the introduction is effective depends on how the team actually practices the focused-based and introduction-based working modes. A developer or operations engineer should only work in one of the working modes at a time. Making developers or operations engineers develop and operate a product in parallel leads to excessive context switches. Each context switch puts cognitive load on the developers or operations engineers. With too much cognitive load, the developers or operations engineers can neither develop nor operate the product. Over time, this might lead to burnout. Therefore, a separation of the development work (focus based) and operations work (interruption based) is required to accommodate the two types of work within a single development team in a sustainable manner.

The rotation within and between the focus-based working mode and interruption-based working mode ensures systematic knowledge sharing within the development or operations team. It is necessary to enable developers to have a broad code base and operational knowledge of services in production. These are the ways of working that truly elevate the value of developers in the marketplace. Not only can the developers develop features, but they can also test, deploy, and operate them in such a way that the features work in real production environments under real data and user load. The T-shape of developer skills gets wider and longer at the same time. New valuable skills are acquired and honed on a regular basis. This is done in a sustainable manner, taking care of the developers' health.

These are the ways of working that enable development teams to accelerate over time. In fact, the knowledge of the code base is growing with each developer. The operational knowledge about services is growing with each developer too. The exchange between development and operational knowledge is fostered by systematic pair rotation. That is, over time, more developers have a holistic context of development and operational aspects applied to feature development at the time of implementation. This leads to a decrease in operational burden in the form of SLO breaches, stakeholder escalations, and customer escalations. This, in turn, leaves more time for feature development to be done with a full context of what is necessary to make the features technically successful right from the get-go. Schematically, this is shown in Figure 7.4.

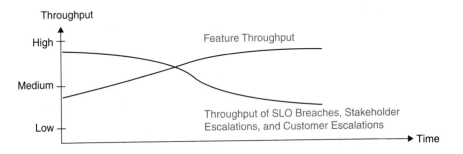

Figure 7.4 *Feature throughput versus throughput of SLO breaches and escalations*

With the ways of working just described, feature throughput of a development team will increase because the team is doing the implementation with the full operational context in mind. This, in turn, leads to a decrease in throughput of interruptions in the form of SLO breaches, stakeholder escalations, and customer escalations. It is a virtuous, mutually reinforcing circle of activities that leads to tangible business benefits over time.

7.3.2 Focus-Based Working Mode

The focus-based working mode needs to be maintained in both the development and operations teams because all of them are working on software development. The development teams develop customer-facing features. The operations teams develop the SRE infrastructure.

The previous section showed that maintaining focus in development teams is done by separating the development and operational activities but not the people. The developers work either on development or on operational activities but rotate regularly between them. This way, focus-based feature work is separated temporally from interruption-based on-call work on the one hand. But on the other hand, everyone is involved in and learning from both types of work.

In operations teams, there will be operations engineers who work on the SRE infrastructure. At the same time, depending on the agreed on-call setup, there may also be operations engineers going on call for product services. This practice of paired working, including pair rotation, will work in either case.

From the knowledge sharing point of view, it is not as critical for the operations engineers implementing the SRE infrastructure to go on call for product services as it is for the developers. Rather, for the operations engineers implementing the SRE infrastructure, being on call for the infrastructure itself is of more importance.

Indeed, if all development teams depend on the SRE infrastructure, its reliability is critical to the organization. How should this reliability be ensured? Should it have its own SLIs and SLOs? Who should be on call for the infrastructure? If SRE should be done for the SRE infrastructure itself, who is the product owner for the infrastructure to make agreements with? These are the questions that the operations teams need to answer.

That is, depending on the agreed on-call setup, the operations teams may have two types of on-call duties.

- On call for the SRE infrastructure. This is not negotiable.

- On call for product services. This depends on the agreed on-call setup with the development teams.

Focus-based work on the SRE infrastructure implementation can be shielded from both on-call duties by employing pairing with pair rotation as exemplified in Section 7.3.1, *Interruption-Based Working Mode*.

7.4 Setting Up On-Call Rotations

With the ways of working clarified, the SRE coaches can take the teams on the next step of the SRE transformation, which is about setting up the on-call rotations for product services. As shown in Section 7.3.1, *Interruption-Based Working Mode*, working in pairs is beneficial. To be successful, on-call pairing needs to be set up properly. How to do this is the subject of this section.

7.4.1 Initial Rotation Period

The first question to discuss in the team is the on-call rotation period. How long does someone go on call? The team will not know the answer at this point. So, what is needed is just an initial statement that seems to make sense to the majority of people in the team. If the statement is difficult to get, a quick vote can take place, carried out by the SRE coaches. Once the initial statement of a rotation period is there, it should be used to start the on-call rotation. After one or two rotation periods, the SRE coaches can conduct a short retrospective to see whether the initial rotation period should be adjusted based on new learnings generated in the meantime.

> **From the Trenches:** Lots of teams choose a calendar week within business hours as an initial rotation period from which to iterate—that is, Monday through Friday, 9 a.m. to 5 p.m.

It is important to reiterate that the rotation period should only be chosen by the operations engineers, developers, and product owner responsible for a service. Development or operations managers should not force the decision or try to unify the on-call rotation periods across teams. Imposing an organization-wide rotation period would lead to demotivation. A unified rotation period is not beneficial. The goal is to always have a knowledgeable person on call for each service, not to have an artificially unified process. To achieve this, full flexibility to schedule the on-call work has to be provided to the people going on call.

With the initial rotation period clarified, an on-call rotation can be set up. The following subsections provide some examples of how on-call rotations can be set up depending on the number of people taking part in a rotation.

7.4.2 One Person On Call

Initially, a development team may start with one person on call reacting to the SLO breaches reported by the SRE infrastructure. That person might never rotate. This is shown in Table 7.3.

Table 7.3 *One Person On Call for All Rotation Periods*

	Rotation Period 1	Rotation Period 2	Rotation Period 3	Rotation Period 4
Main on-call	Person A	Person A	Person A	Person A

There is no backup on-call person for the main on-call person in this setup. In the very early stages, this will be fine as the team is just learning to be on call and doing initial analysis of SLO breaches.

The next evolutionary step is to start rotating a person on call per chosen rotation period (e.g., weekly). This is shown in Table 7.4.

Table 7.4 *One Person On Call, Switching for Each Rotation Period*

	Rotation Period 1	Rotation Period 2	Rotation Period 3	Rotation Period 4
Main on-call	Person A	Person B	Person C	Person D

Still, in this setup there are no back-up on-call people. If the main on-call person becomes unavailable unexpectedly, no one is there to operate the service. Nevertheless, in this setup the operational knowledge gets distributed well among the people on call.

7.4.3 Two People On Call

The next evolutionary step is to have two people on call per rotation period. This is shown in Table 7.5. That is, there are two people on call in every rotation period: person A and person B.

Table 7.5 *Two People On Call, Switching for Each Rotation Period*

	Rotation Period 1	Rotation Period 2	Rotation Period 3	Rotation Period 4
Main on-call	Person A	Person B	Person A	Person B
Backup on-call	Person B	Person A	Person B	Person A

The main on-call person is supposed to be available during the entire rotation period. However, should this person become unavailable unexpectedly, the backup on-call person is there to take over operations until the main on-call person becomes available again.

The main-on call and backup on-call people switch roles on each rotation period. Organizing the on-call rotation with the main and backup on-call people supports the idea of pairing (see Section 7.3.1, *Interruption-Based Working Mode*). So, development teams that have been practicing pair programming for development work are going to find it easy to transition to doing the on-call work in pairs too.

Unlike pair programming, pairing in operations does not yet have a punchy industry term. Pair operations seems to be a new term that would reflect service operations being done in pairs.

7.4.4 Three People On Call

Having two people on call will be sufficient for lots of services. However, sometimes adding a third on-call person might be the next evolutionary step. The need for this might stem, for example, from the necessity to defend tight SLOs in an environment where lots of toil is involved. Alternatively, this setup could be used as a way to introduce more developers to the world of on call.

A setup with three people on call per rotation period is shown in Table 7.6.

Table 7.6 *Three People On Call, Switching for Each Rotation Period*

	Rotation Period 1	Rotation Period 2	Rotation Period 3	Rotation Period 4
Main on call	Person A	Person B	Person C	Person A
Backup on-call 1	Person B	Person C	Person A	Person B
Backup on-call 2	Person C	Person A	Person B	Person C

The main on-call person gets the SLO breaches. If this person becomes unavailable unexpectedly, the SLO breaches get dispatched to backup on-call 1. If backup on-call 1 is not available, backup on-call 2 is dispatched the SLO breaches. Additionally in this setup, if there is a high volume of SLO breaches, some of them can go for investigation to backup on-call 1. In this case, backup on-call 2 still remains in a proper backup capacity.

The main on-call person, backup on-call 1, and backup on-call 2 rotate roles in a round-robin fashion for each rotation period. For example, in Table 7.6, the main on-call person in rotation period 1 is person A. That person becomes backup on-call 2 in rotation period 2.

Further, backup on-call 1 in rotation period 1 is person B. That person becomes the main on-call person in rotation period 2. Likewise, backup on-call 2 in rotation period 1 is person C. That person becomes backup on-call 1 in rotation period 2.

Adding more people on call per rotation period would work in the same way. However, this is not typically seen in the industry.

7.5 On-Call Management Tools

Having clarified the ways on-call rotations can be set up, the next question to explore is tool support for on call. What options are available and what needs should they meet?

In general, operations engineers and developers love tools. Tools make their lives easier, and there is always a shiny new tool to learn, explore, and tell peers about. However, in the context of on-call management as part of the SRE transformation, the first thing to ensure is that people actually react to the SLO breaches. This can be done without professional on-call management tools. In fact, doing so removes the tool learning curve, associated distractions, cost, and time-consuming procurement processes that include intensive data protection checks using applicable laws.

7.5.1 Posting SLO Breaches

For example, the SRE infrastructure can be connected to the organization's chat management service and SLO breaches can be posted there. The people on call can subscribe to the respective chat channels and retrieve the SLO breaches as they appear. Examples of chat management services include Slack, Microsoft Teams, and Basecamp. Figure 7.5 shows how to connect the SRE infrastructure to a chat management service.

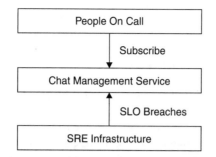

Figure 7.5 *Connecting the SRE infrastructure to a chat management service*

In particular, a dedicated "#slo-breaches" channel can be created per team so that the SLO breaches can be grouped and subscribed to effectively. This is shown in Figure 7.6. At the bottom of the figure, the SRE infrastructure is schematically illustrated. It contains a mapping of the hierarchy: team → services → SLIs → SLOs → SLO breaches.

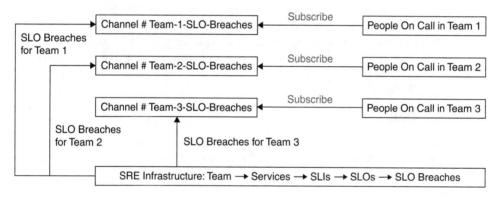

Figure 7.6 *An "#slo-breaches" channel per service owner team*

Above the SRE infrastructure, the team channels are shown. There are three channels for three teams: #team-1-slo-breaches, #team-2-slo-breaches, and #team-3-slo-breaches. The SRE infrastructure pushes the SLO breaches of the services owned by team 1 to the channel #team-1-slo-breaches. It pushes the SLO breaches of the services owned by team 2 to the channel #team-2-slo-breaches. Likewise, the SRE infrastructure pushes the SLO breaches of the services owned by team 3 to the channel #team-3-slo-breaches.

On the right-hand side, the people on call are shown. Depending on the agreed on-call setup, they can consist of only developers, only operations engineers, or a mix of developers and operations engineers. The current people on call for team 1's services subscribe to the channel #team-1-slo-breaches and retrieve the SLO breaches there. The discussions about the SLO breaches can take place in the same channel. Using threaded conversations under SLO breaches provides a good structure for the discussions in the channel. Additional people can be invited to the channel as needed to help bring the services back within the SLOs. Once a rotation period comes to an end and the people on call rotate (see Section 7.4, *Setting Up On-Call Rotations*), the members of the channel change. The people who leave the on-call rotation also leave the channel. The people who join the on-call rotation join the channel #team-1-slo-breaches.

Similarly, the people on call for the services owned by team 2 use the channel #team-2-slo-breaches in the same manner. So do the people on call for the services owned by team 3 using the channel #team-3-slo-breaches.

This solution is much easier to implement overall than using a professional on-call management tool. In the early days of a team learning to react to SLO breaches, the solution is fully sufficient. It does not require any new-tool learning curve by either the people on call or the operations engineers implementing the SRE infrastructure. By contrast, it brings the world of SLO breaches right into the communications tool the organization already uses on a daily basis: the chat management service. Thus, it can be implemented rather quickly. The goal of the SRE coaches is to get a team to a point where they actually react to the SLO breaches. This goal can be achieved using the simple infrastructure solution just described. Once the goal is achieved, the process of reacting to the SLO breaches can be optimized by introducing a professional on-call management tool.

The point is that while on-call management tools are very important and are required at some point, they are absolutely not necessary in the initial stages of the SRE transformation when the focus is on establishing meaningful SLOs and consistent reactions to them by the people on call. The introduction of a professional on-call management tool should be viewed as an optimization of an already working on-call process in the team and not as a prerequisite to establish the process in the first place.

7.5.2 Scheduling

Scheduling the people on call in a simple, unambiguous, and transparent way is an important part of the overall on-call setup. The question "who is on call in team A right now?" should be able to be answered by anyone in the organization on the spot.

Professional on-call management tools offer great scheduling capabilities. They allow a flexible specification of on-call rotations using a graphical user interface or programmatically. The argument from the previous section applies here as well. While required at some point, this functionality is not necessary at the beginning of the SRE transformation when there are one or two people on call in some teams testing the waters of being on call.

At that point, using simple shared calendars is fully sufficient. Popular email management services, among them Gmail and Outlook, offer shared calendars. Shared calendars do not come with a new-tool learning curve as the organization uses calendars on a daily basis already. The shared calendars can also be connected to a chat management service such as Slack or Microsoft Teams. Doing so provides an integrated solution: Both the on-call scheduling and the SLO breaches can be partly handled in the same tool.

There are also more specialized services to manage on-call scheduling within the ecosystems of Slack and Microsoft Teams. For example, Ovvy[2] on Slack and Shifts[3] in Microsoft Teams

---

2. Slack. n.d. "Ovvy." Slack. Accessed January 20, 2022. https://slack.com/apps/APE4PNGQ6-ovvy.

3. Microsoft. n.d. "Get Started in Shifts." Accessed January 20, 2022. https://support.microsoft.com/en-us/office/get-started-in-shifts-Microsoft. n.5f3e30d8-1821-4904-be26-c3cd25a497d6.

offer scheduling services. The same argument holds true here as well. While these specialized services might be nice to use, they are not necessary at the beginning of the SRE transformation.

The simplest and most familiar communication tool landscape already in use provides the fastest on-call implementation and the least time investment in learning new tools. This is what to strive for when the goal is to establish on-call processes in development teams that have never gone on call before.

7.5.3 Professional On-Call Management Tools

Professional on-call management tools established in the industry include PagerDuty and Ops Genie, among others. These are typically paid services that offer rich feature sets to manage on call in small to very large teams. There are also open-source alternatives. Notably, LinkedIn open-sourced its on-call management solution. It is called Oncall[4] and is available on GitHub.

Now, when is the right point in time to switch from a simple infrastructure to a professional on-call management tool? The need should materialize organically. It should become cumbersome to manage on call with the existing simple infrastructure. This typically happens when there is a growing number of people ready to go on call in a growing number of operations and development teams. Table 7.7 shows some of the situations that can serve as signals for introducing a more professional on-call management tool setup.

Table 7.7 *Signals for Introducing a Professional On-Call Management Tool*

Aspect	Process Improvement Trigger	Missing Functionality
SLO breaches targeting	Everyone in an "-slo-breaches" channel gets notified about the SLO breaches. Once in the channel, people often do not leave. Over time, there are more and more people in the channel. They all get notified about the SLO breaches. Better targeting of SLO breaches to the people currently on call is needed.	• Alerting only the people on call about the SLO breaches
Scheduling	The shared calendar provides transparency but is disconnected from SLO breach targeting (see previous aspect in the table). Also, as more and more teams have someone on call, the shared calendar gets cluttered and is less readable to quickly find out who is on call and where. Having a main and a backup on-call person per team exacerbates the situation.	• Scheduling on-call rotations using a dedicated user interface developed for the purpose • Scheduling on-call rotations conveniently for the main and backup on-call people • Connecting scheduling to alert targeting

---

4. LinkedIn. n.d. "Oncall." Accessed January 20, 2022. https://oncall.tools.

Aspect	Process Improvement Trigger	Missing Functionality
Status	The status of services based on SLO fulfillment is clear but not used in aggregation to show the overall status by product or region. So, the question "what is the status of production?" cannot be answered in a self-service manner.	• Displaying services' status by region on a status page • Displaying services' status by product on a status page
Stakeholder notifications	There is a growing number of detected situations that would be great to be distributed to different stakeholders.	• Creating stakeholder groups • Notifying a stakeholder group • Enabling a stakeholder group to subscribe to notifications at will

Once the need for more sophisticated on-call management tools becomes evident, the SRE coaches should initiate a comparison of on-call management tools to be done by the operations teams. The tools should be evaluated using a set of criteria that are important to the organization. The criteria can be

- Cost position based on the projected growth of the organization
- Existing ecosystem fit
- Fulfillment of data protection regulations
- Potential of use by other product delivery organizations within the business
- Scheduling capabilities
- Smart alert dispatching capabilities (deduplication, noise reduction, etc.)
- Stakeholder notification capabilities
- Service status page capabilities, including support by region
- Uptime and latency SLAs
- Offered APIs
- Integrations with existing services used in the organization
- Reporting and analytics capabilities
- Incident management capabilities
- Payment terms
- Data protection provisions
- Security provisions

Introducing a professional on-call management tool requires a significant investment in money and time. Each tool introduces its own terminology that everyone in the team needs to learn. Development teams need to be onboarded to the selected tool as users to be able to manage schedules, retrieve SLO breaches, respond to incidents, notify stakeholders, and so on.

Operations teams need to be onboarded to the selected tool as users, developers, and administrators. They need to figure out how to dock the SRE infrastructure to the selected tool using offered APIs so that the SLO breaches arrive there and are dispatched to the people on call. Finally, stakeholders from different departments need to be onboarded to the selected tool as users to be able to receive stakeholder notifications and view status pages.

That is why introducing a professional on-call management tool only makes sense when the operations and development teams are ready. They are ready when the notion of going on call is not brand new to them because they practice on call already in some way, and questions of on-call process optimization start becoming relevant.

7.6 Out-of-Hours On-Call

When a team talks about setting up on-call rotations (see Section 7.5), questions about out-of-hours on-call support inevitably arise. In this context, it is useful to take a step back and pose the question: Is out of hours on-call support needed at all? If so, to what extent?

In the initial days of introducing on call for SLO breaches in a development team, beginning with on-call duty during business hours is a good starting point. It paves the way to on call for developers who have never done it before and are understandably afraid of being awakened in the middle of the night to fix production issues. Moreover, it allows exploring, and establishing, on call in teams without time-consuming work agreement negotiations with management, the workers council, legal, HR, and others. The negotiations would need to be done for each country, and sometimes each region, where the people on call would work outside of business hours.

Once on-call support during business hours is accepted and established, the question about extending on call outside of business hours becomes relevant. The product owner might be able to approach the question "how much on-call support do we actually need to fulfill user needs?" from the user point of view based on customer complaints and conversations. Additionally, the application performance management facility can provide data about the times of day the product is used most.

What needs to be determined is whether product usage by and product criticality for the customer would require a follow-the-sun approach to on call where knowledgeable staff would need to be available 24x7 for each service. For example, it might be that the product is used by customers in a business setting during their business hours and the vast majority of customers are located within a single time zone. In this case, ensuring on call during these customers' business hours is appropriate and 24x7 on call is not required. In fact, weekend support is not required at all. So, 24x7 is turned into an 8x5 support requirement during these customers' business hours.

Later, if and when the customer base expands to other time zones, the on-call coverage would need to be extended as well. The on-call extension would need to be done based on data. Even if the customer base is distributed across several regions around the world but the product is used mostly during the customers' business hours, full 24x7 support might still not be required. An overlap of the customers' business hours might help reduce the on-call support requirement from 24x7 to, for example, 12x5 or 18x5.

7.6.1 Using Availability Targets and Product Demand

In "Implementing You Build It You Run It at Scale,"[5] Steve Smith suggests using product availability targets and product demand to determine the level of on-call support required by a product. The higher the availability target, the more on-call support is required. For example, a product with a 99.999% availability target would require more on-call support to be provided than a product with only a 99% availability target.

Further, the higher the product demand is, the more support the product requires. Product demand is expressed as the number of production deployments of the application per time unit as requested by the product owner. For example, daily production deployments would be considered high product demand. Monthly production deployments would be considered low product demand.

The availability of the people on call needs to be balanced with the on-call requirement for the product. That is, the business hours of the people on call need to be aligned as much as possible with the time of the required on-call shifts. This is especially possible if the people on call are distributed across time zones.

Further, in "Implementing You Build It You Run It at Scale,"[5] it is suggested to have no out-of-hours on-call rotations for products with low availability targets. It is further suggested to introduce a so-called domain on-call rotation for products with medium availability targets. A domain on-call rotation covers all products belonging to a single domain. People on the domain rotation need to have knowledge of all the products in the domain. For products with a high availability target and high product demand, an out-of-hours on-call rotation per development team is recommended.

7.6.2 Trade-offs

The preceding discussion shows that there are many ways to organize out-of-hours support. It ranges from having no out-of-hours support at all over domain on-call rotations to on-call rotations per development team. Each particular out-of-hours on-call setup is a trade-off decision between the aspects summarized in Table 7.8.

Table 7.8 *Aspects to Consider When Creating an On-Call Setup*

Aspect	Explanatory Questions
Product use	During which times of day is the product currently most heavily used?
	What are the projected times of day the product will be most heavily used based on projected customer base expansion and product use changes within the next 12 months?
Reliability targets	What are the SLOs to be defended?
Product demand	What is the required frequency of production updates?

---

5. Smith, Steve. 2020. "Implementing You Build It You Run It at Scale." *Steve Smith On Tech* (blog). May 19, 2020. https://www.stevesmith.tech/blog/implementing-you-build-it-you-run-it-at-scale.

Aspect	Explanatory Questions
Product maturity	What is the current toil required to defend the SLOs?
	What is the current inflow of customer complaints?
On-call cost	What is the cost of putting operations engineers and developers on call?
	What is the opportunity cost of putting the developers and operations engineers on call (i.e., what else could they do if they did not go on call and what value would it yield)?
On-call staff	How many people with appropriate knowledge are available to go on call per service, per development team, per product, and per domain of products?
On-call times	How many people are available to work during the required on-call times?
	How far can the business hours of the people be aligned with the required on-call times?
Budget	What is the budget for on-call activities? Is it an operations budget? Is it a development budget? Is it a dedicated on-call budget owned by somebody? Is it a capital expenditure or an operating expense budget? How is it accounted for?
Head count	Are there head count limits in the organization for doing on-call work?
Tooling	Is there tooling in place for professional on-call management, including service status reporting?
Knowledge sharing	Are there processes in place for appropriate knowledge sharing to enable team rotations, product rotations, and domain rotations?

All in all, introducing out-of-hours on-call support requires multifaceted decision-making along many dimensions. It is a step change from in-hours on-call that might be practiced initially at the beginning of the SRE transformation. Therefore, the SRE coaches should recommend introducing out-of-hours on-call gradually, in steps. The journey should begin only after in-hours on-call is well understood and practiced in all development and operations teams taking part in the SRE transformation. The first steps could be

- Understanding the most pressing needs for out-of-hours support in terms of time and product areas
- Identifying people who have the knowledge of the product areas identified
- Identifying people who could be on call during the time identified
- Ensuring systematic knowledge sharing procedures enabling people inside and outside the development team to do on call
- Ensuring the availability of an appropriate professional on-call management tool
- Establishing the first out-of-hours on-call rotation for one product

- Establishing hypotheses with measurable signals to measure the effectiveness of out-of-hours on-call (the same way it was done in Section 4.7, *Posing Hypotheses*)
- Iterating on the setup using frequent retrospectives (e.g., every two weeks)

One of the key enablers of out-of-hours on-call is systematic knowledge sharing about the SLOs, SLO breaches, their priorities, and associated actions to bring the services back within the SLOs. This is the subject of the next section.

> **From the Trenches:** Establishing out-of-hours on-call without the systematic knowledge sharing that enables people outside the development teams to do on call only leads to "SLO breach passthrough" to the knowledgeable people in the development teams. It only adds to on-call costs without associated benefits. This equally applies to cases where people doing out-of-hours on-call come from inside or outside the development teams. The rigor of documentation and conversation required for successful out-of-hours on-call has to be equally high in both cases.

7.7 Systematic Knowledge Sharing

To approach the topic of systematic knowledge sharing required to introduce out-of-hours on-call effectively, let us consider the on-call setup illustrated in Figure 7.7. Note that this setup does not need to be considered as something to imitate in a given organization. It should be viewed as a realistic but random example.

The left-hand side of Figure 7.7 shows the local working hours of the development teams. The individual teams may be located in different time zones. During the local working hours, each development team has an on-call rotation. The on-call rotations process the SLO breaches from all production regions. The production regions are individually deployed (e.g., for data protection reasons) and monitored by a central SRE infrastructure. Thus, on call during local working hours is set up in such a way that a development team gets SLO breaches only for the services they own but from all production deployments. The dispatching of the SLO breaches by the SRE infrastructure is done by product or service for all regions where it is deployed in order to target the development team owning the product or service.

Out-of-hours on-call is set up differently. The right-hand side of Figure 7.7 shows three regional on-call rotations. There is an on-call rotation in the United States, one in Asia, and one in Europe. The three regional on-call rotations are there to react to the SLO breaches beyond the development teams' local working hours. Therefore, the dispatching of SLO breaches is done in a different way here. The SLO breaches are dispatched by the SRE infrastructure by region for all products or services deployed in that region in order to target the out-of-hours on-call rotation responsible for the region.

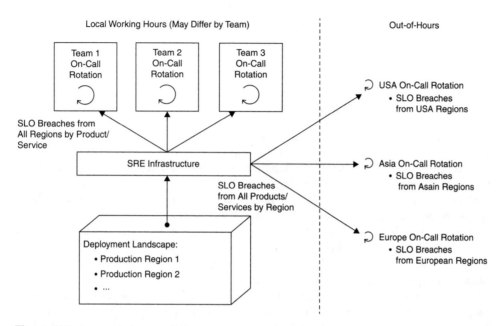

Figure 7.7 *An example on-call setup*

Table 7.9 summarizes the different ways to dispatch the SLO breaches for on-call rotations during business hours and outside of business hours.

Table 7.9 *Example Dispatching of SLO Breaches During and Outside of Business Hours*

	Example Dispatching of SLO Breaches for	
	On-Call Rotations During Business Hours	**On-Call Rotations Outside of Business Hours**
Products/services	Owned by development team	All
Deployment regions	All	Corresponding to the rotation's region

The SRE infrastructure needs to have the flexibility to dispatch the SLO breaches in these ways.

Despite the complexity of the on-call setup shown in Figure 7.7, it may not cover on call 24x7. This should not be considered a drawback in trying to provide as much out-of-hours support as possible. As discussed in Section 7.6, *Out-of-Hours On-Call*, 24x7 support may not be needed. The decision should be made based on data about product usage times and other considerations discussed in Section 7.6.2, *Trade-offs*. More on-call support means more cost but not necessarily more customer satisfaction!

Let us explore the knowledge-sharing needs in the on-call setup illustrated in this section. What would it take to efficiently share knowledge among everyone involved in order to ensure the people are effective at being on call during and outside of business hours? In other words,

- What knowledge is needed before going on call?

- What knowledge is needed while being on call?

- What knowledge needs to be shared after being on call?

7.7.1 Knowledge-Sharing Needs

In the example on-call setup described previously, the development teams have on-call rotations during business hours. Likely, they manage the split between the interruption-based on-call work and the focus-based feature development work using pair rotation as exemplified in Section 7.3.1, *Interruption-Based Working Mode*. Thus, pairing, consisting of performing the work in pairs and pair rotation, is the fundamental knowledge sharing mechanism in the development teams. It is a great enabler for developers getting a broad knowledge of the team's code base, bringing implementation knowledge to operations, and bringing operational insights back to development. However, during pairing, nothing is written down. So, pairing needs to be seen as verbal knowledge sharing only. It only works for the people involved in the process. People not taking part in pairing cannot benefit from the knowledge.

In the example, out-of-hours on-call is done by people outside the development teams. Therefore, additional ways of knowledge sharing are required to enable the people on the out-of-hours on-call rotations to do the on-call work effectively. Note that the development teams and the people on the out-of-hours on-call rotations are located in different time zones. Therefore, live conversations between them might not be as easy to set up during mutual business hours. In fact, there could be no mutual business hours between a development team and an out-of-hours on-call rotation. For example, a development team in India might have no mutual business hours with a U.S.-based on-call rotation. This might even be a rather common case because the example puts the development teams and people on the out-of-hours on-call rotations in opposing time zones by design.

The people on the out-of-hours on-call rotations need to understand the SLOs, typical SLO breaches, what they can do when the breaches occur, what they should do if something unexpected happens, and so forth. This knowledge is often captured in written form in so-called runbooks. However, knowledge documentation does not replace conversation. Regular conversations about the content of the runbooks are required.

Especially in cases where something unexpected happens, the people on call need to be able to quickly find out whether a similar issue was discussed and solved before. Further, they need to be able to ask questions in the relevant knowledgeable community. Internal developer forums like Stack Overflow for Teams[6], if accepted and widely used by the developers, can be of great help for this purpose.

Moreover, the people on call need a general training to prepare for going on call. The training not only explains the structure and procedures of being on call, but might also be a regulatory requirement to complete before a person is allowed to do the on-call work.

---

6. Stack Overflow. n.d. "Knowledge Management Software & Solutions for Collaboration." Accessed January 21, 2022. https://stackoverflow.com/teams.

Finally, with many people doing on-call work, a community of practice starts to emerge. It can be referred to as "SRE CoP" and can act as a forum for exchanging practices in all things SRE in general and in being on call in particular. Different teams will have different ways, tips, and tricks around being on call. These can range from setting up on-call rotations to making runbooks understood. A single team cannot know whether their way of working could be considered a best practice or needs to be adjusted based on other teams' practices. This kind of knowledge sharing can be greatly facilitated in a well-structured community of practice.

That is, a layered approach to knowledge sharing is required to enable on call in an effective and efficient manner. In the following sections, each layer of knowledge sharing is explored in detail.

7.7.2 Knowledge-Sharing Pyramid

The layered approach to knowledge sharing can be explored based on a classification of whether a particular type of knowledge sharing is done on the job (i.e., while on call) or off the job (i.e., when preparing to go on call or improving existing on-call procedures). The classification is shown in Figure 7.8.

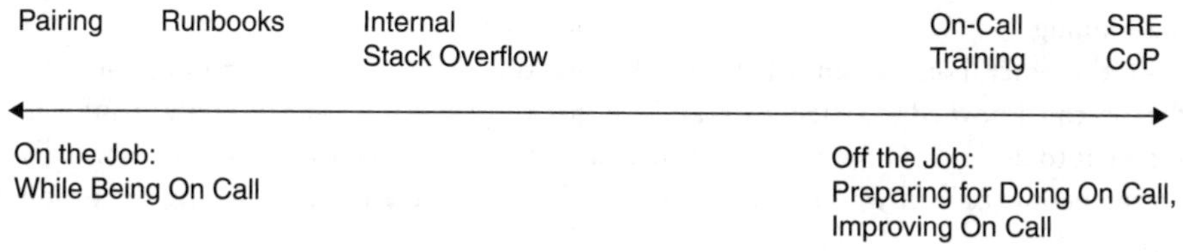

Pairing	Runbooks	Internal Stack Overflow		On-Call Training	SRE CoP

$$\longleftarrow\!\!\!\!-\!\!\!-\!\!\!-\!\!\!-\!\!\!-\!\!\!-\!\!\!-\!\!\!-\!\!\!-\!\!\!\longrightarrow$$

On the Job:
While Being On Call

Off the Job:
Preparing for Doing On Call,
Improving On Call

Figure 7.8 *Knowledge-sharing classification*

The left-hand side of the figure shows the types of knowledge shared while someone is on call. These are pairing, using, and updating runbooks as well as using systems like an internal Stack Overflow to post new questions and read answers to the questions posted before.

The right-hand side of the figure shows the types of knowledge shared while someone is not on call. These include the general on-call training to establish a basic understanding of the ways on call is practiced in the organization, and participation in the SRE CoP to share team practices. Sharing team practices leads to crystallization of best practices for the organization. These, in turn, need to flow into the general on-call training. The SRE coaches need to establish this feedback loop. There is nothing more frustrating than a general on-call training that does not contain the most up-to-date information about working on call. This may seed distrust among new employees in the process documentation they find in the organization in general.

Both types of knowledge sharing can be represented as a pyramid where the upper layers build on top of the lower layers. Figure 7.9 shows this on-call knowledge-sharing pyramid.

Figure 7.9 *On-call knowledge-sharing pyramid*

The on-call training is at the bottom of the pyramid. The training is necessary to obtain general knowledge about the on-call practice. Depending on the industry, it can also represent a regulatory requirement to be allowed to go on call. Generally speaking, the SRE coaches should insist on establishing a formal training requirement so that people would only be allowed to go on call once the training is complete. Associated grants of elevated privileges required for performing the on-call work should also be connected to successful completion of the training.

With the general on-call knowledge established through the on-call training, the next level in the on-call knowledge-sharing pyramid is for the runbooks. They contain information about what to do on SLO breaches in known circumstances. The runbooks are especially useful to the people on call who do not belong to the development team owning the product or service.

Next up in the hierarchy is an internal developer forum like Stack Overflow. It can be consulted once there is an SLO breach whose remedy is not described in the associated runbook. Previously asked questions and answers can be viewed quickly to see whether someone had a similar issue before, was able to fix it, and how. Moreover, new questions can be posted and answered in the right community of knowledgeable developers and operations engineers.

If a quick search on the internal Stack Overflow forum does not lead to a solution to bring the service back within the SLO that is currently broken, an on-call pair can be consulted to discuss the issue. The on-call pair is a backup for the main on-call person. So, consulting the on-call pair should lead to an immediate and qualified conversation about what could be done to restore the service.

Finally, on-call practice sharing across teams can be done well as part of the SRE CoP. Teams can learn from each other and establish best practices that generally apply to most on-call rotations in the organization.

From the Trenches: Developers are used to holding knowledge transfer sessions with each other. In a typical knowledge transfer session, a developer who implemented a component typically talks about the details of the implementation in order to enable other developers to make changes to the component in the future. Because it is a very common practice, the developers might think that similar sessions are all that is needed to enable on-call knowledge transfer.

This is not sufficient, because on-call knowledge transfer is done based on quickly emerging ephemeral incidents and includes people way beyond the development team. The SRE coaches should explain the components of the on-call knowledge-sharing pyramid from the beginning in order to align the understanding and expectations about the effort that need to continuously go into knowledge transfer for a successful on-call practice.

The on-call knowledge-sharing pyramid shows the complex structure of knowledge sharing necessary for establishing effective and efficient on-call service both during and outside of hours. Once established, the pyramid is used by the people on call to drive the knowledge gathering and distribution required to deal with SLO breaches effectively in a systematic manner. Running from the bottom to the top of the pyramid becomes routine for the people on call.

To be sure, not every SLO breach requires running all the way to the top of the pyramid. Most SLO breaches will be possible to tackle using the knowledge provided by the two lowest layers of the pyramid: on-call training and runbooks. A subset of the SLO breaches will require consultation of the internal Stack Overflow or the pair on call. A small number of the SLO breaches will deserve to be discussed in a broader round of the SRE community of practice to share the knowledge with other teams.

The order of the pyramid from bottom to top provides a good structure to systematically pull and push operational knowledge throughout the organization. In the following sections, more details are provided for building up the knowledge-sharing pyramid step by step.

7.7.3 On-Call Training

On-call training should be a component of the onboarding program or bootcamp for new employees. This way, every employee who will take part in on-call rotations will learn the foundations of being on call in the organization as part of their onboarding process.

The training is best done as a combination of the following:

- A small number of short videos explaining the fundamental concepts that do not change frequently
- An on-call wiki as part of the overarching SRE wiki explaining
  - The current ways of working when doing on call
  - Tools being used, where to find them, and how to get access to them
  - Roles doing on call
  - During and out-of-hours on-call setup

- ○ Scheduling and rescheduling of on-call rotations
- ○ Procedure for obtaining the necessary user permissions to perform the on-call work
- ○ Freedom and responsibility split for the on-call work
- ○ Incident response process description
- ○ References to runbooks
- ○ References to the architecture documentation for further reading
- ○ SRE CoP including how to join it
- A reference to postmortems and an invitation to go through them to learn from past incidents
- Watching live incidents unfold in the on-call management tool
- Contact people for further conversations about on call by team
- Simple exercises to gamify the process

In terms of video content creation, it may be beneficial to use online services that can create professional videos from text using AI. This saves time on first-time video creation and all subsequent edits. By just editing the text, the video can be updated in no time. Notably, Synthesia[7] is an online AI video generation service that can be used.

The general on-call training should take a couple of hours to complete. Its purpose is to set the scene and provide an overall general understanding of what it means to be on call and how to perform the on-call work. The training is a process training. It cannot go into the details of a specific product, service, or team.

That is, completing the general on-call training prepares a new employee for going on call but does not qualify them for being an effective on-call person for a particular product or service. Additional in-depth conversations about doing on call for a particular service are required with the team that owns the service. The conversations in the team need to involve the following topics.

- Who is doing on call during and outside of business hours for the service?
- Where are the runbooks for the service?
- What SLOs are set for the service?
  - ○ How do you look them up?
  - ○ What is the procedure for changing them? How do you join an on-call rotation for the service?
- How do you set up the on-call rotation for the service in the on-call management tool?
  - ○ How do you look up who is on call for the service and when?
  - ○ How do you override a previously set up on-call schedule for the service?
- Where do the SLO breaches for the service arrive?
- How is incident management for the service handled?

---

7. Synthesia. n.d. AI video generation platform. Accessed January 21, 2022. https://www.synthesia.io.

- What are the incident priorities for the service?

- Are there postmortems for the service? If so, where are they?

- What is the freedom and responsibility split when doing on call for the service?

The SRE coaches need to facilitate the on-call training at the general and team levels. Further, the effectiveness of the trainings needs to be gauged based on feedback from retrospectives. The SRE coaches should drive the retrospectives when the on-call training is introduced. After that, they should hand the responsibility to the agile coaches or similar roles in the organization.

In regulated environments, doing an on-call training may be a regulatory requirement. In these cases, the on-call training needs to be part of the official training list. It also needs to be part of the training management system subject to regulatory compliance. The system will record training attendance, time, and completion by role. Further, it will prepare the data in such a way that it will be suitable to be presented to an auditor in an audit setting.

7.7.4 Runbooks

When initially introducing on call in a development team, the people on call are developers intimately familiar with the implementation of services they go on call for. The developers were involved in the SLO definition process. They understand the SLO breaches and can connect them to the customer impact. They can also connect the SLO breaches to potential root causes. Further, the developers have all the knowledge to perform failure investigations. All in all, the developers have a very rich and comprehensive context of services they go on call for. If pairing is practiced, this knowledge is spread to other developers. In this setting, written documentation of what to do in case of SLO breaches is desirable but not required to do on call effectively.

The necessity for written documentation arises when people who are further away from the service implementation join the on-call rotations for the service. These people do not have the context necessary for doing on call. They are

1. New developers joining the team owning the service

2. Developers from other teams in case a domain rotation is practiced in the organization

3. Operations engineers doing on call during business hours together with the developers if shared on call between operations engineers and developers is practiced in the organization

4. Operations engineers doing business-hours support by themselves

5. Operations engineers doing out-of-hours support by themselves

The order of the list reflects the distance between service implementation knowledge and a given person. The higher the order number, the larger the distance. The larger the distance, the greater the need for a detailed runbook to do the on-call work effectively.

What makes up a good runbook? A good runbook enables the on-call person with the largest distance from the development team to be effective at reacting to the corresponding SLO breaches. In other words, a good runbook provides a rich context to the people on call who lack it. This certainly can only be verified empirically and arrived at iteratively. If that is the case, the question is where to start.

A good starting point is to create a template for runbooks. The template can be composed based on lots of runbook templates freely available online. A Google search for "runbooks template" returns many good results. A pragmatic starting point could be a runbook template offered by Caitie McCaffrey on GitHub.[8]

By now, the SRE coaches have lots of experience with the operations and development teams as well as some experience with the actual services in operations. Based on that experience, the SRE coaches should trim an existing runbook template off the internet and adjust it to the needs of the organization. As a bare minimum, the following points have to be covered by a runbook template:

1. Timestamp of the last runbook update

2. Name of the person who did the last runbook update

3. Service the runbook is for (with a link to the service catalog, if any)

4. SLO the runbook is for and associated short description (with a link to the SLO definition)

5. Impact on customers of an SLO breach

6. Remediation steps

7. Dashboards about service health, if any

8. Contact details for further support, including availability times with time zones

9. Latest production deployments of the service and code changes for each production deployment (links)

Using a wiki page template is beneficial. Wikis are useful for quick editing and searching. Using a wiki covers points 1 and 2 automatically. Moreover, a wiki records who made which changes and when. This can be beneficial if there are questions about particular runbook entries. Further, a wiki can be connected to a source control system. This way, all changes are also source-controlled like any other source code file. Operations like clone and move become possible, which are useful for future content restructuring activities.

Another benefit of using wikis is that page view statistics are collected and can be analyzed. Analyzing the page views of various runbooks may provide indications about the usefulness of a particular runbook. If a runbook is hardly ever read, it might either not be useful or not be needed. In this case, maintenance of the runbook is not worth the effort. It is worth experimenting with hiding such a runbook and only reinstating it based on requests from the people on call.

With runbooks being available and kept up-to-date, it is easy to think that knowledge sharing can stop there. This is not the case. Conversations about the runbooks are necessary to ensure that everyone on call is on the same page.

---

8. McCaffrey, Caitie. n.d. "Runbook Template." GitHub. Accessed January 21, 2022. https://github.com/CaitieM20/Talks/blob/master/TacklingAlertFatigue/runbook.md.

> **From the Trenches:** It is common for development teams to assume that up-to-date content written in runbooks is sufficient to convey to recipients what is meant. This, however, is not a verified assumption. The further away the recipients are from the developers, the development team, and generally from the last conversation over the runbooks, the more a conversation is necessary on top of the written runbooks update to convey the meaning.
>
> Those who updated the runbooks need to actively seek a conversation with the intended recipients for whom the updates were meant. A five-minute conversation can go a long way toward bringing the recipients on the same page of content understanding in a verified manner. The "Message Not Received"[9] syndrome is guarded against by actively seeking conversations rather than assuming understanding without verifying it.

A good time to have conversations about the runbooks is around the time when the people on call switch. The person going off call may have made some changes to the runbooks. Talking the person going on call through the changes made during the previous shift is a great segue to start the new on-call shift in an up-to-date manner. However, the challenge might be to find a time when the two people would be available to have the conversation. Especially in the case of out-of-hours on-call, the two people might be scheduled to work during mutually exclusive hours.

Thus, if a conversation is not possible, a mitigation to bridge the gap between the updated runbooks and the understanding of the updates by the recipients could be a short video recording. In the video the person who did the runbook update can talk through the changes that were made. A link to the recording needs to be put into the runbook itself for everyone to see. Many video sharing platforms commonly used in product delivery organizations allow for such a recording to be made quickly over a shared screen and embedded in wiki pages. For example, Microsoft Stream[10] and Panopto[11] provide the necessary easy-to-use infrastructure out of the box.

7.7.5 Internal Stack Overflow

If a person on call did the on-call trainings, went on call, received an SLO breach, and went through runbooks in an effort to find a solution for bringing the service back within the SLO, they might be at the end of options for finding a remedy to fix the SLO breach. In situations like that, internal Stack Overflow tools (e.g., Stack Overflow for Teams,[6] Scoold,[12] etc.) can be quite helpful.

---

9. Simon, Phil. 2015. *Message Not Received: Why Business Communication Is Broken and How to Fix It.* Hoboken, NJ: John Wiley & Sons.

10. Microsoft. n.d. "Microsoft Stream – Video Streaming Service." Accessed January 21, 2022. https://www.microsoft.com/en-us/microsoft-365/microsoft-stream.

11. "Panopto." 2015. Panopto Video Platform. September 29, 2015. https://www.panopto.com.

12. "Scoold." n.d. Scoold Q&A. Accessed January 21, 2022. https://scoold.com.

If an internal Stack Overflow tool has been established in the organization, it is used by the developers and operations engineers to post questions and receive answers about development and operational topics. This, however, only works well if the tool is established as the go-to public forum for these topics. That is, while the tool itself is important in terms of functionality and UX, its adoption is what makes it valuable. If there are other prevalent ways of discussing development and operations topics (e.g., on Slack, MS Teams, or email), the internal Stack Overflow loses its significance and usefulness. Occasional conversations elsewhere are fine, but if developers and operations engineers do not see the internal Stack Overflow as the go-to public forum for asking a question, further community building work is necessary.

The work on creating a successful community forum on the internal Stack Overflow needs to be done by the agile coaches in the organization. The SRE coaches should get in touch with the agile coaches and discuss ways to strengthen the community. These could include

- Promoting the internal Stack Overflow as the go-to public forum for discussing development and operations topics
- Discouraging the use of other forums for public online discussions about development and operations topics
- Using gamification such as votes, badges, tags, expertise scores, contributor leaderboards, reputation scores, moderator privileges, and so on to incentivize participation
- Getting informal leaders to use the internal Stack Overflow because they will attract many followers

The SRE coaches cannot be viewed as the drivers of making the internal Stack Overflow a successful initiative. Their focus is firmly on establishing SRE as the primary methodology for doing operations in the organization. For example, establishing a vibrant SRE community of practice is well in scope of the SRE coaches' responsibilities. This is the subject of the next section.

7.7.6 SRE Community of Practice

The establishment of an SRE community of practice (CoP) will make sense when the SRE transformation has reached most of the development and operations teams. Around the time when in-hours on-call is practiced in most teams, the need for sharing on-call ways of working emerges in order to identify best practices. Thus, the initial participants of an SRE CoP will be the people who go on call.

The SRE CoP can get started pragmatically with a list of potential topics that might be interesting to the people practicing on call. The SRE coaches can prepare the list and submit it for voting to those who practice on call as part of their jobs. Topics with the largest number of votes wander to the top of the list. A sample list of topics might be

- SLO definitions (SLOs, SLIs, error budgets)
- Log query language induction
- Log query language advanced concepts

- SRE dashboards for monitoring
- SLO breaches and reacting to alerts
- Extending the SRE infrastructure
- On-call management tooling
- Using workflow automation tools (e.g., Zapier,[13] Power Apps,[14] etc.) for service health checks
- Dashboards with a good UX to support targeted incident resolution
- Ways to speed up incident resolution

The topics can be handled as

- Presentations based on previously prepared slides
- Conversations about past incidents captured in the incident management tool
- Conversations in postmortems
- Freeform conversations about outages, SLOs, dashboards, tools, runbooks, user permissions, on-call rotation setup, and so on

As much as possible, all the presentations and conversations should be recorded, tagged with "SRE," and put on the organization's video sharing platform. Moreover, a wiki page on the SRE wiki needs to be dedicated to the SRE CoP. It should contain a list of previously discussed topics with links to the respective recordings. This is hugely important, because a large share of SRE work is done on rotation, creating a continuous need for onboarding new people.

The SRE CoP members should view the CoP meetings as a way to have serendipitous conversations about the SRE activities in general and on-call work in particular. The meeting frequency of the SRE CoP team members should be decided by the members themselves. Meeting once every two weeks for 30 to 60 minutes seems to be a reasonable starting point.

After a couple of months of informal SRE CoP meetings, the SRE coaches can decide based on feedback from the CoP participants whether the time they spent in the CoP meetings was well invested. If there is a positive response and vibe around the SRE CoP, a lightweight formalization of the CoP may be useful on the way to making it a self-sustaining community and network. The lightweight formalization of the SRE CoP needs to take place along the following dimensions:

- Vision
- Goals
- Leadership
- Membership
- Scope

---

13. Zapier. n.d. "The Easiest Way to Automate Your Work." Accessed January 21, 2022. https://zapier.com.
14. Microsoft. n.d. "Business Apps." Accessed January 21, 2022. https://powerapps.microsoft.com.

- Benefits

- Time investment

- Success measurements

- Sharing successes with a wider audience

These aspects need to be discussed with the SRE CoP members. This strengthens the community as it is going from an ad-hoc series of meetings to something more established based on previous experience. Doing so also ensures good buy-in of the initiative by the people practicing on call. Consequently, they will be the ones recommending other people to join the SRE CoP as more and more people get involved in on-call rotations.

Once finalized, all of these aspects need to be put onto the SRE wiki for everyone to see. A short presentation about the SRE CoP in a forum like a lean coffee session helps spread the word. The presentation should be done by SRE CoP leadership. This also marks the point where the SRE coaches hand over further management of the SRE CoP to its designated leadership.

SRE CoP leadership should, with time, also take over oversight of the SRE wiki content. It should contain all the information necessary to onboard new people onto all SRE-related activities, be it SLO definitions, doing on call during and outside of business hours, and so forth. The wiki can contain short videos explaining the fundamental concepts that rarely change over time, such as why do SRE? The bulk of the content will be wiki pages that can be changed easily at any time. Further, people need to be able to subscribe to changes on the wiki pages they are interested in. This is a powerful way to immediately distribute the content on SRE process changes to the people most interested in the process.

7.8 Broadcast Success

By now, the operations and development teams taking part in the SRE transformation have done a lot.

1. The SLIs and SLOs are defined and iterated upon.

2. The on-call setup agreements are in place.

3. The on-call rotations are set up during business hours and, where necessary, outside of business hours.

4. The people on call react to SLO breaches.

5. Knowledge sharing is systematic with on-call training, runbooks, an internal Stack Overflow, and an SRE CoP.

Clearly, different teams will be at various levels of maturity in SRE practice. This is always the case as change gets absorbed at individual speeds by the team. However, all the teams iterating on the preceding points have come a long way from when production operations was a chaotic, haphazard activity. Gone are the days of misalignment (see Section 2.1) where neither development nor operations effectively operated the product in production, and product management was too far away from any product operations topics. On the contrary, product operations is a very structured activity by now!

This alone is a success worth broadcasting. The SRE coaches should initiate the broadcast using the same channels used for previous broadcasts.

The following questions can guide the SRE coaches in putting together a comprehensive but succinct broadcast on the progress of the SRE transformation.

- What is the typical in-hours on-call setup employed by the majority of teams?

- How is out-of-hours on-call handled at the moment and what are the future plans?

- How are the focus-based and interruption-based working modes accommodated in the development and operations teams?

- What is the content of the new on-call training? How can people sign up for it?

- Where are the runbooks located? Can anybody view them?

- What is the new internal Stack Overflow? Who is using it? What for? How do you sign up for it?

- What is the new SRE CoP? What is it for? Who is part of it? How do you join it?

To this end, some of the SRE transformation hypotheses might have been tested (see Section 4.7, *Posing Hypotheses*). Are there outcomes that the teams got closer to achieving or have already achieved? Are there measurable signals that could be advanced? Are any adjustments of the previously defined hypotheses needed based on new learnings? The answers to these questions should make it into the broadcast presentation. It is important to reinforce the message that the SRE transformation is executed in a data-driven way under the guidance of hypotheses and measurable signals as feedback loops.

If some of the SRE transformation hypotheses were positively tested, the SRE coaches should separately engage with the people they worked with to put SRE onto the portfolio list of organizational initiatives. In particular, the head of operations, head of development, and head of product management need to know that the SRE transformation has indeed moved the dial on the outcomes that were targeted before the transformation began. This builds confidence in the initiative. Additionally, it helps in portfolio prioritization discussions to ensure that the SRE initiative stays there and does not get prioritized lower or deprioritized altogether.

Depending on the situation, the engagement can be done either in person or by email. The SRE coaches should use the stakeholder chart (see Section 5.4.1) created before to determine the stakeholders to engage with and the medium appropriate for the engagement.

7.9 Summary

In this chapter, setting up on-call rotations was at the heart of the discourse. It started with selecting deployment environments to be monitored using SLOs and SLO breaches. The operational responsibilities were introduced, clarified, and delineated from the development responsibilities. To fulfill the development and operational responsibilities, two working modes were defined: focus based and interruption based. Regardless of the on-call setup, developers will need to go on call to the extent agreed. Therefore, the focus-based and interruption-based working modes will need to be put in place in the development teams to enable focused feature development and interruption-driven reactions to SLO breaches at the same time. Pairing is a great means to support both working modes and, most importantly, enable structured, ongoing knowledge sharing between development and operations activities.

Because the operations teams develop and operate the SRE infrastructure and, depending on the on-call setup agreement, may also go on call for product services, the focused-based and interruption-based working modes would need to be set up in the operations teams too.

Further, different ways of setting up on-call rotations depending on the number of people on call were discussed along with the tools required to sustain the practice. Professional on-call management tools are not required at the beginning of the on-call practice where the SLO breaches can be posted to the channels of a chat management service in use.

In addition, aspects especially important to setting up effective out-of-hours on-call were presented. In particular, out-of-hours on-call requires multifaceted knowledge sharing to be successful. To this end, an on-call knowledge-sharing pyramid was introduced. It consists of on-call training, runbooks, an internal Stack Overflow, pairing, and an SRE community of practice. The individual levels of the pyramid were explored to provide guidance to the SRE coaches at large on how to set up knowledge sharing during the SRE transformation.

The chapter concluded with ways to broadcast successes achieved so far. These successes can be significant. By now, the development and operations teams defined SLOs, began reacting to SLO breaches, reached agreements about the on-call setup both during and outside of business hours, set up on-call rotations, and implemented the knowledge-sharing pyramid to enable on call. If this is in place, a big part of the SRE transformation has been achieved. It is possible to start talking about the product delivery organization practicing SRE and achieving outcomes!

In the next chapter, I will explore how the SRE practice in the operations and development teams can benefit nontechnical stakeholders.

Chapter 8

Implementing Alert Dispatching

Alert dispatching is about the efficiency with which alerts about breaches and outages reach the people who can take real action. Recipients can be people who are on call, as well as stakeholders such as those in marketing or management. The people on call would receive alerts about SLO breaches, and their goal would be to *fix* the problem. The stakeholders would receive alerts about high-profile outages so that they can be *informed* about the problem before they start getting calls from angry customers.

The goal of alert dispatching is to precisely target the appropriate recipients and to provide them with all the information they need to take action. It is also about dispatching as few alerts as possible. People on call should only receive alerts about SLO breaches that would severely impact the customer experience. "We do not want to alert you about something you would not react to!" should be the mantra of SRE coaches during the SLO definition process.

This mantra should also be adopted when defining stakeholder notifications. Stakeholders need to be notified only about high-profile outages so that they know they exist and that the operations and development teams are swarming to resolve them. Figure 8.1 depicts alert dispatching to people on call as well as to stakeholders.

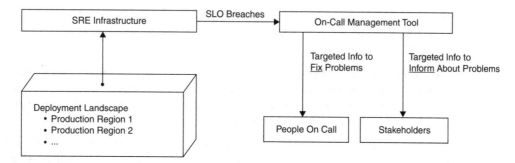

Figure 8.1 *Alert dispatching to the people on call and to the stakeholders*

The left-hand side of the figure shows the deployment landscape. The SRE infrastructure monitors the deployment landscape; when it detects SLO breaches, it forwards them to the on-call management tool, which dispatches alerts regarding the breaches to the people on call. Registered stakeholders can also be informed about relevant outages using the on-call management tool. Stakeholder notifications can be set up to trigger automatically based on some predefined logic, or manually after the people on call have analyzed the breaches.

This chapter provides an in-depth discussion about alert dispatching. First I will cover alert escalations within the product delivery organization, and then I will define stakeholder groups and explain how to set up stakeholder notifications.

8.1 Alert Escalation

In Section 7.4, *Setting Up On-Call Rotations*, I explained how several people can be involved in an on-call rotation. I introduced the notion of having both main on-call and backup on-call people to ensure a timely reaction to SLO breaches in cases where the main on-call person is not available. Propagating alerts from the main on call to the backup on call and beyond is the subject of this section.

Modern on-call management tools allow for sophisticated alert propagation. Propagating alerts from one person to another based on a set of rules is referred to as alert escalation. The set of rules is referred to as the escalation policy. An on-call management tool can reassign an alert between the people on call according to a defined escalation policy.

An escalation policy can reflect the defined on-call setup with the main on-call and backup on-call people. The following options are usually available to set up the details of the escalation policy.

1. Chain of people to be notified. A person can be expressed as follows:

   ○ The current person on call in a defined schedule

   ○ Any responder user

   ○ A defined team of people, in which case all members of the team are notified

   ○ A defined group of people across teams, in which case all members of the group are notified

2. Time span between the alert dispatch to a person in the chain and the alert acknowledgment by anyone before the alert escalation takes place. When the time span is expired, the alert escalation to the next person in the chain is automatically performed. If the alert gets acknowledged before the time span is expired, the escalation policy stops.

3. Number of repeats for the escalation policy. Once the defined chain of people has been iterated through and the alert is still unacknowledged, the escalation policy can be repeated. On repeat, the first person in the chain is notified first, the second one second, and so on.

Figure 8.2 schematically shows a sample escalation policy.

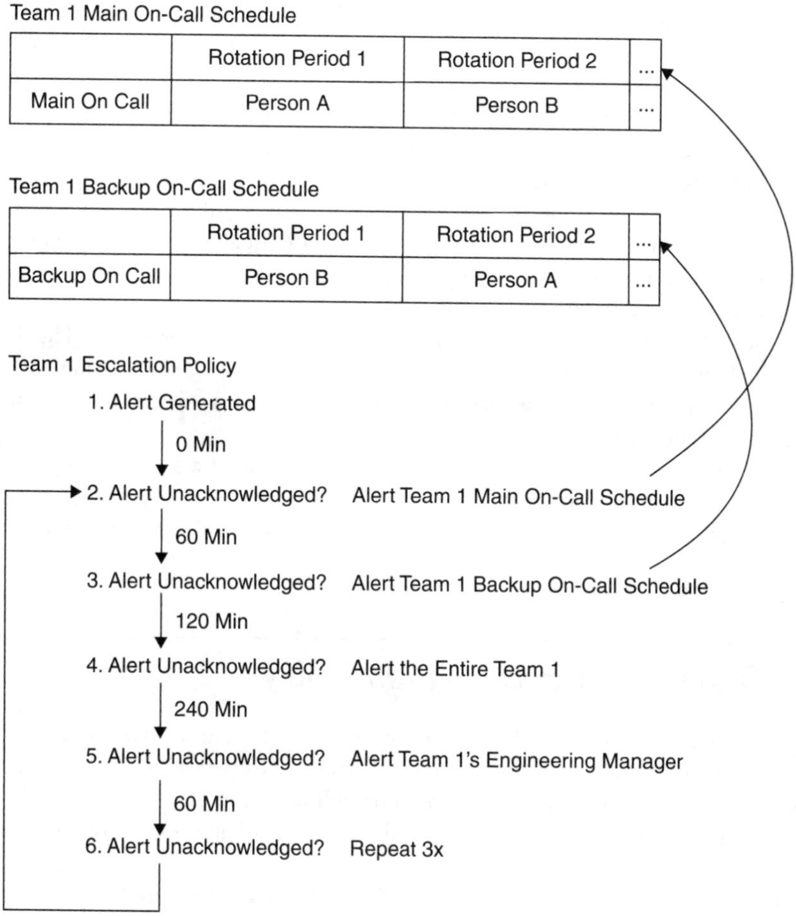

Team 1 Main On-Call Schedule

	Rotation Period 1	Rotation Period 2	...
Main On Call	Person A	Person B	...

Team 1 Backup On-Call Schedule

	Rotation Period 1	Rotation Period 2	...
Backup On Call	Person B	Person A	...

Team 1 Escalation Policy

1. Alert Generated

    0 Min

2. Alert Unacknowledged?   Alert Team 1 Main On-Call Schedule

    60 Min

3. Alert Unacknowledged?   Alert Team 1 Backup On-Call Schedule

    120 Min

4. Alert Unacknowledged?   Alert the Entire Team 1

    240 Min

5. Alert Unacknowledged?   Alert Team 1's Engineering Manager

    60 Min

6. Alert Unacknowledged?   Repeat 3x

Figure 8.2 *A sample escalation policy*

The top of Figure 8.2 shows team 1's main on-call schedule. Two people are on call, one per rotation period. Below the main on-call schedule, the backup on-call schedule is shown. It consists of the same two people on call: Person A and person B rotate their roles between main on call and backup on call by rotation period.

The lower part of Figure 8.2 shows team 1's escalation policy, which consists of six steps. In step 1, an alert is generated as a result of an SLO breach detected by the SRE infrastructure. Immediately after the alert is generated, it is dispatched to the team 1 main on-call schedule (step 2)—that is, to person A or person B, depending on the rotation period. If the main on-call person does not acknowledge the alert within 60 minutes, step 3 of the escalation policy is enacted. In this step, the backup on-call person is alerted according to the backup on-call schedule. Should this person not acknowledge the alert within 120 minutes, step 4 of the escalation policy is enacted.

In step 4, everyone on team 1 is alerted, regardless of whether they are on call or not. Each team member can specify how they prefer to receive the alert; notifications via email, text, mobile app, or phone call, depending on time of day, are commonly available options for dispatching alerts. Should the alert remain unacknowledged within the next 240 minutes, team 1's engineering manager is notified.

If the alert is still unacknowledged 60 minutes later, the repeat option kicks in. This option is set to repeat the escalation policy three times. That is, the on-call management tool goes back to step 2 and runs through the notification chain anew.

The three main options to specify an escalation policy—notification chain, time span to elapse on each escalation step, and number of repeats—are usually available in all on-call management tools. Additional options are also available to fine-tune the escalation policy definition. The additional options vary by tool.

Typically, stakeholder notifications are not subject to an escalation policy. This is because these notifications are sent for informational purposes and not for taking immediate action, such as an acknowledgment. Consequently, it would be difficult to define an escalation policy based on acknowledgment expiry times.

In the atypical case where stakeholder notifications should be acknowledged, they may be defined as acknowledgeable alerts in the on-call management tool. That way, an escalation policy can be defined and the information can be escalated through a chain of stakeholders as required.

8.2 Defining an Alert Escalation Policy

An alert escalation policy needs to be defined for each on-call rotation. The escalation policy is the manifestation of the on-call setup agreement between the operations engineers, developers, and product owner in the on-call management tool. Following this, the escalation policy and the schedules the policy is based upon may contain operations engineers, developers, or a mix thereof.

I recommend starting with a very basic escalation policy and iterate from there based on the feedback from the people on call. The simplest escalation policy for the main on-call and backup on-call people is:

main on-call schedule → backup on-call schedule → repeat once

The alert acknowledgment expiry times for the main and backup on-call people need to be experimented with. The expiry times can vary greatly, ranging from minutes to hours, based on the organization and the criticality of the product.

Once the on-call people work with the simplest escalation policy for a short while and report positive feedback about it, an extension of the escalation policy can be discussed. The extension will necessarily involve people who are not on call in alert-handling activities. Table 8.1 shows who beyond the people on call could be sensibly involved in handling alerts and for what purpose.

Table 8.1 *People in the Escalation Policy Beyond the People On Call*

People in the Escalation Policy Beyond the People On Call	Purpose
Development team	Get the alert acknowledged and worked on by a knowledgeable developer. The developers not on call will look at the alerts during their business hours. All the developers, the respective operations engineers, and the product owner need to agree on whether the escalation policy should include the entire development team. Doing so will interfere with the focus-based working mode (see Section 7.3, Ways of Working) but might still be necessary.
Development team's engineering manager	Get the attention of a higher-up so that they can look for a person who can acknowledge the alert. Having managers in the escalation policy might indirectly motivate the people on call to acknowledge alerts within the agreed time span. This might be a rather contradictory point to be discussed by the operations engineers, developers, product owners, and managers.
Head of development	
Head of operations	

The goal is to fine-tune the escalation policy so that the majority of alerts are acknowledged by the people on call within the defined time spans. In addition, the goal is to have a safety net of the people off call included in the escalation policy to ensure reaction to alerts even if the people on call are unexpectedly unavailable.

> **From the Trenches:** Start with the simplest escalation policy along the lines of "main on-call schedule → backup on-call schedule → repeat once". Experiment with the acknowledgment expiry times for the main and backup on calls. After it is calibrated, think about extending the escalation policy beyond the people on call. Tread carefully to avoid alert fatigue, and iterate based on feedback. Consider the organization's culture when deciding whether to include managers and executives in the escalation policy.

In this context, it is worth being reminded again of the importance of defining the SLOs from the user point of view so that the SLO breaches clearly reflect the impacted customer experience. With the escalation policy potentially including people off call, managers, and executives, it is that much more important to only have SLO breaches that report on customer experiences that were greatly impacted. Technical glitches with unclear connections to customer experience impact do not qualify as SLO breaches!

8.3 Defining Stakeholder Groups

Having discussed alert dispatching for the people on call using alert escalation policies, now I will discuss the dispatching of stakeholder notifications. Stakeholder notifications can be triggered either manually by the people on call or automatically when certain conditions apply. For the stakeholder notifications to be targeted well, two points matter.

1. Stakeholder groups need to be defined with targeting in mind.

2. Stakeholders need to be able to subscribe flexibly to the stakeholder groups of interest.

A stakeholder group needs to be defined in such a way that a certain type of notification can inform the group in an effective manner. For example, for a product delivery organization it might make sense to set up the stakeholder groups shown in Table 8.2.

Table 8.2 *Sample Stakeholder Groups*

Stakeholder Group	Purpose
Product management	To inform the product managers, product owners, and business analysts about ongoing high-profile outages by product and production environment so that they are prepared to talk with marketing, sales, leadership, and customers about it, should conversations arise.
Leadership	To inform leadership about ongoing high-profile outages so that they are prepared to talk to customers about it, should they call.
Marketing and sales	To inform marketing and sales about ongoing high-profile outages by product and production environment so that they can (re-)schedule marketing and sales activities accordingly and be ready to talk to customers.
Partners and customers	To inform partners and customers about ongoing high-profile outages by product and production environment so that they can apply mitigation measures for their products.

Stakeholder subgroups might make sense as well. For example, for the marketing and sales stakeholder group it might make sense to define the subgroups shown in Table 8.3.

Table 8.3 *Sample Marketing and Sales Stakeholder Subgroups*

Marketing and Sales Stakeholder Subgroups	Purpose
Per region for all products	To notify people in marketing and sales about ongoing high-profile outages in all products in a given region. This is useful because marketing and sales staff are typically responsible for all products sold in a given region (e.g., EMEA sales force, American sales force, etc.).

Per product per region	Within a region, individual marketing and sales staff might be dedicated to particular products. To cater to this group of people, stakeholder notifications per product per region are useful to achieve good alert targeting.
For a showcase deployment	Sometimes a global showcase deployment is established in the product delivery organization to be used for all marketing, sales, and customer training purposes. A stakeholder group dedicated to only that deployment might therefore be useful for all marketing, sales, and product training staff around the world.

The SRE coaches should engage product management, marketing, and sales in defining the stakeholder groups. A few representatives from each department would be needed to create an initial set of groups. The way the marketing, sales, and training departments are organized will determine how best to set up the stakeholder groups. The degree of precision needed to enable good notification targeting will also be determined by how the products are marketed and sold. On a whole, geography and product landscape will be the most important dimensions to achieve appropriate stakeholder notification targeting. Table 8.4 shows an example.

Table 8.4 *Example Dimensions for Stakeholder Notification Targeting*

Geography	Product Landscape		
	Product A	Product B	Product C
Production US	Stakeholder group 1	Stakeholder group 2	Stakeholder group 3
Production EU	Stakeholder group 4	Stakeholder group 5	
Production JP	Stakeholder group 6		
Showcase worldwide	Stakeholder group 7		

As shown in Table 8.4, products A, B, and C are sold differently by geography. Therefore, the needs for stakeholder notifications also differ by geography. In the United States, the products are sold individually. The volume of each product sold justifies having dedicated salespeople. Therefore, a stakeholder group per product is needed in the United States. These are stakeholder groups 1, 2, and 3.

In the European Union, product A enjoys good market share. Therefore, there are dedicated sales and marketing people taking care of product A in the European Union. A dedicated stakeholder group is also required for this product in this region. This is stakeholder group 4. Products B and C are primarily sold in a bundle in the European Union. Dedicated marketing and sales people handle bundled sales. Therefore, a corresponding stakeholder group is needed. This is stakeholder group 5.

In Japan, the market for products A, B, and C is small at the moment. Therefore, there are no dedicated marketing and sales people per product. Rather, a small number of people do marketing and sales for the entire product landscape. Following this, only one stakeholder group is needed for Japan. This is stakeholder group 6.

Finally, a showcase deployment is used worldwide for any marketing, sales, and customer training activities to showcase all the products. Everyone in marketing and sales is using that deployment for demos, congresses, and events. A stakeholder group is therefore very important for this particular deployment. This is stakeholder group 7.

As illustrated in the preceding example, the stakeholder groups must be aligned with how sales and marketing is organized and the product is sold. Therefore, the stakeholder groups need to be reconfigured from time to time. This reconfiguration must be offered as a service by the operations teams. The sales and marketing teams need to be able to place the stakeholder group reconfiguration requests and get them fulfilled in a timely manner. During fulfillment, the operations teams also need to inform the people on call about the reconfiguration. This is because the people on call need to know about the stakeholder groups and their purpose to trigger the notifications when necessary.

8.4 Triggering Stakeholder Notifications

Stakeholder notifications can be triggered in a manual, semiautomated, or fully automated manner, as shown in Figure 8.3.

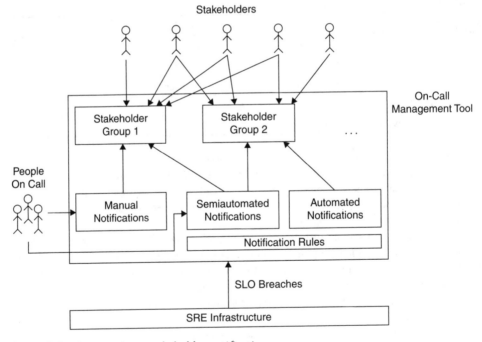

Figure 8.3 *Ways to trigger stakeholder notifications*

The bottom of the figure shows the SRE infrastructure. It detects the SLO breaches and sends them to the on-call management tool. In the on-call management tool, the people on call set up notification rules for automated stakeholder notifications. Additionally, the stakeholder notifications can be sent out in a semiautomated way, by coding up some notification logic in an automated runbook, but triggering execution of the runbook manually, after analysis of SLO breaches.

Moreover, the stakeholder notifications can be triggered manually by the people on call. Here, the right stakeholder groups need to be selected and the notification messages crafted to stakeholders appropriately. To be able to select the stakeholder groups applicable for a notification use case, the current stakeholder groups need to be known to the people on call. A section on the SRE wiki needs to be dedicated to the stakeholder groups and be kept up-to-date by the operations teams.

Once the stakeholder groups are selected for notification in an automated or manual way, the stakeholders subscribed to the groups get notified. Each stakeholder gets the notifications via a medium specified in the on-call management tool. Commonly supported media are email, mobile app push notifications, text messages, and phone calls.

If there are many stakeholder groups, notifications must be ordered between them. How to order stakeholder notifications between stakeholder groups is the subject of the next section.

8.5 Defining Stakeholder Rings

In addition to defining stakeholder groups, it may be useful to also define stakeholder rings in order to stagger the broadcast of information about major outages throughout the organization and beyond. A good way to think about stakeholder rings is to look at the enterprise's organizational chart and determine how the information about major outages should radiate from the people on call to applicable enterprise functions, as well as how it should leave the enterprise and flow to partners and customers. This is where stakeholder rings come in handy. They provide structure to radiate information about major outages within the enterprise and beyond in an orderly manner. That is, both internal and external escalations can be supported using stakeholder rings.

A stakeholder ring has a running number and stakeholder groups associated with it. The number determines the order of the stakeholder ring's notification in the overall stakeholder notification chain. Figure 8.4 shows an example of stakeholder rings.

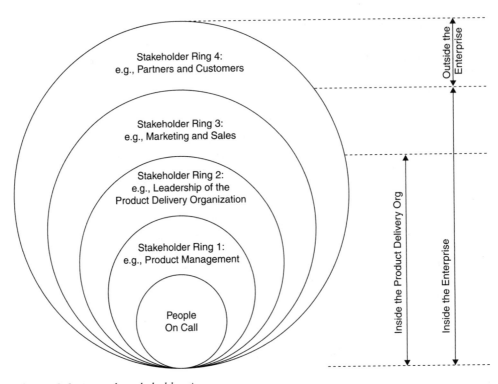

Figure 8.4 *Example stakeholder rings*

The middle of the figure shows the people on call. They obtain SLO breaches from the SRE infrastructure, set up notification rules for automated and semiautomated stakeholder notifications, and send out manual stakeholder notifications.

Exemplified as stakeholder ring 1 in the figure is product management. This stakeholder group is the first to be notified about outages. Based on some stakeholder notification escalation logic, stakeholder ring 2 may need to be notified. In the example, the leadership of the product delivery organization is part of stakeholder ring 2. The notification escalation logic may be based on the projected time to recover from an incident or the severity of the incident, among other factors.

Again, based on some stakeholder notification logic, stakeholder ring 3 may need to be notified. This is the first notification ring situated outside the product delivery organization. In the example, marketing and sales are part of stakeholder ring 3.

The stakeholder notification chain ends with stakeholder ring 4. This is the first notification ring situated outside the enterprise. Notifications to this ring also happen based on some notification escalation logic to be agreed in the product delivery organization and other enterprise functions. This will be a sensitive topic, because communication outside the enterprise might be subject to regulatory compliance and data protection regulations. It further might have an influence on stock price fluctuations and the business's reputation. In the example, partners and customers are part of stakeholder ring 4. Communication to this ring needs to be handled with the utmost of care.

Initially, the SRE coaches need to drive the definition of stakeholder rings 1, 2, and 3, and the agreements necessary for putting them into action. This should result in proper guidance for the people on call for sending stakeholder notifications by stakeholder ring. This guidance needs to be captured in the SRE wiki and confirmed as being understandable and useful by the people on call.

The definition of the stakeholder rings can be supported by setting up a corresponding stakeholder chart. This can be done in a similar fashion as was done at the beginning of the SRE transformation to define stakeholders necessary to rally support for getting SRE into the portfolio of organizational initiatives (see Section 5.4.1, *Stakeholder Chart*). The stakeholder chart for stakeholder rings needs to be part of the SRE wiki for future reference.

Overall, the prerequisites for enacting stakeholder notifications by stakeholder rings are as follows.

1. The initial set of stakeholder rings is defined.

2. The stakeholder rings are assigned stakeholder groups.

3. The agreements to enact the stakeholder rings are in place between the product delivery organization and other affected enterprise functions. These might be marketing, sales, communications, regulatory, and legal. It is important to note that the agreements within the product delivery organization are necessary but not sufficient for this purpose!

4. The guidance for using the stakeholder rings is created for the people on call.

5. The people on call confirm that the guidance is clear and can be used for sending out stakeholder notifications.

Once the prerequisites are fulfilled, the stakeholder notifications can be dispatched accordingly. This is set up and handled by the people on call. As soon as the stakeholder notifications are being sent to the stakeholder rings, the SRE coaches need to establish a feedback loop between the stakeholders receiving the notifications and the people on call who are sending them out, as illustrated in Figure 8.5.

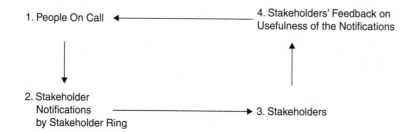

Figure 8.5 *Stakeholders' feedback on stakeholder notifications*

In step 1, the people on call set up automated and semiautomated stakeholder notifications, and they send out manual notifications. In step 2, all the notifications get dispatched to the stakeholders by the stakeholder ring using the on-call management tool. In step 3, the stakeholders receive the notifications. In step 4, the stakeholders are asked to provide feedback on the usefulness of the notifications. The feedback needs to be fed to the people on call.

Acting on the feedback may involve the following activities:

- Adapting stakeholder rings
- Adapting assignment of stakeholder groups to the stakeholder rings
- Adapting stakeholder groups
- Adapting assignment of stakeholders to the stakeholder groups
- Adapting the stakeholder notifications themselves

This is the point where the SRE coaches need to start handing over the responsibility for managing the feedback and stakeholder rings to the operations teams. This requires long-term engagement with people way beyond the product delivery organization within the enterprise. Therefore, it is best done by the people with permanent responsibility for the task.

In addition, the definition of stakeholder ring 4 (see Figure 8.4) should be driven by the operations teams as permanent owners of the stakeholder management process. This is because the definition of stakeholder ring 4 involves communication outside the enterprise. To enable this, many more departments and people need to be involved to ensure proper handling of regulatory, legal, branding, and reputational concerns. Achieving the agreements will take time. The permanent process owners are well suited to doing this by managing relationships with all the necessary departments on a long-term basis.

The people involved in the agreements, and the essence of the agreements themselves, need to be added to the SRE wiki next to the stakeholder chart for stakeholder rings. This is important for transparency, for having a single source of truth about the content of the agreements, for further agreement adaptations, and as an authorization to act for the people on call.

8.6 Defining Effective Stakeholder Notifications

Effective stakeholder notifications have four characteristics, summarized in Table 8.5.

Table 8.5 *Characteristics of Effective Stakeholder Notifications*

#	Characteristic	Explanation
1	Relevance	Effective stakeholder notifications are relevant. This means the dimensions of geography and product landscape are properly taken into account for a particular stakeholder.
2	Timeliness	Effective stakeholder notifications are timely. This means the stakeholders are the first to be informed about an issue directly by the stakeholder notification as opposed to indirectly finding out about it later from a customer, partner, executive, or peer.
		Moreover, the stakeholder notifications arrive in appropriate intervals so that they neither leave the stakeholders wondering what is going on waiting for an update nor overwhelm them with too many updates.

#	Characteristic	Explanation
3	Conciseness	Effective stakeholder notifications are concise. This means the notifications contain all the details necessary to fully inform a particular stakeholder about a particular issue, and only those details. In the majority of cases, the information is sufficient so as not to require the stakeholder to reach out to other people for more details.
4	Brackets	Effective stakeholder notifications are sent out in brackets. The first message of the bracket is about the announcement of a major outage. The last message of the bracket is about the announcement of the end of the major outage. Messages between the first and last brackets inform recipients about the progress being made on the way to recovery. Each message before the final message specifies roughly when the next stakeholder notification will be broadcast.

That is, an effective stakeholder notification is embedded in the overall stakeholder experience of the outage. Based on ongoing feedback from the stakeholders, the notifications need to be adapted to improve the four dimensions listed in Table 8.5.

Table 8.6 and Table 8.7 are examples of very simple stakeholder notification brackets for an outage.

Table 8.6 *First Stakeholder Notification in a Bracket*

First Stakeholder Notification	
Recipients	Stakeholder ring 1
Geography	Worldwide
Product landscape	All products
Message	No data uploads from most point-of-sale devices used for the showcase deployment after the most recent cloud deployment. Next notification is planned in max. 4 hours as events warrant.
Timestamp	01.12.2020 3.00pm UTC

Table 8.7 *Last Stakeholder Notification in a Bracket*

Last Stakeholder Notification	
Recipients	Stakeholder ring 1
Geography	Worldwide
Product landscape	All products
Message	Data uploads for all point-of-sale devices used for the showcase deployment are reinstated. A deployment with a bug fix was performed. Missing data since the outage will be reuploaded within 24 hours. No further communication planned for the issue.
Timestamp	01.12.2020 3.51pm UTC (Time to recovery: 51 minutes)

The message in Table 8.6 notifies the stakeholders from stakeholder ring 1 about data uploads from most point-of-sale devices used for the showcase deployment not taking place. This impacts many product demonstrations by product management, marketing, sales, and others. In stakeholder ring 1, only product management might be included.

The notification escalation logic might dictate notifying stakeholder ring 2 if the outage is not fixed within an hour. Stakeholder ring 2 might contain marketing and sales. However, as shown in Table 8.7, 51 minutes after the first notification is dispatched the last stakeholder notification is sent announcing full recovery from the outage. Therefore, stakeholder ring 2 is no longer notified in this case.

To kick off the process of defining stakeholder notifications for a service, the SRE coaches should start with the service's operations engineers, developers, and product owner. The starting point is to look at the defined SLOs and ask the following questions.

- Which of the defined SLOs, when broken, would represent a major service outage?

- Which roles would need to know about the outage?

- Why would they need the information about the outage?

- What would they do with the information about the outage?

- How do you craft a succinct message for the people to communicate the information about the outage in a self-contained and actionable way?

- Are there other scenarios not covered by SLOs that would represent major service outages?

The answers to these questions will give rise to the definition of an initial set of stakeholder notifications. Next, the SRE coaches need to organize a feedback session with people in all the roles intended to receive the notifications. For example, someone from marketing and someone from sales should be invited if some stakeholder notifications are intended for marketing and sales.

In the meeting, the SRE coaches should briefly explain the approach to stakeholder notifications. Then they should present the initial set of stakeholder notifications and ask the invitees to comment on each of them along the four characteristics of effective notifications outlined in Table 8.8.

Table 8.8 *Feedback Questions on Stakeholder Notifications*

#	Characteristic	Question
1	Relevance	Do you find the stakeholder notification relevant?
2	Timeliness	When would you like to receive the first notification?
3	Conciseness	Is the message concise and does it contain everything you would need to act on or be informed about without having to reach out to other people for more information?
4	Brackets	The stakeholder notification will be sent out in a bracket. The first notification will announce the outage, and the last one will announce the end of the outage. There may be some notifications between the first and last ones regarding the progress being made on the way to recovery from the outage. Is this way of being informed suitable for you? How frequently would you like to be updated on progress?

Based on the feedback, the initially defined stakeholder notifications can be adapted and extended. This is a great way to ensure that when the stakeholder notifications start arriving, their relevance, timeliness, conciseness, and brackets will make sense to the recipients. The defined notifications need to be put onto the SRE wiki in a new subsection, "Stakeholder notifications." The corresponding links need to be distributed to the people on call.

The people on call also need to add to their runbooks references to the stakeholder notification definitions in the SRE wiki. In the next runbook review, the stakeholder notifications need to be discussed to ensure that the people on call who were not involved in defining the notifications have sufficient context to send them out in a proper way. A recording of the conversation, if one took place online, can be embedded into the runbook for later reference by other people going on call.

8.7 Getting the Stakeholders Subscribed

Once the stakeholder groups, stakeholder rings, and stakeholder notifications are defined, set up in the on-call management tool, and reflected in runbooks, the SRE coaches need to engage with the respective recipient roles to explain the setup and associated tools. The central question to explore and get answered for the stakeholders at this point is: How do you subscribe to the stakeholder notifications?

For the stakeholder rings within the product delivery organization, the subscription to the stakeholder notifications will be handled via the on-call management tool. Typically, on-call management tools offer dedicated user accounts for stakeholders.

The stakeholder rings residing beyond the product delivery organization but still within the enterprise should be able to use either the on-call management tool or other, more common means, such as email or RSS feed. Stakeholders with a technical background might choose to receive stakeholder notifications in the on-call management tool, whereas those without such a background might prefer to receive them via email.

For stakeholder rings residing beyond the enterprise, the on-call management tool will not be a suitable option. This is because external partners and customers would have to have user accounts in order to use the tool. Usage is typically billed per user, which is not practical from a financial standpoint in the case of large numbers of partners and customers. Additionally, partners and stakeholders should not be forced to learn a new tool just to get stakeholder notifications from a service they selected to use. Therefore, it should be possible to receive stakeholder notifications via a common means of working on the internet, such as email, SMS, mobile push notifications, or RSS feed.

8.7.1 Subscribing Using the On-Call Management Tool

The SRE coaches should prepare the operations teams to run onboarding sessions for subscribers to stakeholder notifications in the on-call management tool. The onboarding sessions need to be targeted to nontechnical users. For example, onboarding product management leadership will be different from onboarding operations engineers and developers, which was previously done. If possible and practical, the onboarding sessions need to be conducted without using specific SRE or on-call management tool terminology.

With the onboarding of stakeholders, the number of user accounts in the on-call management tool will grow significantly. The operations teams need to plan capacity for increased administration efforts. At the same time, they need to create self-service onboarding documentation for stakeholders on the SRE wiki. The usefulness of the self-service documentation should be verified by the stakeholders. An indirect measure of the usefulness is the number of page views of the documentation pages on the SRE wiki over time.

Moreover, the operations teams need to plan a budget to cover procurement of new stakeholder licenses. To do so, they should estimate the number of stakeholder licenses required based on the stakeholder rings and stakeholder groups currently defined. A hiring projection for the enterprise might be another hint.

8.7.2 Subscribing Using Other Means

For subscribers using a more common means than the on-call management tool, it needs to be checked whether the tool offers the ability to subscribe to stakeholder notifications without having to create a user account.

Otherwise, an add-on to the SRE infrastructure sitting on top of the on-call management tool will be required. The add-on will need to take the stakeholder notifications residing inside the tool and dispatch them to the stakeholders using a means such as email or SMS, for instance.

Depending on the on-call management tool's technical setup, an add-on like that might be possible to implement without custom development by using workflow automation tools such as, for example, Zapier[1] or Power Automate.[2] Otherwise, custom development may be required to notify stakeholders using a means beyond the on-call management tool. There are products on the market that might be useful in this regard. For example, Statuspage[3] from Atlassian allows stakeholder notifications to be sent via email, mobile push notifications, and Twitter, among other methods.

The operations engineers should create corresponding self-service stakeholder onboarding documentation on the SRE wiki. The documentation should first explain to enterprise stakeholders how to subscribe and then explain to the enterprise's employees how to subscribe stakeholders outside the enterprise.

8.8 Broadcast Success

By now, many more people in many diverse roles have been involved in SRE activities. In fact, nontechnical roles that are far away from operations and development are now taking part in ongoing SRE activities as well! Information about outages is radiated throughout the enterprise in an ordered manner. Moreover, information about major outages is properly distributed to

---

1. Zapier. n.d. "The easiest way to automate your work." Accessed January 21, 2022. https://zapier.com.
2. Microsoft. n.d. "Power Automate." Accessed January 21, 2022. https://flow.microsoft.com.
3. Atlassian. n.d. "Statuspage." Accessed January 21, 2022. https://www.atlassian.com/software/statuspage.

partners and customers outside the enterprise under considerations of regulatory, legal, financial, and reputational concerns.

This creates a new level of alignment on operational concerns within the enterprise and beyond. Certainly, this is a success that needs to be broadcast! The SRE coaches should organize this broadcast. Channels that proved successful for broadcasting in the past should be reused.

The following questions can guide the SRE coaches in putting together a concise broadcast on the progress of the SRE transformation.

- How was the information about outages distributed within the enterprise and beyond in the past?

- How is the information about outages distributed within the enterprise and beyond with the new alert dispatching?

- What are the typical escalation policies for alerts on SLO breaches?

- What are the defined stakeholder groups?

- What are the defined stakeholder rings?

- What is the stakeholder notification escalation logic through the stakeholder rings?

- How many stakeholders have subscribed to notifications by the stakeholder group?

- What is the feedback on the stakeholder notifications from the stakeholders?

Having some of the stakeholders be part of the broadcast and telling a good story about how their work was improved with the introduced stakeholder notifications is a great way to build credibility right into the broadcast.

In addition, the current state of progress on the SRE transformation hypotheses should be highlighted in the presentation (see Section 4.7, *Posing Hypotheses*). Are there outcomes that have been achieved and can be measured using the defined measurable signals? Do the hypotheses need to be adapted? Is there a need for new hypotheses?

A set of next steps defined for the SRE transformation is a good way to finish the broadcast. The recording of the broadcast should be put onto the internal video sharing platform, tagged with "SRE," and linked from the SRE wiki.

Finally, the stakeholders of the SRE transformation should be informed about the achievements in accordance with the defined stakeholder chart.

8.9 Summary

In this chapter, I discussed alert dispatching in a broad sense. Alerts on SLO breaches are dispatched to the people on call so that they can fix the issues and bring the services back within the SLOs. Propagation of the alerts on SLO breaches between the people on call and beyond is done using an escalation policy.

Another category of alerts are notifications for stakeholders within the enterprise. These are dispatched to the stakeholders by relevance so that they are informed about major outages before the impact becomes visible to the outside world. Stakeholder notifications can be sent in an automated, semiautomated, or manual fashion. For the stakeholder notifications to be targeted well, stakeholder groups need to be defined. For the stakeholder notifications to radiate between the stakeholder groups in a properly ordered manner, stakeholder rings need to be defined. A stakeholder ring can contain several stakeholder groups. The stakeholder notification escalation logic between the rings needs to be defined as well.

A special agreement between the product delivery organization and other relevant enterprise functions needs to be established to notify stakeholders outside the enterprise. These stakeholders are typically partners and customers. Making notifications outside the enterprise will have regulatory, financial, reputational, and business implications. It therefore needs to be done with the utmost of care. At the same time, communicating proactively about outages is a great way to build trust with the stakeholders.

Chapter 9

Implementing Incident Response

By now the teams have defined SLOs in an iterative manner, implemented on-call rotations to react to SLO breaches, and set up stakeholder notifications to keep stakeholders abreast of major outages. With that, the basics of an incident response process are laid down in the product delivery organization: Incidents are being detected and worked on by the teams, and the stakeholders are being informed about major outages before customers complain.

The next evolutionary step in the incident response process is to define an incident classification scheme and set up appropriate responses based on incident class. This involves combining all the tools involved in streamlining the work, broadcasting the service status, and implementing postmortems with effective learning procedures. These points are the subject of this chapter.

9.1 Incident Response Foundations

To begin, let us look at the widely available definitions of the terms "incident" and "incident response." According to Wikipedia, "An incident is an event that could lead to loss of, or disruption to, an organization's operations, services or functions."[1]

According to Digital Guardian, "Incident response is a term used to describe the process by which an organization handles a data breach or cyberattack, including the way the organization attempts to manage the consequences of the attack or breach (the 'incident')."[2]

The ITIL framework, discussed in Chapter 1, defines an incident as "an unplanned interruption to or quality reduction of an IT service. The service level agreements (SLA) define the agreed-upon service level between the provider and the customer."[3]

ITIL specifies a detailed incident response process. It includes five steps:

1. Incident identification

2. Incident logging

1. Wikipedia. 2021. "Incident management." https://en.wikipedia.org/wiki/Incident_management.

2. Digital Guardian. 2015. "What Is Incident Response?" https://digitalguardian.com/blog/what-incident-response.

3. BMC Blogs. n.d. "ITIL Incident Management: An Introduction." Accessed January 21, 2022. https://www.bmc.com/blogs/itil-v3-incident-management.

3. Incident categorization

4. Incident prioritization

5. Incident response

   ○ Initial diagnosis

   ○ Incident escalation

   ○ Investigation and diagnosis

   ○ Resolution and recovery

   ○ Incident closure

With the SRE methodology in place, the preceding steps are covered to some degree. The goal of defining an incident response process is to strengthen the points where necessary to achieve a robust and repeatable process for handling incidents. The process needs to be defendable in audits of various kinds. This generally means it needs to be written down and adhered to. Further, the evidence of process adherence needs to be produced on request.

In light of the ITIL incident response process, the discussions in the previous chapters were focused on the following:

- Incident identification and logging by means of defining SLOs and SLO breaches

- Incident diagnosis, investigation, resolution, and recovery by means of analyzing SLO breaches and fixing the services to bring them back within the SLOs

- Incident escalation by means of escalation policies

What the discussions in the previous chapters were not directly focused on are incident categorization and prioritization. This is the subject of the next section.

9.2 Incident Priorities

So far, the SLOs and, consequently, the SLO breaches were not assigned explicit priorities. This does not mean the teams did not prioritize them internally. They probably did, in order to know which SLO breaches are more important than others and to act accordingly. To strengthen the incident response process, more consistent, explicit, and transparent SLO prioritization needs to take place.

To kick off the process, the SRE coaches need to initiate a generic definition of incident priorities for the product delivery organization. The teams will use the generically defined incident priorities to categorize their SLOs accordingly within the unique context of their domain. This will result in cross-domain standardization of incident priorities used by all the teams in the organization. Whenever someone is talking about an incident with a given priority, it will mean the same to everyone. That is, what is sought are generic, organization-wide incident priorities, and a mapping between them and team-local SLOs (see Figure 9.1).

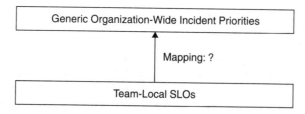

Figure 9.1 *Organization-wide incident priorities versus team-local SLOs*

With the mapping, the teams will be able to set incident priorities for SLOs in a uniform manner across the organization, as illustrated in Figure 9.2.

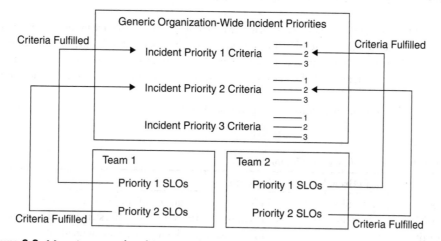

Figure 9.2 *Mapping team-local SLOs to the organization-wide incident priorities*

The upper part of Figure 9.2 shows the generic organization-wide incident priorities. Three incident priorities are defined, and each definition has a set of criteria. A broken SLO must fulfill the criteria of an incident priority for it to be assigned.

The lower part of Figure 9.2 shows two teams. Team 1, on the left, analyzed their SLOs and the organization-wide incident priorities. Following this, they categorized their SLOs. Some SLOs, when broken, fulfill the incident priority 1 criteria. Other SLOs, when broken, fulfill the incident priority 2 criteria. Incident priorities 1 and 2 are therefore assigned to the corresponding SLOs.

The same analysis and categorization of broken SLOs into incident priorities is done in team 2, depicted in the lower-right part of the figure. Teams 1 and 2 operate in different domains. Following this, their SLOs and SLO breaches have different meanings within their domains. However, the incident priorities assigned to the broken SLO are uniform for both teams. Whenever a priority 1 incident occurs based on an SLO breach, it fulfills the same generic criteria in both teams.

In terms of tool support, setting incident priorities is supported by all common on-call management tools available on the market. Moreover, the incident priorities can be used as criteria to notify the stakeholders. This can be done by stakeholder groups and stakeholder rings.

9.2.1 SLO Breaches Versus Incidents

The organization-wide incident priorities need to be defined in a distinct way without overlap between them. This is necessary to ensure unique assignments of SLOs to the incident priorities. Based on the unique incident priority assigned to an SLO, all incidents based on the breaches of that SLO should be assigned the incident priority. The people on call can do this either automatically or manually. Figure 9.3 illustrates the cardinalities of the relationships between the incident priority, SLO, and SLO breaches.

Incident Priority $\underset{1}{\overline{\hspace{3cm}}}_{1}$ SLO $\underset{1}{\overline{\hspace{3cm}}}_{n}$ SLO Breaches

Figure 9.3 *Incident priority versus SLO breaches*

An SLO has exactly one incident priority assignment. An SLO can have many SLO breaches. All SLO breaches of an SLO get the SLO's incident priority assigned when the breach occurred. As the incident unfolds, the people on call may change its priority based on the situational context and their judgment of the matter. The incident priority may get lowered or elevated as a result.

At this point, it is important to delineate the SLO breaches and incidents. Table 9.1 compares the two.

Table 9.1 *SLO Breaches Versus Incidents*

	SLO Breach	Incident
Where It Is Created as an Entity	In the SRE infrastructure	In the on-call management tool based on the SLO breach trigger from the SRE infrastructure. That is, the SLO breach precedes and triggers an incident.
Incident Priority	The SLO incident priority (does not get changed during an incident)	On incident creation, the incident priority is based on the SLO's incident priority. During the incident, the incident priority can be changed based on the decisions by the people on call.
Incident Priority Assignment	Ideally done as part of the SLO definition process	On incident creation based on an SLO breach trigger from the SRE infrastructure, incident priority assignment can be done automatically (preferred) or manually. After incident creation, incident priority assignment can be done by the people on call manually or semiautomatically via runbook automation.

Figure 9.4 points out how an SLO breach turns into an incident. The lower part of the figure shows the SRE infrastructure. For each SLO, the infrastructure contains a mapping between the SLO and its incident priority. The SRE infrastructure needs to support the incident priority

specification. The SRE coaches need to stage the implementation of that feature in the SRE infrastructure by the operations teams to be done in time for the incident priorities being defined by the teams owning the services.

In step 1, the SRE infrastructure detects an SLO breach. Following that, the SRE infrastructure sends the details of the SLO breach (e.g., deployment, endpoint, SLI, etc.) together with the SLO incident priority to the on-call management tool.

In step 2, the on-call management tool creates an incident based on the SLO breach. In step 3, the incident is assigned the SLO's incident priority passed by the SRE infrastructure. If the SRE infrastructure does not pass an SLO incident priority for the SLO breach, the on-call management tool does not assign a priority to the created incident, and it is up to the people on call to manually assign the priority later. In step 4, the on-call management tool notifies the people on call who can assign the priority. Finally, the people on call can start investigating the SLO breach.

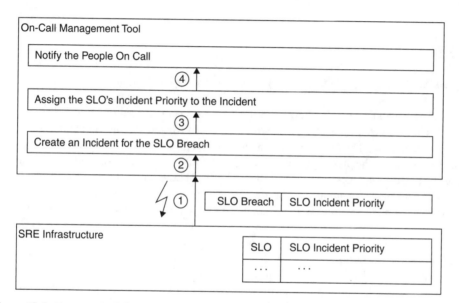

Figure 9.4 *From an SLO breach to a dispatched incident*

9.2.2 Changing Incident Priority During an Incident

During an incident investigation, the people on call may change the incident priority based on ongoing learnings, refined context, and new details. Figure 9.5 illustrates an example of how the incident priority can change during an incident.

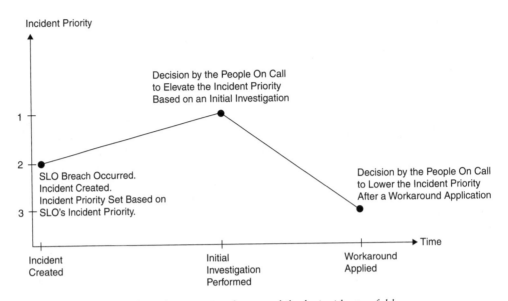

Figure 9.5 *Example of incident priority changes while the incident unfolds*

On the left-hand side of Figure 9.5, an incident was created based on an SLO breach. The SLO breach is detected by the SRE infrastructure, which triggers the on-call management tool to create an incident. The on-call management tool creates the incident and notifies the people on call according to the previously set schedules and notification methods. While the incident is being created, its priority is set to that of the SLO's. The SLO's incident priority is passed to the on-call management tool along with the SLO breach trigger, which is set to 2.

The people on call are notified and begin investigating the SLO breach. After an initial investigation, they decide that the situation is worse than the incident priority indicated; that is, more customers will be affected and for a longer period than originally thought when the SLO's incident priority was set. A hotfix will have to be rolled out as soon as possible. Therefore, the people on call decide to elevate the incident priority from 2 to 1.

The people on call continue the investigation. It turns out that a workaround might be able to be applied very quickly to temporarily alleviate the user impact. If it works, the hotfix may not have to be rolled out immediately. After the workaround is applied, the broken use case starts working again. To reflect this, the people on call decide to lower the incident priority.

9.2.3 Defining Generic Incident Priorities

Incident priorities need to be defined so that it is easy for a person on call to dynamically decide on an incident priority as the incident unfolds. The decisions may need to take place in the middle of the night. Therefore, the set of criteria for an incident priority should be very short. Generally, more than five criteria per incident priority will slow down the decision-making process for the people on call, and should be avoided.

Each criterion should be defined in a succinct and precise manner reflecting the terms commonly used in the organization and understood by everyone unambiguously.

To drive the definition of generic incident priorities, the SRE coaches need to start with the operations teams. They might already have some incident priority definitions (e.g., because of ITIL implementation). If so, they need to be examined to ensure they are suitable for the purpose at hand: classifying and unifying the meaning and associated actions for various incidents in production.

The SRE coaches with the operations teams need to propose a small set of incident priorities with a proportionally small set of criteria describing each priority. The incident priorities should provide direction on the following dimensions.

- Which actions must be taken?

- Who has to be informed about the issue and the actions being taken?

Purely as an example, the incident priorities proposed might look like those shown in Table 9.2.

Table 9.2 *Sample Incident Priorities*

#	Criteria	Incident Priority 1	Incident Priority 2	Incident Priority 3
1	Hotfix	Yes	No	No
2	Postmortem	Yes	No	No
3	Management notification	Yes	Yes	No
4	Stakeholder notifications	Yes	Yes	Yes
5	Status update	Every two hours	Every four hours	Every six hours
	Generic example	No log-on possible to any application	More than 70% drop in average daily user log-ons to an application in a data center	Demo data not available in the showcase deployment

Incident priority 1 describes situations that require an immediate hotfix rollout and a later postmortem. The product delivery organization's management team and the stakeholders need to be notified about the outage. The teams themselves select the stakeholder groups when assigning priorities to the SLOs. Incidents with a priority of 1 represent outages with severe customer impact. Therefore, these incident status updates need to be broadcast to the stakeholders every two hours.

A generic example of an incident with priority 1 would be when no log-on to any application is possible (think: Amazon or Twitter log-on does not work). Concrete examples of priority 1 incidents will be defined team by team in their respective domains when they go through their SLOs to find the ones that, when broken, would correspond to the five criteria in Table 9.2.

Next, incident priority 2 describes situations that do not require a hotfix to be rolled out. Likewise, no postmortem is required. However, these situations deserve some attention from management and stakeholders. Therefore, notifications to them are required and need to be sent out every four hours.

A generic example of a priority 2 incident is when an application experiences a more than 70% drop in average daily user log-ons in a data center. In this situation, the reasons for the drop in log-ons may be manifold. It might be because a festival being held in the region is taking people away from their work, and therefore they are not using the application because the application only applies to situations in business settings. It might be because internet connectivity in the region was impacted due to a natural disaster. Or it might be because of a network slowdown in the region with the cloud provider of choice, which can be rectified only by the cloud provider itself. In situations like these, the stakeholders and the management team need to be aware of the outage and receive a progress update every four hours. More, however, cannot be done by the product delivery organization if the reasons for the drop in number of log-ons are beyond their control.

Also, for priority 2, the concrete examples of potential incidents will be defined by individual teams. They will identify these use cases by looking at their SLOs and correlating them to the five criteria for the priority 2 incident.

Finally, incident priority 3 describes situations where no hotfix, postmortem, or management notification is required. However, the issue at hand is affecting the work of customers or stakeholders to the point where specific stakeholder notifications need to be broadcast to make them aware of the issue ahead of time. The issue is not that pressing. Therefore, status updates every eight hours should be sufficient.

For example, if the demo data suddenly becomes unavailable in the showcase deployment that product management, marketing, and sales use for demonstration purposes, they need to be notified about it. Other stakeholders who do not use the showcase deployment do not need the notification.

As with the other two incident priorities, the incident priority 3 use cases become concrete when the teams browse through their SLOs and classify them according to the five criteria in Table 9.2.

The SRE coaches should ensure that the initial proposal of generic incident priorities does not contain more than five priorities. Each priority should not be defined using more than five criteria. Simplicity and unambiguity are more important than precision and detailedness here. With the initial proposal of generic incident priorities, the SRE coaches should run feedback sessions with some development teams who are ready to start thinking about that. A development team is ready for the definition of incident priorities when they

- Have defined SLOs in an iterative manner

- Have an on-call rotation in place

- Use the on-call management tool

- Are looking to streamline their incident response process by prioritizing SLO breaches

With feedback from a couple of development teams, the generic incident priorities should be revised and refined. If the changes are not small, another round of review with the involved development and operations teams needs to take place until the priorities are finally agreed upon.

The moment when the incident priorities can be declared as finalized needs to be chosen carefully. This is because many development teams will start classifying their SLO breaches based on the incident priority definitions. Later changes to the definitions will require effort in all development teams that build on top of them. Although the teams should be open to the changes in general, it is best not to change defined generic incident priorities frequently.

The purpose of the incident priorities is also to prioritize the processing of incidents by the people on call in case more than one incident is occurring. As the incident priority numbers suggest, priority 1 incidents are processed first, priority 2 incidents are processed second, and priority 3 incidents are processed third. Following this, in cases when more than one incident is occurring, the time to recover from priority 1 incidents will be shorter than that required to recover from priority 2 incidents. Likewise, the time to recover from priority 2 incidents will be shorter than that required to recover from priority 3 incidents.

The final definition of the generic incident priorities, and how to use them, needs to be put onto the SRE wiki. This way, the teams can easily reference the definition while prioritizing their SLOs.

9.2.4 Mapping SLOs to Incident Priorities

With the generic incident priorities defined, the SRE coaches should bring the topic of prioritizing the SLO breaches to the development teams that are ready, in order to streamline the incident response process. This can be done in the regular SRE coaching sessions.

For example, let us imagine a team responsible for services that can send notifications to users via different media channels, such as an in-app overlay in mobile apps, notification center entries, email, and so on. The team might have SLOs for the use cases shown in Table 9.3.

Table 9.3 *Sample SLO Use Cases in a Team*

#	SLO Use Case	SLI
1	Application cannot register with notification services	Availability
2	Application cannot notify its users	Availability
3	Notifications arrive with a delay	Latency
4	Notification preferences cannot be set	Availability
5	Notifications are sent in the wrong language	Correctness
...	...	...

For each SLO, the team needs to decide what incident priority they think is appropriate when the respective SLO gets broken. For instance, the team might make these decisions using the sample incident priorities from the previous section, as shown in Table 9.4.

Table 9.4 *Sample Assignment of SLOs to Incident Priorities*

#	SLO	Incident Priority
1	Application cannot register with notification services	2
2	Application cannot notify its users	2
3	Notifications arrive with a delay	3
4	Notification preferences cannot be set	None
5	Notifications are sent in the wrong language	None

The team decided not to use incident priority 1 for any SLOs because the services sending notifications to users are not critical in the product's domain. Incident priority 2 is set for SLO 1 and SLO 2: when an application cannot register with notification services or cannot notify its users. These use cases require stakeholders and management to be notified about the issues so that they are informed before customer escalations occur.

Incident priority 3 is assigned to SLO 3: when notifications arrive with a delay. Some stakeholders need to know about this because for their application use cases, the arrival of notifications in near-real time is important. For example, for marketers demonstrating the notification services to customers, it is important for a sample notification to arrive within 4 to 8 seconds of it being sent. Otherwise, the demonstration might lose its credibility.

Finally, for SLOs 4 and 5, no incident priority is set. The team made that decision because in cases when notification preferences cannot be set or notifications are set in the wrong language, no stakeholder needs to be notified. This is because these use cases are rarely exercised in practice, and the notification preferences are rarely changed. Typically, this happens once, when an application is set up. Notifications sent in the wrong language happen very rarely based on the experience in the team. If they happen, they usually can be fixed quickly. The people on call will still work on the breaches of SLOs 4 and 5 but only after the incidents with defined priorities have been resolved.

The exercise of setting the incident priorities undertaken by the team might give rise to additional requests to the SRE infrastructure. For example, a team might conclude that a use case, when broken once, would warrant a priority 4 incident. However, when broken more than three times within an hour, it would warrant a priority 2 incident. Requests like this should be carefully collected and put onto the SRE infrastructure backlog for the operations teams to prioritize and work on. Additionally, the need to support new SLIs or new ways to measure existing SLIs can be uncovered while deciding on incident priorities for SLOs.

The SLOs' incident priorities set by the teams need to be set in the SRE infrastructure. The priorities need to be made public for reference by everyone in the product delivery organization. The reference to the SLO priorities in the SRE infrastructure also needs to be added to the runbooks so that they are readily available for the people on call.

Additionally, it is beneficial to have the reference to the SLO incident priorities available on the SRE wiki. This is because verbose comments about the reasons for choosing an incident priority can be added there. The reasons are very valuable because they enable the development teams to get feedback on their incident priority choices by the stakeholders who might be affected.

Moreover, for the teams themselves, it is important to keep a record of why incident priority choices were made, both to put everyone on the same page and for onboarding new team members. Without recorded reasons for incident priority choices, it is often difficult to explain them later. This may well be necessary because an incident priority choice governs the actions by the people on call while responding to severe incidents. Why a certain action was performed during an outage is a common question in postmortems. The ability to refer not only to the incident priority but also to the reasons that led to the decision about the priority is very valuable in this context. Therefore, the SLOs' incident priority choices should be recorded similar to architectural decisions, which can be recorded in a lightweight manner using, for example, architectural decision records.[4]

9.2.5 Mapping Error Budgets to Incident Priorities

It may be possible to generically map domain use cases in the teams to incident priorities as a function of error budget depletion for a given SLO breach. In this case, the SRE infrastructure could assign the incident priorities automatically to SLO breach-based incidents instead of the teams manually setting them in advance. Table 9.5 shows an example.

Table 9.5 *Mapping Error Budget Depletion Thresholds to Incident Priorities*

Incident Priority	Use Case Expressed as Error Budget Depletion Threshold on SLO Breach
Priority 1	20% of the error budget is left within a given time unit, and with the current error budget depletion trend, the error budget will be exhausted prematurely.
Priority 2	40% of the error budget is left within a given time unit, and with the current error budget depletion trend, the error budget will be exhausted prematurely.
Priority 3	60% of the error budget is left within a given time unit, and with the current error budget depletion trend, the error budget will be exhausted prematurely.
Priority 4	80% of the error budget is left within a given time unit, and with the current error budget depletion trend, the error budget will be exhausted prematurely.

Another example might be to map the error budget depletion velocity per time unit to incident priorities, as shown in Table 9.6.

---

4. ADR GitHub. n.d. "Architectural Decision Records." Accessed January 21, 2022. https://adr.github.io.

Table 9.6 *Mapping Error Budget Depletion Velocity to Incident Priorities*

Incident Priority	Use Case Expressed as Error Budget Depletion Velocity on SLO Breach
Priority 1	More than 75% of the monthly error budget was depleted within five consecutive minutes.
Priority 2	More than 50% of the monthly error budget was depleted within 10 consecutive minutes.
Priority 3	More than 25% of the monthly error budget was depleted within 15 consecutive minutes.
Priority 4	More than 25% of the monthly error budget was depleted within 20 consecutive minutes.

Although technically feasible, this seems to be too mechanical to be applied generally and reflect reality well. However, this kind of logic might be an idea to explore to set incident priorities for the SLO breaches whose SLOs do not have an explicit incident priority assigned. It would represent a default incident priority similar to default SLOs (see Section 6.7, *Default SLOs*).

An additional reason for the aforementioned approach not being generally applicable is that it requires everything to be measured through proper SLIs and nothing through resource-based alerts. Achieving that level of maturity requires an extensive SRE infrastructure, which will not be available at the beginning of the SRE transformation. Therefore, to begin, expressing incident priorities using team-based use cases created based on a definition of generic incident priorities will be a more viable option.

The SRE coaches should be able to see the possibility for the error budget depletion-based incident priority setting when working with all teams on setting the SLO incident priorities. If the possibility is crystallizing, the coaches should invite some representatives from the operations and development teams to brainstorm the matter.

9.2.6 Mapping Resource-Based Alerts to Incident Priorities

When the SRE coaches guide a team through their SLOs to define incident priorities for them, only the use cases covered by the SLOs are considered. To broaden the scope of coverage by the incident priorities, the SRE coaches should also encourage the teams to go through the resource-based alerts they might have and assign incident priorities to them, as well. The assignment works much the same way as with the SLOs.

The resource-based alerts go directly to the on-call management tool, bypassing the SRE infrastructure. Therefore, the incident priority can be set either automatically based on logic to be implemented in the on-call management tool, or manually by the people on call.

The defined incident priorities for the resource-based alerts, along with the associated reasoning, should be put onto the SRE wiki next to the incident priorities for SLOs. The corresponding runbooks should be updated as well.

As the SRE infrastructure matures and starts supporting the use cases currently covered by the resource-based alerts, these alerts should be replaced with proper SLOs. Doing so enables a whole host of improvements out of the box. These are shown in Figure 9.6.

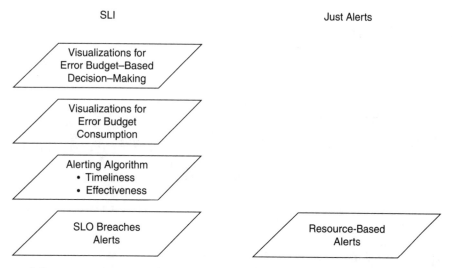

Figure 9.6 *SLIs versus resource-based alerts*

With the switch from resource-based alerts to alerts on SLO breaches, the alerting algorithm implemented in the SRE infrastructure is used to send out the alerts. It does not alert immediately on every SLO breach, but rather implements features of timeliness, effectiveness, and others to strike a good balance in order to reduce alert fatigue. Moreover, visualizations of error budget depletions are enabled. Likewise, additional visualizations for error budget–based decision–making are unlocked.

To make sure the development teams know about the new features in the SRE infrastructure that can be used to switch from resource-based alerts to the SLIs and SLOs, the operations teams need to establish appropriate broadcast mechanisms. The new features need to be well described for self-service consumption in the SRE wiki. Presentations of the new features need to take place within the SRE CoP. The recordings of the presentations need to be embedded in the SRE wiki. Occasionally, broader presentations such as lean coffee sessions need to be done as well to announce bigger infrastructure enhancements, allowing whole sets of resource-based alerts to be replaced by SLIs and SLOs in many teams.

The SRE coaches need to make sure the teams understand the difference between resource-based alerts and SLIs/SLOs. It needs to be clear that the goal is to reduce the number of resource-based alerts and increase the use of SLIs/SLOs over time. That is, the goal is to move from just alerts to proper indicators (SLIs) that support user-centric reliability decision-making in a data-driven way. Doing so is also recommended in *Implementing Service Level Objectives*.[5]

---

5. Hidalgo, Alex. 2020. *Implementing Service Level Objectives: A Practical Guide to SLIs, SLOs & Error Budgets*. Sebastopol, CA: O'Reilly Media.

9.2.7 Uncovering New Use Cases for Incident Priorities

In the previous sections, the existing SLOs and resource-based alerts were mapped to generic incident priorities resulting in a classification of outages across SLO breaches and resource-based alerts. Regardless of the outage reporting source, the actions to be taken are normalized based on the incident priority.

In addition to mapping the existing SLOs and resource-based alerts to the generic incident priorities, the definition of the priorities can be used as a source of inspiration to define new alert use cases not yet covered. This is shown in Figure 9.7.

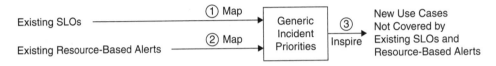

Figure 9.7 *Using generic incident priorities to inspire new alert use cases*

The SRE coaches should encourage the teams to use the incident priority definitions to uncover new use cases (see point 3 in Figure 9.7). This can be done as follows.

1. Take the definition of generic incident priorities.

2. For each incident priority, think about new use cases in the team's domain not covered by existing monitoring that would warrant actions stipulated by the priority.

3. For each use case discovered in this way, think about how it could be monitored:

   ○ Could it be monitored by a new SLO of an existing SLI?

   ○ Could it be monitored by a new SLO of a new SLI?

   ○ Could it be monitored by a new resource-based alert?

An analysis like this is going to uncover the need for new SLIs or new ways to measure existing SLIs to be supported by the SRE infrastructure. These requests should go directly to the SRE infrastructure backlog for the operations teams. To cover the use cases that are relevant but not yet supported by the current SRE infrastructure, resource-based alerts should be defined and handled as described in the previous section.

9.2.8 Adjusting Incident Priorities Based on Stakeholder Feedback

So far, the development teams defined the incident priorities for SLOs and resource-based alerts. This is the necessary starting point for defining priorities. The next step is to get stakeholder feedback on the priorities and adjust them as necessary. The SRE coaches need to organize these feedback sessions. The sessions are necessary to reconcile the views of service providers and service consumers regarding the incident priority of a given outage.

Service provider teams defined the incident priorities based on their understanding of the importance of a given functionality to an average consumer of the service. Because of the plurality of service consumers, each potentially operating in a separate subdomain, different consumers will have different views on the incident priority for an outage of a given functionality, as illustrated in Figure 9.8.

Figure 9.8 *Service provider's and service consumers' views on incident priorities*

Coming back to the example with notification services from Section 9.2.4, *Mapping SLOs to Incident Priorities*, sending notifications to users might be implemented in several teams. In the domain of service consumer 1, sending notifications to users might be the most critical functionality. If it does not work, the functionality has to be reinstated immediately. Therefore, the service consumer 1 team would like to assign incident priority 1 to outages indicating that user notifications cannot be sent (referencing the sample incident priority 1 from Section 9.2.3, *Defining Generic Incident Priorities*).

Service consumer 2's team might be consuming the notification services in an entirely different domain. In that domain, sending notifications might be a nice add-on feature. If it does not work, the core functionality is not affected. This team would like to assign incident priority 3 to incidents indicating that user notifications cannot be sent (referencing the sample incident priority 3 from Section 9.2.3, *Defining Generic Incident Priorities*).

To the service provider, it seems appropriate to set the incident priority of outages indicating that the user notification cannot be sent to 2. The different views on the incident priority are summarized in Table 9.7.

Table 9.7 *Sample Views on the Incident Priority of an SLO Breach*

SLO Breach Use Case	Service Provider's View on the Incident Priority	Service Consumer 1's View on the Incident Priority	Service Consumer 2's View on the Incident Priority
Application cannot notify users	2	1	3

Certainly, Table 9.7 will be different depending on the domains and the number of service consumers taking part in the feedback session. Generally, the feedback session is for the service provider team to reflect on their incident priority decision using the priorities the service consumer teams would like to set to the functionality in question.

In a bigger service network of a microservices architecture or a public API used by many third parties, it will not be possible to ask all the stakeholders. It follows that the feedback on the incident priorities will be orientational at most. Still, iterating on the orientational feedback is better than soliciting no feedback at all.

The final decision about the incident priority after considering the feedback from the stakeholders remains with the service provider team. It is their service and service incidents, after all. The final decision needs to be reflected in the SRE infrastructure and be made public.

Based on the decision, the service consumer teams might implement a different strategy for coping with a given outage. The strategy might be defined along the dimensions shown in Table 9.8.

Table 9.8 *Strategy Dimensions for Coping with Dependent Service Outages*

Strategy Dimension	Explanation
Adaptive capacity	The amount of adaptive capacity between a service consumer and a service provider can be increased if the incident priority from the consumer point of view should be higher than that set by the service provider. This is because the service provider will fix the respective outages with lower priority than the priority wished for by the service consumer. This is going to lead to a longer time to recover from the outages. During that time, the users of the service consumer need to be kept operational with degraded functionality.
Stakeholder notifications	If the incident priority from the consumer point of view should be higher than that set by the service provider, the service consumer might wish to implement a stakeholder group to notify their people on call when there is an outage in the service provider. The people on call in the service consumer team will evaluate the outage notification and, if degraded functionality cannot be provided, might decide to notify their own stakeholders about the outage, rephrasing it for their domain.

Overall, the incident priority set in a particular use case will need to be evaluated as part of postmortems. Additionally, as discussed in Section 9.2.2, *Changing Incident Priority During an Incident*, incident priority can be changed dynamically as incidents unfold. This needs to be taken into account when deciding on the initial incident priority for a use case. This also needs to be made clear to the stakeholders when soliciting their feedback.

9.2.9 Extending the SLO Definition Process

In the teams that defined incident priorities for their existing SLOs once, the SLO definition process can be extended in the future. Right after a new SLO is set, its associated incident priority can be set by the team using the generic incident priority definitions.

It needs to be noted that this is only beneficial for the teams that are further ahead on the SRE transformation journey. Teams that are only defining initial SLOs are not yet ready for incident priority definition. They are fully absorbed by the technicalities and newness of the SLO-based approach to reliability (see Section 6.6, *Defining Initial SLOs*). Trying to define incident priorities in addition to the initial SLOs themselves is a distraction at the moment.

Moreover, the incident priorities are there to prioritize the processing of the SLO breaches by a team. If a team is just learning how to react to SLO breaches, does not have an on-call rotation, and has not repeatedly encountered a problem with many SLO breaches waiting to be processed at the same time, the time has not yet come for the team to define incident priorities. Doing so would only confuse the team with additional new terminology and tools at a time when they should be learning to master the basics of reacting to SLO breaches.

9.2.10 Infrastructure

With SLO breach-based alerts and resource-based alerts being the origins for incidents, the entire infrastructure setup is growing a bit more complex. It is shown in its entirety in Figure 9.9. The bottom of the figure shows three pieces of infrastructure. The application performance management facility observes the resources and generates resource-based alerts on thresholds. Some of them go to the on-call management tool for incident creation. Others go to the SRE infrastructure for SLO breach recording. The SRE infrastructure records the SLO breaches; augments them with the necessary parameters, including SLO incident priority; and sends them to the on-call management tool for incident creation. The SLO breaches can additionally be triggered by the logging facility based on log query results.

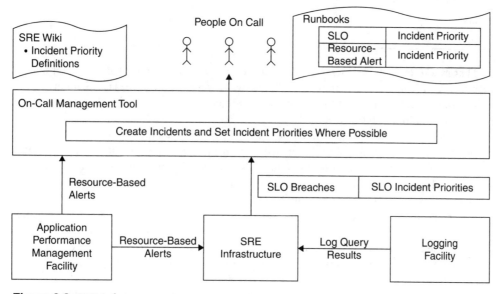

Figure 9.9 *SRE infrastructure setup*

The middle of Figure 9.9 shows the on-call management tool. It creates incidents based on resource-based alerts from the application performance management facility or SLO breaches from the SRE infrastructure. Where possible, the on-call management tool automatically assigns the incident priority. In the figure, this is done for the SLO breaches.

Once an incident is created, it is dispatched to the people on call, who use runbooks to manually set incident priorities where necessary and applicable. The SRE wiki is used for general reference of incident priority definitions. The actions associated with setting each incident priority are specified there in a generic fashion. The associated actions are important to have handy because the people on call can dynamically change the incident priority as the incident unfolds, which should prompt a change of actions.

9.2.11 Deduplication

Incidents originate from SLO breaches and resource-based alerts. Both have a characteristic that they may occur many times for the same root causes as the incident unfolds. For resource-based alerts, an alert is sent every time a resource threshold is reached. For example, for an alert on CPU consumption in a virtual machine, the alert settings may be done as shown in Table 9.9.

Table 9.9 *Example Settings for a Resource-Based Alert on CPU Consumption*

Setting	Operator	Value
Host	=	ABC
CPU	>	90%
Aggregation	Average	15 minutes
Evaluation frequency	=	5 minutes
Alert	=	Immediate
Name	=	"CPU > 90% on host ABC"

That is, a resource-based alert like this will fire every time the average CPU consumption is over 90% for 15 minutes. The sampling will be done every 5 minutes for the last 15 minutes. The alert with the name "CPU > 90% on host ABC" will be generated immediately after the sampling if the condition is fulfilled.

As shown in the previous section, the alert will be turned into an incident in the on-call management tool. The incident will be dispatched to the people on call, who will start looking into the reasons for the high CPU consumption. If they cannot fix the issue within 15 minutes, a second incident will arrive for the same issue. If the issue is not fixed within 15 minutes, a third incident will arrive for the same issue, and so on.

This behavior only increases cognitive load for the people on call without adding any value. To avoid an accumulation of incidents with the same root causes, most on-call management tools provide features for incident deduplication. Typically, text pattern matching for a field in the incident can be used to do the deduplication. In the preceding example, the name of the alert, "CPU > 90% on host ABC", can be used to deduplicate the incidents.

The on-call management tool can be instructed to only have one open incident with the alert name "CPU > 90% on host ABC" at all times. This way, the people on call will not be bombarded with a growing number of incidents with the same root cause. Typically, on-call management tools add a counter to the incidents that shows how many times deduplication took place. The people on call can use the counter to look up the number of times the alert threshold was broken in production while the fix was being prepared to solve the incident.

Alert deduplication can be applied to the incidents that are based on the SLO breaches in the same way. The number of deduplications necessary for SLO breach–based incidents will be smaller than that for resource-based incidents. This is because of the special alerting algorithm implemented by the SRE infrastructure. SLO breaches are not alerted upon immediately. Rather, the alerting algorithm implements features like timeliness, effectiveness, and so forth to reduce alert fatigue. Table 9.10 shows an example of settings for an SLO breach–based alert regarding endpoint availability.

Table 9.10 *Example Settings for an Availability SLO Breach*

Setting	Operator	Value
Endpoint	=	@GET /api/data/{tenant}
SLI	=	Availability
SLO	=	99.7%
Error budget depletion for alert	>	200%
Error budget depletion window	=	60 minutes
Evaluation frequency	=	5 minutes
Alert snooze	=	120 minutes
Name	=	"Availability of get data API"

This SLO breach–based alert is for availability of endpoint "@GET /api/data/{tenant}". The availability SLO for the endpoint is set to 99.7%. Therefore, the error budget is 100% − 99.7% = 0.3%. For an alert to be fired, the error budget depletion within the last 60 minutes needs to be 200% of the hourly error budget: 0.3% x 2 = 0.6%. This is evaluated every five minutes. Once an alert is fired, the evaluation is snoozed for 120 minutes. After that it is automatically resumed.

In this case, the alerting algorithm only alerts when the proportionate hourly error budget was depleted more than 200% in the last hour (timeliness). Once alerted, the algorithm snoozes alerts of the same SLO breach for two hours (effectiveness).

Figure 9.10 shows the overall incident deduplication procedure for SLO breaches and resource-based alerts.

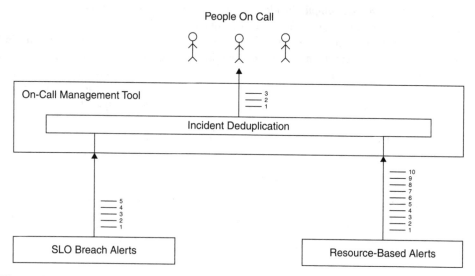

Figure 9.10 *Incident deduplication*

The numerous resource-based alerts get fed to the on-call management tool. Less numerous SLO breach alerts are also fed to the on-call management tool. The tool deduplicates all the incoming alerts based on the deduplication rules. The rules need to be specified by the people on call ahead of time. Using the deduplication rules, only a fraction of the incoming alerts turn into real incidents that are dispatched to the people on call. This is absolutely necessary to avoid alert fatigue, reduce cognitive load, improve the time to recover from real incidents, and keep motivation high.

The deduplication rules need to be mentioned in the runbooks to ensure that the deduplication logic is understood by anyone who joins an on-call rotation.

9.3 Complex Incident Coordination

So far, the incident priorities were defined. They help the people on call prioritize their work when several incidents pile up. Moreover, they help standardize actions taken for all incidents of a given priority across the product delivery organization. The incident priorities, however, typically do not say a lot about the complexity of an incident in terms of, for example, the number of teams required to resolve it. This dimension is explored in this section.

9.3.1 What Is a Complex Incident?

Whenever an incident cannot be solved in a team where it originated and has to be distributed to other teams for further processing, it can be referred to as complex. That is, a complex incident involves more than one team to be resolved. According to PagerDuty,[6] additional criteria may apply to complex incidents, such as the availability of multiple uncorrelated symptoms, several experts working on the same analysis, and so on. In the majority of cases, complex incidents will be assigned incident priority 1.

In large-scale outages, a complex incident may involve dozens of teams. These teams have to be coordinated to provide an overall streamlined incident response. That is, coordination is needed to enable an effective and efficient swarming of the teams on the problem at hand to reduce the time to recover from the incident. By means of coordination, during the incident the teams should be highly aligned but loosely coupled. These are the tenets of a good modern software delivery organization anyway, which need to be applied in the "war context" of resolving a complex incident.

The coordination of a complex incident needs to be done in such a way that

- All the teams involved have the same shared context of the incident (alignment on a single source of truth)

- Every team knows what they need to do as part of the overall incident response (alignment)

- Every team has enough autonomy to do their part of the work (loose coupling)

- The stakeholders are informed appropriately by stakeholder ring

- The incident is documented well on an ongoing basis to

  ○ Efficiently onboard new teams and experts to incident resolution

  ○ Be able to conduct an incident postmortem after the resolution

---

6. PagerDuty. n.d. "Complex Incidents." PagerDuty Incident Response Documentation. Accessed January 24, 2022. https://response.pagerduty.com/before/complex_incidents.

9.3.2 Existing Incident Coordination Systems

In order to drive complex incident coordination, in the past entire systems were developed by governments and professional groups such as firefighters, natural disaster rescuers, and medical emergency units. Notably, in the United States, an Incident Command System was developed. According to Wikipedia, "The Incident Command System (ICS) is a standardized approach to the command, control, and coordination of emergency response providing a common hierarchy within which responders from multiple agencies can be effective."[7] That is, the standardization of command, control, and coordination is at the heart of ICS. In the context of complex software incidents, coordination is especially important to enable efficient team swarming on the problem at hand.

In terms of software operations, PagerDuty[8] defined a similar system with specific roles to coordinate complex incident response. According to PagerDuty, the roles shown in Table 9.11 are needed.

Table 9.11 *PagerDuty Incident Response Roles*

PagerDuty Role	Purpose
Incident commander	Overall driver of the incident toward resolution
Deputy incident commander	Supports the incident commander with detail coordination
Scribe	Ensures the incident is documented on an ongoing basis
Internal liaison	Ensures internal stakeholders are informed appropriately
Customer liaison	Ensures customers are informed appropriately
Subject matter expert	Domain expert responsible for a part of the system

The SRE coaches need to initiate an engagement with the operations teams to study existing incident response systems such as ICS, that from PagerDuty, and any others. Together, they need to assess the complexity of the product delivery organization at hand and work to propose an appropriate process including roles to drive the coordination of complex incidents. The proposed process needs to cover the following fundamental questions.

1. When is incident coordination required?

2. Who initiates incident coordination?

3. Who is making decisions?

4. How are the decisions communicated?

5. Who is in charge of receiving the communicated decisions?

6. Who has to follow the decisions?

---

7. Wikipedia. 2021. "Incident Command System." November 1, 2021. https://en.wikipedia.org/wiki/Incident_Command_System.

8. PagerDuty. n.d. "Different Roles." PagerDuty Incident Response Documentation. Accessed January 24, 2022. https://response.pagerduty.com/before/different_roles.

7. What is the freedom versus responsibility for the teams involved?

8. Who is responsible for communication?

9. Who is responsible for documentation?

10. Who is responsible for running the incident postmortem?

Before answering these questions, the SRE coaches should poll the people who have been going on call on how complex incidents have been handled so far. There was no explicitly defined incident response process. So, the complex incidents were resolved in an ad-hoc manner. Knowing how it was done is invaluable input to define an incident response process that would have the potential to sustainably improve the status quo. The goal is to define a repeatable and reliable process for handling complex incidents in an efficient and effective manner.

9.3.3 Incident Classification

So far, incidents were classified by priority. Depending on the definition, the incident priority may dictate the actions to be taken as part of incident resolution, such as hotfix rollout and management notification (see Section 9.2.3, *Defining Generic Incident Priorities*). That is, the incident priority may determine *what* needs to be done during incident resolution.

The first question in the preceding list, "When is incident coordination required?", is about incident classification along a new dimension. The new dimension is about *how* to do incident resolution in an organized fashion. Would it take a single team to perform the actions? Would it require a full-blown incident response with all roles suggested by PagerDuty fulfilled by distinct people to perform the actions? Would it take some setup in between? This should be possible to express using the new dimension.

The new dimension can be expressed by extending the criteria defining the generic incident priorities. This will yield a longer single list of criteria. Alternatively, the new dimension can be expressed using a new distinct unit. The unit can be referred to as the incident severity.

At this point, it is important to note that the names of incident dimensions such as incident severity and incident priority are not standardized in SRE or in software operations at large. The names are used in this book to illustrate the concepts and not in an attempt to standardize the terminology. With that, the difference between incident priority and incident severity can be summarized as shown in Table 9.12.

Table 9.12 *Incident Dimensions*

#	Incident Dimension	Example Definition
1	Incident priority	What needs to be done during the incident?
2	Incident severity	How should it be done organizationally?

To reiterate, the two incident dimensions can also be expressed using a single unit, such as incident priority, combining the "what" and the "how" in a single set of criteria. Common on-call management tools are flexible in this regard. The next section illustrates a distinct definition of incident severity.

9.3.4 Defining Generic Incident Severities

Like with generic incident priority definitions, incident severities also need to be defined in a generic way. Table 9.13 shows an example of how three incident severities can be defined in an organization.

Table 9.13 *Sample Incident Severities*

#	Criteria	Incident Severity "Critical"	Incident Severity "Error"	Incident Severity "Warning"
1	Users affected	Majority	About 50%	Minority
2	Teams required	> 2	2	1
3	Team coordinator required	Yes	Yes	No
	Example	No log-on possible to any application	Sporadic user auto log out of applications	Demo data not available in the showcase deployment

The incident severity needs to be set by the people on call in order to invoke a certain incident response process. In the preceding example, the "critical" incident severity means the majority of users are affected, more than two teams are required to work on the incident, and the teams have to be coordinated by a dedicated team coordinator.

An example of an incident with a "critical" severity would be if no log-on is possible to any application. Setting the incident severity level to "critical" invokes the highest level of incident response. All roles to be defined in the incident response process will have to be involved in the resolution of the incident.

The "error" incident severity means that about 50% of users are affected. To resolve the incident two teams will be required, and the teams will need to be coordinated by a dedicated coordinator. An example of an incident with an "error" severity would be when users are sporadically logged out of applications involuntarily. In this case, the incident response might not require all roles defined in the incident response process to be involved in the resolution of the incident. For example, with two teams involved, a dedicated person responsible only for communication might not be required. The communication responsibilities might be with the incident coordinator.

The third incident severity in Table 9.13 is "warning." This severity represents an incident where only a minority of users are affected. The incident can be resolved by a single team, so no external team coordination is required. An example of an incident with a "warning" severity would be when demo data is not available in the showcase deployment used by sales and marketing for customer demonstrations.

Finally, it needs to be defined which incident severity should be set in borderline cases where the severity criteria do not correspond to the incident at hand in a very clear way. For example, if three teams need to be involved in an incident but only a minority of users are affected, neither of the severities defined earlier would apply. It can be recommended to set a higher severity in ambiguous cases, to be on the safe side. Following this, the "critical" severity would be set.

Another example would be if only one team needs to be involved in an incident with a majority of the users being affected. Also in this case, neither of the severities defined earlier would apply. Still, a "critical" severity should be set.

The SRE coaches need to work with the operations teams to define the incident severities. As part of the work, a decision needs to be made as to whether the severity should be expressed as a separate dimension or as additional criteria in incident priorities. The on-call management tool in use might influence this decision.

9.3.5 Social Dimension of Incident Classification

The definitions of incident priority and severity from the previous sections are rule based. The rules suggest that the people on call should assign incident priority and severity by and large irrespective of the wider circumstances or context. Therefore, the rules are not particularly context sensitive.

However, in reality, the definitions of incident priority and severity quite often have a social dimension associated with them. The social dimension adds to the rule-based definitions of priority and severity. That social dimension may manifest itself in the rules being overridden in a given situation.

For instance, the "warning" incident severity from the previous section states that it applies only to incidents that affect a minority of the users. Based on that, it is possible to imagine an incident that affects only one customer due to a failure in a service owned by a single team. So, the incident should be assigned a "warning" severity. However, the single customer affected by the incident could turn out to be a really important customer. Therefore, the people on call might want to be extra cautious and, as an exception, set the severity of the incident to "critical," causing a full-blown incident response to unfold.

This poses a couple of questions. The first question is the definition of customer importance. That property is not defined in the incident response process. In fact, customer classification is not part of the incident response process at all. The second question concerns the decision maker on the undefined property of customer importance. Who should make a decision about the importance of a given customer? That is also not defined in the incident response process.

To take the example further, it is possible to imagine that the important customer has a powerful advocate in the product delivery organization. For instance, a senior vice president of product can be in close touch with the customer and be called to immediately fix the issue. Following that, the senior VP may consult the on-call management tool, find the corresponding incident, and join the conference bridge where the incident response is unfolding. On the call, the senior VP may outrank everyone and demand that the most senior engineers join the call.

This breaks the entire incident response process that was carefully set up before. First, the senior VP takes over incident command, overriding the incident coordinator. Second, the senior VP commands people currently not on call to troubleshoot the incident. Third, the senior VP, unaware of the incident response process details, is likely to break the incident stakeholder communication rules. The SRE coaches need to think through situations like this in advance and systematically prepare the organization for a structured incident response in an attempt to minimize the likelihood of such chaotic situations occurring.

That is, the social dimension of incident classification will influence the rule-based definitions of incident priority and severity. This is a very important aspect to be aware of. The impact of the social dimension will differ depending on the organizational culture. The least impact will be felt in performance-oriented cultures. The most impact will be felt in power-oriented cultures, with the impact in rule-oriented cultures possibly situated in the middle. In any case, the rule-based definitions of priority and severity will not be rock-solid and clear in all situations for the lifetime of an organization. The SRE coaches need to take this into consideration during the SRE transformation.

Due to the social dimension diluting the rules of priority and severity definitions, there is a school of thought for doing away with coarse level incident classifications, such as priorities and severities, and leaving the matter to human judgment in full context of the situation. Notably, there is a Learning from Incidents in Software (LFI)[9] community, led by Nora Jones, John Allspaw, Richard Cook, and others. It is rooted in resilience engineering for safety in complex systems and the Safety-II[10] perspective on safety. The Safety-II perspective places safety in the context of complex adaptive systems. It attempts to achieve safety by enabling as many things as possible to go right. The contrasting Safety-I perspective places safety in the context of linear systems constructed of individual components. It attempts to achieve safety by preventing as many things as possible from going wrong.[10] The LFI community is there to "reshape how the software industry thinks about incidents, software reliability, and the critical role people play in keeping their systems running."

According to the LFI community, the idea of counting incidents is not the right path to achieve safety. This is because a sufficiently complex online system could potentially give rise to an infinite number of outages indefinitely.

Further, according to the LFI community, the idea of dividing incidents into categories might not be that relevant to the impact of those incidents. However, the field is not yet developed to a point where traditional incident classification using, for example, incident priority and severity can be eliminated. Some kind of incident classification is required so that the organization knows where to allocate its attention.

Finally, the incident classification needs to support the people on call to rapidly figure out what can be successfully ignored and what to focus on immediately.

9.3.6 Incident Priority Versus Incident Severity

In cases where the incident priority (e.g., what needs to be done) and incident severity (e.g., how to do it organizationally) are defined as separate dimensions, their cross product also needs to be defined. The definition needs to make clear whether every permutation of incident priority and severity should be possible. Following the examples of incident priorities and severities from previous sections, the cross product shown in Table 9.14 can be considered.

---

9. LFI. n.d. "Learning from Incidents in Software." Accessed January 24, 2022. https://www.learning-fromincidents.io.

10. Jones, Christian E.L., Denham L. Phipps, and Darren M. Ashcroft. 2018. "Understanding Procedural Violations Using Safety-I and Safety-II: The Case of Community Pharmacies." *Safety Science* 105 (June): 114–120. https://doi.org/10.1016/j.ssci.2018.02.002.

Table 9.14 *Incident Priority Versus Incident Severity*

		Incident Severity		
		Severity "critical"	*Severity "error"*	*Severity "warning"*
Incident Priority	Priority 1	Possible?	Possible?	Possible?
	Priority 2	Possible?	Possible?	Possible?
	Priority 3	Possible?	Possible?	Possible?

In general, every permutation of incident priorities and severities should be possible. An incident with a "critical" severity involving many teams and therefore requiring a full-blown incident response can have a priority of 3. For example, when demo data is not available in the showcase deployment, the appropriate incident priority would be 3 because it would not affect customers. However, if the entire global sales and marketing force is affected and now is unable to make important demonstrations for closing big new deals, the appropriate severity for such an incident is "critical." In this case, it is appropriate to run a full-blown incident response to reinstate the showcase deployment as soon as possible.

Conversely, an incident with a "warning" severity only taking place in a single team can have a priority of 1, requiring an immediate hotfix to be rolled out. For example, in a seldom sporadic authentication issue with an authentication service owned by a single team, there might be a single SLO breach covering the use case. The SLO breach gets converted into an incident in the on-call management tool, and the incident gets assigned to the person on call in the team owning the authentication service.

The person on call analyzes the SLO breach and concludes that it can be fixed by a quick configuration change, which can be rolled out to all production environments within minutes using a fully automated deployment pipeline. The action is taken immediately and the service is restored soon after. The incident priority of 1 is justified because the hotfix was required and appropriate management and stakeholder notifications were necessary. Also, a postmortem will be required. The "warning" incident severity is justified too because only a minority of the users were affected due to the issue occurring infrequently and sporadically, and because the incident resolution could be driven autonomously by a single team.

9.3.7 Defining Roles

With the incident severities defined, the highest severity level will require all roles defined in the incident response process to be involved in incident resolution. Role definition is the subject of this section.

As discussed in Section 9.3.2, *Existing Incident Coordination Systems*, the roles are needed to fulfill four areas:

1. Coordination

2. Communication

3. Documentation

4. Execution

The SRE coaches need to work with the operations teams to propose a set of roles and associated responsibilities. Purely as an example, the initially proposed roles might look like those shown in Table 9.15.

Table 9.15 *Example Incident Response Roles, Responsibilities, and Skills*

Role	Responsibilities	Skills
Incident coordinator	Decision-making Team coordination Team well-being Running postmortem	Decision-making Emotional intelligence People motivation People coordination Communication
Incident communicator	Communication toward teams Communication toward internal stakeholders Communication toward external stakeholders Incident documentation Postmortem documentation Postmortem results communication	Communication Technical writing Liaising with stakeholders
Technical expert	Technical analysis Solution proposal Solution implementation Postmortem participation	Technical expertise Communication

It might happen that additional people would be necessary for decision-making. For example, a project manager might be needed because of their knowledge of the impact of changing timelines on other internal and external stakeholders. Additionally, an operations engineer might be needed because of their knowledge of an incident's impact on first level support distributed around the world. Furthermore, in organizations where management team members are usually involved in decisions affecting customers because they know the impact of the decisions on the organization's reputation, a management team member might be needed.

The SRE coaches and operations engineers need to take these points into account when proposing the roles to be involved in the incident response process. They also need to carefully consider these decisions in light of the existing organizational culture. At the same time, the decisions on roles represent a good opportunity to influence the company culture. A well-arranged devolvement of decision-making power away from the management teams and to the teams doing the work might be supported by a well-thought-out role structure as part of the incident response process.

When it comes to naming the roles, the most appropriate role names in the context of a given organization can be freely chosen. The role name "incident coordinator" is chosen in the preceding example to deliberately point out the need for coordination tasks within the context of a team of fully responsible people on call. In the industry, the role name "incident commander" is used more often than "incident coordinator." Having the word "commander" in the role name might suggest to the people on call that they are fully commanded by the incident commander. It might suggest that the incident would be owned by the incident commander and the individual experts are "contracted" by the commander to carry out individual tasks of their incident.

With the choice of "incident coordinator" as the role name, this perception will be countered. It should be clear that ownership of the incident is not with the incident coordinator alone. Rather, it is with the entire team assigned to the incident. Every individual on the team contributes something to the incident resolution. The incident coordinator contributes coordination, the incident communicator contributes information distribution to get everyone on the same page, the technical experts contribute technical skills, and so on.

Although it might be just a question of naming a role, the decision should not be dismissed as something very minor. People associate names with meanings based on their training, previous experience, and culture. Especially in a multicultural setting, which is common in modern software delivery organizations, different people have different backgrounds and therefore might associate different meanings with names. Moreover, depending on the culture, the attitude toward roles might be different. In some cultures, having a role assigned in the project is regarded highly. Other cultures might not place as much emphasis on roles.

For these reasons, naming the incident response roles should be given appropriate consideration within the culture of a particular product delivery organization. Naming the roles should not be dismissed as a mere annoyance that bears no consequences whatsoever.

In terms of defining responsibilities, a detailed list is required to communicate the expectations. In a given product delivery organization, the list should include the tools to be used, by purpose. Moreover, where applicable, the list of responsibilities should include the behavioral aspects of working with other roles.

Generally, the list of responsibilities does not include what a particular role should not do. However, on occasion it might be useful to include this as well to avoid ambiguity. Especially when a role culturally tends to do something that should not be done in the context of incident response, adding a note regarding what should not be done by the role is appropriate. For instance, it might happen that culturally the incident coordinators would tend to distribute stakeholder notifications very broadly in an attempt to reach everyone in the organization. Again, culturally, this might cause many people to "reply all" to find out more. In this case, the incident coordinator's list of responsibilities should contain a note discouraging broad distribution of stakeholder notifications.

Another aspect to be considered is partial responsibilities. Notably, each role has a partial responsibility in running incident postmortems. The incident coordinator is the overall driver of a postmortem. They are responsible for the postmortem write-up and appropriate communication about the postmortem to different stakeholders. The technical experts contribute the technical knowledge and firsthand experience of events that occurred during the incident.

The list of skills in Table 9.15 corresponds to the responsibilities by and large. Notably, the incident coordinator needs to possess emotional intelligence skills to motivate and coordinate people, make calm decisions under stress, manage and resolve conflict, and keep team morale high.

The incident coordinator does not need to possess technical skills. They only need to be technical enough to be able to communicate well about technical topics to audiences with different levels of technical understanding. Finally, the technical experts need to possess sound technical knowledge in a product area they are responsible for.

9.3.8 Roles Required by Incident Severity

With the definition of the roles involved in the overall incident response process, role assignment by incident severity needs to take place. For exemplary purposes, such a role assignment by incident severity is shown in Table 9.16.

Table 9.16 *Incident Response Roles by Incident Severity*

#	Role	Incident Severity "Critical"	Incident Severity "Error"	Incident Severity "Warning"
1	Dedicated incident coordinator	Yes	Yes	No
2	Dedicated incident communicator	Yes	No	No
3	Dedicated technical expert	Yes	Yes	Yes

In Table 9.16, the incident severity "critical" invokes all roles defined in the incident response process to be available in a dedicated manner. That is, a dedicated incident coordinator is required for team coordination and decision-making, a dedicated incident communicator is required for all communication activities, and dedicated technical experts are required for executing the decisions, finding technical solutions, and implementing them.

The incident severity "error" requires a dedicated incident coordinator. Because the resolution of such incidents only involves two teams, the incident coordinator also performs the role of incident communicator. A dedicated incident communicator is not required here.

Finally, the incident severity "warning" requires neither incident coordinator nor communicator. Here, the person on call in a team performs coordination activities within the team and communication activities outside the team as determined by the incident priority. The single source of truth about the incident is within the team in this case. Thus, outside coordination is unnecessary.

9.3.9 Roles On Call

With the roles involved in the incident response process defined, an on-call rotation needs to be set up for each role. For the technical experts, the on-call rotations are defined already by team or domain (see Section 7.4, *Setting Up On-Call Rotations*). For other roles, on-call rotations need to be defined in the same way. This is shown in Table 9.17.

Table 9.17 *Example Roles On Call*

	Rotation Period 1	Rotation Period 2	Rotation Period 3	Rotation Period 4
Incident Coordinator	Person A	Person A	Person B	Person B
Incident Communicator	Person C	Person C	Person D	Person D
Team 1 Technical Expert	Person E	Person F	Person G	Person E

The incident coordinator and communicator rotate every second rotation period (e.g., every two weeks). Team 1's technical experts rotate every rotation period (e.g., every week). It needs to be pointed out that each role involved in the incident response process needs to get an on-call rotation. This means project managers and management team members also need to be on call should they be defined in a decision-maker role in the incident response process.

When on call, the technical experts will set the severity of an incident assigned to them based on their judgment of the situation at hand and the incident severity definitions. If the incident severity selected requires team coordination, the technical expert will add the incident coordinator rotation to the incident. The on-call management tool will automatically select the current incident coordinator based on the rotation and add them to the incident.

Furthermore, the incident coordinator will add additional role rotations to the incident depending on the incident severity. For example, the incident communicator rotation may be added; as a result, the on-call management tool will add the current incident communicator to the incident.

The technical experts will have an escalation policy defined to propagate unacknowledged incidents through a predefined chain of technical experts in an attempt to get the incident acknowledged (see Section 8.2, *Defining an Alert Escalation Policy*). Such escalation policies can be defined for any role's on-call rotation. For example, an escalation policy for the incident coordinator rotation can help get unacknowledged incidents acknowledged by an incident coordinator.

9.3.10 Incident Response Process Evaluation

The incident response process proposed by the SRE coaches and operations teams consists of a complex incident definition, roles, responsibilities, incident priorities, and possibly, incident severities. The interplay of these entities can be checked against the incident response process criteria outlined in Section 9.3.2, *Existing Incident Coordination Systems*. Exemplarily, this is shown in Table 9.18.

Table 9.18 *Sample Incident Response Process Evaluation*

#	Incident Response Process Criterion	Sample Fulfillment
1	When is incident coordination required?	For incidents with severity set to "critical" or "error"

#	Incident Response Process Criterion	Sample Fulfillment
2	Who initiates the incident coordination?	A person on call by setting the incident severity to "critical"
3	Who is making decisions?	The incident coordinator but not in a rigid command and control manner
4	How are the decisions communicated?	In a dedicated channel created for the incident automatically by the on-call management tool
5	Who is in charge of receiving the communicated decisions?	The people on call in the development and operations teams
6	Who has to follow the decisions?	The people on call in the development and operations teams
7	What is the freedom versus responsibility for the teams involved?	Freedom: • Select technical solutions Responsibility: • Receive decisions from the incident coordinator • Execute on the decisions • Report on the execution status
8	Who is responsible for communication?	Incident severity "critical": incident coordinator Incident severity "error": incident communicator
9	Who is responsible for documentation?	The incident communicator
10	Who is responsible for running the incident postmortem?	The incident coordinator

The proposed incident response process needs to undergo a thorough review. The operations teams need to own the process and should initiate the review. To do so, the process needs to be documented in draft form on the SRE wiki. This way, the reviewers will be able to comment on the process easily. Furthermore, the changes proposed and made by anyone will be fully transparent. The list of reviewers needs to include everyone who has been going on call so far. These are the people who have been coordinating complex incidents in some ad-hoc manner. They are best equipped to assess how much the proposed incident response process would streamline the resolution of complex incidents.

Based on the reviews that were received, the process adaptations need to be incorporated by the operations teams. If the adaptations were significant, another review round needs to be initiated. Once the process has been hardened by the reviews, it needs to be applied a couple of times in a complex incident resolution to test it in real, high-pressure situations. This will provide additional feedback to further improve the process before declaring it generally enacted in the product delivery organization.

In order to do so, volunteers in all defined roles should be found and asked to drive the next complex incident responses following the incident response process at hand.

9.3.11 Incident Response Process Dynamics

Using the incident response process should be easy. To facilitate ease of use, a decision diagram showing the process dynamics may be helpful. An example diagram is shown in Figure 9.11. It can be used by all incident response roles to prepare for incident response ahead of time. Additionally, it can be used by all roles during incident response to act in line with the process. Certainly, the on-call management tool automates implementation of the diagram to a great extent.

Aesthetically, it is important for the diagram to fit on a single A4-size sheet of paper. A longer diagram will inevitably evoke feelings of an overly complex process. This would be the opposite of what the diagram is trying to achieve, which is facilitation of a process that is easy to use.

The top of the diagram shows the following four triggers for incidents:

- First level support when they cannot fulfill a customer request

- Anyone else who found a bug in production

- An SLO breach from the SRE infrastructure

- A resource-based alert from the application performance management facility

Following this, incidents can be created by a human manually, or through automation. Manual incident creation can be done by the first level support or anyone who found a bug in production (steps 1 and 2 in Figure 9.11). Once an incident is created manually, it is automatically assigned to the incident coordinator rotation (step 3). The incident coordinator on call needs to acknowledge the incident (step 4). If that does not happen within a defined time frame, the incident coordinator rotation's escalation policy will kick in, if defined.

Once an incident coordinator acknowledges the incident, they need to assess it and decide on the best suitable technical expert to look at the issue at hand. Following that decision, the incident coordinator assigns the incident to the technical expert selected or to a rotation of technical experts closest to the issue (step 5).

The upper-right part of Figure 9.11 shows the path of automated incident creation. An incident can be created automatically based on an SLO breach or resource-based alert (steps 6 and 7). Once the incident is created automatically, it is assigned to a technical expert rotation that was specified as a parameter passed to the on-call management tool as part of the incident creation request. This is shown in step 8. In step 9, a technical expert from the technical expert rotation needs to acknowledge the incident (step 10 indicates the same action, but taken after step 5). If this does not happen within a defined time frame, the technical expert rotation's escalation policy will kick in, if defined.

Once a technical expert has acknowledged the incident, they need to assess the issue at hand and decide on the incident priority (e.g., what needs to be done) and the incident severity (e.g., how to do it organizationally). This is shown in steps 11 and 12. Depending on the severity chosen, further actions differ (step 13).

For the incidents with severity "critical," the next step is to assign the incident to the incident coordinator rotation because many teams need to be coordinated and decisions made to coordinate the teams (step 14). Once the incident coordinator has acknowledged the incident (step 17), the incident communicator rotation needs to be added to the incident to take care of communication to all teams and stakeholders. This is done manually in step 18.

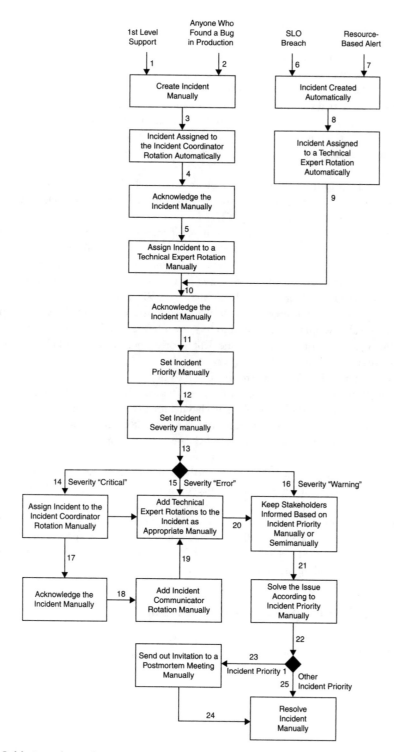

Figure 9.11 *Sample incident response process diagram*

For the incidents with severity "error," more technical experts need to be added to the incident as appropriate (step 15). For the incidents with severity "warning," the stakeholders need to be informed in accordance with the incident priority. This can be done in a manual or semimanual manner (step 16). Step 20 represents the same action for the incidents with the severities "critical" and "error." The incident priority may also dictate the frequency of stakeholder notifications.

In step 21, the actual solution for the issue at hand will be developed by the technical experts working on the incident. The incident priority may determine how the solution should be rolled out. For instance, incident priority 1 might require a hotfix to be rolled out, while lower incident priorities might indicate less invasive work such as, for example, changes of cloud or infrastructure settings.

Next, incident priority 1 might dictate a postmortem to be initiated. This can be done in the form of sending out a meeting invite before resolving the incident (step 23). Otherwise, the incident can be resolved straight away (step 25).

It is important to note that the flow diagram in Figure 9.11 does not contain lots of branches. Nor does it contain any circles. This is important. The incident response is, by definition, performed in high-stress situations, often outside of business hours. The simpler the process, the higher the probability that it will be followed to resolve complex incidents because it helps streamline the response rather than making it more complicated.

Additionally, it is important to indicate which actions are performed manually and which ones automatically. Manual actions need to be known to the people on call to actually perform them at the right time. For example, the incident priority and severity should be set before starting to resolve the issue and not the other way around.

Further, automated actions need to be known to the people on call to understand how the automation works and moves the steps in the flow diagram. For example, the on-call management tool might automatically create a new channel for each incident in the chat management service used in the organization. This needs to be known to the people on call in order to avoid a situation where each of them would create a dedicated channel for the issue, invite everyone else, and start disparate discussions.

Through iteration, the operations team needs to adapt the process to make it simpler and increasingly suitable, striking a good balance between structure and flexibility. Structure is required to align and coordinate different teams and people. Flexibility is required to enable each team to act autonomously and quickly, avoiding delays due to waiting for coordination commands from the incident coordinator. The balance between structure and flexibility is required in order to achieve a reliable and repeatable incident response process that supports the organization in responding to complex incidents.

9.3.12 Incident Response Team Well-Being

In Section 9.3.7, *Defining Roles*, I explained that one of the incident coordinator's responsibilities is team well-being. This responsibility deserves special consideration. It is rarely described in the literature but has a great impact on the success of an organization's incident response.

When an incident unfolds, a team of the people on call is dynamically assembled. Over time, a complex incident might involve a dozen or more people. It is the incident coordinator's responsibility to not only coordinate the people but also ensure their well-being as individuals and as a team.

Fulfilling this responsibility isn't always a straightforward task. For instance:

- The incident coordinator may not personally know all the people on call who have been assigned to the incident.

- These people may have never worked together as a team.

- Some of them may be working beyond normal business hours after having spent an exhausting day at work.

To top it all off, if the incident severity is "critical," the entire team is, by definition, working in a high-pressure environment. The financial consequences of every second of the outage may increase the pressure.

To ensure the team's well-being under such circumstances, a structured preparation is required. This may involve the following aspects:

- Social

- Etiquette

- Emotional

- Equality

- Source of truth

- Blame handling

Each aspect is explained in Table 9.19.

Table 9.19 *Aspects to Ensure the Well-Being of Incident Response Teams*

Aspect	Explanation
Social	The incident coordinator should take part in the SRE CoP activities to get to know the people on call personally and become familiar with what they are typically doing when they are on call.
	Furthermore, they should check the rotations of other roles from time to time to see whether new names appear, and if so, should try to meet the new people personally or in a 1:1 video call.
	The incident coordinator might organize an informal incident coordinator lunch (e.g., once every two weeks) where the people who go on call can have lunch together in a relaxed atmosphere before meeting in a high-pressure incident response setting. The purpose of the lunch is for the team members to get to know one another personally to establish a human connection. That purpose should be made known to the people in advance.
	Certainly, work conversations can happen during the incident coordinator lunch as well, but it should not be the primary focus. The incident coordinator should lightly moderate the conversation. Work topics should be collected to be elaborated upon in other meetings. Conversations about hobbies, vacations, aspirations, family, and so on should be welcomed.

Aspect	Explanation
Etiquette	The incident coordinators can work together to establish rules of etiquette for the people on call to follow during incident response situations. The rules should describe the individual and team behaviors the incident coordinators aspire to see and facilitate during incidents. The etiquette can include the language choice and the type of language (e.g., colloquial, formal) for the incident response team members to use with stakeholders based on stakeholder ring.
	The language choice is important for multicultural teams that have a dominant number of people who speak a language that others do not. It needs to be stated that a language everyone can understand, often English, is the only language to be used during the incident response. There is nothing more frustrating for people working in the middle of the night to suddenly see in the chat window a discussion unfold in a language they cannot understand. In cases like that, the incident coordinator or incident communicator needs to intervene and politely ask everyone to return to leading the discussion in the language stated in the etiquette rules.
	Further, the etiquette can include details about when and how often team members can take breaks. The incident coordinator should attempt to detect situations in which people are going without breaks for hours on end and ask them to take a short break to clear their mind. Clear suggestions on what to do and not do during the short break might be helpful as well—for instance, do have a bite to eat, grab some water, and stretch a bit; do not use a computer or phone.
	At the same time, the incident coordinator should clearly state in writing when the person leaving for a break is expected to be back on call. This is important for everyone involved to know. Other people's decisions to take a break might depend on that.
	The etiquette may involve a statement that people are expected to use web cameras during online calls. This needs to be known in advance because people might look different when they are at home in the middle of the night than they do when they're at the office during business hours. Knowing that online calls are supposed to be conducted with webcams prompts people to quickly groom themselves a bit before going on on-call duty outside business hours.
	Although this might add a couple of minutes to the time to recover from incidents, it might be worth it because it would strengthen the human connection among the team members when discussing the incident. It also gives people a chance to refresh in the middle of the night instead of jumping on the call in a sleepy state of mind.
	Additionally, the etiquette may require that people taking part in the incident resolution participate in the incident postmortem that will take place shortly after the incident is resolved.

Aspect	Explanation
Emotional	Generally, the incident coordinator should sense the team's, individuals', and their own emotional state for relieving stress, overcoming challenges, resolving conflicts, and acting empathetically. In other words, exercising emotional intelligence is very important for the incident coordinator. Generally, emotional intelligence consists of four characteristics: self-management, self-awareness, social awareness, and relationship management.[11] All of these are important in the context of incident response. The incident coordinator needs to detect when they or the incident response team members might become emotionally aroused. Following this, they need to manage the situation by calming themselves and the people around them when conversations heat up. Big, open conflicts should be avoided. If the incident coordinator detects the need to talk to a team member or a small group of team members about their on-call behavior, they should not do it in writing, but rather in a video call with webcams or a phone call. During the call, the incident coordinator should provide clear direction for expected behavior during future incidents. Any improvements and analyses of the situation should be discussed later as part of the incident postmortem. Further, the incident coordinator needs to ensure they and the people around them are in a stable emotional state when making decisions. Delaying a decision by a couple of minutes to come to a calm emotional state might be helpful. (Good preparation for being able to do so quickly in a heated moment is a regular practice of mindfulness," which is the practice of purposely bringing one's attention in the present moment without judgment."[12]) Generally, the decisions should be made based on undisputable data as much as possible. The decision-making should be documented well for potential future analysis as part of the incident postmortem. The incident coordinator should watch the conversation unfold. If the conversation becomes too stiff or threatens to become emotionally laden, for example, the incident coordinator might consider defusing the tension using humor and laughter. These are great stress relievers in general but need to be used considerately in the context of incident response and multicultural settings. Using emojis in chat conversations adds emotion to text. When used appropriately, emojis can have the desired effect of causing humor and laughter in moderation in an attempt to lighten up a tense situation. In this context, it is important to keep the humor and laughter within limits and to avoid sarcasm. Especially in a multicultural setting, humor is perceived differently. While lightweight humor will be universally acceptable, sarcasm will probably not and should therefore be avoided.

11. HelpGuide. 2018. "Improving Emotional Intelligence (EQ)." November 2, 2018. https://www.helpguide.org/articles/mental-health/emotional-intelligence-eq.htm..
12. Wikipedia. 2022. "Mindfulness." January 19, 2022. https://en.wikipedia.org/wiki/Mindfulness.

Aspect	Explanation
Equality	The incident coordinator should not treat people they know personally in a different way than others. The incident coordinator might have a trustful relationship with the people they know or have worked with in the past. However, this should not affect how they work with other members of the incident response team. Everybody should be treated in the same way.
	The people on call who do not know the incident coordinator personally should not feel like some off-the-record conversations take place with other team members. That can cause feelings of suspicion because the people who do not know the incident coordinator personally may not know that other people do. They therefore might develop conspiracy theories around why the incident coordinator seems to treat other people differently.
	The situation might be exacerbated if a person who does not know the incident coordinator personally arguably possesses better technical knowledge. Thinking along the lines of why the incident coordinator seemingly listens more to the team members with arguably inferior technical knowledge distracts the team member from working on the incident response.
	The incident coordinator needs to be aware of this possibility and actively work to ensure that everyone is treated in the same way and everything is transparent to everyone.
Single source of truth	The incident response is likely to unfold in a chat channel of a chat management service like Slack or Microsoft Teams. In this context, it is very important to lead the entire conversation between the incident coordinator and other team members in a single designated chat channel. That channel should also include references to online meetings taking place so that anyone can jump into a running meeting on demand without searching for a meeting link.
	The channel should contain the entire conversation from the incident trigger to the resolution. It should be the single source of truth regarding the state of the incident at any given time.
	The incident coordinator should actively reject any attempts to talk to them on any matters other than personal in any other channels or private chat conversations. Politely, the incident coordinator should refer everyone to the designated incident channel because it has to be the single source of truth for everyone. The same applies to the incident communicator.

Aspect	Explanation
	It also needs to be clear to everyone who creates the designated channel for an incident, when to do it, and how to enable others to find it. Often the on-call management tool can create a channel per incident automatically and include the incident number in the channel name. This is beneficial because the channel is created the moment the incident is created. Moreover, with the channel name referencing the incident number from the on-call management tool, the search for the channel is simplified. The link to the channel is also available inside the incident itself in the on-call management tool.
	Adding people to the designated incident channel could also be automated to some extent based on the list of responders for the incident in the on-call management tool. Beyond some possible automation, the incident coordinator will need to add missing people manually to the channel.
	When channel creation is not automated, the incident coordinator needs to be responsible for timely channel creation and naming according to a naming convention; for example, "inc-id-dd-mm-yy-short-reason". The naming convention simplifies the search for the channel. Also in this case, all the necessary people need to be added manually to the channel.
No blame	This will be part of the etiquette, but it is so important that it deserves to be flagged as a separate top-level aspect here. In high-pressure situations where people also work after business hours, any hint of blame might result in a breakdown of morale among the incident response team. It is the incident coordinator's responsibility to sense and detect blameful situations.
	Once they are detected, the incident coordinator should publicly but politely and calmly state that blame is not part of the etiquette. The team should focus on the problem at hand to rapidly find a solution and resolve the incident. An ability to discuss other matters will be provided at the incident postmortem.
	Also, the incident postmortem needs to be a safe place to discuss the incident without fear of being punished or blamed. The incident coordinator needs to nourish and foster a blameless culture during the incident postmortems as well as while the incident is being worked on.

In fact, coordinating complex incidents every time with a new, dynamically allocated team is a dynamic reteaming exercise of sorts that incident coordinators need to master. In *Dynamic Reteaming: The Art and Wisdom of Changing Teams*,[13] Heidi Helfand discusses how to restructure teams dynamically. However, the advice is for reteaming more static and long-lived teams such as development teams.

---

13. Helfand, Heidi. 2020. *Dynamic Reteaming: The Art and Wisdom of Changing Teams*. Sebastopol, CA: O'Reilly Media.

Incident response teams are the opposite. By definition, they are dynamic and short-lived. The differences between development and incident response teams are summarized in Table 9.20.

Table 9.20 *Development Teams Versus Incident Response Teams*

Characteristic	Development Teams	Incident Response Teams
Working hours	Business hours	24/7
Regular daily number of working hours	8	Defined?
Teams dynamically formed for a short-lived mission	No	Yes
Teams disband after fulfilling a short-lived mission	No	Yes

Table 9.20 shows that development teams regularly work for eight hours during business hours. By contrast, incident response teams are on call 24/7. However, it is sometimes not clearly defined how long a person on call should be working on an incident. What if an incident takes 24 hours to resolve and the expertise of a person on call is required the entire time? Careful definition of on-call shifts in the on-call management tool is required to avoid burnout among incident response team members. Also, when a deeply knowledgeable person on call goes off duty in the middle of a raging incident, a very detailed on-call shift handover procedure needs to take place. This needs to be ensured by the incident coordinator.

Furthermore, unlike development teams, the nature of incident response teams is that they are formed dynamically with a purpose to fulfill a short-lived mission to resolve the incident. After the mission is fulfilled, the team is disbanded. Mastering team dynamics in the context of incident response poses new challenges not encountered with teams operating in more stable environments. It takes lots of experience on the part of incident coordinators to master the art of handling team dynamics in an incident response context. It would be great to see this aspect explored well in the industry in the future across several dimensions: geography, culture, time of work, incident duration, familiarity of team members with one another, technical expertise, duration of tenure at the company, and so on.

9.4 Incident Postmortems

I mentioned incident postmortems many times in the preceding chapters as rituals conducted at the end of an incident. This section explores how incident postmortems can be introduced in a product delivery organization in an effective manner. For an incident postmortem to be effective, its value needs to be greater than the time investment to conduct it. Although this ratio is difficult to calculate quantitatively, a qualitative assessment may be possible. Let us begin by looking at some existing definitions of incident postmortem.

According to PagerDuty, "A postmortem (or post-mortem) is a process intended to help you learn from past incidents. It typically involves an analysis or discussion soon after an event has taken place."[14]

According to OpsGenie, "A postmortem is a written record of an incident that contains information such as incident impact, mitigation steps, root cause, and follow-up actions. The goal of a postmortem is to understand all root causes, document the incident for future reference, discover patterns, and enact effective preventative actions to reduce the impact or likelihood of recurrence."[15]

The original Google SRE book *Site Reliability Engineering: How Google Runs Production Systems* states, "A postmortem is a written record of an incident, its impact, the actions taken to mitigate or resolve it, the root cause(s), and the follow-up actions to prevent the incident from recurring."[16]

From these incident postmortem definitions, some criteria for an effective postmortem can be derived. These criteria are postmortem timeliness, learning, record, and actions. They are explained in the next section.

9.5 Effective Postmortem Criteria

A successful postmortem is based on the criteria described in Table 9.21.

Table 9.21 *Effective Postmortem Criteria*

Criterion	Explanation
Timeliness	The incident postmortem needs to be conducted soon after the incident has been resolved. A good practice is to ensure that the people on call take a break after the stress of a high-severity incident. A break of 24 to 48 hours seems to be a good time frame to recover from an incident but still keep the details of what happened top of mind.
	Following this, a timely postmortem is conducted within a window of 24 to 72 hours after the incident has been resolved. Conducting the postmortem later is still valuable, but because people tend to forget the details of what happened as time goes by, the value of a later postmortem may diminish over time.

14. PagerDuty. 2017. "What Is an Incident Post-Mortem?" May 8, 2017. https://www.pagerduty.com/resources/learn/incident-postmortem.

15. Atlassian Support. n.d. "Create a Postmortem Report." Accessed January 24, 2022. https://docs.opsgenie.com/docs/postmortems.

16. Murphy, Niall Richard, Betsy Beyer, Chris Jones, and Jennifer Petoff. 2016. *Site Reliability Engineering: How Google Runs Production Systems*. Sebastopol, CA: O'Reilly Media, Inc.

Criterion	Explanation
Learning	The value of an incident postmortem is in the learning it generates. The learning can take different flavors. On the one hand, direct action items to fix immediate issues represent one-time learning episodes. On the other hand, there are a number of additional opportunities beyond the immediate action items to inject learnings into the product delivery organization.
	These are runbook updates, incident response process updates, on-call training updates, employee onboarding program updates, on-call rotation updates, SLO updates, SRE CoP presentations, architecture upgrades, responsibility updates, organizational structure updates, hiring practices, supplier selection, and many more. The goal is to look beyond what happened during the incident and take the entire socio-technical setup of the organization into the realm of the analysis.
	This is where the long-term value of postmortems really lies. It is in the facilitation of a broader update of organizational processes and practices based on postmortem conversations in an efficient and effective manner. The facilitation needs to be done consistently and professionally to be able to reach all parties in the organization.
	Agile coaches are in a good position to drive the facilitation as part of continuous improvement activities. They are also in a good position to bridge the immediate incident postmortem conversations with the overarching organizational processes, practices, and activities at large.
Record	A written record of a postmortem is required for future reference to enable learning for people who did not take part in the postmortem meeting. Clear technical writing is essential to motivate the people to read and learn from a postmortem that was conducted by others. Opaque and unstructured postmortems will not be read and learned from, which devalues the process to nearly zero.
	In addition to writing, as much as possible other media should be used to record postmortems. Whenever a postmortem is conducted in an online meeting, it should be recorded. The recording should be uploaded onto the organization's video sharing service. Once uploaded, the recording should be tagged with "SRE" and "postmortem" tags. Moreover, the sound should be extracted and the pure audio recording should be placed onto the organization's audio sharing service.
	Having the postmortem content in different media formats is very valuable because different people prefer consuming content using different media. Offering the postmortem content in writing, on video, and in audio enhances the likelihood that the content will be consumed by different audiences in the organization.
	Indeed, think about it: Would it not be cool to listen to another team's postmortem while driving to work? It would! Thus, the possibility to do so should be offered to everyone in the product delivery organization to enhance learning.

Criterion	Explanation
Actions	Clearly defined action items are an essential part of incident postmortems. Each action item needs to have a driver. Being a driver may mean to work on the action item directly or it may mean to orchestrate the work of others on different parts of the action item. Moreover, each action item needs to have a review date. On that date the driver of the action item, the incident coordinator, and, if necessary, an agile coach should review the progress achieved so far. If the action item is not yet done, they should set a new review date.
	The action items from postmortems need to be entered into the work item management tool where all the other work is specified. They also need to be linked to a defect work item that will exist for the incident. The defect work item will contain a link to the incident in the on-call management tool. This way, full traceability is established, which might be necessary for regulatory compliance purposes.
	In addition, all the postmortem action items need to be identifiable as such in the work item management tool. This can be achieved, for instance, by attaching a common tag such as "postmortem" to all the postmortem action items. Ensuring proper handling of the postmortem action items in the work item management tool is another reason to involve the agile coaches in the postmortem process.
	A product delivery organization may establish a prioritization scheme for action items from postmortems. For instance, some action items from incidents with priority 1 and severity "critical" could be declared as action items to be put at the top of each affected team's backlog. Another way to establish a prioritization scheme for action items from postmortems would be to selectively allow any action item coming from any postmortem to be declared to be put at the top of each affected team's backlog.
	Regardless of how the prioritization scheme is set up, the lead time for postmortem action items is an indicator of organizational learning velocity based on postmortem efforts.

Now that you understand what makes a successful postmortem based on the criteria described in Table 9.21, let us take a deep dive into the details of initiating, running, and bringing a postmortem efficiently to conclusion in order to improve the overall system of work.

9.5.1 Initiating a Postmortem

Postmortems need to be initiated by a role in the incident response process that has the respective responsibility. For instance, the example role "incident coordinator" from Section 9.3.7, *Defining Roles*, has that responsibility.

Further, the responsibility for creating a postmortem record needs to be clarified. For instance, the responsibility to record the postmortem in writing and through the use of other media is with the example role "incident communicator" from Section 9.3.7, *Defining Roles*.

However, the incident communicator only takes part in incidents with severity "critical." If no incident communicator was part of the incident, the incident coordinator needs to either take care of the postmortem record or ask someone to do so. For instance, an agile coach may support the incident coordinator in this regard.

Generally, the availability of an agile coach in the postmortem is beneficial for several reasons. An agile coach can help

- Create the incident record using different media (writing, video, audio)
- Bridge what happened during the incident with overall organizational processes and practices
- Ensure proper handling of the postmortem action items in the work item management tool
- Follow up on the postmortem action items
- Identify common themes across postmortems

The incident coordinator needs to clarify the responsibilities of an agile coach when inviting them to the incident postmortem.

Initiating a postmortem is not necessary for every incident. The incident response process needs to clearly define incidents that require an incident postmortem to be conducted. The incident priority criteria can specify which incidents need to have an associated postmortem after incident resolution. For instance, the sample incident priority 1 from Section 9.2.3, *Defining Generic Incident Priorities*, requires an incident postmortem.

The sample incident priorities 2 and 3 do not. This does not mean incidents with priority 2 and 3 cannot have a postmortem. The incident coordinator or the people on call can still decide to have one if they think it is necessary.

9.5.2 Postmortem Lifecycle

After the decision to initiate a postmortem is made, the postmortem lifecycle begins. The lifecycle can be divided into three phases: activities before, during, and after the postmortem. The activities by phase are summarized in Table 9.22.

Table 9.22 *Postmortem Lifecycle Activities*

Before Postmortem	During Postmortem	After Postmortem
<ul><li>Invite participants</li><li>Clarify responsibilities</li><li>Construct the timeline</li><li>Run automated incident conversation analysis</li></ul>	<ul><li>Establish the Prime Directive</li><li>Clarify responsibilities</li><li>Refine the timeline</li><li>Review the timeline</li><li>Derive immediate action items</li><li>Derive action items for improvements in broader processes and practices</li></ul>	<ul><li>Create or complete work items for action items in the work item management tool</li><li>Follow up on action items in line with agreed review dates</li><li>Present the postmortem</li><li>Finish the postmortem write-up</li></ul>

Before Postmortem	During Postmortem	After Postmortem
• Create an initial postmortem write-up • Clarify people issues	• Prioritize action items • Assign action items • Agree on review dates for action items • Agree on forums where the postmortem needs to be presented and by whom • Solicit quick feedback on postmortem effectiveness	• Upload the postmortem video recording, if any • Upload the postmortem audio recording, if any • Distribute the postmortem content • Solicit periodic feedback on the outcomes achieved through the postmortem

The following sections explore the activities in each phase in detail.

9.5.3 Before the Postmortem

The first activity before the postmortem begins is to invite the necessary participants to the postmortem meeting in a timely fashion for a suitable time frame. Once they are invited, the incident coordinator needs to clarify responsibilities by postmortem phase so that each participant knows in advance what to do before, during, and after the meeting.

Reconstructing the Timeline

One of the major activities before the meeting is the reconstruction of the postmortem timeline. This can initially be done by the incident participants working individually on a shared timeline. Later the reconstructed timeline will be refined and discussed jointly in the postmortem meeting. The incident coordinator needs to request the incident participants to work on the timeline reconstruction before the meeting.

To facilitate the timeline reconstruction, the on-call management tool typically records all the events that took place in the tool during the incident. Additionally, many modern on-call management tools are able to illustrate the events on a graphically represented timeline. The timeline shows the events in chronological order: who did what manually and when, what was done automatically and when, and so on.

What is more, some on-call management tools contain a postmortem builder. Some tools also allow adding conversations from a chat management service to the postmortem builder in a selective manner. This way, the reconstruction of the incident timeline can be done in a semiautomated way. The actual events and the selected chat conversations can be added automatically. The accompanying narrative, screenshots, and figures can be added manually.

Despite the availability of a postmortem builder in an on-call management tool, a decision about where the incident postmortems should be stored needs to be made as part of the incident response process definition. For example, it might be decided to store postmortems close to runbooks. The storage location might be the SRE wiki. Alternatively, the storage location might be a dedicated shared source control repository or a dedicated work item type.

In any case, the decision about where the incident postmortems are stored needs to be documented and used across the product delivery organization to store postmortems in a uniform way. Also, before the postmortem meeting when the incident participants reconstruct a shared incident timeline individually, everyone needs to work on the same document stored at a designated location. Merging separately created incident timelines during the postmortem meeting is an antipattern that needs to be avoided!

Having Conversations Analyzed

Timeline reconstruction can also be supported by having the human conversations in the chat management tool, by email, and in the online video conferencing tool analyzed automatically. This can be done using tools that recently became available for the purpose. A notable example of such a tool is Jeli.[17]

Jeli creates a graphical timeline representation of the human conversations that took place in different tools it can connect to. Next, it allows the user to tag some phrases that would indicate a particular event during the incident. For example, the user can create tags like "incident trigger," "missing knowledge," "bug fix suggestion," and so on for some phrases on the visually created timeline.

Armed with the tags, Jeli traverses the entire timeline, applying the tags throughout, analyzing potential causalities, and trying to detect abnormalities in the incident response process based on the incident participants' conversations. The result is a set of insights on some strong and problematic areas of the incident response process. The automatically created insights can be brought to the postmortem meeting for discussion.

Drafting the Postmortem Write-Up

Before the postmortem, the incident coordinator needs to ask the person responsible for the postmortem write-up to draft it initially. The draft needs to be started at the agreed postmortem location (e.g., on-call management tool, SRE wiki, source control repository, etc.). The initial draft should also be distributed to the postmortem participants before the meeting so that they can have a quick look. This way, prior to the meeting, everyone's thinking is already directed to one of the most significant deliverables of the postmortem process. Mentally, people start finding holes and flaws in the draft write-up. These points are great conversation starters during the postmortem meeting.

Taking Care of People Issues

Interpersonal issues that surfaced during the incident need to be handled with the utmost of care. It is critical that these issues are taken care of before the postmortem meeting. This is so important that an already planned postmortem meeting should be delayed if known interpersonal issues have not been clarified yet. This is because making angry people with grudges against each other talk about what happened publicly in front of other people might escalate, become very emotional, and even derail the entire postmortem meeting.

To avoid such tense situations, before the postmortem meeting the incident coordinator should find a way to talk individually to the people who might have interpersonal issues with others. Ideally, this can be done offline. However, if done online, it is critical to run the meeting with webcams on both sides. Talking about emotional issues without seeing each other's emotions expressed on the face is detrimental to the purpose of the conversation, which is to find ways to resolve the conflict.

Taking emotional cues from faces is indeed what can help people lead the conversation in a way so that the right points are suitably discussed at the right time and depth in order to approach a resolution to the conflict. For example, if the incident coordinator finds someone

---

17. Jeli. 2020. Jeli Incident Analysis Platform. November 29, 2020. https://www.jeli.io/.

visibly very angry with someone else, they might refrain from digging into the details of the incident before giving the person time to vent about their frustrations.

In such a situation, zooming in to the incident details quickly would probably backfire, leave the person in an angry state, make them feel like they are unheard, and make them become angry with the incident coordinator. At worst, the person may not want to even join the postmortem meeting because they would not want to meet the person they are angry with and talk through what happened in a public setting. To avoid this, the incident coordinator may need to spend a significant amount of time silently listening to what the angry person has to say until the tension seemingly subsides. At this point, it might be possible to steer the conversation to the issues at hand.

In other cases, if the incident coordinator notices that a person is only slightly irritated with someone else's behavior, they would need to confirm this. After listening to the person for a short while, the incident coordinator might say: "You seem to be slightly irritated about what the other person said. At the same time, I have a feeling that you are not very angry about that. I would need to know whether this is the case to understand the size of the issue we have at hand from your point of view. Would you be able to let me know whether my observation is correct?"

The preceding sentences are constructed based on the "Nonviolent Communication"[18] approach by Marshall B. Rosenberg. According to the approach, a useful way to have fruitful interpersonal conversations is to use the formula: observations → feelings → needs → requests. This means state your observations; discuss the feelings evoked by the observations; explain what you need and why it is important; and then ask the other person to do something, being very specific in your request.

The "Nonviolent Communication" approach has proven to be useful in a wide range of contexts: business, personal, within groups, during negotiations, and more.[19] It can surely be applied successfully for resolving interpersonal issues in the context of incident postmortems.

Once the incident coordinator has talked to the people on an individual basis, they need to talk to them in a small group setting. In lots of cases, the group will consist of the two people who have issues with each other, plus the incident coordinator who invited them to the meeting and is leading the conversation. This conversation is important to have because the two people should not meet and talk to each other for the first time in a public setting during the incident postmortem meeting. Rather, the first conversation between the conflicting parties should take place in a more private meeting.

In the meeting, the incident coordinator is well advised to follow the "Nonviolent Communication" approach. They should state the observations that were made both during the incident and during the individual conversations that took place later. Following that, the incident coordinator should express the feelings they have after the individual conversations. Then the needs should be expressed along the lines of the necessity to continue to work together well as a team. The incident coordinator should finish by requesting the conflicting parties to express their viewpoints openly and have a conversation about how they might be able to work together in the future. Finally, the incident coordinator should hand over the floor to one of the conflicting parties to continue.

---

18. Rosenberg, Marshall B., and Deepak Chopra. 2015. *Nonviolent Communication: A Language of Life: Life-Changing Tools for Healthy Relationships*. Encinitas, CA: Puddle Dancer Press.

19. Wikipedia. 2022. "Nonviolent Communication." January 2, 2022. https://en.wikipedia.org/wiki/Nonviolent_Communication.

Typically, after the conflicting parties have discussed the matter, they can find a suitable way to work together in the future. In acute cases in which the incident coordinator's efforts have not yielded the desired conflict resolution, it might be appropriate to involve the corresponding line managers in the conversation. This, however, should be the very last resort: The line managers are totally out of context and would need to be brought up-to-date by the incident coordinator, all while the incident postmortem meeting still cannot take place in a timely manner as envisioned by the incident response process.

In any case, every attempt needs to be undertaken to clear the air before the postmortem meeting. Emotionally laden situations during the meeting should be avoided at all costs.

To be sure, the incident coordinator may not know about all the interpersonal issues that existed between the people during the incident. This is also not the goal. The goal is to tackle the most significant issues and ensure that the biggest tensions are defused and the people can work together again to have an incident postmortem that would lead to positive outcomes. The outcomes can be manyfold: improved interpersonal relationships between the incident participants, improved processes, improved tech, and more.

To help the people on call feel more comfortable opening up about an interpersonal issue, the incident coordinator needs to make every attempt to establish an interpersonal connection with them prior to a real incident. An effective strategy for doing so is to have a regular incident coordinator lunch, introduced in Section 9.3.12, *Incident Response Team Well-Being*.

9.5.4 During the Postmortem

Once the pre-postmortem activities are finished, the postmortem meeting can begin in a well-prepared manner. If possible, the meeting should be recorded in full. The incident coordinator should open the meeting with a greeting and a heartfelt thank-you to everyone for detecting, tackling, and resolving the incident. Right after that, the incident coordinator should explain the agenda points of the meeting to put everyone on the same page about what the team will be doing in the course of the meeting. See Section 9.5.2, *Postmortem Lifecycle*, for an example of a detailed postmortem meeting agenda.

Prime Directive

The first point on the agenda needs to be to put the participants in the right mindset. The right mindset needs to be blameless at the core. "We are not here to blame each other" is the message the incident coordinator must convey. To facilitate this, a so-called retrospective prime directive can be used. The prime directive was published by Norman L. Kerth in *Project Retrospectives: A Handbook for Team Reviews*.[20] It reads as follows:

"Regardless of what we discover, we understand and truly believe that everyone did the best job they could, given what they knew at the time, their skills and abilities, the resources available, and the situation at hand."

The prime directive gained popularity in the agile community. It is a good practice to show it prominently at the beginning of the postmortem meeting. Many great visualizations of the prime directive are available online that can be easily retrieved with a Google image search for

---

20. Kerth, Norman. 2013. *Project Retrospectives: A Handbook for Team Reviews*. Boston: Addison-Wesley.

"retrospective prime directive." Alternatively, the prime directive can be handwritten on a whiteboard, printed on a big wall poster, or set in large text on a presentation slide. Whatever the medium, the goal is to have the prime directive prominently shown to all the meeting participants.

The incident coordinator needs to explain that the text is a retrospective prime directive widely used in the agile community. If it is new to the meeting participants, the incident coordinator can read it verbatim. Otherwise, reading the prime directive in full would be tedious and unnecessary. The incident coordinator can show the prime directive and just say it is there to ensure that the team is aware that the postmortem meeting is not meant to blame, but rather to accept what happened and generate as much learning as possible from it. After the meeting, it will be about putting the learning into action and later assessing the outcome of the actions performed.

If the postmortem meeting is conducted offline and the prime directive is handwritten on a whiteboard, it is great to leave the whiteboard intact for the duration of the meeting and use other whiteboards for other purposes. This way, the prime directive stays visible during the meeting, symbolically conveying the meaning that it is applicable throughout. In case of tension, the incident coordinator can refer to the prime directive at any time by just pointing to it.

Reviewing the Timeline

The next big point on the agenda declared by the incident coordinator is to refine and review the timeline, ensuring that it reflects everyone's views on what happened and in which order. Before starting, the incident coordinator needs to reiterate the responsibilities that were distributed before. It should be clear who should take notes, who should contribute which knowledge, and who should moderate the discussion.

With the work conducted before the postmortem meeting to reconstruct the timeline, there is a great context for the discussion! The timeline should be examined event by event and pondered for factual correctness. The narrative in particular, if already available, should be checked for correctness by everyone involved.

It is helpful to ask some templated questions at appropriate points during the timeline review discussion.

- Do you think the incident priority was set to the correct value?
- Do you think the incident severity was set to the correct value?
- Is this abbreviation generally understood in the product delivery organization?
- Is this the best visualization of the data to illustrate the point?
- Can the visualization be understood by people who did not take part in the incident?
- Are the log queries for the visualizations shown stored and linked from the write-up?
- Will the majority of people have access to the queries?
- Should this passage go into the external write-up of the postmortem?

Any action items that might come up during the discussion are very useful because they originate in a deep context. They need to be put to the side; for example, on a dedicated whiteboard, in bullet point form. The action items should not disrupt the discussion on the timeline. The person responsible for taking notes should quickly record them while letting the discussion proceed.

Generating Action Items

Once the timeline has been refined and reviewed, it is time to generate the action items. A good starting point for action item generation are the corresponding side notes that were made as bullet points during the timeline discussion. The immediate action items can be generated off the notes.

Once the immediate action items have been generated, the team needs to review the timeline again with the goal of coming up with additional action items that would lead to improvements in people collaboration, processes, and tech.

The next step is to review broader organizational processes and practices that would need improvement based on what happened during the incident. Because there might be too many organizational processes and practices to review, and some practices might be manifested actions rooted in the organizational culture, this is the fuzziest source for action item generation. Also, because the action items would address wider organizational processes, practices, and possibly cultural norms, they themselves might end up being fuzzy. Finding the right balance of sourcing and creating good action items in this context is where the value lies for the product delivery organization. This is one of the things that make the postmortem-inspired change stick.

The generation of the postmortem action items is based on three input sources, summarized in Figure 9.12.

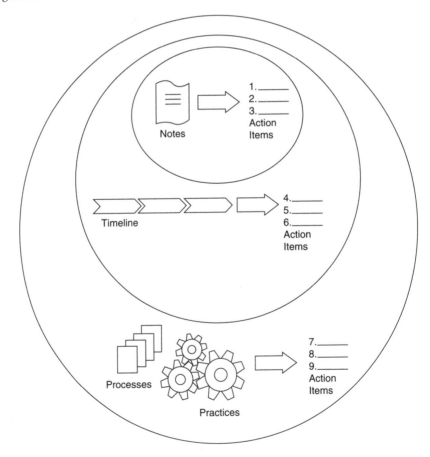

Figure 9.12 *Input sources for postmortem action items*

The notes taken give rise to immediate action items. The deliberate timeline review to generate action items yields additional action items. A broader review of processes and practices generates the final set of action items.

To support the process of generating action items from broader processes and practices, the following checklist might be helpful.

1. Incident response process
   a. Does any runbook need to be updated?
   b. Does the on-call training need to be updated? (See Section 7.7.3, *On-Call Training.*)
   c. Does the on-call rotation setup need to be updated?
   d. Does the incident classification with priorities and severities need to be updated?
   e. Does any SLO need to be updated/added/removed?
   f. Does any SLI need to be updated/added/removed?
   g. Does any stakeholder notification need to be updated/added/removed?

2. SRE infrastructure
   a. Does any dashboard need to be updated/added/removed?
   b. Does the alerting algorithm need to be updated?
   c. Does the tool chain need to be updated?
   d. Does the SRE wiki need to be updated/extended?

3. Architecture
   a. Is there a dependency between services that can be loosened?
   b. Does an aspect of architecture governance need to be updated/introduced?

4. Organizational
   a. Does any responsibility need to be made clearer?
   b. Does the organizational structure need to be updated?
   c. Does the employee onboarding program need to be updated?
   d. Does the workload need to be reduced to avoid burnout of some people?

5. Collaboration
   a. Are there interpersonal issues to be solved preventing collaboration?
   b. Do the collaboration practices between departments need to be updated?

6. Customer support
   a. Does the interaction between the first level support and the customers need to be updated?

7. Hiring
   a. Does the list of skills required for a particular role need to be updated?
   b. Does the list of technologies required for a particular role need to be updated?

8. Procurement
   a. Does the list of supplier selection criteria for custom software development need to be updated?
   b. Does the list of supplier selection criteria for software components/services need to be updated?

The goal is to take a wide-ranging view of what can be improved in the organization at large (the overall system of work) based on the incident at hand. In particular, the agile coaches working at all levels of the organization might be able to suggest improvement points in areas that are not immediately obvious to be related to the incident.

Once the list of action items has been compiled, they need to be prioritized. The prioritization should be undertaken as a group exercise by the postmortem participants. Once prioritized, each action item needs to be augmented by two important points.

- Who will be the driver of the action item? This needs to be one of the postmortem participants.

- What is a reasonable review date for when progress on the action item can be checked? The review is done by the incident coordinator and the driver. Other people can join on demand.

At the end of the postmortem meeting, this yields the table shown in Figure 9-13.

Incident A: postmortem action item list

Priority	ID	Title	Driver	Review date	State
1	...	...	...	DD.MM. YYYY	New

Figure 9-13 *Incident A's postmortem action items*

The action items need to be entered into the work item management tool in such a way that a table like that can be easily invoked, for example, using a single hyperlink. This way, an overview of outstanding action items by postmortem can be easily generated. The overview will be important for review purposes.

Postmortem Distribution

One of the final steps in the postmortem meeting is to decide how the postmortem learnings should be distributed and by whom. The incident coordinator, agile coach, and incident participants spent quite some time learning from the incident and identifying improvements across many dimensions to act on the learnings. Now is the time to distribute the learnings throughout the organization in an efficient and effective manner.

The first decision that needs to be made at this point is whether the postmortem needs to be made public outside the organization in addition to being publicized internally. The goal of external communication is to inform the public. If it is decided to do so, the external postmortem needs to be composed in writing based on the internal postmortem write-up. This external postmortem write-up needs to be drafted by the incident communicator, or another appointee if the incident communicator was not part of the incident.

In the external postmortem write-up, all the people's names, internal service references, and action item tables need to be removed and replaced by the entities recognizable outside the organization; for example, company name, externally offered services, and general statements about actions taken based on the learnings from the postmortem. The narrative needs to be shortened and cleaned up to only refer to something that can be recognized outside the organization.

Next, the external postmortem write-up should be reviewed by a group of people defined in the incident response process, and then published using the medium stated in the incident response process. Typically, an external postmortem write-up is published on the organization's website in the service status section.

For internal postmortem distribution, the goal is to facilitate the learnings from the postmortem throughout the organization. To do so, potential forums where the internal postmortem write-up can be presented need to be identified and decided upon. Typically, postmortems can be presented to a broader audience in meetings such as lean coffee sessions. Furthermore, postmortems can be presented to a more focused audience in meetings like the SRE CoP.

Because the goal of postmortem presentations is to facilitate the learnings for others, the internal postmortem write-up should specifically include a section on this. The section can be titled "What and how can others learn from the incident?" and should contain specific pointers to what people can do in their contexts to prevent a similar incident from happening with their services. For instance, the following statements might prompt people to take action.

- Check the availability of sufficient adaptive capacity to a prominent dependency X in your services.

- Check the availability of the description of the applicable auto-scaling rules by service in your runbooks.

- Ensure that a dashboard exists for your data processing pipelines showing the pipeline steps and the status of passing each step for each data set.

- Check the people who are on the on-call rotations scheduled for outside business hours.

Addressing people directly by using "your" is a good way to short-circuit the distance between the incident that happened to someone else's services and the person listening to the postmortem presentation or reading the postmortem write-up. The question of "What do I learn from someone else's incident?" gets answered directly in this way. If people get a clear checklist for what they can do to draw learnings from the incident, the entire nebulosity is gone. Instead, a clear path is paved. This approach is much more likely to spur action.

Sometimes it might be beneficial to present a postmortem in a forum applicable to the bulk of postmortem action items because the people in the forum will be involved in the work on the action items later. Getting them generally familiar with the postmortem helps create a shared understanding of what happened in production and why. It allows the people to ask questions from within their context. It builds momentum for the right intellectual and emotional connections with the topic at hand for the people to actually take action.

For example, if the postmortem action items contain several architecture-related refactorings in different teams, presenting the postmortem in a round of architects helps set the scene for the refactoring work to come. This is a much better context than just contacting individual architects with action items not created by them and asking them to do something on priority.

Additionally, if there is an SRE-related newsletter or an engineering blog, it needs to be decided whether a reference or a short article should be placed there to spread the information about the postmortem even further.

All the postmortem distribution activities should be captured as regular postmortem action items. This way, the action item tracking system would apply, ensuring that the discussed activities do not fall through the cracks and get forgotten.

Quick Feedback

At the end of each postmortem meeting, about three minutes should be left for quick feedback on whether the meeting made sense to the participants. This feedback can be enabled using red, yellow, and green sticky circles, for instance. The participants can use the circles to indicate whether the postmortem meeting was not effective (red), somewhat effective (yellow), or very effective (green). The circles can be put on a whiteboard in the offline setting; in the online setting, they can be put on a shared presentation slide or a shared board in an online collaboration tool.

Each participant would get one vote to cast. Once the votes are cast, a visual picture of the team's shared opinion about the postmortem meeting emerges. For instance, if seven participants took part in the meeting and the voting turned out to be as shown in Figure 9.14, the overall mood is that the meeting can indeed be improved.

Red circles	Yellow circles	Green circles
2	3	2

Figure 9.14 *Postmortem meeting quick feedback requiring action*

This is great feedback for the incident coordinator and agile coach to work on after the meeting. Instead of making the meeting run long due to a discussion about how postmortem meetings can be improved, the participants can be asked to send in or explain additional thoughts on postmortem meeting effectiveness afterward. If necessary, the agile coach can call for an additional meeting to discuss postmortem meeting conduct improvements.

If, however, the voting turned out as shown in Figure 9.15, no additional meeting is required.

Red circles	Yellow circles	Green circles
0	1	6

Figure 9.15 *Positive postmortem meeting quick feedback*

The agile coach can simply talk to the person who put a yellow circle after the meeting to understand their perspective and feed it into the postmortem practice. This is the case where the generally positive feedback provides confirmation to the incident coordinator and agile coach that the postmortem meeting practice is on the right track.

9.5.5 After the Postmortem

Once the postmortem meeting is over, the action items contain a clear path to further action. First, the action items in the work item management tool need to be checked for completeness. In all likelihood, not all the details were spelled out clearly enough during the postmortem meeting for the description to be understood thereafter by people who did not take part in the meeting. The action item descriptions in the on-call management tool need to be completed immediately after the meeting, while the conversations and context are fresh in the minds of the action item drivers. The action item drivers should take care of this.

Next, the agile coaches should schedule the action item review meetings according to the review dates agreed to in the postmortem meeting. This way, people's calendars are blocked for the purpose and a reminder for the action items is reflected in the calendars. Importantly, at the end of each review meeting, the meeting participants need to agree to a new review date. Again, the agile coaches need to schedule the next review meeting right afterward. This kind of relentless follow-up is absolutely necessary to drive the topics to conclusion. In the absence of this kind of rigorous follow-up system, the value of postmortems diminishes, the motivation to perform them declines, and morale suffers. The follow-up system is the driving force behind organizational learning based on knowledge from postmortems.

In addition to the action item review meetings, the agile coaches should book slots in the agreed forums to present the postmortem. This can be as easy as making a note on the forum's wiki page. However, it needs to be done right after the postmortem meeting to get a slot within a week or two in order to make the presentation while the incident is still fresh in people's minds. Presenting a postmortem more than two weeks after the postmortem meeting will convey less emotion and therefore trigger less action. Timely presentations should be preferred!

Before the presentations can be done, the internal postmortem write-up needs to be finalized. Clear and succinct technical writing goes a long way toward conveying the information in a structured manner, prompting people to act. This needs to be done by the incident communicator or someone else who was designated instead.

Some technical preparations need to be done as well. The postmortem meeting video recording needs to be uploaded onto the internal video sharing service and tagged accordingly. The postmortem audio recording needs to be uploaded onto the internal audio sharing service and tagged accordingly as well. This needs to be done by the agile coach.

Depending on the decision in the postmortem meeting, the owners of respective newsletters need to be contacted to include a piece about the postmortem. Finally, if it has been decided to publicize the postmortem externally, the external write-up needs to be prepared and the respective review process initiated. This needs to be done by the incident communicator.

9.5.6 Analyzing the Postmortem Process

The previous sections explored how the postmortem process can be initiated in a product delivery organization. Running the process takes time and effort. Therefore, analyzing its effectiveness to get an understanding of the outcomes achieved through the process is important to get a handle on the outcome versus effort ratio. This can be used to drive postmortem process improvement. How to do it is the subject of this section.

Action Item Lead Time and Cycle Time

In *Generating Action Items*, the process of postmortem action item generation was discussed. Once the action items are in the work item management tool, their lead and cycle times can get calculated. These lead and cycle times are important for the SRE coaches and agile coaches to get an indication of the speed of learning based on the postmortem activities. Both times are illustrated in Table 9.23.

Table 9.23 *Postmortem Action Items' Lead and Cycle Times*

		Postmortem Action Item			
	Is created	*Is scheduled*	*Is started*	*Is finished*	*Is reviewed*
State	New	Ready	In work	Implemented	Done
			← ——————— Cycle time ——————— →		
	← ——————————— Lead time ——————————— →				

The postmortem action item cycle time begins when the actual work on a given topic has started. It ends when the work has been finished, reviewed, and declared appropriately done. The cycle time indicates how long it takes to actually work on a particular topic.

The postmortem action item lead time is longer than its cycle time. This is because the lead time includes two additional time periods. First, it is the time the action item spends in the New state when it is created but not yet scheduled to be worked on. Second, it is the time the action item spends in the Ready state when it is scheduled to be worked on but the actual work has not begun yet.

Modern work item management tools provide a means to automatically obtain lead times and cycle times for the stored work items based on their state change times. Moreover, the lead times and cycle times can be obtained in aggregation. The corresponding visualizations are also often available out of the box. Notably, the cumulative flow diagrams provide good visualizations that can be used for trend analysis.

The postmortem action items can be tagged by category. Examples of categories may include tech, process, infrastructure, collaboration, and organizational. Once they are categorized, lead time and cycle time analysis can be undertaken by category.

The agile coaches do not need to be very precise about the lead time and cycle time numbers for postmortem action items. Although all sorts of mathematical analysis is possible, only bigger trends will be useful in practice. For example, if the average lead time for process-related postmortem action items is growing over time, it can be used as a data-driven impetus for discussion about why the pace of process changes is decelerating. The action items are from postmortems of real-world incidents, after all. So, there must be an urgency associated with process changes inspired by the postmortems. Why is the average lead time growing in this case? The value lies in answering questions like that, not in creating perfectly plotted cumulative flow diagrams or something similar.

Another example of useful postmortem action item analysis by category is to look at big differences between the lead time and cycle time. If this is detected, it means it takes a lot of time for the work from a category of postmortem action items to actually get started. Using this data-driven insight for discussion among the incident coordinators, agile coaches, and people involved in the work category can be beneficial.

For instance, if there is a big difference between the lead and cycle times of architecture-related postmortem action items, a discussion among the incident coordinators, agile coaches, architects, and product owners might be fruitful. It might happen that the teams struggle with prioritization of feature work versus tech work. This might lead to the realization that it might make sense for the team to create an error budget policy. The error budget policy may include a clause about the prioritization of postmortem action items.

The prioritization is important because if a team did nothing other than work on the post-mortem action items, the services owned by the team may asymptotically approach perfect reliability. Because only working on the postmortem action items will not be a viable option for the team from a business point of view, the error budget policy governs the balance of the work split.

The error budget policy may then get introduced and enacted accordingly. Sometime later, the average lead time trend of architecture-related postmortem action items can be analyzed again to see whether the introduction of the error budget policy led to the lead time reduction.

Generally speaking, appropriately short postmortem action items' lead and cycle times by category provide an indication that the organization is learning from postmortems at a suitable speed. Another indication of learning are the postmortem content consumption statistics. This is the subject of the next section.

Content Consumption Statistics

The postmortem process outlined previously generates text, video, and audio content. The content is produced by the postmortem participants to be used by others in the product delivery organization. That is, content consumption indicates whether the usefulness of the postmortem process goes beyond the immediate postmortem participants, their teams, and the teams affected by the postmortem action items. It indicates whether the quality and attractiveness of the postmortem content are high enough for teams not affected by the incident to take notice and start learning from other peoples' service outages.

How can the content consumption be measured? All of the content is digital. Therefore, its consumption can be measured using standard web content measurements based on content type and using metrics, as shown in Table 9.24.

Table 9.24 *Postmortem Content Consumption Metrics*

Content Type	Content Consumption Metrics
Internal postmortem write-up	Monthly page visits by postmortem
	Traffic source breakdown
	Top visited postmortems
	Number of postmortem email subscribers

Content Type	Content Consumption Metrics
Internal postmortem video	Monthly watch time by video
	Average view duration
	Video rewatches
	Top watched postmortems
	Number of postmortem video channel subscribers
Internal postmortem audio	Monthly listens
	Top listened episodes
	Number of postmortem audio channel subscribers
Internal postmortem presentations	Number of people attending the presentations
	Number of questions asked in the presentations
External postmortem write-up	Monthly page visits by postmortem
	Inbound web links by postmortem
	Traffic source breakdown
	Top viewed postmortems
	Number of postmortem subscribers by offered medium

All the metrics in Table 9.24 are only interesting as bigger trends. The trends should be available out of the box from the content publishing infrastructure. By no means should the product delivery organization invest anything in creating custom infrastructure to collect the metrics and trends. Let us explore them one by one.

The consumption of an internal postmortem write-up published on a web page such as a wiki page can be analyzed using metrics used for blog content analysis. The central metric here is the number of monthly page visits. If a postmortem is never visited, its usefulness remains within the circle of postmortem participants and the teams affected by the postmortem action items. The write-up does not break that circle to benefit other teams in the product delivery organization. Therefore, the primary metric for the SRE and agile coaches to look at is the monthly page visits by postmortem. Finding ways to get the postmortem write-ups viewed is part of ongoing postmortem process improvement within the SRE transformation.

> **From the Trenches:** At the beginning of the postmortem process introduction when the initial postmortem write-ups start appearing, the number of postmortem page views will be very low. The SRE and agile coaches should be prepared for this. It will take dedicated work to shape the postmortem process and associated culture to reach a point where teams begin to want to learn from other teams' service outages.

Another metric is the traffic source breakdown. This only becomes relevant once the page view metrics indicate reasonable user engagement. Also, not every wiki engine provides this metric. If it is possible to collect, the traffic source breakdown is useful to see how the users are reaching a particular postmortem. Is it through a general wiki search? A link to the postmortem posted on the organization's chat management service? Or by navigating to the postmortem section on the SRE wiki and accessing it there? Knowing how users most commonly reach the postmortem is useful for the SRE and agile coaches to better pave those ways in an attempt to build more user engagement.

For example, if the biggest traffic source for postmortem write-ups turns out to be the organization's chat management service, a dedicated channel for postmortems might be useful to create. A link to every new postmortem write-up can be posted to the channel by the incident communicator. The channel can be advertised in the organization so that the people interested in postmortems can join it and get the information that way.

The next metric is the top visited postmortems. This metric also only becomes relevant once the page view metrics indicate reasonable user engagement. It is interesting to know what kind of write-up, topic, and service outage attracts the most visitors. Perhaps the narrative was written much better than in other postmortems. Perhaps the services that experienced the outage are of central importance. All this intelligence might provide the SRE and agile coaches with ideas on how to adapt the postmortem process to output write-ups for increased user engagement.

Finally, the last metric is the number of postmortem email subscribers. This is an indication of whether people actively subscribe to email notifications about new postmortem write-ups being available for review. A low number of email subscribers does not necessarily mean low engagement with postmortem write-ups. The page views might indicate otherwise. In this case, the email as a distribution channel of postmortem write-up content may not be suitable. Other distribution channels may lead to greater engagement with the content.

Consumption of an internal postmortem video can also be measured using a number of metrics. The most important metric is the monthly watch time. If a postmortem video is never watched, it is not useful. However, it does not mean the postmortem is not useful. If the corresponding postmortem write-up page view is appropriate, it may mean that video as a medium is not embraced by the users. If, however, the monthly video watch time indicates reasonable consumption, other video metrics become relevant.

The average view duration indicates how long the users engage with the video. This metric trend can be used to understand whether engagement with the video content is meaningful. For example, if the trend shows one-minute engagement of a 60-minute video, it can be concluded that the engagement is not significant enough for some learning to take place. If the average view duration is longer, the next metric of video rewatches might be worth looking at. The rewatches indicate the parts of the video the viewers rewatched.

For instance, the periods 1:20–1:30 and 3:50–4:20 might be the most rewatched parts of the postmortem video. This insight might provide ideas about what the users found most interesting or what they least understood. This can trigger a wide range of follow-up actions to ensure the knowledge is provided to the teams.

Further, the metric of most-watched postmortems can give insight into what kind of video content resonates most with the users. Finally, the number of postmortem video channel subscribers indicates how many people actively seek to be notified about new postmortem videos being published. Correlating this with monthly watch time might provide insight into whether the channel subscribers are active.

The internal postmortem audio recording has similar metrics as the ones described for the postmortem write-ups and videos. It is about the number of monthly listens, the episodes listened to the most, and the number of postmortem audio recording subscribers. The same conclusions can be drawn from these metrics' trends as well.

An interesting set of statistics can be applied to postmortem presentations. The number of people attending the presentations is a good indication of whether people are interested in learning from postmortems in general. The number of questions asked by presentation is an indication of whether the people listen and pay attention, which is the prerequisite for learning.

Finally, a set of metrics can be applied to the externally published postmortem write-ups as well. Using the metrics, external consumption of the published content can be measured and used for analysis. The metrics provide an external view of the relevance of outages.

The monthly page visits indicate whether the postmortems are read at all. The inbound web links indicate which websites link to the externally published postmortem. This might uncover new user interest groups, which might be useful for marketing purposes. The same applies to the traffic source breakdown.

The top viewed externally published postmortems provide an indication of the most useful content pieces for the public user base at large. If subscriptions to external postmortem write-ups are offered by different channels such as email, RSS, and webhooks, the effectiveness of each channel can be analyzed based on the respective number of postmortem subscribers. Channels that are not used may not need to be offered in the future.

Soliciting Feedback on Outcomes

Another way to analyze the postmortem process is to solicit feedback on whether the postmortem activities yield real outcomes. The feedback can indicate whether some of the outcomes achieved by the teams are materializing through application of the postmortem process; that is, whether the outcomes materialize through processing the postmortem action items in a reasonable time frame and feeding the postmortem learnings into the right processes and groups in the product delivery organization. If not for the postmortem process, the outcomes would probably not materialize or would materialize much later, or it would be much more difficult to bring them about.

Such feedback can be obtained from the teams on a periodic basis. It can be organized using a periodic poll with a short number of carefully crafted questions to evaluate the postmortem. An associated retrospective needs to be run afterward by the agile coaches. Initially, the poll and retrospective should be conducted about once per month in order to adapt the postmortem process quickly so that it starts yielding outcomes.

Later, the frequency can be reduced to once every two or three months as the process matures. The poll should go to all the incident response roles, and specifically to the people who have taken part in the incident response since the last feedback round. The same applies to the participants of the retrospective after the poll.

If possible, the poll questions should be constructed in such a way that a trend analysis over time can be made. This is going to be the case if the questions can be categorized and the categories stay relatively stable over time. Examples of poll questions by category are summarized in Table 9.25.

Table 9.25 *Example Questions to Measure Postmortem Process Outcomes*

Category	Example Poll Question
Tech	Did your team achieve a technical improvement based on a postmortem action item in the last three months?
Process	Did your team implement or notice any process improvement based on a postmortem action item in the last three months?
People	Did your team implement or notice responsibility clarifications based on a postmortem action item in the last three months?

When constructing the new poll questions for a period since the last poll, the agile coaches should look at postmortems that took place during that period. It is great to orient the questions around those postmortem themes and action items. This will make the poll tangible to the people who will receive it. They were part of the incidents and incident postmortems. They defined the action items. Now they are asked to comment on the outcomes achieved by the process.

A positive feedback trend by category is an indication that the postmortem outcomes seem to be appropriate.

9.5.7 Postmortem Template

It is a good practice to have a postmortem template defined as part of the incident response process. This way, the postmortem write-ups are done in a consistent manner across the product delivery organization. However, because the value of a postmortem write-up is often in a good narrative of how the incident unfolded, a good postmortem template needs to strike a balance between structure and freeform.

A good collection of postmortem templates can be found on GitHub.[21] The templates from the collection have a lot in common. Generally, it is recommended to include the following sections in a postmortem template:

1. Title (sentence)
   a. Incident ID (number)
   b. Incident priority (number)
   c. Incident severity (number)
   d. Detection date and time including time zone
   e. Resolution date and time including time zone
2. Summary of what happened (narrative paragraph)
3. Incident response team (list)
   a. Incident coordinator (name)
   b. Incident communicator (name)
   c. Technical experts (list of names)

---

21. GitHub. 2021. "Dastergon/Postmortem-Templates: A Collection of Postmortem Templates." December 23, 2021. https://github.com/dastergon/postmortem-templates.

4. One-time quick fix

    a. Detection (narrative)

    b. Customer impact (narrative)

    c. Identified root causes (narrative)

    d. Immediate resolution (narrative)

5. Sustainable improvement

    a. Lessons learned (narrative)

    b. Action items (list)

    c. What and how can others learn from the incident? (checklist)

The last template section is particularly about making the postmortem useful for people who did not participate in the incident. It directly answers a question asked by many at the beginning of the incident response process: "Why should I spend time listening to other teams' service outages?" Having the postmortem template provide the reasoning head-on is a good initial answer to that question. Seeing the actual postmortem write-ups containing useful information for others to learn from the incident reinforces the message.

In a microservices architecture where teams own one or more services belonging to a domain implemented using similar tech stacks, potential technical issues can be similar. Therefore, a team that suffered an outage might be in a good position to advise other teams on what they can do to ensure the same kind of outage would not happen to their services. This kind of advice is exactly the point of the "What and how can others learn from the incident?" section of the postmortem template. Structuring the advice using a checklist lowers the barrier of adoption for postmortem readers.

The same applies to process issues. When a product delivery organization is introducing an incident response process, the teams will go through similar adjustments. Therefore, problems related to issues that occur in a team, such as on-call rotations, knowledge sharing, and adherence to defined procedures, might be applicable to other teams as well. Advice for ensuring that the process issues that occurred in one team do not occur in other teams should also be put into the "What and how can others learn from the incident?" section of the postmortem. Providing the advice in a checklist form is a great way to pave the way for the reading teams to take action.

The operations teams together with the SRE coaches should define an initial postmortem template that is simple and concise. From there the template should be evolved based on the ongoing retrospectives and feedback. Also, silent feedback in the form of postmortem template sections being consistently left blank or containing very little useful information should be taken into account. These sections need to be removed, renamed, or clarified.

Once the postmortem practice gains some momentum and there are good examples of postmortem write-ups, they should be presented on the SRE wiki for people to learn from. Indeed, excellently written postmortem write-up sections can be linked to from the postmortem template in order to show what good looks like by means of example.

9.5.8 Facilitating Learning from Postmortems

The previous sections showed the importance of learning as the central theme for the relevance of postmortems. Who needs to learn what, when, and how should be on top of agile coaches' minds when attending postmortem meetings. This thought process yields action items for various teams and groups in the product delivery organization.

In addition to that, the agile coaches can sift through the postmortems and discover patterns. Common themes can be found that come up again and again in different situations, with different teams and services. Tackling the common themes might require some bigger initiative to be started and executed throughout the organization.

Initiatives like that are home turf for agile coaches. They know how to pull the strings in the organization to convince the decision makers, get the ball rolling, and roll out a change in many teams within a reasonable amount of time. Following are some examples of such initiatives.

- A growing number of incidents took place where one of the root causes is inefficient resource management in applications not running in containers. Most of the teams do not have the applications packaged and deployed in containers. The necessary containerization would be a bigger change that involves container knowledge ramp-up, build procedure changes, deployment changes, and new ways of debugging. It requires money and time investments. Such an initiative can be driven by agile coaches throughout the organization.

- A growing number of incidents took place at night with an unacceptably long time to recover because the teams only go on call during business hours. The people on the teams do not have a provision in their work contracts to work outside business hours. Additionally, there is no desire in the teams to work at night. It is a bigger change that involves the HR, workers' council, legal, and regulatory departments. It requires money and time investments. It might involve organizational changes. Certainly, it will involve culture changes. Such an initiative can also be driven by agile coaches together with the team managers.

All in all, finding common themes across postmortems with a view to identify bigger initiatives for the organization is a useful activity that should be undertaken by the agile coaches on a cadence. Doing so every quarter seems to be reasonable.

9.5.9 Successful Postmortem Practice

As stated earlier, for an incident postmortem to be effective, its value needs to be greater than the time investment to conduct it. The time investment of the people on call and the agile coaches in conducting the postmortems, preparing the records using different media, and driving the action items needs to have a positive ratio to the outcomes achieved.

It is possible to qualitatively measure the ratio using some means. These are summarized in Table 9.26.

Table 9.26 *Postmortem Practice Measurements*

#	Measurement	Explanation
1	The trend of repeatedly occurring incidents for the same root causes is on decline.	Although this outcome cannot be fully attributed to the postmortem activities, it is a reasonable indicator of postmortem effectiveness.
2	Feedback on postmortem effectiveness from the people on call is generally positive.	First, quick feedback using red, yellow, and green circles at the end of postmortem meetings indicates that the meetings themselves make sense. Next, periodic feedback on postmortem outcomes by category indicates that the teams achieve satisfactorily good outcomes through the postmortem process.
3	The trend of postmortem content consumption is on the rise.	A growing number of people attending postmortem presentations is an indication that the culture of learning is developing. People find it valuable to spend time learning from other teams' service outages. A growing number of postmortem write-up page views, video recording watches, and audio recordings listens is an indication that the postmortem content is useful and engaging for the people.
4	The average lead time for postmortem action items is not increasing.	If the average lead time for postmortem action items across the organization is not increasing, it is an indication that the organization is learning from postmortems at a relatively constant velocity.

The postmortem practice is successful in a product delivery organization if the four measurements in Table 9.26 exhibit positive trends. An organization can reach a point where the work on postmortems is so ubiquitous and useful that people cannot imagine stopping it. Once that feeling sets in, people are genuinely learning from the postmortems and the learning is measurably contributing to positive outcomes in terms of product reliability.

The practice of postmortems is undergoing a lot of debate in the SRE community. This is because extracting effective learning from incident postmortems is still a problem not adequately solved in a consistent way in the software community at large. Notably, the online community Learning from Incidents in Software[9] is a good resource for learning about how incident postmortems are practiced in different organizations with high reliability requirements.

9.5.10 Example Postmortems

There are lots of opportunities to learn from postmortems by different companies online. This section presents some online resources with postmortems.

An example postmortem of a 66-minute Shakespeare Search outage at Google can be found in the original Google SRE book *Site Reliability Engineering: How Google Runs Production Systems.*[16]

The SRE Weekly[22] newsletter contains a section called "Outages" that includes a list of outages that happened during the week with links to their descriptions. Some links go to well-elaborated incident postmortem write-ups. For instance:

- A 47-minute outage of all customer-facing Google services[23] that required Google OAuth access. User request authentications could not be verified. This resulted in serving 5xx errors on virtually all authenticated traffic.

- A 48-minute Slack outage[24] during which users could not connect to Slack. Interestingly, people are invited to email Slack at feedback@slack.com to request a copy of the root cause analysis report.

In addition, many online services store their postmortems publicly online in a well-structured manner. Some examples include the following:

- Amazon Web Services[25]

- Microsoft Azure[26]

- Cloudflare[27]

- PagerDuty[28]

Finally, a maintained collection of postmortems classified by category is available on GitHub.[29]

Using these resources, a great deal of learning can be had by seeing how the most advanced software companies on the planet cope with outages and write up postmortems for the public. The external postmortems only refer to the services exposed for public consumption. Certainly, there are corresponding internal postmortems too. They refer to internal services not visible outside, and include detailed action items for specific teams and individuals owning the services.

---

22. *SRE Weekly.* n.d. "Scalability, Availability, Incident Response, Automation." Accessed January 19, 2022. https://sreweekly.com.

23. Google. n.d. "Google Cloud Status Dashboard." Accessed January 24, 2022. https://status.cloud.google.com/incident/zall/20013.

24. Speck, Tiny. n.d. "Slack System Status." Slack. Accessed January 24, 2022. https://status.slack.com/2020-05-12.

25. Amazon Web Services Inc. n.d. "Post-Event Summaries." Accessed January 24, 2022. https://aws.amazon.com/premiumsupport/technology/pes/.

26. Microsoft. n.d. "Azure Status History." Accessed January 24, 2022. https://status.azure.com/en-us/status/history.

27. Cloudflare. n.d. "Cloudflare Postmortems." Accessed January 24, 2022. https://blog.cloudflare.com/tag/postmortem.

28. PagerDuty. n.d. "Incident History." Accessed January 24, 2022. https://status.pagerduty.com/history.

29. GitHub. n.d. "Dan Luu: A Collection of Postmortems." Accessed January 24, 2022. https://github.com/danluu/post-mortems.

9.6 Mashing Up the Tools

The incident response process is greatly supported by a variety of tools discussed in the previous sections. The process can be streamlined a great deal by mashing up the tools in use. Lots of modern tools support integrations with each other. In this section, an exploration of useful tool mashups is done conceptually without referencing concrete tools individually. The exploration will be applicable to different tool landscapes composed of modern tools. Examples of possible tool landscapes are presented at the end of the section.

Previous chapters showed the central importance of the on-call management tool. This tool is at the heart of SRE practice and incident response. It is the tool used by the entire product delivery organization and stakeholders beyond. It could indeed be referred to as the operation's central nervous system. If so, then in analogy to the human nervous system, the tools connecting to the on-call management tool could be referred to as the operation's peripheral nervous system.

9.6.1 Connecting to the On-Call Management Tool

Figure 9.16 shows which tools could connect to the on-call management tool.

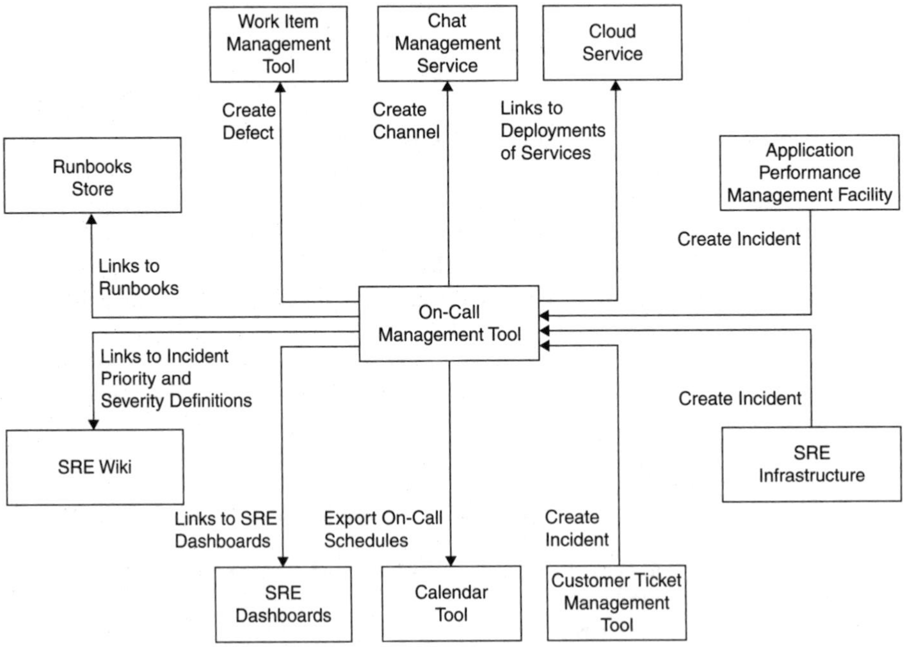

Figure 9.16 *Tool connections with the on-call management tool*

Table 9.27 follows the circle in Figure 9.16 clockwise, explaining each connection with the on-call management tool.

Table 9.27 *Explanations of Tool Connections with the On-Call Management Tool*

Tool	Explanation of the Connection to/from the On-Call Management Tool
Work item management tool	The on-call management tool gets connected to the work item management tool to synchronize incidents with work items. Whenever an incident is created in the on-call management tool, a respective defect work item is created automatically in the work item management tool. Whenever the status of the incident gets changed, the status of the defect gets changed as well. The synchronization is done to have transparency in the work item management tool of what teams are working on. Furthermore, the synchronization enables tracing from work items to code changes, which might be required for regulatory compliance.
Chat management service	The on-call management tool gets connected to the chat management tool to automate the creation of chat channels for incidents. Whenever an incident gets created, a respective channel gets created with the incident ID in the channel name. This supports the "single source of communication truth" for the incident.
Cloud service	The on-call management tool gets connected to the cloud service to link to specific respective deployments for each incident. This enables the people on call to quickly go into the deployment to perform incident analysis.
Application performance management facility	The application performance management facility gets connected to the on-call management tool in order to automatically create incidents based on the resource-based alerts.
SRE infrastructure	The SRE infrastructure gets connected to the on-call management tool in order to automatically create incidents based on the SLO breaches with a priority assigned to the SLO.
Customer ticket management tool	The customer ticket management tool gets connected to the on-call management tool in order to automatically create incidents based on customer complaints about functionality not working in the product.
Calendar tool	The on-call management tool gets connected to the calendar tool in order to export on-call rotation schedules to shared or individual calendars. This way, the people on call can have an overview of SRE-related and all other appointments in a single calendar of choice.
SRE dashboards	The on-call management tool links to the SRE dashboards from within incidents to reduce the time it takes for the people on call to find the right dashboard for analysis purposes.

Tool	Explanation of the Connection to/from the On-Call Management Tool
SRE wiki	The on-call management tool links to the SRE wiki in order to provide quick links to the definitions of incident priorities and severities.
Runbooks store	The on-call management tool links to the runbooks from within incidents to reduce the time it takes for the people on call to find the right runbook for a particular service to start taking action.

Mashing up the tools allows users to work seamlessly without having to log in to many tools separately. This is achieved using single sign-on, which is supported by many modern tools. Additionally, depending on the depth of the mashup, working in a tool might allow the work in other tools to be performed within a single window. For example, when working in the on-call management tool, it might be possible to open a defect work item in the work item management tool without leaving the on-call management tool itself. Another example would be to be able to view the on-call schedules from the on-call management tool in the calendar tool of choice without leaving the calendar.

9.6.2 Connections Among Other Tools

The integrations described in the previous section revolve around the on-call management tool. In addition, integrations among the tools connecting to the on-call management tool are possible as well. Examples of such connections are presented in Table 9.28.

Table 9.28 *Tool Connections Beyond the On-Call Management Tool*

Connection From	Connection To	Purpose
Work item management tool	Calendar	Export of timeline schedules (e.g., for portfolio level work items)
	SRE dashboards	Implementation of a service catalog based on dedicated work items; such a service catalog work item can be a well-described representation of a deployed service and can contain a link to the SRE dashboards for the service
Chat management service	On-call management tool	Incident creation
	Customer ticket management tool	Customer ticket creation
Customer ticket management tool	Work item management tool	Creation of new work items to describe customer requests for new features or for changes in existing features (not bugs)

Connection From	Connection To	Purpose
SRE wiki	Runbooks store	Links to runbooks for overview purposes
	Work item management tool	Link to the work item management tool to explain how the incidents from the on-call management tool are reflected there
	Chat management service	Link to the chat management service to explain the channel creation policy for incidents
	Cloud service	Link to the cloud service to explain where the services are deployed, by region
	Application performance management facility	Link to the application performance management facility to explain what it does in the SRE context
	Customer ticket management tool	Link to the customer ticket management tool to explain how it can be used by the first level support to create incidents in the on-call management tool
	Calendar tool	Link to the shared calendars where the on-call schedules are exported to from the on-call management tool
	SRE dashboards	Links to the SRE dashboards by team and by service
Runbooks	SRE wiki	Reference to the definition of incident priorities and severities

Using the connections from Table 9.28, a tight mashup of tools can be created. The goal is to have the right information ready for consumption for the right person at the right time. To achieve this goal, story maps can be useful (see Section 6.2.4, *User Story Mapping*). They allow for a user-centric analysis of specific user journeys through the tools. Based on the analysis, tool connections can be set up wherever technically possible.

9.6.3 Mobile Integrations

An important aspect of tool connection is integration using mobile apps. Sometimes deep tool integrations that are available in web tools are not possible in the respective mobile apps for phones and tablets. This, however, is an important aspect because working using mobile phone and tablet apps is as common as working on laptops.

If possible, the tool landscape should be integrated equally on mobile devices and laptops. This enables rather seamless switching between mobile and stationary working modes. This switching is a common necessity. Imagine a person on call getting an incident alert from the on-call management tool while grocery shopping. The alert arrives on the person's phone. The initial glance at the issue is done then and there: in the shop and on the phone. The person on call acknowledges the incident on the phone. Next, after checking out, the person on call puts their groceries into their car, gets into the car, pulls out their tablet, and performs an initial analysis of the incident. Confident that the incident is not a large-scale disaster, the person on call drives home and resolves the incident shortly after on their work laptop.

9.6.4 Example Tool Landscapes

Table 9.29 exemplarily shows two tool landscapes that might be available in product delivery organizations. Example tool landscape 1 is leaning toward Microsoft products. Example tool landscape 2 is leaning toward Atlassian products. Generally, many combinations of the products are possible.

Table 9.29 *Example Tool Landscapes*

Tool	Example Tool Landscape 1	Example Tool Landscape 2
On-call management tool	PagerDuty	Ops Genie
Work item management tool	Azure DevOps	JIRA
Chat management service	Microsoft Teams	Slack
Cloud service	Azure	AWS
Application performance management facility	Azure Monitor	Datadog
Customer ticket management tool	ServiceNow	JIRA Service Management
Calendar tool	Outlook	Google Calendar
SRE dashboards	Power BI	Datadog
SRE wiki	Azure DevOps	Confluence
Runbooks store	Azure DevOps source-controlled wiki	Bitbucket

Typically, SRE is introduced in an established organization where some of the tools are already in use. Adding new tools within the existing tool landscape should be done considering the integration possibilities among the tools. Deep integrations greatly streamline the incident response process by reducing the cognitive overhead of tool switching. This contributes to a pleasant and efficient working environment for the people on call.

9.7 Service Status Broadcast

The incident response process established so far involves the definition of incident priorities, incident severities, incident response roles, complex incident coordination, and a postmortem process. The next step for establishing a reliable incident response process is to provide transparency about the ongoing incidents and services they affect.

This transparency can be provided using a service status page. The service status page should contain all the services deployed in production by region. For each service, the service status should be displayed. The service status should reflect the availability of incidents with a certain priority and severity that affect the service. Which incident priorities and severities should lead to a service status page change is a matter of definition. The definition needs to be universal for the entire product delivery organization. It needs to be owned by the operations teams.

For example, it can be decided that incidents with priorities 1 and 2, regardless of their severity, change the status of a service on the status page to "impacted." The absence of such incidents associated with a service makes it appear in the status "healthy" on the status page. An example of a service status page is schematically illustrated in Figure 9.17.

```
Service Status Page

Deployment: Production Europe

Impacted Services            Stakeholder Notifications

    • Service 1                 • Service 1
                                  Incident Priority: 1
    • Service 2                   Notification: Data Uploaded in the Last 24h
                                  Not Visible in App1. Investigations Ongoing.
                                  Date: 12.12.2021
                                  Time: 7am


Healthy Services             • Service 2
                               Incident Priority: 2
    • Service 3                 Notification: Sporadic Log-On Failures. Root
                               Causes Understood. Fix in Preparation.
    • Service 4                 Date: 12.12.2021
                               Time: 1pm
    • Service 5
```

Figure 9.17 *Example service status page*

The example status page shows impacted and healthy services deployed in production in Europe. Services 1 and 2 are impacted; services 3, 4, and 5 are healthy. On the right-hand side of the status page the stakeholder notifications are listed. Service 1 has an incident with priority 1 where the data uploaded in the last 24 hours is not visible in application 1. Service 2 has an incident with priority 2 where sporadic log-on failures occur that have been understood and are being fixed.

This is the kind of service status broadcast that is necessary to put everyone in the organization, and beyond, on the same page feeding off the single source of truth regarding service status.

Common on-call management tools include a status page. The content of the page is generated automatically based on the services known to the on-call management tool, the incidents associated with each service, and the mapping of the incident classification to the service status on the status page.

Moreover, some on-call management tools support the creation of multiple status pages. Each status page can include a set of services and be targeted for a user group with user permissions set accordingly. This way, a dedicated status page can be created for different groups of people. For example:

- A status page for the product delivery organization containing all external and internal services
- A status page for stakeholders containing all external and some relevant internal services
- A status page for external users containing all external services

An example of a status page for external users from Microsoft Azure can be viewed at https://status.azure.com. An example of a status page for external users from Amazon Web Services can be viewed at https://status.aws.amazon.com.

In addition to the status page capabilities included in the on-call management tools, there are separate products dedicated to showing and distributing service status. Notably, Statuspage[30] from Atlassian can be used as a standalone tool. It can be seen in action showing the status of the Statuspage services[31] themselves.

From the Trenches: Development teams might be very used to working in the chat management service resolving issues with their services on request. This workflow might be so entrenched that, initially, the teams might have difficulty understanding why it is actually beneficial to broadcast their service status.

After all, they have been working without it for years, helping anyone with a service issue raised in any channel of the chat management service. In other words, sarcastically the teams might be asking: Is it not sufficient to have conversations about service outages spontaneously in 10 Slack channels in parallel? The teams might not realize that the number of requests they get in various channels can be reduced significantly if the service status is broadcast consistently with the single source of truth from the on-call management tool, distributed via the status page. With this in mind, the SRE coaches should take time to explain the reasons for broadcasting the service status. They should not assume that the reasons for having a service status page would be immediately apparent to the development teams.

The stakeholders, on the other hand, typically understand the need for a status page very well. It is they, after all, who need to chase the teams in the chat management tool asking for service status. Therefore, the stakeholders are usually eager to start using the status page as soon as it goes live.

Another important functionality of a status page is its ability to distribute service status updates using different media such as email, text messages, web hook notifications, RSS, or Atom feeds. This ensures that interested users can get service status updates via a preferred medium of choice. What is more, it typically reduces the volume of support emails and calls

---

30. Atlassian. n.d. "Statuspage." Accessed January 21, 2022. https://www.atlassian.com/software/statuspage.

31. Atlassian. n.d. "Statuspage Status." Accessed January 24, 2022. https://metastatuspage.com.

obtained by first level support asking for service status because that information can be obtained more quickly in a self-service manner.

The structure of services displayed on a service page needs to reflect the business view of what is offered. Therefore, many on-call management tools offer the possibility to create hierarchical structures of services. For example, a logical data ingestion service can be defined and linked to all the actual services deployed in production to ensure data ingestion can take place. This way, the logical data ingestion service status can be shown on the status page as an aggregation of statuses of all the linked services. On demand, users can drill down into the linked services individually.

9.8 Documenting the Incident Response Process

Documentation of the incident response process needs to take place first and foremost on the SRE wiki. It is important that the following content is crafted well:

- Incident response purpose
  - Overview
  - Expected outcomes
- Incident response roles
  - Responsibilities by role
  - Skills by role
- Incident classification
  - Incident priorities
  - Incident severities
- How to drive a complex incident response?
  - Process dynamics
  - Team well-being
- Stakeholder notifications
  - Stakeholder groups
  - Stakeholder rings
- Incident postmortem process
  - Responsibilities
  - Activities before postmortem
  - Activities during postmortem
  - Activities after postmortem
  - Postmortem template
  - Outcome feedback

- Service status pages

  ○ Mapping of incident classification to service state changes on the status page

- Tools

- Continuous process improvement

Clear and succinct technical writing is required to make the process understood and followed. Based on the SRE wiki content, the incident response process needs to become part of the on-call training (see Section 7.7.3, *On-Call Training*).

Additionally, the incident response process may well be subject to regulatory compliance. In this case, the content of the SRE wiki might need to be exported into a document that might need to be officially reviewed, signed, and archived. Upon significant changes to the process, the document may need to be officially updated.

Moreover, evidence of adherence to the defined process may need to be produced as well. With the incident timeline events stored permanently in the on-call management tool, availability of runbooks, and postmortems, the foundations for producing the necessary process adherence evidence should be available.

9.9 Broadcast Success

By now, an entire incident response process for handling complex incidents has been put in place. The organization now has a repeatable and reliable process to uniformly classify incidents by incident priority and severity, as well as respond to the incidents appropriately by classification. What is more, the organization drives improvements of many kinds based on the learnings from the incidents via the incident postmortem process. Finally, it qualitatively assesses the outcomes achieved through application of the postmortem process in regular feedback sessions.

This is a big achievement, without a doubt. It is certainly a reason to broadcast the success to a wider audience in the product delivery organization. In order to prepare for the broadcast, the progress on the SRE transformation hypotheses defined at the beginning of the transformation should be checked first (see Section 4.7, *Posing Hypotheses*). In fact, by now the SRE capabilities in some, or most, of the teams should be developed to the point where there is enough data to test the hypotheses using defined measurable signals. It is likely that some, or most, of the hypotheses can be tested positively!

If so, this is a huge fact to highlight during the presentation because it provides data-driven evidence that the SRE process envisioned at the beginning of the SRE transformation actually works in the organization as intended! All the stakeholders who helped get the SRE transformation into the portfolio of organizational activities (see Section 5.4.6, *Getting SRE into the Portfolio*) should be notified about the good news. It was they who had the courage to believe in SRE when it was just a handful of ideas to improve operations in the product delivery organization. It was they who defended SRE in the difficult portfolio prioritization discussions based on their beliefs without evidence at hand. Now that the evidence is there, the stakeholders should join in the celebration. The level of engagement appropriate by stakeholder should be informed using the defined stakeholder chart (see Section 5.4.1).

The SRE coaches should set up the broadcast. The broadcast communication channels that worked well in previous broadcasts should be reused.

The following questions can guide the SRE coaches in preparing a convincing presentation about the progress of the SRE transformation.

- How was complex incident response driven before the introduction of the incident response process?

- How is complex incident response driven now, explained in a high-level overview form?

- What are the defined incident response roles? What are their responsibilities and required skills?

- What is the process of taking on a role defined in the incident response process?

- What is the incident classification and how does it work?

- What are the incident priorities and severities?

- What is the mapping between the SLO breaches and incidents?

- What is a complex incident?

- How do you drive a complex incident response?

- How do you notify the stakeholders?

- What is an incident postmortem?

- How do you run an incident postmortem?

- What is a service status page?

- What are the tools involved and how are they mashed up?

- What are some examples of outages that were handled well using the defined incident postmortem process in the last three months?

- What are the current measurements of measurable signals from the SRE transformation hypotheses? (Publicly acknowledge everyone who contributed to driving the work on hypotheses. This will be everyone involved in the SRE transformation.)

The presentation can be concluded by specifying next steps for the SRE transformation. The recording should be tagged with "SRE" and linked to from the SRE wiki.

9.10 Summary

This chapter started on the basis of good SRE foundations in the development and operations teams established in previous activities; that is, the teams organized in on-call rotations to consistently react to the SLO breaches and informed stakeholders organized in groups and rings about major outages. Missing was a reliable and repeatable incident response process for complex incidents. These are the incidents that affect customers in particularly adverse ways and require the involvement of many teams to be resolved.

In the course of the chapter, such an incident response process was defined. It started with the definition of incident classification in the form of incident priorities. The generic incident priorities were defined as an example. It was shown how SLOs can be mapped to the generic incident priorities. Furthermore, the mapping of SLO breaches to incidents was clarified as well.

Further, it was shown how the generic incident priorities can be analyzed to uncover new use cases not covered by existing SLOs. The analysis might uncover some missing SLOs to be added. It may also uncover some cases that are currently not yet supported by the SRE infrastructure to be expressed as SLIs. In these cases, resource-based alerts can be created and new feature requests can be added to the SRE infrastructure backlog to support new kinds of SLIs.

Next, complex incidents were defined as incidents that require more than one team to be resolved. Following that, roles needed to handle the complex incidents in a well-structured manner were introduced. The dynamics of complex incident handling were explored. They necessarily need to be simple so that the people on call can follow and be supported by the process under the most mentally challenging circumstances. Additionally, aspects of incident response team well-being were discussed.

Following on, the incident postmortem process was introduced. It was shown that generating, facilitating, and spreading learning is the central value of the process. Facilitating learning using different means such as postmortem write-ups, presentations, video recordings, audio recordings, and action items is necessary to cast the learning net as wide and deep as possible. Measuring the outcomes generated by the learning from postmortems is difficult to do purely quantitatively. However, it is possible to do it in combination with qualitative measurements. A collection of outcome polls; associated retrospectives; statistics on write-up, video, and audio recording views; as well as meeting attendance numbers can shed light on the trends of success for achieving outcomes via the postmortem process.

Mashing up tools and providing service status on self-service status pages round up an efficient incident response process. Implementing such a process in a product delivery organization ensures a reliable and repeatable way of responding to complex incidents. Augmented by appropriate documentation, the process can be used and defended in a regulatory compliance context.

Establishment of the incident response process marks a point on the SRE transformation journey where the basic SRE foundations are in place. From this point onward, enhancements of the basic foundations are implemented. The first enhancement is to climb a step up on the SRE concept pyramid (see Section 3.5) and set up an error budget policy per team. This is the subject of the next chapter.

Chapter 10

Setting Up an Error Budget Policy

A team's error budget policy can be defined only after solid basic SRE foundations are in place—that is, the SLOs have been defined, the SLO breaches have been analyzed, and the SLOs have been adapted several times based on ongoing analysis of the SLO breaches. At this point, there is empirical evidence that the defined SLOs actually make sense in that they reflect the user experience impact well. Conversely, the error budgets also make sense. Solid mastery of the basic SRE concepts and the associated SRE practice in a team is the prerequisite for embarking on a journey to set up an error budget policy. With this in mind, this chapter explains the elements of an effective error budget policy and best practices for setting one up.

10.1 Motivation

Once a team has a solid SRE foundation in place, it is time to start discussing the team's error budget policy. At this point, the team might think SRE is fully established and no further refinement is needed. Therefore, it might require effort for the SRE coaches to motivate the team to optimize the established SRE practice in the form of an error budget policy.

This motivation can be sourced from the SRE concept pyramid defined in Section 3.5, *SRE Concept Pyramid*. The error budget policy sits just below the top level of the pyramid and it represents the second-to-the-top level of SRE maturity. Therefore, defining an error budget policy is a step toward maturing the SRE practice in the team. In the initial step, it should also be motivated as such.

But how would the introduction of an error budget policy mature the SRE practice in a team? It would do so by formalizing the consequences of breaching SLOs in terms of engineering capacity allocation to reliability. It would also strike an agreement between the operations engineers, developers, product owner, and possibly some management stakeholders about when and to what extent the team's capacity should be dedicated to reliability work.

Dedication of the team's capacity to feature work is done naturally by the product owner. Dedication of the team's capacity to reliability work has not been agreed to so far. With the definition and enactment of an error budget policy, an agreement in this regard will be worked out and enforced.

For example, the original thinking behind an error budget policy from Google's *Site Reliability Workbook* is to stop new feature releases until reliability work is implemented to bring the services back within the SLOs: "If the service has exceeded its error budget for the preceding four-week window, we will halt all changes and releases other than P0 issues or security fixes until the service is back within its SLO. P0 is the highest priority of bug: all hands on deck; drop everything else until this is fixed."[1]

The argument is that it does not make sense to add new features to a service in which existing features do not run reliably. This seems plausible. However, this thinking was challenged later in *Implementing Service Level Objectives*.[2] The authors argue that halting new feature releases of services until they are within their SLOs leads to a big rush of new feature releases later. Once the services are brought within the SLOs, every team is pushing many new features at once. This snowballs into a large number of changes in production, all done within a very short period of time. In turn, this greatly increases the likelihood of failures and, therefore, of premature error budget exhaustion. In fact, it might make a product delivery organization that usually releases software in small batches release software in a way similar to a giant release of a monolith.

These different views on what the error budget policy should contain demonstrate that an error budget policy should be crafted carefully, individually, and on a team-by-team basis. The policy should reflect the views of operations engineers, developers, and the product owner. It should guide data-driven decision-making regarding reliability investments and time allocation to reliability work in the respective team.

With an error budget policy, the team takes a longer-term view of reliability that goes beyond immediate fixes of individual SLO breaches and incident resolutions. In fact, the error budget policy gets enacted when the SLO breaches occur so many times that the error budget is depleted prematurely according to a definition of what premature means. The error budget policy should contain clauses about the type of work to take up and when to schedule the work to make the services reliable in terms of SLO fulfillment in a timely fashion.

The goal of the error budget policy is to make definitions, reach agreements, and stipulate action to support two principles from Google's *Site Reliability Workbook*:[1]

- "Manage by service level objectives (SLOs)"
- "SRE needs SLOs with consequences"

The error budget policy is, indeed, about defining the consequences that will have a noticeable and transparent effect on the engineering capacity allocation to reliability within the product delivery organization.

> **Key Insight:** An error budget policy is about defining consequences of breaching SLOs that will have a noticeable and transparent effect on the engineering capacity allocation to reliability within the product delivery organization.

The introduction of an error budget policy in a team needs to be accompanied by an introduction of terms frequently used in this context. This terminology is explained in the next section.

---

1. Beyer, Betsy, Niall Richard Murphy, David K. Rensin, Stephen Thorne, and Kent Kawahara. 2018. *The Site Reliability Workbook: Practical Ways to Implement SRE*. Sebastopol, CA: O'Reilly Media.

2. Hidalgo, Alex. 2020. *Implementing Service Level Objectives: A Practical Guide to SLIs, SLOs & Error Budgets*. Sebastopol, CA: O'Reilly Media.

10.2 Terminology

Achieving meaningful error budgets in a team requires looking at error budget depletion graphs to see which SLOs are broken so frequently that their corresponding error budgets get depleted prematurely. Premature error budget depletion is a matter of definition. It may be defined to mean error budget exhaustion before the end of an error budget period, or it may be defined to mean a high speed of error budget depletion within a given time frame (e.g., 50% of a monthly error budget depleted within a week). Other definitions are also possible.

In addition to premature error budget depletion, additional terms are frequently used in error budget policies. These are summarized in the following SRE cheat sheet.

SRE Cheat Sheet:

Term	Definition
Error budget grant	The error budget afforded by the SRE infrastructure based on an SLO. Once it is granted, the infrastructure keeps track of the remaining error budget based on the occurring SLO breaches.
Error budget period	A fixed period of time for which the SRE infrastructure grants an error budget.
Error budget grant period	Same as error budget period.
Error budget depletion	The consumption of the error budget. Each SLO breach depletes a small bit of the error budget.
Error budget exhaustion	The depletion of the error budget to zero.
Premature error budget depletion	The depletion of the error budget to an agreed level before the end of an agreed period. For example, the agreed error budget level can be 10% or 50%. The agreed period can be the entire error budget period of four weeks or just one week. Following this, premature error budget depletion can be defined as 90% of the monthly error budget depleted within four weeks, or 50% of the monthly error budget depleted within one week.
Premature error budget exhaustion	The depletion of the error budget to zero before the end of an agreed period.
Error budget policy	An agreed document stating what the team will do in terms of reliability work prioritization in case of premature error budget depletion.

The next sections explore the introduction of an error budget policy in a step-by-step manner. The exploration begins with the error budget policy structure.

10.3 Error Budget Policy Structure

An error budget policy needs to be structured well so that readers quickly understand the agreement to prioritize reliability work over other work in a team. To provide this structure, an error budget policy template can be defined in the product delivery organization.

The error budget policy template needs to specify the required parts of an error budget policy and leave enough room for additional freeform specifications to provide a good degree of freedom to the teams for expressing their prioritization of reliability work. Table 10.1 summarizes the required parts of an effective error budget policy.

Table 10.1 *Error Budget Policy Parts*

#	Part	Explanation
1	Scope	What are the services in scope for the error budget policy?
2	Purpose	What is the purpose of the error budget policy?
3	Conditions	What concrete conditions require the error budget policy to be enacted?
4	Consequences	What are the concrete consequences to be drawn for each condition where the error budget policy applies?
5	Escalation policy	In case of disagreements about conditions, actions, and reliability work prioritization in general, who will break the ties and how?
6	Agreed by	Who was involved in the error budget policy agreement?
7	Next review date	When will the error budget policy be reviewed next?

The scope of an error budget policy is typically all the services owned by a team. As such, defining the scope usually does not involve extensive discussions. This is different for the error budget policy purpose. It may take a while to clarify and agree on its purpose. The SRE coaches should steer the discussion toward the key insight that an error budget policy is fundamentally defined in order to influence the prioritization of reliability work in the team: that is, the consequences of insufficient reliability using directions for reliability work prioritization.

Parts 3 and 4 in Table 10.1, conditions and consequences, represent the heart of the error budget policy. These refer to the concrete error budget depletion conditions under the policy and the consequences to be drawn for each condition in terms of reliability work prioritization.

Part 5, escalation policy, specifies who will break the tie if the people on call do not agree on a certain case to which the error budget policy should apply or a certain consequence to be drawn in a given case. There will always be room for interpretation in an agreement such as an error budget policy. Not every possible case that may occur in the future can be foreseen. However, once new cases occur where the error budget policy might need to be applied, which is not very clear based on the current wording in the policy, someone needs to be designated to quickly make a decision based on the situation at hand. Later, the error budget policy needs to be reviewed and improved as part of the postmortem process.

Often, an engineering manager or operations manager would be defined as the go-to person to break ties as part of the error budget policy's escalation policy. At times more senior people in a product delivery organization, such as a vice president of engineering, vice president of operations, or CTO, might be more appropriate. The scope of the error budget policy should inform the designation of the most relevant tiebreaker.

The escalation policy may also outline a procedure for breaking ties. For example, the SRE practice at Google is set up in such a way that the people with the role "SRE" can refuse the responsibility for services that consistently violate their error budgets. In this case, the responsibility is handed over to the development teams that own the services. A detailed description of such a procedure needs to be made in the escalation policy part of the error budget policy.

Part 6 of the error budget policy needs to specify people who were involved in its definition, review, and agreement. This is important information for the people on call who are enacting the policy. Because the policy might contain some measures that could be unpopular in a given set of circumstances, it needs to be clear to the people on call whose air cover they enjoy when acting a certain way.

The final part of the error budget policy is the next planned review date. An error budget policy review should be conducted as a retrospective to assess the policy's effectiveness based on feedback. It therefore can be driven by an agile coach. The next planned review date for the policy should be defined at the end of the retrospective. The date can additionally be defined as a function of an event, such as an outage with a certain priority.

No further structure beyond Table 10.1 needs to be part of the error budget policy template. The template should explicitly encourage the teams to experiment and add parts to their error budget policies to cater to their unique needs in expressing the prioritization of reliability work over feature work.

This kind of lightweight structure also makes the error budget policies of different teams sufficiently comparable. The ability to compare different teams' error budget policies might be handy when several policies are looked at simultaneously, such as during an incident postmortem. Furthermore, a common lightweight structure of error budget policies across teams is helpful for quick orientation for people to get up to speed when they change teams.

10.4 Error Budget Policy Conditions

The previous section introduced the specification of the error budget depletion conditions and consequences that should be at the heart of an effective error budget policy. The conditions can be categorized as follows:

- Error budget spend
- Error budget burn rate
- Dependency handling

Example conditions for each of these categories are specified in Table 10.2.

Table 10.2 *Example Error Budget Policy Conditions*

Condition Category	Example Conditions
Error budget spend	A. Premature error budget exhaustion before the end of the current error budget period (e.g., the current month)
	B. A certain percentage of the error budget depleted in the current error budget period (e.g., 70% in a monthly error budget period, 80% for a contractually agreed SLA in a monthly error budget period)
	C. A certain percentage of the error budget in the current error budget period depleted by a single incident
	D. A certain percentage of the quarterly error budget depleted by a certain type of outage
Error budget burn rate	E. A certain percentage of the error budget granted for the current error budget period depleted within 24 hours (e.g., 30% - indicating a fast burn rate)
	F. A certain percentage of the error budget granted for the current error budget period depleted within seven days (e.g., 50% - indicating a relatively slow burn rate)
Dependency handling	G. A certain percentage of the error budget granted for the current error budget period depleted due to failures in a dependent service (e.g., 50%)

If possible, the conditions should be specified in such a way that they can be alerted upon by the SRE infrastructure. This makes the triggers for enacting the error budget policy automated. For instance, example conditions A, B, E, and F from the table above can be turned into automated alerts by the basic SRE infrastructure. On the contrary, example conditions C, D, and G are more difficult to automate and require SRE infrastructure add-ons. Each condition in the error budget policy needs to be specified in terms of being triggered automatically or manually.

Manual conditions need to be triggered by the people on call. Therefore, a procedure must be established in each team for the manual error budget policy conditions to be checked on a regular basis. For example, this can be done every time an on-call shift rotation takes place. The person going on call can quickly review the team's error budget policy, identify the manual conditions, and check whether they apply. Doing so at the beginning of the on-call shift helps keep the manual conditions fresh in the person's mind during their shift.

Ensuring that the error budget policy conditions are actually triggered, either automatically or manually, is an important step toward making the policy relevant. In fact, the policy can only be effective and lead to outcomes if it is triggered according to the specified conditions. Having the error budget policy defined but not triggered will quickly bring the motivation of the people on call to deal with it to zero.

10.5 Error Budget Policy Consequences

When defining the consequences for conditions governed by an error budget policy, an attempt should be made to define them in an automatable and traceable manner, if possible. Doing so will enable automated checks whether or not the consequences are executed as agreed.

To be sure, error budget policy consequences will contain lots of qualified statements to be interpreted by humans. However, wherever possible, automatable and traceable clauses should be defined to enable automated analysis.

The error budget depletion consequences may be categorized. The following categories might be useful:

- Assigning people
- Conducting activities
- Stopping activities

Example consequences for each category are presented in Table 10.3.

Table 10.3 *Example Error Budget Policy Consequences*

Consequence Category	Example Consequences
Assigning people	A. Assign a certain percentage of engineers on the team to reliability work until certain conditions apply.
	B. Escalate to a higher-up to influence the assignment of engineers to reliability work.
Conducting activities	C. Conduct a postmortem.
	D. Create an action item.
	E. Prioritize an action item in a certain way.
	F. Get an action item done within a certain amount of time.
	G. Engage with the owner of a dependent service (internal team or external company).
	H. Communicate the error budget state to certain parties.
Stopping activities	I. Stop new feature releases to the staging environment.
	J. Stop new feature releases to the production environments.

Consequence D can be fully automated. In fact, some on-call management tools support so-called runbook automation that can automatically create work items in a connected work item management tool.

Consequences I and J can also be automated. This would require corresponding features to be made available in the SRE and deployment infrastructure. Other consequences, such as A, B, C, E, F, G, and H, cannot be automated. However, some of these consequences, such as C, E, and F, are traceable.

10.6 Error Budget Policy Governance

The cross-product of policy conditions and consequences yields the overall set of actions governed by the error budget policy. The more data-driven the conditions and consequences can be, the more traceability and transparency can be associated with a given policy. This is illustrated in Figure 10.1.

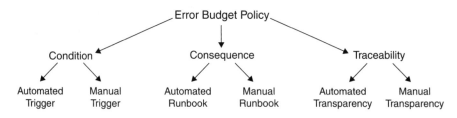

Figure 10.1 *Error budget policy governance*

The error budget policy consists of conditions and consequences. Further, it has some level of traceability. The conditions can be triggered either automatically or manually. Likewise, the consequences can be executed using either automated or manual runbooks. The resultant traceability will be a combination of automated and manual steps providing transparency.

As an example, let us consider a clause in an error budget policy. A policy condition may be about the availability of dead letters in a queue. Such dead letters represent queue messages that a message processor could not process successfully. The associated consequence may be to create an action item and get it prioritized and turned around within a week. Table 10.4 shows how the clause could be specified to enable traceability.

Table 10.4 *Example Error Budget Policy Clause*

Condition	The error budget for dead letters in the message queue "data_inflow" is exhausted prematurely before the end of the current error budget period.
Automated Trigger	An alert is sent to the people on call when the error budget is exhausted before the end of the current error budget period.
Consequence	• Raise an action item to be prioritized at the top of the team backlog. • Link the action item to the error budget policy. • Finish the work on the backlog item within a week.
Automated Runbook	The consequence is partly coded up in an automated runbook. The action item is created and linked to the error budget policy automatically. The people on call need to get the action item prioritized.
Traceability	• Check for work items in the work item management tool linked to the error budget policy. • Check the action item lead time.

In the error budget policy clause shown in Table 10.4, the SRE infrastructure alerts can trigger the condition in a fully automated manner. This is great because the people on call will be notified automatically about the condition without having to keep the clause in mind. The consequence of the clause can be semiautomated. The envisioned action item can be created and linked automatically using runbook automation. The prioritization of the action item needs to be driven manually. The traceability of the clause is there because the action item lead time can be obtained automatically from the work item management tool. The entire process is illustrated in Figure 10.2.

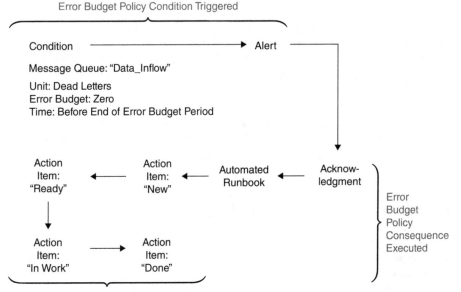

Figure 10.2 *Error budget policy execution*

The top of Figure 10.2 shows the condition of the error budget policy. Once the SRE infrastructure detects the condition, an alert is generated and dispatched to the people on call in the given team. That is, the policy condition trigger is fully automated.

Next, the alert is acknowledged by a person on call, and then the on-call management tool runs an automated runbook that creates an action item. The action item moves to the "New" state; once the action item is prioritized, it moves to the "Ready" state. When the actual work on the action item begins, it moves to the "In Work" state. Finally, once the work on the action item is finished, it moves to the "Done" state.

Thus, the error budget policy consequence is executed. The execution is automatically traceable using the action item state changes. It is also transparent because anybody in the product delivery organization can view the action item and its lead time in the work item management tool.

In general, the value of an error budget policy for a product delivery organization is in the consequences executed on its basis. If no consequences are executed on the basis of an error budget policy, the prioritization of reliability work is not influenced and hence no value is generated. The transparency of actions taken on the basis of an error budget policy is great to have to assess the policy's effectiveness. The more data-driven the transparency is, the more objective the policy's effectiveness assessment will be.

This is not to say that the entire error budget policy can be specified in an automatable and traceable manner. If this were possible, the error budget policy could be fully coded up in a programming language. Although that would be great to have, it is not a realistic expectation. An error budget policy should address complex socio-technical cases, which do not always lend themselves to programming. Wherever possible, though, error budget policy clauses should be specified in an automatable and traceable way to simplify the enactment and measurement of the policy's effectiveness.

In terms of measuring a policy's effectiveness, a lot of the measurement will be qualitative and done in periodic error budget policy reviews conducted as retrospectives. Because some error budget policy clauses will not be automatable and traceable, the policy's effectiveness will be determined to a significant extent by simply how serious the team takes the policy. This, in turn, will be determined by the team's SRE culture. As mentioned at the beginning of this chapter, an error budget policy resides near the top layer of the SRE concept pyramid. Not every team will reach that level. The effort to define and enact an error budget policy needs to be extended only in teams with mature SRE culture, thereby maximizing the chances of successful policy application leading to good reliability outcomes.

10.7 Extending the Error Budget Policy

In Section 10.3, *Error Budget Policy Structure*, I discussed the required parts of an effective policy template and hinted that teams must have freedom to extend the policy in order to prioritize the reliability work in the way they see fit.

In that context, the conditions in an error budget policy should ideally be expressed in terms of error budget depletion. However, if a team wants to deviate from that, they should be free to do so. It is more important to have an error budget policy in place that is working effectively based on conditions expressed using means other than functions of error budget depletion than it is to have no error budget policy at all. Even worse is to have an error budget policy that does not get enacted. This is because in that case, the time taken by many people to agree on the policy was fully wasted.

The need for policy conditions to be specified not just as functions of error budget depletion may stem from the fact that the team may have resource-based alerts—for example, "CPU is over 80%" or "Memory is over 90%"—in addition to SLOs. The SRE infrastructure might not yet support all the necessary SLIs or ways to measure existing SLIs to express every reliability concern of every service in the product delivery organization. Therefore, some resource-based alerts might still be there to fill in the gaps.

Following this, the error budget policy might contain conditions that are rooted in resource-based alerts. For example, such conditions might be

- High CPU consumption over extended time periods
- Sudden increase in dead letters in dead letter queues
- Sudden active message count increase in message queues
- High background job restart numbers

What is more, the teams might specify additional points in an error budget policy that only seem distantly related at first. For example, a team might list phases in the release lifecycle and specify different error budget policies by phase. This might happen when each phase takes a significant amount of time because the team's production release cadence is rather infrequent. Often in this context, many teams release to production together at the same time.

Table 10.5 shows an example of release lifecycle phases and their respective durations.

Table 10.5 *Example Release Lifecycle Phases and Their Durations*

Release Lifecycle Phase	Possible Duration
Planning	Several days
Development	Several months
Rollout to staging	Several days
Testing for regulatory compliance	Several days to several weeks
Hotfix rollout to all production environments	Several days
Feature release rollout to all production environments	Several weeks

For instance, the teams in the product delivery organization might plan releases using so-called Program Increment (PI) plannings as suggested by the Scaled Agile Framework (SAFe[3]). In this case, the teams might also be organized in so-called Agile Release Trains (ARTs) as suggested by the framework. Given this, a PI planning includes all members of all teams belonging to an ART. The planning is executed like a conference that runs for several days. During that time, all the team members are expected to focus on the planning activities. It follows that the teams might want to specify the policy conditions in their error budget policies that specifically apply during the PI planning.

This might sound counterproductive. The error budget policy should govern the team's actions to ensure reliability in production regardless of the release lifecycle phase. After all, there is always a previous release running in production whose reliability has to be ensured. Why on earth would any other activity, like PI planning, have an influence on ensuring reliability in production according to the error budget policy?

This is the point in the SRE transformation when the SRE coaches need to pay very close attention to other established frameworks like the Scaled Agile Framework in the product delivery organization. It may happen that, culturally, frameworks like SAFe are very powerful. In that case, an intersection between SAFe and SRE needs to be found. Out of the box, there might be no intersection, initially causing tension.

Indeed, the Scaled Agile Framework does not mention SRE. In fact, searching for "SRE" on the SAFe website results in zero search results at the time of this writing. The opposite holds true as well. The SRE community never talks about SAFe. Now, introducing SRE in an environment where SAFe is culturally strong requires creation of a bridge between the two. The first stepping-stone on that bridge might be the error budget policy.

---

3. Leffingwell, Dean. 2012. "PI Planning." Scaled Agile Framework. August 7, 2012. https://www.scaledagileframework.com/pi-planning.

That is, if a team wants to create specific error budget policy clauses that reflect how they currently work under the Scaled Agile Framework, the SRE coaches should let them do so. It is more important to start building a bridge between SAFe and SRE in a team than to create a canonically perfect error budget policy according to SRE. In fact, if the Scaled Agile Framework dictates that all the team members should focus on PI planning for a couple of days and the SRE framework dictates that they should focus on reliability at the same time, it might be the error budget policy that breaks the tie!

The SRE coaches should show empathy, accept the environment the teams operate in, and use the error budget policy clauses to think about how SRE could be accommodated better in the given environment. The SRE coaches should initiate these conversations with the agile coaches. For example, the way the PI plannings are conducted might be adapted to accommodate more error budget policy activities to be done at the same time.

Another topic of conversation with the agile coaches could be about testing for regulatory compliance. As shown in Table 10.5, testing can take several days to several weeks. Also, all the team members might be required to work full time to run tests for regulatory compliance. This time, it is the regulatory compliance regime that might require the teams to act this way. Digging deeper, it might actually be the regulatory compliance regime specifically installed at the product delivery organization to meet the regulatory requirements imposed by industry standards. However, other ways of meeting regulatory requirements might be possible. For instance, meeting the requirements using more automation holds the potential to free people from being bound to the testing activity for a lengthy amount of time. This way, more activities from the error budget policies can be done at the time of regulatory compliance testing.

An additional topic of conversation between the SRE coaches and agile coaches based on Table 10.5 is the speed of rollouts. If the team members want to include the staging, hotfix, and production rollouts as distinct release phases in the error budget policy, it is a clear indication that the rollouts are rather painful for the team. The reasons for this need to be uncovered. Following this, appropriate changes need to be initiated in the teams. The changes will be in the area of deployment and test automation. Additionally, changes may be made to the architecture, to rearchitect a monolith into smaller, independently deployable units. This will be a bigger change that may require a longer period of time to execute.

Once the independently deployable units become available, the next conversation between the SRE and agile coaches might be related to release cadence. With smaller, independently deployable units, smaller development phases can be initiated, leading to more frequent releases.

The entire transformation of how regulatory compliance is ensured, staging and production rollouts are done, the development cadence is planned, and the release cadence is carried out can be executed as a bigger transformation initiative called, for example, "Continuous Delivery transformation" or "DevOps transformation." Due to the size and effort of the transformation, it will need to be established at the portfolio level of the organizational initiatives. This can be achieved similar to how the SRE transformation was established at the portfolio level of initiatives, as explained in detail in Section 5.4.6, *Getting SRE into the Portfolio*.

This discussion demonstrates how the SRE transformation influences other established processes and methodologies existing in a product delivery organization. Indeed, during the SRE transformation, an intersection of SRE with the existing processes and methodologies needs to be found and established. This is illustrated in Figure 10.3.

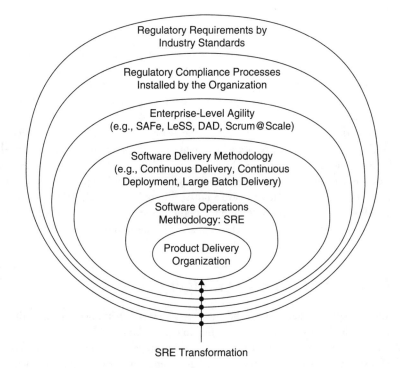

Regulatory Requirements by
Industry Standards

Regulatory Compliance Processes
Installed by the Organization

Enterprise-Level Agility
(e.g., SAFe, LeSS, DAD, Scrum@Scale)

Software Delivery Methodology
(e.g., Continuous Delivery, Continuous
Deployment, Large Batch Delivery)

Software Operations
Methodology: SRE

Product Delivery
Organization

SRE Transformation

Figure 10.3 *SRE being woven into existing processes during the SRE transformation*

As Figure 10.3 depicts, the SRE transformation touches several established processes and methodologies. While the SRE transformation is being injected into the organization, the transformation passes layers of existing processes and methodologies. For example, beyond SRE as the software operations methodology being established lies a software delivery methodology that determines the way teams deliver software to production.

The methodology could be one of continuous delivery, always keeping the software in a releasable state but doing the actual production releases on some frequent cadence in agreement with the business. Alternatively, the software could be delivered to production using a continuous deployment methodology, in which every change is deployed to production automatically after passing all the tests on a deployment pipeline. It could also be delivered in large batches, whereby a release consists of software developed by many teams over several months. As shown in Table 10.5, the way teams deliver software to production may have an influence on the content of the error budget policy. This is exactly the intersection point between SRE and the software delivery methodology.

Beyond the software delivery methodology is the enterprise-level agility methodology. This is about making agility in the enterprise go beyond the development teams to the areas of portfolio management, compliance management, large customer solution creation, budgeting, and organizational KPIs. Popular frameworks for achieving enterprise-level agility are SAFe, Large-Scale

Scrum (LeSS),[4] Disciplined Agile Delivery (DAD),[5] and Scrum@Scale.[6] As shown in Table 10.5, these frameworks may also influence the way the teams structure their error budget policies.

Beyond the enterprise-level agility methodology are the regulatory compliance processes installed by the product delivery organization to meet regulatory requirements set by industry standards. These processes may impose certain tests to be performed and certain documentation to be produced in specific ways at specific times. This as well may have an influence on the way the teams decide to structure their error budget policies.

Thus, considering the overall environment the teams are operating in, the SRE coaches should give them, within limits, freedom to systematize and set guidelines for their reliability work in the error budget policy. In fact, the SRE coaches should only provide a single boundary condition for the error budget policy content: That is, an error budget policy should define consequences of breaching SLOs that will have a noticeable and transparent effect on the engineering capacity allocation to reliability. Should the team members want to express the engineering capacity allocation to reliability by the release phase, they need to be free to do so.

10.8 Agreeing to the Error Budget Policy

The operations engineers, developers, and product owner of a team need to agree on the error budget policy, as do the people who are specified in the escalation policy to break ties in case of disagreements. It is beneficial to drive this agreement in stages to involve the right people at the right time for the appropriate amount of time. Agreement can be staged in the following way.

1. The operations engineers and developers create an error budget policy draft using their technical knowledge.

2. The product owner gets involved to review the error budget policy draft from the user and business point of view.

3. The people specified in the escalation policy get involved to review the error budget policy from the clarity, specificity, precision, and data-driven measurements point of view.

The SRE coaches should initiate and drive the process. First, they should invite the operations engineers and developers for the services in the scope of the error budget policy for a discussion rooted in the services' past incidents and bigger outages. The discussion will be fairly technical. At the beginning of the discussion, the SRE coaches should reiterate the context and motivation and explain how the discussion will be facilitated.

The facilitation can start by reviewing and discussing examples of other teams' error budget policies. The first example can be drawn directly from Google's *Site Reliability Workbook*.[1] Further examples may come from other teams' error budget policies if they exist at the time.

4. The LeSS Company B.V. n.d. "Overview – Large Scale Scrum (LeSS)." Accessed January 24, 2022. https://less.works.

5. Project Management Institute Inc. n.d. "Disciplined Agile®." Accessed January 24, 2022. https://www.pmi.org/disciplined-agile.

6. Scrum Inc. 2019. Scrum@Scale. August 23, 2019. https://www.scrumatscale.com.

Discussing the examples will lead to conversations about what the error budget policy might look like for the team. The SRE coaches need to channel the conversations toward creation of an error budget policy draft. Elaboration of conditions and consequences should take center stage. Moreover, the draft will be affected by other frameworks and methodologies established in the product delivery organization by which the team owning the services is influenced.

The SRE coaches should pay close attention to the influence on the team exercised by other frameworks and methodologies to learn some specific aspects and use the learnings in error budget policy discussions with other teams. Moreover, these aspects provide a good basis for discussions with agile coaches to drive broader organizational improvements.

The SRE coaches should see the discussion converge by achieving agreement on the error budget policy draft by the operations engineers and developers. Once this agreement has been reached, the SRE coaches should invite the product owner to the discussion of the draft.

At this point, the technical discussions are over, the conditions addressed by the error budget policy are clear, and the corresponding consequences are defined. The product owner can now review the current error budget policy draft from the customer and business point of view. That is, does the error budget policy strike a good balance between the reliability work and the new feature work to provide an optimal user experience and business benefit? Does it dictate that the team should work on reliability when required to ensure a good user experience for existing features? Does it allow the team to work on new features when the reliability of existing features is up to standard? These checks by the product owner also contribute to the error budget policy being written in a way that can be understood by people without deep technical expertise. This is especially required by the people specified in the escalation policy.

Once the product owner is in agreement with the operations engineers and developers about the content of the error budget policy draft, the SRE coaches should invite the people specified in the escalation policy to a discussion of the draft. These people should check the policy for precision, completeness, clarity, and vernacular to make the agreement as unambiguous as possible. Furthermore, they should check whether the conditions and consequences are specified in such a way that programmatic evaluation is enabled as far as possible.

Once the operations engineers, developers, product owner, and people from the escalation policy agree to the error budget policy, it needs to be stored. This is the subject of the next section.

10.9 Storing the Error Budget Policy

Generally speaking, an error budget policy is a team-specific document. However, it might be beneficial to store it publicly. For example, a section in the SRE wiki might be a good place to store the error budget policies of all teams in a transparent manner. Storing the policies publicly has several advantages.

- Having an effective error budget policy is an advanced SRE practice. Therefore, it may take a long time for teams to start adopting it. For the same reason, there are not a lot of examples on the web to learn how an effective error budget policy can be created. Being able to learn from other teams in the product delivery organization by analyzing their policies is a great catalyst for other teams to adopt the concept.

- During postmortems, when several teams are involved in an outage, it is beneficial to enable the postmortem participants to look up the error budget policies of the involved teams in parallel. This might generate new postmortem action items to adapt existing policies. The process might also prompt the creation of a new error budget policy for a team that does not yet have one in place.

- People specified in the escalation policy approving a team's error budget policy need easy access to it. Furthermore, these stakeholders may need to approve the error budget policies of several teams. For example, a VP of engineering may be on the escalation policy list of several teams' error budget policies. Such stakeholders would prefer a central location for all the error budget policies from all teams they are involved with.

In terms of the storage medium, storing the error budget policy in a source-controlled wiki may be a good option. It combines the transparency of a changelog with the ease of editing a wiki. Additionally, if an error budget policy is stored on a wiki page within a larger application lifecycle management system, the work items linked to the wiki page may be displayable on the page automatically along with details such as their state, last update date, and owner. This contributes to an additional degree of transparency as to whether the conditions and consequences, which can be expressed as work items, are executed as stated in the policy.

As an aside, storing the error budget policy on a wiki provides pageview statistics, typically out of the box. The SRE coaches and agile coaches can use these to get an understanding of whether the error budget policy is referenced at all.

However, despite these advantages, if a team would like to keep their error budget policy private, the SRE coaches should respect that decision. To reiterate, having an effective error budget policy in place is an advanced SRE practice. Developing this capability and underpinning culture should be done with care by being empathetic to the circumstances of individual teams.

Once the error budget policy is stored, its location needs to be announced to everyone who contributed to achieving the error budget policy agreement. The next step is to put the policy into action. This is the subject of the next section.

10.10 Enacting the Error Budget Policy

Once the error budget policy is agreed, the SRE coaches should invite the team for an explicit kick-off to enact it. This is because it is fairly easy for an error budget policy to remain a document that gets forgotten as the day-to-day work takes over people's attention.

The team should decide on the date of the enactment. From that date onward, the error budget policy governs decisions about reliability work prioritization in the team. The date should be chosen in such a way that automatic policy checks that are feasible are set up beforehand.

This means that all the conditions and consequences from the error budget policy that lend themselves to automatic processing should be set up to be triggered and executed in an automated fashion. This may include setting up new alerts in the SRE infrastructure and notifications in the on-call management tool. Furthermore, it may include setting up automated runbooks in the on-call management tool. As part of the process, new feature requests to the SRE infrastructure may be raised to increase the degree of automation in the future.

Finally, the team needs to check the next error budget policy review date and update it as needed. How an error budget policy review can be done is the subject of the next section.

10.11 Reviewing the Error Budget Policy

It is beneficial to run error budget policy reviews in the form of retrospectives. This is because retrospectives provide a structured way to solicit process feedback in a short time frame without lots of preparation. This is exactly what is needed in an error budget policy review. The review is not only about sharpening the defined clauses. To a greater degree the review is about finding out whether the defined error budget policy is effective in that it delivers outcomes in terms of reliability work prioritization.

Running a retrospective well and in a professional manner is the home turf of agile coaches. Therefore, it is great to engage an agile coach to run an error budget policy review as a retrospective. The agile coach should invite the people who agreed on the policy and the people who were going on call for the services under the policy since the last retrospective. The invitation should be sent about two weeks before the actual retrospective to accommodate people's schedules.

In the retrospective, the effectiveness of the error budget policy should be discussed. The following questions may guide the discussion.

- Does the error budget policy get enacted at all?

  ○ If the error budget policy does not get enacted, what could be the reasons for that? For example, are the triggers for enacting the policy automated as much as possible?

  ○ If the error budget policy does get enacted, is it transparent?

- Are the conditions specified to trigger the error budget policy appropriate?

- Are the consequences specified for each condition executed as envisioned?

- What are the outcomes of the application of the consequences?

  ○ Does reliability work prioritization happen as intended?

  ○ If so, does the prioritization lead to reliability improvements?

- Do the conditions and consequences need any updates?

  ○ Create new conditions/consequences.

  ○ Update existing conditions/consequences.

  ○ Delete existing conditions/consequences.

The retrospective should define action items to improve the policy based on the discussion in the meeting. Importantly, it should define who will update the actual error budget policy, how the update will be communicated, and to whom.

The retrospective should conclude with agreeing on the date of the next error budget policy review. In addition, it could be specified as a function of an event. For instance, it can be specified as: "The next review date is on DD.MM.YYYY or after a priority 1 outage involving the services in scope, whichever comes first." This kind of specification makes sense because the purpose of an error budget policy is to drive reliability work prioritization so that priority 1 outages do not occur by and large. If they do, the policy is not effective. Thus, it needs to be reviewed.

10.12 Related Concepts

There are a number of additional concepts that might be useful in the context of error budget policies. They can be found in the literature and in online articles. In this section, an overview of the concepts is provided to establish a more comprehensive view of the current state of thinking in the area of error budget policies. They are summarized in Table 10.6.

Table 10.6 *Additional Concepts in the Context of Error Budget Policies*

Concept	Explanation
Code Yellow	At Google, a state of Code Yellow[7] can be declared. It means that everyone affected needs to stop working on features and start working on reliability. Code Yellow is applied during the teams' business hours.
	In an error budget policy, declaring Code Yellow can be specified as a consequence for a condition. Specifying Code Yellow in the error budget policy has the advantage that the exit criteria from that working mode are automatically specified by the condition that triggered it. When the condition does not apply anymore, the Code Yellow working mode does not apply either.
Code Red	LinkedIn also has a state of Code Yellow. In addition, it has a state called Code Red. Code Red[8] is Code Yellow applied around the clock. That is, declaring Code Red means that everyone affected needs to stop working on features and start working on reliability around the clock.
	Code Red can be specified as a consequence in an error budget policy.
Silver bullet	In *Implementing Service Level Objectives*, the concept of a silver bullet is introduced. It applies when the error budget policy specifies that new feature releases are prohibited until there is a certain level of error budget available again.
	In this case, there may be an agreement in the error budget policy to have a certain small number of silver bullets available per year (e.g., three). The business can use the silver bullets to allow a new feature release despite the policy forbidding new feature releases. When the agreed number of silver bullets is used within a year, the business cannot lift the ban on new feature releases.

---

7. Coursera. n.d. "A Hypothetical Policy Scenario – Consequences of SLO Misses." Accessed January 24, 2022. https://www.coursera.org/lecture/site-reliability-engineering-slos/a-hypothetical-policy-scenario-1DpVG.
8. Palino, Todd. 2018. "Code Yellow: When Operations Isn't Perfect." DevOps.Com. April 13, 2018. https://devops.com/code-yellow-when-operations-isnt-perfect.

Thaw tax	*Implementing Service Level Objectives*[2] also introduces the concept of thaw tax. Thaw tax also applies when the error budget policy declares a ban on new feature releases. It works as follows. For every day a new feature release was done despite the fact that the error budget policy declared a ban on new feature releases, a daily thaw tax is added to the day. So, for each day that violated the ban, the number of ban days gets increased by 1 + thaw tax. The thaw tax is defined in the error budget policy and is designed to extend the time when only reliability work is allowed in case of error budget policy violations.
	For example, imagine the thaw tax is agreed to be half a day. Further, imagine the error budget policy declared a ban on new feature releases as a consequence to a policy condition. The condition gets fulfilled, and the ban on new feature releases gets declared. During the ban, three new feature releases are done on three different days. For each day, the thaw tax of half a day is added. This means that each day now counts as 1 day + ½ day thaw tax = 1.5 days.
	Thus, for three days when new feature releases were done despite the ban, 3 x 1.5 = 4.5 days of ban time are added. During these days, only reliability work is allowed.
Error budget top-up	Nobl9[9] applies a concept of error budget top-up to situations in which a team's error budget depletion is found to be due to the team's external dependencies. The dependencies can be in another team's services within the same product delivery organization or in external companies' services. So, when a team depletes some error budget that is then attributed to its external dependency, the lost error budget is topped up.
	No further details of the concept are provided by Nobl9. However, the error budget top-up needs to be done within the current error budget period. Otherwise, hoarding of the error budget will take place, which does not reflect the number of errors allowed by the respective SLO.

The SRE coaches need to assess whether it would be beneficial to introduce and realistic to execute any of these concepts in a given product delivery organization. Code Yellow and Code Red would require an organization-wide agreement. Once declared, it applies to all the affected teams. This means a team's error budget policy containing a Code Yellow or Code Red consequence may have an influence on other teams. The other teams need to be prepared to work according to the Code Yellow or Code Red working mode based on another team's error budget policy.

The silver bullet, thaw tax, and error budget top-up concepts can be applied within the context of a team. The silver bullet and thaw tax require some transparent means to keep the current score. Questions like "How many silver bullets are left within a year?" and "How many thaw tax days were added last month?" must be answerable in a self-service manner to cater to full transparency.

The error budget top-up concept requires the corresponding SRE infrastructure to be able to make the top-ups with precision. Additionally, the concept might lead to not creating the

---

9. Nobl9. n.d. "Intro to Error Budget Policies." Accessed January 24, 2022. https://nobl9.com/resources/intro-to-error-budget-policies.

necessary urgency for teams to select and consume the dependent services in such a way that their error budget does not get depleted prematurely. The SRE coaches need to find ways to mitigate this.

The aforementioned concepts must be weighed based on need, cost of introduction, and cost of execution. They can be considered to be advanced concepts. Therefore, their introduction should be contemplated only after there is basic working practice of defining and executing simple error budget policies.

10.13 Summary

The error budget policy is the second concept from the top of the SRE concept pyramid (see Section 3.5). Being an advanced concept, it is not as widespread as the basic SRE concepts of SLIs, SLOs, and error budgets. Solid mastery of the basic SRE concepts and the associated SRE practice in a team is the prerequisite for embarking on a journey to set up an error budget policy.

This chapter showed how an effective error budget policy can be set up in a team that is ready. It began with motivating the error budget policy setup. The motivation is in formalizing an agreement among the operations engineers, developers, product owner, and some others about reliability work prioritization in a team. When enacted, the agreement governs the actions of the people on call and others geared to reinstate service reliability in terms of SLO fulfillment.

The structure of an error budget policy was also discussed in this chapter. At the heart of an effective error budget policy is a set of conditions and consequences. The conditions specify concrete cases in which the error budget policy applies. The consequences specify actions to be taken for each condition toward prioritizing the respective reliability work.

The conditions can be expressed as a function of error budget depletion. Alternatively, they can be specified based on resource consumption. Where applicable, both conditions and consequences should be expressed in such a way that programmatic processing is possible. This ensures that some conditions can be triggered automatically and that some consequences can be executed automatically. This way, the transparency of error budget policy execution is ensured.

For conditions and consequences that do not lend themselves to automatic processing, a procedure needs to be established in the team to enact the clauses in a manual way. In particular, these clauses may be influenced by other governance frameworks established in the product delivery organization for scaling agility, delivering software, ensuring regulatory compliance, and so on.

The chapter concluded with a discussion of regular error budget policy reviews, noting that they should be conducted as retrospectives by agile coaches. This enables the team to assess policy effectiveness and initiate policy improvements in a structured but flexible manner on a cadence.

With the error budget policy, the basic SRE foundations are enhanced by formalizing and agreeing to the reliability work prioritization procedure in a team. The next logical enhancement of the SRE foundations is the introduction of error budget–based decision–making. This is the subject of the next chapter.

Chapter 11

Enabling Error Budget–Based Decision–Making

Error budget–based decision–making is the topmost concept in the SRE concept pyramid (see Section 3.5). It rests on all the other concepts beneath: error budget policies, SLOs, and SLIs. Enabling error budget–based decision–making puts a product delivery organization in a true position to steer reliability efforts on many levels in a data-driven way. With that, which reliability decisions can be driven by error budget–based decision–making? The answer to this question is very wide ranging. It is explored in the next section.

11.1 Reliability Decision-Making Taxonomy

The following decision categories can be supported by error budget–based decision–making in the realm of reliability:

- Prioritization decisions
- Development decisions
- Deployment decisions
- Conversation decisions
- Test decisions
- Requirement decisions
- Budget decisions
- Legal decisions

Table 11.1 provides decision examples and associated questions for each decision category.

Table 11.1 *Decision Categories Supported by Error Budget–Based Decision–Making*

Decision Category	Decision Examples and Associated Questions

Prioritization	• Decision to enact the error budget policy:
	  ○ Have the error budget policy conditions in terms of error budget depletion been met?
	• Decisions to adapt the error budget policy:
	  • Does enactment of the error budget policy entail error budget depletion that leads to an unsatisfactory reliability user experience?
	  • Does the error budget policy get enacted too late for error budget depletion to be within the scope of a satisfactory reliability user experience?
	• Decisions to prioritize services in most need of reliability improvements:
	  ○ Which services consistently exhausted their error budgets prematurely across all SLIs in the last three error budget periods?
	  ○ Which services exhausted their availability error budgets prematurely in the last three error budget periods?
	  ○ Which services exhausted their latency error budgets prematurely in the last three error budget periods?
	  ○ What are the most critical SLIs by service?
	  ○ Which services are the fastest premature error budget exhausters by SLI in the last three error budget periods?
	  ○ Is the service customer facing?

Development	• Decisions to consume an API:
	  ○ What is the defined reliability of the API?
	  ○ What are the defined SLOs for the API?
	  ○ What are the defined SLAs for the API?
	  ○ Are the defined SLOs and SLAs sufficient to provide a good user experience for the use cases intended to be implemented?
	  ○ What is the historical adherence to the defined SLOs and SLAs in the target deployment environments?
	• Decision to implement adaptive capacity between services:
	  ○ What is the adherence to the defined SLOs over time in the target environment exhibited by the service considered to be consumed?

Decision Category	Decision Examples and Associated Questions
	• Decision to check whether implemented reliability improvements have led to reduced error budget depletion: ○ Did the error budget depletion of a service reduce in the error budget period after the implemented reliability improvement compared to previous periods?
Deployment	• Decision about denying a production deployment: ○ Does a service's error budget depletion pattern correspond to an error budget policy condition with the consequence of denying production deployments? • Decision about denying a deployment into a nonproduction environment: ○ Are SLO sets defined as entry criteria for allowing new deployments into a nonproduction environment?
Conversation	• Decision to talk to a team owning a dependent service to get the SLOs of the dependent service tightened: ○ Does a new customer use case resulting in a new interaction between a team's service and a dependent service require tighter SLOs for the dependent service?
Reliability	• Decisions to set SLOs for a team's service: ○ What are the SLOs and SLAs of internal dependent services? ○ What are the SLAs of external dependent services? ○ What is the level of adaptive capacity currently implemented between a team's service and dependent services?
Test	• Decisions to choose a hypothesis to test using chaos engineering: ○ Which services are the slowest availability error budget depletors? ○ Which services did not exhaust the latency error budget prematurely in the last three error budget periods? ○ Which services depleted the least availability error budget in the last three error budget periods? ○ Which services depleted the least latency error budget in the last three error budget periods? ○ Which services have the tightest SLOs defined?

Decision Category	Decision Examples and Associated Questions

Requirement	• Decisions to add new BDD scenarios:
	
	   ○ For which SLIs are the error budgets depleted most by service in the last error budget period?
	
	   ○ Based on the postmortem analyses of the last three error budget periods, which new BDD scenarios can be added to test the use cases frequently broken in production in other deployment pipeline environments that precede production?

Budget	• Decisions to allocate more SREs to a team:
	
	   ○ Which team consistently exhausted some of their error budgets prematurely in the last three error budget periods?
	
	   ○ Does the team have an on-call rotation?
	
	   ○ How many people are practicing SRE in the team?
	
	   ○ What is the 12-month trend of customer support ticket numbers for the services owned by the team?
	
	• Decision to allocate more SREs to an organizational unit:
	
	   ○ The same questions as in the previous decision but at the organizational unit level
	
	• Decisions to allocate a (project) budget for reliability improvements:
	
	   ○ How many services consistently exhausted some of their error budgets prematurely in the last three error budget periods?
	
	   ○ How many services are showing a growing 12-month trend of customer support ticket numbers?
	
	• Decision to allocate a business plan cost position for cost of outages:
	
	   ○ What is the time to recovery trend for a set of services that generate a given amount of revenue per time unit?

Legal	• Decisions to set SLAs for own services:
	
	   ○ What are the SLOs set for own services?
	
	   ○ What is the historical adherence to the SLOs set for own services?
	
	   ○ Is there room to tighten the SLAs? Could they be defended?
	
	   ○ What is a reasonable safety margin between the SLOs and SLAs for a given service?

Decision Category	Decision Examples and Associated Questions
	• Decisions to agree to contractual penalties for breaking SLAs:
	○ What is the incident time to detection trend?
	○ What is the incident time to recovery trend?
	○ What is the potential monthly revenue loss given the current incident number trend and time to recovery trend?
Regulatory	• Decisions to use SRE data points in regulatory audits:
	○ Where are the defined SLIs, SLOs, and SLAs stated by service?
	○ Who decided on the defined SLIs, SLOs, and SLAs? Where are the decision records signed by all the decision makers?
	○ Where are the contracts with customers and partners containing the SLAs?
	○ Where is the data evidencing the fulfillment of the defined SLOs and SLAs?
	○ Where are the consequences of breaking SLOs and SLAs stated?
	○ Who decided on the consequences? Where are the decision records signed by all the decision makers?
	○ How can someone view the current state of SLO and SLA fulfillment for any service?

Table 11.1 shows the gamut of decisions and questions that can be answered using error budget–based decision-making. It is truly remarkable that tracking the error budget depletion of services gives rise to the possibility to make decisions in a data-driven way in so many diverse areas! Indeed, the decisions range from technical to legal and cover all phases of the software delivery lifecycle.

This is evidence that it is worth climbing the SRE concept pyramid (see Section 3.5) all the way to the top. Implementing the SLIs, SLOs, error budgets, and error budget policies at the lower layers of the pyramid is undoubtedly a great and necessary thrust toward reliability in any product delivery organization. At the same time, the full potential of SRE is ignited with error budget–based decision-making at the top of the pyramid. The SRE coaches should therefore encourage teams not to stop the SRE transformation midway up the pyramid. Rather, the teams should climb the pyramid all the way to the top, reaping the full benefits of data-driven reliability decision-making in the decision categories specified in the table.

In order to enable error budget–based decision-making, the SRE infrastructure needs to implement a set of SRE indicators. The indicators should be accessible to everyone in the product delivery organization in a self-service manner, and they should be self-explanatory. This is the prerequisite for winning people's hearts and minds to use the indicators in order to make error budget–based decisions. What the SRE indicators are and how to implement them is the subject of the next section.

11.2 Implementing SRE Indicators

The previous section covered the impressive range of decisions that can be made in a data-driven fashion using error budget–based decision–making. Usefully, most of the decisions can be made, or at least supported, using a standard set of SRE indicators. Implementation of the indicators is the subject of the next sections.

11.2.1 Dimensions of SRE Indicators

The SRE indicators have a common set of dimensions. It is worth getting an overview of the dimensions before discussing the indicators themselves. Table 11.2 provides this overview.

Table 11.2 *Dimensions of SRE Indicators*

Dimension	Explanation
SLI	Most SRE indicators need to show data classified by SLI or across a set of SLIs.
SLO	Most SRE indicators need to show data classified by SLO or across a set of SLOs.
Error budget period	All SRE indicators need to show data over time. A commonly useful time period is the error budget period. Showing data by error budget period or across error budget periods is beneficial in the SRE context.
Deployment environment	Most SRE indicators need to show data by deployment environment. Sometimes showing data across deployment environments is beneficial as well. Most common environments will be production environments. However, it can also be useful to explore preproduction environments using SRE indicators.

Depending on the need to show data in a certain way, an SRE indicator can implement any number of the dimensions in Table 11.2. The SRE infrastructure implementing the indicators needs to be able to visualize data across all the dimensions. The SRE coaches need to work with the operations teams owning the SRE infrastructure to introduce the indicators, explain the purpose behind them, and establish tight feedback loops with users during implementation.

In the following sections, the SRE indicators are introduced one by one.

11.2.2 "SLOs by Service" Indicator

Displaying a list of SLOs by service might be the most pragmatic SRE indicator. However, the usefulness of such a list should not be underestimated. Making the list available to everyone in the product delivery organization to be pulled in a self-service manner has many advantages.

1. The transparency of SRE activities increases significantly.

2. The reliability levels defined by team and service become accessible to everyone.

3. Decisions to consume a service API can be supported by the list.

4. Decisions to implement adaptive capacity between services can be supported by the list.

5. Decisions to set SLOs for own services can be supported by the list.

6. Decisions to set SLAs for own services can be supported by the list.

7. The amount of communication between the operations teams owning the SRE infrastructure and the development teams consuming it is reduced.

An example list of SLOs by service is shown in Figure 11.1. The list settings appear on the right-hand side of the figure. A team, service, SLI, and deployment can be selected as entities known from the previous chapters. Additionally, the default SLOs (see Section 6.7) can be set to be shown or hidden in the list. (To recap, default SLOs can be applied automatically to the endpoints that do not have explicit SLOs defined. A default SLO can be defined by a team for an SLI. Based on the definition, the SRE infrastructure assigns the default SLOs to the endpoints where explicit SLOs are absent.)

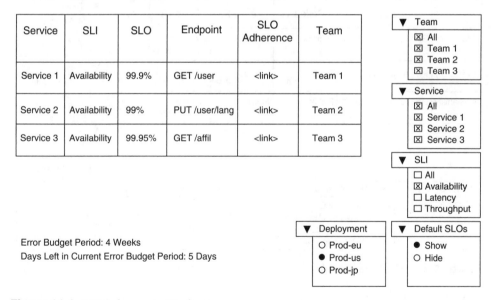

Figure 11.1 *"SLOs by service" indicator*

The lower-left corner of Figure 11.1 shows two static fields: The first one states that the error budget period duration is four weeks, and the second one states that there are five days left in the current error budget period. The two fields serve as an orientation for the people new to SRE and how it is set up in the organization.

In the table shown in Figure 11.1, three services are listed. Service 1 has an availability SLO of 99.9% set for the endpoint "GET /user". The service and the SLO are owned by team 1. Using the link in the SLO adherence column, the user can navigate to the SLO adherence indicator, described in the next section, showing the SLO adherence over time.

Similarly, service 2 has an availability SLO of 99% set for the endpoint "PUT /user/lang". The service and the SLO are owned by team 2. The link in the SLO adherence column takes the user to further data about adherence to the SLO over time.

Likewise, service 3 has an availability SLO of 99.95% set for the endpoint "GET /affil". The service and the SLO are owned by team 3. Using the link in the SLO adherence column, further information can be obtained regarding whether the team successfully defends the SLO over time.

11.2.3 SLO Adherence Indicator

The "SLOs by service" indicator from the previous section references SLO adherence. It is implemented by the SLO adherence indicator, which shows adherence to the SLO by the service over time in the selected deployment environment. Adherence can be represented well in tabular form, as shown in Figure 11.2.

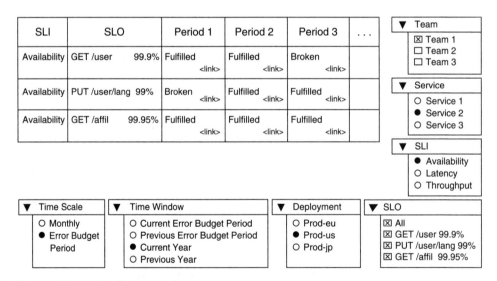

Figure 11.2 *SLO adherence indicator*

On the right-hand side and below the table in Figure 11.2, the table settings are shown. Team, service, SLI, SLO, deployment, time window, and time scale settings can be set by the user. The settings in the table select all SLOs for service 2's availability SLI in the "Prod-us" deployment to be shown for the current year by error budget period. These settings yield the table shown at the top of Figure 11.2.

There are three error budget periods in the selected time window. Each period has a dedicated column in the table. The respective table cell states whether the error budget was fulfilled or broken. Additionally, each table cell contains a link to the respective SLO error budget depletion indicator that can be used for further exploration. How the exploration can be done is the subject of the next section.

The SLO adherence indicator can support decisions to consume an API and implement a certain level of adaptive capacity when consuming the API. Furthermore, the indicator can support decisions when setting SLOs and SLAs for own services by showing the SLO adherence of dependent services.

11.2.4 SLO Error Budget Depletion Indicator

The SLO error budget depletion indicator shows SLO error budget depletion over time. To be generally useful for a wide range of purposes, the indicator should enable the user to select the service, SLI, SLO, and deployment environment, as well as the time window and time scale. Notably, a 24-hour time window with an hourly time scale is useful for analyzing immediate error budget depletion. A yearly time window with an error budget period time scale is useful for analyzing long-term error budget depletion trends. An error budget time window with a weekly time scale is useful for analyzing the error budget depletion trend in the current error budget period.

This section shows two ways to implement the SLO error budget depletion indicator: as a graph and as a table.

Graph Representation
Figure 11.3 shows an example of an SLO error budget depletion graph with settings that can be changed to slice and dice the data.

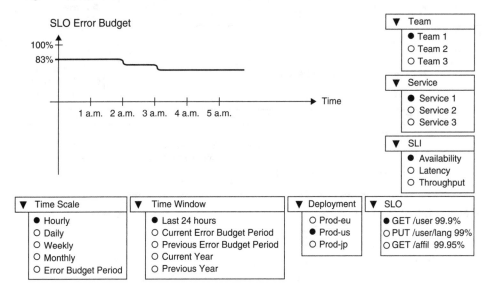

Figure 11.3 *SLO error budget depletion indicator graph over the last 24 hours*

The right-hand side and bottom of Figure 11.3 show the graph settings. These need to be set in order to make the graph show the data the user is looking for. In the team drop-down list, team 1 is selected. In the service drop-down list, service 1 is selected. In the SLI drop-down list, the availability SLI is selected. In the SLO drop-down list, the availability SLO of 99.95% for the endpoint "GET /affil" is selected. The endpoint returns user affiliations. Further in the drop-down list deployment, the US production deployment "Prod-us" is selected. In the time settings at the bottom of the figure, the time window of the last 24 hours to be shown on an hourly scale is selected.

With these selections, the graph shows the error budget depletion in the last 24 hours. It starts at 0 a.m. with 83% of the error budget available. At around 2 a.m. and 3 a.m. there is a little bit of error budget depletion. From 3 a.m. onward there is no further error budget depletion.

Figure 11.4 shows another SLO error budget graph with the current error budget period time window and weekly time scale. Except for the time settings, all the other settings on the right-hand side of the graph are the same as in Figure 11.3.

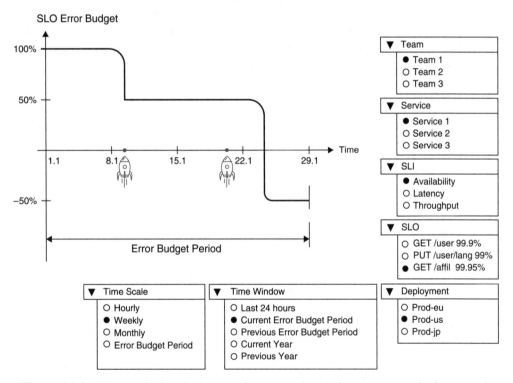

Figure 11.4 *SLO error budget depletion indicator graph over the current error budget period*

The four weeks shown in the graph are the weeks of January 1, 8, 15, and 22. During the week of January 1, there is no error budget depletion. At the beginning of the week of January 8, there is a serious outage that depletes 50% of the error budget. In order to fix the outage, a deployment to the environment "Prod-us" was made.

After that, there is no error budget depletion until the week of January 22. Right before the beginning of that week, there is another deployment to the "Prod-us" environment. Soon after the deployment, there is a more serious outage than the previous one. The outage consumes 100% of the error budget in a single day! It might be attributed to the deployment performed shortly before.

When the outage began, error budget depletion was at 50%. After the 100% error budget depletion, the service ended up being at −50% of the error budget. The service did not deplete the error budget any further until the end of the error budget period. It therefore finished the error budget period at the −50% error budget mark. Such a service should definitely be considered for reliability work prioritization in the next error budget period. The graph in Figure 11.4 can be used to prompt a corresponding discussion.

The preceding graphs can be implemented using business intelligence or data analytics software such as Power BI, Qlik Sense, or Tableau. This requires expertise that might not be available in the operations team owning the SRE infrastructure. Therefore, to start, less sophisticated graphing of SLO error budget depletion can be implemented.

The goal is to enable people to make error budget–based decisions as quickly as possible. This can be achieved using simpler graphs than the one shown in Figure 11.4. Speed trumps graph feature fidelity in this case. For instance, providing a dedicated error budget depletion graph per service, SLI, SLO, and deployment for the current error budget period is sufficient for quickly enabling error budget–based decision–making. Although this approach yields a large number of individual graphs, they may be produced quickly.

Moreover, navigation across the graphs can be simplified by using an easy-to-remember naming convention for the graph URLs. For example, the naming convention "/service/SLI/deployment" can be remembered easily. Navigating to such a URL would take the user to a web page with the error budget depletion graphs for all the SLOs set for the service, SLI, and deployment specified in the URL. The graphs would show the data for the current error budget period on an hourly time scale, for instance.

Finally, the links to each graph can be put onto a single wiki page. This way, anyone can navigate to the wiki page to get to the error budget depletion graph of any service.

> **From the Trenches:** The speed with which graphs can be created is more important than graph feature fidelity. The SRE coaches should work with the operations teams to get the simplest error budget depletion graphs implemented as quickly as possible. Once the basic graphs are available, the SRE coaches should engage with the teams to start the process of error budget–based decision–making. In the meantime, the operations teams can work on extending the fidelity of the graphs, iterating on the feedback from the teams, and improving the overall UX.

Table Representation

Error budget depletion data can also be presented in tabular form, as shown in Figure 11.5. When doing so, the same table settings as those in Figure 11.3 and Figure 11.4 are useful.

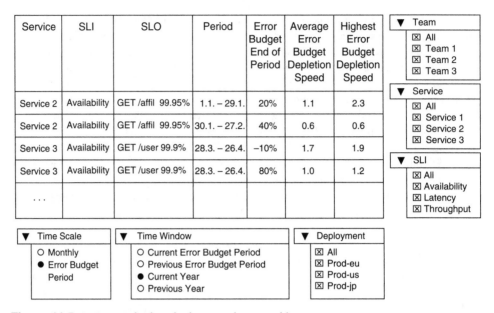

Figure 11.5 *SLO error budget depletion indicator table*

On the right-hand side and at the bottom of Figure 11.5, the team, service, SLI, deployment, and time settings can be set. For example, in the figure, all teams, services, SLIs, and deployments are selected. On the time settings, the current year divided by error budget periods is set. With these settings, a list of services with their SLO error budget depletion data is presented.

Each service row in the table displays the SLI, SLO, and error budget period; the error budget remaining at the end of the error budget period; and the average and highest error budget depletion speeds in the given error budget period.

Each column in the table in Figure 11.5 can be used to order the table. Column ordering is useful for answering different questions during decision-making. For example, the table can be used when deciding which hypotheses to choose for testing using chaos engineering. A hypothesis is defined based on the definition of a system's steady state. The steady state can be determined using error budget depletion. In this context, the following questions about the least depleted error budgets can be answered easily by ordering the table using the "highest error budget depletion speed" and "error budget end of period" columns.

- Which services are the slowest availability error budget depletors?

- Which services depleted the least availability error budget in the last three error budget periods?

- Which services depleted the least latency error budget in the last three error budget periods?

Furthermore, decisions to add new behavior-driven development (BDD) scenarios for regular testing can be supported by answering questions about the most depleted error budgets. For instance, the following question can support the ideation process for new BDD scenarios: "For which SLIs are the error budgets depleted most by service in the last error budget period?" The question can be answered by ordering the table in Figure 11.5 by error budget end of period, SLI, and service.

Moreover, reliability prioritization decisions can be supported by the table in the Figure 11.5. For instance, the fastest error budget depletors for the most recent error budget period or across error budget periods can be easily determined by ordering the column "highest error budget depletion speed" in descending order. The top 10 table rows can be prioritized for reliability improvements in the next planning period of teams owning the respective services.

The average and highest error budget depletion speeds for the columns in the table are calculated using dedicated formulae. For example, the speed with which the error budget is depleted can be determined using the following formula:

> Error budget depletion speed = Percentage of error budget depleted / Time span of depletion

Within an SLO error budget period, several incidents can occur. Each incident will have its own error budget depletion speed. In this case, the average error budget depletion speed per error budget period is determined using the following formula:

> Average error budget depletion speed per period = Sum of error budget depletion speed for all incidents in the period / Number of incidents in the period

The highest error budget depletion speed per error budget period is determined using the following formula:

> Highest error budget depletion speed per period = Max error budget depletion speed of all incidents in the period

In this context, the period can be an error budget period or any other period chosen using the time settings in the table shown in Figure 11.5. Table 11.3 provides examples of error budget depletion speed calculations.

Table 11.3 *Error Budget Depletion Speed Calculations*

Error Budget Period	Incident	Percentage of Error Budget Depleted	Time Span of Depletion in Hours	Error Budget Depletion Speed
1	1	70	52	70 / 52 = 1.3% per hour
1	2	50	26	50 / 26 = 1.9% per hour
1	3	25	70	25 / 70 = 0.4% per hour

The three incidents in Table 11.3 occurred within error budget period 1. Therefore, the average and highest error budget depletion speeds in error budget period 1 can be calculated as follows.

Average error budget depletion speed = (1.3 + 1.9 + 0.4) / 3 = 1.2% per hour
Highest error budget depletion speed = Max (1.3, 1.9, 0.4) = 1.9% per hour

This makes the error budget periods comparable based on the average error budget depletion speed. The same way financial quarters can be good or bad depending on quarterly financial results, error budget periods can be successful or unsuccessful depending on premature error budget exhaustion or average error budget depletion speed.

A high error budget depletion speed, such as in incident 2 in Table 11.3, gives evidence of the outage's large blast radius. A large blast radius gives evidence of the lack of adaptive capacity in the system. With the presence of adaptive capacity, a system can be robust: A fault, error, or failure in one part of the system does not propagate rapidly to other parts of the system; rather, the damage is contained and the partial functionality is preserved, preventing complete failures.

Adaptive capacity can be introduced in the system using so-called stability patterns for distributed systems. These are described in depth in the book *Release It!: Design and Deploy Production-Ready Software*[1] by Michael T. Nygard. In the book, a robust system is defined as follows: "A robust system keeps processing transactions, even when transient impulses, persistent stresses, or component failures disrupt normal processing. This is what most people mean by 'stability'. It's not just that your individual server or applications stay up and running but rather that the user can still get work done."

Thus, calculating error budget depletion speed is an important indicator to identify system parts lacking adaptive capacity. System parts identified in this way can be prioritized for implementation of stability patterns. Referring to the table shown in Figure 11.5, service 3 with the error budget depletion speed of 1.9% per hour is the fastest error budget depletor in the most recent error budget period. Moreover, service 3 ended the error budget period with an error budget of −10%. It should therefore be prioritized e.g. for stability pattern implementation in the owner team's next planning period.

Analysis of error budget depletion speed versus time span of depletion is an interesting topic. What is better in terms of reliability in the user experience: burning through the error budget quickly over a short period of time or doing so slowly over a long period of time? Table 11.4 shows two incidents that depleted the same error budget but within completely different time spans.

Table 11.4 *Fast Versus Slow Error Budget Depletion over Time*

Incident	Percentage of Error Budget Depleted	Time Span of Depletion in Hours	Error Budget Depletion Speed
A	80	2	80 / 2 = 40% per hour
B	80	336	80 / 336 = 0.2% per hour

---

1. Nygard, Michael T. 2018. *Release It!: Design and Deploy Production-Ready Software*. Raleigh, NC: Pragmatic Bookshelf.

Incident A depleted 80% of the error budget within two hours. Incident B also depleted 80% of the error budget but within 336 hours, which corresponds to two weeks or half of a four-week error budget period. Incident A's error budget depletion speed is 40% per hour. By contrast, incident B's error budget depletion speed is only 0.2% per hour.

Just by comparing the error budget depletion speeds, it can be said that incident 1 presumably tapped into a system area with a greater lack of adaptive capacity. If the adaptive capacity were there, 80% of the error budget would probably not be depleted within two hours.

But what can be said about 80% error budget depletion within two weeks? It can be said that the time to recover from the incident was very long. Because the incident was a slow error budget burner, the error budget depletion presumably did not trigger alerts. As a result, the incident was detected much later, after the error budget burn started. A customer support ticket graph might be helpful to understand the impact of the incident from the customer point of view (see Section 11.2.9, *Customer Support Ticket Trend Indicator*).

Generally speaking, it is difficult to compare the reliability user experience impact of incidents A and B based purely on error budget depletion speeds. An in-depth analysis of error budget burn rates as a topic is available in *Implementing Service Level Objectives: A Practical Guide to SLIs, SLOs, and Error Budgets*.[2]

11.2.5 Premature SLO Error Budget Exhaustion Indicator

Premature SLO error budget exhaustion is an important indicator of unreliability. The core of SRE decision-making can be done based on knowledge of services and endpoints exhausting SLO error budgets prematurely across error budget periods. It is about data-driven decisions to determine where reliability investments are immediately required and where new feature investments can be made because service reliability is satisfactory. Two types of information visualization are useful here: a graph for exploratory purposes and a table for focused decision-making. In the next sections, a premature SLO error budget exhaustion graph and a corresponding table are explored.

Graph Representation

The premature SLO error budget exhaustion graph is useful for analyzing services in which repeated premature error budget exhaustion occurred. Figure 11.6 illustrates such a graph.

2. Hidalgo, Alex. 2020. *Implementing Service Level Objectives: A Practical Guide to SLIs, SLOs & Error Budgets*. Sebastopol, CA: O'Reilly Media.

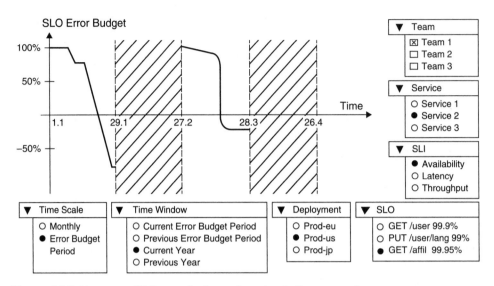

Figure 11.6 *Premature SLO error budget exhaustion indicator graph*

The right-hand side and bottom of the graph in Figure 11.6 display the graph settings. Using these settings, it is possible to select a team, service, SLI, SLO, deployment, time window, and time scale. The settings correspond to the settings discussed for other graphs in the previous sections. In the graph in Figure 11.6, teams 1, 2, and 3 are selected, as is the availability SLO of 99.95% for the endpoint "GET /affil" of service 2 in the "Prod-us" deployment. The data is set to be shown for the current year on the error budget period scale.

With the selected settings, the graph shows four error budget periods. The graph curves are only shown for the two error budget periods during which premature error budget exhaustion occurred: 1.1 to 29.1 (January 1–29) and 27.2 to 28.3 (February 27–March 28). The other two error budget periods are covered with a slanted line pattern. There is no premature error budget exhaustion there. Therefore, these error budget periods are out of focus for the analysis in question.

The patterns of premature error budget exhaustion are rather different by error budget period. In the first error budget period, two incidents occurred. The first incident depleted the error budget by about 25% within a rather short time frame. The second incident was running for a rather long time. It depleted around 150% of the error budget, sending it firmly into a negative area of the graph. As a result of the incident, the first error budget period ends with an error budget shortage of around –75%.

In the second error budget period, premature error budget depletion did not occur. However, in the third error budget period, it came back again. The period started with slow error budget depletion over several weeks. Around halfway into the error budget period, an incident occurred that depleted almost 100% of the error budget on a single day. The incident was troubleshooted quickly so that no further depletion occurred until the end of the error budget period. Moreover, in the next error budget period, premature error budget depletion did not occur either.

An analysis of the graph can support the decision-making for prioritization of services in most need of reliability improvements. Questions such as the following can be answered using the graph.

- Which services exhausted their availability error budgets prematurely in the last three error budget periods and what was the error budget depletion pattern?

- What were the premature error budget exhaustion patterns for latency error budgets in the last year for the services owned by a given organizational unit?

These questions are exploratory by nature. The exploration is supported well using the graph settings. The data can be sliced and diced by organizational units expressed as teams, and services; as well as by SLIs, SLOs, time windows, and time scales.

Technically, the premature SLO error budget depletion graph can be implemented using the same infrastructure used for the SLO error budget depletion indicator (Section 11.2.4). It might also be possible to merge both graphs by offering the user an additional setting: "show only premature error budget exhaustion periods." This setting would enable the user to only see time scale periods when premature error budget exhaustion occurred. All the other periods would be covered with a slanted line pattern as shown in Figure 11.6.

Table Representation

A tabular representation of services exhausting SLO error budgets prematurely is very useful for supporting reliability prioritization decisions in a service network. Which services have the greatest need for reliability improvements can be read directly from the table, as illustrated in Figure 11.7.

Service	SLI	SLO	Period	Error Budget End of Period	Time to Error Budget Exhaustion	Average Error Budget Depletion Speed	Deployment	Team
Service 2	Availability	GET /affil 99.95%	1.1. – 29.1.	–70%	3 days	0.6.	Prod-us	Team 1
Service 2	Availability	GET /affil 99.95%	30.1. – 27.2.	–30%	5 days	1.7.	Prod-us	Team 1
Service 3	Availability	GET /user 99.9%	28.3. – 26.4.	–43%	8 days	1.5.	Prod-us	Team 2
Service 3	Availability	GET /user 99.9%	28.3. – 26.4.	–51%	20 days	2.1.	Prod-eu	Team 2

▼ Team
- ☒ All
- ☒ Team 1
- ☒ Team 2
- ☒ Team 3

▼ Service
- ☒ All
- ☒ Service 1
- ☒ Service 2
- ☒ Service 3

▼ SLI
- ☒ All
- ☒ Availability
- ☒ Latency
- ☒ Throughput

▼ Time Scale
- ○ Monthly
- ● Error Budget Period

▼ Time window
- ○ Current Error Budget Period
- ○ Previous Error Budget Period
- ● Current Year
- ○ Previous Year

▼ Deployment
- ☒ All
- ☒ Prod-eu
- ☒ Prod-us
- ☒ Prod-jp

Figure 11.7 *Premature SLO error budget exhaustion indicator table*

The right-hand side and bottom of Figure 11.7 show the table settings. The settings, teams, services, SLIs, deployments, and time settings can be adjusted. The table itself is composed of nine columns: service, SLI, SLO, time scale period, error budget at the end of the period, time to error budget exhaustion, average error budget depletion speed, deployment, and team. Each column can be sorted in ascending or descending order. Using column ordering, lots of questions can be answered that help in reliability prioritization decision-making.

There are four rows in the table in Figure 11.7. The rows are sorted in ascending order by error budget period. In the first row, service 2 exhausted an availability error budget in prod-us deployment prematurely within three days and finished the error budget period on 29.1 (January 29) with a –70% error budget shortage. In the second row, service 2 exhausted the same availability SLO in the same deployment prematurely within five days in the next error budget period. This time, the error budget shortage was at –30% at the end of the error budget period on 27.2 (February 27).

In the third row, service 3 exhausted an availability error budget prematurely. It happened in the Prod-us deployment. The error budget period finished at the –43% error budget shortage mark on 26.4 (April 26). Interestingly, the same service exhausted the same availability error budget prematurely in the Prod-eu deployment as well. There, the error budget shortage was at the –51% mark at the end of the error budget period on 26.4 (April 26). The error budget in Prod-us was exhausted within eight days. By contrast, the error budget in Prod-eu was exhausted within 20 days.

The following observations can be made by analyzing the table.

- The biggest, most recent availability error budget depletor is service 3. In error budget period 28.3–26.4 (March 28–April 26), it depleted 43% + 51% = 94% more error budget than allowed by the SLO across two deployments, Prod-us and Prod-eu.

- Service 2 had issues with premature availability error budget exhaustion in the January and February error budget periods. However, in March and April, service 2 did not exhaust any availability error budget prematurely.

- Following this analysis, service 3 should be prioritized for reliability improvements. In general, the following kind of prioritization-related questions can be answered by using the table.

  ○ Which services consistently exhausted their error budgets prematurely across all SLIs in the last three error budget periods?

  ○ Which services exhausted their availability error budgets prematurely in the last two error budget periods?

  ○ Which services exhausted their latency error budgets prematurely in the last year?

  ○ Which services were the fastest to deplete their error budgets by SLI?

Furthermore, the table can be used when deciding which team should have more SREs allocated to it. Questions like "Which team is consistently exhausting some of their error budgets prematurely in the last three error budget periods?" can be answered directly by the table.

Finally, the table can support decisions about project budget allocation for reliability improvements. In this context, questions like "How many services are consistently exhausting some of their error budgets prematurely in the last three error budget periods?" can be answered by selecting the table settings accordingly.

Beyond that, the table column "average error budget depletion speed" indicates the speed with which the error budget was exhausted. Sorting the column in descending order brings the services with the fastest premature error budget exhaustion to the top of the table. (Refer to Section 11.2.4, for explanations of how the average error budget depletion speed is calculated.) These services can be selected for reliability prioritization.

Technically, the premature SLO error budget depletion table can be implemented using the same infrastructure used for the SLO error budget depletion indicator (Section 11.2.4). It might also be possible to merge both tables by offering the user an additional setting: "show only premature error budget exhaustion periods." The setting would enable the user to only see time scale periods where premature error budget exhaustion occurred.

The SRE indicators presented so far revolve around SLOs. A similar set of indicators can be created for SLAs. Technically, the depletion of an SLA error budget is the same as that of an SLO. However, an SLA error budget depletion indicator needs to have somewhat different settings to be useful. These and other nuances are the subject of the next sections that introduce SRE indicators for SLAs.

11.2.6 "SLAs by Service" Indicator

A list of SLAs by service is an important indicator of a product delivery organization's contractual obligations to customers and partners. There are two points of interest here: contractual SLAs written in customer contracts, and corresponding endpoint-level SLAs. The endpoint-level SLAs have to be fulfilled in order for the contractual SLAs to be fulfilled in turn. This is exemplarily shown in tabular form in Figure 11.8.

The right-hand side of the table in Figure 11.8 shows the table settings. SLIs, contractual SLAs, services, and deployments can be selected using these settings. On selection of a contractual SLA, the services drop-down list is automatically filtered by services that are involved in ensuring the SLA.

The bottom of Figure 11.8 statistically displays the error budget period of four weeks. Below that, the number of days left in the current error budget period, 5, is shown. These numbers are important for orientation.

The table settings in Figure 11.8 let the table show a list of services that have latency SLAs on the endpoint level for the contractually agreed latency SLA "data roundtrip under 15 seconds for 90% of workflows" in the deployment "Prod-us." There are two services that fulfill these criteria: service 1 (two SLAs) and service 2 (two SLAs).

Service	SLI	SLA	Endpoint	SLA Adherence	Team
Service 1	Latency	5 sec for 95% of Calls	GET /tenant/{id}/studies/{id}/attachments	\<link\>	Team 1
Service 1	Latency	10 sec for 90% of Calls	POST /tenant/{id}/studies/{id}/attachments	\<link\>	Team 1
Service 2	Latency	3 sec for 93% of Calls	GET /tenant/{id}/query/{id}/status	\<link\>	Team 2
Service 2	Latency	7 sec for 91% of Calls	POST /tenant/{id}/study/{id}/queries	\<link\>	Team 2

▼ SLI
- ☐ All
- ☐ Availability
- ☒ Latency
- ☐ Throughput

▼ Contractual SLAs
- ☒ Data Roundtrip Under 15 sec for 90% of Workflows
- ☐ Data Ingested in 5 min for 99.9% of Workflows

Error Budget Period : 4 Weeks
Days Left in Current Error Budget Period : 5 Days

▼ Deployment
- ☐ All
- ☐ Prod-eu
- ☒ Prod-us
- ☐ Prod-jp

▼ Service
- ☒ All
- ☒ Service 1
- ☒ Service 2
- ☒ Service 3

Figure 11.8 *"SLAs by service" indicator*

Service 1 has a latency SLA of five seconds for the endpoint "GET /tenant/{id}/studies/{id}/attachments." Using the link in the SLA adherence table, the user can navigate to a page to see adherence to the SLA over time. Similarly, service 1 has another latency SLA defined for the endpoint "POST /tenant/{id}/studies/{id}/attachments" to return within 10 seconds in 90% of the calls within a given error budget period.

Service 2 also has two latency SLAs defined in a similar manner shown in the table. The four latency SLAs in the table spread across service 1 and service 2 are required to be defended in order to fulfill the overarching contractual SLA "data roundtrip under 15 seconds for 90% of workflows." Teams 1 and 2 owning services 1 and 2, respectively, need to set up on-call rotations appropriately to react to SLA breaches in a timely manner.

The table enables a number of decisions to be supported by its data. For instance, decisions to consume an API, define SLAs for own services, and determine the level of adaptive capacity required between the services can be informed by the data in the table.

Furthermore, the table leads to a reduction of communication between different parties within the product delivery organization. This is because anyone can pull the data about the contractually agreed SLAs and their breakdowns into endpoint-level SLAs in a self-service manner. This satisfies the information needs of different roles without increasing the communication overhead.

11.2.7 SLA Error Budget Depletion Indicator

SLA error budget depletion is useful for various stakeholders. Because SLAs are agreed to contractually, and consequently, adherence to them is directly linked to contractual penalties, the SLA error budget depletion graph will have lots of nontechnical stakeholders. These are people from the legal and regulatory departments as well as general managers. They are looking for answers to questions along the lines of the following.

- "How far away are we from contractual penalties due to SLA breaches?"

- "How can we avoid contractual penalties due to SLA breaches?"

- "Did we have to pay contractual penalties due to SLA breaches in the last quarter?"

In an attempt to answer questions like these, and others, the SRE infrastructure needs to implement an SLA error budget depletion graph. This is the subject of the next section.

Graph Representation

Figure 11.9 shows an SLA error budget depletion graph. On the right-hand side and below the graph, the graph settings are shown. The first setting in the upper-right corner is the SLI. The setting below the SLI is the contractual SLA. The contractual SLA is almost never agreed to at the level of individual services. In most cases, it is an aggregate number for a bigger piece of functionality recognizable by customers and partners.

For example, in Figure 11.9, "data roundtrip" is the functionality agreed to contractually using SLAs. The data roundtrip needs to take less than fifteen seconds for 90% of executed workflows.

At this point, there is a new additional aspect to consider. In the common case of services being offered in a shared way to a wide variety of customers (SaaS), the services will be subject to many contracts. The contracts might be identical. However, each customer will have their own unique contract with the service provider.

In this context, if the contractually agreed SLA with customer A reads "the data roundtrip needs to take less than 15 seconds for 90% of executed workflows," it refers to all the workflows executed for customer A and only customer A. In fact, if all the other workflows for other customers took more than fifteen seconds, the contracts with those other customers would be broken. However, the contract with customer A would not be broken.

In this case, the SRE infrastructure needs to provide a means to differentiate customers. It can be implemented using another setting whereby all the customers would be listed and a customer can be selected. The legal stakeholders in particular would need customer selection if they have to deal with individual contracts with customers in a dedicated manner.

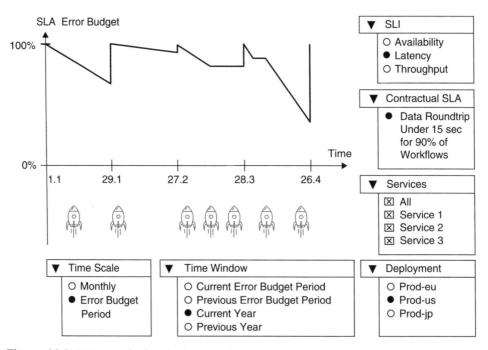

Figure 11.9 *SLA error budget depletion indicator graph*

However, dealing with individual contracts with customers in a dedicated manner might not be feasible. This is especially the case in larger economies of scale where a SaaS is offered to thousands of customers. Every customer will have a standard contract with the SaaS provider. Based on the standard contract, refunds due to SLA breaches can be credited in an automated fashion upon customer request. The refunds are typically calculated based on a given service credit formula.

This contractual provision will make contract handling manageable for the legal department. In this case, differentiation between the customers on the SLA error budget depletion graph is not needed.

The next setting on the graph in Figure 11.9, below the contractual SLA setting, is a list of services. The list of services needs to be populated based on what has been selected in the contractual SLA setting. In most cases, each contractual SLA is an aggregation of individual services' SLAs. The mapping between a contractual SLA and the individual services it affects should be known to the SRE infrastructure. Therefore, the drop-down list of services affected by a selected contractual SLA should be populated automatically.

If all services are selected, the graph shows the average SLA error budget depletion of all services involved in defending the contractually agreed SLA. If an individual service is selected, the graph shows the SLA error budget depletion for that service. If a set of services is selected, the graph shows the average SLA error budget depletion for that set of services. This might be useful when analyzing services related to a technical domain. For instance, it might make sense to look at the SLA error budget depletion of all networking services together.

Below the services drop-down list, a deployment can be selected. To the left of the deployment drop-down list, time settings can be chosen. The selectable time windows refer to error budget periods and years. The selectable time scales refer to months and error budget periods.

The settings on the graph are selected as follows. The graph shows the latency SLA error budget depletion of the contractual SLA "Data roundtrip under 15 seconds for 90% of workflows" in the deployment "Prod-us" for the current year depicted by the error budget period.

Four SLA error budget periods are shown on the graph. Error budget period 1 starts on January 1, error budget period 2 starts on January 29, error budget period 3 starts on February 27, and error budget period 4 starts on March 28. That is, an SLA error budget period is four weeks long. At the beginning of each error budget period, the SLA error budget is fully replenished.

Additionally, the graph shows deployments as icons made during the selected time window in the selected deployment environments. The deployments shown are for the services selected. Because all services are selected in the services drop-down list, the deployment of any service from the list leads to the deployment icon shown on the graph.

In error budget period 1, a single deployment was made. During that period, about 20% of the SLA error budget was depleted. At the beginning of error budget period 2, another deployment was made. After that deployment, SLA error budget depletion slowed down significantly.

In error budget period 3, three deployments were made. After the first deployment, the SLA error budget depletion curve got steeper again. The second deployment in the period brought error budget depletion to a halt. The third deployment in the period did not lead to error budget depletion.

In error budget period 4, two deployments were made. After the first deployment, SLA error budget depletion got very strong. It went from about 90% to about 30% within about three weeks. Still, it was possible to finish the error budget period without exhausting the SLA error budget prematurely.

The SLA error budget depletion graph can be used to check whether implemented reliability improvements have led to reduced SLA error budget depletion over time. This can be done conveniently by looking at SLA error budget depletion by error budget period.

Moreover, the SLA error budget depletion graph is useful for data-driven preparations for contract negotiations about SLAs by looking at historical adherence to the currently defined SLAs for the services relevant in upcoming negotiations.

Table Representation

SLA error budget depletion can also be presented in tabular form. This is useful for obtaining the detailed data necessary for quick decision-making. Figure 11.10 shows an SLA error budget depletion table.

On the right-hand side and at the bottom of the table, the table settings are shown. The SLI, contractual SLAs, services, deployments, time window, and time scale can be set using these settings. In Figure 11.10, the contractual latency SLA "Data roundtrip under 15 seconds for 90% of workflows" is selected. Error budget depletion is selected to be shown for all services involved in the "Prod-us" deployment for the current year divided by error budget periods.

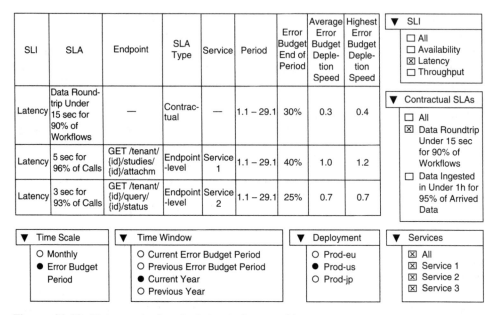

SLI	SLA	Endpoint	SLA Type	Service	Period	Error Budget End of Period	Average Error Budget Depletion Speed	Highest Error Budget Depletion Speed
Latency	Data Round-trip Under 15 sec for 90% of Workflows	—	Contractual	—	1.1 – 29.1	30%	0.3	0.4
Latency	5 sec for 96% of Calls	GET /tenant/{id}/studies/{id}/attachm	Endpoint-level	Service 1	1.1 – 29.1	40%	1.0	1.2
Latency	3 sec for 93% of Calls	GET /tenant/{id}/query/{id}/status	Endpoint-level	Service 2	1.1 – 29.1	25%	0.7	0.7

▼ SLI
- ☐ All
- ☐ Availability
- ☒ Latency
- ☐ Throughput

▼ Contractual SLAs
- ☐ All
- ☒ Data Roundtrip Under 15 sec for 90% of Workflows
- ☐ Data Ingested in Under 1h for 95% of Arrived Data

▼ Time Scale
- ○ Monthly
- ● Error Budget Period

▼ Time Window
- ○ Current Error Budget Period
- ○ Previous Error Budget Period
- ● Current Year
- ○ Previous Year

▼ Deployment
- ○ Prod-eu
- ● Prod-us
- ○ Prod-jp

▼ Services
- ☒ All
- ☒ Service 1
- ☒ Service 2
- ☒ Service 3

Figure 11.10 *SLA error budget depletion indicator table*

The resultant table shows contractual and endpoint-level error budget depletion by error budget period. The first SLA shown in the table is contractual. The error budget period of 1.1 (January 1) finished with 30% of the error budget remaining. At 0.3% per hour, the average error budget depletion speed in the error budget period was rather low. At 0.4% per hour, the highest error budget depletion speed in the period was low as well.

The two SLAs at the bottom of the table are endpoint-level SLAs. Their remaining SLA error budget at the end of the error budget period of 1.1 (January 1) is 40% and 25%, respectively.

This kind of data is useful during SLA negotiations. The remaining error budget at the end of the error budget periods shows the room available for negotiation of tighter SLAs. If a significant error budget consistently remains across a significant number of error budget periods, the SLA negotiators might agree to tightening the SLAs.

11.2.8 SLA Adherence Indicator

SLA adherence is referenced from within the SLAs by service indicator (Section 11.2.6) where the user can obtain a list of SLAs defined contractually. In order to explore the relevant SLAs in more detail, the user can look at SLA adherence by following a link. The link takes the user to the SLA adherence indicator that illustrates SLA fulfillment over time in a tabular form. This is shown in Figure 11.11.

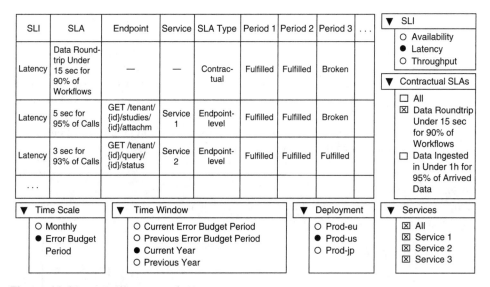

SLI	SLA	Endpoint	Service	SLA Type	Period 1	Period 2	Period 3	...
Latency	Data Round-trip Under 15 sec for 90% of Workflows	—	—	Contrac-tual	Fulfilled	Fulfilled	Broken	
Latency	5 sec for 95% of Calls	GET /tenant/{id}/studies/{id}/attachm	Service 1	Endpoint-level	Fulfilled	Fulfilled	Broken	
Latency	3 sec for 93% of Calls	GET /tenant/{id}/query/{id}/status	Service 2	Endpoint-level	Fulfilled	Fulfilled	Fulfilled	
...								

▼ SLI
- ○ Availability
- ● Latency
- ○ Throughput

▼ Contractual SLAs
- ☐ All
- ☒ Data Roundtrip Under 15 sec for 90% of Workflows
- ☐ Data Ingested in Under 1h for 95% of Arrived Data

▼ Time Scale
- ○ Monthly
- ● Error Budget Period

▼ Time Window
- ○ Current Error Budget Period
- ○ Previous Error Budget Period
- ● Current Year
- ○ Previous Year

▼ Deployment
- ○ Prod-eu
- ● Prod-us
- ○ Prod-jp

▼ Services
- ☒ All
- ☒ Service 1
- ☒ Service 2
- ☒ Service 3

Figure 11.11 *SLA adherence indicator*

On the right and at the bottom of Figure 11.11, the table settings are shown. SLI, contractual SLA, service, and deployment can be selected using these settings. Furthermore, the time window and time scale can be set in a flexible manner. Based on these settings, the table shows a list containing two types of SLAs: contractual SLAs and a corresponding list of endpoint-level SLAs. Adherence to each SLA of any type is shown in columns by time scale period on the right-hand side of the table.

In Figure 11.11, both the latency SLI and the contractual latency SLA of "Data roundtrip under 15 seconds for 90% of workflows" are selected. Adherence to the SLA is selected to be shown by all services contributing to the workflow in the "Prod-us" deployment in the current year divided by error budget periods.

The resultant table shows the contractual SLA on top. In error budget periods 1 and 2, the SLA was fulfilled. However, in error budget period 3, the SLA was broken. Two endpoint-level SLAs contribute to the contractual SLA in this case. The first endpoint-level SLA is fulfilled in error budget periods 1 and 2 and is broken in error budget period 3. The second endpoint-level SLA is fulfilled in all the error budget periods. Following this, it becomes clear that the contractual SLA got broken in error budget period 3 because the first endpoint-level SLA got broken in that period.

The SLA adherence indicator table is useful when making decisions about consuming an API or implementing adaptive capacity between services.

11.2.9 Customer Support Ticket Trend Indicator

The customer support ticket trend is useful for getting a hint about the customer's perception of system reliability. The trend indicates customer support ticket numbers over time. Although a high number of customer support tickets can merely be considered a hint about system reliability, it is still a valid indicator.

Whereas other SRE indicators reflect adherence to an internally defined number such as an SLO or SLA, customer support tickets directly reflect the level of customer satisfaction with the product. After all, happy customers just use the product instead of raising customer support tickets! A growing trend in customer support tickets is therefore a measure worth looking into.

Together with other SRE indicators, the customer support ticket trend should be taken into account to assess system reliability. The trend can be visualized as a graph and as a table. Both visualizations are explored in the next two sections.

Graph Representation

Figure 11.12 shows a sample customer support ticket graph that can be provided by the SRE infrastructure.

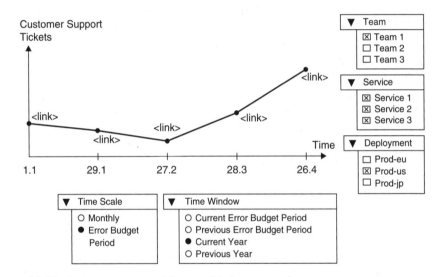

Figure 11.12 *Customer support ticket trend indicator graph*

On the right-hand side and at the bottom of Figure 11.12, the graph settings are displayed. In the upper-right corner, a team can be selected. Team selection determines the services shown in the service drop-down list below. If a team is selected, the service drop-down list only displays the services owned by the selected team. If no team is selected, the service drop-down list displays all the services known to the SRE infrastructure.

Multiple services can be selected. Likewise, multiple deployments can be selected in the deployment drop-down list. Time window and time scale selections can also be made. The data can be displayed on a yearly basis or by error budget period.

In the graph depicted at the top of Figure 11.12, the selected time window is the current year displayed on the error budget period scale. Following this, four error budget periods can be seen on the graph. In the first error budget period, the number of customer support tickets declined.

The same trend occurred during the second error budget period. In the third and fourth error budget periods, the trend was reversed. At the end of the fourth error budget period, the number of customer support tickets was at an all-time high.

The data points at the beginning of each error budget period are hyperlinked. The hyperlinks lead to the tool that manages the customer support tickets. This connection is very important in order to help users navigate to the actual lists of support tickets. Looking at the plain numbers on the graph can only be a starting point for analysis and a trigger to understand the background of the tickets.

Do many customer support tickets from different customers in an error budget period refer to the same technical issue? Are there several technical issues mostly referred to by the customer support tickets? Are there technical issues that are mentioned by many customer support tickets across the error budget periods? Questions like these will be raised by the people analyzing the graph. Only if these questions can be answered on the spot is the customer support ticket graph valuable.

That is, the customer support ticket graph needs to not only pull the data from the tool managing the customer support tickets, but also link back to it using deep links, taking users to the appropriate ticket lists. Each customer support ticket in the list needs to be viewable to obtain the full details of the reported issue.

Customer support tickets can generally refer to different types of issues. Some issues will be clearly attributed to broken functionality. Others may refer to inadequate user experiences that are not related to reliability. Yet others may refer to missing features that make accomplishing the intended user tasks impossible or very cumbersome.

Depending on the tool that manages the customer support tickets, it may be possible to categorize the tickets. Ticket categorization is very helpful in order to ensure that the ticket numbers on the graph are not skewed by the tickets that do not refer to reliability issues. If ticket categorization is possible, the customer support ticket graph should only count the tickets referring to reliability issues. Moreover, the links on the data points of the graph should correspondingly lead to the lists filtered for tickets that refer to the reliability issues.

The tickets might be further classified using priorities or severities. If it is possible to retrieve this classification from the tool that manages the customer tickets, it can greatly enrich the customer support ticket graph's informational content. If the graph can display the ticket classification along with the ticket numbers, further analysis becomes possible. For instance, the number of customer support tickets of the highest priority and severity by error budget period can be seen and correlated with the deployments made in that period.

Additional decisions can also be made using the customer support ticket graph. For example, the effectiveness of the error budget policy can be partially measured by looking at the customer support tickets. How did enactment of the error budget policy correlate with the ticket numbers? In error budget periods where the error budget policy was enacted, the customer ticket numbers might be expected to rise. In periods where the error budget policy did not need to be enacted, the ticket numbers might be expected not to rise.

Is this the customer ticket growth pattern that is observed? If so, does it mean the applicable error budget policies are effective? If this is not the observed pattern, does it mean that the applicable error budget policies are not effective? Having the customer ticket numbers plotted by error budget period considerably supports the teams and SRE coaches looking for evidence of the error budget policies' effectiveness.

Another question that can be approached using the customer ticket numbers is whether the error budget policy is enacted too late for error budget depletion to be within the scope of satisfactory user experience. If after premature error budget exhaustion and corresponding error budget policy enactment there is no subsequent drop of customer support tickets, it is an indication worth noticing. If this pattern is recurring, it is an indication worth investigating.

Table Representation

Budget and effort allocation decisions can be efficiently supported by customer support ticket trends displayed in a tabular form. Such a table is shown in Figure 11.13. The table settings correspond by and large to those known from the customer support ticket trend indicator graph discussed in the previous section.

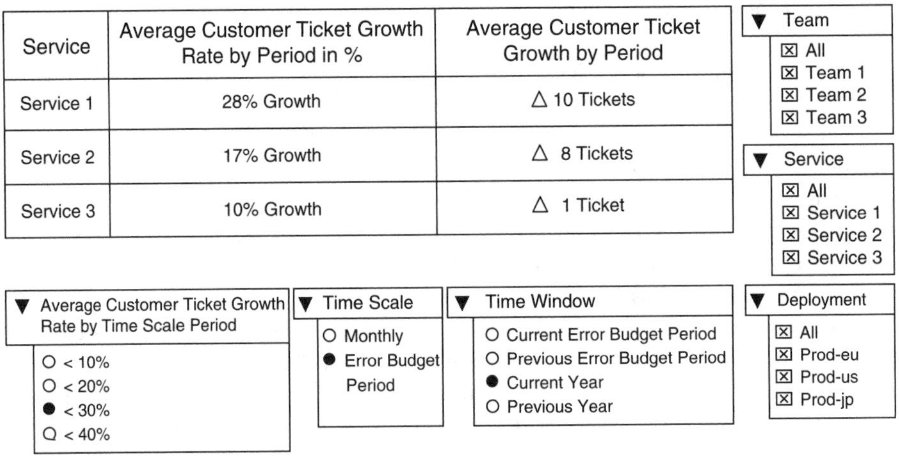

Figure 11.13 *Customer support ticket trend indicator table*

Budget allocation decisions often require data from the entire organization. Therefore, the "all" setting in the team drop-down list will be useful. If it is selected, the "all" setting in the service drop-down list is selected automatically as well.

In the lower-left corner of Figure 11.13, a new setting is shown. It represents the average customer ticket growth rate by the time scale period in the selected time window.

For example, in the case of three time scale periods (P1, P2, and P3), there are two transitions between them: transition P1 → P2 and transition P2 → P3. The customer ticket growth rate in the P1 → P2 transition is averaged with that in the P2 → P3 transition. This number is compared with the setting "< 30%" selected in the figure. The resultant list of services is displayed in the table at the top of the figure.

In the list of services shown in the figure, service 1 has the highest average customer ticket growth rate, 28%, across error budget periods in the current year. This results in an average delta of 10 tickets added from time scale period to time scale period. Service 2 has the second highest average customer ticket growth rate, 17%, across error budget periods in the current year. An average of eight tickets is added between the time scale periods. The last in the list is service 3.

It averages a 10% customer ticket growth rate between the time scale periods, which yields one additional ticket on average.

The service list in the figure can help with budget allocation decisions. When allocating a budget to a new project that will use existing services, the list can help estimate the cost of customer support. Each customer support ticket needs to be processed and solved. Knowing the number of services with a growing 12-month trend of customer support tickets provides an indication of the potential number of tickets to be solved on a yearly basis. The cost of processing and solving the tickets can be estimated based on historical cost data.

Moreover, if the list shown is very long, it might be an indication that the new project should not be started until the services at the top of the list have improved their reliability. It might be more beneficial to start the new project a bit later based on services that are more reliable than to do so earlier given the data showing unsatisfactory customer support ticket trends.

The service list in the figure can also be used to support SRE head count allocation decisions. It might turn out that the teams owning the services from the top of the list simply lack SRE capacity. In a product delivery organization where the developers perform the SRE work, it might mean the teams need to get an additional developer head count. In a product delivery organization where there are dedicated SREs in the teams, it might mean a dedicated SRE needs to be allocated to a team.

In any case, the service list supports decision-making using real data coming from customers interacting with the services and expressing their concerns. If the service list can be augmented by customer ticket categorization and classification, it extends the decision-making support.

11.2.10 "On-Call Rotations by Team" Indicator

An important SRE indicator is the presence of on-call rotations by team, the number of services covered by the rotations, and the number of people involved in the rotations. This data gives an overview of the on-call coverage set up by a team to support the services they own. The data can be presented in tabular form, as shown in Figure 11.14.

Rotation #	Covered Time Periods	Covered Services	Number of People
1	7a.m. – 7p.m. UTC	Service 1	2
2	8a.m. – 4p.m. UTC 7a.m. – 9p.m. UTC	Service 2, Service 3	2
3	1a.m. – 5a.m. UTC	Service 1	1
4	1a.m. – 4a.m. UTC	Service 2	1
5	2a.m. – 5a.m. UTC	Service 3	1

▼ Team
- ○ Team 1
- ● Team 2
- ○ Team 3

▼ Service
- ☒ Service 1
- ☒ Service 2
- ☒ Service 3

▼ Time Window
- ○ Current Error Budget Period
- ○ Previous Error Budget Period
- ● Current Year
- ○ Previous Year

▼ Deployment
- ○ Prod-eu
- ● Prod-us
- ○ Prod-jp

Figure 11.14 *"On-call rotations by team" indicator*

On the right-hand side and at the bottom of Figure 11.14, the table settings are shown. Using the settings, the team, service, deployment, and time window can be set. In Figure 11.14, all the services owned by team 2 in the "Prod-us" deployment are selected. The table shows team 2's on-call rotations for the current year.

There are five rotations covering services 1, 2, and 3. Service 1 is covered by rotation 1 from 7 a.m. to 7 p.m. UTC and the rotation consists of two people. Service 1 is further covered by rotation 3 from 1 a.m. to 5 a.m. and the rotation consists of one person.

Services 2 and 3 are covered by rotation 2 from 8 a.m. to 4 p.m. and from 7 p.m. to 9 p.m. Rotation 2 consists of two people: a primary on-call person and a backup on-call person. Service 2 is covered after business hours by rotation 4, from 1 a.m. to 4 a.m. Service 3 is covered after-hours by rotation 5, from 2 a.m. to 5 a.m. Each of these rotations consists of a single person.

None of the services is covered by on-call rotations 24/7. This might not be necessary. An in-depth discussion about the level of on-call support required by different services is available in Section 7.6, *Providing On-Call Support Outside of Business Hours*.

In order to implement the table in Figure 11.14, the SRE infrastructure needs to connect to the on-call management tool. It contains all the data necessary for the table. The data can be accessed using APIs offered by most of the modern on-call management tools. Some also provide reporting capabilities that enable users to generate a view of the data that resembles the table in Figure 11.14.

Decisions to allocate SREs to a team can be supported by the "on-call rotations by team" indicator. If a team does not have an on-call rotation at all, it is a clear indication that the reliability of the services owned by the team is endangered. The SRE coaches need to work with teams that do not have any on-call rotations to find out why they don't and to support them in setting up their first on-call rotation. In this context, the SRE coaches need to work with the team managers to ensure the teams in most need of SRE manpower obtain it first.

Another discovery using the on-call rotations table can be related to insufficient on-call time coverage by existing rotations for important services. Services with a high availability target (e.g., greater than 99.99% availability) and a high production deployment frequency (e.g., daily) might require 24/7 on-call coverage. The table clearly shows the times of day when on-call coverage is not available for a service.

By contrast, the data in the on-call rotations table may indicate broad on-call time coverage for services with a rather low availability target and production deployment frequency. For instance, on-call coverage of 16/7 (i.e., 16 hours a day, 7 days a week) for a service with an availability target of less than 99% and a production deployment frequency less than monthly will not be necessary. The on-call rotation coverage can be used in a more effective way for a service with a higher availability target and a higher production deployment frequency.

Another signal using the on-call rotations indicator may be a rather low number of people in the teams involved in the on-call work. For instance, in the table consisting of five rotations, up to seven people are involved. This number roughly corresponds to an agile team size owning a full lifecycle of a service. This is something to strive for: Nearly every team member should go on call to experience and support production operations of services they develop.

If the number of people involved in on-call rotations is rather low for a team, the SRE coaches should engage with the team to find out why. They should coach the team to gradually involve more and more people in the on-call work.

11.2.11 Incident Time to Recovery Trend Indicator

The time to recover from incidents is the time between incident creation and incident resolution. Both measures are automatically tracked by modern on-call management tools. Therefore, the time to recover from incidents might be available as a graph out of the box in the on-call management tool. Such a graph is shown in Figure 11.15.

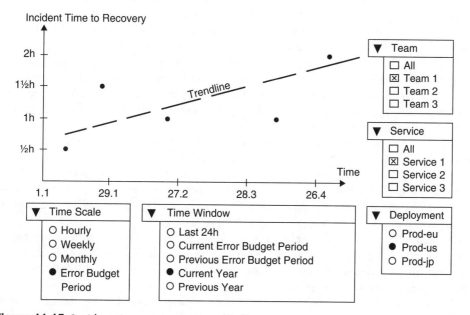

Figure 11.15 *Incident time to recovery trend indicator*

On the right-hand side and at the bottom of Figure 11.15, the graph settings are shown. Using the settings, the team, service, deployment, time window, and time scale can be set. In the figure, service 1 owned by team 1 in the "Prod-us" deployment is selected. The window is set to the current year on the error budget period time scale.

With these settings, the graph in the figure shows the time to recover from incidents that occurred with service 1. In the first error budget period, two incidents occurred. The first incident was recovered from within 30 minutes, the second within 90 minutes. In the second error budget period, a single incident occurred. It was recovered from within 60 minutes. In the third error budget period, no incidents occurred with service 1. In the fourth error budget period, again a single incident occurred. Like the previous incident, it was recovered from within 60 minutes. In the final error budget period, another incident occurred. At two hours, it had the longest time to recover from an incident in the current year.

The five data points on the graph yield a trendline with an upward trend. Using the insight of the upward trending time to recover from service 1 incidents, SLA negotiations where service 1 is involved can be supported by the data. The upward trending time to recover from service 1 incidents does not leave room for negotiation of tighter SLAs for service 1. With tighter SLAs, more SLA breaches need to be assumed to be on the safe side for negotiation purposes. More SLA breaches mean more incidents to resolve.

If team 1 has a growing incident recovery time trend with the current SLAs and incidents, it needs to be assumed for SLA negotiation purposes that the trendline would become steeper if the SLAs were tightened. Team 1 would be occupied with a growing number of incidents and longer times to recover from them. Following this, team 1 will not be able to defend the tightened SLAs.

If, however, the incident recovery time is trending firmly downward, it might indicate that a growing number of incidents due to the tightened SLAs might not overwhelm the team. In this case, the next set of data the SLA negotiation team needs to look at is historical SLA adherence (Section 11.2.8). If the SLA adherence data shows that team 1 was able to defend the current SLAs successfully, the next dataset to look at is SLA error budget depletion (Section 11.2.7).

If SLA error budget depletion shows some SLA error budget remaining across error budget periods, it provides the SLA negotiators with the necessary confidence to consider a contractual agreement to a slightly tightened set of SLAs. All the historical data provides evidence that team 1 may be able to defend the tightened SLA.

The incident time to recovery trend can also be used for making decisions to allocate a business plan cost position for an estimated cost of outages. In order to do so, revenue generated by a set of services needs to be known or estimated. Following this, the graph in Figure 11.15 can be used to find out the number of incidents and incident time to recovery trend for the set of services. Selecting an appropriate time frame of, for example, one year yields the data required for estimation.

For example, let us assume a set of services offering data analytics capabilities generating $1 million per year on a monthly subscription basis with contractually agreed chargebacks in case of unavailability. A chargeback is paid per 30 minutes of unavailability proportionally to 50% of the customer's monthly subscription cost.

Selecting the data analytics services in the graph in Figure 11.15 and setting the time window of the previous year might yield the following data.

There were 10 outages in the previous year. The time to recover from the outages is trending upward, averaging three hours.

Assuming all customers were affected by the 10 outages, the cost of outages can grossly be calculated as follows: 10 outages x 3-hour average = 30 hours of outages in the previous year. To calculate the chargebacks to all customers, the hourly revenue generated by the services needs to be calculated first. This can be done as follows: $1,000,000 / 365 days / 24 hours = $114 per hour. The chargebacks for the 30 hours of outages are then calculated as 30 hours x $114 x 1/2 = $1,710.

Because the time to recover from outages is trending upward and the number of future outages is unknown, a higher chargeback cost should be put into the business plan. To be on the safe side, the cost position for the estimated costs of outages could be stated as $5,000 per year.

11.2.12 Least Available Service Endpoints Indicator

Another supporting SRE indicator for reliability prioritization decisions is the least available service endpoints in a given time period. It can be used complementary to the premature SLO error budget exhaustion indicator (Section 11.2.5.2).

The least available service endpoints indicator can be presented well in tabular form. Such a table is shown in Figure 11.16. The table settings allow the user to set the team, service, deployment, time windows, and time scale.

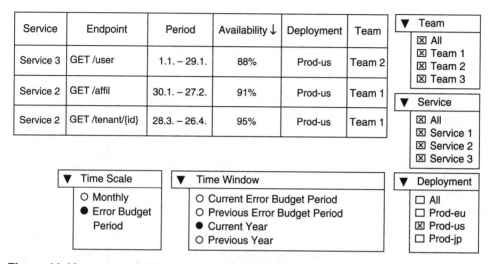

Figure 11.16 *Least available service endpoints indicator*

In the table, all teams and services are selected. The selected deployment is "Prod-us." The chosen time window is the current year on the error budget period time scale. Given the settings, the table shows three service endpoints. The endpoints are sorted by availability in a given error budget period in ascending order.

The least available endpoint is "GET /user" with availability of 88%. The second least available endpoint is "GET /affil" with availability of 91%. The third least available endpoint is "GET /tenant/{id}" with availability of 95%. Using the data, decisions to prioritize the endpoints in order to increase availability can be supported.

First, the premature SLO error budget exhaustion indicator (Section 11.2.5) can be used to determine the endpoints consistently breaking their availability SLOs. This list can be further filtered or ordered by the data from the table in Figure 11.16. The result is a list of services that consistently exhaust their availability SLO error budgets prematurely and are least available in a given time period. The job of a product owner to prioritize service availability improvements is greatly supported by the resultant service list.

The table in Figure 11.16 could be technically implemented using the infrastructure for the SLO error budget depletion indicator visualized as a table (Section 11.2.4). It might even be merged with that indicator by providing the user with additional table settings to switch some table columns on and off.

Apart from that, the data from the table can be used verbatim for a weekly availability newsletter to the product delivery organization. It only requires a deep link containing the necessary table settings in order to get the data generated for a particular newsletter issue. The link can be directly included in the newsletter as it stays valid as long as the underlying data is available.

11.2.13 Slowest Service Endpoints Indicator

Another supporting SRE indicator for reliability prioritization decisions is the slowest service endpoints in a given time period. It can be used complementary to the premature SLO error budget exhaustion indicator (Section 11.2.5.2).

The slowest service endpoints indicator can be presented well in tabular form. Such a table is shown in Figure 11.17. The table settings allow the user to select the team, service, deployment, time windows, and time scale.

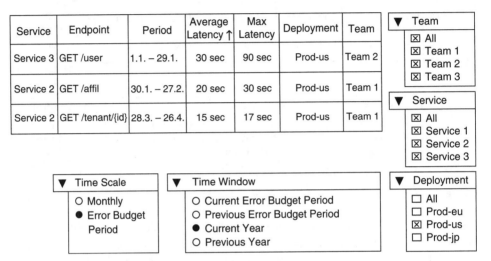

Service	Endpoint	Period	Average Latency ↑	Max Latency	Deployment	Team
Service 3	GET /user	1.1. – 29.1.	30 sec	90 sec	Prod-us	Team 2
Service 2	GET /affil	30.1. – 27.2.	20 sec	30 sec	Prod-us	Team 1
Service 2	GET /tenant/{id}	28.3. – 26.4.	15 sec	17 sec	Prod-us	Team 1

▼ Team
- ☒ All
- ☒ Team 1
- ☒ Team 2
- ☒ Team 3

▼ Service
- ☒ All
- ☒ Service 1
- ☒ Service 2
- ☒ Service 3

▼ Time Scale
- ○ Monthly
- ● Error Budget Period

▼ Time Window
- ○ Current Error Budget Period
- ○ Previous Error Budget Period
- ● Current Year
- ○ Previous Year

▼ Deployment
- ☐ All
- ☐ Prod-eu
- ☒ Prod-us
- ☐ Prod-jp

Figure 11.17 *Slowest service endpoints indicator*

In the table, all teams and services are selected. The selected deployment is "Prod-us." The chosen time window is the current year on the error budget period time scale. Given the settings, the table shows three service endpoints. The endpoints are sorted by average latency in a given error budget period in descending order.

The slowest endpoint is "GET /user" with average latency of 30 seconds. The second slowest endpoint is "GET /affil" with average latency of 20 seconds. The third slowest endpoint is "GET /tenant/{id}" with average latency of 17 seconds. Using the data, decisions to prioritize the endpoints in order to reduce latency can be supported.

First, the premature SLO error budget exhaustion indicator (Section 11.2.5) can be used to determine the endpoints consistently breaking their latency SLOs. This list can be further filtered or ordered by the data from the table in the figure. The result is a list of services that consistently exhaust their latency SLO error budgets prematurely and are the slowest in a given time period. The job of a product owner to prioritize service latency improvements is greatly supported by the resultant service list.

The table in Figure 11.17 could be technically implemented using the infrastructure for the SLO error budget depletion table (Section 11.2.4). It might even be merged with that table by providing the user with additional table settings to switch some table columns on and off.

11.3 Process Indicators, Not People KPIs

The SRE indicators need to be treated as the indicators of the reliability engineering process being executed in the organization. They should not be used as key performance indicators (KPIs) for evaluating people. This is important, because if they are used to evaluate people, the people are likely to be inclined to tweak the SRE indicator data to be evaluated in favorable terms.

The SRE coaches need to ensure that the leadership team and people managers are aware of this important aspect. Following this, they must make it clear to the entire product delivery organization that the SRE indicators will not be used for people evaluation purposes. Consequently, no one in the product delivery organization should fear that the SRE indicators may be used for performance appraisals. Only then can unskewed data quality and data evaluation be expected, ensured, and achieved.

Skewing the data shown by the SRE indicators is actually not that difficult. For example:

- The number of customer tickets per service is subject to the way the tickets are created.

- The number of SLO breaches is subject to the way the SLOs are set.

- The time to recovery from incidents is subject to the way the recovery is determined.

Therefore, like every other process indicator, the SRE indicators are subject to Goodhart's law: "Any observed statistical regularity will tend to collapse once pressure is placed upon it for control purposes."[3] The law was later generalized by Marilyn Strathern: "When a measure becomes a target, it ceases to be a good measure."[3] This happens because people anticipate the adverse consequence of missing the target. Following this, they might be inclined to take action, altering the measures in order to hit the target.

In order to ensure that the people in the product delivery organization do not spend valuable engineering time trying to alter the data, it should be clear to everyone that the SRE indicators do not influence individual careers. In fact, services are owned by teams. Therefore, the SRE indicators need to be owned by the teams.

Following this, the SRE indicators are a great topic for discussion in team meetings. If the indicators show improvement potential, which will be the case virtually every time they are looked at, it is the team's job as a whole to discuss, define, and implement the improvements. Finally, it is also the team's job to use the SRE indicators after the improvements have been implemented to measure whether the envisioned outcomes were indeed achieved.

11.4 Decisions Versus Indicators

As described in Section 11.1, *Reliability Decision-Making Taxonomy*, a large number of decisions can be supported by error budget–based decision–making using the SRE indicators from

---

3. Wikipedia. n.d. "Goodhart's law." Accessed January 27, 2022. https://en.wikipedia.org/wiki/Goodhart%27s_law.

the previous sections. Table 11.5 provides a summary of which decisions can specifically be supported by which SRE indicators. In addition, the table states the primary roles making the decisions using the indicators.

Table 11.5 *Decisions Supported by the SRE Indicators*

Category	Supported Decisions	SRE Indicators	Primary Roles
Prioritization decisions	Decision to prioritize services in most need of reliability improvements Decision to enact or adapt the error budget policy	Premature SLO error budget exhaustion indicator (Section 11.2.5) SLO error budget depletion indicator (Section 11.2.4) SLO adherence indicator (Section 11.2.3) Customer support ticket trend indicator (Section 11.2.9) Least available service endpoints indicator (Section 11.2.12) Slowest service endpoints indicator (Section 11.2.13)	Product owners, developers, operations engineers
Development decisions	Decision to consume an API Decision to implement adaptive capacity between services Decision to check the effectiveness of reliability improvements	"SLOs by service" indicator (Section 11.2.2) SLO error budget depletion indicator (Section 11.2.4) SLO adherence indicator (Section 11.2.3) "SLAs by service" indicator (Section 11.2.6) SLA adherence indicator (Section 11.2.8)	Developers, architects
Deployment decisions	Decision about denying a deployment into an environment	SLO error budget depletion indicator (Section 11.2.4)	Developers, operations engineers

Category	Supported Decisions	SRE Indicators	Primary Roles
Conversation decisions	Decision to talk to a team owning a dependent service to get the SLOs tightened	"SLOs by service" indicator (Section 11.2.2) SLO error budget depletion indicator (Section 11.2.4) SLO adherence indicator (Section 11.2.3)	Developers, architects, product owners
Reliability decisions	Decision to set SLOs for own service	"SLOs by service" indicator (Section 11.2.2) SLO adherence indicator (Section 11.2.3) "SLAs by service" indicator (Section 11.2.6) SLA adherence indicator (Section 11.2.8)	Operations engineers, developers, product owners
Test decisions	Decision to choose a hypothesis to test using chaos engineering	"SLOs by service" indicator (Section 11.2.2) SLO adherence indicator (Section 11.2.3) SLO error budget depletion indicator (Section 11.2.4)	Developers, operations engineers
Requirement decisions	Decision to add new BDD scenarios	SLO error budget depletion indicator (Section 11.2.4)	Product owners, developers
Budget decisions	Decision to allocate more SREs to a team or organizational unit Decision to allocate a budget for reliability improvements Decision to allocate a business plan cost position for outages	SLO adherence indicator (Section 11.2.3) Premature SLO error budget exhaustion indicator (Section 11.2.5) "On-call rotations by team" indicator (Section 11.2.10) Customer support ticket trend indicator (Section 11.2.9) Incident time to recovery trend indicator (Section 11.2.11)	Development managers, operations managers

Category	Supported Decisions	SRE Indicators	Primary Roles
Legal decisions	Decision to set SLAs for own services Decision to agree to contractual penalties of breaking SLAs	"SLOs by service" indicator (Section 11.2.2) SLO adherence indicator (Section 11.2.3) "SLAs by service" indicator (Section 11.2.6) SLA adherence indicator (Section 11.2.8) SLA error budget depletion indicator (Section 11.2.7) Incident time to recovery trend indicator (Section 11.2.11)	Legal counsel, general managers, product owners
Regulatory decisions	Decision to use SRE data points in regulatory compliance audits.	"SLOs by service" indicator (Section 11.2.2) SLO adherence indicator (Section 11.2.3) "SLAs by service" indicator (Section 11.2.6) SLA adherence indicator (Section 11.2.8)	Compliance managers, regulatory process owners, auditors

The variety of decisions in the table is impressive. They range from prioritization, development, and deployment to legal and regulatory. In the following section, frequent decision-making workflows using SRE indicators are presented in detail. The workflows demonstrate error budget–based decision–making in action.

11.5 Decision-Making Workflows

In this section, the SRE indicators will be used to demonstrate how error budget–based decision–making can be practiced to support the most important and frequent reliability decisions, such as the following:

- Decision to consume an API
- Decision to tighten a dependent service's SLO
- Decision to invest in new features versus reliability

- Decision to set an SLO

- Decision to set an SLA

- Decision to allocate SRE capacity to a team

- Decision to select a hypothesis for chaos engineering

Each decision can be made using a workflow supported by a set of SRE indicators. These workflows are explained in the next sections.

11.5.1 API Consumption Decision Workflow

A decision to consume an API can be supported by a three-step workflow. The workflow is rooted in three questions.

1. Which SLOs are defined for a service?

2. What is the adherence to the SLOs?

3. What is the SLO error budget depletion trend?

Answering the questions is directly supported by three SRE indicators defined in the previous sections and shown in Table 11.6.

Table 11.6 *Three-Step Workflow Supporting an API Consumption Decision*

Step	SRE Indicator	Explanation
1	"SLOs by service" indicator (Section 11.2.2)	Shows the SLOs defined for a service whose APIs are considered to be consumed
2	SLO adherence indicator (Section 11.2.3)	Shows the adherence to the defined SLOs over time
3	SLO error budget depletion indicator (Section 11.2.4)	Shows the error budget depletion trend that can be used for exploration purposes

The three-step decision-making workflow supported by the three SRE indicators is illustrated in Figure 11.18.

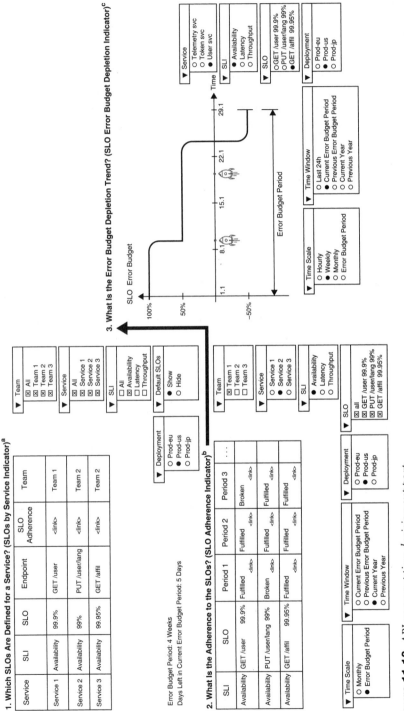

Figure 11.18 *API consumption decision support*

[a] See Figure 11.1 for larger version of this part of the figure.
[b] See Figure 11.2 for larger version of this part of the figure.
[c] See Figure 11.4 for larger version of this part of the figure.

When considering consuming an API exposed by a service, the first thing to find out is whether there are any SLOs defined for the API. This can conveniently be done using the "SLOs by service" indicator (step 1 in Figure 11.18). The table settings enable the user to easily find the right service, select the target deployment of interest, and explore the SLOs by SLI.

If there is no SLO defined for the API considered for consumption, the workflow cannot be executed. The team considering API consumption needs to get in touch with the team owning the service and ask them to set SLOs for the API. This is a great opportunity to define the SLOs together, discussing the customer use cases intended to be fulfilled.

If there are SLOs defined for the relevant API, they can be analyzed for their suitability to fulfill the intended customer use cases. In the next step, SLO adherence by the service over time can be viewed by clicking on the link in the SLO adherence column of the "SLOs by service" indicator table.

The link takes the user to the SLO adherence indicator (step 2 in the Figure 11.18). The SLO adherence indicator is automatically filtered to display the right SLO. In the table, the user will be able to see a preselected set of time periods. Each time period has a dedicated column that indicates whether the SLO was fulfilled or broken in the period. The user can change the table settings, especially the preselected time settings, to get the SLO adherence data displayed in the relevant time window on a relevant time scale.

In order to dig deeper into the data and explore SLO adherence, the user can view the error budget depletion trend on a fine-grained scale shown by the SLO error budget depletion graph. The user is taken to the graph automatically by following the link in the respective cell of the SLO adherence table. The graph shows error budget depletion over time (step 3 in the Figure 11.18).

Using the error budget depletion graph, the user can see the historic error budget depletion trend by error budget period. Although an SLO may be fulfilled in an error budget period, the error budget may be nearly exhausted. By contrast, although an SLO may be broken in an error budget period, the error budget may be only marginally in the negative. The error budget depletion graph is a perfect tool for doing exploratory analysis of this sort.

Using the three-step workflow and looping through the steps as required, the user can learn a great deal about the historical reliability of the API considered for consumption. The following questions become clarified.

- What are the SLOs defined for the API?

- What is the historical adherence to the defined SLOs in the intended target environments?

- What was the error budget depletion trend in the error budget periods where the SLO was fulfilled?

- What was the error budget depletion trend in the error budget periods where the SLO was broken?

- How does the error budget depletion trend correlate with the service deployments?

- How quickly is the error budget depletion stopped on average?

This wealth of reliability knowledge about the service considered for consumption enables a very conscious decision-making process. It is worth noting that this reliability knowledge is accumulated using the SRE indicators before any API integration work begins. This is in stark contrast to the current approaches in which the APIs are often integrated without any deep dive into their historical reliability.

Moreover, if the reliability of the API intended to be consumed turns out to be sufficient to make the decision to start the integration, the accumulated reliability knowledge can also be used to determine the level of adaptive capacity necessary between the services. If the SLOs are generally fulfilled and the error budget depletion trend shows no significant depletion, less investment in adaptive capacity might need to be done. If, on the other hand, the SLOs are broken from time to time or the error budget depletion trend shows significant depletion in general, a solid investment in adaptive capacity is justified. Circuit breakers, bulkheads, backpressure, and other stability patterns need to be implemented to provide degraded service to users when the dependent service is not reliable. The need to invest in these technical capabilities becomes transparent to the product owner as opposed to just being claimed by the developers.

If the defined SLOs are not sufficient to fulfill the new customer use cases intended to be enabled by service integration, there is a need for a conversation between the teams to see whether the SLO could be tightened. Crafting that conversation is the subject of the next section.

11.5.2 Tightening a Dependency's SLO Decision Workflow

After a team has looked at an SLO definition of another team's APIs that they are considering consuming, adherence to the SLO in the target environment, and SLO error budget depletion, they might conclude that the SLO needs to be tightened. This might be necessary because of a new customer use case that would be enabled by the two services being integrated in a new way (e.g., service A calling service B: A → B). The use case would only then satisfy the user if service B tightens applicable SLOs of the endpoints considered to be consumed by service A. For instance, the use case might require a certain low latency of service B response that, if exceeded, would prompt the user to leave.

Let us assume there are two teams, A and B, each respectively owning one service, A and B. In this case, team A should check whether historically there is some error budget left at the end of most error budget periods for service B's APIs considered to be consumed. This can conveniently be done using the SLO error budget depletion indicator shown in Figure 11.19.

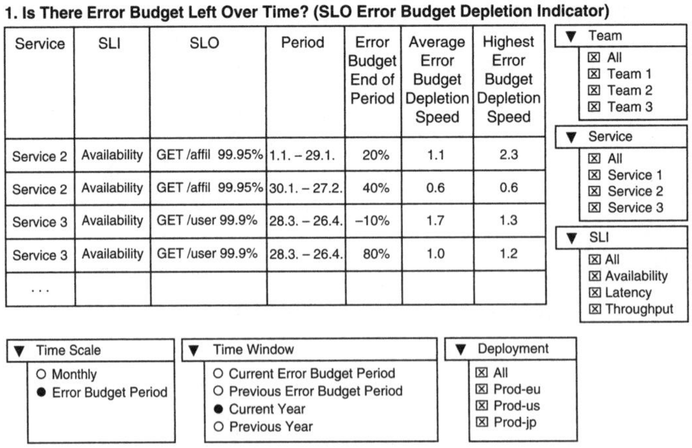

1. Is There Error Budget Left Over Time? (SLO Error Budget Depletion Indicator)

Service	SLI	SLO	Period	Error Budget End of Period	Average Error Budget Depletion Speed	Highest Error Budget Depletion Speed
Service 2	Availability	GET /affil 99.95%	1.1. – 29.1.	20%	1.1	2.3
Service 2	Availability	GET /affil 99.95%	30.1. – 27.2.	40%	0.6	0.6
Service 3	Availability	GET /user 99.9%	28.3. – 26.4.	–10%	1.7	1.3
Service 3	Availability	GET /user 99.9%	28.3. – 26.4.	80%	1.0	1.2
...						

▼ Team
- ☒ All
- ☒ Team 1
- ☒ Team 2
- ☒ Team 3

▼ Service
- ☒ All
- ☒ Service 1
- ☒ Service 2
- ☒ Service 3

▼ SLI
- ☒ All
- ☒ Availability
- ☒ Latency
- ☒ Throughput

▼ Time Scale
- ○ Monthly
- ● Error Budget Period

▼ Time Window
- ○ Current Error Budget Period
- ○ Previous Error Budget Period
- ● Current Year
- ○ Previous Year

▼ Deployment
- ☒ All
- ☒ Prod-eu
- ☒ Prod-us
- ☒ Prod-jp

Figure 11.19 *Decision support to tighten a dependency's SLO*

If most of the error budget periods end with some representative error budget remaining, team A can confidently initiate a conversation with team B using that data. For example, the GET /affil endpoint of service 2 exhibits such an error budget depletion pattern across error budget periods. In the error budget period of 1.1 (January 1), the remaining error budget at the end of the period is 20%. In the error budget period of 30.1 (January 30), the remaining error budget at the end of the period is 40%.

Team A should explain the new customer use case that can be satisfied using service integration A → B, if service B could tighten some of their SLOs. Team A should further show service B's historical error budget depletion data. The remaining error budget at the end of the error budget periods should be discussed between the teams, and questions such as the following should be explored: Could the SLOs be tightened as required without causing additional effort for team B due to the currently remaining error budget? Would some additional reliability implementation be required in team B in order to defend the tightened SLOs? Would any changes to service B's on-call rotation coverage be required?

If, however, most of the error budget periods do not end with any noteworthy error budget remaining, team A should still approach team B to discuss what could be done to get service B's reliability to where it would need to be to support the new customer use case. If the availability SLOs get broken, for example, adding some adaptive capacity against service B's dependencies might be helpful. If the latency SLOs get broken, for example, optimizing database indices might be helpful. Whatever the measure, it is in team A's interest to make service B more reliable. Therefore, team A might offer to perform some inner source work in team B's codebase in order to improve service B's reliability more quickly.

This way, a whole new level of conversations is enabled between the teams. It is DevOps at its core: Developers talk about operations in their daily development work. Moreover, developers make implementation decisions based on operations data.

> **From the Trenches:** The new conversations between the teams do not happen just because of the availability of SRE indicators. To get the new conversations going, they need to be facilitated by the SRE coaches. Initially, this means going team by team as part of the regular SRE coaching meetings.
>
> In the meetings, the SRE coaches need to inquire about the plans to consume APIs owned by other teams. Based on the plans, the coaches need to facilitate the decisions to consume the APIs using the SRE indicators. They need to demonstrate the new decision-making workflows, such as the API consumption decision workflow (Section 11.5.1) and tightening a dependency's SLO decision workflow (Section 11.5.2).
>
> This will need to be repeated a couple of times by each team. Depending on the ease of use of the SRE indicators and the effectiveness of the conversations between the teams, the new way of considering API consumption will start making its way into ongoing practice.

If team A does not manage to convince team B to tighten the relevant SLOs, they need to make a decision. If there is an alternative to service B, they might consider consuming another service to achieve the same purpose. If there is not, they might consider changing the user journey in order to make the reliability of service B less relevant to the outcome the user seeks to achieve.

In any case, the aforementioned decision workflow enables team A to make the API consumption decision in a very conscious manner well ahead of time, before any significant integration effort is underway.

11.5.3 Features Versus Reliability Prioritization Workflow

Decisions regarding investing in new features versus reliability for a given period of time in the future are at the heart of SRE. These decisions constitute the core prioritization workflow exercised regularly by the product owners. The SRE indicators provide a great deal of support in making these decisions in a data-driven manner.

A decision to invest in features versus reliability can be supported by a five-step workflow. The workflow is rooted in the following five questions.

1. Which service endpoints break the error budgets in most error budget periods?

2. Which service endpoints have the least time to error budget exhaustion and the least error budget available (i.e., most error budget shortage) at the end of error budget periods?

3. Which service endpoints have the highest error budget depletion speed?

4. Which service endpoints are the least available?

5. Which service endpoints are the slowest?

Answering the questions is directly supported by the five SRE indicators defined in the previous sections and outlined in Table 11.7.

Table 11.7 *Five-Step Workflow Supporting a Decision to Invest in Features Versus Reliability*

Step	SRE Indicator	Explanation
1	SLO adherence indicator (Section 11.2.3)	Shows the adherence to the defined SLOs over time by error budget period
2	Premature SLO error budget exhaustion indicator (Section 11.2.5)	Shows service endpoints that exhaust the SLO error budgets prematurely, as well as the time to error budget exhaustion and the error budget shortage at the end of each error budget period
3	SLO error budget depletion indicator (Section 11.2.4)	Shows the error budget depletion speed by service endpoint
4	Least available service endpoints indicator (Section 11.2.12)	Shows the least available service endpoints
5	Slowest service endpoints indicator (Section 11.2.13)	Shows the slowest service endpoints

Each indicator returns a set of service endpoints. In order to limit the returned results, it is advisable to take a certain number of services (e.g., three) from the top of each indicator's result list. This will yield a manageable number of the most critical service endpoints to be taken for reliability improvements.

The five-step decision-making workflow supported by the five SRE indicators is illustrated in Figure 11.20.

In workflow step 1, the sorted list returned by the error budget adherence indicator table represents the endpoints that consistently break their error budgets over many error budget periods. These services require reliability investments the most. Adding new features to the services will almost certainly result in users perceiving the features as being unreliable.

In workflow step 2, the sorted list returned by the premature error budget exhaustion indicator table represents the endpoints that have the least time to error budget exhaustion and the least error budget available (or the most error budget shortage) at the end of each error budget period. The endpoints with the least time to error budget exhaustion experience outages so severe that the entire monthly error budget gets exhausted within several days.

In contrast to the endpoint list from step 1 where the endpoints that consistently broke their error budgets over several error budget periods are shown, the list from step 2 contains endpoints with very rapid error budget exhaustion in at least one error budget period. Certainly, the endpoint lists from steps 1 and 2 may have correlations. This is also the goal of shortlisting distinct endpoints across the five indicators of the five-step workflow that are in most need of reliability improvements. The longer the list, the more time needs to be invested in reliability. The shorter the list, the more time can be invested in features. This is error budget–based decision–making at its best!

The endpoint list from workflow step 2 additionally contains endpoints with the least error budget available (or the most error budget shortage) at the end of an error budget period. That is, the available error budget will be negative because the list only contains the endpoints that exhausted the error budget prematurely. The list answers the question of how far negative the error budget is at the end of an error budget period. This measure does not necessarily correlate with the time required to exhaust the error budget. The error budget might not be depleted to exhaustion over a large part of the entire error budget period and then plunge into deep negative numbers right at the end.

The deeper the plunge into the negative, the more investment in reliability is required by the respective service. Such error budget depletion indicates a serious issue, such as a hard dependency that is unreliable. It needs to be dealt with in order to ensure a good user experience for the respective use cases in the future.

In workflow step 3, a similar question is explored. The sorted list returned by the SLO error budget depletion indicator contains endpoints with the highest error budget depletion speed. Unlike the list from workflow step 2 where the error budget depletion speed is considered in terms of error budget exhaustion, here the error budget depletion speed is viewed in general. An endpoint may not exhaust the error budget in an error budget period. This, however, does not prevent the endpoint from having the highest error budget depletion speed among all services regardless of whether they exhausted the error budget or not.

1. What Are the Top Three Service Endpoints Breaking the Error Budgets in Most of the Error Budget Periods? (SLO Adherence Indicator)[a]

SLI	SLO	Period 1	Period 2	Period 3	...
Availability	GET /user 99.9%	Fulfilled <link>	Fulfilled <link>	Broken <link>	
Availability	PUT /user/lang 99%	Broken <link>	Fulfilled <link>	Fulfilled <link>	
Availability	GET /affil 99.95%	Fulfilled <link>	Fulfilled <link>	Fulfilled <link>	

▼ Team: ☒ Team 1 ☒ Team 2 ☒ Team 3
▼ Service: ● Service 1 ● Service 2 ○ Service 3
▼ SLI: ● Availability ○ Latency ○ Throughput
▼ SLO: ☒ all ☒ GET /user 99.9% ☒ PUT /user/lang 99% ☒ GET /affil 99.95%
▼ Time Scale: ○ Monthly ● Error Budget Period
▼ Time Window: ○ Current Error Budget Period ○ Previous Error Budget Period ● Current Year ○ Previous Year
▼ Deployment: ○ Prod-eu ● Prod-us ○ Prod-jp

2. What Are the Top Three Endpoints with the Least Time to Error Budget Exhaustion and the Least Error Budget Available at the End of Each Error Budget Period? (Premature SLO Error Budget Exhaustion Indicator)[b]

Service	SLI	SLO	Period	Error Budget End of Period	Time to Error Budget Exhaustion	Average Error Budget Depletion Speed	Deployment	Team
Service 2	Availability	GET /affil 99.95%	1.1.–29.1.	–70%	3 days	0.6.	Prod-us	Team 1
Service 2	Availability	GET /affil 99.95%	30.1.–27.2.	–30%	5 days	1.7.	Prod-us	Team 1
Service 3	Availability	GET /user 99.9%	28.3.–26.4.	–43%	8 days	1.5.	Prod-us	Team 2
Service 3	Availability	GET /user 99.9%	28.3.–26.4.	–51%	20 days	2.1.	Prod-eu	Team 2

▼ Time Scale: ○ Monthly ● Error Budget Period
▼ Time Window: ○ Current Error Budget Period ○ Previous Error Budget Period ○ Previous Year
▼ Deployment: ☒ All ☒ Prod-eu ☒ Prod-us ☒ Prod-jp

▼ Team: ☒ All ☒ Team 1 ☒ Team 2 ☒ Team 3
▼ Service: ☒ All ☒ Service 1 ☒ Service 2 ☒ Service 3
▼ SLI: ☒ All ☒ Availability ☒ Latency ☒ Throughput

3. What Are the Top Three Endpoints with the Highest Error Budget Depletion Speed? (SLO Error Budget Depletion Indicator)[c]

Service	SLI	SLO	Period	Error Budget End of Period	Average Error Budget Depletion Speed	Highest Error Budget Depletion Speed
Service 2	Availability	GET /affil 99.95%	1.1.–29.1.	20%	1.1	2.3
Service 2	Availability	GET /affil 99.95%	30.1.–27.2.	40%	0.6	0.6
Service 3	Availability	GET /user 99.9%	28.3.–26.4.	–10%	1.7	1.3.
Service 3	Availability	GET /user 99.9%	28.3.–26.4.	80%	1.0	1.2
...						

▼ Time Scale: ○ Monthly ● Error Budget Period
▼ Time Window: ○ Current Error Budget Period ○ Previous Error Budget Period ● Current Year ○ Previous Year
▼ Deployment: ☒ All ☒ Prod-eu ☒ Prod-us ☒ Prod-jp

▼ Team: ☒ All ☒ Team 1 ☒ Team 2 ☒ Team 3
▼ Service: ☒ All ☒ Service 1 ☒ Service 2 ☒ Service 3
▼ SLI: ☒ All ☒ Availability ☒ Latency ☒ Throughput

4. What Are the Top Three Least Available Endpoints? (Least Available Service Endpoints Indicator)[d]

Service	Endpoint	Period	Availability ↓	Deployment	Team
Service 3	GET /user	1.1.–29.1.	88%	Prod-us	Team 2
Service 2	GET /affil	30.1.–27.2.	91%	Prod-us	Team 1
Service 2	GET /tenant/[id]	28.3.–26.4.	95%	Prod-us	Team 1

▼ Time Scale: ○ Monthly ○ Error Budget Period
▼ Time Window: ○ Current Error Budget Period ○ Previous Error Budget Period ● Current Year ○ Previous Year

▼ Team: ☒ All ☒ Team 1 ☒ Team 2 ☒ Team 3
▼ Service: ☒ All ☒ Service 1 ☒ Service 2 ☒ Service 3
▼ Deployment: ☐ All ☐ Prod-eu ☒ Prod-us ☐ Prod-jp

5. What Are the Top Three Slowest Endpoints? (Slowest Service Endpoints Indicator)[e]

Service	Endpoint	Period	Average Latency	Max Latency	Deployment	Team
Service 3	GET /user	1.1.–29.1.	30 sec	90 sec	Prod-us	Team 2
Service 2	GET /affil	30.1.–27.2.	20 sec	30 sec	Prod-us	Team 1
Service 2	GET /tenant/[id]	28.3.–26.4.	15 sec	17 sec	Prod-us	Team 1

▼ Time Scale: ○ Monthly ● Error Budget Period
▼ Time Window: ○ Current Error Budget Period ○ Previous Error Budget Period ● Current Year ○ Previous Year

▼ Team: ☒ All ☒ Team 1 ☒ Team 2 ☒ Team 3
▼ Service: ☒ All ☒ Service 1 ☒ Service 2 ☒ Service 3
▼ Deployment: ☐ All ☐ Prod-eu ☒ Prod-us ☐ Prod-jp

Figure 11.20 *Decision support to invest in features versus reliability*

[a] See Figure 11.2 for larger version of this part of the figure.
[b] See Figure 11.7 for larger version of this part of the figure.
[c] See Figure 11.5 for larger version of this part of the figure.
[d] See Figure 11.16 for larger version of this part of the figure.
[e] See Figure 11.17 for larger version of this part of the figure.

For instance, if an incident consumes 50% of the monthly error budget within an hour, it might be the fastest error budget depletion across all services within six months. In the error budget period where the incident occurred, the service that experienced the incident might end the error budget period with 10% of its error budget still available. Other services within six months might exhaust their error budgets prematurely. However, none of the other incidents might reach the error budget depletion speed of 50% of the monthly error budget per hour.

Detecting cases like this in workflow step 3 using the SLO error budget depletion indicator is a great way to identify service issues that require reliability improvements. By definition, rapid error budget depletion correlates with rapid user experience deterioration. This justifies reliability improvements to be prioritized over new feature development from the business point of view.

In workflow steps 4 and 5, the two most important SLIs are considered: availability and latency. In workflow step 4, a sorted list of the least available endpoints is shown using the least available endpoints indicator table. In workflow step 5, a sorted list of the slowest endpoints is shown using the slowest service endpoints indicator table. The two lists will almost certainly have a significant correlation with the other lists from the previous workflow steps. Still, it is beneficial to have the lists as a safety net in order to avoid missing important endpoints in need of reliability improvements due to the SLOs not yet being fully calibrated to reflect the user experience.

The lists from workflow steps 4 and 5 are not necessarily dependent on SLOs. They are barebones measures of the most important characteristics for the majority of services. If a service is not available, it is not reliable. This is true for all services. Likewise, if a service is available but so slow that it is considered unavailable, the service is not reliable. This is also true for most services.

In summary, the five-step workflow to find services in most need of reliability improvements yields service endpoints of the characteristics shown in Table 11.8.

Table 11.8 *Characteristics of Service Endpoints in Most Need of Reliability Improvements*

Workflow Step	Indicator	Depends on SLO	View Across Error Budget Periods	Characteristic
1	SLO adherence indicator (Section 11.2.3)	Yes	Yes	Long-term error budget breakers
2	Premature SLO error budget exhaustion indicator (Section 11.2.5)	Yes	No	Short-term fastest error budget exhausters Short-term biggest error budget shortage by error budget period

Workflow Step	Indicator	Depends on SLO	View Across Error Budget Periods	Characteristic
3	SLO error budget depletion indicator (Section 11.2.4)	Yes	No	Short-term fastest error budget depletors
4	Least available service endpoints indicator (Section 11.2.12)	No	No	Short-term least available endpoints
5	Slowest service endpoints indicator (Section 11.2.13)	No	No	Short-term slowest endpoints

The resultant list of distinct endpoints is definitely worth prioritizing for reliability improvements. Following the five-step workflow outlined in this section, the product owners can make fine-grained, data-driven decisions to improve reliability in service endpoints where it matters most. The rest of the development capacity can be used to build new customer-facing features.

The service instrumentation in terms of reliability enabled by the use of the five SRE indicators is unique. It is fair to say that the vast majority of product owners today do not have access to this kind of data and, consequently, prioritization workflows. The reliability investments are therefore done in a less systematic manner based on conversations with the architects and developers.

Using the five-step workflow, these conversations are put onto a solid data-driven foundation. The architects and developers can make their case in a more convincing manner. The product owners do not need to rely only on the statements by the architects and developers to make prioritization decisions. They can actively dive into the data themselves and become an eye-level conversation partner with the technical members of the team about reliability prioritization.

The results are better decisions, reliability improvements where it matters most, and ultimately, timely establishment of a good user experience where users suffered most in the past.

11.5.4 Setting an SLO Decision Workflow

As discussed in Section 6.6.1, *What Makes a Good SLO?*, an SLO needs to have a number of characteristics to be good. Most importantly, a good SLO needs to reflect well on the user experience of a specific step in a specific user journey and, when broken, lead to a fast and clear understanding of how the user experience is impacted. That is, setting an SLO needs to be rooted in user experience.

Technically the user experience when interacting with a service depends on the reliability of the service itself and the reliability of dependent services. The topic of calculating SLOs for a service based on the SLOs of dependent services is explored in depth in *Implementing Service*

Level Objectives[2] and "The Calculus of Service Availability."[4] In "The Calculus of Service Availability," the authors state that "you're only as available as the sum of your dependencies."

However, dependent services can be of different kinds. Some dependent services are mandatorily required to be available for a service to work reliably. Other dependent services might become unavailable for some time without impacting the reliability of the service itself because of the adaptive capacity implemented between the services. Furthermore, the service might mitigate the unavailability, slowness, and so on of some of the dependent services by providing reliable but degraded functionality to its users.

Another dimension to think about is that the dependent services might become unavailable either at the same time or at different times. These temporal effects may impact the service level that can be offered to users. Following the aforementioned considerations, in the presentation on SLO Math[5] by Steve McGhee, there is a statement: "You can build more reliable things on top of less reliable things."

Digging deeper, some dependent services might have SLOs or SLAs published. Others might not. Furthermore, some dependent services might have the historical adherence to the SLOs or SLAs published. Others might not.

This discussion shows that setting an SLO is not a fully straightforward process. The aim is to set the SLO in such a way that it reflects the user experience well. This can be done empirically by setting an initial SLO to a seemingly appropriate value and iterating quickly based on SLO breaches. While iterating on SLO breaches is an inherent part of achieving a good SLO, setting an initial SLO can be supported well by data.

In a service network, the SLOs and SLAs of dependent services owned by the product delivery organization should be public information, as should the historical adherence to the SLOs and SLAs. This data can be used to estimate the impact of the dependent services' reliability on the service whose SLOs are being set.

As to the dependent services not owned by the product delivery organization, some of them may have SLAs exposed. Historical adherence to the SLAs might be exposed as well. That is, the process of setting an SLO for a service can be supported by analyzing the available data on and the historical adherence to the SLOs and SLAs of internal and external dependent services.

If a service has SLOs and SLAs defined, it is worth looking at both of them and their adherence. SLOs are typically set at a higher service level than SLAs. This is done in order for the SLOs to be higher internal targets than contractually agreed SLAs. This arrangement is schematically illustrated in Figure 11.21.

---

4. Sloss, Benjamin Treynor, Mike Dahlin, Vivek Rau, and Betsy Beyer. 2017. "The Calculus of Service Availability." *Queue* 15(2):49–67. https://doi.org/10.1145/3084693.3096459.

5. McGhee, Steve. 2021. "SLO Math." YouTube, May 16, 2021. https://www.youtube.com/watch?v=-lHPDx90Ppg.

Figure 11.21 *Setting SLOs versus SLAs*

When the SLOs as high internal targets get broken, they do not lead to contractual consequences agreed to by the SLAs, as the SLAs are more relaxed external targets. Thus, a service with SLOs and SLAs has two targets. The first target is to provide a high service level expressed by the SLOs. The second target is to provide, at least, a more relaxed service level than the SLOs, expressed by the SLAs. This is illustrated in Figure 11.22.

That is, good adherence to the SLOs means good adherence to the SLAs, as they are more relaxed targets. Insufficient adherence to the SLOs does not mean insufficient adherence to the SLAs. A service might break the SLOs but defend the SLAs, thus fulfilling contractual obligations.

A decision to set an SLO for a service can be supported by a four-step workflow to be executed for each dependent service. The workflow is rooted in the following four questions.

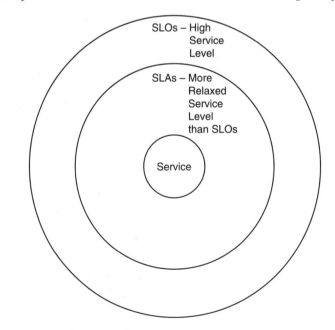

Figure 11.22 *Service with SLOs and SLAs set*

1. Does the dependent service have SLAs? What are they?

2. Are the SLAs fulfilled over time?

3. Does the dependent service have SLOs? What are they?

4. Are the SLOs fulfilled over time?

Answering the questions is directly supported by four SRE indicators defined in the previous sections and shown in Table 11.9.

Table 11.9 *Four-Step Workflow Supporting a Decision to Set an SLO*

Step	SRE Indicator	Explanation
1	"SLAs by service" indicator (Section 11.2.6)	Shows the SLAs defined for a service, if any
2	SLA adherence indicator (Section 11.2.8)	Shows the adherence to the defined SLAs over time by error budget period
3	"SLOs by service" indicator (Section 11.2.2)	Shows the SLOs defined for a service, if any
4	SLO adherence indicator (Section 11.2.3)	Shows the adherence to the defined SLOs over time by error budget period

Using the indicators, it may be possible to find out the highest service level offered by a dependent service. The service levels could be categorized as follows:

• Undefined: if neither SLOs nor SLAs are set for the service

• Low: if SLAs and SLOs are defined but broken

• Medium: if SLAs are defined and fulfilled

• High: if SLOs are defined and fulfilled

The four-step workflow supported by the four SRE indicators is illustrated in Figure 11.23.

In workflow step 1, the SLAs defined for a service can be found. This can be done using the "SLAs by service" indicator for services owned by the product delivery organization. For external services, the SLAs, if any, will be part of the contract with the service provider. The relevant parts of the contract are often available as part of the master service agreement referenced on the service provider's website.

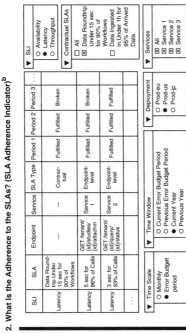

Figure 11.23 *Decision support to set an SLO*

[a] See Figure 11.8 for larger version of this part of the figure.
[b] See Figure 11.11 for larger version of this part of the figure.
[c] See Figure 11.1 for larger version of this part of the figure.
[d] See Figure 11.2 for larger version of this part of the figure.

In workflow step 2, adherence to the SLAs over time can be seen. Also here, for services owned by the product delivery organization, the SLA adherence indicator can be used. For external services, SLA adherence, if any, may be listed on the service provider's website.

Workflow steps 3 and 4 are applicable only to the services owned by the product delivery organization. This is because the external services do not expose their internal SLOs. In workflow step 3, the SLOs defined for a service can be found. In workflow step 4, the SLO adherence over time can be seen.

The four-step workflow needs to be repeated for each dependent service. Using the data about the highest service level ensured by each dependent service, an analysis can be done to see how it affects overall reliability depending on whether the dependency is strong, soft, or something in between. Based on the analysis, an initial SLO can be set and iterated upon based on the SLO breaches reported by the SRE infrastructure.

11.5.5 Setting an SLA Decision Workflow

Setting an SLA involves two parts: technical and contractual. Technically, if a service has a well-defined SLO already, it can and should be used as a basis for the technical SLA definition. In this case, the SLA will be a relaxed version of the SLO. Otherwise, the technical decision to set an SLA can be supported as discussed in Section 11.5.4, *Setting an SLO Decision Workflow*. The highest service level ensured by each dependent service will be determined using that workflow.

The contractual part of setting an SLA will involve negotiations with customers and partners. The negotiations can be supported by data provided by the SRE indicators. What is important in the negotiations is knowledge of the risk that can be accepted by the product delivery organization. Specifically, it is about the risk of the following:

- Tightening an SLA in the contract
- Contractual penalties of breaking the SLA

The risk of tightening an SLA in the contract could be estimated using the workflow outlined briefly in Section 11.2.11, *Incident Time to Recovery Trend Indicator*. The workflow consists of three steps. It is rooted in the following three questions.

1. What is the incident time to recovery trend?
2. If the incident recovery time trend is declining, what is the SLA adherence trend?
3. If the historical SLA adherence is acceptable, what is the typically remaining SLA error budget by error budget period?

Answering the questions is directly supported by three SRE indicators from the previous sections, shown in Table 11.10.

Table 11.10 *Three-Step Workflow Supporting a Contractual Decision to Tighten an SLA*

Step	SRE Indicator	Explanation
1	Incident time to recovery trend indicator (Section 11.2.11)	Shows the historical incident recovery time trend
2	SLA adherence indicator (Section 11.2.8)	Shows the historical SLA adherence
3	SLA error budget depletion indicator (Section 11.2.7)	Shows the historical SLA error budget depletion

The three-step workflow supported by the three SRE indicators for estimating the risk of tightening an SLA is illustrated in Figure 11.24.

In workflow step 1, the incident time to recovery trend is determined for the teams and services involved in the SLA negotiations. The incident time to recovery trend is an indicator of whether a team might be overburdened if their SLAs were to be tightened. The trend shows the recovery time from the incidents based on the current SLAs. If the SLAs were to be tightened, more incidents need to be assumed, to be on the safe side for negotiation purposes. If the current incident time to recovery is trending upward, the assumption for negotiation purposes needs to be that more incidents in the teams would lead to even longer times to recovery. That is, more incidents and longer times to recover from them need to be assumed with the growing incident time to recovery trend. These circumstances do not provide firm ground to sign a contract in confidence that the team can defend the tightened SLAs.

If, however, the current incident time to recovery trend is steadily declining, it might be an indication that more incidents, assumed to happen due to the tightened SLAs, could be handled by the team. In order to explore this question, in workflow step 2, the SLA adherence trend can be seen. If the historical adherence to the SLAs is appropriate in that the SLAs were successfully defended in most of the error budget periods of the selected time window, it might be another indication that the team might be able to defend the tightened SLAs.

In order to test this hypothesis, in workflow step 3, the remaining SLA error budget at the end of the error budget periods can be looked at. If the error budget remaining at the end of the selected error budget periods is significant (e.g., over 25%), there is a reason to believe that tightening the SLAs will not overburden the team. Indeed, three indicators hint at that.

1. The team's incident time to recovery is trending downward.

2. The adherence to the current SLAs is sufficient.

3. The remaining SLA error budget by error budget period is significant.

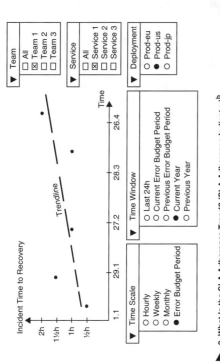

Figure 11.24 *Decision support to tighten an SLA*

[a] See Figure 11.15 for larger version of this part of the figure.

[b] See Figure 11.11 for larger version of this part of the figure.

[c] See Figure 11.10 for larger version of this part of the figure.

The three-step workflow needs to be repeated for all teams involved in defending the SLAs in question. If the workflow yields a positive result for all the teams involved, a decision backed up by data can be made to contractually agree to tighten the SLAs. The data provides confidence to believe that the teams will be able to defend them.

Another risk estimation that needs to be done during SLA negotiations is that of contractual penalties for breaking the SLAs. The estimation can be supported by the incident time to recovery trend indicator. If the incident time to recovery is trending upward, the SLA negotiators do not have a lot of room for negotiation. Indeed, if SLAs are broken, it takes the teams longer and longer to recover from them. The longer the recovery, the more the SLA error budget is depleted and, consequently, the larger the impact of contractual penalties will be.

In this situation, the SLA negotiators cannot take risks. They can only agree to some minimum contractual penalties. If, on the other hand, the incident time to recovery is trending downward, there might be room for taking a slightly higher risk by negotiating penalties on a slightly larger scale. This is because with the lower time to recovery, SLA error budget depletion during the incidents is getting smaller. As the contractual penalties of breaching the SLAs tend to be based on SLA error budget depletion, the diminishing SLA error budget depletion trend avoids large penalties from being invoked.

That is, a product delivery organization can agree to larger penalties being contractually signed knowing that these terms will not be invoked due to incident time to recovery trending downward. Agreeing to larger penalties due to SLA breaches may open room for negotiating other terms of the contract in favor of the product delivery organization. For instance, a higher price for using the offered services might be possible to negotiate, strengthening the overall business case.

11.5.6 Allocating SRE Capacity to a Team Decision Workflow

Personnel decisions regarding SRE capacity allocation to a team are subject to a number of constraints. Budget availability constraints, budget distribution difficulties, situations that are difficult to untangle due to ambiguous statements by different people claiming the budget and head count, high-stakes conversations including blame, and other constraints might stand in the way of transparent decision-making. SRE indicators provide good assistance in making SRE capacity allocation decisions in a data-driven manner.

A decision to allocate SRE capacity to a team can be supported by a four-step workflow. The workflow is rooted in the following four questions.

1. What is the SLO adherence by error budget period by the services owned by the team?

2. How many people are involved in the on-call rotation, if any?

3. What is the customer support ticket trend for the services owned by the team?

4. What is the incident time to recovery trend in the team?

Answering these questions is directly supported by four SRE indicators defined in the previous sections and shown in Table 11.11.

Table 11.11 *Four-Step Workflow to Support a Decision to Allocate SRE Capacity*

Step	SRE Indicator	Explanation
1	SLO adherence indicator (Section 11.2.3)	Shows the adherence to the defined SLOs over time by error budget period
2	"On-call rotations" by team indicator (Section 11.2.10)	Shows the number of people involved in on-call rotations by team
3	Customer support ticket trend (Section 11.2.9)	Shows the customer support ticket growth trend for services owned by a team
4	Incident time to recovery trend (Section 11.2.11)	Shows the incident time to recovery trend for a team

The four-step decision-making workflow supported by the four SRE indicators is illustrated in Figure 11.25.

Signs that a team needs more SRE capacity allocated in order to adequately support the services they own in production are

- The SLO adherence by error budget period is low.

- The on-call rotations by the team are not adequately manned.

- The customer support ticket trend for the services owned by the team is growing.

- The incident time to recovery trend is growing.

Using the data from the four SRE indicators, the signs can be read and used in decision-making conversations. To be sure, the SRE indicators data can only assist in these conversations. The data alone should not determine personnel and budget allocation decisions directly! Once the decisions are made, SRE capacity allocation can be executed in different ways depending on the SRE setup in the product delivery organization.

If developers perform the SRE work in the teams, a decision to add a developer to the team might be made. Alternatively, a decision to reallocate the ownership of services might be made in order to provide each team with enough capacity for doing the SRE work. If the operations engineers also perform the SRE work for product services, a decision might be made to allocate an operations engineer to a team.

The preceding workflow should also be used to check the effectiveness of the decision a couple of months down the road. The answers to the questions from the workflow should be a bit different at that point. Forming hypotheses on the basis of the workflow and checking them periodically is a good way to check the effectiveness of the SRE personnel and budget allocation decisions.

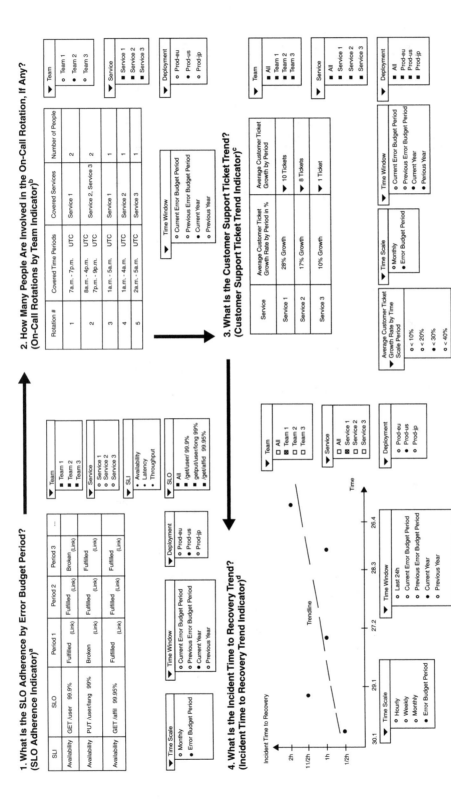

Figure 11.25 *Decision support to allocate SRE capacity to a team*

[a] See Figure 11.2 for larger version of this part of the figure.

[b] See Figure 11.14 for larger version of this part of the figure.

[c] See Figure 11.13 for larger version of this part of the figure.

[d] See Figure 11.15 for larger version of this part of the figure.

11.5.7 Chaos Engineering Hypotheses Selection Workflow

Chaos engineering is a software discipline formed at the end of the 2010s with the purpose of increasing system resilience. It is defined by Principles of Chaos Engineering as "the discipline of experimenting on a system in order to build confidence in the system's capability to withstand turbulent conditions in production."[6] "Hope is not a strategy"[7] is a traditional SRE saying that aligns well with chaos engineering's philosophy of experimentation.

In Section 1.3, *Why Does SRE Work?*, the scientific method was discussed as the reason why SRE works. The scientific method also lies at the heart of chaos engineering applied in the context of running experiments to generate knowledge about system resilience. An experiment in chaos engineering is designed as a four-step process, outlined in Table 11.12.

Table 11.12 *Chaos Engineering Experiment Structure*

Step	Description	Explanation
1	Define a steady state of the system	This can be defined using relevant business metrics measured in real time showing that the system is healthily working as expected from the user point of view.
2	Form a hypothesis	A hypothesis about the steady state remaining grossly unchanged when some harm is inflicted to the system. The hypothesis can be specified using, for example, the <capability> / <outcome> / <measurable signal> triple (see Section 4.7, *Posing Hypotheses*). The capability in this case is the planned harm to the system. The expected outcome is the maintenance of the steady state. The measurable signal specifies how the steady state will be measured during the experiment.
3	Simulate real-world events	This is the phase of inflicting the harm to the system planned in the hypotheses. It can include all kinds of adversary technical actions. For instance, shutting down a data center region, multiplying the network latency in a network, and random shutdown of services are typical examples of how real-world events are simulated.
4	Test the hypothesis	In this phase, the actual system state during the harm infliction is compared to the steady state defined in the first step. If the steady state is maintained despite the harm, the hypothesis is proved. The learning is that the system is as reliable as hypothesized before. If the steady state is not maintained, the hypothesis is disproved. The learning is in the new system weaknesses that got uncovered. These need to be prioritized to improve the system reliability.

---

6. "Principles of Chaos Engineering." n.d. Principles of Chaos Engineering. Accessed January 25, 2022. https://principlesofchaos.org.

7. Murphy, Niall Richard, Betsy Beyer, Chris Jones, and Jennifer Petoff. 2016. *Site Reliability Engineering: How Google Runs Production Systems*. Sebastopol, CA: O'Reilly Media.

It is important to note that chaos experiments are not for use cases in which the harm inflicted to the system is expected to significantly change its steady state. For these use cases, reliability improvements can be implemented and tested as part of the regular development process. This should be done first, before chaos engineering can be applied in a beneficial manner.

Chaos experiments need to involve actual unknowns. Using a hypothesis, a genuine guess needs to be made that can only be tested in real life by running the experiment. Hypotheses around use cases arising from system complexity, where the outcome of inflicting harm is not obvious in advance, are a good area for exploration using chaos engineering.

In essence, chaos engineering is applied best in system areas hardened well using traditional software engineering and thought to be reliable, possibly based on data from production. The question posed by the chaos experiments is whether the previous reliability was due to the fact that the system was not exposed to enough harm and a new kind of harm would reveal unreliability.

That is, chaos engineering is about running well-defined experiments based on well-defined hypotheses. This is contrary to what might be suggested by the term "chaos," which would represent random, unsupervised, unanticipated, or wild experiments, breaking production. The chaos engineering experiments can be executed in production or another internal environment of choice. The purpose of running the experiments is to reveal chaos in a controlled manner ahead of time before it erupts unexpectedly in the face of users.

Steps 1, 2, and 4 for designing a chaos engineering experiment can be supported by the SLOs. Table 11.13 explains how this can be done.

Table 11.13 *Supporting Chaos Engineering Experiment Design Using SLOs*

Step	Description	Explanation		
1	Define a steady state of the system	The steady state of the system can be defined in terms of SLO error budget depletion. For instance, it can be defined as follows in a simplified way. Steady state: The weekly latency SLO error budgets for all endpoints of service 1 do not get exhausted prematurely.		
2	Form a hypothesis	A hypothesis can be defined using SLO error budget depletion. For instance, using the <capability> / <outcome> / <measurable signal> triple, the hypothesis can be defined as follows.		
		Capability	25% latency increase in network A between services 1 and 2 for 24 hours	
		Outcome	The weekly latency SLO error budgets for all endpoints of service 1 do not get exhausted prematurely despite the latency increase.	
		Measurable signal	Latency SLO error budget depletion using the SLO error budget depletion indicator	
3	Simulate real-world events	This is done as usual without resorting to SLOs.		

Step	Description	Explanation
4	Test the hypothesis	Testing the hypothesis defined in step 2 involves comparing the latency SLO error budget depletion levels at the end of the week in which the experiment was conducted to the granted weekly latency SLO error budgets of service 1. This is done using the SLO error budget depletion indicator.

That is, a steady state of the system can be defined using SLOs. A hypothesis to test can also be defined using the SLOs. Testing the hypothesis can be done using SRE indicators. In addition, the search for hypotheses to test using chaos engineering experiments can be supported by the SRE indicators as well.

A decision to select a hypothesis can be supported by a three-step workflow. The workflow is rooted in the following three questions.

1. Which SLOs are defined for which services?

2. What is the adherence to the SLOs on different time scales?

3. Are there any unusual error budget depletion patterns for successfully defended SLOs?

The goal is to find services that consistently defend their SLOs successfully and try to break them using chaos experiments; and, on an exploratory basis, to investigate the error budget depletion patterns aiming to find cases where the error budget defense is strong but the reasons for that are either unknown or opaque.

Answering the questions is directly supported by three SRE indicators defined in the previous sections and shown in Table 11.14.

Table 11.14 *Three-Step Workflow to Support a Chaos Engineering Hypothesis Selection Decision*

Step	SRE Indicator	Explanation
1	"SLOs by service" indicator (Section 11.2.2)	Shows the SLOs defined for a service, if any
2	SLO adherence indicator (Section 11.2.3)	Shows the adherence to the defined SLOs over time by error budget period
3	SLO error budget depletion indicator (Section 11.2.4)	Shows the error budget depletion trend that can be used for exploration purposes

The three-step decision-making workflow supported by the three SRE indicators is illustrated in Figure 11.26.

1. Which SLOs Are Defined for Which Services? (SLOs by Service Indicator)[a]

Service	SLI	SLO	Endpoint	SLO Adherence	Team
Service 1	Availability	99.9%	GET /user	<link>	Team 1
Service 2	Availability	99%	PUT /user/lang	<link>	Team 2
Service 3	Availability	99.95%	GET /affil	<link>	Team 3

Error Budget Period : 4 Weeks
Days Left in Current Error Budget Period : 5 Days

▼ Team
☒ All
☒ Team 1
☒ Team 2
☒ Team 3

▼ Service
☒ All
☒ Service 1
☒ Service 2
☒ Service 3

▼ SLI
☐ All
☐ Availability
☐ Latency
☐ Throughput

Default SLOs
● Show
○ Hide

▼ Deployment
○ Prod-eu
● Prod-us
○ Prod-jp

2. What Is the Adherence to the SLOs on Different Time Scales? (SLO Adherence Indicator)[b]

SLI	SLO	Period 1	Period 2	Period 3	...
Availability	GET /user 99.9%	Fulfilled <link>	Fulfilled <link>	Broken <link>	
Availability	PUT /user/lang 99%	Broken <link>	Fulfilled <link>	Fulfilled <link>	
Availability	GET /affil 99.95%	Fulfilled <link>	Fulfilled <link>	Fulfilled <link>	

▼ Time Scale
○ Monthly
● Error Budget Period

▼ Time Window
○ Current Error Budget Period
○ Previous Error Budget Period
● Current Year
○ Previous Year

▼ Team
☒ Team 1
☒ Team 2
☒ Team 3

▼ Service
○ Service 1
● Service 2
○ Service 3

▼ SLI
○ Availability
○ Latency
○ Throughput

▼ SLO
☒ All
☒ GET /user 99.9%
☒ PUT /user/lang 99%
☒ GET /affil 99.95%

▼ Deployment
○ Prod-eu
● Prod-us
○ Prod-jp

3. Are There Any Unusual Error Budget Depletion Patterns for Successfully Defended SLOs ? (SLO Error Budget Depletion Indicator)[c]

SLO Error Budget

100%
50%
–50%

1.1   8.1   15.1   22.1   29.1   Time

Error Budget Period

▼ Time Scale
○ Hourly
● Weekly
○ Monthly
○ Error Budget Period

▼ Time Window
○ Last 24h
● Current Error Budget Period
○ Previous Error Budget Period
○ Current Year
○ Previous Year

▼ Service
○ Telemetry svc
○ Token svc
● User svc

▼ SLI
● Availability
○ Latency
○ Throughput

▼ SLO
○ GET /user 99.9%
○ PUT /user/lang 99%
● GET /affil 99.95%

▼ Deployment
○ Prod-eu
● Prod-us
○ Prod-jp

Figure 11.26 *Chaos engineering hypothesis selection decision support*

[a] See Figure 11.1 for larger version of this part of the figure.
[b] See Figure 11.2 for larger version of this part of the figure.
[c] See Figure 11.4 for larger version of this part of the figure.

Workflow step 1 allows finding system areas where reliability is quantitatively defined using SLOs. Workflow step 2 allows finding system areas where the SLOs are successfully defended. Workflow step 3 enables exploratory work to find unusual error budget depletion patterns for successfully defended SLOs. For example, an SLO may be successfully defended in all error budget periods being looked at with a significant remaining error budget at the end of each period. However, there could be some small but regular error budget depletion blips in each period. The blips cannot be explained easily by looking at the error budget depletion trends of dependent services. A hypothesis can be formed around the blips that they might be due to a cloud provider's infrastructure service scale-out mechanisms not being tuned optimally. This hypothesis can be tested using a chaos experiment.

At the end of a chaos experiment, if a hypothesis is proven wrong, the steady state of the system is significantly changed. This provides the teams owning the respective services with valuable data to improve service reliability. Additionally, the data might give rise to the creation of new or the adaptation of existing SLOs.

In "How to Use Chaos Engineering to Break Things Productively,"[8] there is a suggestion for structuring chaos experiments. It is summarized in Table 11.15.

Table 11.15 *Structuring Chaos Engineering Experiments*

	Known	**Unknown**
Known	Testing for "Known Knowns" • Awareness: exists • Understanding: exists	Experimenting for "Known Unknowns" • Awareness: exists • Understanding: does not exist
Unknown	Checking "Unknown Knowns" • Awareness: does not exist • Understanding: exists	Looking at "Unknown Unknowns" • Awareness: does not exist • Understanding: does not exist

An example of a "Known Known" is a cloud service auto-restart on service shutdown with the auto-restart setting switched on. When switching on the setting, there is an understanding that a service restart can happen. The reason to switch on the auto-restart setting provides awareness of the situations where the restart is necessary.

An example of a "Known Unknown" can be the time frame for a cloud service auto-restart on service shutdown with the auto-restart setting switched on. The time frame might be significant for the reliability of important use cases. There is awareness that the service auto-restart will happen. However, there is no understanding of how long it would take due to, for example, the cloud provider not publishing an SLA for the auto-restart duration.

8. Bocetta, Sam. 2019. "How to Use Chaos Engineering to Break Things Productively." *InfoQ*, September 2, 2019. https://www.infoq.com/articles/chaos-engineering-security-networking.

An example of an "Unknown Known" is when a cloud service is deployed in a shared service plan with many other services sharing resources such as memory, storage, and so on. The cloud provider may have a recommendation for the maximum number of services in the plan to optimize resource consumption and avoid resource starvation by the deployed services. However, there might be no native way to enforce the recommended limit. In this case, after a service auto-restart, it is unknown whether the service will get enough resources allocated by the service plan. In fact, resource starvation might be the reason for the service auto-restart in the first place. The understanding of the situation is there but it is beyond perception what would actually happen in terms of resource allocation after the service auto-restart.

An example of an "Unknown Unknown" is when there is no experience with a cloud service auto-restart in case of a simultaneous failure in the cloud provider's compute service. The failure could be small scale or encompass an entire data center region. According to the cloud provider's SLAs, this can happen. However, it was not experienced in the past. There is no understanding and very little awareness of what would happen in this case.

The "Known Unknowns" and "Unknown Knowns" can be uncovered by analyzing the SLO error budget depletion in an exploratory manner using the SLO error budget depletion indicator (Section 11.2.4) as well as studying the corresponding incident postmortems. The "Known Knowns" are most evident and might therefore not need a deeper analysis to find. The "Unknown Unknowns" are least evident and might be difficult to uncover despite the deep analysis.

In "Chaos Engineering: the history, principles, and practice,"[9] the Failure as a Service company Gremlin argues that chaos experiments should be performed in the following order:

1. Known Knowns

2. Known Unknowns

3. Unknown Knowns

4. Unknown Unknowns

In general, the use of the SLO error budget depletion indicator (Section 11.2.4) greatly supports the process of finding hypotheses for chaos engineering experiments that can be used to learn about the reliability of and improving the system under test.

11.6 Summary

This chapter showed how error budget–based decision–making can be used to make data-driven decisions for a wide variety of topics. The topics range from development and prioritization to budget and legal decisions. The decisions can be supported by a number of SRE indicators. Most indicators provide different views on error budget depletion over time. For SLOs, these are the "SLOs by service" indicator, SLO error budget depletion indicator, premature SLO error budget exhaustion indicator, and SLO adherence indicator. For SLAs, similarly there are the

---

9. Gremlin. n.d. "Chaos Engineering: the history, principles, and practice." Accessed January 25, 2022. https://www.gremlin.com/community/tutorials/chaos-engineering-the-history-principles-and-practice.

"SLAs by service" indicator, SLA error budget depletion indicator, and SLA adherence indicator.

In terms of implementation, the SRE indicators are visualized as graphs or tables. Graphs are useful for explorative decision-making. Tables provide a more concentrated view on the data for focused decision-making. The SRE indicators' graphs and tables can be used in combination to drive decision-making workflows. Some of the most common and frequently used workflows are the API consumption decision workflow, tightening a dependency's SLO decision workflow, features versus reliability prioritization workflow, and setting an SLO decision workflow. By following the workflows, an entirely new level of transparency and objectivity is induced in the typically difficult decision-making process on the respective topics.

The availability of the SRE indicators is only the first step toward error budget–based decision–making in teams. The SRE coaches need to familiarize the teams with the individual indicators and with the workflows that can be executed using them. Executing the workflows in the domain of a given team fosters an understanding and familiarity with the SRE indicators by the team members. This is the prerequisite for the workflows to be run by the teams on a standalone and regular basis.

With error budget–based decision–making in place, the entire SRE concept pyramid (Section 3.5) is fully implemented in the product delivery organization. The next step on the SRE transformation journey is to embed the pyramid in a more formal organizational structure. An implementation of a suitable organizational structure for SRE is required in order to sustain the SRE practice over the long term. This is a big step, indeed. It involves considering lots of dimensions and options, which are explored in depth in the next chapter.

Chapter 12

Implementing Organizational Structure

The SRE practice achieved so far fulfills the promise of the SRE transformation in that it enables the product delivery organization to operate software reliably at scale. The SRE practice can be introduced without a reorganization or the introduction of new formal roles. This is the right strategy, as it allows the organization to find its way of practicing SRE through experimentation, working collaboratively across existing organizational boundaries.

Thinking about the organizational structure before experimenting with SRE would require the organization to make decisions that would be difficult to change later without the necessary practical SRE experience. However, once the SRE practice has been proven effective through experimentation and is on the way to becoming solidified, questions regarding the right organizational structure to support and sustain SRE over the long term need to be considered.

The questions in Table 12.1 may drive a discussion about implementing an organizational structure for SRE.

Table 12.1 *Questions Driving SRE Organizational Structure*

Category	Questions
Roles and responsibilities	• What are the responsibilities in the realm of SRE? • What are the roles in the realm of SRE? • What are the necessary skills by role?
Business vision	• What are the long-term business goals with SRE? • What is the long-term vision for the SRE infrastructure? • Is ROI expected for SRE activities?
Leadership	• What kind of leadership is needed for SRE? • Is business/product/technical leadership needed? • Is a new C-level/VP-level leader needed?

Category	Questions
Career	• What are the career paths by role in the realm of SRE? • How do you attract people to SRE from inside and outside the organization? • How do you switch to an SRE career from another role?
Organizational	• What should be the organizational visibility of SRE? • Should SRE become a new dedicated organizational unit? • What are the reporting lines by role in the realm of SRE? • What should be the formal authority by role? • What should be the formal power by role? • How do you measure the success of SRE?
Budget	• Should SRE get its own dedicated budget? • Who should be responsible for the budget? • Who should be responsible for budget distribution? • What are the salaries by role and location in the realm of SRE?
Planning	• How many people by role would be needed in the realm of SRE in the next one to three years? • Where in the world would the people need to be hired? • Is fully remote work acceptable by role?
Regulatory	• How formal is the SRE practice? • Can SRE be used for audit purposes? • Does SRE help fulfill regulations for software operations?
Decision-making	• Which organizational decisions should be governed by SRE? • Which organizational decisions should be supported by SRE? • Which organizational decisions are out of scope for SRE?

These questions are multidimensional and have wide implications on organizational structure, budget distribution, and people's careers. Therefore, it is important to deliberately start discussing the questions late in the SRE transformation journey, once the organization is practicing SRE successfully.

The questions will come up naturally during the SRE transformation. The SRE coaches should monitor the discussions as much as possible. If serious discussions around organizational structure arise before the organization is solidly practicing SRE, the SRE coaches should advise the people to hold off on making decisions in this area.

Depending on the situation, it might be difficult for the SRE coaches to stop these discussions because they simply might not be involved in them. At this point, the coaches' connections to the managers who put SRE into the portfolio of organizational initiatives might come in handy. Organizational matters are always discussed at the management level. So, the managers will know organizational structure discussions around SRE. This gives the coaches an opportunity to state their point of view, explaining whether the SRE practice is mature enough to justify a change in the organizational structure.

12.1 SRE Principles Versus Organizational Structure

To start the organizational structure discussion, it is worth going back to the original SRE principles to see how they might influence the matter. The SRE principles from the *Site Reliability Workbook*[1] are

1. Operations is a software problem.

2. Manage by service level objectives (SLOs).

3. Work to minimize toil.

4. Automate this year's job away.

5. Move fast by reducing the cost of failure.

6. Share ownership with developers.

7. Use the same tooling, regardless of function or job title.

Additionally, there are three more principles for practicing SRE. They are

1. SRE needs SLOs with consequences.

2. SREs must have time to make tomorrow better than today.

3. SRE teams have the ability to regulate their workload.

When looking at the principles, an important aspect to notice is that the organizational structure for implementing SRE is not on the list. This means the SRE principles can be implemented by software delivery organizations using different organizational structures.

Indeed, this is what can be seen based on conversations in the book *Seeking SRE: Conversations About Running Production Systems at Scale*[2] by David N. Blank-Edelman. Some companies, like Google, have central SRE teams. Others, like Amazon, have the SRE responsibilities fully embedded in the actual development teams. Yet others, like Facebook, have a separate SRE

---

1. Beyer, Betsy, Niall Richard Murphy, David K. Rensin, Stephen Thorne, and Kent Kawahara. 2018. *The Site Reliability Workbook: Practical Ways to Implement SRE.* Sebastopol, CA: O'Reilly Media.

2. Blank-Edelman, David N. 2018. *Seeking SRE: Conversations About Running Production Systems at Scale.* Sebastopol, CA: O'Reilly Media.

organization, but the actual SREs are working mostly embedded in the development teams for longer periods.

It follows that a discussion about a suitable organizational structure needs to be led separately from the SRE principles. The organization needs to fulfill the SRE principles using an organizational structure that suits it. Fulfillment of the SRE principles comes first; the organizational structure to do so is secondary.

> **SRE Myth:** SRE can only be done with a central SRE team.

> **SRE Myth:** A dedicated SRE team is required to do SRE.

By contrast, does the organizational structure influence the fulfillment of the SRE principles? It does, indeed! The organizational structure certainly steers how people work together. For some, it simplifies collaboration and communication; for others, it impedes it. The influence is highly dependent on the organization and the people who work there.

Therefore, general advice to set up the right organizational structure to fulfill the SRE principles would not be valuable. What is valuable is to demonstrate options to implement organizational structures that can fulfill the SRE principles. The options need to be evaluated for applicability in a given organization.

One of the central questions that must be decided in this context is who builds and runs the services. While the answer to the build part of the question can usually be provided in a straightforward manner, the answer to the run part might not be as clear. There are different options to consider. These are explored in the next section.

12.2 Who Builds It, Who Runs It?

The title of this section is inspired by the line expressed by Amazon CTO Werner Vogels in an interview for ACM Queue[3] from 2006: "You build it, you run it. This brings developers into contact with the day-to-day operation of their software. It also brings them into day-to-day contact with the customer. This customer feedback loop is essential for improving the quality of the service."

"You build it, you run it" is a way to give the responsibility for running the services to those who build them; that is, the development teams themselves. It maximizes the incentives for development teams to invest in reliability. This is because the developers are on call 24/7 for their services and do not necessarily enjoy being awakened in the middle of the night to fix bugs. Thus, they will do everything they can in terms of reliability implementation and testing to prevent that from happening. Beyond Amazon, the "you build it, you run it" model is employed by Netflix as well as many other companies.

---

3. "A Conversation with Werner Vogels." n.d. ACM Queue. https://queue.acm.org/detail.cfm?id=1142065.

12.2.1 "Who Builds It, Who Runs It?" Spectrum

"You build it, you run it" describes one end of the "who builds it, who runs it?" spectrum. At the other end is the opposite way of running services. It can be referred to as "you build it, ops run it." The phrase was probably coined by Steve Smith in a blog post[4] with the same name, as part of the "Who Runs It"[5] blog post series. With "you build it, ops run it," the development teams are responsible for building services and the operations teams are responsible for running them in production. The development teams are not directly incentivized for implementing reliable services. This is because they do not go on call for their services running in production. This responsibility is fully with the operations teams.

The "who builds it, who runs it?" spectrum is illustrated in Figure 12.1.

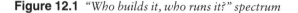

Figure 12.1 *"Who builds it, who runs it?" spectrum*

In addition to the "you build it, you run it" option on the left-hand side and the "you build it, ops run it" option on the right-hand side, two additional options are shown in the middle of the figure:

- "You build it, you and SRE run it"
- "You build it, SRE run it"

With "you build it, SRE run it," a dedicated SRE team is established. It is staffed with people who possess development and operations knowledge. That is, they can develop services like developers and operate them like operations engineers with a software development background. The development team builds the services and the SRE team runs them. For the SRE team to take a service into operation the service needs to fulfill strict reliability criteria. Also, once the SRE team is operating the service, the reliability criteria need to stay fulfilled. If the service consistently fails to stay within its error budgets, the SRE team returns the service to the development team, which then has to run the service until service reliability is reinstated.

The "you build it, SRE run it" model is employed at Google for most popular Google services. For emerging new services, the "you build it, you run it" model is employed by default at Google. If and when the service gains popularity, the development team may solicit support from an SRE team, which will assess the service and decide whether they will operate it.

The last model to discuss on the "who builds it, who runs it?" spectrum is "you build it, you and SRE run it." With this, a shared on-call model is established. The developers who build the services are on call for the services together with SREs from the SRE team. The details of the

4. Smith, Steve. 2020. "You Build It Ops Runs It." *Steve Smith On Tech* (blog). October 4, 2020. https://www.stevesmith.tech/blog/you-build-it-ops-runs-it.

5. Smith, Steve. 2020. "Who Runs It." *Steve Smith On Tech* (blog). October 4, 2020. https://www.stevesmith.tech/blog/who-runs-it.

shared on-call responsibility split may vary by team. The split may be 50:50, with the developers and SREs on call for the services for an equal amount of time; or it may be 25:75 or 75:25. Generally, any split is possible as long as each party is contributing a share of time greater than zero.

Facebook employs the "you build it, you and SRE run it" model. At Facebook, SREs are called Production Engineers (PEs), and they belong to a separate Production Engineering organization but necessarily sit together with the development team they are currently supporting. The support is long term; however, the PEs are encouraged to regularly change the development teams they support. Team mobility and cross-pollination are important characteristics of the PE engagement model at Facebook.

12.2.2 Hybrid Models

Beyond the options shown in Figure 12.1, some additional hybrid models are possible. For example:

- "You build it, ops sometimes run it"

- "You build it, you run it but some specific use cases are additionally monitored by ops"

- And others

The "you build it, ops sometimes run it" model is described in a blog post[6] of the same name. It is a combination of the "you build it, you run it" and "you build it, ops run it" models. With "you build it, ops sometimes run it," some services are run by the development teams and others are run by the operations teams. The decision for which services should be run by which team can be based on the service availability target.

Services with high availability targets need to be run by the development teams due to high business demand and the need to recover from incidents quickly. Services with low availability targets can be run by the operations teams because they have lower business demand, and therefore a longer time to recover from incidents might be acceptable.

The "you build it, you run it but some specific use cases are additionally monitored by ops" model refers to the development teams generally running their services in production. On top of that, there are very specific cross-team use cases that are monitored by ops. For example, the bulk of users might take a specific path through the application that crosses the boundaries of many teams. The ops team may be responsible for monitoring that particular path. In case of failures, the ops team will try to figure out which teams are more likely able to fix the issues and notify the respective people on call from those teams.

Because the teams run their services themselves, they may already be aware of the issues and are working on them. The value of the additional monitoring by ops is in the additional ability to detect cross-team issues that inhibit execution of the most frequently used or most critical workflows in the system.

---

6. Smith, Steve. 2020. "You Build It Ops Sometimes Run It." *Steve Smith On Tech* (blog). October 4, 2020. https://www.stevesmith.tech/blog/you-build-it-ops-sometimes-run-it.

12.2.3 Reliability Incentives

A fundamental difference between the models from the "who builds it, who runs it?" spectrum lies in the level of incentives for the development teams to implement reliability in their services. The distribution of incentives is shown in Figure 12.2.

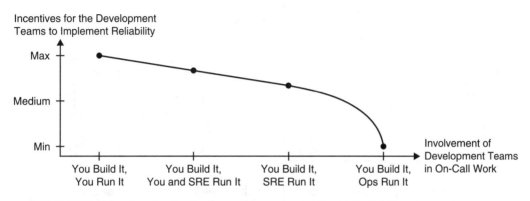

Figure 12.2 *Incentives for the development teams to implement reliability*

With "you build, you run it," the development teams have the most incentive to implement reliability into their services. This is because they are the ones who bear the full brunt of the 24/7 on-call rotation.

The incentives may diminish slightly with the "you build it, you and SRE run it" shared on-call model. Here, only part of the 24/7 on-call responsibility is borne by the development teams. Another diminishment of incentives takes place with the "you build it, SRE run it" model. In this model, the developers do not go on call if their services fulfill the agreed reliability criteria. If the criteria are not met, the development teams are asked to reinstate the reliability. Only when the error budgets are exceeded repeatedly does the SRE team stop running the services and hand over the responsibility to the development team.

A downright drop in incentives for the development teams to implement reliability takes place with the "you build it, ops run it" model. This is shown on the right-hand side of Figure 12.2. In this model, the typical divide between development and operations becomes apparent. The development teams simply hand over the built services to the operations teams to run them in production. The operations teams do the 24/7 on-call rotation. This means the development teams never go on call. There are no reliability criteria to be fulfilled by the services for the operations team to operate them. Rather, the services are always operated by the operations teams regardless of their reliability.

Following on the distribution of incentives from Figure 12.2, one can compare how much skin in the game of running services the developers have depending on the model. This is illustrated in Figure 12.3.

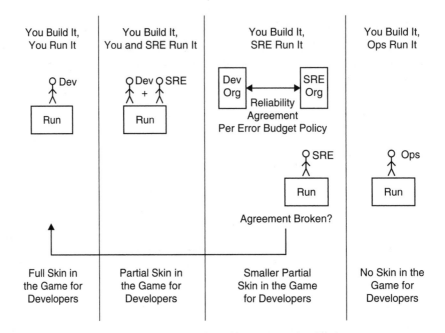

Figure 12.3 *Extents of skin in the game of running services for developers*

With "you build it, you run it," the developers have full skin in the game of running services. With the shared way of running services in "you build it, you and SRE run it," developers have partial skin in the game. With "you build it, SRE run it," developers have less skin in the game of running services as they are generally not on call as long as the services stay within error budgets. Finally, with "you build it, ops run it," the developers do not have any skin in the game of running services.

"You build it, ops run it" is a traditional way of running software. The issues with this model are what has made DevOps in general and SRE in particular grow in popularity in the software industry. Typical issues are summarized in Table 12.2.

Table 12.2 *Issues with the "You Build It, Ops Run It" Model*

Issue	Explanation
Long incident resolution times	The operations teams possess limited knowledge about services in production. Therefore, they cannot resolve lots of incidents directly. Rather, the development teams need to be consulted. First, it takes time to get the incidents to the development teams. Second, it takes time to get the incidents prioritized by the development teams. The development teams are never on call. Therefore, work on the incidents almost never starts immediately once an incident occurs. All this adds up to long incident resolution times.

Issue	Explanation
Large number of workarounds	It takes a long time for the development teams to resolve an incident. However, customers often cannot wait that long. Therefore, the operations teams create workarounds in production to get the services working on a temporary basis. Once the development teams fix the issues, the fixes might interfere with the existing workarounds during or after the deployment.
Lack of knowledge synchronization	The knowledge gap between the development and operations teams is very large. They literally live in two different worlds. To bridge the two worlds, extensive knowledge synchronization is required. In practice, this is rarely achieved.
Limited adaptive capacity in the architecture	The services are architected with insufficient adaptive capacity. Therefore, they are not resilient to failure in production. A failure easily becomes cascading. The failure blast radius is not limited by technical means, such as stability patterns.
Limited telemetry	The logging is insufficient for fast investigations of product failures in production because it is implemented by the developers who never go on call. Based on the insufficient logging and available black box resource consumption metrics, the operations teams can build dashboards and implement alerts that can only superficially reflect the state of services under operation.
Limited understanding of infrastructure and service interplay	Because the operations teams possess limited knowledge about the services in production, their understanding of the interplay between the services and the underlying infrastructure is also limited. The interplay requires special knowledge of deployment, traffic, security, authentication, and authorization infrastructure. That knowledge is typically not available with the operations teams in the depth necessary for effective and fast incident resolution.
Collaboration issues during incident response	The development and operations teams generally have different ways of working. Moreover, the development teams do not have access to production. The operations teams do. Therefore, in all likelihood the operations teams will have a different set of tools than the development teams. These factors will lead to collaboration issues between the development and operations teams during incident response.

Due to the issues outlined in Table 12.2 (additional details are available in Section 2.1, *Misalignment*), more and more companies are moving to the left of the "who builds it, who runs it?" spectrum. Where a particular product delivery organization should position itself on the spectrum to the left of the "you build it, ops run it" model is a question that does not have a generic answer. Rather, it needs to be explored in the unique context of a given organization.

The exploration needs to be done using a set of criteria to thoroughly compare the models. Such criteria are presented in the next section.

12.2.4 Model Comparison Criteria

When comparing "who builds it, who runs it?" models, many criteria can be taken into account. The criteria need to be selected in such a way that they help a product delivery organization choose a suitable model. The following set of comparison criteria is exemplary but representative:

- Involvement of the development teams in the on-call work

- Knowledge synchronization between teams

- Incident resolution times

- Service handover for operations

- Establishment of a distinct SRE organization

- Ownership of the SRE infrastructure

- Availability targets and product demand

- Funding

- Cost

These are explained one by one in Table 12.3. The explanations focus on the "you build it, you run it," "you build it, you and SRE run it," and "you build it, SRE run it" models. The "you build it, ops run it" model and its shortcomings were already explained in detail in the previous section.

Table 12.3 *Criteria to Compare Models from the "Who Builds It, Who Runs It?" Spectrum*

Comparison Criteria	Explanation
Involvement of the development teams in the on-call work	The level of the development teams' involvement in the on-call work determines their incentives for implementing reliable services. If the incentives are to be maximized, the development teams need to be on call as in the "you build it, you run it" or "you build it, you and SRE run it" model. With the incentives maximized, the development teams care deeply about issues such as adaptive architecture, extensive product telemetry, robust automated testing, infrastructure knowledge build-up (deployment, traffic, debugging, security, authentication, authorization), SLOs reflecting user experience well, and so on.
Knowledge synchronization between teams	Knowledge synchronization between the people developing and operating the services is required to a greater extent if the people are not on the same team. The least amount of knowledge synchronization effort is in the "you build it, you run it" model. The most is in the "you build it, SRE run it" model.

Comparison Criteria	Explanation
Incident resolution times	Incident resolution times are shorter and there is a shorter distance between the people on call and the people who implemented the service. Therefore, the shortest incident resolution times are in the "you build it, you run it" model. The longest are in the "you build it, SRE run it" model. That said, in most cases, incident resolution times in the "you build it, SRE run it" model will be fast enough because the SRE team is staffed with engineers with a development and operations background who understand and want to defend the error budgets of a service.
Service handover for operations	Service handover for operations is required in the "you build it, SRE run it" model. It has to be set up appropriately for a given service deployment frequency. In the "you build it, you run it" model, the handover is not required in a strict sense because the team implementing the service also operates it. In the "you build it, you and SRE run it" model, a lightweight handover may be needed to bring the SRE team up to speed on service changes.
Establishment of a distinct SRE organization	The "you build it, you and SRE run it" and "you build it, SRE run it" models require an SRE team to be set up. The SRE team can be set up as a new team in the existing development organization or as a new team in the existing operations organization. Another option is to set up a new organization for SRE and run all the SRE activities there. The activities may include internal SRE advisory, SRE consulting, service co-design, SRE coaching, SRE infrastructure ownership, shared on call for services, and full production ownership for services. The SRE advisory, consulting, co-design, coaching, and infrastructure may even be offered externally as a service to other companies. That is, an SRE organization may generate its own revenue both internally and externally. It will have its own goals and may develop its own culture within the broader culture of the product delivery organization.
Ownership of the SRE infrastructure	Ownership of the SRE infrastructure needs to be clarified. In the "you build it, you run it" model, the infrastructure for the development teams needs to be owned by a dedicated team. It is typical for the team owning the SRE infrastructure to be in the operations organization.

Comparison Criteria	Explanation
	In the "you build it, you and SRE run it" and "you build it, SRE run it" models, ownership of the SRE infrastructure can be in different places in the organization. If there is a dedicated SRE organization, it will own the infrastructure. Alternatively, if the SREs are within the operations organization, that organization will own the infrastructure. If the SREs are within the development organization, either the development or operations organization may own the infrastructure.
Availability targets and product demand	In "Implementing You Build It, You Run It at scale,"[7] Steve Smith proposes to use availability targets and product demand requirements to choose the operations support approach for a service. The argument is that services with high availability targets and high product demand should be operated by the "you build it, you run it" model due to its maximization of operability incentives for the development teams, minimization of knowledge synchronization and incident resolution times, and the absence of service handovers for operations.
	This thinking might be extended to selecting a model on the "who builds it, who runs it?" spectrum by service availability targets and product demand. Generally, the "you build it, you and SRE run it" and "you build it, SRE run it" models can also support well the services with high availability targets and product demand.
Funding	The funding in the "you build it, you run it," "you build it, you and SRE run it," and "you build it, ops run it" will be a capital expenditure (CAPEX). Salaries of developers and SREs will represent the majority of investment in that area. The CAPEX budget will undergo regular funding renewals.
	The cost of tool licenses such as the on-call management tool or the application performance management facility will be OPEX.
Cost	Most of the cost will come from the salaries of developers and SREs. Generally, the cost can be considered high. It can be optimized by creating on-call rotations for services either in a dedicated or domain-specific manner depending on the service availability target and product demand.

12.2.5 Model Comparison

The models from the "who builds it, who runs it?" spectrum can be compared using the comparison criteria from the previous section. This is shown in Table 12.4.

---

7. Smith, Steve. 2020. "Implementing You Build It You Run It at Scale." *Steve Smith On Tech* (blog). May 19, 2020. https://www.stevesmith.tech/blog/implementing-you-build-it-you-run-it-at-scale.

Table 12.4 *Comparison of Models from the "Who Builds It, Who Runs It?" Spectrum*

Criterion	You Build It, You Run It	You Build It, You and SRE Run It	You Build It, SRE Run It	You Build It, Ops Run It
Involvement of the development teams in the on-call work	Max	Continuous	None if services within error budgets	None
Knowledge synchronization between teams	None	Partially required	Required	Not practical
Incident resolution times	Min	Short	Short	Max
Service handover for operations	Not applicable	Partially required	Required	Required
Establishment of a distinct SRE organization	Not applicable	May be an option	May be an option	Not applicable
Ownership of the SRE infrastructure	Ops org	Either SRE or ops org	Either SRE or ops org	Ops org
Availability targets and product demand	Highest targets and demand	Highest targets and demand	Highest targets and demand	Lower targets and demand
Funding	CAPEX	CAPEX	CAPEX	OPEX
Cost	High	High	High	Low

In summary, it can be said that the "you build it, ops run it" model bears lower cost but does not exhibit characteristics necessary for operating the services reliably at scale. The other three models—"you build it, you run it," "you build it, you and SRE run it," and "you build it, SRE run it"—bear higher cost but are suitable for ensuring reliable service operations at scale. These three models represent quite comparable alternatives.

The differences between the "you build it, you run it," "you build it, you and SRE run it," and "you build it, SRE run it" models are mainly in the involvement of the development teams in the on-call work and in the reporting line of the SRE teams. The two aspects are interrelated. They are explored in the next sections.

12.3 You Build It, You Run It

With the "you build it, you run it" model, the development teams operate their services in production. To do so, they use the SRE infrastructure provided by the operations teams. This is shown in Figure 12.4.

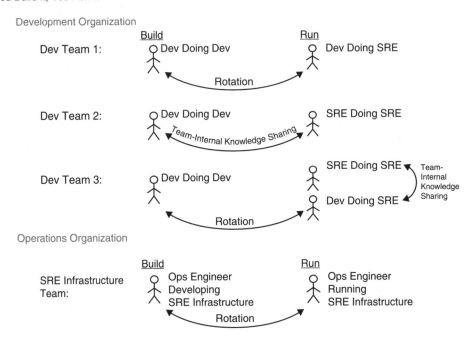

Figure 12.4 *"You build it, you run it" model*

In the upper part of Figure 12.4, the development organization is shown. The organization is responsible for building and running services. This can be done in slightly different ways team by team. In the development organization, three development teams are shown. These teams fulfill the SRE responsibilities slightly differently.

Development team 1 does not have a dedicated SRE role. Rather, the responsibilities for running services are borne by the entire team, with developers working on certain SRE aspects on rotation. For example, the developers may go on call on a rotation basis. A distinct characteristic of the team 1 setup is that there is no dedicated SRE role or person in the team.

Development team 2 is organized differently. There is a dedicated SRE role in the team, and the role is assumed by a dedicated person. The developers on the team build the product and the SREs run it. Team-internal knowledge sharing procedures ensure the development knowledge flows from developers to SREs and vice versa.

That is, the distinct characteristic of team 2 is that there is a dedicated SRE as part of the development team. The SRE takes part in all the team activities: daily standups, backlog grooming, demos, retrospectives, concept discussions, and so on. Therefore, knowledge between the SRE and the developers flows naturally for the most part, with ongoing team rituals and activities. It is distinctly not the kind of knowledge sharing that would be required in the "you build it, ops run it" model. The operations engineers in that model are not part of the development teams. They have to run the services without the rich context of the team that built them.

> **Key Insight:** If there is a dedicated team-internal SRE as part of the development team to run the services owned by the team in the "you build it, you run it" model, knowledge between the SRE and the developers flows naturally for the most part, with ongoing team rituals and activities. The SRE is a full member of the development team and takes part in all the team rituals and activities like every other team member.

Development team 3 is organized as a combination of how development teams 1 and 2 work. Team 3 has a dedicated SRE running the services. Additionally, the developers join the SRE to run the services on rotation. Operational knowledge between the SRE and the developer flows naturally as part of shared on-call work when they run the services together.

In the lower part of Figure 12.4, the operations organization is shown. Here, there is an SRE infrastructure team that builds and runs the SRE infrastructure. It is very typical for the SRE infrastructure team to run the infrastructure by the same people who implemented it. Generally, however, every setup discussed with development teams 1, 2, and 3 in the figure is applicable here as well.

It is important to note that in the "you build it, you run it" model, the different setups to run the services in a team can be decided flexibly team by team. What is more, a team can change the setup over time to suit their unique circumstances. For example, a team might start without a dedicated SRE, with the operations work done by the developers on rotation. At some point, the team might decide to add a dedicated SRE to better cope with the operations work due to the rising popularity of the service. Later, when the SRE leaves the organization to pursue other opportunities elsewhere, the team may switch back to running the service without a dedicated SRE. At some point in the future, when a new SRE has joined the team, they might organize a shared on call with the SRE and one of the developers on rotation running the service.

The flexibility is there. The decisions can be made quickly by the team. The development managers need to support the teams in implementing how they prefer to work within the "you build it, you run it" model. The support needs to come in the form of head count allowance, budget availability, and hiring activities.

"You build it, you run it" is a very scalable model. It scales easily as the number of development teams in the development organization grows. For example, in an organization where the development teams are organized according to domain-driven design principles, each team owns a largely independent subdomain. This way, very scalable organizations can be built without extensive dependencies between the teams. Because each team is expected to run their own services, the teams are founded and, most importantly, staffed with this aspect in mind from the beginning. No other organizational changes are required to scale the operations. The SRE infrastructure is shared by all the teams.

Table 12.5 summarizes the different ways of running the "you build it, you run it" model.

Table 12.5 *Ways of Running the "You Build It, You Run It" Model*

	You Build It, You Run It		
Who Operates Services Within the Development Team?	Developers operate the services.	SRE operates the services.	SRE and developers operate the services.
Are SREs Full Development Team Members?	N/A	Yes	Yes
What Is the Reporting Line of SREs?	N/A	Development manager → Head of development	Development manager → Head of development
What Are the Incentives of SREs?	N/A	Incentives are aligned with the development team goals.	Incentives are aligned with the development team goals.
What Is the Scalability?	Scale the number of development teams.	Scale the number of development teams. Each team gets a dedicated SRE.	Scale the number of development teams. Each team gets a dedicated SRE.

In the next section, let us dive deep into another model on the "who builds it, who runs it?" spectrum: "You build it, you and SRE run it."

12.4 You Build It, You and SRE Run It

There are two distinct characteristics of the "you build it, you and SRE run it" model: the existence of an SRE team and a shared on-call rotation. The SRE team runs a shared on-call rotation for services in production with the developers of the respective development teams. The SRE team itself can organizationally be placed in the development, operations, or a dedicated SRE organization. In this section, these three alternatives are explored.

12.4.1 SRE Team Within the Development Organization

In Figure 12.5, a "you build it, you and SRE run it" model is illustrated in which the SRE team is placed in the development organization.

You Build It, You and SRE Run It: SRE Team within Development Organization

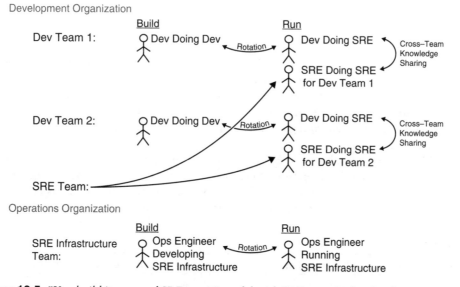

Figure 12.5 *"You build it, you and SRE run it" model with SRE team within development organization*

The upper part of Figure 12.5 shows the development organization. In the development organization there are three teams: development team 1, development team 2, and the SRE team. The SRE team consists of SREs who support individual development teams. One SRE supports development team 1 and another SRE supports development team 2. The support consists of running a shared on-call rotation with the developers from the respective teams.

Development team 1 has a developer on rotation running the services owned by team 1 together with an SRE from the SRE team. Likewise, development team 2 has a developer on rotation running the services owned by team 2 together with another SRE from the SRE team.

The SRE team decides which SRE supports which development team. Furthermore, the SRE team decides on the duration of stay of a particular SRE with a particular development team. Generally, the duration is rather long-term. The SRE learns about the services they support in a long-term engagement with the development team. They support the team in all SRE-related matters. They are, indeed, essential members of the development team's incident response process.

Still, the SRE does not become a full member of the development team. They do not take part in all the development team's ceremonies. Rather, organizationally the SRE remains a member of the SRE team. Rotating SREs between the development teams is a regular matter in the SRE team.

A general agreement between the development teams and the SRE team needs to govern the SRE engagements. Depending on the agreement, the SRE team might be given the freedom to decide when to start and stop supporting a development team. Given the choice, the SRE team will make the level of reliability of the services to be supported be the crucial factor when deciding to engage with a development team. The SRE team might be able to postulate reliability criteria that will have to be fulfilled by the services owned by a development team for the SRE team to support them. Moreover, the SRE team might be able to postulate withdrawal criteria that, when fulfilled, will lead to the withdrawal of SRE support from a development team.

In terms of "you build it, you and SRE run it" model scalability, if the number of SREs in the SRE team is smaller than the number of development teams, some development teams will have to operate according to the "you build it, you run it" model. This poses a question of scaling the "you build it, you and SRE run it" model. In order to scale it, the number of SRE teams needs to be grown in line with growing the number of development teams in the development organization.

To estimate the number of SRE teams needed to support a given number of development teams, an SRE team size of eight can be assumed. This corresponds to a general agreement in the software industry that the number of members in an agile team should be less than 10. With this assumption, scaling the number of SRE teams will need to be done as shown in Table 12.6.

Table 12.6 *Example of Scaling the Number of SRE Teams*

Number of Development Teams	Number of SRE Teams
1	
3	1
5	
7	
9	
11	2
13	
15	
17	
19	3
21	
23	

With the number of SRE teams above two and growing, the development organization needs to start asking questions about its purpose. Is the purpose of the development organization to build and run products? If so, the number of SRE teams can grow within the development organization. Otherwise, the question of the right home for the SRE teams should be discussed. Would it be appropriate to host the SRE teams in the operations organization? Would it be more future-oriented to create a separate SRE organization and host the SRE teams there? These are the questions explored in the next sections.

12.4.2 SRE Team Within the Operations Organization

"You build it, you and SRE run it" can be implemented with the SRE team being placed in the operations organization. Such a setup is shown in Figure 12.6.

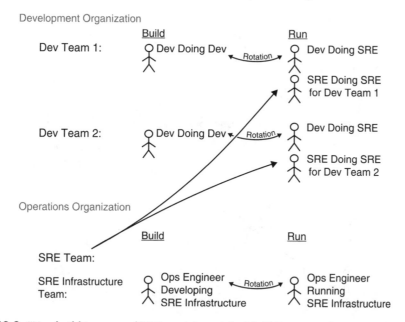

Figure 12.6 *"You build it, you and SRE run it" model with SRE team within operations organization*

The upper part of Figure 12.6 shows the development organization. It consists of development teams 1 and 2. The lower part of the figure shows the operations organization. It consists of the SRE team and the SRE infrastructure team. The SRE infrastructure team builds and runs the SRE infrastructure. The SRE team supports the development teams from the development organization.

In this setup, development team 1 is supported by one SRE and development team 2 is supported by another SRE. It is important to note that the support happens in a cross-organizational manner. This means that in this setup, the SRE team will have more organizational power to determine which development teams are supported. By the same token, the SRE team will have more organizational power to withdraw support from a development team.

The support agreement by the SRE team for the development teams will be more formal. This will be reflected in the development teams' error budget policies. In fact, the SRE team may want to put in place a new error budget policy or adapt an existing one to capture the SRE support agreement before engaging with a development team.

12.4.3 SRE Team in a Dedicated SRE Organization

"You build it, you and SRE run it" can also be implemented with the SRE team being placed in a dedicated SRE organization. Such a setup is shown in Figure 12.7.

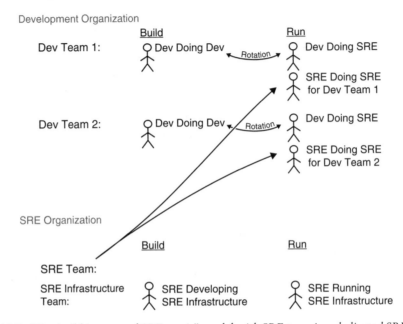

Figure 12.7 *"You build it, you and SRE run it" model with SRE team in a dedicated SRE organization*

The upper part of Figure 12.7 shows the development organization. It consists of development teams 1 and 2. The lower part of the figure shows a dedicated SRE organization. It consists of the SRE team and the SRE infrastructure team.

The SRE infrastructure team builds and runs the SRE infrastructure. The engineers building the infrastructure are likely to be called SREs as they reside in the SRE organization. The SRE team also consists of SREs. The SREs from the SRE team support the development teams from the development organization.

Within the SRE organization, rotation between the SRE team and the SRE infrastructure team will be encouraged. This way, the SREs gain broad and deep knowledge both within the SRE infrastructure and outside where it is used by development teams from different subdomains.

Thus, the SRE organization becomes a dedicated hub of SRE knowledge where the infrastructure, best practices, knowledge sharing, incident response, and, indeed, an SRE culture are bred and cultivated.

From there, the SRE organization can grow into a more substantial entity offering reliability services to the development teams. Examples of some services are shown in Table 12.7.

Table 12.7 *Services Offered by the SRE Organization*

Service	Explanation
SRE advisory	Reliability advice for organizations and teams. Typically, this would be done without formal deliverables.
SRE consulting	Concrete reliability consulting for teams. Typically, some concrete deliverables will be negotiated.
Services co-design	Designing services together with a team, with a focus on reliability.
SRE transformation	Providing SRE coaches to run the SRE transformation within an organization or a team.
Shared on call	Providing SREs to implement the "you build it, you and SRE run it" on-call model in a team
Dedicated on call	Providing SREs to implement full production ownership for an organization with strictly defined entry and exit criteria expressed in terms of service reliability
SRE infrastructure	SRE infrastructure as a service provided for use by other organizations on a subscription basis

All seven engagement models are possible. The SRE organization is the organizational unit to explore these opportunities. If the services can be offered successfully internally, they might also be offered externally. If successful, the SRE organization will generate its own external revenue and may turn a profit in its own right. This would represent a classic example of service externalization after honing and proving the capabilities internally.

Finally, Figure 12.7 does not show the operations organization. This is because all the activities related to running the services are within the SRE organization. However, supporting tool work such as tool procurement, licensing, and management will remain in the operations organization. This applies to tools required by SRE, such as the on-call management tool, application performance management facility, logging facility, and chat management service.

12.4.4 Comparison

The three ways of implementing the "you build it, you and SRE run it" model can be summarized and compared as shown in Table 12.8.

Table 12.8 *Ways of Running the "You Build It, You and SRE Run It" Model*

	You Build It, You and SRE Run It		
SRE Team Placement in the Product Delivery Organization	SRE team within development organization	SRE team within operations organization	SRE team in a dedicated SRE organization
SRE Team Reporting Line	Development manager → Head of development	Operations manager → Head of operations	Head of SRE

	You Build It, You and SRE Run It		
SRE Team Incentives	Aligned with the development organization's goals	Aligned with the operations organization's goals	Aligned with the SRE organization's goals
SRE Team Head Count	Part of the development organization's head count	Part of the operations organization's head count	SRE organization's own head count
SRE Team Budget	Part of the development organization's budget	Part of the operations organization's budget	SRE organization's own budget
SRE Team Cost Accounting	Cost accounting within the development organization	Cost accounting within the operations organization or cross-organizational cost accounting	Cost accounting within the SRE organization or cross-organizational cost accounting or by service offered
SRE Team KPIs	Set by the development organization	Set by the operations organization	Set by the SRE organization
Scalability	Scale the number of SRE teams	Scale the number of SRE teams	Scale the number of SRE teams

The location of the SRE team in the product delivery organization greatly influences the reporting line, team incentives, head count allowance, budget allowance, cost accounting, and team KPIs. The only constant that does not change regardless of SRE team location is the scalability aspect. "You build it, you and SRE run it" requires at least one SRE from the SRE team to be dedicated to a development team. Following this, the number of SRE teams needs to be scaled with the number of development teams supported.

In the following sections, the differences with the SRE team being placed in different organizations within the product delivery organization are explored in detail.

12.4.5 SRE Team Incentives, Identity, and Pride

In terms of the SRE team incentives being aligned with the goals of the organization the team belongs to, in the development organization the SRE team goals will be more product-centric and product-specific. In the operations organization, the goals will be expressed in more operational terms, such as time to recover from incidents. In the SRE organization, the goals will be expressed in SRE terms, such as error budget depletion.

Every organization has its own vernacular and, indeed, subculture. Putting the SRE team into a particular organization needs to be done with this aspect in mind. The team will have some shared mindset with other teams in the same organization.

What is more, the SRE team identity will be influenced by the organization it is in. In the development organization, the SRE team identity might be related to the products they support. In the operations organization, it might be related to the efficiency of recovery from incidents and the low number of high-profile incidents. In the SRE organization, it might be related to the user experience in terms of reliability provided when the services are within their error budgets.

Based on the team identity influenced by the organization the team is in, team pride will develop. In the development organization, the SRE team might take pride in the reliability of specific products being delivered. That is, given two different development organizations with one SRE team in each of them, each SRE team might take pride in the reliability of the specific products delivered by the respective development organization they are in. The SREs on these teams might specifically care a lot about the products themselves and individual features, not only about reliability in general.

In the operations organization, the SRE team might take pride in the very low number of high-profile incidents of the products they support. The specific products being supported might not be the focus of their pride. Rather, the team might take pride in the general stability in production where products are deployed and used.

In the SRE organization, the SRE team might take pride in the well-calibrated error budgets that reflect the user experience in terms of reliability very well. This enables the SREs and developers to have the luxury to sleep well at night with the confidence that the users are happy as long as the services are within the error budgets.

The SRE team identity and pride are shaped by several factors. These include people in other teams within the same organization, offline and online watercooler conversations, and the company office space. Additionally, the factors include topics in the organization's all-employee meetings and rituals established in the organization, such as planning cycles, release cadence, expert talks, team outings, generally accepted level of discipline, and so on.

Moreover, the leader of the organization has a profound effect on all the teams within. Knowingly or not, the leader shapes the culture of the organization to a significant extent.

In summary, the SRE team identity and pride might be influenced by the organization the team is in. This is shown in Table 12.9.

Table 12.9 *SRE Team Identity and Pride*

SRE Team Placement in the Product Delivery Organization	SRE team within the development organization	SRE team within the operations organization	SRE team in a dedicated SRE organization
Team Identity and Pride	Might be product-specific	Might be incident-specific	Might be specific to user experience in terms of reliability

On the whole, people are influenced by their environment to a great extent. This includes the organizational environment of the team the people are in, which may have an impact on people's behavior, motivation level, mood, communication patterns, and stress levels. All these factors need to be taken into account when making a decision about SRE team placement within the product delivery organization.

12.4.6 SRE Team Head Count and Budget

In terms of the SRE head count and budget, the big question is where the funding for the SRE team would come from. Generally, it may come from a budget increase for the entire division or the product delivery organization within the division. Alternatively, the funding may come from an optimization of the division's or product delivery organization's existing budget.

Figure 12.8 is an example of the overall funding flow options throughout the company. In the figure, the entire organizational hierarchy is illustrated. It starts at the top level of the company and goes to the division the product delivery organization is in. From the product delivery organization, the hierarchy goes all the way down to the development, operations, and, potentially, SRE organizations.

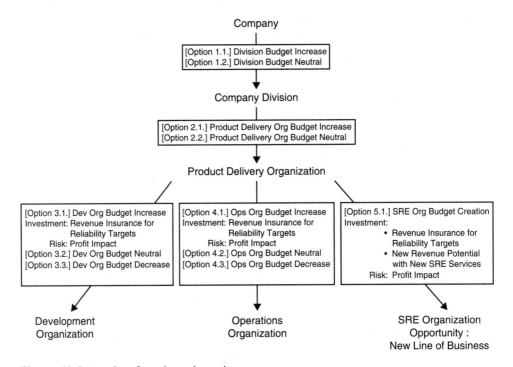

Figure 12.8 *Funding flow throughout the company*

At the company level, a division budget increase may be an option to fund the SRE team (option 1.1). Any budget increase will need to be justified by a business case. The business case for investing in the SRE team may be supported by two aspects: insurance and revenue.

1. [Insurance] The investment in the SRE team is revenue insurance for reliability targets. (This thinking is attributed to Steve Smith, who coined the term "production support as revenue insurance for availability targets" in "You Build It, You Run It".[8]) The reliability targets are expressed as SLOs for different SLIs. To defend them, an SRE team needs to be funded. The funding is a premium for insurance that protects the existing company revenue from reliability damage. That is, the insurance covers a revenue impact risk from reliability damage.

2. [Revenue] The investment in the SRE organization is to seize the opportunity to start a new line of business offering new SRE services. These are SRE advisory, consulting, service co-design, transformation, shared on call, dedicated on call, and SRE infrastructure as a service.

It is likely that a business case calculation will be required to raise a division budget increase and carry it through all the necessary processes within the company. Alternatively (option 1.2), the funding of the SRE team will be done in a budget-neutral manner for the division. "Budget neutral" is a financial term that refers to a program or project that has no impact on the budget. In this case, a reallocation of the division's existing budget needs to take place to find room for SRE team funding.

Either through the division budget increase (option 1.1) or the division budget reallocation (option 1.2), the budget of the product delivery organization may get increased (option 2.1). Also here, a business case calculation will be required. Alternatively, some reallocation of the existing product delivery organization budget may lead to sufficient room to fund the SRE team (option 2.2).

It is important to note that the existing budget reallocation at any level in the organization may come at the expense of other running or planned activities. If this is the case, the respective managers might argue about budget and head count. This needs to be anticipated. The SRE coaches should attempt to smooth the waves as much as possible. A solid explanation of what the SRE team is for and a plausible business case might be able to support the rational side of the argument. War stories of past incidents that were not handled well, consequently impacting customers and the company's reputation, might support the emotional side of the argument.

In the product delivery organization, the existing budgets of the development and operations organizations may increase, decrease, or remain neutral. If the SRE team is to be placed in the development organization, its budget may be increased to fund the SRE team fully (option 3.1). Alternatively, the budget may be increased to only partially fund the SRE team (also option 3.1). The remainder of the funding may need to be found in a budget-neutral manner through reallocation of people and projects.

Although difficult to realize, it might also happen that the entire SRE team would need to be funded in a budget-neutral way in the development organization (option 3.2). Moreover, the funding may decrease to fund the SRE team in the operations organization or to fund a new SRE organization (option 3.3).

Similar budget allocation procedures take place if the SRE team is to be placed in the operations organization. The operations organization's budget may be increased to fund the SRE

---

8. Smith, Steve. 2020. "You Build It You Run It." *Steve Smith On Tech* (blog). April 7, 2020. https://www.stevesmith.tech/blog/you-build-it-you-run-it.

team fully (option 4.1). The funding might come from the delivery organization's budget or from a decrease in the development organization's budget. Alternatively, the operations organization's funding increase may fund the SRE team only partially (also option 4.1). The remainder of the funding may need to be found using budget reallocation activities in the operations organization.

It might happen that the SRE team would need to be funded entirely in a budget-neutral manner in the operations organization (option 4.2). Leadership might do this in an attempt to accelerate the SRE transformation in the operations organization. However, this could be a dangerous move. It might lead to the operations engineers previously conducting manual operations work being retitled as SREs and their team being renamed as the SRE team. Apart from the name swapping, not a lot might get changed.

The title change might lead to higher wage expectations by the operations engineers. However, it will not lead to the operations engineers supporting the development teams adequately in shared on call as part of the "you build it, you and SRE run it" model. Development and debugging skills are essential for an SRE. An operations engineer who was doing manual operations work might not possess these skills. The SRE coaches should watch this space closely and not spare any effort to prevent such a situation from happening.

In "Aim for Operability, not SRE as a Cult,"[9] Steve Smith says: "In 2020, I learned of a sysadmin team that were rebranded as an SRE team, received a small pay increase… and then carried on doing the same sysadmin work." To counter this state of affairs, an SRE team must be staffed with engineers combining development and operations capabilities. This is the core reason and the justification for SREs commanding higher wages than operations engineers. The SRE methodology can be learned and the experience applying it can be gained. However, it only works effectively on top of sound development and operations capabilities.

This discussion shows how budget decisions might impact the SRE transformation. The intentions of managers holding the budgets and financial controllers controlling the budgets might clash with the views of SRE coaches driving the SRE transformation. The SRE coaches should therefore cultivate relationships with the managers and financial controllers to establish an understanding of SRE necessary to make appropriate budget allocation decisions.

Coming back to the budget allocation options, the operations organization's budget may also be decreased to fund the SRE team in the development organization or fund a new SRE organization (option 4.3). Generally, if the SRE team is to be placed in the new SRE organization, the budget may come either from the product delivery, development, or operations organization, or from a partial combination thereof. The SRE organization is new, and its budget needs to be created for the first time (option 5.1). Therefore, it is a pure investment case motivated by the need of revenue insurance for reliability targets and the desire to pursue the opportunity to open a new revenue stream with new SRE services.

In summary, within the product delivery organization, funding for the SRE team may come from a budget increase for the development or operations organization. The increase might cover the full cost or only part of the cost of the SRE team. As an alternative, the funding might come from an optimization of the development or operation organization's existing budget. The different options are summarized in Table 12.10.

---

9. Smith, Steve. 2020. "Aim for Operability, Not SRE as a Cult." *Steve Smith On Tech* (blog). October 20, 2020. https://www.stevesmith.tech/blog/aim-for-operability-not-sre-as-a-cult.

Table 12.10 *SRE Team Funding Options*

SRE Team Placement in the Product Delivery Organization	SRE team placement in the product delivery organization	SRE team within development organization	SRE team within operations organization	SRE team in a dedicated SRE organization
SRE Team Head Count and Budget	SRE team head count and budget	Budget increase to fully/partially cover cost or no budget increase for the development organization	Budget increase to fully/partially cover cost or no budget increase for the operations organization	Budget increase to fully/partially cover cost or no budget increase for the product delivery organization

In terms of head count allowance, the head count is generally dictated by the budget. However, there may be cases in which financial controls impose a head count limit in addition to the budget limit. This might be motivated by the organizational KPIs that measure ratios such as revenue versus head count and profit versus head count.

If a head count limit exists for an organization, it may reduce the maneuvering room for hiring people. For instance, an organization might not be able to hire two junior people fresh out of university instead of a senior person, not because doing so would break the budget limit, but rather because it would break the head count limit. Moreover, even if a senior person leaves a team, it might not be possible to replace them with two junior people even if it could be done in a budget-neutral manner.

To be on the safe side, the question of head count limit needs to be discussed alongside the budget for the SRE team. The head count limit might indeed turn out to be different depending on whether the SRE team should be placed in the development, operations, or a separate SRE organization. If so, this factor might contribute to decision-making about where to place the SRE team in the product delivery organization. It should therefore be taken seriously. The SRE coaches should be aware of this and try to ensure that the factor head count limit does not lead to decisions that are counterproductive to the SRE transformation.

This discussion shows the importance of SRE coaches being connected to financial controllers. If a good collaboration can be established, it may lead to meaningful exchanges, resulting in decisions that are appropriate from the financial point of view and that support the SRE transformation well.

12.4.7 SRE Team Cost Accounting

SRE team cost accounting depends on where the team is located within the product delivery organization. If the SRE team is within the development organization, the cost accounting happens with the development organization itself. The development organization has a cost center within the product delivery organization. The SRE team cost is attributed to that cost center like every other team within the development organization.

If the SRE team is within the operations organization, the cost accounting might be done in two different ways. For instance, it may be done within the operations organization itself, which means the cost is allocated to the operations organization's cost center.

Alternatively, the development and operations organizations may have agreed to attribute the cost of SREs to the development organization. That is, organizationally the SREs are within the operations organization, and their salaries are paid by the operations organization. However, the time the SREs spend supporting the development teams (nearly all their work time) is charged to the development organization based on a negotiated transfer price. This is paid by the development organization's cost center to the operations organization's cost center, which means there is cross-organizational cost accounting within the product delivery organization. This is illustrated in Figure 12.9.

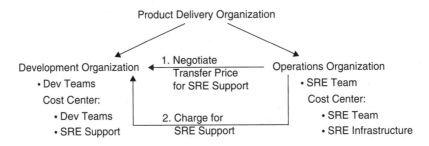

Figure 12.9 *Cross-organizational cost accounting for SRE services*

The top of Figure 12.9 shows the product delivery organization, and below it, the development and operations organizations. The development organization contains development teams and the operations organization contains the SRE team. The operations organization negotiates a transfer price for SRE support with the development organization (step 1 in Figure 12.9). Typically, the price would be a flat hourly rate for an SRE supporting a development team. The rate would be flat regardless of the actual hourly salary of a given SRE. It would cover an average hourly rate of an SRE and possibly some contribution to the SRE infrastructure cost.

Based on the negotiated transfer price, the operations organization charges the development organization for the hours during which the SREs from the SRE team supported the development teams each month. Thus, the development organization's cost center contains the costs for the development teams and the SRE support. The operations team's cost center contains the SRE team and SRE infrastructure costs.

Finally, if the SRE team is within a dedicated SRE organization, there are two ways to do cost accounting. First, the SRE team cost may just be accounted for within the SRE organization. Alternatively, the SRE organization may negotiate a transfer price for SRE support with the development organization and charge accordingly on a monthly basis.

Additionally, the SRE organization may offer many services beyond pure on-call support as part of the "you build it, you and SRE run it" model. These services may be priced and accounted for in different ways. This is illustrated in Table 12.11.

Table 12.11 *Price Models for Different SRE Services*

Service	Possible Price Model Within the Company
SRE advisory	Project price
SRE consulting	Project price

Service	Possible Price Model Within the Company
Services co-design	Transfer price based on negotiated rates
SRE transformation	Project price or transfer price based on negotiated rates
Shared on call	Transfer price based on negotiated rates
Dedicated on call	Price based on services supported
SRE infrastructure	Software as a service recurring pricing

That is, when the SRE organization becomes a service provider with many offerings, its pricing structure and cost accounting become more complex and need to be defined for each offering individually.

12.4.8 SRE Team KPIs

The SRE team KPIs will be influenced greatly depending on the organization the team is in. Similar to the discussion in Section 12.4.5, *SRE Team Incentives, Identity, and Pride*, the KPIs for the SRE team in the development organization may be rooted in products under development. For the SRE team in the operations organization, the KPIs may be rooted in incidents. For the SRE team in the SRE organization, the KPIs may be rooted in reliability user experience. Example KPIs by organization are shown in Table 12.12.

Table 12.12 *Example SRE Team KPIs*

SRE Team Placement in the Product Delivery Organization	SRE Team Within the Development Organization	SRE Team Within the Operations Organization	SRE Team in a Dedicated SRE Organization
SRE team KPIs	Rooted in products under development	Rooted in incidents	Rooted in reliability user experience
Example KPI 1	97% of customer complaints about product A are not related to reliability.	Mean time between failures (MTBF) is less than two weeks.	90% of supported services are within error budgets.
Example KPI 2	NPS score of at least 75 for product B	Mean time to recovery (MTTR) from an incident is less than a day.	95% of incidents with supported services consume less than 30% of the monthly error budget.
Example KPI 3	Reliability engineering implemented in new product C from the outset	Number of incidents is on a decline quarterly,	95% of customer complaints for supported services are not related to reliability.

The example KPIs for the SRE team within the operations organization are undergoing criticism in the industry. According to *Implementing Service Level Objectives*,[10] counting incidents is not useful because many incidents with a small user experience impact might be less impactful than a single incident with a severe user experience impact. So, having a small number of incidents is not always better than having a large number of incidents!

Classifying the incidents is very difficult because incidents in complex systems are very often unique. There are multiple and different causes for incidents in complex systems each time they fail. The root causes can be technical and people-related. Thus, counting the incidents by classification is difficult too.

Measuring MTTR can hide the user experience in terms of reliability. While MTTR might be short and get shorter over time, the reliability user experience might not improve. This is counterintuitive but can be demonstrated well using an example (based on a similar example provided in *Implementing Service Level Objectives*[10]). Imagine six incidents occurring in period 1. Each incident is recovered from within 30 minutes. The MTTR for the six incidents in period 1 is 30 minutes. The downtime in period 1 is 6 incidents x 30 minutes = 180 minutes.

Now imagine period 2. In that period, there is only one incident. The incident was recovered from within 120 minutes. The MTTR for period 2 is 120 minutes. The downtime in period 2 is 120 minutes.

A comparison of the two periods based on MTTR, downtime, and reliability user experience yields the situation shown in Table 12.13.

Table 12.13 *MTTR Versus Reliability User Experience*

	MTTR	Downtime	Reliability User Experience
Period 1	30 minutes	180 minutes	Worse than in period 2
Period 2	120 minutes	120 minutes	Better than in period 1

Period 1 has the lowest MTTR but the longest downtime. Period 2 has the highest MTTR but the shortest downtime. Following this, the reliability user experience in period 2 is better than that in period 1.

Furthermore, in Resilience as a Continuous Delivery enabler,[11] it is argued that "Optimising For Robustness – prioritising MTBF over MTTR – is an antiquated, flawed approach to IT reliability that results in Discontinuous Delivery and an operational brittleness that begets failure." When an organization optimizes for robustness measured by MTBF, it tends to control changes in production using end-to-end testing, change advisory boards, and change freezes. These practices slow down the speed of delivery. They are employed on the assumption that slowing down changes in production would lead to a reduction of failures, thus improving MTBF. This assumption was shown to be incorrect by research from Accelerate.[12] The research showed that

10. Hidalgo, Alex. 2020. *Implementing Service Level Objectives: A Practical Guide to SLIs, SLOs & Error Budgets*. Sebastopol, CA: O'Reilly Media.

11. Smith, Steve. 2017. "Resilience as a Continuous Delivery Enabler." *Steve Smith On Tech* (blog). November 19, 2017. https://www.stevesmith.tech/blog/resilience-as-a-continuous-delivery-enabler/.

12. Forsgren PhD, Nicole, Jez Humble, and Gene Kim. 2018. *Accelerate: The Science of Lean Software and DevOps: Building and Scaling High Performing Technology Organizations*. Portland, OR: IT Revolution Press.

high-performance software delivery organizations achieve speed and stability of delivery at the same time. That is, the faster an organization goes, the more stable the software delivery is. This is because of the presence of adaptive capacity in the software and infrastructure. The adaptive capacity and on-call practices enable low MTTR and support low MTBF.

By contrast, organizations slowing down changes using end-to-end testing, change advisory boards, and change freezes tend to underinvest in adaptive capacity such as adaptive architecture, automated infrastructure provisioning, telemetry, and on-call practices. However, "success is the result of the presence of adaptive capacity, not the absence of failures," according to John Allspaw in The Future of Monitoring.[13]

The questions attempted to be answered by counting incidents and measuring MTTR and MTBF should actually revolve around the reliability user experience. Instead of MTTR and MTBF, these questions can be answered in a more targeted manner by SLOs, error budgets, and error budget depletion rates.

12.5 You Build It, SRE Run It

A distinguishing characteristic of the "you build it, SRE run it" model is the existence of an SRE team that runs services on their own. That is, in this model the SRE team is fully responsible for running services that were developed by the development teams.

With this comes another distinguishing characteristic of the "you build it, you and SRE run it" model. It is an agreement between the SRE team and the development team whose services are run in production about the minimum reliability to be exhibited by the services for the SRE team to run them. With that, the SRE team only runs services of sufficiently high reliability. If the services do not meet the reliability criteria from the agreement, they are not taken into operation by the SRE team. Likewise, if the services stop meeting the reliability criteria from the agreement after being taken into operation by the SRE team, the SRE team can return the services to the development team to operate and improve reliability.

The agreement between the SRE team and the development team should be based on the error budget policy. It is the right place to specify and sign off on actions to be taken in cases of premature error budget depletions.

The SRE team itself can organizationally be placed either in a development, an operations, or a dedicated SRE organization. In this section, these three alternatives are explored.

12.5.1 SRE Team Within a Development Organization

In Figure 12.10, a "you build it, SRE run it" model is illustrated in which the SRE team is placed in the development organization.

---

13. Schlossnagle, Theo. 2015. "The Future of Monitoring: Q&A with John Allspaw." Circonus. September 4, 2015. https://www.circonus.com/2015/09/the-future-of-monitoring-qa-with-john-allspaw.

You Build It, SRE Run It: SRE Team within Development Organization

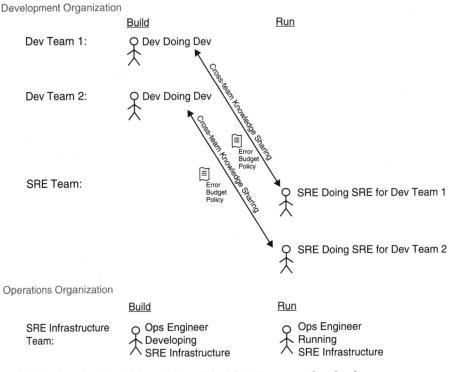

Figure 12.10 *"You build it, SRE run it" model with SRE team within development organization*

The upper part of Figure 12.10 shows the development organization. It consists of two development teams and one SRE team. Development teams 1 and 2 focus on building the product. The SRE team operates the product for development teams 1 and 2. In order to operate the product, there is ongoing cross-team knowledge sharing between the SRE team and development teams 1 and 2.

The SRE team only operates services that stay within defined limits of error budget depletion. The limits are laid down in the error budget policies. There is an error budget policy for development team 1. Likewise, there is another error budget policy for development team 2. It contains agreements between the teams about the kinds of error budget depletion that are acceptable for the SRE team to operate the respective services.

If the services are within the error budget depletion limits specified in the error budget policy, the SRE team keeps operating the services. Otherwise, the SRE team hands over the service operation responsibility to the development team. In this case, the service operation model is switched from "you build it, SRE run it" to "you build it, you run it."

The lower part of Figure 12.10 shows the operations organization. In the operations organization is an SRE infrastructure team that builds and runs the SRE infrastructure the SRE team uses to run the services developed by the development teams.

12.5.2 SRE Team Within an Operations Organization

"You build it, SRE run it" can also be implemented by putting the SRE team into the operations organization. This is illustrated in Figure 12.11.

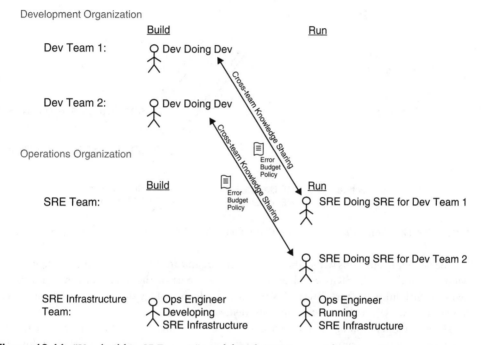

Figure 12.11 *"You build it, SRE run it" model with SRE team within operations organization*

The upper part of Figure 12.11 shows the development organization. The development teams in the development organization are building the product. The operations organization in the lower part of the figure operates the services and owns the SRE infrastructure.

The SRE infrastructure team is responsible for building and running the SRE infrastructure. The SRE team is responsible for running the services developed by the development teams. The error budget policies regulate the relationship between the SRE team and the development teams in terms of error budget depletion. Consistent premature error budget depletion can lead to the SRE team handing over the service operations responsibility to the respective development team until reliability is improved.

12.5.3 SRE Team in a Dedicated SRE Organization

"You build it, SRE run it" can also be implemented in an organizational structure with a dedicated SRE organization. Such a setup is shown in Figure 12.12.

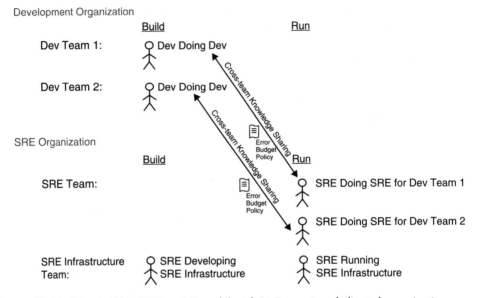

Figure 12.12 *"You build it, SRE run it" model with SRE team in a dedicated organization*

The development teams within the development organization in the upper part of Figure 12.12 build the product. The SRE organization in the lower part of the figure runs the services and owns the SRE infrastructure. The infrastructure is built and run by the SRE infrastructure team. It is staffed by SREs with infrastructure knowledge.

The actual operation of product services is done by the SRE team. It is staffed by SREs with the knowledge necessary to go on call for the product services developed by the development teams. To keep the knowledge up-to-date, regular cross-team knowledge sharing between the SRE team and development teams is carried out.

The error budget policies are used to regulate the levels of service reliability necessary to be fulfilled by the services to be operated by the SRE team. Otherwise, the SRE team can hand over the service operations responsibility to the respective development team.

12.6 Cost Optimization

The models from the "who builds it, who runs it?" spectrum bear different costs. The model comparison (Section 12.2.5) showed that "you build it, ops run it" is a low-cost model of running operations that comes with lots of disadvantages. Further, the comparison showed that "you build it, you run it," "you build it, you and SRE run it," and "you build it, SRE run it" are all high-cost models. They score well on important criteria such as involvement of the development teams in the on-call work, knowledge synchronization between teams, incident resolution times, service handover for operations, and availability targets.

The availability targets offer leeway for cost optimization for the high-cost models. In Implementing You Build It You Run It at scale,[14] a notion of team on-call rotations versus domain on-call rotations is explored. For services with high availability targets, a team on-call rotation is recommended. Such a rotation can be implemented with the "you build it, you run it" and "you build it, you and SRE run it" models. The cost of a team on-call rotation is high. It is justified by the high availability targets the rotation is tasked to protect.

For services with medium availability targets, a cost optimization is suggested. It is achieved by setting up a domain rotation instead of a team on-call rotation. A domain rotation supports several services from different teams that share a logical knowledge domain. That is, a person on call from a domain rotation needs to react to the SLO breaches of services owned by several teams. That can only work effectively if the person has solid knowledge of services from the domain regardless of the team owning a particular service.

That is, if there are three teams in the domain rotation, there may be one person on call for the three teams at any given time. By contrast, with team on-call rotations there would be three people on call for the three teams at any given time. This is illustrated in Figure 12.13.

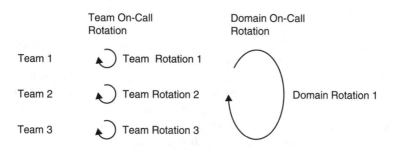

Figure 12.13 *Team on-call rotation versus domain on-call rotation*

Thus, the cost optimization with the domain on-call rotations comes from putting fewer people on call per set of teams within a domain. It is justified by the medium availability targets the domain on-call rotation is tasked to protect. With lower availability targets, the error budgets are bigger. The bigger the error budgets, the longer the time to recover from incidents that can be had without depleting the error budgets prematurely. This means the people on call on a domain rotation would generally have a bit more time to recover from incidents than their counterparts on team rotations protecting high availability targets.

A rather common attempt to optimize the cost of running the "you build it, you run it" model is to introduce a thin layer of a few people with a 24/7 on-call rotation. This is illustrated in Figure 12.14.

14. Smith, Steve. 2020. "Implementing You Build It You Run It at Scale." *Steve Smith On Tech* (blog). May 19, 2020. https://www.stevesmith.tech/blog/implementing-you-build-it-you-run-it-at-scale.

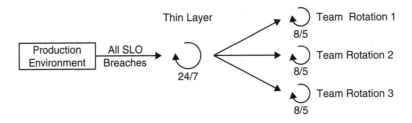

Figure 12.14 *Thin layer of people receiving all the SLO breaches*

The people from the thin layer are tasked with receiving the SLO breaches from all the teams. Once received, the SLO breaches are triaged. Some SLO breaches can be reacted to by the thin layer using runbooks. The remaining breaches, which cannot be reacted to by the thin layer due to lack of knowledge or capacity, are forwarded to the respective team on-call rotations. The team on-call rotations are typically not available 24/7, but rather on an 8/5 (eight-hour weekdays) or 8/7 (eight-hour weekdays and weekends) basis.

The cost optimization strategy here is to only pay the after-hours support cost to a small number of people from the thin layer. This cost optimization strategy will not be effective, because it weakens the reliability incentives for the development teams. The teams know they will never be the first line of defense against unreliability. Mentally, they will have the people from the thin layer in mind as the ones doing production support 24/7. They will not see themselves as the enablers and guardians of reliability in production. It follows that the investments in adaptive capacity, evolutionary architecture, and runbooks will suffer greatly as a result.

The setup with the thin layer on-call rotation may only work as a cost optimization technique if the thin layer is dedicated responsible for very specific customer use cases that are cross-team, well-expressed using SLOs, and well-documented in runbooks.

Another way to generally optimize cost is to strictly implement only those features in the SRE infrastructure that can be commonly used in the majority of teams in the product delivery organization. This way, the economy of scale for the SRE infrastructure investment is enabled. Special feature requests benefiting only one team will need to be implemented by the requesting team themselves, in most cases. Alternatively, the team could wait until more teams get interested in the functionality so that a common implementation in the central SRE infrastructure is justified.

12.7 Team Topologies

The team topologies explored in the previous sections can be summarized as an intersection of the models from the "who builds it, who runs it?" spectrum and the relevant departments within the product delivery organization. The summary is shown in Table 12.14.

Table 12.14 *Team Topologies*

	You Build It, You Run It	You Build It, You and SRE Run It	You Build It, SRE Run It
Development Organization	Option 1: No dedicated SRE role. SRE is a responsibility borne by all developers on rotation. Option 2: Dedicated SRE role in the team. Option 3: Dedicated SRE role in the team and a dedicated developer on rotation.	Option 1: SRE team in the development organization. SRE infrastructure team in the operations organization. No SRE organization.	Option 1: SRE team in the development organization. SRE infrastructure team in the operations organization. No SRE organization.
Operations Organization	SRE infrastructure team	Option 2: SRE team and SRE infrastructure team in the operations organization. No SRE organization.	Option 2: SRE team and SRE infrastructure team in the operations organization. No SRE organization.
SRE Organization	N/A	Option 3: SRE team and SRE infrastructure team in the SRE organization. SRE tool chain procurement and administration in the operations organization.	Option 3: SRE team and SRE infrastructure team in the SRE organization. SRE tool chain procurement and administration in the operations organization.

12.7.1 Reporting Lines

Following the team topologies, the reporting lines of the developers, SRE infrastructure engineers, and SREs can be determined. These are illustrated in Table 12.15. Mentioned option numbers refer to the team topology options from the previous section.

Table 12.15 *Reporting Lines*

	You Build It, You Run It	You Build It, You and SRE Run It	You Build It, SRE Run It
Development Organization Reporting Line	Developers (option 1) SREs (options 2, 3)	Developers SREs (option 1)	Developers SREs (option 1)
Operations Organization Reporting Line	SRE infrastructure engineers	SREs (option 2) SRE infrastructure engineers (options 1, 2)	SREs (option 2) SRE infrastructure engineers (options 1, 2)
SRE Organization Reporting Line	N/A	SREs (option 3) SRE infrastructure engineers (option 3)	SREs (option 3) SRE infrastructure engineers (option 3)

The reporting lines are important, as they determine the organizational goals, incentives, and KPIs for the teams and people. For example, in an organizational setup with no dedicated SREs where developers fulfill the SRE responsibilities on rotation (option 1 in the "you build it, you run it" model), all the people working in a team have the same product goals, incentives, and KPIs. These need to reflect all the product aspects, including reliability. Ensuring product reliability becomes everybody's goal.

In another organizational setup, inserting a reporting line, or organizational boundary, between the developers and SREs might be done deliberately to incentivize development and SRE teams on different aspects. Development teams can be focused on product functionality, and SRE teams can be focused on product reliability.

In this setup, developers and SREs working together are forced to find a good balance and appropriate activities to satisfy one another's goals. Depending on the goals, the balance might be beneficial for the overall product or it might not be. The usefulness of the balance will be determined by how well the goals of the development and SRE teams interlock. This, in turn, will be determined by how well the development and SRE organizations work together in the goal-setting process. Moreover, the usefulness of the balance will be determined by how deeply rooted the SRE culture is in the product delivery organization.

12.7.2 SRE Identity Triangle

In this context, the question of the SREs' identity plays a big role. Should the SREs have a more product-centric identity, incident-centric identity, or reliability user experience–centric identity? In combination, the SREs should have identity that encompasses the product, incidents, and reliability user experience. This is shown as a triangle in Figure 12.15.

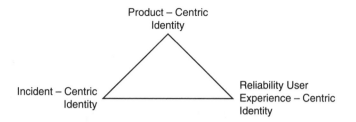

Figure 12.15 *SRE identity triangle*

The focus of SREs within the SRE identity triangle will be influenced by the organization they are in. Let us explore the SRE identity triangle in the context of the development, operations, and SRE organizations.

A possible SRE identity within the development organization is shown in Figure 12.16.

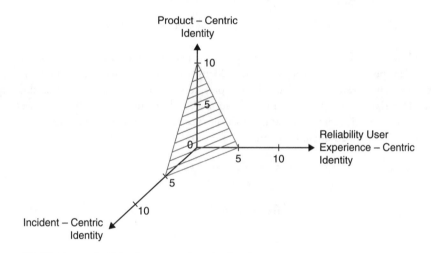

Figure 12.16 *Example SRE identity within the development organization*

The focus of the identity is product-centric. The reliability user experience and incidents are also an important part of the identity, but within the scope of the product the SREs are working on. The product itself is very important to SREs here. Within the product, the reliability user experience and incidents are the second most important product aspects. Note that the triangle may turn out to be somewhat different, but the defining characteristic of the product-centric identity is that it has the highest score on the product axis.

A possible SRE identity within the operations organization is shown in Figure 12.17.

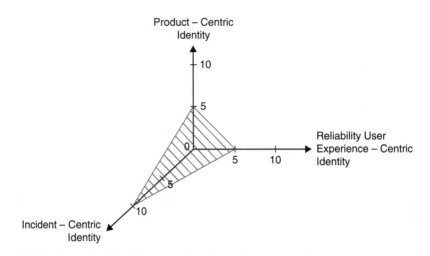

Figure 12.17 *Example SRE identity within the operations organization*

The identity here leans toward incidents. The absence of incidents, efficient response to incidents, and proper incident postmortems are in focus here. The product and reliability user experience are also important. These aspects are expressed more in terms of incidents in this type of identity. The triangle itself may turn out to be somewhat different, but the defining characteristic of the incident-centric identity is that it has the highest score on the incident axis.

Finally, a possible SRE identity within the SRE organization is shown in Figure 12.18.

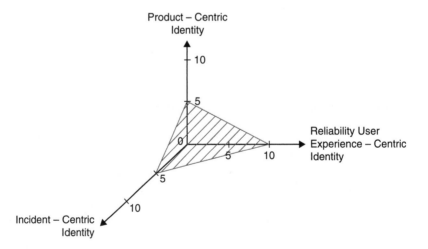

Figure 12.18 *Example SRE identity within the SRE organization*

This identity gravitates toward reliability user experience. The user experiencing the product as reliable is the focus of this identity. The product itself and the incidents are important, but these aspects are expressed and measured in terms of reliability user experience. The triangle may turn out to be somewhat different, but the defining characteristic of the reliability user experience–centric identity is that it has the highest score on the reliability user experience axis.

The SRE identity triangle can be used before deciding on the organizational structure for SRE to inform the options in terms of SRE identities that might get shaped. After the decision on the organizational structure has been made, the SRE coaches should present the SRE identity triangle to the developers and, if available, the SREs. This should kick off a discussion about the identity that would be appropriate for the people within the chosen organizational setup.

It will certainly be the people practicing SRE who will determine and develop the ingredients of the SRE identity and culture that will become prevalent in the product delivery organization. The SRE identity triangle might be a useful tool to support the discussions. It will certainly not work as a tool for managers to impose a certain identity or culture on the people practicing SRE.

12.7.3 Holacracy: No Reporting Lines

When drawing reporting lines for SREs, a new method of organizing enterprises deserves special attention: holacracy. Wikipedia defines it as follows: "Holacracy is a method of decentralized management and organizational governance, which claims to distribute authority and decision-making through a holarchy of self-organizing teams rather than being vested in a management hierarchy."[15]

A holacracy enterprise does not have bosses or traditional management levels. Rather, it is managed by agile self-organizing networks. Holacracy.org is a good resource to learn how this could be achieved.

Further, in a new book, A Radical Enterprise: Pioneering the Future of High-Performing Organizations,[16] Matt Parker examines holacracy enterprises. He states: "The fastest growing and most competitive organizations in the world have no bureaucracies and no bosses. They have recently doubled in number, and currently comprise around 8% of the world's corporations."

Some of the pioneering radical enterprises include

- Haier,[17] the largest home appliance retailer by sales volume in the world, with 80,000 staff members

- Morning Star,[18] the largest tomato processor in the world, with 400 staff members

- Buurtzorg,[19] the best home health-care provider in the Netherlands, with 15,000 staff members

15. Wikipedia. 2022. "Holacracy." January 10, 2022. https://en.wikipedia.org/wiki/Holacracy.

16. Parker, Matt K. 2022. *A Radical Enterprise: Pioneering the Future of High-Performing Organizations.* Portland, OR: IT Revolution Press.

17. Wikipedia. 2022. "Haier." January 7, 2022. https://en.wikipedia.org/wiki/Haier.

18. Wikipedia. 2021. "The Morning Star Company." November 1, 2021. https://en.wikipedia.org/wiki/The_Morning_Star_Company.

19. Wikipedia. 2020. "Buurtzorg Nederland." May 8, 2020. https://en.wikipedia.org/wiki/Buurtzorg_Nederland.

The radical enterprises consist of thousands of micro-enterprises. Each micro-enterprise is fully autonomous, self-organized, self-managed, self-allocating, and self-linking to other micro-enterprises.

A radical enterprise is based on radical collaboration. Radical collaboration is achieved through freely given commitments of intrinsically motivated peers. That is, it is always voluntary. In *A Radical Enterprise*,[16] Matt Parker states four imperatives of radical collaboration:

1. Team autonomy in terms of practice, allocation or role, and schedule

2. Managerial devolution or decentralization of power in terms of governance, compensation, and so on

3. Deficiency gratification in terms of human deficiency needs such as the need for predictability, choice, equity, and positive self-image, and the need for others to believe in us

4. Candid vulnerability as the opposite of defensive reasoning

Radical enterprises succeed through the fusion of the four imperatives. That said, at the time of this writing, it is unclear how SRE could be introduced in a radical enterprise or holacracy. What can be said with certainty is that it will take a new approach to be explored through experimentation.

Because no industry experience with introducing SRE in a holacracy is known, this topic is not touched upon in subsequent sections. It remains very relevant for the industry, though, and should therefore be researched.

12.8 Choosing a Model

The process of choosing a model from the "who builds it, who runs it?" spectrum can be influenced by several factors. For one, if SRE is introduced in a greenfield product initiative, there is no existing organizational setup to consider or transit from. The model comparison from Section 12.2.5 can be used to choose the most appropriate setup.

If, on the other hand, there is an existing organization for operations, it is the transition from the current setup to a new one that is in focus. The model comparison is still useful. However, it only compares the models from the "who builds it, who runs it?" spectrum without considering the transformation aspects and costs of a given transition.

12.8.1 Model Transformation Options

The current organizational setup for operations may range from unorganized to any of the four models from the "who builds it, who runs it?" spectrum. With this, a number of transitions emerge. They are summarized in Table 12.16. The rows of the table show the origin of the transitions and the columns show the transition targets.

Table 12.16 *Model Transition Options Within the "Who Builds It, Who Runs It?" Spectrum*

		Transition TO				
		Unorganized	*"You build it, ops run it"*	*"You build it, SRE run it"*	*"You build it, you and SRE run it"*	*"You build it, you run it"*
	Unorganized	-	Possible	Possible	Possible	Possible
	"You build it, ops run it"	No reason	-	Possible	Possible	Possible
Transition FROM	"You build it, SRE run it"	No reason	Unlikely	-	Possible	Possible
	"You build it, you and SRE run it"	No reason	Unlikely	Possible	-	Possible
	"You build it, you run it"	No reason	Unlikely	Possible	Possible	-

The first analysis in Table 12.16 reveals that transitioning from any setup to an unorganized setup is not a practical option. This is because there is no reason to fall into chaos. However, the opposite transition, from an unorganized setup to any other setup, is possible. Indeed, any setup from the "who builds it, who runs it?" spectrum is better than running operations in an unorganized way.

Moreover, the transition to the "you build it, ops run it" model is unlikely to be done from "you build it, SRE run it," "you build it, you and SRE run it," or "you build it, you run it." This is because these three models score better than "you build it, ops run it" in the model comparison (Section 12.2.5) on important criteria such as the following:

- Involvement of the development teams in the on-call work
- Knowledge synchronization between teams
- Incident resolution times
- Service handover for operations
- Availability targets
- Product demand

All the other transitions in the "you build it, SRE run it," "you build it, you and SRE run it," and "you build it, you run it" columns are possible. In fact, the choice between these models could be made on a service basis. It does not necessarily have to be the model for all services in the product delivery organization.

Another dimension of making a transition illustrated in Table 12.16 is concerned with the reporting lines of the people involved. The organizational reporting lines have an influence on the distribution of authority, power, and decision-making. In terms of decision-making in operations in general and in SRE in particular, the organizational power of advocating for reliability is important, when the data from production shows reliability investment is needed.

The cross-product of the reporting lines and the model from the "who builds it, who runs it?" spectrum is the two-dimensional decision that needs to be made to choose a suitable organizational setup for SRE. This is explored in the next section.

12.8.2 Decision Dimensions

Let us consider what is difficult and what is easy to change about the "who builds it, who runs it?" decision. This is shown in Table 12.17.

Table 12.17 *Decision Changes Within the "Who Builds It, Who Runs It?" Spectrum*

		This Model Can Be Decided by Service. The Decision Can Be Changed Easily.		
		You Build It, You Run It	*You Build It, You and SRE Run It*	*You Build It, SRE Run It*
The reporting lines are decided for the product delivery organization. **The decision is difficult to change.**	Development organization reporting line for SREs	Possible option	Possible option	Possible option
	Operations organization reporting line for SREs	Possible option	Possible option	Possible option
	SRE organization reporting line for SREs	-	Possible option	Possible option

When choosing a model from the "who builds it, who runs it?" spectrum, one consideration is that the decision is two-dimensional. One dimension is "who runs it?": "you build it, you run it," "you build it, you and SRE run it," "you build it, SRE run it," or some hybrid thereof. This is shown at the top of Table 12.17. The decision can be made by service, team, product, and so on, and can be easily changed.

Indeed, a service may initially be operated by the development team ("you build it, you run it"). Later, the development team may team up with the SRE team to operate the service jointly using shared on call ("you build it, you and SRE run it"). At some point, the same service may be operated fully by the SRE team supported by the reliability agreement anchored in the error budget policy ("you build it, SRE run it").

The other dimension of choosing a model from the "who builds it, who runs it?" spectrum is organizational. This is shown on the left-hand side of Table 12.17. The decision is weighty. It is made for the entire product delivery organization, and it entails drawing reporting lines for SREs. Therefore, this decision is difficult to change later.

Figure 12.19 illustrates the two-dimensionality of the decision.

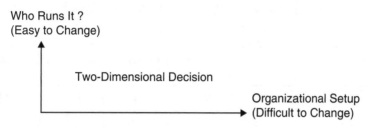

Figure 12.19 *Dimensionality of the "who builds it, who runs it?" model decision*

While the "who runs it?" dimension of the decision is important to get right from the beginning, should it turn out to be wrong it can be corrected easily later. The organizational dimension of the decision is more important to get right from the beginning, because should it turn out to be wrong, it cannot be corrected easily later.

The decision to create a new SRE organization is especially difficult to reverse. Indeed, setting up a new SRE organization means installing a new director or VP role for SRE in the product delivery organization. This is shown in Table 12.18.

Table 12.18 *New Director or VP for a New SRE Organization*

	You Build It, You Run It	You Build It, You and SRE Run It	You Build It, SRE Run It
Development Organization Reporting Line for SREs	-	-	-
Operations Organization Reporting Line for SREs	-	-	-
SRE Organization Reporting Line for SREs	-	New director or VP	New director or VP

With a new director or VP role for SRE created within the product delivery organization, the question is to whom the newly created role should be reporting. Should the new role be reporting to a CTO, CIO, head of the product delivery organization, or head of the product area? What would be the implications of choosing one over the others? Let us consider possible options.

12.8.3 Reporting Options

Table 12.19 exemplarily summarizes eight possible organizational hierarchies that embed an SRE director or an SRE VP into an existing organization. The table only contains direct solid line reporting structures. Other nuances such as dotted line reporting, leadership team membership questions, and so on are not considered as they are highly contextual in organizations.

Table 12.19 *Reporting Options*

Option 1	Option 2	Option 3	Option 4	Option 5	Option 6	Option 7	Option 8
CTO-Bound SRE Organization		*CIO-Bound SRE Organization*		*Head of Product Delivery Organization–Bound SRE Organization*		*Head of Product Area–Bound SRE Organization*	
CEO	CEO	CEO	CEO	CEO	CEO	CEO	CEO
↑	↑	↑	↑	↑	↑	↑	↑
CTO	CTO	CIO	CIO	Head of product delivery org	Head of product delivery org	Head of product area	Head of product area
↑	↑	↑	↑				
↑	↑	↑	↑	↑	↑	↑	↑
↑	↑	↑	↑	↑	↑	↑	↑
↑	↑	↑	↑	↑	↑	Head of product delivery org	Head of product delivery org
↑	↑	↑	↑	↑	↑		
↑	↑	↑	↑	↑	↑		
↑	↑	↑	↑	↑	↑	↑	↑
SRE VP	↑	SRE VP	↑	SRE VP	↑	SRE VP	↑
↑	↑	↑	↑	↑	↑	↑	↑
SRE director	SRE director	SRE director	SRE director	SRE director	SRE director	SRE director	SRE director
↑	↑	↑	↑	↑	↑	↑	↑
SRE teams	SRE teams	SRE teams	SRE teams	SRE teams	SRE teams	SRE teams	SRE teams

Options 1 and 2 illustrate a CTO-bound SRE organization. In option 1, an SRE director reports to an SRE VP and the SRE VP reports to the CTO. Option 2 does not have an SRE VP. Rather, the SRE director reports directly into the CTO.

Options 3 and 4 illustrate a CIO-bound SRE organization. In option 3, an SRE director reports to an SRE VP, and the SRE VP reports to the CIO. In option 4, there is no SRE VP. Rather, the SRE director reports to the CIO.

Options 5 and 6 illustrate an organization in which the head of the product delivery organization reports directly to the CEO. In option 5, the SRE director reports to the SRE VP, and the

SRE VP reports to the head of the product delivery organization. In option 6, there is no SRE VP. Rather, the SRE director reports directly to the head of the product delivery organization.

Finally, options 7 and 8 demonstrate an organization divided by product areas. The head of a product area oversees several product delivery organizations. In option 7, the SRE VP reports to the head of the product delivery organization. In option 8, there is no SRE VP. Here, the SRE director reports directly to the head of the product delivery organization.

Given these options, what would be the differences between them? In *The Software Architect Elevator: Redefining the Architect's Role in the Digital Enterprise*,[20] Gregor Hohpe proposes a model for reverse engineering organizations. It attempts to decode how the IT function of an enterprise is viewed depending on whom the CIO is reporting to. In this context, the model defines four types of organizations: IT as a cost center, IT as an asset, IT as a partner, and IT as an enabler. The focus of a given organization type is shown in Table 12.20.

Table 12.20 *Four Types of IT Organizations*

	IT as a Cost Center	IT as an Asset	IT as a Partner	IT as an Enabler
Focus on	Cost reduction	Return on investment	Business value	Speed and innovation

This model can be used to position the SRE organization as well. How to do it is the subject of the next section.

12.8.4 Positioning the SRE Organization

Inspired by four types of IT organizations, four types of SRE organizations can be defined in a similar vein: SRE as a cost center, SRE as an asset, SRE as a partner, and SRE as an enabler. This is shown in Table 12.21.

Table 12.21 *Four Types of SRE Organizations*

	SRE as a Cost Center	SRE as an Asset	SRE as a Partner	SRE as an Enabler
Focus on	Cost reduction	Reliability asset	Reliability business value	Enabling business through reliability
Strategy	Reduce cost	Optimize the asset	Exploit revenue	Nurture

If SRE is viewed as a cost center, the focus will be on reducing the cost incurred by the SRE organization. There might be pressure to cut costs on a yearly basis by innovating within the organization. Other measures, such as cutting the positions once people have left the SRE organization and thus reducing the head count, might be employed as well. In this context, it will be nearly impossible to get an additional budget beyond the initial allocation. This is a difficult

20. Hohpe, Gregor. 2020. *The Software Architect Elevator: Redefining the Architect's Role in the Digital Enterprise*. Sebastopol, CA: O'Reilly Media.

position for the SRE director or VP to be in. They should attempt to reposition the organization differently. Any other option—SRE as an asset, partner, or enabler—is a better alternative.

If SRE is viewed as an asset, the investments in SRE will be made in pursuit of economies of scale. This means the SRE infrastructure and SRE coaching will be packaged as products from the beginning. The products will be geared to be sold to different product delivery organizations within the enterprise. The self-service features of the products will be of central importance. This is because these features will drive revenue without adding cost. Self-service onboarding onto the SRE infrastructure, self-service use of the infrastructure features, self-service paved roads for stepwise SRE adoption in teams, and so on will be prioritized. Product management's goal in this case will be to create infrastructure that is applicable to the bulk of operability use cases that users can fulfill in a self-service manner. Implementing bespoke feature requests to fulfill special corner cases, offering bespoke consulting services, and so on will not be in focus, because they do not contribute to the strategy of asset optimization.

If SRE is viewed as a partner of business creation, the inception of new revenue streams using SRE will be in focus. In addition to the generic SRE infrastructure that can be sold as a product, bespoke consultancy services will be on the agenda as well. For instance, SRE advisory, SRE consulting, services co-design, SRE transformation, shared on-call services, and dedicated on-call services will be offered to diversify the SRE revenue streams. That is, the SRE organization will be shaped into a full-fledged business that provides the SRE infrastructure as a core offering and a number of bespoke consultancy services complementing it. It will be an attractive value proposition because it can satisfy nearly any demand for SRE from a single source. The various services on offer can be attractively packaged and rendered in a variety of ways to fit and grow the market.

To be sure, the services will be offered both internally and externally. A business interested in the offered SRE services can, for example, initially buy services co-designed to inject reliability thinking into ongoing architectural discussions. Following that, SRE advisory and some SRE consulting can be bought to establish a strategic direction for reliability in the organization and evaluate it exemplarily on some of the services with the most reliability needs. On successful evaluation, the SRE transformation service can be bought to kick-start the SRE transformation in the organization. Offerings like that are rare at the time of this writing. In the decade of the 2020s, it may be possible to build a successful business with these services.

Finally, if SRE is viewed as a business enabler, the focus will be on nurturing the capability internally. In such a setting, reliability is one of the central unique selling points of the products offered. Examples are life safety critical systems and trading systems. With these systems, service unavailability may lead directly to either life-threatening or business-threatening conditions. For instance, in the medical domain, a service supporting remote surgery using robotics needs to be highly available because its malfunction may lead to patient harm. In the financial domain, a service supporting high trade volumes of securities needs to be highly available because its malfunction may render the financial exchange and its customers bankrupt in minutes.

By contrast, services in a social network or video streaming domain do not command people safety or business threat to a similar extent. They undoubtedly need to be reliable to adequately support the business, but the consequences of a service malfunction are less severe.

Nurturing SRE capability will mean investing heavily in adaptive capacity, operability, and incident response, as well as achieving low time to recovery from incidents, low lead time to changes in production, and low production deployment failure rates. Companies doing this score best on the DORA DevOps Quick Check[21] and turn out to be the industry leaders in DevOps according to DORA's research program.

12.8.5 Conveying the Value to Executives

The SRE director or VP needs to be aware of the organizational dynamics described in the previous section that arise based on the way SRE is viewed in the product delivery organization. They should work to move the SRE organization toward being viewed as a partner or a business enabler. In order to achieve this, steady engagement with the higher-ups is essential. Depending on the organizational setup, the head of the product delivery organization, head of the product area, CTO, or CIO needs to be engaged. The CEO needs to be engaged as well.

The SRE director or VP needs to be well-prepared for a conversation with a higher-up. They need to have data demonstrating the value delivered through SRE activities. The value can be expressed through the incidents detected and fixed internally before any customer notices the degradation. As demonstrated in "You Build It You Run It,"[8] the value can be demonstrated in financial terms by projecting the ongoing revenue protected. An estimate of the revenue protected through SRE activities is a powerful way to illustrate the SRE value in financial terms that are understandable to C-level executives. The protected revenue can be expressed on a monthly basis or cumulatively by year depending on the level of the conversation.

Further, reputational damage protection is another good aspect to be used in conversations with executives about the value of SRE. It is difficult to express quantitatively, but it can be well-articulated qualitatively.

Having both quantitative and qualitative data well-prepared in an interactive dashboard goes a long way toward convincing executives of the value delivered by SRE. The interactivity of the dashboard supports a free-flowing conversation. Discussed scenarios may be possible to see or simulate immediately in the dashboard. Access to the dashboard should be provided to every executive in the organization. This way, access to the value provided by SRE is available at a glance for all executives in a self-service manner.

Moreover, the value of SRE can be expressed as the time taken to resolve incidents that did get noticed by customers. In "You Build It You Run It,"[8] the time to recovery is connected to financials as the amount of expected revenue lost during incident recovery.

Taken together, the amount of ongoing revenue protected and the amount of revenue lost during recovery from incidents visible to customers represent a suitable financial framework that can be used to demonstrate the value of SRE. The higher the ongoing amount of protected revenue and the lower the projected revenue loss, the higher the value of SRE. SRE investment decisions can also be based on this financial framework.

---

21. Google Cloud. n.d. "DORA DevOps Quick Check." Accessed January 26, 2022. https://www.devops-research.com/quickcheck.html.

> **From the Trenches:** Conveying the value of SRE to executives is best done in financial terms; that is, expressing the amount of ongoing revenue protected and the amount of revenue lost during recovery from customer visible incidents. Investments in SRE can be justified by a growing revenue that needs to be protected and a reduction in the revenue projected to be lost during recovery from incidents.

Moreover, the value can be expressed as the ability to know the current level of reliability of the system in production in terms of, for instance, SLA adherence. Cumulative SLA error budget depletion dashboards are a good way to put executives into a position to experience the reliability levels in units accessible to them. The financial consequences of breaking the SLAs will be known to most of the executives because it was they who contractually negotiated the consequences with the partners. Thus, the SLAs' error budget depletion trends and projections of whether the error budgets will be depleted to zero prematurely make the value of SRE tangible to executives.

12.9 A New Role: SRE

Depending on the model chosen from the "who builds it, who runs it?" spectrum, a new role for the people practicing SRE may well need to be introduced in the product delivery organization. The need to create the new role needs to be clear and transparent to motivate and catalyze the introduction. Thus, the first question to answer about the new role is why it is needed. This is the subject of the next section.

12.9.1 Why Is a New Role Needed?

The answer to the question of why a new role is needed can be approached by looking at a general definition of role as a concept. According to Britannica: "A role is a comprehensive pattern of behaviour that is socially recognized, providing a means of identifying and placing an individual in a society."[22]

Projecting this onto the SRE space, it can be said that an envisioned SRE role is a comprehensive pattern of behavior and reliability practice that is socially recognized in the product delivery organization, providing a means of identifying people who do operations. That is, the roots of the need to introduce a new SRE role lie in the identification and social recognition of the people who do operations according to the SRE principles and practices.

As discussed in Section 12.2, *Who Builds It, Who Runs It?*, and Section 12.7, *Team Topologies*, there are many different ways to follow the SRE principles and practice SRE in a product delivery organization. They are summarized in Table 12.22.

---

22. Britannica, The Editors of Encyclopaedia. 2020. "role." *Encyclopedia Britannica*, March 3, 2020. Accessed May 2, 2022. https://www.britannica.com/topic/role.

Table 12.22 *Ways to Practice SRE*

	You Build It, You Run It	You Build It, You and SRE Run It	You Build It, SRE Run It
Development Organization Reporting Line for SREs	A. SRE practiced by developers on rotation B. Dedicated people practicing SRE C. SRE practiced by developers on rotation + Dedicated people practicing SRE	SRE practiced by developers on rotation + Dedicated people practicing SRE	Dedicated people practicing SRE
Operations Organization Reporting Line for SREs	Dedicated people practicing SRE (SRE infrastructure)	SRE practiced by developers on rotation + Dedicated people practicing SRE	Dedicated people practicing SRE
SRE Organization Reporting Line for SREs	-	SRE practiced by developers on rotation + Dedicated people practicing SRE	Dedicated people practicing SRE

With the "you build it, you run it" model, several options of practicing SRE exist. With option A, the developers practice SRE on rotation. With option B, dedicated people in the development teams practice SRE full time. With option C, the developers practice SRE on rotation and additionally there are dedicated people in the development teams practicing SRE.

In all the other cells in Table 12.22, there are dedicated people practicing SRE. In order to identify and socially recognize them in the product delivery organization, an SRE role needs to be introduced.

The only option where there are no dedicated people practicing SRE permanently is option A of the "you build it, you run it" model with developers performing SRE activities on rotation. With this option, it may be possible to do without an SRE role. In this case, the SRE activities are just a set of operational responsibilities fulfilled by the developers. The responsibilities need to be clearly written down to align everyone's expectations and create accountability.

The decision not to introduce an SRE role may stem from the desire to stay away from the idea of "SRE as a cargo cult." The cult is well-delineated from the valuable SRE practice in "Aim for Operability, Not SRE as a Cult."[23] It encourages focusing on operability and using the SRE principles as a philosophy as opposed to being focused on SRE teams and certifications as a panacea to solve problems in operations.

This discussion is similar to that of a DevOps role. Should a DevOps role be introduced or should DevOps be considered an overarching philosophy to follow? By looking at the job advertisements on Indeed.com, thousands of companies are actively looking for thousands of DevOps engineers and even more DevOps managers. Further research on Indeed reveals that at

---

23. Smith, Steve. 2020. "Aim for Operability, Not SRE as a Cult." *Steve Smith On Tech* (blog). October 20, 2020. https://www.stevesmith.tech/blog/aim-for-operability-not-sre-as-a-cult.

the time of this writing, there are more job ads for SRE engineers than for DevOps engineers. However, the numbers are comparable, differing in the range of 25%. In terms of job ads for SRE managers versus DevOps managers, there is an entire order of magnitude more job ads looking for DevOps managers than for SRE managers.

This data might be interpreted in such a way that in the software industry at large, the SRE role is considered more of an engineering role but not necessarily a managerial role. The DevOps role, on the other hand, is considered in both lights: engineering and managerial. What can be inferred from the data is that there is room for confusion in role definitions. The confusion is fueled by many online publications, including the blog post "Isn't SRE Just DevOps?"[24] which states "SRE is a job title. DevOps isn't."

Why are so many companies looking for DevOps engineers and DevOps managers, then? This is also where the cargo cult begins. If there are so many companies looking for SRE engineers and DevOps managers, is that what should be followed in your own organization?

The answer is that every organization needs to consciously define its own naming, meaning, responsibilities, and accountability for each of its roles. Moreover, the overall set of roles in a domain needs to be coherent and transparent and offer progression paths among them. This is where the involvement of HR professionals is beneficial. They can help design a set of roles that cover software operations in line with sound organizational development practices.

To be sure, the general industry trends will absolutely need to be considered. At the same time, following the cargo cult blindly needs to be avoided. The best engineers might be able to recognize based on the job ads alone whether an organization is following SRE as a philosophy or as a cargo cult. It will become apparent in the first interview. The best engineers look for work substance and not for job titles. They will continue their job search until they find a company that puts serious meaning into the SRE role.

> **From the Trenches:** It is beneficial to introduce the SRE role in any model from the "who builds it, who runs it?" spectrum in order to give SRE activities an umbrella in the organization that can be recognized on par with other activities, such as architecture and development. Moreover, dedicated role definitions and dedicated people assigned to the roles may be required from the regulatory compliance point of view.

The introduction of an SRE role in a conscious manner with a clear definition of responsibilities, skills, and accountability in the context of a given organization has the following benefits:

- Identification and social recognition of people practicing SRE in the product delivery organization
- Recognition of different ways SRE can be practiced:
  ○ By developers on rotation
  ○ Full-time dedicated SRE practice

---

24. Müeller, Michael. 2021. "Isn't SRE Just DevOps?" *Container Solutions* (blog). January 10, 2021. https://blog.container-solutions.com/isnt-sre-just-devops-maturity-matrix.

○ Full-time dedicated SRE infrastructure implementation and operations

- Fulfillment of regulatory compliance requirements in terms of roles and responsibilities in operations

- Enablement of a new SRE career path

Now that the need for a new SRE role has been clarified, the next step is to detail the role. This can be done by considering four aspects: role definition, role naming, role assignment, and role fulfillment. These are explored in the next sections.

12.9.2 Role Definition

In terms of defining an SRE role, the *Site Reliability Workbook*[1] provides a great graph that shows the levels and phases of a Google SRE team engagement during the lifetime of a service (see Figure 12.20).

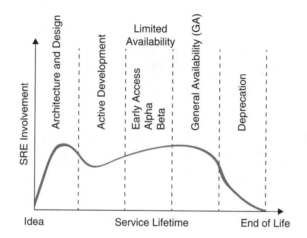

Figure 12.20 *SRE team engagement phases during service lifetime*

The graph illustrates very well that SREs need to be involved in all technical phases of the service lifecycle. Additionally, it can be said that SRE involvement is also beneficial before the technical phases begin. That is, when a service is being conceived by the product owners in the ideation and evaluation phases, SRE involvement can provide valuable insights into reliability before decisions are made to further invest in technical implementation.

The design thinking phases, Empathize → Define → Ideate → Prototype → Test, can benefit from the involvement of an SRE. Specifically, input into the prototype and test phases can be augmented with reliability thinking in late iterations. The goal of late test iterations is to harden assumptions about the envisioned product being desirable, fulfilling a burning need, and confirming the conditions of product use, user thinking, behavior, and feeling. The hardening can be done in more depth if reliability aspects are explicitly included.

To be sure, the system architecture does not need to be known at this stage. Rather, the reliability aspects that can be discussed here include the most critical user workflows, the most critical reliability aspects of the workflows, and the frequency of workflow execution. In fact, involving SREs at this stage is about starting the discussion about the SLI and SLO definitions much earlier than usual.

Typically, the teams have SLI/SLO discussions for the first time somewhere around the active development phase shown in Figure 12.20. Doing so is generally great. However, it is even better to discuss and test reliability assumptions before the architecture and design phase begins. This is because feedback on the assumptions comes earlier and can be used as input for creating the appropriate architecture and software design.

The overall involvement of SREs starting from the design thinking phase over the technical implementation phase all the way to operations is shown in Figure 12.21.

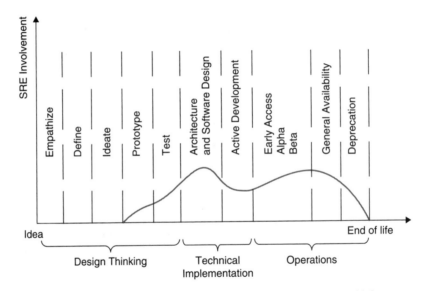

Figure 12.21 *SRE team engagement phases from design thinking to end of life*

In the empathize, define, and ideate design thinking phases, SRE involvement is not needed. In the prototype and test phases, SRE involvement grows. The involvement culminates in the architecture and software design phase. It further drops during the active development phase, and rises again toward the alpha and beta release phases. Finally, the involvement drops a bit in the general availability phase, and then subsides during service deprecation.

The majority of the phases in Figure 12.21 do not run linearly. They are depicted on an axis only for the purpose of illustrating the SRE involvement levels. In reality, the design thinking and technical implementation phases run in a nonlinear, iterative, incremental, and flexible manner. Moreover, different features being worked on in parallel are typically in different phases of the service lifecycle depicted in the figure. The operations phase is the most linear, but it is characterized by a constant parallel inflow of new features and existing feature updates, making it very dynamic.

In terms of responsibilities and skills, an SRE role can generically be defined as shown in Table 12.23.

Table 12.23 *SRE Role Responsibilities and Skills*

Responsibilities	Skills
• Maintain system availability	• Software engineering
• Maintain system scalability	• Software operations
• Define and agree on SLIs and SLOs	• Debugging and troubleshooting
• Support SLA negotiations	• Distributed systems
• Define and agree on error budget policy	• Large-scale, high-traffic systems
• Make error budget–based decisions	• Infrastructure as code
• Set up monitoring	• Being driven and self-motivated
• Set up alerting	• Blameless continuous improvement
• On call during business hours	• Emotional intelligence
• On call outside of business hours	• Ability to perform well on call
• Maintain runbooks	• Technical communication
• Take part in postmortems	• Stakeholder communication
• Enhance SRE infrastructure	• Technical documentation
• Take part in chaos engineering	• Ability to work well in short-lived incident response teams
• Run disaster recovery drills	
• Review service implementations	
• Review architectures and designs	
• Improve release procedures	
• Support team onboarding onto SRE	
• Participate in SRE CoP	
• Contribute to technical road map	
• Support first level support	
• Support user testing	
• Support requirement engineering	

In a concrete SRE role definition for a given product delivery organization, the technical stack used should play a prominent role. However, when hiring internal and external people for the SRE role, the skills to command the given technical stack should be considered a plus but not necessarily a must-have. It is the general skill set, aptitude, and motivation for SRE that are hard to find on the market. Given these, a new technical stack can be learned rather quickly by a suitable individual.

The role definition in Table 12.23 assumed the role name "SRE" for simplicity purposes. Role naming, however, should be a conscious decision made in the product delivery organization. This is the subject of the next section.

12.9.3 Role Naming

Several role names can be found in the industry describing people practicing SRE to an acceptable extent. These are summarized in Table 12.24.

Table 12.24 *Current Industry Roles Practicing SRE*

Role Name	Explanation
Site reliability engineer (SRE)	The original role name introduced and used by Google. Most commonly used role name for people practicing SRE.
DevOps engineer	A common role name for the people doing operations, implementing deployment infrastructure, and performing deployments. The name originates from the DevOps movement.
Production engineer	The role name used at Facebook by the people running the services dedicatedly using the "you build it, you and SRE run it" model.
Reliability engineer	Similar to site reliability engineer (SRE)
Cloud site reliability engineer	Same as site reliability engineer (SRE)

Now, if an SRE transformation has been executed in its pure sense in a given product delivery organization, it should be natural to name the new role "SRE." However, if the transformation in operations has not been explicitly driven as "an SRE transformation," there is more freedom to think about role naming. The examples in Table 12.24 might provide some ideas in that regard.

In general, as discussed in Section 12.9.1, *Why Is a New Role Needed?*, avoiding the cargo cult when introducing and naming new roles is important. A product delivery organization must have genuine reasons for naming a role. Delving deeper into SRE work specialization, the role names in Table 12.25 might additionally be taken into consideration.

Table 12.25 *SRE Role Names*

Role Name	Explanation
Site reliability infrastructure product owner (SRE Infrastructure PO)	The SRE infrastructure can and should be developed as a full-fledged product using product thinking. To do so, a dedicated product owner is required.
Site reliability infrastructure engineer (Infrastructure SRE)	Software engineers implementing the SRE infrastructure used by the development teams can have a dedicated role name. This is justified because the work they do differs from that of an SRE using the infrastructure in a development team.
Site reliability platform engineer (Platform SRE)	In a larger product delivery organization, an explicit domain platform may be developed. People working on the domain platform may face unique operational challenges. Therefore, SREs working on the platform development teams may deserve an explicit role name.
Site reliability application engineer (Application SRE)	In a larger product delivery organization, an explicit domain platform may be available that is used by customer-facing applications. People doing SRE on the applications development teams may be given a dedicated role name due to unique SRE challenges with the applications.

It is worth noting that there are other established role names in operations, such as production support engineer, production systems engineer, technical support engineer, IT administrator, IT support administrator, and IT systems administrator. These roles typically do not practice SRE. Therefore, they should not be taken into consideration when brainstorming potential SRE role names.

Role naming should not be dismissed as a minor aspect of new role introduction. This is because people associate meanings with role names. The association happens based on people's backgrounds, culture, geography, local job market, work experience, and company. Culture in particular might play a significant role in these associations. In today's multicultural workplace, this is even more the case.

Culture may also determine the attitude people have toward roles in general and role names in particular. Some cultures regard roles highly as a statement of status. Other cultures do not place that much emphasis on roles, let alone role names. In any case, role names appear on people's CVs and are shown publicly in professional social networks such as LinkedIn. This makes role names significant, regardless of culture.

Furthermore, especially in the SRE arena, people with the job title "SRE" are notoriously remunerated better than other role names in operations. This aspect will also be significant to everyone regardless of culture.

For these reasons, naming the SRE role(s) should be given appropriate consideration within the culture mix of a particular product delivery organization. Naming the SRE role(s) should not be dismissed as something insignificant that bears no consequences.

In the remaining chapters of the book, we will use the role name "SRE" for simplicity. This should not influence the decision to name the role differently in a given product delivery organization.

12.9.4 Role Assignment

It is notorious in the industry that if SRE is followed as a cult, occasionally IT administrators might get a different job title and a small pay raise. Otherwise, nothing would change.

As mentioned in Section 12.4.6, *SRE Team Head Count and Budget*, this is evidenced well in "Aim for Operability, Not SRE as a Cult":[22] "In 2020, I learned of a sysadmin team that were rebranded as an SRE team, received a small pay increase … and then carried on doing the same sysadmin work. This is for decision makers who have been told SRE will solve their IT problems…"

To counter this kind of situation, assignment of the SRE role to a person should be done using a properly defined procedure. For existing employees in the product delivery organization transitioning to SRE from another discipline, including IT administration, there needs to be a transition path. These employees need to begin practicing SRE before they are assigned the SRE role. This way, it can be evaluated whether the person can indeed follow the SRE principles and practices. SRE role assignment becomes a culmination in recognition that the person has demonstrated the ability to practice SRE appropriately.

This does not mean the person needs to master the SRE practice perfectly and stand the test of time before being assigned the SRE role. What it does mean, though, is that the person needs to show aptitude for becoming a good SRE by applying the SRE principles and practices on real products in real life for an appropriately short amount of time.

SRE role assignment for people outside the product delivery organization, both from inside and outside the company, will be done based on a job interview. Once the hiring decision has been made, the interviewee can join the product delivery organization with the SRE role. Therefore, the job interview needs to enable an effective and efficient assessment of the interviewee's aptitude for the SRE role within the product delivery organization.

Multistage interviews for SRE roles are the norm in the industry. In an initial interview, often conducted online, the interviewee presents their background, previous and current work assignments, motivation to join the product delivery organization, and career aspirations. If the initial interview goes well, the second interview is conducted to assess the interviewee's technical abilities, on-call attitude, and capacity to work in a team in different circumstances.

The second interview may and should contain hands-on coding exercises. Technical interview platforms such as HackerRank[25] offer great possibilities for employers to set up coding exercises relevant to their technical stack. The platform offers a wide variety of predefined exercises to choose from. Additionally, custom exercises can be created as well.

The interviewees can take the coding exercises on the platform itself from within their web browser. The exercises can be set up in a time-bound manner. To prepare for an interview, the interviewees can use the HackerRank platform to practice using predefined exercises categorized by role, technical stack, time range, and so on.

Evaluation of the coding exercise on the HackerRank platform can and should be done in a code review manner. The interviewee can talk the interviewers through the written code and explain software design choices, difficulties encountered, and solutions found. The platform allows the interviewers to go back in time and see how the interviewee was writing the code. A discussion about this can deepen the understanding of the interviewee's thinking process.

All these features contribute a great deal to the interviewer's ability to assess the interviewee's technical capabilities from different angles. Once the second interview has been successfully passed, a third interview often involves conversations with future team members. The aim of the third interview is to assess the interviewee's suitability to work well in the team. Every team member gets an opportunity to talk to the candidate and make up their mind about whether hiring the candidate would enrich the team.

Only after all three interviews have been successfully passed is the candidate extended an offer to join the product delivery organization as an SRE. This kind of rigorous assessment process is required to ensure that the best candidates get hired, and thereby make a great contribution to the reliability of products.

12.9.5 Role Fulfillment

As discussed in Section 12.2, *Who Builds It, Who Runs It?*, there are different ways to fulfill the SRE role. They generally fall into three categories:

- Dedicated SRE for services (full time)

- SRE on rotation for services (full time when on call, off-duty when not on call)

- Dedicated SRE for SRE infrastructure (full time)

---

25. HackerRank. 2019. "HackerRank." September 13, 2019. https://www.hackerrank.com.

A summary of the SRE role fulfillment options is shown in Table 12.26.

Table 12.26 *SRE Role Fulfillment Options*

	You Build It, You Run It	You Build It, You and SRE Run It	You Build It, SRE Run It
Development Organization Reporting Line for SREs	• SRE role on rotation • Dedicated SRE role • SRE role on rotation + Dedicated SRE role	SRE role on rotation + Dedicated SRE role	Dedicated SRE role
Operations Organization Reporting Line for SREs	Dedicated SRE role (SRE infrastructure)	SRE role on rotation + Dedicated SRE role	Dedicated SRE role
SRE Organization Reporting Line for SREs	-	SRE role on rotation + Dedicated SRE role	Dedicated SRE role

The nature of the SRE role on rotation is that developers perform the SRE activities full time when on call and are off-duty when not on call. Overall, this setup caters to the developers practicing on call in a part-time manner. Interestingly, when developers apply the SRE principles when they are not on call developing code, they implicitly still practice SRE.

Outside of business hours, SRE role fulfillment needs to be enabled by HR appropriately. Being on call outside of business hours means being available to work after business hours. Even if there is no incident while being on call outside of business hours, the readiness to be on standby needs to be compensated. If there are incidents while being on call outside of business hours, the work needs to be compensated appropriately.

The compensation can be monetary, additional time off, or a combination thereof. The following compensation building blocks could be considered:

- Higher base salaries for the people on call outside of business hours

- Payment for being on standby outside of business hours

- Payments for working on incidents outside of business hours

- Time off following an on-call shift on standby outside of business hours

- Time off following an on-call shift resolving incidents outside of business hours

- Payment for keeping the services within error budgets

An effective outside of business hours on-call compensation model is critical to keep SREs who do this type of work motivated and to ensure the service reliability required by the SLAs. Moreover, in some countries there are labor laws and regulations that have to be considered when designing an out-of-hours on-call compensation model.

In the cross-border teams that are common today in the IT industry, people from several countries can easily find themselves working as a virtual team resolving an incident in a data center located in yet another country. In this setting, all the local labor laws and regulations need to be considered so that every person on the virtual team is compensated appropriately based on their country of residence. That said, though, because the people are working together for the same company resolving the same incident, they need to know that the company's out-of-hours compensation model honors the work equally, irrespective of the SRE's country of residency.

That is, the locally perceived value of the out-of-hours compensation needs to be more or less the same regardless of where the SREs live. The value can be brought about through different means. In some countries, monetary compensation might be valued more than time off. In other countries, equal value might be placed on both monetary and time-off compensation. In yet other countries, time off might be valued more than additional payments for out-of-hours on-call work. It is the job of HR to find out the local preferences and set up the compensation policies accordingly.

An agreed, a documented and enacted out-of-hours on-call compensation model is required in order to discuss the matter in a binding way during job interviews. It is equally necessary for internal employees transitioning to SRE to know how they will be compensated.

> **From the Trenches:** When a product delivery organization is in the process of introducing out-of-hours on call for the first time, there may be a lengthy gray period during which the out-of-hours on-call work is required but not yet properly compensated. While discussions about the compensation are ongoing, the actual out-of-hours on-call work is required to keep the SLAs.
>
> In this context, it is common in larger product delivery organizations to find long-term SREs who are willing to be on call outside of business hours without a clearly agreed and enacted compensation model. The managers of the SREs may have legal and other difficulties compensating the effort with monetary payments. However, compensating the effort with additional time off in lieu of additional payments typically can be enabled immediately.
>
> Doing so is highly recommended. Leaving the SREs to resolve incidents outside of business hours without any extra compensation will snowball into burnout, resentfulness, and attempts to find another job elsewhere.

12.10 SRE Career Path

With the introduction of SRE as a new role in the product delivery organization, an entirely new career path is introduced. The career path needs to be designed as a series of progressive steps. An SRE can take these steps to grow the following aspects of their career:

- Scope of work

- Responsibility

- Influence

- Accountability

- Compensation

12.10.1 SRE Role Progressions

Career paths are often designed as a three-step progression. This can be applied to the SRE career path as well. Introduction of a junior, senior, and principal SRE is an appropriate progression that will be suitable for the majority of product delivery organizations. For example, the career path shown in Table 12.27 could be offered for the junior, senior, and principal SREs.

Table 12.27 *Example SRE Career Path*

	Junior SRE	Senior SRE	Principal SRE
Scope of Work	• Drive the agreements on SLIs, SLOs • Drive the agreements on error budget policy • Set up monitoring • Set up alerting • Go on call • Implement reliability improvements	• Drive the agreements on SLIs, SLOs • Drive the agreements on error budget policies • Set up monitoring • Set up alerting • Go on call • Implement reliability improvements • Drive SRE CoP • Review architecture • Review design • Shape tech road map • Support user testing • Support SRE hiring	• Drive the agreements on SLIs, SLOs • Drive the agreements on error budget policies • Negotiate SLAs • Go on call • Drive SRE hiring • Drive tech road map • Drive new practices • Support SRE budgeting • Coach other SREs • Mentor other SREs • Evolve SRE discipline • SRE consulting • SRE advisory • SRE transformation • Represent reliability within and across business lines
Responsibility	Reliability of services owned by a single development team	Reliability of services from a domain	Reliability of services owned by a business line. Support new revenue generation with SRE services.
Influence	Developers on the team and the operations team supporting the team	All development teams belonging to the domain and the operations team supporting the domain	All development and operations teams belonging to the business line. Teams being consulted and advised.

	Junior SRE	Senior SRE	Principal SRE
Accountability	Keep the SLO and SLA error budgets for the team services.	Keep the SLO and SLA error budgets for the domain services.	Keep the SLA error budgets for the business line services. Participate in SRE consulting and advisory projects.
Relevant Work Experience	> 1 year	> 3 years	> 5 years

A junior SRE is responsible for the reliability of services owned by a single development team. They drive the agreements on SLIs, SLOs, and the error budget policy for the team with all the necessary stakeholders. Further, a junior SRE sets up monitoring and alerting and goes on call for the services owned by the team. They implement reliability improvements in the services themselves and the tools in use. A junior SRE is held accountable for the services staying within their SLO and SLA error budgets by error budget period. They are remunerated with a base SRE salary and agreed on-call compensation. To be considered for a junior SRE position, the person needs to have at least one year of relevant work experience. The relevant work experience might be in software engineering, automation, or operations.

A senior SRE has more responsibility. They are responsible for the reliability of services in an entire domain. A domain typically corresponds to an organizational unit within the product delivery organization. For instance, all the applications implementing food dispatching services in a food delivery organization would represent a food dispatching domain a senior SRE can be responsible for. A senior SRE has all the responsibilities of a junior SRE plus additional work scope. The additional scope consists of driving the SRE community of practice (CoP); reviewing the architecture, design, and implementation of services within the domain; shaping the technical road map; supporting user testing activities from design thinking; and hiring junior SREs.

A senior SRE is held accountable for the services from the domain staying within their SLO and SLA error budgets. To be considered for a senior SRE position at least three years of relevant work experience may be required. The experience should be in a variety of domains, such as software engineering, operations, and SRE.

Finally, a principal SRE is responsible for the reliability of services in an entire business line. A business line is an organizational unit with its own profit and loss (P&L) statement. In other words, it is an own business within an enterprise or the entire business in the case of a smaller company. Like the junior and senior SREs, the principal SRE agrees to SLIs, SLOs, and error budget policies as well as goes on call for some services in the business line. Apart from that, there are distinct new responsibilitiies for the principal SRE.

These responsibilities include negotiating SLAs with customers and partners, driving SRE hiring, and driving new practices such as chaos engineering, disaster recovery drills, and AI ops. Furthermore, a principal SRE is expected to explore new revenue potential with SRE services, such as SRE consulting, advisory, and transformation. These can be offered both internally and externally.

Moreover, the principal SRE is expected to mentor and coach other SREs in the company across all existing product delivery organizations. Mentoring SREs means sharing knowledge and experience. Coaching SREs means guiding them on their way to defined professional goals.

Finally, the principal SRE represents reliability as a discipline within and across the business lines. Active participation in relevant internal and external events and conferences and maintaining a professional network of peers in different companies is expected from a principal SRE. Leveraging the network of peers, the principal SRE is expected to evolve SRE as a discipline, devising and incubating novel concepts and their implementation.

The principal SRE is held accountable for keeping the SLA error budgets for all services owned by the business line. Moreover, the accountability extends to participation in the SRE consulting and advisory projects that explore new revenue potential. To be considered for a principal SRE position, at least five years of relevant work experience is required. The relevant work experience in this case is in SRE, software engineering, automation, operations, team management, engineering management, technical consulting, advisory, and innovation management.

In terms of remuneration of the on-call duty for all the three SRE roles, an aspect of social justice needs to be taken into account in an appropriate way. For instance, single parents agreeing to be on call outside of business hours may be compensated differently than others. Likewise, people with several children of preschool age might be compensated differently than others.

The definitions of the junior, senior, and principal SRE roles provide a transparent path for people to grow their SRE skills and capabilities. Additionally, they enable hiring managers and HR to create appropriate job requisitions and assess candidates' skills for suitability to fulfill one of the roles. Performance reviews of existing SREs can be done using the SRE role definitions as well.

There is another important aspect that gets covered with the definition of the SRE role profiles. It is that of comparison between the traditional roles in operations and the new SRE roles. The traditional roles in operations are IT administrator, support engineer, IT systems support engineer, and technical support engineer, among others. With the introduction of SRE and SRE roles, a growing tension is experienced by the people in the traditional roles in operations about how they should and would be compared to as well as fit in the brave new world of SRE.

With the definition of the SRE role profiles, the comparison becomes easy to do. Everyone in a traditional operations role can assess their skills, abilities, and current work responsibilities against those of a junior, senior, or principal SRE. The same applies to the comparison of compensation. The SRE role profiles should make it evident why SREs can command higher wages than traditional operations roles such as IT administrator.

12.10.2 SRE Role Transitions

In addition to role definitions, the definition of an SRE career path needs to include the progression criteria between the junior, senior, and principal SRE roles. That is, it needs to be clear to a junior SRE what they would need to do to attain a senior SRE role. Likewise, it needs to be clear to a senior SRE what they would need to do to attain a principal SRE role.

The role progressions should be designed using a set of criteria. As an example, in order to transition from a junior to a senior and from a senior to a principal SRE, the following would need to apply.

- The SRE has performed for more than six months some of the work usually performed by the SRE role sought to be attained.

- The SRE has been able to influence people beyond their current immediate scope of responsibility.

- The SRE's communication and interpersonal skills allow for connection with a wide range of people and roles on the technical topics presented appropriately case by case.

- The SRE's work feedback in the last six months by their line manager and others demonstrates potential for assuming more responsibility and accountability.

- The SRE is actively seeking to assume more responsibility and accountability.

- In order to attain the principal SRE role: The SRE has served as a mentor to at least one SRE who provided generally positive feedback about the mentorship.

HR needs to make these transition criteria transparent to the SREs. This way, the SREs have a clear preparation plan to drive their own promotions: The SRE role definitions and the transition criteria between them are clear.

In addition to the transition between the SRE roles, a transition from another professional discipline to SRE needs to be designed as well. In this context, it is desirable to design typical transition paths to SRE from the disciplines where potential candidates would be coming from. Specifically, a transition path from traditional operations to SRE and from development to SRE can be designed to pave the way for the people who want to make the switch.

Paving the way to SRE can be facilitated using training, development, coaching, and mentorship programs. The mentorship program can, for example, be organized in such a way that HR serves as an intermediary between the people seeking SRE mentorship and the SREs willing to be mentors.

In terms of head count and budget planning, the hiring managers and HR need to have some orientation as to the number of SREs and which roles might be required in a product delivery organization in a given time frame. Table 12.28 provides an indication in this regard.

Table 12.28 *SRE Head Count by Role*

	Junior SRE	Senior SRE	Principal SRE
Number of People	Roughly corresponds to the number of development teams	Roughly corresponds to the number of product domains	Roughly corresponds to the number of product lines

With these indicative numbers of how many SREs in a particular role would be needed, HR can work to put succession plans in place in order to quickly fill critical open positions internally. The indicative numbers in Table 12.28 can also be used by the hiring managers to request the corresponding budget.

In summary, the introduction of a well-thought-out SRE career path has many advantages. People who join the product delivery organization have a clear promotion path in front of them that they can use to grow their SRE careers. This is beneficial to people joining from outside and inside the product delivery organization.

In fact, the availability of an SRE career path may be a decisive factor for an individual to join the organization. This is especially true in a job market where only a few companies offer SRE career paths because SRE as a discipline is by and large still very young. The SRE career path thus helps a company differentiate itself from other companies, attract young SREs, retain key existing SREs, and decrease turnover rates.

12.10.3 Cultural Importance

The introduction of a new SRE career path with several SRE roles represents a big new opportunity for many people to develop their careers in a product delivery organization. Depending on the culture, assuming a new role may bear a lot of social status value. This needs to be kept in mind when introducing a new SRE career path in a given country.

In some cultures, being assigned a role provides a sense of pride to the bearer and at the same time a sense of subordinacy to others when it comes to discussing and making decisions about the topics associated with the role. In discussions, the benefit of the doubt will be given to the role bearer. Moreover, discussions in which the role bearer is present will go differently than when the role bearer is absent. This is because the people who do not bear the role have such reverence for someone with the role that they do not express themselves freely in professional conversations on the subject matter.

Hierarchical cultures like this are common. Given the international nature of today's software delivery teams, there is a high likelihood that people originating from a hierarchical culture will be part of the team. The opposite holds true as well. There is a high likelihood that people from a less hierarchical culture will be part of the team.

In a less hierarchical culture, the role bearer is not met with any kind of reverence for the fact that they bear the role. They are part of the team like everyone else who does not have the role. Everyone including the role bearer has to prove their SRE knowledge based on sound decision-making, deductive derivation, and appropriate behavior following the SRE practice. In discussions, people express themselves regardless of whether the role bearer is present.

Hierarchical cultures are common in Asia. Less hierarchical cultures are common in Northern Europe. Do people from a hierarchical and less hierarchical culture hit it off immediately in the workplace and understand each other easily? Not really. Does communicating using online video calls or video chat help with cross-cultural understanding? Not really.

It follows that cross-cultural understanding needs to be developed before teams consisting of people from different cultures can work together well. It is the responsibility of HR to point out this aspect to the employees and offer training to understand the cultures of the people on the teams. Notably, The Culture Map[26] by Erin Meyer provides good background information on culture. It breaks down cultures into how people communicate, evaluate work, persuade each other, lead teams, decide, trust, disagree, and schedule time.

HR, line managers, and SRE coaches need to highlight the topic of cross-cultural understanding of roles as being important to all SREs. This is necessary to cultivate trustful working relationships between SREs and others. Trust is absolutely necessary for SRE work, especially in the context of stressful on-call work both during and outside of business hours.

---

26. Meyer, Erin. 2016. *The Culture Map: Decoding How People Think, Lead, and Get Things Done Across Cultures*. New York: PublicAffairs.

12.11 Communicating the Chosen Model

Once a model from the "who builds it, who runs it?" spectrum has been chosen and the reporting line for SREs has been decided, the decision needs to be communicated. The communication needs to be staged appropriately. This is shown in Figure 12.22. First, communication about the future organizational SRE setup needs to take place within the product delivery organization's leadership team.

The leadership team debated the chosen model before. Now is the time to reiterate the final decision to ensure one final time that everyone is on the same page. After all, it is the leadership team as a whole that has accountability for the decision. The decision dictates the allocation of future funds to SRE, which in turn means diverting some funds from other areas. This needs to be transparent to and agreed by the product delivery organization's leadership team.

The SRE coaches should try to sense the level of agreement within the leadership team. In case of a very weak agreement, the SRE coaches should advise the team not to proceed with further communication. Instead, the decision should be brought for further debate until a stronger agreement can be reached.

Once a strong agreement on the chosen organizational SRE setup has been reached in the leadership team, further communication to the current and future line managers of the people practicing SRE should take place. This can be done in a single short meeting. Once the line managers know about the change, the current line managers of the people practicing SRE should let them know about the upcoming organizational change in short, private conversations.

Next, a bigger communication to the people practicing SRE, as well as their current and future line managers, should be made in a dedicated meeting, in the form of a presentation that reveals the business goals supported by SRE, the reasons for the chosen SRE setup in the organization, what it would mean for everyone in the meeting, and how the rollout of the setup is planned to unfold.

The presentation should be held by the head of the product delivery organization or a C-level executive. After the presentation, the presenter, other members of the leadership team, HR, and the SRE coaches should make themselves available to answer questions posed by the audience. People will ask questions regarding their careers, transition plans, remuneration, packages, and so on.

Soon after the meeting, the presentation should be repeated in a more condensed form in an all-employee meeting of the product delivery organization. This way, there is a small amount of time between the new SRE model announcements to the people affected by the change and to others in the product delivery organization. This keeps to a minimum the grapevine rumors that will inevitably spread among employees.

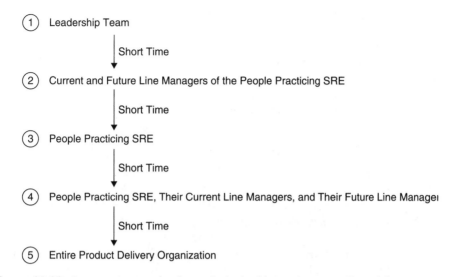

① Leadership Team

　　　│ Short Time
　　　▼

② Current and Future Line Managers of the People Practicing SRE

　　　│ Short Time
　　　▼

③ People Practicing SRE

　　　│ Short Time
　　　▼

④ People Practicing SRE, Their Current Line Managers, and Their Future Line Manager

　　　│ Short Time
　　　▼

⑤ Entire Product Delivery Organization

Figure 12.22 *Communicating the chosen "who builds it, who runs it?" model*

The goal of staging the communication is to bring the entire product delivery organization on the same page in an ordered manner in the shortest amount of time. In all likelihood, the chosen SRE model will be similar to the product delivery organization's current SRE practice anyway. Organizationally, the line managers of SREs may change. This is the area in which the most change can be expected.

In any case, the introduction of the chosen model and line management changes should not be done in a flashy manner. How to introduce these changes more organically is the subject of the next section.

12.12 Introducing the Chosen Model

The introduction of the chosen model depends on the changes from the status quo that may have to be done in order to achieve the agreed target state for the product delivery organization. The changes can happen along four dimensions:

1. Changes of the model on the "who builds it, who runs it?" spectrum

2. Organization changes

3. Reporting structure changes

4. Role changes

The change options on the "who builds it, who runs it?" spectrum were discussed in depth in Section 12.8.1, *Model Transformation Options*. The changes of organization, reporting structure, and roles are discussed in the following sections.

12.12.1 Organization Changes

In terms of the target reporting structure changes for SREs, several transition options are possible for moving people between the development, operations, and SRE organizations. The options are illustrated in Figure 12.23.

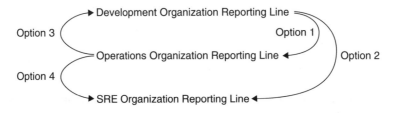

Figure 12.23 *Reporting structure change options*

If the people practicing SRE currently report within the development organization, their reporting may change to be within the operations organization (option 1) or the newly created SRE organization (option 2). If the people practicing SRE currently report within the operations organization, their reporting may change to be within the development organization (option 3) or the newly created SRE organization (option 4).

The new SRE organization needs to be properly established. To kick off the process, the head of the SRE organization needs to run an all-employee meeting laying down the foundations. Following is a sample agenda:

- Introduce themselves
- Introduce the vision for the SRE organization
- Introduce the teams within the SRE organizations
- Introduce the working mode with other departments
- Introduce the freedom and responsibility split for the teams
- Introduce the organizational KPIs for the SRE organization
- Introduce the roles in the SRE organization
- Introduce people in the key roles
- Introduce the SRE career path
- Introduce the envisioned head count of the organization
- Introduce the open positions by team
- Encourage everyone to suggest suitable people they know for the open positions
- Introduce the way how the key people can be contacted by anyone
- Introduce standing meetings:

    ○ All-employee meeting

    ○ SRE CoP

- Introduce SRE publications:

    ○ Blog

    ○ Availability newsletter

- Introduce immediate new initiatives:

    ○ Set the purpose

    ○ Appoint the initiative leader

    ○ Define success hypotheses

- Talk about the envisioned on-call practice

- Talk about docking the SRE onto the regulatory compliance

- Introduce the employee performance review process

- Introduce the key supporting people from other departments:

    ○ HR

    ○ Procurement

    ○ Workers council

    ○ Legal

- List open topics

- Open the stage for questions and answer all of them thoroughly

The first all-employee meeting should take place soon after the SRE organization has been introduced to everyone in the product delivery organization. The goal of the meeting is to start building a connection and, most importantly, trust between the head of the SRE organization and the employees. In order to run the meeting in an effective manner with the content outlined in the preceding list, the head of the SRE organization needs to start preparing well ahead of time. Timely preparation is required in order to allow for sufficient time to agree to the content with the necessary stakeholders across departments.

The SRE coaches working closely with all the teams can gauge the pulse, assess the mood, and listen to the concerns of the team members in light of the upcoming changes. Working closely with the head of the SRE organization, the coaches can let them know the concerns raised by the teams and discuss ways to address them. Moreover, the SRE coaches can help the head of the SRE organization adjust the strategy and tactics accordingly.

Naturally, when the head of the SRE organization takes over the reins, the connection between them and the employees will not be that strong. Through an open dialogue with the employees, honest reactions to feedback, and respective ongoing strategy and tactics adaptations, the connection can be strengthened and turned into a trustful relationship. This must be the primary goal of the head of the SRE organization from the beginning.

This is because with trust, it becomes much easier to master decision-making, execution, adherence to policies, and so on in an organization. Time-wasting processes to meticulously check the execution of agreed procedures by micromanaging employees become unnecessary in organizations with high trust. In fact, in The Speed of Trust: The One Thing that Changes Everything,[27] Stephen M. R. Covey goes so far as to say that "trust — and the speed at which it is established with clients, employees, and all stakeholders — is the single most critical component of a successful leader and organization."

Finally, in some countries, organization changes are subject to labor laws dictating the involvement of a so-called workers' council. The workers' council represents the interests of the employees in an enterprise. Before an organization change can be offered to an employee, the workers' council has to agree to it. The workers' council checks the offer for appropriateness in terms of such things as skills, responsibilities, salary, and career path match. In addition, the workers' council takes into account other aspects such as the treatment of minorities, consideration of females for higher positions, and investment in innovation.

Once the workers' council has agreed to an organization change for an employee, the offer to join the organization can be extended to the employee. Transitioning an employee to a new organization is a three-step process: (1) product delivery organization management needs to agree to extend the offer; (2) the workers' council needs to agree to management's offer; and (3) the employee needs to agree to management's offer agreed to by the workers' council.

Based on this description of the process, it may appear that it would take a long time to transition all the SREs to a designated organization. While this might be true in some cases, internal transfers of people into similar roles can be agreed by management and the workers' council fairly quickly, if there are no hardship cases.

12.12.2 Reporting Structure Changes

In terms of line management changes, in order to transition an SRE from one manager to another, the recommended approach is to use three meetings:

1. Meeting between the SRE and their current line manager

2. Meeting between the SRE and their current and future line managers

3. Meeting between the SRE and their new line manager

The meeting between the SRE and their current line manager should take place before the establishment of the SRE organization is announced to everyone who will be part of the new organization (see Section 12.11, *Communicating the Chosen Model*). In the meeting, the current line manager should outline the plans by the leadership team to establish a new SRE organization. The reasons for establishing the new organization need to be explained, the envisioned position of the employee therein needs to be discussed, and the new line manager in the new organization needs to be introduced as part of the conversation. At the end of the meeting, the

---

27. Covey, Stephen R., and Rebecca R. Merrill. 2008. *The SPEED of Trust: The One Thing That Changes Everything*. New York: Simon and Schuster.

SRE needs to have a clear picture of the new SRE organization they will be part of and their place therein.

The meeting between the SRE and their current and future line managers needs to take place right after a bigger round with all the SREs and their current and future line managers where the new SRE organization is introduced. The purpose of the second meeting is to discuss the actual transition from the current line managers to the future line managers. In this meeting, concrete topics such as the transition time frame, role, remuneration, and career path changes need to be discussed. At the end of the meeting, the SRE needs to have a clear picture of what will happen in the immediate future to execute the line management change.

The meeting between the SRE and the new line manager needs to take place right after the line management change has taken place. The purpose of this meeting is to welcome the SRE to the new organization, and discuss the SRE's goals, role assignments, career path aspirations, and frequency of one-on-one meetings with the line manager.

Staggering the line management transition with three meetings should give the SRE plenty of opportunity to ask questions, clarify doubts, and feel taken care of during the entire process. The first meeting with the current line manager is especially important because it provides the SRE with the opportunity to raise concerns with the future line manager.

Not everyone can work well together, and if there is history of a difficult working relationship between the SRE and the future line manager, the current line manager should take it seriously. They should work with the target organization, which can be the development, operations, or SRE organization, to find another line manager for the SRE in order to ensure a great start that is untarnished by previous difficulties.

12.12.3 Role Changes

Another big area to be taken care of is that of roles and role changes. The introduction of a new SRE career path with dedicated roles such as junior, senior, and principal SREs could coincide with the organization changes for SREs. In this case, the big question when changing the organization is which role will be assigned to a particular person currently practicing SRE without bearing an official role.

What are the criteria for assigning a particular SRE role? How does role assignment influence the area of responsibility, influence, and remuneration of a person? The answers to these questions lie in the SRE role definitions from Section 12.10.1, *SRE Role Progressions*. Each individual practicing SRE needs to be assessed based on the role definitions. With this, some individuals will clearly fall into the junior, senior, or principal role grade. In these cases, role assignments can proceed accordingly. Salary adjustments can be undertaken likewise.

In borderline cases when an individual's skill set and responsibility are not covered by any of the defined roles, the line manager needs to discuss possible options. The content of the discussion with the SRE needs to be the individual's career aspirations, current skills and responsibilities, and future skills and responsibilities required to fulfill the aspirations. With the career aspirations clarified, the line manager needs to discuss the options with their manager and HR. A decision needs to be made whether to assign a slightly higher or a slightly lower role to the individual compared to what they currently do.

A respective salary negotiation needs to take place as well. An especially difficult situation arises when the newly designated role for the SRE would pay a lower salary than the current one.

This situation should be avoided. HR should have a means in place to match the current salaries of SREs. It cannot be expected that people will accept a pay cut as part of the transition to a new organization.

The opposite situation may arise as well. It could happen that in a borderline case it was decided to assign a new role to the SRE that has higher levels of responsibility than the work performed to date. Also, the skills possessed by the SRE would need to grow to match the new role. The new role would generally pay a higher salary than what the SRE earns today. In this case, HR can have provisions that would raise the SRE's salary not in one go, but rather in a series of steps. Each step would need to be earned by the SRE following a plan agreed between the SRE and their new line manager.

12.13 Summary

This chapter showed that implementing an organizational structure to fulfill SRE responsibilities requires a systematically deliberate approach. It involves far more than the notorious renaming of the operations teams to SRE. There are many options and several dimensions to consider. Using the "who builds it, who runs it?" spectrum introduced in the chapter, the dimension of operational responsibilities can be explored. The models from the spectrum such as "you build it, ops run it," "you build it, SRE run it," "you build it, you and SRE run it," and "you build it, you run it" represent different reliability incentives for the development teams. These incentives drive the investment in reliability done by the development teams on an ongoing basis during product implementation.

The fewest reliability incentives for the development teams are with the "you build it, ops run it" model. With this model, the developers never go on call. Thus, they do not have skin in the game to make the services run reliably in production. An increase in reliability incentives is with the "you build it, SRE run it" model. With this model, there is an error budget policy agreement between the developers and SREs stating the service levels required to be fulfilled by the services for the SREs to run them. Otherwise, the developers run the services.

The next increase in incentives comes with the "you build it, you and SRE run it" model. This model represents shared on call staffed by an SRE and a developer. Together, they run the services. The most reliability incentives for the development teams are with the "you build it, you run it" model in which the developers always go on call for their services in production. Doing so, they will want to be disturbed as little as possible. Thus, they will diligently implement reliability into services while implementing features.

The models from the "who builds it, who runs it?" spectrum can be implemented with different reporting lines. The SREs can report within the development, operations, or a dedicated SRE organization. This choice influences the SRE identity that will be created. The identity can be represented using a triangle of product, incidents, and reliability user experience. SREs reporting within the development organization may have an inclination toward the product-centric identity. SREs reporting within the operations organization may have an inclination toward the incident-centric identity. SREs reporting within the dedicated SRE organization may have an inclination toward the reliability user experience–centric identity.

Once a model from the "who builds it, who runs it?" spectrum and a reporting line for SREs have been chosen, the changes need to be introduced and rolled out in the product delivery organization. As part of the rollout, an SRE career path can be defined to recognize SRE as an official role. The SRE career path can provide several grades for the SRE role, such as junior, senior, and principal SRE. Careful assignment of the respective SRE role grade to the people practicing SRE needs to happen considering the individuals' current skills, current and future responsibilities, and career aspirations.

With the organizational structure for SRE implemented, the SREs have a permanent home in the product delivery organization. SRE is now established both as a practice and as a formal organizational structure!

Part III

Measuring and Sustaining the Transformation

The SRE foundations have been established. The basic foundations with SLIs, SLOs, and error budgets were established first, followed by advanced foundations with error budget policies and error budget decision-making. Creation of an organizational structure for SRE, including a corresponding career path, put the established SRE foundations onto firm organizational footing. In this part of the book, we bring the transformation to a conclusion by measuring its success, fostering sustainability of the SRE movement in the organization, and taking a look at the road ahead.

Chapter 13

Measuring the SRE Transformation

In this chapter, the success of the SRE transformation is measured. The outcomes are measured both quantitatively and qualitatively, reflecting the complex nature of the transformation. Because it is a very multidimensional process, the transformation must be measured across many dimensions. This chapter shows how to do this.

13.1 Testing Transformation Hypotheses

The starting point of measuring the success of the SRE transformation is to evaluate the hypotheses defined at the beginning of the journey. The hypotheses were established in Section 4.7, *Posing Hypotheses*, and they were defined by role: executives, managers, product owners, developers, and operations engineers. To define a hypothesis, a triple <capability> / <outcome> / <measurable signal> was used.

In terms of <capability>, all roles were looking to establish SLIs, SLOs, error budgets, and error budget policies in the organization, and they hoped to achieve diverse outcomes. Each outcome was envisioned to be measured using distinct measurable signals. These are shown collectively in Table 13.1, along with ways to test the signals.

Table 13.1 *Testing SRE Transformation Hypotheses*

#	Measurable Signal	Way to Test the Signal
1	Yearly customer churn rate due to reliability issues 12 months into the SRE transformation has been reduced by 50% compared to the previous 12-month period.	Reasons for customer churn are stored in the customer relationship management (CRM) tool used by the enterprise. Customer churn rates are stored there as well. Thus, the data in the CRM tool can be used for this calculation.
2	A customer escalation is defined unambiguously.	A customer escalation is an incident in the on-call management tool initiated by the first level support mentioning a concrete customer or a customer group.

#	Measurable Signal	Way to Test the Signal
3	The number of customer escalations six months into the SRE transformation has been reduced 50% compared to the previous six-month period.	This can be calculated based on the incident data in the on-call management tool and customer escalation records before the SRE introduction.
4	Reliability work is clearly identifiable in team backlogs.	Work items created based on incident postmortem action items are in the work item management tool. They are either tagged accordingly or linked to the incident postmortems themselves. Other kinds of reliability work might not be easily identifiable in the team backlogs.
5	The average lead time for reliability work prioritization in the fourth quarter of the SRE transformation is at least 25% shorter than in the second quarter.	For the work items created based on the incident postmortem action items, the lead time for prioritization should be available out of the box in the work item management tool. Based on this data, the comparative lead time calculation can be done.
6	Eight months into the SRE transformation developers go on call for their services at defined times and in defined circumstances.	The on-call management tool contains data about the on-call rotations in all teams. The roles of people who go on call by rotation can be looked up in a role management repository. The agreements between development and operations regarding the on-call responsibility split are available in error budget policies.
7	Six months into the SRE transformation any development team can be involved in an ongoing production incident within two hours of the request.	This can be measured by analyzing incident timelines during incident postmortems. The discussion around the timelines should reveal the necessary data.
8	Twelve months into the SRE transformation the median production deployment failure rate and median production deployment recovery time of the last three months have been reduced 50% compared to the three months before the transformation started.	This can be measured using Continuous Delivery indicators defined in Measuring Continuous Delivery.[1] The data to construct the indicators is available in the deployment framework and on-call management tool used. Some custom development is likely needed to construct and visualize the indicators from the data.

---

1. Smith, Steve. n.d. *Measuring Continuous Delivery.* Accessed January 26, 2022. https://leanpub.com/measuringcontinuousdelivery.

#	Measurable Signal	Way to Test the Signal
9	The number of issues brought to the attention of managers concerning production rollouts in the fourth quarter of the SRE transformation is at least 40% less than in the second quarter.	This can be measured by interviewing the managers and comparing the data from the two time periods.
10	Teams can sustain SRE activities on their own without ongoing coaching 24 months into the SRE transformation.	Deployment of the SRE coaches in the teams can be tracked by month. Likewise, the effort extended by the SRE coaches in the teams can be tracked by month.
11	Customer complaints do not occur repeatedly about the same issues for longer than a week 24 months into the SRE transformation.	This can be measured using the customer support tickets processed by the first level support. Customer support tickets linked to the same incident in the on-call management tool represent customer complaints that occur repeatedly about the same issue.
12	Teams adapt their SLOs and error budget policies regularly 18 months into the SRE transformation	Changes in SLOs can be tracked in the SRE infrastructure. It is a system of record with history implemented using source code control mechanisms.

Testing the hypotheses in a data-driven way is a great way to objectively assess the SRE transformation's success. Measurable signal #3, which concerns customer escalation numbers, is a very prominent measure. Let us look at it in some more detail in the next section.

13.2 Outages Not Detected Internally

One of the major reasons for introducing SRE in the first place might have been frequent high-profile customer escalations. These occurred because there might have been no party in the product delivery organization both responsible for and capable of operating the product with the necessary rigor. The operations teams operated the product without sufficient internal knowledge, mostly in a black box manner based on resource-based alerts. The development teams were not involved in operations, as they were fully focused on feature development. The product owners blindly relied on operations to run the services in production.

It is apparent that in this context, many outages have not been detected internally but have been reported by customers through escalations. Now that the SRE transformation has reached a point where the SRE foundations are in place in the product delivery organization, how has this changed? Is there a significant drop in outages that was not detected internally compared to before?

This question is easy to answer based on the data in the on-call management tool. Every incident is permanently recorded there. Incidents initiated manually by the first level support can be considered customer escalations because they get initiated based on the customer support tickets. The data about the incidents from before the SRE introduction should be available in some other system or record, possibly in the work item management tool. This way, a comparison can be made based on ground truth data.

If the number of outages not detected internally is nearly as high as before the SRE introduction for a system of comparable size, the SRE transformation is not going to be considered successful. Note that this measure is so significant that it will overshadow all the other measurable signals from the previous section. Only if a very significant drop in the number of outages not detected internally can be observed will the SRE transformation have a visible positive effect on the product delivery organization that is perceivable outside the transformation process.

It can be safely said that the drop needs to be greater than 50% to justify the effort that went into the SRE transformation. Indeed, if the effort to introduce SRE was so high and involved nearly everyone in the product delivery organization, the expectations for the return on the investment are accordingly high, and rightly so.

Following on, another measurement of SRE transformation success can be made using native SRE means: error budget depletion rates. This is the subject of the next section.

13.3 Services Exhausting Error Budgets Prematurely

Services exhausting error budgets prematurely are tracked using the premature SLO error budget exhaustion indicator (Section 11.3.4). Using the indicator data, a table similar to Table 13.2 can be generated for overview purposes.

Table 13.2 *Overview of Fulfilled and Broken SLOs by Error Budget Period*

	Error Budget Period 1	**Error Budget Period 2**	**Error Budget Period 3**
Service 1	Five SLOs were within the error budgets. Three SLOs broke the error budgets.	Six SLOs were within the error budgets. Two SLOs broke the error budgets.	Seven SLOs were within the error budgets. One SLO broke the error budgets.
Service 2	Two SLOs were within the error budgets. Two SLOs broke the error budgets.	Three SLOs were within the error budgets. Two SLOs broke the error budgets.	Five SLOs were within the error budgets. Zero SLOs broke the error budgets.

Service 1 increased the number of SLOs that stayed within the error budgets from five to six to seven in the three error budget periods shown in Table 13.2. However, in each error budget period, there were SLOs that broke the error budgets.

Service 2 had SLOs that broke the error budgets in error budget periods 1 and 2. In error budget period 3, service 2 successfully defended all five of its SLOs. It therefore stayed within the granted error budgets.

Therefore, service 1 has to be prioritized for reliability improvements. It does not fully fulfill the reliability requirements stated by its SLOs.

If a significant number of services operated by the product delivery organization deplete their error budgets prematurely, the SRE transformation will not be considered successful. The goal of the SRE transformation is not only to build up the infrastructure to monitor error budget fulfillment and flag services that are breaking the error budgets. That is necessary but not sufficient. The goal is to permeate the product delivery organization at a deeper level. It is about achieving the organizational, technical, and people changes that prompt the kind of reliability actions in the teams that lead to the majority of services staying within their error budgets on a consistent basis.

As a rule of thumb, more than 50% of services owned by the product delivery organization need to consistently stay within their error budgets for the SRE transformation to be considered successful so far. This number is surely not the end. More transformation effort is required to get the number to climb to over 90%.

In general, performing an overall assessment quantitatively where possible and qualitatively otherwise is a good way to measure the success of the SRE transformation. Following this, the next dimension to look at can be the executives' perceptions of the SRE transformation outcomes. This is done in a qualitative manner in the next section.

13.4 Executives' Perceptions

Executives' perceptions of the outcomes of the SRE transformation are an important measure. Although subjective, they determine how SRE is viewed by the people not involved in the day-to-day operations of services. Importantly, the executives' views will determine the funding allocated to future SRE activities. This funding may determine the head count allocated to SRE and smaller investments that might be possible, such as for tools, experiments, training, and attendance at conferences.

Executives' perceptions will be based on two input sources: the customer escalations experienced by the executive, and the opinions of the executives' direct reports.

A perceived drop in high-profile customer escalations an executive has recently been involved in will frame SRE in a positive light. An executive's direct reports might talk about SRE streamlining responsibilities around operations, leading to faster recovery from incidents as well as improving alignment between operations, development, and product management. This too will frame SRE in a positive light for the executive.

This kind of assessment is qualitative but is still as valuable as data-driven approaches for measuring other dimensions of the transformation. To be sure, it might happen that the executives' perceptions deviate from reality based on evaluation of the hypotheses from Section 13.1, *Testing Transformation Hypotheses*. The deviation can be in both directions. That is, the executives may perceive SRE as unsuccessful while the hypotheses' measurable signals may show otherwise. And vice versa: The executives may perceive SRE as successful while the hypotheses' measurable signals may show that it is not.

This is a good case for mixing the transformation's qualitative and quantitative assessments. Ideally, the SRE coaches would present the hypotheses data to the executives and their direct reports in an attempt to dig deeper and discover the ground truth. Although it might be difficult to get executives' time for this exercise, it is still worth a try. At the very least, it should be possible to arrange a session like this with the executives' direct reports.

In the next section, we will look at another qualitative way to measure perceptions of the transformation's success.

13.5 Reliability Perception by Users and Partners

The entire effort to operate the services in production in a reliable manner is for the sake of the customers and partners actually using the services and, while doing so, perceiving them as being reliable. A perception of reliability is also a perception of trust.

According to The Site Reliability Workbook:[2]

1. "If a system isn't reliable, users won't trust it."

2. "If users don't trust a system, when given a choice, they won't use it."

3. "… if a system has no users, it's worth nothing."

This is even more important today, when more and more data and processes are stored and implemented in software systems with an increasing choice for users.

In this context, the Net Promoter Score (NPS) can be used to gauge user and partner perceptions of product reliability. NPS is the percentage of system users who are likely to recommend the system to others. It is calculated based on a rating question such as "On a scale of 0 to 10, how likely are you to recommend the system to a friend or colleague?"

After the rating question, typically there is a more open-ended question along the lines of the following.

- "What is the reason for the score?"

- "What was disappointing in your experience with the system?"

- "Which features do you value most?"

Here lies the opportunity to inject a reliability-related question. It can be posed in a closed-ended or open-ended way. For example:

- "On a scale of 0 to 10, how reliable is the system?" (closed-ended)

- "Do you perceive the system to be reliable?" (closed-ended)

- "What is your experience with system reliability?" (open-ended)

---

2. Beyer, Betsy, Niall Richard Murphy, David K. Rensin, Stephen Thorne, and Kent Kawahara. 2018. *The Site Reliability Workbook: Practical Ways to Implement SRE*. Sebastopol, CA: O'Reilly Media.

The SRE coaches can get in touch with the marketing department to find out whether an NPS survey can be created that includes a reliability question. If this is possible, the marketing department can set up the survey and send it out to customers. This way, another qualitative assessment of perception of the SRE transformation's success can be made.

13.6 Summary

The SRE foundations have been established in the organization. Measuring the foundations is an important part of the SRE transformation. Indeed, what are the measurable outcomes of the transformation so far?

The measurements should start in a quantifiable manner. First, the hypotheses defined at the beginning of the transformation should be tested. This can be done using the measurable signals and data about incidents in the on-call management tool. The number of outages not detected internally is a significant measure of success. This number has to drop at least 50% for the transformation to be considered successful and for the effort to establish the SRE foundations to be justified.

Another quantifiable measure of transformation success native to SRE is the number of services that consistently deplete their error budgets prematurely. If the number is significant, the transformation is only successful in establishing the indicators. However, so far the transformation is not successful in influencing the teams to invest in reliability based on the indicator data. More effort is required by the SRE coaches and the teams to get there.

Following this, qualified measurements of SRE transformation success should be made. The executives' perceptions of the transformation are important. Among other things, they might influence further investment in SRE. Finally, the perception of product reliability among users and partners is of utmost importance. In fact, it is they who must be the final judges of reliability. By working together with the marketing department, the SRE coaches can include reliability questions in NPS surveys. This way, reliability perception can be measured together with user willingness to promote the product in general.

Having measured the SRE transformation's success, in the next chapter we will explore ways to further sustain the SRE movement.

Chapter 14

Sustaining the SRE Movement

In the previous chapters, I discussed the motivation for embarking on the SRE transformational journey, as well as how to establish the SRE foundations and measure their success. This chapter is dedicated to sustaining the SRE movement.

14.1 Maturing the SRE CoP

The SRE CoP is a communal force behind driving SRE awareness, best practice exchange, and cross-team knowledge fertilization. Importantly, once the SRE coaches start disengaging from the teams (see Section 5.9.3, *Team Engagements Over Time*), it indeed remains the only driving force behind SRE operating in a cross-team manner.

Therefore, every attempt should be made to support and firmly establish the SRE CoP while the SRE coaches are engaged in the initiative. Ways to do so were revealed in *Formalizing the CoP* in Chapter 7. It is about electing the SRE CoP leadership and setting its vision, goals, and scope. Furthermore, it is about measuring SRE success in a suitable manner, making the CoP known to existing and new employees, and connecting it well to other ongoing activities in the product delivery organization.

For instance, bigger achievements in the SRE arena should be shared not only within the CoP but also outside, in larger rounds such as lean coffee sessions and brown bag lunches. Moreover, the SRE CoP can publish SRE material for consumption by others interested in operations. Regular publications such as newsletters and blog posts on SRE can be driven by the SRE CoP. How to do this is the subject of the next several sections.

14.2 SRE Minutes

At SREcon Americas 2020, Zach Thomas gave a talk titled "The Smallest Possible SRE Team."[1] During the talk, he suggested an idea that garnered a lot of attention among conference attendees. The idea is about spreading the knowledge about SRE within the product delivery organization in a way that does

---

1. Thomas, Zach. 2020. "SREcon20 Americas – The Smallest Possible SRE Team." YouTube, December 23, 2020. https://youtu.be/XEcGBGBzNRA.

not consume lots of time for producers and consumers of the information. It is about creating SRE micro-content.

This content is referred to as SRE minutes. Table 14.1 offers some example topics.

Table 14.1 *Topics for SRE Minutes*

Topic	Explanation
Availability	What does counting the nines mean?
Time series	How do you plot a time series graph using a log query?
SLO	How do you set an SLO using the SRE infrastructure?

An SRE minute is about a paragraph long. It can be written within minutes and read within seconds. This way of distributing SRE knowledge is more effective than having meetings to explain the SRE concepts. It also scales well with even the smallest number of people driving SRE in the organization. Indeed, as Zach Thomas said in his talk, "the pen is mightier than a bunch of meetings."

Each SRE minute is stored on a page within the SRE wiki. It gets distributed via email to a distribution list within the product delivery organization or posted to suitable channels in the organization's chat management service. Setting the frequency of distribution to once a week seems just about right. Production of the SRE minutes can be done on rotation by the SRE CoP members.

The SRE minutes contribute to sustaining the SRE movement because they bring SRE topics to the top of employees' minds in a consistent and subtle way.

14.3 Availability Newsletter

Another way to create awareness about one of the most relevant SLIs, availability, is to establish an availability newsletter. The newsletter can contain a list of the most and least available endpoints and services in production for a chosen period. Each newsletter issue can be stored on a page within the SRE wiki. It can then be distributed similar to SRE minutes, either via email or by posting it to the relevant channels in the organization's chat management service.

The newsletter can be distributed more broadly than the SRE minutes. While the goal of the minutes is to educate the product delivery organization on SRE concepts, the goal of the availability newsletter is to create awareness of current product availability in production. This should be of interest to more people than those who would like to learn SRE concepts.

In fact, product availability can be directly linked to revenue. Therefore, the business stakeholders may also be interested in the newsletter. The production and distribution of the newsletter can be driven by the SRE CoP members. The newsletter can be distributed weekly or every two weeks.

14.4 SRE Column in the Engineering Blog

Many software engineering organizations have engineering blogs. They serve as a means of distributing relevant and important information within the product development community. Bigger engineering blogs have columns that contain information about a specific topic. For instance, there may be columns about continuous delivery, databases, and product management, among others.

SRE can be established as a new column on the engineering blog. It can cover numerous topics, such as, for example, what is going on in different teams in terms of SRE adoption, central changes to the SRE infrastructure, and postmortems of the most impactful recent outages. The column would bring the topic of operations to the forefront of engineering news coverage and distribution. This would be new, as engineering blogs are typically more focused on development topics.

As with the SRE minutes and availability newsletter, the SRE column can be driven by the SRE CoP community members. They can contribute relevant articles on rotation. Having a useful SRE column on the engineering blog will take more time than producing SRE minutes or the availability newsletter. This needs to be taken into account before the initiative gets started.

Having a column on the blog means contributing fresh, well-written content on a regular basis. Posts would be around 200 to 400 words. The narrative may not be easy to produce for people who do not write frequently. At the same time, posting an SRE column on rotation represents a good opportunity for people to develop technical writing skills without lots of time pressure.

14.5 Promote Long-Form SRE Wiki Articles

A good way to promote SRE knowledge is to write long-form articles for the SRE wiki. These articles should be from one to three pages long. The topics can flow naturally based on conversations between the SRE coaches and the teams. Additionally, discussions at the SRE CoP meetings can prompt good ideas for these articles to highlight a topic in depth. The articles can be written as the need arises, not necessarily on a strict schedule. They should be written so that readers can understand the content on their own.

Following are some ideas for topics:

- How do you refine SLOs iteratively?

- How do you separate development and on-call activities on rotation within a development team?

- How do you use the join operator in the log query language?

- What are the typical log query language queries for analyzing issues in a data pipeline?

- How do you debug high latency in the networking infrastructure?

To promote the articles, a brief synopsis of each one can be included in the SRE column on the engineering blog. New articles can be announced during SRE CoP meetings, and the SRE channel in the organization's chat management service can be used to post links to the new articles. Some SRE minutes might be suitable for promoting some of the articles as well.

Once a new article has been published, a dedicated effort needs to be made to make it known. That is, the goal is not to produce the content en masse, but rather occasionally, with high quality, and to spread it as widely as possible. A dedicated readership may form over time. Through commentary on the articles, the SRE community can strengthen and grow.

14.6 SRE Broadcasting

With the SRE minutes, availability newsletter, SRE column on the engineering blog, and articles on the SRE wiki, an entire broadcasting system can be put in place. The purpose of the broadcasting system is to keep reliability topics top of mind in the product delivery organization.

The broadcasting system needs to be calibrated in such a way that the SRE-related information does not overwhelm people, leading to SRE fatigue. Rather, an attempt should be undertaken to stagger information delivery in such a way that it arrives in the right portions at the appropriate time when people are most likely to consume it. This could be achieved as shown in Table 14.2.

Table 14.2 *SRE Broadcasting Schedule*

Content	Frequency	Weekday	Distribution
SRE minutes	Once a week	Fridays	Email, chat
Availability newsletter	Once a week/once every two weeks	Mondays	Email, chat
SRE column on engineering blog	Once every two weeks/ monthly	Wednesdays	Blog subscriptions, chat
SRE wiki articles	Occasionally	Thursdays	Wiki subscriptions, SRE column on engineering blog, chat

The SRE minutes should be broadcast about once a week. This is ideally done on Fridays because it implies a quick, casual read. Thus, it coincides with the Friday afternoon mood of heading into the weekend.

The availability newsletter should be broadcast once a week or once every two weeks. The frequency may be chosen depending on production deployment lead times. If it takes a long time to deploy a service to production, its availability will not be improved quickly. Consequently, broadcasting service unavailability frequently would not improve service availability.

Pillorying the service owners is not the goal of the availability newsletter. Rather, it is to create a shared understanding of the availability bottlenecks in the organization. This needs to be timed in congruence with the organization's speed of making changes in production. In terms of the publishing day, Monday seems to be the most appropriate because it gives the teams an entire workweek to improve the availability of the service.

The SRE column on the engineering blog should be published about once every two weeks or once a month. It is an infrequent SRE information broadcast mixed with lots of other topics on the blog relevant to the product delivery organization. Therefore, the people reading the engineering blog posts are looking to grasp much more information than just topics related to SRE.

Publishing the engineering blog posts on Wednesdays provides people with enough time to consume the information until the end of the week. Also, on Wednesdays people are fully in the working mode and are discussing all sorts of work-related matters. This coincides well with the mood conveyed by the engineering blog posts reporting from different corners of the product delivery organization.

Finally, SRE wiki articles should be published occasionally on the SRE wiki. They can be published on Thursdays in order to allow enough time to finish reading the article before the end of the workweek for those who are immediately interested in the topic at hand. For others, the weekend ahead represents a good opportunity to go through the article without the presence of day-to-day work pressures.

These broadcasts can help sustain the SRE movement well. The SRE movement can also be sustained by combining SRE data with other data sources. This is the subject of the next section.

14.7 Combining SRE and CD Indicators

Another way to sustain the SRE movement is to combine the SRE indicators with Continuous Delivery indicators that may already exist in the product delivery organization. The Continuous Delivery indicators are defined in *Measuring Continuous Delivery*.[2] They measure the stability and throughput of a product delivery organization's technical value streams using five indicators:

1. Deployment stability indicator

2. Deployment throughput indicator

3. Build stability indicator

4. Build throughput indicator

5. Mainline throughput indicator

The stability indicators are composed of failure rate and failure recovery time. The throughput indicators are composed of lead time and interval. Applied to the five indicators in the preceding list yields the indicator components shown in Table 14.3.

---

2. Smith, Steve. n.d. *Measuring Continuous Delivery*. Accessed January 26, 2022. https://leanpub.com/measuringcontinuousdelivery.

Table 14.3 *Stability and Throughput Indicator Components*

Stability Indicator	Indicator Component 1	Indicator Component 2
Deployment stability indicator	Deployment failure rate in a (production) environment	Deployment failure recovery time in a (production) environment
Deployment throughput indicator	Deployment lead time in a (production) environment	Interval between deployments in a (production) environment
Build stability indicator	Mainline build failure rate	Mainline build failure recovery time
Build throughput indicator	Mainline build lead time	Interval between mainline builds
Mainline throughput indicator	Mainline commit lead time	Interval between mainline commits

Using the indicators, it is possible to automatically analyze deployment pipelines that exist in the product delivery organization. The analysis can detect bottlenecks in the technical value streams at any point, starting from developer workstations all the way to any production environment.

The bottlenecks might be in mainline throughput (e.g., long mainline commit lead times or long intervals between mainline commits); build throughput (e.g., long build lead times or long intervals between builds); or deployment throughput (e.g., long deployment lead times or long intervals between deployments).

Furthermore, the bottlenecks might be detected in deployment stability (e.g., high deployment failure rates or long deployment failure recovery times in a production environment), or they may be detected in build stability (e.g., high mainline build failure rates or long mainline build failure recovery times).

The detected bottlenecks can also be prioritized automatically, depending on how severe they are considered in the product delivery organization. The teams can then feed the prioritized bottlenecks into the backlog prioritization. For instance, the least stable pipelines in terms of failure rates and recovery times can be prioritized for improvements. Likewise, the slowest pipelines in terms of lead times between the pipeline environments and intervals between deployments, builds, or commits can be prioritized for improvements. This process is described in more detail in "Data-Driven Decision Making – Product Development with Continuous Delivery Indicators."[3]

The Continuous Delivery indicators support the product owners with data for making prioritization decisions in the area of development efficiency. However, they do not extend into the area of operations. This is where the SRE indicators from Chapter 11 come into play!

---

3. Ukis, Vladyslav. 2020. "Data-Driven Decision Making – Product Development with Continuous Delivery Indicators." *InfoQ*, February 26, 2020. https://www.infoq.com/articles/data-driven-decision-product-development.

14.7.1 CD Versus SRE Indicators

The Continuous Delivery and SRE indicators measure development and operations processes, respectively. A comparison of the indicators is summarized in Table 14.4.

Table 14.4 *Continuous Delivery Versus SRE Indicators*

Process →	Development Process	Operations Process
Indicators	Continuous Delivery indicators	SRE indicators
Measurements	Development process efficiency	Reliability in production
Main question	How do you build the product efficiently?	How do you operate the product reliably in production?
Data for investments	In development efficiency	In product reliability

Now, the question would be how to glue the Continuous Delivery and SRE indicators in a meaningful way so that they reinforce each other and help teams decide whether to invest in development efficiency versus product reliability.

The Continuous Delivery indicators can spot the bottlenecks in development process efficiency. The SRE indicators can spot the bottlenecks in product reliability. Which side is more important? When? Where should more investment be made? How do you compare the bottlenecks of the two disciplines? Are they related? If so, how?

These questions have not been properly answered yet in the software delivery community. In "Data-Driven Decision Making – Optimizing the Product Delivery Organization,"[4] an initial attempt is made to do so. However, it only states that applying the Continuous Delivery indicators together with the SRE indicators enables a product delivery organization to optimize for efficiency and reliability at the same time. Additionally, it states that if product hypotheses from hypothesis-driven development[5] are added, the organization can optimize for effectiveness at the same time.

Taken together, the data from the hypotheses' measurable signals, the Continuous Delivery indicators, and the SRE indicators enable product owners to make prioritization trade-offs in a data-driven way by[4]

- Investing in features to enhance product effectiveness and/or

- Investing in development efficiency and/or

- Investing in service reliability

4. Ukis, Vladyslav. 2020. "Data-Driven Decision Making – Optimizing the Product Delivery Organization." *InfoQ*, April 20, 2020. https://www.infoq.com/articles/data-driven-decision-optimize-delivery.

5. O'Reilly, Barry. 2014. "How to Implement Hypothesis-Driven Development." Thoughtworks, October 18, 2014. https://www.thoughtworks.com/insights/articles/how-implement-hypothesis-driven-development.

14.7.2 Bottleneck Analysis

Within each bucket (product effectiveness, development efficiency, and service reliability), prioritization can be driven using the respective indicators. Cross-bucket, however, the prioritization drivers are less obvious. Let us consider an example of the Continuous Delivery indicators and SRE indicators each demonstrating two different bottlenecks. This is shown in Table 14.5.

Table 14.5 *Bottlenecks Uncovered by the Continuous Delivery and SRE Indicators*

	Continuous Delivery Indicators	**SRE Indicators**
Bottlenecks	Bottleneck 1: Production deployment failure recovery time is two hours on average. Bottleneck 2: Production deployment feature lead time is two days on average.	Bottleneck 3: The authentication service broke the latency error budget in three consecutive error budget periods. Bottleneck 4: The notifications service broke the availability error budget in the last two error budget periods.

The prioritization between bottlenecks 1 and 2 is about development process efficiency optimization. What is more important: the production failure recovery time reduction or the production deployment feature lead time reduction? The product owner can make the prioritization decision based on customer feedback.

Furthermore, the prioritization between bottlenecks 3 and 4 is about product reliability improvements. What is more important: the authentication service latency reduction or the notifications service availability increase? Also here, the product owner can make the prioritization decision based on customer feedback.

The customer feedback can be gleaned from automated customer behavior analysis using web analytics. Additionally, the customer experience can be understood by analyzing the customer support tickets. If the web analytics show that the customers abandon the log-on process because it takes too long, prioritizing bottleneck 3 gains importance.

Moreover, if the web analytics show that the notifications do not lead to a significant increase in customer engagement, the availability of the notifications service is not that important. Following this, bottleneck 4 does not need to be prioritized for the time being.

Further on, if the customer support tickets show lots of complaints about service downtime correlated with the average failure recovery time of two hours, prioritization of bottleneck 1 gains importance. On the product demand side, the product owner may not view the average production deployment feature lead time of two days as leading to significant revenue loss or amounting to significant opportunity cost. Therefore, prioritization of bottleneck 2 will not be deemed important for the moment.

Therefore, prioritization decisions can be made based on the combined data summarized in Table 14.6.

Table 14.6 *Bottleneck Analysis*

	Continuous Delivery Indicators	**SRE Indicators**
Bottleneck analysis	Bottleneck 1: There are lots of customer support tickets complaining about service downtime. [Prioritize!]	Bottleneck 3: Customers are abandoning the log-on process. [Prioritize!]
	Bottleneck 2: There is no significant revenue loss and no significant opportunity cost.	Bottleneck 4: Notifications do not lead to a significant increase in customer engagement.

Based on the bottleneck analysis in Table 14.6, bottlenecks 1 and 3 will get prioritized. It is important to note that this kind of systematic analysis of bottlenecks is rarely done in the software industry. There are several reasons for this. First, the Continuous Delivery indicators are not commonly established in product delivery organizations. Second, the SRE indicators are even less common due to SRE being a rather new discipline.

Third, even if the Continuous Delivery indicators and SRE indicators are established, bottleneck detection may not be done automatically. It takes time to manually find bottlenecks based on raw data from the indicators. Finally, even if the bottlenecks are detected automatically, the bottleneck analysis may not be automated. Also here, it takes time to manually analyze bottlenecks to reach prioritization decisions in a data-driven way.

This shows that the software industry has a long way to go before data-driven prioritization decisions are easier to make for product owners and transparent to everyone else. When it comes to the sought-after connection between Continuous Delivery indicators and SRE indicators, it may be helpful to look at error budget depletion. In the preceding example, bottleneck 1 may be connected to some significant error budget depletion. Therefore, it probably would either need to be manifested on the SRE indicators, or prompt the need to adapt existing SLOs or set new ones.

Another question is whether it would be possible to predict some of the SRE indicators based on the Continuous Delivery indicators. Can high production deployment failure rates and long production deployment feature lead times be the predictors of some SRE indicators' deterioration? They might be. At the very least, it is definitely worth it to formulate structured hypotheses around these questions and rigorously test them. Perhaps the DevOps Research and Assessment (DORA) research program[6] would take on this task to shed some light on questions like this. Doing so would advance the software industry at large.

Generally speaking, combining the Continuous Delivery and SRE indicators would help sustain the SRE movement in a product delivery organization. It would move SRE into the spotlight of prioritization decisions in the organization.

14.8 SRE Feedback Loops

The SRE foundations described in this book have been established with lots of feedback loops. This is what made advancements in the SRE transformation successful along the way.

---

6. DORA. n.d. "DORA Research Program." Accessed January 26, 2022. https://www.devops-research.com/research.html.

Implementing an SRE transformation means changing the technical, social, and cultural fabric of software operations in a product delivery organization. In this context, a successful step is always a combination of hard and soft changes coming together in such a way that the majority of people affected by the step accept it as positive and necessary. This can only be achieved with small and frequent feedback loops measuring the transformation process on various dimensions.

To recap, Table 14.7 summarizes the feedback loops used along the way.

Table 14.7 *SRE Feedback Loops*

Artifact	Defined By	Feedback By
SLI/SLO	Operations engineers, developers, product owners	SLO breaches reported by the SRE infrastructure and analyzed by the people on call
Stakeholder groups	Developers, product owners, operations engineers	Stakeholders
Stakeholder rings	Operations engineers	Stakeholders
Generic incident priorities	Operations teams	Development teams
Generic incident severities	Operations teams	People on call
Incident priorities by team	Operations engineers, developers, product owners	Stakeholders
Incident response process	Operations teams	People on call
Runbooks	People on call	People on call
Status pages	Operations teams	Stakeholders
Postmortem process	Operations teams	Postmortem participants
SLAs	Operations engineers, developers, product owners, legal, management	Customers

The established SRE processes will evolve. The processes need to continue to evolve using feedback loops. This is the fastest and surest path to successful introduction and acceptance of process changes.

14.9 New Hypotheses

At the beginning of the SRE transformation, a set of hypotheses was posed (see Section 4.7, *Posing Hypotheses*). These hypotheses were used along the way to measure the impact of the transformation. Once most of the initial hypotheses have been tested positively (see Section 13.1, *Testing Transformation Hypotheses*), it is time to define some new ones. This provides motivation and a framework for measuring progress in a data-driven way to further optimize the SRE process in order to achieve a new level of sophistication. For example, the new hypotheses in Table 14.8 might be posed to drive SRE process optimization.

Table 14.8 *New Hypotheses to Drive SRE Process Optimization*

Stakeholders	Example Hypotheses		
	Capability	*Outcome*	*Measurable Signals*
Executives	Service catalog	Available services are presented hierarchically along with information useful for legal, sales, and marketing.	The service catalog is used in a self-service manner by legal, sales, and marketing at least once a month.
Product owners	Error budget–based decision-making	Fast prioritization decisions are supported by operational data.	SRE indicators are available and used: • "SLOs by service" indicator (Section 11.2.2) • SLO error budget depletion indicator (Section 11.2.4) • Premature SLO error budget exhaustion indicator (Section 11.2.5) • SLO adherence indicator (Section 11.2.3) • "SLAs by service" indicator (Section 11.2.6) • SLA error budget depletion indicator (Section 11.2.7) • Least available service endpoints indicator (Section 11.2.12) • Slowest service endpoints indicator (Section 11.12.13)
Developers	Error budget policy	Error budget depletion leads to clear agreed action.	Actions for error budget depletion cases are described and agreed in a team's error budget policy. The team's error budget policy is enacted as agreed.
Operations engineers	SLAs	Reliability commitments to customers are clear.	SLAs are defined and agreed contractually with customers. SLAs' error budget depletion can be tracked using dashboards and alerts.
Managers	SRE career path	People can get on the SRE career path in a defined manner.	The SRE career path is defined. At least one person per year hops on the SRE career path.

Stakeholders	Example Hypotheses		
	Capability	*Outcome*	*Measurable Signals*
SRE coaches	SRE supports regulatory compliance	Regulatory compliance in terms of operations is supported by SRE.	The SRE process is described formally. The SRE process adherence can be evidenced. The SRE process is used in all audits concerning operations.

Generally, the approach of driving bigger changes using hypotheses is a proven way to achieve alignment at the right time and enable progress measurements in a data-driven way. Whenever existing hypotheses have been exhausted, new ones can be defined supporting continuous improvement. Always having SRE hypotheses defined is a great way to sustain and drive the SRE movement!

14.10 Providing Learning Opportunities

SRE is one of the youngest disciplines within software engineering. It changes rapidly as more and more organizations become practitioners and contribute their experience to the existing body of knowledge, theory, and practice. In this context, it is important for employers to provide learning opportunities to the people practicing SRE in their organizations. Learning the latest best practices and connecting with leading practitioners worldwide helps organizations be at the forefront of doing operations in a modern way.

Being offered opportunities to learn motivates people in the software industry at large. These people are used to rapidly changing work practices. In fact, they expect the practices to change. At the same time, they also expect some working time to be allocated to learning about and adopting the changes. This certainly applies to SRE.

The following SRE online courses and conferences can be recommended.

- Online Courses:

  ○ "Site Reliability Engineering: Measuring and Managing Reliability"[7] at Coursera (or at Pluralsight)

  ○ "Site Reliability Engineering (SRE) Foundation"[8] at Cloud Academy

- Conferences:

  ○ SREcon[9] by Usenix

---

7. Coursera. n.d. "Site Reliability Engineering: Measuring and Managing Reliability." Accessed January 26, 2022. https://www.coursera.org/learn/site-reliability-engineering-slos.

8. Cloud Academy. n.d. "Site Reliability Engineering (SRE) Foundation." Accessed January 26, 2022. https://cloudacademy.com/learning-paths/site-reliability-engineering-sre-foundation-1759.

9. "SREcon." 2017. USENIX. August 25, 2017. https://www.usenix.org/srecon.

   ○ DevOps Enterprise Summit[10] by IT Revolution

   ○ QCon[11] by InfoQ

SREcon is fully focused on SRE. It requires some basic SRE knowledge to be able to follow the tracks. The conference highlights the latest and greatest on SRE being practiced in organizations ranging from startups to large enterprises.

The DevOps Enterprise Summit is focused particularly on enterprises running DevOps transformations. SRE is only a part of the summit, not necessarily a dedicated separate track. As the saying goes, the DevOps Enterprise Summit is a conference run for horses by horses. The unicorns, on the other hand, are more present at QCon.

QCon is a general software engineering conference highlighting the latest trends in software engineering. Some QCon conferences run a dedicated SRE track, others sprinkle SRE presentations throughout the agenda.

Bringing fresh news from any of the conferences and presenting them internally is a great way to spread the latest SRE knowledge, practices, and tools. Doing so should be a requirement to get the budget to go to a conference. Apart from improving the conference budget ROI, it also contributes to sparking interest in everything new around SRE with people who would not normally travel to conferences.

14.11 Supporting SRE Coaches

The last way to sustain the SRE movement is about supporting the SRE coaches. The coaches deal with a large number of teams and people to drive the SRE transformation forward. Naturally, different people have different backgrounds, opinions, and views. Trying to align people toward shared SRE goals depletes the SRE coaches' energy.

What is more, the SRE coaches may occasionally get involved in serious disagreements. People may be openly against SRE and express their opinions vocally. This may have an influence on other people and, thus, might represent an impediment to the overall SRE transformation.

In order to be able to navigate the complex maze of emotions and difficult situations with a large number of people, the SRE coaches must exercise emotional intelligence skills on a daily basis. At times, they may need emotional support themselves. What is important in this context is the availability of some kind of support system for the coaches to bring them through occasional rough patches.

The support system should not be underestimated. Without it, the SRE coaches might reach the brink of collapse. Alternatively, they might decide to quit the coaching job. Something like this should be avoided at all costs. On the one hand, it has a severe impact on the health of the SRE coaches. On the other hand, it may have a severe impact on the SRE transformation itself.

Changing SRE coaches before even the basic SRE foundations are established requires finding a replacement, which can be incredibly difficult. As discussed in Section 5.3, *SRE Coaches*,

---

10. IT Revolution Events. n.d. "DevOps Enterprise Summit 2022." Accessed January 12, 2022. https://events.itrevolution.com.

11. InfoQ. n.d. "QCon Software Development Conferences." Accessed January 26, 2022. https://qconferences.com.

the set of knowledge, skills, and experiences required from an internal SRE coach is extensive, pretty unique, and difficult to find. External SRE coaches are not only very hard to find but also very expensive, making this option barely viable.

If two SRE coaches were driving the SRE transformation and one of them quits, placing the entire burden of the transformation on a single person is very risky. For one, the person might simply not be able to handle the load. Even if this were possible, the transformation pace will slow down. This, in turn, will have an impact on the motivation of the teams to undergo the transformation. If the teams do not see at least some transformation success rather quickly, their motivation to continue will dwindle.

Thus, establishing a support system for the SRE coaches is an important part of sustaining the SRE movement. Such a support system needs to have three parts:

1. A group of confidants whom the SRE coaches can turn to privately at will

2. A day-off policy that can be used on top of vacation to recharge the batteries

3. A budget that can be used for engaging occasional external support, getting training, and experimenting with tools

The most important part of the support system is the establishment of a group of confidants who can privately discuss ongoing people issues with the SRE coaches. In some countries, the group of confidants is established by voting as part of the so-called workers' council in an enterprise. The workers' council negotiates with enterprise management on behalf of employees.

If there is no workers' council, product delivery organization leadership can issue a call for confidants. Anyone in the organization can apply to become a confidant candidate. The candidates can then be voted on by everyone in the organization. This way, a group of confidants can be elected in a low-key way without introducing an official workers' council.

The SRE coaches must be absolutely certain that the confidants will keep the discussed issues private. The SRE coaches will use the confidants as a sounding board and not as a way to find solutions. They will unload the emotional burden of the SRE transformation during these conversations. The purpose of the conversations is to relieve the emotional pressure the SRE coaches may find themselves being exposed to. As a result, new positive energy is released that is vital for the SRE coaches to drive the SRE transformation further in full strength.

The second part of the support system is setting up a day-off policy that the SRE coaches can draw on to recharge their batteries after handling emotionally charged situations. The day-off policy should be separate from the vacation policy. For instance, the day-off policy may add 10% to the SRE coaches' annual vacation time. This way, if an SRE coach takes 20 vacation days per year, they get an additional two days off per year that they may use on request.

Requesting additional days off should be easy. For instance, an informal conversation between the SRE coach and their manager about the recent work undertaken with the teams followed by a request to take a day off should be sufficient.

The third and final part of the support system for the SRE coaches is the availability of a budget that can be drawn on in order to engage occasional external support, get training, and experiment with tools. This can be useful for diving deep into a topic in the form of a one-day workshop that can be run by a freelancer specializing in the area. For instance, a workshop about learning the best ways to set up an on-call management tool in a large enterprise may be conducted by an external consultant.

In terms of training, the SRE coaches need to be on the very cutting edge of SRE practice. They need to consume as much material on SRE as possible, and they should make connections with other SRE coaches running SRE transformations in other companies. In other words, they need to be embedded in the SRE community at large. To do so, the SRE coaches need to attend and present at conferences; read, comment, and write on blogs; be active in SRE communities online; and have meetings with other SRE coaches from other companies. Doing so requires a budget. It is a great support for the SRE coaches if the budget is clarified and granted up front to minimize budget approval process overhead on every request.

A budget is also needed to run experiments with tools. While establishing the SRE foundations, lots of tools need to be selected to form a tool landscape best suitable for the product delivery organization. Many tools offer free trials to evaluate functionality. Sometimes, though, a deep evaluation either takes longer than the trial period offered or requires features that are not part of the trial period. In these cases, short-term tool evaluations require payments, which can be handled by drawing on the budget that may be made available to the SRE coaches.

In summary, a support system for the SRE coaches consisting of a group of confidants, a day-off policy, and a budget can go a long way toward sustaining the SRE movement. It is the SRE coaches, after all, who represent the leadership of the movement. Supporting the coaches contributes directly to enabling a sustainable spread of SRE in the product delivery organization.

14.12 Summary

This book has shown that SRE is not established by proclamation. Rather, an organization moves to SRE by taking a journey. This chapter showed how the journey can be sustained beyond establishing the SRE foundations.

The first pillar of sustaining the SRE movement is about creating a broadcast system to keep reliability topics top of mind in the product delivery organization. This can be done in a comprehensive way by developing short SRE minutes, an availability newsletter, an SRE column on the engineering blog, and occasional SRE articles.

The second pillar is to establish the Continuous Delivery indicators in conjunction with the SRE indicators. This enables simultaneous optimization of development process efficiency and product reliability. In particular, it may be possible to correlate the Continuous Delivery indicators of production deployment failure rate and recovery time with the SRE error budget indicators.

The third pillar of sustaining the SRE movement is about providing learning opportunities for everyone involved and, especially, creating a support system for the SRE coaches as the major transformation drivers.

The fourth pillar is about continuing to use feedback loops and hypotheses to drive the transformation forward. In this spirit, outlining the road ahead for the SRE transformation is the subject of the next chapter.

Chapter 15

The Road Ahead

This is the last chapter of this book. The chapter name is borrowed from the book *The Road Ahead*[1] written by Bill Gates in 1995. The book was about his view of the then undiscovered territory of the information highway. Similarly, the purpose of this chapter is to provide a view on the yet undiscovered territory on the SRE transformation journey.

The foundational pieces of SRE have been put in place in all development and operations teams using the methodologies and efforts described in this book. The operations teams provide and maintain the SRE infrastructure. The development teams use it. The people in the development and operations teams go on call in rotations according to the team's agreed on-call setup. For complex incidents, the incident response process is defined and used to drive the resolution of outages in a reliable and repeatable manner. Teams make reliability investment decisions in a data-driven way based on error budget depletion data. The organizational structure for SRE ensures the long-term sustainability of the SRE practice and provides a career path to people practicing SRE. The software delivery organization leadership are happy with the way operations have improved. High-profile customer escalations have become very rare. All thanks to SRE.

Now that the SRE foundations have been firmly established, they can be enhanced to foster the efficiency and effectiveness of the SRE organization. This is the road ahead on the SRE transformation journey. The road is schematically mapped in Figure 15.1.

The middle of Figure 15.1 shows the SRE concept pyramid. It was established in this book along with the organizational structure for SRE. There are three new elements in the figure. To the left of the SRE concept pyramid is the service catalog to foster transparency and ownership of services. To the right are the contractual service-level agreements (SLAs) to guarantee reliability levels for customers and partners. Finally, at the top of the pyramid is the regulatory compliance that is mandatory in many industries and can be fulfilled using the SRE concepts, processes, and practices.

---

1. Gates, Bill. 1999. *The Road Ahead*. New York: Viking Press.

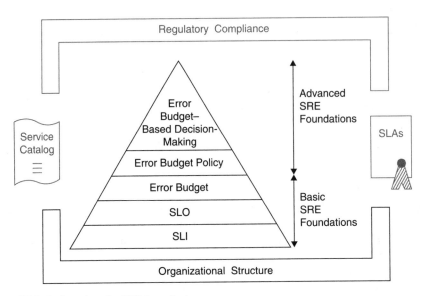

Figure 15.1 *Enhancing the SRE foundations*

In the following sections, service catalog, SLAs, and regulatory compliance are explored one by one to explain their role in the SRE transformation journey moving forward.

15.1 Service Catalog

The first area to look at in order to drive the SRE transformation further is the hierarchical representation of services on the status pages. Is the current hierarchy optimally representing services from the business point of view? Can it be easily understood by stakeholders?

Is there a corresponding service catalog available? Is the service catalog used for looking up services at each hierarchy level in terms of purpose, ownership, on-call rotations, SLOs in aggregation, SLAs in aggregation, and so on?

Is there an overarching service operating model based on the service catalog? If not, the introduction of a well-thought-out service catalog should be pursued.

The service catalog should reflect the ground truth deployed in all production environments. This means it must be created partly automatically to ensure its content is fully synchronized with all service deployments in all production environments. Beyond the ground truth from production, the service catalog should contain a list of services in preparation with an indication of production environments the services are planned to be deployed to.

Using the catalog, it should be possible in a self-service manner to obtain information about the services planned to be deployed to production and the services already deployed in all the production environments. Each service in the service catalog needs to have at least the following attributes:

- Unique ID

- Description

- Hierarchy level

- Owner team

- Set of depployment environments the service is available in

- Set of deployment environments the service is planned to be made available in

- Service hosting environment

- Specification of consumed and produced data

- On-call rotation

- SLOs including historical adherence data

- SLAs including historical adherence data

The extent of the attributes' usefulness will depend on the service's hierarchy level. For a service at the lowest level of the hierarchy, all the attributes in the preceding list can be specified in a detailed manner. At higher levels of the hierarchy, some attributes will be specified only in an overview form.

For example, a service visible to customers for storing data might be a logical aggregate of many technical services. Such an aggregate will appear in the service catalog at the highest level. Attributes such as service hosting environment and on-call rotation are not valuable to be specified at that level. By contrast, the SLOs and SLAs of such an aggregate service are very valuable to have in the service catalog. The legal, business development, sales, marketing, strategy, and leadership folks require this information so that they can understand the current service levels at their operational level of abstraction.

In fact, the service catalog is the only place where these parties could get this kind of information! That is, the service catalog connects the business stakeholders, the services in production, and their reliability in a unique way.

The ownership of maintaining the manual parts of the service catalog needs to be clearly agreed and accepted by the service owner teams. A service catalog with stale information is of very limited value. Only a service catalog with up-to-date information can be used for informational and decision-making purposes. The SRE coaches should drive the service catalog creation, automation, ownership, and maintenance aspects in a way similar to introducing the SRE foundations back in the day.

15.2 SLAs

SLAs are another big area of enhancing the SRE foundations. The SLAs need to be defined based on the SLOs previously arrived at through iteration. Offered SLAs need to be more relaxed than existing SLOs. This way, when the SLOs are fulfilled, the SLAs are automatically fulfilled. Conversely, when the SLOs get broken, it does not immediately mean the SLAs are broken as well.

A leeway between the SLOs and SLAs provides an error budget window. Only when the error budget window is burned through will the SLAs get broken. Thus, defining the SLAs based on the SLOs is a good way to be confident that the SLAs offered can be defended and upheld.

With the introduction of SLAs, the maturity of the SRE practice increases as now there are contractual penalties associated with not fulfilling the service reliability goals. Moreover, the SLAs, being specified in legal contracts, are almost always defined at the highest level of the service catalog where big service aggregates reside. The distribution of the SLA error budgets by SLI to the individual services, and consequently to the teams, will require negotiations between the teams that have not taken place before.

The SRE infrastructure will need to be extended to provide alerting on SLA breaches to different stakeholders. Unlike alerts on SLO breaches, the SLA breaches might be interesting to business stakeholders. Notably, the legal department may well be interested in being notified in a timely manner about the SLA breaches to be able to prepare for any contractual penalty negotiations they might entail.

Contractually, SLAs might be defined by customer segment. For instance, several tiers of premium customers might be defined and associated with an SLA set by tier. This might be a great way to generate revenue. Technically, only a minor extension of the SRE infrastructure is required to enable this.

15.3 Regulatory Compliance

Many industries operate under the regulatory regimes that impose regulations on the products that can be placed on the market. Some regulatory regimes go a step further and also impose regulations on the product development process used to manufacture the products. Much like hardware products, software products in regulated industries are subject to regulations in the same fashion. These regulations can also extend beyond the product development process into the realm of product operations.

Generally, the regulations are country-specific. For example, medical products in the medical domain are subject to Food and Drug Administration (FDA) regulations in the United States. Avionics products in the avionics domain are subject to European Union Aviation Safety Agency (EASA) regulations in the European Union.

Beyond the regulations, there are also industry certifications that companies can acquire. These certifications are often asked for in public tenders for bigger IT projects. That is, only companies that have the certifications can take part in the tenders. For example, the ISO/IEC 27001 standard for managing information security is a voluntary certification that companies can acquire. The certification, however, is often required to take part in public tenders.

Acquiring such a certification is similar to complying with a regulatory regime. A large number of controls need to be fulfilled by the organization, product development, and product operations processes. A yearly audit by external auditors from a certification body accredited in the region is established to renew the certification on a yearly basis.

Ensuring regulatory compliance was traditionally done using document-based processes supported by tools. With the establishment of SRE, new processes, practices, responsibilities, and infrastructure were introduced in the product delivery organization. There is a lot of potential in finding out how the established SRE process and organization can be used to ensure regulatory compliance in a way that is more efficient than with document-based processes.

Generally speaking, the introduction of SRE turned the subject of product operations into a data-driven practice with transparent decision-making. This will be welcomed by auditors. To approach the matter, a number of questions need to be explored.

- Which operations regulations may apply to a given product delivery organization?

- What is required by the regulations? Why?

- How are the regulations met today?

- How can the regulations be met using SRE?

- Would the use of SRE streamline the process of ensuring necessary regulatory compliance?

These questions need to be answered to understand the potential for streamlining how regulatory compliance is ensured and reducing the effort of doing so in a product delivery organization.

15.4 SRE Infrastructure

The SRE infrastructure discussed in this book supports two basic SLIs applicable to a vast majority of services: availability and latency. As part of enhancing the SRE foundations, the infrastructure should be extended to support additional SLIs beyond availability and latency. The support for additional SLIs should be implemented in a generic manner benefiting all development teams with a single infrastructure implementation. This is the prerequisite for unleashing an economy of scale based on SRE infrastructure investment.

Moreover, the SRE infrastructure was developed so far with a view to provide as many teams as possible with the necessary features as quickly as possible. This was the right approach to take to get the SRE practice established in the organization quickly. The next step for the SRE infrastructure is to become a genuine internal product where product thinking is applied in much the same way as is done for external products.

To be sure, user centricity was the central aspect of infrastructure feature prioritization up to now. This needs to be the case in the future as well. That is, feature prioritization and implementation need to be only one step ahead of the teams requesting and using them. This caters to a very tight feedback loop between feature implementation and usage. The infrastructure evolves based on the feedback loop measuring the usage of its features.

In this lane, the users of the SRE infrastructure need to be properly defined. Are they developers? Are they operations engineers? Are they product owners? Are they stakeholders? A user journey for each user needs to be modeled using user story maps. The requirements for each user journey need to be clearly and completely defined. Testing for the infrastructure requirements needs to be implemented using a suitable testing framework.

Importantly, monitoring of SRE infrastructure services needs to be established in a way that the monitoring components are independent from the SRE infrastructure services. Monitoring the SRE infrastructure services using the services themselves is very risky. This is because when the SRE infrastructure services go down, their monitoring goes down as well.

In terms of feature implementation, there are many vectors of optimization in the SRE infrastructure. The alerting algorithm can be refined beyond the basic timeliness and effectiveness features, visualizations can be optimized in terms of UX for productivity, anomaly detection can be implemented, and so on. This area is eagerly explored by the software tool industry. So, making effective use of free and commercial off-the-shelf tools and infrastructure components may speed up the lead time for new SRE infrastructure features.

15.5 Game Days

In Chapter 9, *Implementing Incident Response*, the incident response process was set up. In order to keep the organization prepared to use the process in an effective manner, it needs to be exercised in staged situations. Defined process roles, incident classification, on-call rotations, stakeholder notifications, incident states, ways of communication, runbooks, postmortem procedures, and so on need to be implemented throughout the organization on a regular basis. Otherwise, in a real emergency, adherence to the defined incident response process might be patchy simply because people might not remember the details.

The situation is similar to fire emergency procedures. The procedures are defined and put on the walls of the building for people to see. However, unless fire drills occur regularly, the building will not be evacuated according to procedures. People might panic and use elevators, ignore the fire alarm buttons at the exits, and so on. The regular fire drills remind people in a staged setting how building evacuation should take place.

In the world of software, such fire drills are often referred to as game days. The name "game day" suggests that on a given day a simulation of real-world adverse events will be conducted. The purpose of a game day is to test products, services, monitoring systems, processes, and team responses in terms of incident process adherence and effectiveness. Ultimately, game days contribute to improving reliability as perceived by the user.

Regular game days help build organizational "muscle memory" of how to respond to adverse events. Often they are associated with chaos engineering. Indeed, chaos engineering experiments can be executed on a game day.

Introducing regular game days is another way to strengthen the SRE practice in a product delivery organization. The game days can be incubated, launched, and sustained by the SRE community of practice.

This marks the end of the SRE transformation journey for this book. Finalizing the book with so much potential to make SRE practice more efficient and effective makes it evident that what has been achieved so far is not the end of the overall journey. More technical and nontechnical books are required to further pave the way for organizations establishing SRE.

The SRE introduction programs themselves could become more differentiated depending on the culture of the organization from the Westrum model.[2] While this book focused on introduc-ing SRE in rule-oriented and performance-oriented organizational cultures, it would be helpful to research how the introduction of SRE can be driven in power-oriented cultures.

Moreover, introducing SRE in a holacracy organization (see Section 12.4.3) with no bosses and bureaucracies is unexplored terrain as a whole.

Finally, there is a lot of fundamental research required to bring SRE as a discipline to the next level. The research agenda is outlined well by Niall Murphy in "What SRE Could Be. How Do We Get To SRE 2.0?"[3]

That is, SRE overall remains a great field to explore to advance the software industry at large! Go explore!

---

2. Westrum, R. 2004. "A Typology of Organisational Cultures." *Quality and Safety in Health Care* 13 (suppl_2): ii22–27. https://doi.org/10.1136/qshc.2003.009522.

3. Murphy, Niall. 2022. "What SRE Could Be? How do we get to SRE 2.0?" USENIX ;login: (blog). Accessed June 2, 2022. https://www.usenix.org/publications/loginonline/what-sre-could-be.

Appendix

Topics for Quick Reference

This appendix contains a list of topics described in reference form for quick lookup while reading the book and thereafter. The topics are

- SRE wiki content
- Runbook template content
- Incident response process content
- Postmortem lifecycle
- Operations teams' responsibilities
- SRE online communities
- SRE newsletters
- SRE conferences
- SRE indicators
- Decision-making workflows

SRE Wiki Content

- Why SRE?
- SRE foundations to onboard people new to SRE in a self-service manner
- How do you dock services of any type onto the SRE infrastructure?
- How do you use the logging facility?
- How do you use the application performance management facility?
- How do you use the on-call management tool?

- Runbooks
  - ○ Reference to the runbook template
  - ○ References to the actual runbooks
  - ○ Good examples of runbooks
- Incident response process
  - ○ Definition of stakeholder groups
  - ○ Definition of stakeholder rings
  - ○ Definition of generic incident priorities
  - ○ Definition of incident severities
  - ○ Definition of roles involved in incident response
  - ○ How do you get into a role?
- References to service status pages
- References to incident priority definitions for SLOs, including reasons
- Incident priority definitions for resource-based alerts, including reasons
- Incident postmortems
  - ○ Reference to the incident postmortem template
  - ○ References to the actual incident postmortem write-ups, videos, and audio
  - ○ Good examples of postmortem write-ups
- References to on-call rotations by teams in the on-call management tool
- How do you report a bug found in the SRE infrastructure?
- How do you file a new feature request for the SRE infrastructure?
- SRE transformation broadcasts (embedded recordings)
- List of SRE coaches in the organization
- SRE minutes
- Availability newsletter issues

Runbook Template Content

- Timestamp of the last runbook update
- Name of the person who did the last runbook update
- Service the runbook is for (with a link to the service catalog, if any)

- For each SLO covered by the runbook:

  ○ Short description (with a link to the SLO definition)

  ○ Impact on customers when the SLO gets broken

  ○ SLO incident priority

  ○ Remediation steps

- For each resource-based alert covered by the runbook:

  ○ Short description

  ○ Impact on customers

  ○ Remediation steps

- Dashboards about service health, if any

- Contact details for further support, including availability times with time zones

  ○ Can be specified using applicable on-call rotations in the on-call management tool

- Alert deduplication tags

- Link to the definition of generic incident priorities in the SRE wiki

- Link to the definition of incident severities, if any, in the SRE wiki

- Latest production deployments of the service and code changes for each production deployment (links)

Incident Response Process Content

- Why the incident response process?

- Incident response roles

  ○ Responsibilities by role

  ○ Skills by role

- Incident classification

  ○ Incident priorities

  ○ Incident severities

- How do you drive a complex incident response?

- Incident postmortem process

  ○ Responsibilities

  ○ Activities before postmortem

○ Activities during postmortem

○ Activities after postmortem

○ Postmortem template

○ Outcome feedback

- Service status pages

  ○ Mapping of incident classification to service state changes on the status page

Postmortem Lifecycle

Effective postmortems require that a series of steps be undertaken before, during, and after the actual postmortem meeting. These are presented in a concise form in Table A.1.

Table A.1 *Postmortem Lifecycle*

Before Postmortem	During Postmortem	After Postmortem
1. Invite participants	1. Prime directive	1. Create or complete work items for action items in the work item management tool
2. Clarify responsibilities	2. Clarify responsibilities	
3. Construct the timeline	3. Refine the timeline	2. Follow up on action items in line with agreed review dates
4. Automated incident conversation analysis	4. Review the timeline	3. Present the postmortem
5. Initial postmortem write-up	5. Derive immediate action items	4. Finish the postmortem write-up
6. Clarify people issues	6. Derive action items for improvements in broader processes and practices	5. Upload the postmortem video recording, if any
	7. Prioritize action items	6. Upload the postmortem audio recording, if any
	8. Assign action items	7. Distribute the postmortem content
	9. Agree on review dates for action items	8. Provide periodic feedback on the outcomes achieved through postmortems
	10. Agree on forums where the postmortem needs to be presented and by whom	
	11. Quick feedback on postmortem effectiveness	

Operations Teams' Responsibilities

The operations teams' responsibilities under the SRE framework are as follows:

- Development of the SRE infrastructure
- Maintenance of the SRE infrastructure
- Operations of the SRE infrastructure
- Documentation of the SRE infrastructure
- Promotion of the SRE infrastructure
- Logging facility administration, licensing, and procurement
- Application performance management facility administration, licensing, and procurement
- On-call management tool administration, licensing, and procurement
- Management of agreements for stakeholder notifications outside the enterprise
- Support of SRE CoP
- Ownership of the incident response process
- Possibly going on call for product services as agreed to with development teams as part of the SRE organizational structure setup

SRE Online Communities

There are a number of online communities related to SRE. As the SRE practices evolve in the industry at large, it is necessary to stay on top by being active in these communities. Table A.2 is a summary of communities that can be joined.

Table A.2 *SRE Online Communities*

#	Community	Medium	How to Join
1	SREcon	Slack	Access is provided on attendance of one of the SREcon conferences[1]
2	DevOps Enterprise Summit	Slack	Access is provided on attendance of one of the DevOps Enterprise Summit conferences[2]

---

1. USENIX. 2022. "SREcon." July 08, 2022. https://www.usenix.org/srecon.

2. IT Revolution. n.d. "DevOps Enterprise Summit 2022." Accessed January 12, 2022. https://events.itrevolution.com.

#	Community	Medium	How to Join
3	SRE From Home	Slack	Follow the link to join the Slack workspace on the SRE From Home home page[3]
4	"Learning from Incidents in Software" (LFI)	Slack	Follow the link at the bottom of the LFI GitHub page[4] to find instructions for requesting access
5	#sre tag on LinkedIn	LinkedIn	Follow the #sre tag on LinkedIn[5]
6	DevOps at Scale	LinkedIn	Request access on LinkedIn[6]
7	Site Reliability Engineers (SRE)	LinkedIn	Request access on LinkedIn[7]

SRE Newsletters

I am aware of two online newsletters related to SRE. They are summarized in Table A.3.

Table A.3 *SRE Newsletters*

#	Newsletter	Frequency	How to Join
1	SRE Weekly	Weekly	Sign up at https://sreweekly.com
2	DevOps Weekly	Weekly	Sign up at https://www.devopsweekly.com

SRE Conferences

Professional conferences offer broad and deep coverage of SRE topics. They are listed in Table A.4.

Table A.4 *SRE Conferences*

#	Conference	Region	Conduct	How to Attend
1	SREcon	Global	Online and offline	Sign up on the SREcon conferences home page[1]

3. Catchpoint. n.d. "SRE From Home." Accessed January 27, 2022. https://www.srefromhome.com.

4. Jones, Nora. n.d. "GitHub – Norajones/LFI-Slack: Documents and Resources for the 'Learning from Incidents in Software' Slack Workspace." GitHub. Accessed January 27, 2022. https://github.com/norajones/LFI-Slack.

5. LinkedIn. n.d. "#sre. " Accessed January 27, 2022. https://www.linkedin.com/feed/hashtag/sre.

6. LinkedIn. n.d. "DevOps at Scale." Accessed January 27, 2022. https://www.linkedin.com/groups/4200099.

7. LinkedIn. n.d. "Site Reliability Engineers (SRE)." Accessed January 27, 2022. https://www.linkedin.com/groups/8811337.

#	Conference	Region	Conduct	How to Attend
2	DevOps Enterprise Summit	Global	Online and offline	Sign up on the DevOps Enterprise Summit conferences home page[2]
3	QCon	Global	Online and offline	Sign up on the QCon home page[8]

SRE Indicators

Table A.5 summarizes the SRE indicators defined in the book.

Table A.5 *SRE Indicators*

#	SRE Indicator	Visualization	Explanation
1	"SLOs by service" indicator (Section 11.2.2)	Table	Shows defined SLOs
2	SLO error budget depletion indicator (Section 11.2.4)	Graph, Table	Shows SLO error budget depletion over time
3	Premature SLO error budget exhaustion indicator (Section 11.2.5)	Graph, Table	Shows SLOs where the error budget was exhausted prematurely before the end of a given error budget period
4	SLO adherence indicator (Section 11.2.3)	Table	Shows adherence to SLOs over time
5	"SLAs by service" indicator (Section 11.2.6)	Table	Shows defined SLAs
6	SLA error budget depletion indicator (Section 11.2.7)	Graph, Table	Shows SLA error budget depletion over time
7	SLA adherence indicator (Section 11.2.8)	Table	Shows adherence to SLAs over time
8	Customer support ticket trend indicator (Section 11.2.9)	Graph, Table	Shows customer support ticket trends over time
9	"On-call rotations by team" indicator (Section 11.2.10)	Table	Shows on-call rotation setup by team
10	Incident time to recovery trend indicator (Section 11.2.11)	Table	Shows incident time to recovery trends over time

8. "QCon Software Development Conferences." n.d. QCon Software Conferences for Senior Software Engineers. Accessed January 26, 2022. https://qconferences.com.

#	SRE Indicator	Visualization	Explanation
11	Least available service endpoints indicator (Section 11.2.12)	Table	Shows the least available endpoints in a given period
12	Slowest service endpoints indicator (Section 11.2.13)	Table	Shows the slowest endpoints in a given period

Decision-Making Workflows

The decision-making workflows explored in the book using the SRE indicators are summarized in Table A.6.

Table A.6 *Decision-Making Workflows*

#	Decision-Making Workflow	Purpose
1	API consumption decision workflow (Section 11.5.1)	Can be used before integrating with an API to make a conscious decision about reliability aspects of the integration ahead of time
2	Tightening a dependency's SLO decision workflow (Section 11.5.2)	Can be used to facilitate conversations between teams when a dependent service's SLO needs to be tightened
3	Features vs. reliability prioritization workflow (Section 11.5.3)	Can be used to prioritize feature development against reliability improvements in a data-driven manner
4	Setting an SLO decision workflow (Section 11.5.4)	Can be used to support setting an SLO for a service considering reliability of dependent services
5	Setting an SLA decision workflow (Section 11.5.5)	Can be used to support setting an SLA for a service both technically and contractually
6	Allocating SRE capacity to a team decision workflow (Section 11.5.6)	Can be used to support decisions about SRE capacity allocation to teams and departments
7	Chaos engineering hypotheses selection workflow (Section 11.5.7)	Can be used to find reliable parts of the system to test for hardness using chaos experiments

Index

Numerics

100% availability, 50–52

A

Adzic, G., *Fifty Quick Ideas to Improve Your User Stories*, 99
agile/agility
  coach, 272
  delivery, 1
  enterprise-level, 318
AIDA marketing funnel, 92
  agreement, 95–96
  awareness, 92
  desire/understanding, 93–94
  engagement, 96
  interest, 93–94
alert(s), 25, 34, 108, 152, 166–167, 168–169. *See also* reacting to alerts on SLO breaches
  deduplication, 246–248
  dispatching, 211–212
    escalation policy, 212–215
    stakeholder groups, 216–217
    stakeholder notifications, 216, 217–219, 222–226
    stakeholder rings, 219–222
  error budget, 54
  escalation, 212–214
  mapping to incident priorities, 240–241
alignment
  mis-, 22–30
  organizational, 67–68
  SRE, 23–17, 29, 100
    on-call rotation and, 62
    concept pyramid and, 59–63
    error budget policies and, 62–63
    SLOs, 60–62
allocating SRE capacity to a team decision workflow, 380–381
Allspaw, J., 253
  The Future of Monitoring, 421

API, 33, 363–366
  application performance management facility, 149–150. *See also* infrastructure
automation
  DevOps and, 6
  incident response, 260–262
availability, 148, 149, 150–151, 159–160. *See also* SLI(s) (service level indicator/s)
  error budget, 49, 50–52
  newsletter, 476
  SLO, 17
  targets, 194
awareness, ways of promoting, 92
  availability newsletter, 476
  broadcasting, 478–479
  CoP (community of practice), 475
  long-form wiki articles, 477–478
  SRE column in the engineering blog, 477
  SRE minutes, 475–476
  success stories, 172–173, 208–209, 226–227

B

backlog, 30
  incident detection and resolution, 36
  product development, 25–26, 29
BDD (behavior-driven development), 336
Blank-Adelman, D. N., *Seeking SRE: Conversations About Running Production Systems at Scale*, 393
bottleneck analysis, 482–483
bottom-up buy-in, 90, 117
  development team, 119–121
  operations team, 117–119
bridging, 78
broadcasting
  service status, 299
  success stories, 302
  system, 478–479

Register Your Product at informit.com/register

Access additional benefits and save up to 65%* on your next purchase

- Automatically receive a coupon for 35% off books, eBooks, and web editions and 65% off video courses, valid for 30 days. Look for your code in your InformIT cart or the Manage Codes section of your account page.

- Download available product updates.

- Access bonus material if available.**

- Check the box to hear from us and receive exclusive offers on new editions and related products.

InformIT—The Trusted Technology Learning Source

InformIT is the online home of information technology brands at Pearson, the world's leading learning company. At informit.com, you can

- Shop our books, eBooks, and video training. Most eBooks are DRM-Free and include PDF and EPUB files.

- Take advantage of our special offers and promotions (informit.com/promotions).

- Sign up for special offers and content newsletter (informit.com/newsletters).

- Access thousands of free chapters and video lessons.

- Enjoy free ground shipping on U.S. orders.*

* Offers subject to change.
** Registration benefits vary by product. Benefits will be listed on your account page under Registered Products.

Connect with InformIT—Visit informit.com/community

twitter.com/informit

 Pearson